HUMAN RESOURCE MANAGEMENT

DEREK TORRINGTON, LAURA HALL, CAROL ATKINSON, STEPHEN TAYLOR

TENTH EDITION

Pearson

Harlow, England • London • New York • Boston • San Francisco • Toronto • Sydney • Dubai • Singapore • Hong Kong
Tokyo • Seoul • Taipei • New Delhi • Cape Town • Sao Paulo • Mexico City • Madrid • Amsterdam • Munich • Paris • Milan

Pearson Education Limited
Edinburgh Gate
Harlow CM20 2JE
United Kingdom
Tel: +44 (0)1279 623623

Web: www.pearson.com/uk

First published in Great Britain under the Prentice Hall Europe imprint in 1987 (print)
Second edition published in 1991 (print)
Third edition published 1995 (print)
Fourth edition published 1998 (print)
Fifth edition published 2002 (print)
Sixth edition published 2005 (print)
Seventh edition published 2008 (print)
Eighth edition published 2011 (print)
Ninth edition published 2014 (print and electronic)
Tenth edition published 2017 (print and electronic)

ISBN: 978-1-292-12909-9 (print)
         978-1-292-12911-2 (PDF)
         978-1-292-19152-2 (ePub)

British Library Cataloguing-in-Publication Data
A catalogue record for the print edition is available from the British Library

Library of Congress Cataloging-in-Publication Data

Names: Torrington, Derek, 1931- author. | Hall, Laura, 1952- author. |
   Taylor, Stephen, 1965- author.
Title: Human resource management / Derek Torrington, Laura Hall, Carol
   Atkinson, Stephen Taylor.
Description: Tenth Edition. | New York : Pearson, 2017. | Revised edition of
   Human resource management, 2014.
Identifiers: LCCN 2016043893| ISBN 9781292129099 (print) | ISBN 9781292129112
   (pdf) | ISBN 9781292191522 (epub)
Subjects: LCSH: Personnel management.
Classification: LCC HF5549 .T675 2017 | DDC 658.3-dc23
LC record available at https://lccn.loc.gov/2016043893

10 9 8 7 6 5 4 3 2 1

21 20 19 18 17

Print edition typeset in Sabon MT Pro 10/12.5 pt by SPi Global

Printed in Slovakia by Neografia

NOTE THAT ANY PAGE CROSS REFERENCES REFER TO THE PRINT EDITION

BRIEF CONTENTS

CONTENTS

Contents

GUIDED TOUR

Learning Objectives work in conjunction with the chapter-ending Summary Propositions to quickly show you what you will learn about in the chapter and help you compare how well you have understood the learning you undertake.

Window on Practice boxes provide you with examples of real organisational practice, survey results, anecdotes and quotations and court cases, helping you to build up your knowledge of real-World practice and prepare you for life after study.

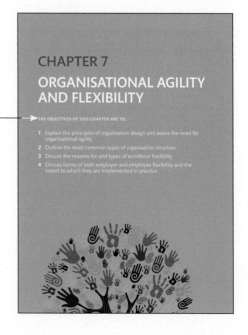

Activity boxes encourage you to regularly review and critically apply your learning, either as an individual or within a group. These have been developed for both students with little or no business experience, as well as those with more practical knowledge.

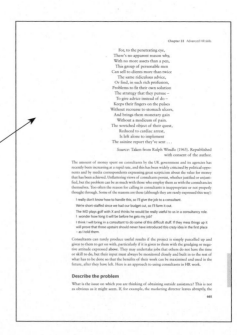

Regular **quotes** throughout help to enliven and contextualise the subject.

Summary Propositions provide a useful revision tool enabling you to recap and check your understanding of the chapter. In conjunction with the chapter-opening Learning Objectives, you can quickly determine whether you are prepared enough to move on, or need further study.

General Discussion Topics are useful both as a basis for group discussion within tutorials or study groups, as well as activities to help develop your better understanding of the topics covered within the chapter.

Theory into Practice case studies or learning activities that enable you to put your learning into practice within a realistic scenario. Improve your employability by answering the associated questions and developing a better understanding of business practice.

Further Reading sections provide guided access to some key readings in the area, and help you to further develop your skills and learning.

Some chapters list relevant **Web Links** that can help expand your understanding of the topics covered within the chapter.

Detailed **References** provide quick and easy access to the research behind the chapter and additional sources of information to support your learning.

A detailed **Glossary** is included at the end of the book, for quick reference to key terms and definitions within each chapter.

PREFACE

Peter Drucker, the early and highly respected management guru, once said that management was largely about making things difficult for other people. HR is a management function which many people regard as making life difficult for them. This text has evolved steadily over thirty-five years to this tenth edition. Our objective has always been to track the development of the personnel/HR function and its activities in a way that fits with the changing approaches to the teaching of the subject in universities. There is no doubt that academic research and teaching has an important impact on practice. We see our role as to help the teaching and learning process to assist those working, or aspiring to work, in HR or kindred roles. Our hope is that those who read this text will move on to work in a way that seems less like making things difficult for other people and more like making their employment more satisfying, and make a success of the jobs they share. At the same time, some people sometimes do need to have their working lives made more difficult!

Despite the increasingly global nature of HR activities, we live and work in Britain and basing a text in a specific context gives it more substance and meaning to its readers. To paraphrase Shakespeare, the writer brings a shape to things unknown, giving them a local habitation and a name. Things that were understood in isolation fit together and acquire new meaning when applied in a specific setting. The time of writing and revising the text was through the Summer of 2016, before and immediately after the referendum that produced a vote in favour of the United Kingdom leaving the European Union. Being a member state has always been the background to our writing, but we see no need to make alterations. It is clear that the process of withdrawal will be protracted and the implications for employment practice are going to be limited. We are confident that the book will remain up to date and relevant throughout its lifetime.

Our structure is of seven distinct parts with thirty-three chapters, each with objectives, summary propositions, general discussion topics, theory into practice (or putting it into practice), further reading and references; Part 7 is different. We have had feedback from a number of people who use the text in their teaching with the result that we have reverted to our practice in editions five (2002) to seven (2008) of having a skills section at the end of each part, with skills of particular relevance at that point. They have been refocused with the title of 'Employability: skills in . . .'. This is a key theme in contemporary UK universities, with an emphasis on ensuring that their students will be effective in the workforce alongside their academic credentials. We also have a new chapter on advanced HR skills, which concludes Part 7. We set it clearly apart from the rest, where the treatment is of basic skills that can to some extent be learned and practised away from the workplace. We see advanced skills as those often associated with more senior roles, like chairing meetings or managing consultants, in which experience is an essential element in acquiring *skilfulness*.

As before there are several design features to assist readers in using and learning from the text, including the following:

a   Integrated **Window on practice boxes** provide a range of illustrative material throughout the text, including examples of real company practice, survey results, anecdotes and quotations, and court cases.

b   Integrated **Activity boxes** encourage readers to review and critically apply their understanding at regular intervals throughout the text, either by responding to a question or by undertaking a small practical assignment, individually or as part of a group. In recognition that this text is used on both professional and academic courses, most of the exercises reflect the fact that many students will have little or no business experience. Others may appear to exclude students who are not in employment by asking readers to consider an aspect in their own organisation; however, the organisation could be a college or university, the students' union, a political body or sports team.

c **Discussion topics** at the end of each chapter comprise two or three short questions intended for general discussion in a tutorial or study group.

d **Theory into practice** at the end of chapters enables readers to review, link and apply their understanding of the chapter to a business scenario. For skills chapters, 'Theory into practice' becomes 'Putting it into practice' as an indicator that these are generally more practical than traditionally academic.

e **Web links** are given as appropriate at various points in the text. These are links to other websites containing useful information relating to the topics covered.

f **Further reading** for each chapter suggests further relevant readings, with guidance on their value.

g **Each part** of the text includes a brief introduction explaining its scope and purpose.

h **Chapter objectives** to open and **Summary propositions** to conclude each chapter set up the readers' expectations and review their understanding progressively.

i **References** are given in full at the end of each chapter to aid further exploration of the chapter material, as required.

j **Glossary**: we close with a short glossary of terms taken selectively from the text.

PUBLISHER'S ACKNOWLEDGEMENTS

We are grateful to the following for permission to reproduce copyright material:

Figures

Figure 4.2 from *Strategic Human Resource Management*, New York: John Wiley & Sons, Inc. (Fombrun, C., Tichy, N.M., and Devanna, M.A. 1984) p. 41, © John Wiley and Sons 1984, reproduced with permission of John Wiley and Sons Inc.; Figure 4.3 from Human resources and sustained competitive advantage: A resource-based perspective, *International Journal of Human Resource Management*, 5(2), p. 318 (Wright, P.M., McMaham, G.C., and McWilliams, A. 1994), reprinted with the permission of Taylor and Francis Ltd, www.tandf.co.uk/journals; Figure 4.4 from Front-line managers as agents in the HRM performance causal chain: theory, analysis and evidence, *Human Resource Management Journal*, 17(1), pp. 3–20 (Purcell, J. and Hutchinson, S. 2007), p. 7, Figure 1, reproduced with permission of Wiley-Blackwell; Figure 7.1 from Manpower strategies for flexible organisation, *Personnel Management*, August, pp. 28–9 (Atkinson, J. 1984); Figure 14.1 from Major influences on employee attendance: A process model, *Journal of Applied Psychology*, 63, p. 393 (Steers, R.M. and Rhodes, S.R.), copyright 1978 by the American Psychological Association, reprinted by permission.

Tables

Table 4.1 adapted from Linking competitive strategies with human resource management practices, *Academy of Management Executive*, 1 (3) (Schuler, R.S. and Jackson, S.E. 1987), Academy of Management, reproduced with permission of the Academy of Management; Table 7.1 from Organisational learning and organisational design, *The Learning Organisation*, 13, pp. 25–48 (Curado, C. 2006), © 2006 Emerald Publishing Group Ltd; Table 8.1 adapted from What is (or should be) the difference between competency modelling and traditional job analysis? *Human Resource Management Review*, 19(1), pp. 53–63 (Sanchez, J. and Levine, E. 2009), Copyright © 2009 Elsevier Ltd. All rights reserved. With permission from Elsevier; Table 12.1 adapted from *The Managerial Grid*, Houston, Texas: Gulf Publishing (Blake, R.R. and Mouton, J.S. 1964); Table 12.2 adapted from *Management of Organizational Behavior: Utilizing Human Resources*, 5th ed., Englewood Cliffs, NJ: Prentice-Hall International (Hersey, P. and Blanchard, K.H. 1988) © Copyright material, adapted and reprinted with the permission of Center for Leadership Studies, Escondido, CA 92025; Table 17.1 after *Cranet Survey on Comparative Human Resource Management*, Cranet (2011) Table 6, p. 62; Table 18.1 after *Major learning trends and indicators for 2013 and beyond within the Asia Pacific Region*, Singapore: Cegos (Blain, J. 2013) p. 27; Table 23.1 after Employers move on equal pay, *IDS Report*, No. 897, January, pp. 10–8 (IDS 2004).

Text

Case Study on pp. 21–2 from Why we no longer need HR departments, Marr B. (2013), www.linkedin.com/pulse/20131118060732-64875646-why-we-no-longer-need-hr-departments; Extract on p. 76 from Human resource management strategies under uncertainty, *Cross Cultural Management: An International Journal*, 13(2), pp. 171–86 (Fields, D., Chan, A., Aktar, S., and Blum, T. 2006), © 2006 Emerald Publishing Group Ltd; Extract on pp. 74–5 from Exploring the fit perspective, *Human Resource*

Management, 52(1), pp. 124–44 (Samnani, A. and Singh. P. 2013), © John Wiley and Sons 2013, reproduced with permission of John Wiley and Sons Inc.; Extract on p. 94 adapted from Labour shortages: Double digit wage increases, *Financial Times*, 11/12/2012 (Jacob, R.), © The Financial Times Limited. All Rights Reserved; Extract on pp. 177–9 adapted from Globalisation of HR at function level: Four UK-based case studies of the international recruitment and selection process, *International Journal of Human Resource Management*, 18(5), pp. 845–67 (Sparrow, P. 2007), reprinted with the permission of Taylor and Francis Ltd, www.tandf.co.uk/journals; Extract on p. 260 adapted from Telling an untold story: On being a follower rather than a leader, *EGOS Colloquium, Barcelona* (Ford, J. and Harding, N. 2009); Extract on pp. 519–21 adapted from Pandora's Pay Packet, *Financial Times*, 14/05/2001 (Kellaway, L.), © The Financial Times Limited. All Rights Reserved.

Cover

Quotation on front cover from *People Management Magazine*, November 2016: www.peoplemanagement.co.uk.

PART 1

HUMAN RESOURCE MANAGEMENT IN A CHANGING WORLD

CHAPTERS

For those entering the HR profession this text aims to introduce you to the interconnectedness of the discipline. Part 1 puts in place the totality of HRM in six ways. Chapter 1 describes the nature of HRM, a specialism which is everywhere and in everything. Chapter 2 sketches in the background of the global context within which we operate, as what you do in your small corner has to make sense not only in your business but in the local, national and international situation. A closer look at this issue is provided in Chapter 3, which reviews how HR practice varies across different countries. Chapter 4 deals with strategy, which not only sets the course of the business but also ensures that it is right, and how it could be implemented.

Implementation requires planning: the story of Chapter 5 is analytics or the application of statistics to many aspects of HR work; to deal with a question or a problem you need some information to know what it is and then you need some data with which to measure it. We close Part 1, in Chapter 6, with a bundle of basic skills for employability and effectiveness in HR work. At the end of each chapter you will find a case study in Putting it into practice which will help you to put these ideas into context and explore them more thoroughly.

Part 1 is the biggest section, but what you read and learn here will be a constant reference point throughout the rest of the text. We sincerely hope it works well for you.

CHAPTER 1
THE NATURE OF HUMAN RESOURCE MANAGEMENT

THE OBJECTIVES OF THIS CHAPTER ARE TO:

1 Define the term 'human resource management'
2 Explain the different ways in which the term 'human resource management' is used
3 Set out the main objectives of the human resource function
4 Review the historical evolution of the modern HR function
5 Discuss links between HRM activity and business performance

Human resource management (HRM) is the basis of all management activity, but it is not the basis of all business activity. A business may depend fundamentally on having a unique product, like the Dyson vacuum cleaner, or on obtaining the necessary funding, like the London bid to stage the Olympic Games, or on identifying a previously unnoticed market niche, like Saga Services. The basis of management is always the same: getting the people of the business to make things happen in a productive way, so that the business prospers and the people thrive.

All organisations have to draw on a range of resources to function and to achieve their objectives. They need access to capital to finance their operations, land and premises to operate from, energy, equipment and raw materials in order to manufacture a product or deliver a service. They also require access to some form of distribution network so that they can publicise, sell or dispense their goods and services. In addition, human resources are required in order to provide organisations with know-how, ideas and manpower. In a competitive market economy the effectiveness and efficiency with which an organisation manages its relationship with the suppliers of all these kinds of resources determines its success. And the scarcer the resource and the more critical it is to a particular organisation's operations, the greater the skill, time and effort needed in order to manage the relationship.

There was a time when most people employed by organisations were required simply to provide manual labour. Relatively little skill, experience or intelligence was needed to do the jobs. The requisite training was cheap and speedy to provide, and payment methods unsophisticated. Finding people to do the work was rarely a problem and there were no restrictions of significance when it came to firing those who were not satisfactory or who displeased managers in some other way. This remains the situation in some industries and in some parts of the world, but in industrialised countries it is now increasingly rare. Instead we have a situation in which the majority of jobs require their holders to have mastered some form of specialised skill, or at the very least to possess attributes which others do not share to the same extent. The demand for higher-level skills has grown particularly quickly, there being a need for many more people to fill professional and managerial jobs than was the case twenty years ago. Moreover, almost all informed commentators believe that these established trends will accelerate in the future (UKCES 2012, Ross 2016).

Just as the workforce has changed, so have the methods used to manage its members. The more specialised their roles, the harder it has become to find individuals with the right skills, qualifications, attributes and experience to undertake them. It has also become harder to keep people once they are employed because competitors are always keen to secure the services of the most talented people by offering them a better deal. Employing organisations have had to acquire a capacity for developing people effectively, together with increasingly sophisticated approaches to recruitment, selection, retention, employee relations and performance management. Further sophistication is required thanks to the substantial body of employment regulation that now governs the management of the employment relationship in most industrialised countries. The process becomes more complex still in the case of organisations that employ people in different countries. Not only do they have to grapple with a range of often diverse legislative and public policy regimes, but also have to find ways of effectively managing people whose expectations vary significantly for cultural reasons.

These developments have led all over the world to the evolution of a more complex human resource management function, charged with overseeing all aspects of managing the relationship between an organisation and its people in a professional and productive manner (Lawler & Boudreau 2015). The management of people, however, can never be a responsibility shouldered by specialists alone. It is an area of management activity that all managers must share if it is to be carried out effectively and contribute to the achievement of competitive advantage.

In this chapter we introduce HRM by setting out its purpose and showing how the effective management of people helps organisations to achieve their objectives. We go on to examine the historical development of HR work and speculate on how this may evolve further in the future. The final part of the chapter introduces thinking about the extent and nature of the link between HR activities and organisational effectiveness and performance.

WINDOW ON PRACTICE

In 2008, twenty-five years after it was first planned, Terminal Five at Heathrow Airport in London finally opened its doors to passengers. The total cost of the building was £4.3 billion. The new terminal was exclusively for the use of British Airways, which had been planning for several years to move all its existing operations from the various other terminals at Heathrow into Terminal Five and had gone so far as to contribute £330 million to its flamboyant interior design. The day before the opening an article in the *Financial Times* reported executives' concerns that the look of the place would raise expectations too high, but that it was 'beyond imagination to contemplate failure' (Blitz 2008). Yet spectacular failure was what followed.

In the first few days of operation over 300 flights scheduled to depart from Terminal Five were cancelled, very long queues formed at check-in and transfer desks, while some 28,000 passengers found themselves separated from their luggage. The immediate cost to British Airways was £16 million, but the long-term direct costs were authoritatively estimated to be around £150 million (BBC 2008a), let alone vast further losses resulting from a deterioration in the airline's already poor brand image.

And why did this debacle happen? It appears that the major reason was simply extraordinarily poor management of people. The major immediate problem arose because the staff were not properly trained to use the equipment at Terminal Five and were unprepared when it came to solving the technical 'glitches' that quickly appeared once the baggage handling machinery started operating. In addition long delays were caused on the first day as a result of staff being unable to find the staff car park or get through security screening on schedule. Later on, as flights began to arrive, staff simply failed to 'remove luggage quickly enough at the final unloading stage' (BBC 2008b).

Matters were not helped by the persistence over a long period of very poor employment relationships at British Airways. Done and Willman (2008) reported that the failure of the airline to solve this fundamental problem was the real underlying cause of the Terminal Five debacle. An unnamed Heathrow executive said that they had all been expecting an outbreak of 'fuck'em disease' as the new terminal opened and some staff simply decided 'not to work very hard'. British Airways' staff were neither committed to the success of the operation nor to their employer. Goodwill was in short supply, leading staff to be intransigent and uncooperative when effort, positive enthusiasm and flexibility were what was required.

Defining HRM

The term 'human resource management' (HRM) is not easy to define. This is because it is commonly used in two different ways. On the one hand it is used generically to describe the body of management activities covered in texts such as this. Used in this way 'HRM' is really no more than a more modern and supposedly imposing name for what used commonly to be labelled 'personnel management.' On the other hand, the term is equally widely used to denote a particular approach to the management of people which is clearly distinct from 'personnel management'. Used in this way 'HRM' signifies more than an updating of the label; it also suggests a distinctive philosophy towards carrying out people-oriented organisational activities: one which is held to serve the modern business more effectively than 'traditional' personnel management. We explore the substance of these two meanings of human resource management in the following subsections, referring to the first as 'HRM mark 1' and the second as 'HRM mark 2'.

HRM mark 1: the generic term

The role of the HR functions is explained by identifying the key objectives to be achieved. Five objectives form the foundation of HR activity in most contemporary organisations.

Staffing objectives

HR managers are first concerned with ensuring that the business is appropriately staffed and thus able to draw on the human resources it needs. This involves designing organisation structures, identifying under what type of contract different groups of employees (or subcontractors) will work, before recruiting, selecting and developing the people required to fill the roles: the right people, with the right skills, to provide their services when needed. There is a need to compete effectively in the employment market by recruiting and retaining the best, affordable workforce that is available. This involves developing employment packages that are sufficiently attractive to maintain the required employee skills levels and, where necessary, disposing of those judged no longer to have a role to play in the organisation. The tighter a key employment market becomes, the harder it is to find and then to hold on to the people an organisation needs in order to compete effectively. In such circumstances increased attention has to be given to developing competitive pay packages, to the provision of valued training and development opportunities and to ensuring that the experience of working in the organisation is, as far as is possible, rewarding and fulfilling. Recent years have seen organisations take a more strategic approach, at least in their rhetoric, towards the meeting of staffing objectives. They are, for example, increasingly seeking to differentiate and position themselves in their labour markets vis-à-vis competitors by managing their reputations as employers, by engaging in employer branding exercises and by seeking to be recognised as 'employers of choice'.

Performance objectives

Once the required workforce is in place, HR managers seek to ensure that people are well motivated and committed so as to maximise their performance in their different roles. Training and development have a role to play, as do reward systems to maximise effort and focus attention on performance targets. In many organisations, particularly where trade unions play a significant role, HR managers negotiate improved performance with the workforce. The achievement of performance objectives also requires HR specialists to assist in disciplining employees effectively and equitably where individual conduct and/or performance standards are unsatisfactory. Welfare functions can also assist performance by providing constructive assistance to people whose performance has fallen short of their potential because of illness or difficult personal circumstances. Last but not least, there is the range of employee involvement initiatives to raise levels of commitment and to engage employees in developing new ideas. It is increasingly recognised that a key determinant of superior competitive performance is a propensity on the part of an organisation's employees to demonstrate discretionary effort. Essentially this means that they choose to go further in the service of their employer than is strictly required in their contracts of employment, working longer hours perhaps, working with greater enthusiasm or taking the initiative to improve systems and relationships. Willingness to engage in such behaviour cannot be forced by managers. But they can help to create an environment in which it is more likely to occur. A term that is currently very fashionable in HR circles is 'employee engagement', an idea which encapsulates what is required if organisations are successfully to enhance individual performance. Engaged employees know what is expected of them, have a sense of ownership of their work, are satisfied (hopefully very satisfied) with their jobs and, as a result, prepared to contribute positively both with their effort and their ideas.

Change-management objectives

A third set of core objectives in nearly every business relates to the role played by the HR function in effectively managing change. Frequently change does not come along in readily defined episodes precipitated by some external factor. Instead it is endemic and well-nigh continuous, generated as much by a continual need to innovate as from definable environmental pressures. Change comes in different forms. Sometimes it is merely structural, requiring reorganisation of activities or the introduction of new people into particular roles. At other times cultural change is sought in order to alter attitudes, philosophies or long-present organisational norms. In any of these scenarios the HR function can play a central role. Key activities include the recruitment and/or development of people with the necessary leadership skills to drive the change process, the employment of change agents to encourage acceptance of change and the construction of reward systems which underpin the change process. Timely and effective employee involvement is also crucial because 'people support what they help to create'. However, it must also be remembered that change, particularly when imposed without genuine employee involvement, is also a major potential source of conflict in organisations. This can be minimised if plenty of time is available, but a degree of conflict is inevitable where groups of staff lose out in some way as a result of change. The effective management of conflict and its avoidance through careful management of expectations and involvement in decision making are thus also significant features of an effective HR manager's role.

Administration objectives

The fourth type of objective is less directly related to achieving competitive advantage, but is focused on underpinning the achievement of the other forms of objective. In part it is simply carried out in order to facilitate an organisation's smooth running.

Hence there is a need to maintain accurate and comprehensive data on individual employees, a record of their achievement in terms of performance, their attendance and training records, their terms and conditions of employment and their personal details. However, there is also a legal aspect to much administrative activity, meaning that it is done because the business is required by law to comply. Of particular significance is the requirement that payment is administered professionally and lawfully, with itemised monthly pay statements being provided for all employees. There is the need to make arrangements for the deduction of taxation and national insurance, for the payment of pension fund contributions and to be on top of the complexities associated with Statutory Sick Pay and Statutory Maternity Pay, as well as maternity and paternity leave. Additional legal requirements relate to the monitoring of health and safety systems and the issuing of contracts to new employees. Accurate record keeping is also central to ensuring compliance with a variety of other legal obligations such as the National Minimum Wage and the Working Time Regulations. HR professionals often downgrade the significance of effective administration, seeking instead to gain for themselves a more glamorous (and usually more highly paid) role formulating policy and strategy. This is a short-sighted attitude. Achieving excellence (i.e. professionalism and cost effectiveness) in the delivery of the basic administrative tasks is important as an aim in itself because it can provide a source of competitive advantage vis à vis other organisations who struggle administratively. Moreover, as Stevens (2005: 137) demonstrates, sound administration in HR matters is important to achieve if 'potential legislative risks' are to be minimised. It also helps the HR function in an organisation to gain and maintain the credibility and respect that are required in order to influence other managers in the organisation. In this respect it can be persuasively argued that efficient administration is a prerequisite if the HR function is to make a really significant contribution in the three other areas outlined above.

Reputational objectives

Until recently it seemed that the above four objectives between them provided a comprehensive summary of what HRM in contemporary organisations seeks to achieve. It is now becoming clear that it is appropriate to add a fifth core objective. In many organisations, particularly larger companies whose names are synonymous with valuable brands, the need to build and maintain a positive reputation has become a central corporate objective. This need has grown steadily in recent years as the media environment has become increasingly competitive, and particularly since the advent of social media, which by its nature is very difficult to influence, let alone control. The notion that the HR function should properly be concerned with helping to maintain an organisation's wider corporate reputation links up with the ideas both of those who conceive of the HR role as being primarily about effective risk management (see Stevens 2005) and those who take a particular interest in the ethics of HR practices (see Pinnington *et al.* 2007, Klikauer 2014).

In organisations with a high public profile and which are obliged to compete hard in order to survive, HR managers can find themselves thinking in risk management terms. Their main role, put simply, is to ensure that the organisation:

- avoids damaging, negative media coverage on account of its employment practices,
- is not required to defend itself in an employment tribunal,
- does not develop an image as a poor employer in its key labour markets,
- retains a good relationship with regulatory authorities,

- avoids disruptive strikes and other forms of industrial action,
- maintains positive relationships with customers and suppliers.

There is a particular need nowadays for managers in private sector organisations to reassure those whose job is to assess the long-term financial viability of the organisation that it is competently managed and is well placed to meet the challenges that lie ahead in both the short and the longer term. This includes fund managers who decide where to invest their clients' money as well as the financial journalists and advisors who influence them. The ability to attract and retain a strong management team is central to achieving this aspect of organisational effectiveness, as is the ability of the organisation to plan for the future by having in place effective succession planning arrangements and robust systems for the development of the skills and knowledge that will be key in the future. Above all, financial markets need to be assured that the organisation is stable and is thus a safe repository for investors' funds.

The HR function also plays a central role in building an organisation's reputation as an ethically or socially responsible organisation. This happens in two distinct ways. The first involves fostering an understanding of and commitment to ethical conduct on the part of managers and staff. It is achieved by paying attention to these objectives in recruitment campaigns, in the criteria adopted for the selection of new employees and the promotion of staff, in the methods used to develop people and in performance management processes. The second relates to the manner in which people are managed. A poor ethical reputation can be gained simply because an organisation becomes known for treating its staff poorly. In recent years well-known brands of fast food chain in the UK have suffered because of their use of zero hours contracts, while several large multinationals have had their reputations stained by stories in the media about the conditions under which their employees in developing countries are required to work.

WINDOW ON PRACTICE

In 2015 undercover reporters working for the *Guardian* got themselves jobs in a warehouse operated by the retailer Sports Direct, a company whose approach to HRM had attracted negative publicity in the past. The reporters found that a range of seemingly unethical and potentially unlawful employment practices were in use by managers in the warehouse. They recorded instances of employees being 'fined' fifteen minutes' pay when they were just one minute late for work, of unpaid overtime, and mandatory searches of staff leaving the warehouse which took some time and were unpaid. This meant that in practice staff at the warehouse were not being paid the National Minimum Wage. They reported that there was a list of 800 sports brands that employees were not permitted to wear, that workers were harangued by tannoy for not working fast enough, and that 80% of them were employed on zero-hours contracts. The company also operated a 'black mark' system, sacking people who notched up six such marks in any six-month period: 'Offences that could lead to the receipt of a black mark included "periods of reported sickness"; "errors", "time wasting, in the form of excessive toilet breaks or chatting", "horseplay" and "using a mobile phone in the warehouse".' Union officials told the reporters that there was a climate of fear in operation in the warehouse that resulted in staff being too frightened to ask for time off even when their children were too sick to attend school. The story was placed on the front page of the *Guardian* alongside a picture of Sports Direct's owner, Mike Ashley.

The impact of this story was very substantial. Within days, Sports Direct's share price fell by 15%, wiping £600 million off the company's value and it was labelled 'a scar on British business' by the Institute of Directors. MPs raised the issue of the company's conduct in the House of Commons, announcing that Mr Ashley would soon be summoned to answer questions before a Select Committee.

Sports Direct responded quickly to the allegations, giving its warehouse staff a pay rise and promising to investigate the allegations fully. Mike Ashley released a statement saying that it was now his intention to turn his organisation into the best employer on the high street. Time will tell whether or not this is actually achieved. In the meantime the experience of Sports Direct serves as a cautionary tale for other employers, showing what can happen to a corporation's reputation if it fails to treat its staff properly.

Source: Guardian, December 2015.

ACTIVITY 1.1

Each of the five types of HR objective is important and necessary for organisations in different ways. However, at certain times one or more can assume greater importance than the others. Can you identify types of situation in which each could become the most significant or urgent?

HRM mark 2: a distinctive approach to the management of people

The second meaning commonly accorded to the term 'human resource management' denotes a particular way of carrying out the range of activities discussed above. Under this definition, a 'human resource management approach' is something qualitatively different from a 'personnel management approach'. Commentators disagree, however, about how fundamental a shift is signified by a movement from personnel management to human resource management. For some, particularly those whose focus of interest is on the management of collective relationships at work, the rise of HRM in the last two decades of the twentieth century represented something new and very different from the dominant personnel management approach in earlier years. A particular theme in their work is the contention that personnel management is essentially *workforce centred*, while HRM is *resource centred*. Personnel specialists direct their efforts mainly at the organisation's employees; finding and training them, arranging for them to be paid, explaining management's expectations, justifying management's actions, satisfying employees' work-related needs, dealing with their problems and seeking to modify management action that could produce an unwelcome employee response. The people who work in the

Table 1.1 Personnel versus HRM

	Personnel management	**Human resource management**
Time and planning perspective	Short term, reactive, ad hoc, marginal	Long term, proactive, strategic, integrated
Psychological contract	Compliance	Commitment
Control systems	External controls	Self-control
Employee relations perspective	Pluralist, collective, low trust	Unitarist, individual, high trust
Preferred structures/systems	Bureaucratic/mechanistic, centralised, formal defined roles	Organic, devolved, flexible roles
Roles	Specialist/professional	Largely integrated into line management
Evaluation criteria	Cost minimisation	Maximum utilisation (human asset accounting)

organisation are the starting point, and they are a resource that is relatively inflexible in comparison with other resources, like cash and materials. Although indisputably a management function, personnel management is not totally identified with management interests. Just as sales representatives have to understand and articulate the aspirations of the customers, personnel managers seek to understand and articulate the aspirations and views of the workforce. There is always some degree of being in between management and the employees, mediating the needs of each to the other.

HRM, by contrast, is directed mainly at management needs for human resources (not necessarily employees) to be provided and deployed. Demand rather than supply is the focus of the activity. There is greater emphasis on planning, monitoring and control, rather than mediation. Problem solving is undertaken with other members of management on human resource issues rather than directly with employees or their representatives. It is totally identified with management interests, being a general management activity, and is relatively distant from the workforce as a whole. David Guest (1987) emphasised the differences between the two approaches in his model illustrating 'stereotypes of personnel management and human resource management' (see Table 1.1).

The evolution of the modern HRM

Most large organisations have established a specialist HR function which is tasked with the efficient and effective management of the relationship that the organisation has with its employees. There is nothing at all new about the existence of such a function, managers specialising in people management having been employed at senior levels in organisations for centuries. Over time the nature of the role has evolved very significantly as have the labels that have conventionally been given to such managers, and the process of steady evolution continues today. However, this process has never totally seen the abandonment of earlier concerns. Instead as time goes by and new issues have come to the fore, the HR function has tended to add further layers to its activities. Significant legacies from each stage in the evolution of modern HRM have remained in the function's bloodstream and hence retain some significance.

Theme 1: social justice

The origins of HRM lie in the nineteenth century, with the work of social reformers such as Lord Shaftesbury and Robert Owen. Their criticisms of the free enterprise system and the hardship created by the exploitation of workers by factory owners enabled the first personnel managers to be appointed and provided the first frame of reference in which they worked: to ameliorate the lot of the workers. Such concerns are not obsolete. There are still regular reports of employees being exploited by employers flouting the law, and the problem of organisational distance between decision makers and those putting decisions into practice remains a source of alienation from work.

In the late nineteenth and early twentieth centuries some of the larger employers with a paternalist outlook began to appoint welfare officers to manage a series of new initiatives designed to make life less harsh for their employees. Prominent examples were the progressive schemes of unemployment benefit, sick pay and subsidised housing provided by the Quaker family firms of Cadbury and Rowntree, and the Lever Brothers' soap business. While the motives were ostensibly charitable, there was and remains a business as well as an ethical case for paying serious attention to the welfare of employees. This is based on the contention that it improves commitment on the part of staff and leads potential employees to compare the organisation favourably with *competitors*. The result is higher productivity, a longer-serving workforce and a bigger pool of applicants for each job. It has also been argued that a commitment to welfare reduces the scope for the development of adversarial industrial relations. The more conspicuous welfare initiatives promoted by employers today include employee assistance schemes, childcare facilities and health-screening programmes.

Theme 2: humane bureaucracy

The second phase marked the beginnings of a move away from a sole focus on welfare towards the meeting of various other organisational objectives. Personnel managers began to gain responsibilities in the areas of staffing, training and organisation design. Influenced by social scientists such as F. W. Taylor (1856–1915) and Henri Fayol (1841–1925), personnel specialists started to look at management and administrative processes analytically, working out how organisational structures could be designed and labour deployed so as to maximise efficiency. The humane bureaucracy stage in the development of personnel thinking was also influenced by the Human Relations School, which sought to ameliorate the potential for industrial conflict and dehumanisation present in too rigid an application of these scientific management approaches. Following the ideas of thinkers such as Elton Mayo (1880–1949), the fostering of social relationships in the workplace and employee morale thus became equally important objectives for personnel professionals seeking to raise productivity levels.

Theme 3: negotiated consent

Personnel managers next added expertise in bargaining to their repertoire of skills. In the period of full employment following the Second World War, labour became a scarce resource. This led to a growth in trade union membership and to what Allan Flanders, the leading industrial relations analyst of the 1960s, called 'the challenge from below'. Personnel specialists managed the new collective institutions such as joint consultation committees, joint production committees and suggestion schemes set up in order to accommodate the new realities. In the industries that were nationalised in the 1940s, employers were placed under a statutory duty to negotiate with unions representing employees. To help achieve this, the government encouraged the appointment of personnel officers and set up the first specialist courses for them in the universities. A personnel management advisory service was also set up at the Ministry of Labour, which still survives as the first A in ACAS (the Advisory, Conciliation and Arbitration Service).

Theme 4: organisation

The late 1960s saw a switch in focus among personnel specialists, away from dealing principally with the rank-and-file employee on behalf of management, towards dealing with management itself and the integration of managerial activity. This phase was characterised by the development of career paths and of opportunities within organisations for personal growth. This too remains a concern of HR specialists today, with a significant portion of time and resources being devoted to the recruitment, development and retention of an elite core of people with specialist expertise on whom the business depends for its future. Personnel specialists developed techniques of manpower or workforce planning. This is basically a quantitative activity, boosted by the advent of information technology, which involves forecasting an organisation's likely future skills needs and taking steps to ensure that they are met in practice.

Theme 5: human resource management

The term 'human resources' was commonly used by social scientists in contrast to 'natural resources' for much of the twentieth century (see Ginzberg 1958), and a journal called *Human Resource Management* was launched at Michigan University in 1961. But the term 'HRM' only came to be used commonly in organisations in the 1980s when courses with that name began to be offered as part of MBA programmes at leading American business schools. Before long 'HRM' replaced 'personnel management' and is now almost universally used in organisations across the world. The change of label coincided with the decline of trade union influence in many organisations and, consequently, with the seizing by managers of the opportunities that this decline gave them. Previously, across most industrialised countries, industry-level collective bargaining systems had prevailed through which terms and conditions of employment were negotiated by trade unions and employer's associations on behalf of almost everyone in the country who worked in that industry. As a result pay, along with many other rules and management policies, were the same throughout a whole industry in each country, meaning that these were not issues about which local managers could make decisions. With the decentralisation of bargaining and the rise in many industries of non-union firms, managers in the private sector found themselves free and able to develop their own, local policies and practices. Some chose to adopt a macho approach, particularly during recessionary periods when employees were in no position to resist the introduction of efficiency and cost-saving measures, leaner organisational structures and downsized workplaces. Others sought to enhance their profitability and competitiveness by seeking to gain employee commitment and by investing in their people. Either way, it was not long before organisations began to take an explicitly strategic approach to the management of human resources, setting objectives and seeking in a more proactive way to achieve these. As time went by the same kind of approaches were increasingly used in the public sector too, so that by the turn of the millennium it was the norm for organisations to employ human resource managers, officers and assistants whose aim was to add value by carrying out the four areas of activity we set out above in as efficient and effective a manner as possible. The objective, quite explicitly, was to make a major contribution to the achievement and maintenance of competitive advantage.

Theme 6: A 'new HR'?

Some writers and commentators have recently begun to argue that we are now witnessing the beginning of a new sixth stage in the evolution of personnel/HR work. While there is by no means a clear consensus about this point of view, it is notable that leading thinkers have identified a group of trends which they believe to be sufficiently dissimilar, as a bundle, from established practices to justify, at the very least, a distinct title. Bach (2005: 28–9), for example, used the term 'the new HR' to describe 'a different trajectory' which is now beginning to become discernible. Others have started using the term 'HR 2.0', likening recent developments to a new and improved edition of a software package. A number of themes are identified including a more global perspective, a tendency for issues relating to legal compliance to move up the HR management agenda and the rise of multi-employer networks which Bach calls 'permeable organisations'. Here, instead of employees having a single, readily defined employer, there may be a number of different employers, or at least more than one organisation which exercises a degree of authority over their work. Examples are found in public–private partnerships, joint ventures, franchises, situations where work is outsourced by one organisation to another, in the employment of agency workers and where strong supply chains are established consisting of smaller organisations which are wholly or very heavily reliant on the custom of a single large client corporation.

Another apparently new trajectory can be summarised as an approach to the employment relationship which views employees and potential employees very much as individuals or at least small groups rather than as a single group and which seeks to engage them emotionally. It is associated with a move away from an expectation that staff will demonstrate commitment to a set of corporate values which are determined by senior management and towards a philosophy which is far more customer-focused. Customers are defined explicitly as the ultimate employers and staff are empowered to act in such a way as to meet their requirements. This involves encouraging employees to empathise with customers, recruiting, selecting and appraising them according to their capacity to do so. In turn, and this is what seems to make 'the new HR' different from established HRM, managers are starting to refer to the staff and line managers who they 'serve' as their 'internal customers', a client group which they aim to satisfy and which they survey regularly as a means of establishing how far this aim is in fact being achieved. Another term that is becoming very much more commonly used in HR is 'strategic business partner'. The image conjured up here is of the HR manager as internal consultant, assisting clients in the achievement of their objectives and expecting to be judged on results.

The practice of viewing staff as internal customers goes further still in some organisations with the use of HR practices that borrow explicitly from the toolkit of marketing specialists (see Edwards and Bach 2013). We see this in the widespread interest in employer branding exercises (see Chapter 8) where an organisation markets itself in quite sophisticated ways, not to customers and potential customers, but to employees and potential employees.

Gratton (2004) shows how highly successful companies such as Tesco go further still in categorising job applicants and existing staff into distinct categories which summarise their principal aspirations as far as their work is concerned in much the same way that organisations seek to identify distinct market segments to use when developing, designing, packaging and marketing products and services. Such approaches aim to provide an 'employee value proposition' which it is hoped will attract the right candidates, allow the appointment of highly effective performers, motivate them to provide excellent levels of service and subsequently retain them for a longer period of time.

Lepak and Snell (2007) also note a move in HR away from 'the management of jobs' and towards 'the management of people', which includes the development of employment strategies that differ for different groups of employees. Importantly this approach recognises the capacity that most people have to become emotionally engaged in their work, with their customers, with their colleagues and hence (if to a lesser extent) with their organisations. The employment relationship is not just a transactional one in which money is earned in exchange for carrying out a set of duties competently, but is also a relational one which involves emotional attachments. The 'new HR' understands this and seeks to manage people accordingly.

Cardy *et al.* (2007) are also keen to advocate the repositioning of the HR function as one which is focused on providing services to 'internal customers' who the aim is to satisfy. Like Gratton they argue in favour of a degree of segmentation. They also take the concept of 'customer equity' long used by marketing analysts and apply it to the employment relationship, developing the notion of 'employee equity'. The argument they advance is complex, but at base they advocate thinking about employment from the perspective of the employee and to take steps which serve to:

- increase the value employees perceive that they derive from the relationship (value equity);
- improve the reputation of the organisation as an employer (brand equity);
- establish and maintain high levels of loyalty with employees (retention equity).

Saunders and Hunter (2009) adopt the same philosophy, but focus on the practicalities of transforming a traditionally-focused HR function into one which sees managers and employees at all levels as customers who the function needs to satisfy if it is to achieve its wider, longer-term objectives.

What we appear to be seeing here is a repositioning of HR thinking and activity. The aim is the same, namely to help the organisation achieve its objectives, but the means are different. Instead of simply devising and then operationalising HR strategies and policies which suit the short-term, current, financial needs of the organisation, there is an increased recognition that this cannot be done successfully over the longer term without the active engagement and support of people. In a world where many are employed because of their knowledge, in which skills that employers seek are often scarce and in which employees enjoy substantial protection from the law, there are major limits imposed on the extent of management's freedom to manage people at will. The most successful organisations are thus those which are best able to recruit good people, retain them and motivate them. This means looking after their interests and involving them as far as is possible in decision making – often using technologies that enable collaborative decision making. Hence we see the evolution of thinking based around internal customers, collaboration, partnership and employee engagement which are characteristic of the new HR trajectory.

ACTIVITY 1.2

Lynda Gratton (2004) reports that Tesco use the following five 'identities' to categorise their staff. The way that they are managed and the reward packages that are available to them can thus be tailored so as to be more appropriate to the needs and aspirations of each individual:

- work–life balancers;
- want it all;
- pleasure seekers;
- live to work;
- work to live.

Which of these categories best describes you as far as your present employment is concerned? What about friends and members of your family? Choose any two of the categories and think about in what ways it would make sense to manage people in each group differently from one another.

HRM and the achievement of organisational effectiveness

As Storey *et al.* (2009: 4) point out, unless HR activity can be shown to add value to an organisation, there is no point in devoting time and resources to it except insofar as is necessary 'to comply with prevailing employment laws or to meet minimum operational requirements in hiring, firing, labour deployment and the like'.

So for the past two decades the theme which has dominated the HR research agenda has been the study of links between HR practices and organisational effectiveness.

Two main types of research have been carried out extensively in this field:

1 The first involves establishing correlations between superior business performance as measured against a range of indicators and the presence of HR practices in thousands of organisations. Major examples of this kind of research are the studies carried out by Mark Huselid (1995) in the USA and by David Guest and his colleagues (2003) in the UK.

2 The second involves seeking to establish through interviews in successful case study organisations what factors have contributed to their growth, profitability, quality of service, etc. This type of work has been carried out by researchers such as Jeffery Pfeffer (1994, 1998) in the USA and by John Purcell in the UK.

Both streams of research have produced strong, if by no means inconclusive, evidence to suggest that organisations which adopt appropriate, sophisticated, 'good-practice' HR practices are more likely to meet their business objectives over the long term than those which do not. What these business objectives are varies from organisation to organisation and industry to industry. For major private-sector corporations the aim is to gain and maintain sustained competitive advantage. For smaller organisations in the private and voluntary sectors growth or survival are key objectives. In the public sector organisational effectiveness and meeting government targets are the key objectives defined in terms of meeting a service need as cost-efficiently as possible and to the highest achievable standard of quality. In all these situations good HR management can be shown to correlate with the achievement of core business objectives, particularly when skills are in relatively short supply or where the potential contribution made by individual employees to the success of an organisation is substantial.

What is less clear is exactly through what processes HR makes this contribution. There are a number of possibilities, none of which are mutually exclusive:

- Good management and the establishment of a positive employment relations climate means that an organisation is better able than its competitors to recruit, retain and motivate staff. Superior performance results because the best performers want to work for the organisation, because they are motivated to work hard and demonstrate commitment once employed, and because there is less resistance to change and a greater capacity to seize opportunities when they arise.

- Effective HRM alongside good management of other functions allows an organisation to develop and maintain a strong and positive corporate reputation. This enables it to raise money with relative ease when it is needed and also helps to ensure that managers of investment funds and financial advisors see it or its shares as a desirable place to put their clients' money. The maintenance of a positive reputation in the media is also an important objective as this helps to maintain and grow the customer base. A reputation for ethical management is increasingly important in this context.

- There is a big difference between the rhetoric of HRM, which is positive and people centred, and the experienced reality in many organisations. In the real world HRM is focused on reducing labour costs and extracting greater value for organisations from their human resources. This leads to the intensification of work and more efficient operations, and it is these which account for the apparent link between HRM and measures of corporate financial performance.

- The relationship between HR and business performance is in fact the other way around. The presence of a correlation does not mean that there is any causal relationship. Any HR contribution to the maintenance of superior business performance is limited. Having gained its competitive advantage, an employer has the resources to develop good HR practices.

Fleetwood and Hesketh (2010) rightly warn against uncritical acceptance of the findings of studies that link HR practices to business outcomes. Ultimately, they point out, it is the people who work in organisations who are generally responsible for the achievement of sustained superior business performance. At best all HR practices and policies can do is play 'an enabling role' in this process and in many organisations there is little evidence to suggest that the average employee's commitment or level of engagement is linked particularly closely to the formal 'architecture' of HRM.

Purcell *et al.* in 2003 and in subsequent publications also stress the inadequacy of thinking that assumes having in place a range of 'good practice' HR policies and practices will lead inexorably to the achievement of sustained, superior business performance. Their research strongly suggests that this can help, but they argue that what really makes the difference in practice are sufficient numbers of line managers who are both willing and able to give life and meaning to the policies and practices. These are the people with whom employees interact on a day-to-day basis, and unless they buy in to the ideas that underpin progressive HRM and manage their teams accordingly, the chances that well-chosen HR policies will have any serious impact on organisational performance are very limited. Purcell *et al.* (2003) point out that poor implementation of policies and practices by line managers who have not bought into them is often worse for the organisation than not having any policies at all.

The central importance of the mediating role played by line managers in the delivery of HRM was further stressed by Purcell and Hutchinson (2007) in their identification of a 'people management–performance causal chain' and by Nishii and Wright (2008) in their 'process model of HRM' (see Den Hartog and Boon 2013). Both argue that an important distinction must be made between 'intended HR practices', how these are actually perceived by employees and what impact they actually have in practice. Without effective communication and, crucially, the active support of line managers in implementing the policies, there is little chance that the desired outcomes will ever materialise. It follows that all managers in an organisation must take a good deal of responsibility for the delivery of HRM practices if they are to add value in any meaningful way.

Increasingly, others play a role too as HRM in organisations is less and less shaped by generalist HR managers alone. In larger organisations there is scope to employ people to specialise in particular areas of HRM. Some, for example, employ employee relations specialists to look after the collective relationship between management and employees and to provide advice about legal developments. Further common areas of specialisation are training and development, recruitment, reward management, and health and safety. In all these areas there is an increasing tendency for the term 'consultant' to be used instead of 'officer' or 'manager', indicating a shift towards a situation in which line managers determine the services *they* want rather than these being prescribed by a central HR function. Indeed, it is not at all uncommon nowadays for these aspects of HR work to be undertaken on behalf of organisations by subcontractors or independent consultants rather than by directly-employed HR officers.

While responsibility for making sure that HRM really does add value for an organisation rests with all managers, it typically remains the role of HR managers with a generalist remit to shape the policies and practices that are ultimately implemented. Subsequently, their job is not merely to enable, but also actively to promote the effective implementation of these practices. It may be an enabling role, but it is nonetheless a crucial one. And on the question of which types of approaches are most likely to underpin superior business performance, the research that has been carried out over the last twenty years is fairly conclusive. The need, quite simply, is for organisations to achieve the core HR objectives described above more effectively than their competitors are able to. When this is achieved the result tends to be high levels of trust, a strong sense of shared purpose and an enhanced capacity for recruiting, retaining, motivating and engaging an excellent workforce that is both willing and able to adapt to changed circumstances when necessary. Purcell *et al.* (2003), like other researchers, stress the role that a bundle of progressive HR practices can play in bringing about these outcomes (Figure 1.1):

- giving people career development opportunities;
- giving people influence over their own area of work;
- making jobs challenging and interesting;
- providing good training;
- appraising people regularly on their individual performance;
- teamworking;

Figure 1.1
HRM roles and
objectives

- involving employees in decision making;
- providing a good work–life balance;
- employing line managers 'who are good at leadership and who show respect'.

A further potential contribution made by the HR function involves recognising the significance of the organisation's people as an effective barrier preventing would-be rivals from expanding their markets into territory that your organisation holds. The term 'human capital' is more and more used in this context to signify that the combined knowledge and experience of an organisation's staff are a highly significant source of competitive advantage largely because they are difficult for competitors to replicate easily. Attracting, engaging, rewarding, developing and retaining people effectively is thus vital. Failing to do so enables accumulated human capital to leak away into the hands of competitors, reducing the effectiveness of commercial defences and making it harder to maintain competitive advantage.

SUMMARY PROPOSITIONS

1.1. It is possible to identify two distinct definitions of the term 'human resource management'. The first describes a body of management activities, while the second signifies a particular approach to carrying out those activities.

1.2. HR managers are concerned with meeting five distinct sets of organisational objectives: staffing, performance, change management, administration and reputation.

> 1.3. HRM activities are carried out in various ways through various forms of organisational structure. In some larger organisations HR generalists work alongside specialists in particular HR disciplines.

1.4. HRM can be characterised as one of the more recent in a series of incarnations that personnel practitioners have developed since the origins of the profession over 100 years ago.

1.5. The HRM function contributes to the achievement of different dimensions of organisational effectiveness. Prominent are the gaining and maintaining of competitive advantage, the fostering of a positive standing in financial markets and the development of a reputation for corporate social responsibility.

GENERAL DISCUSSION TOPICS

1. What are the major advantages and disadvantages associated with HR managers seeing employees as 'internal customers' who need to be satisfied?

2. How far do you agree with the view that an HR function which achieves administrative excellence adds value to an organisation just as much as one which focuses on improving its employees' performance?

3. To what extent is your organisation successful in translating its 'intended HR outcomes' into 'actual HR outcomes'? What could it do to make it more successful?

THEORY INTO PRACTICE

The following is an opinion piece by the business writer Bernard Marr. In it the author puts a case against typical HRM departments.

Why we no longer need HR departments

The time has come for HR (Human Resources) departments to call it a day. HR departments often portray themselves as a valued business partner for management and staff alike. However, how can anyone take a department seriously that refers to people as 'resources'?

Nothing matters more to companies than the people who work there. Companies are nothing without the right people! And I am sure that not one, single individual wants to be referred to as a 'human resource'.

So, the first point I want to make is that the name is wrong: very wrong. It signals to everyone that *this* department manages 'human resources' in a top-down fashion, i.e. managing humans in a similar way to other resources such as finance, property or machines. If departments can't see that this is sending out the wrong messages, then they don't deserve to be there anyway.

➤ Another issue is that HR departments are trying to serve two masters – which, in most cases, is not very successful. On the one hand, they are there to provide support for the employees and, on the other hand, they are there for the company and the senior management to help manage (and monitor, discipline, appraise, etc.) employees. This conflict of interest can cause friction and in many instances HR departments swing to the 'support the company' side, rather than the 'support the employees' side.

There is more. We can argue about whether the name is right or wrong, or whether the focus should be on the company or on the employees, but what really matters is whether HR delivers value. I have recently seen a number of companies that shut their HR departments down completely; outsourced the function or reduced it to a minimum. The reason they have done it, and not suffered any significant throw-back, is because HR wasn't delivering any real value. Most of their time was taken up with bureaucratic and administrative tasks or legal issues. If HR doesn't deliver some unique benefits then outsourcing it makes a lot of business sense.

Other companies, however, have invested in the 'people function'. They realize that they need people who ensure that the company finds, recruits, retains and develops its people. So here is what I recommend:

1 Don't call it HR!

2 Put two teams in place: a *'people analytics' team* and a *'people support' team*.

3 The role of the *people support team* is, as the title suggests, supporting all employees in the organization – from the front line to the senior leadership team. The tasks of this team include: helping employees with their development; ensuring staff engagement; identifying issues with morale and culture and generally looking after the well-being of the people in the business.

4 The role of the *people analytics team* is to look at people more scientifically and support the company with insights and analytics. The kind of questions this team would help to answer includes: What are our talent gaps? What makes a good employee in our company and how do we best recruit them? Which employees have got the highest potential? How can we predict staff turnover? Etc.

5 Outsource or automate the non-value adding part of HR.v

Questions

1 What is the essence of Bernard Marr's case against HR departments and common HR practices?

2 Many of the criticisms of HRM expressed in this article are commonly held by managers in organisations. Why do you think this?

3 What arguments could be deployed to counteract the major points Mr Marr makes?

4 What is your view of the alternative approach that is set out in the second part of the article?

Source: www.linkedin.com/pulse/20131118060732-64875646-why-we-no-longer-need-hr-departments.

FURTHER READING

Legge, K. (1995) *Human Resource Management: Rhetorics and Realities*. London: Macmillan.

This seminal book provides a rigorous discussion of the differences between personnel management and HRM, as well as introducing and considering a series of other debates about the nature of HRM and its purpose for organisations.

Withers, M., Williamson, M. and Reddington, M. (2010) *Transforming HR: Creating Value through People*. Oxford: Butterworth–Heinemann/Elsevier.

A very accessible book which develops many of the themes we have introduced in this chapter, going on to explore the particular contribution the HR function can make in the contemporary business environment.

'Human Resource management and Performance' by Paul Boselie (2013), in *HRM & Performance: Achievements and Challenges,* edited by Jaap Paauwe, David Guest and Patrick Wright.

Boselie's chapter sums up most effectively the current state of ongoing research into the extent and nature of the link between HRM activity and the achievement of superior business performance. Paauwe *et al.* examine the same issues at much greater length in their recent book.

REFERENCES

Bach, S. (2005) 'Personnel management in transition', in S. Bach (ed.), *Managing Human Resources: Personnel Management in Transition* (4th edn.). Oxford: Blackwell.

BBC (2008a) 'BA's terminal losses top £16 million', BBC News Website, 3 April.

BBC (2008b) 'What did go wrong at Terminal 5?', BBC News Website, 30 March.

Blitz, R. (2008) 'The trouble with great expectations', *Financial Times,* 26 March.

Boselie, P. (2013) 'Human resource management and performance', in S. Bach and M. Edwards (eds), *Managing Human Resources* (5th edn.). Chichester: Wiley.

Cardy R., Miller, J. and Ellis, A. (2007) 'Employee equity: Toward a person-based approach to HRM', *Human Resource Management Review,* Vol. 17, pp. 140–51.

Den Hartog, D. and Boon, C. (2013) 'HRM and Leadership', in S. Bach and M. Edwards (eds), *Managing Human Resources* (5th edn.). Chichester: Wiley.

Done, K. and Willman, J. (2008) 'Goodwill of staff is often in short supply', *Financial Times,* 5 April.

Edwards, M. and Bach, S. (2013) 'Human resource management in transition', in S. Bach and M. Edwards (eds), *Managing Human Resources* (5th edn.). Chichester: Wiley.

Fleetwood, S. and Hesketh, A. (2010) *Explaining the Performance of Human Resource Management*. Cambridge: Cambridge University Press.

Ginzberg, E. (1958) *Human Resources: The Wealth of a Nation*. New York: Simon & Schuster.

Gratton, L. (2004) *The Democratic Enterprise: Liberating Your Business with Freedom, Flexibility and Commitment*. Harlow: Pearson Education.

Guest, D.E. (1987) 'Human resource management and industrial relations', *Journal of Management Studies,* Vol. 24, No. 5.

Guest D.E. Micie, J., Conway, N. and Sheehan, M. (2003) 'Human resource management and corporate performance in the UK', *British Journal of Industrial Relations,* Vol. 41, No. 2, pp. 291–314.

Huselid, M. (1995) 'The impact of human resource management practices on turnover, productivity and corporate financial performance', *Academy of Management Journal,* Vol. 38, No. 3.

Johnson, L. (2008) 'The truth about the HR department', *Financial Times,* 29 January.

Klikauer, T. (2014) *Seven moralities of human resource management.* Basingstoke: Palgrave.

Lawler, E. and Boudreau, J. (2015) *Global Trends in Human Resource Management: A Twenty Year Analysis.* California: Stanford University Press.

Legge, K. (1995) *Human Resource Management: Rhetorics and Realities.* London: Macmillan.

Lepak, D. and Snell, S.A. (2007) 'Employment sub-systems and the HR architecture', in P. Boxall, J. Purcell and P. Wright (eds), *The Oxford Handbook of Human Resource Management.* Oxford: Oxford University Press.

Nishii, L. and Wright, P. (2008) 'Variability within organizations: Implications for strategic human resource management', in D. Brent Smith (ed), *The People Make the Place: Dynamic Linkages between Individuals and Organizations.* New York: Taylor and Francis.

Patterson, M.G., West, M.A., Lawthom, R. and Nickell, S. (1998), 'Impact of people management practices on business performance', *Issues in People Management,* No. 22. London: IPD.

Paauwe, J., Guest, D. and Wright, P. (eds) (2013) *HRM and Performance: Achievements and Challenges.* Chichester: Wiley.

Pfeffer, J. (1994) *Competitive Advantage through People.* Boston: Harvard Business School Press.

Pfeffer, J. (1998) *The Human Equation.* Boston: Harvard University Press.

Pinnington A., Macklin, R. and Campbell, T. (eds) (2007) *Human Resource Management: Ethics and Employment.* Oxford: Oxford University Press.

Purcell, J., Kinnie, N., Hutchinson, S., Rayton, B. and Swart, J. (2003) *Understanding the People and Performance Link: Unlocking the Black Box.* London: CIPD.

Purcell, J. and Hutchinson, S. (2007) 'Front-line managers as agents in the HRM-performance causal chain: theory, analysis and evidence', *Human Resource Management Journal,* Vol. 17, No. 1, pp. 3–20.

Ross, A. (2016) *The Industries of the Future.* New York: Simon & Schuster.

Saunders, J. and Hunter, I. (2009) *Led Design: Planning the New HR Function.* London: Gower.

Stevens, J. (ed) (2005) *Managing Risk: The Human Resources Contribution.* London: LexisNexis Butterworths.

Storey, J., Ulrich, D. and Wright, P. (2009) 'Introduction', in J. Storey, D. Ulrich and P. Wright (eds), *The Routledge Companion to Strategic Human Resource Management.* London: Routledge.

UKCES (2012) *Working Futures 2010–2020: Evidence Report 41.* UK Commission for Employment and Skills.

Withers, M., Williamson, M. and Reddington, M. (2010) *Transforming HR: Creating Value through People* (2nd edn.). London: Butterworth Heinemann/Elsevier.

CHAPTER 2
THE GLOBAL CONTEXT FOR HUMAN RESOURCE MANAGEMENT

THE OBJECTIVES OF THIS CHAPTER ARE TO:

1 Define and account for the development of globalisation
2 Set out the significance of globalisation for industry and the labour market
3 Examine the major consequences of globalisation for HRM
4 Explain why the global business environment is characterised by increasing uncertainty, volatility and unpredictability

In 2008 the UK economy, like those of most western industrialised countries, entered the sharpest and most prolonged downturn we had experienced since the 1930s. In an eighteen-month period our economy contracted by 6%, after which the recovery was slow and hesitant. At the time of writing (early 2016) the UK economy is growing steadily again and is slightly bigger than it was before the recession. Unemployment is falling, but productivity is poor, while debt levels remain high. There remains an underlying lack of confidence in the business community reflecting doubts about the world's future economic security. While prospects are looking good for some economies (e.g. the USA, Canada and India), growth remains low elsewhere (e.g. Japan and Northern Europe) and is slowing in China. Elsewhere many more serious economic difficulties are being faced due to sharp reductions in oil, gas and other commodity prices (e.g. Russia and Brazil) and continued financial problems in the most heavily indebted Eurozone countries such as Spain, Portugal and Greece. Meanwhile, political instability across much of the Middle East is creating further economic apprehension. In short, no one can be at all confident about what now lies ahead for the world economy.

Uncertainty and unpredictability are, however, nothing new. Long before our most recent economic travails they had long established themselves as dominant features of the evolving context in which organisations do business. And looking forward, even without the intervention of that unwelcome downturn in the fortunes of the world economy, it was always likely that the global business environment would become increasingly volatile for several decades to come. In this chapter our aim is to explain why this is the case and to set out what the key consequences are for the management of the HR function in organisations. At the same time we will introduce some other significant, long-term and well-established trends in the business environment – all linked to globalisation – which together are tending to make HR work more challenging.

Globalisation

The term 'globalisation' tends to be used in rather different ways by different people depending on their perspective (Scholte 2005). For some, it can be used interchangeably with the term 'internationalisation' to signify in general terms an increase in cross-border relations between peoples and governments. From this perspective the trend towards greater globalisation simply means the development of more international exchange and greater interdependence. Others see 'globalisation' as representing a more profound development. It is more than increased international activity, instead being used to signify a new development best described as 'international economic integration'. It is thus seen as representing a process of movement away from a world economic system which is dominated by national and regional economies for the most part trading internally, to one in which pretty well anyone based anywhere across the globe can sell things to anyone else. A third definition stresses universalism, by which is meant a dilution of national identity and separateness as people of all backgrounds increasingly share a similar global culture and set of aspirations, buy the same products and live under similar types of governmental and economic system. A fourth definition sees globalisation as Americanisation, sometimes conceived as the development of an American global empire. It thus focuses on the significance of capitalism, western-style representative government, liberalism, bureaucracy and rationalism in the establishment of a 'new world order'. The growing international power of US-based corporations is also often stressed by those who adopt this perspective. A fifth characterisation stresses a change in our perceptions of distance. Globalisation, according to this definition, is about the world becoming 'smaller' due to modern transportation and communications technologies which allow readier and much more affordable contact between people across national borders. For the purposes of thinking about the evolving global business environment it is helpful not to have any single definition of the term 'globalisation' in mind, but instead to accept that a variety of significant trends are observable and that they are having a differential impact on the lives of different people. 'Globalisation' is thus best conceived of as an umbrella term covering a variety of developments.

It is not possible to say when globalisation started because a degree of international economic exchange has been carried on for many centuries. Some argue that before the First World War economies such as the UK's were more globally integrated than they are in the modern era (Wes 1996: 5), but most agree that the process of globalisation that we observe today properly got going in the decades after 1945 as the Western countries recovered from the Second World War and steadily transformed into much more affluent, consumer-oriented societies. They started to trade more and more with one another and to welcome investment in their economies by overseas-based corporations. This period also saw the rapid rise of economies such as those of Japan, Taiwan, South Korea, Hong Kong and Singapore, expanding the number of consumers who were in a position to participate in international economic exchange. There was then a big acceleration after 1990 following the fall of the Berlin wall, the rise of capitalism in China, the adoption of a more western-oriented economic policy in India, the very rapid development of some economies in the Middle East, and the move towards liberal democratic forms of governance in South Africa and across much of South America. The full integration of these economies into the world trading system brought about its transformation – a process that is still very much ongoing (see Dicken 2015 for an excellent account of this process). At the same time across much of the industrialised world, governments adopted more liberal trading regimes and started to promote much more competition in their home markets.

The practical consequences of these trends have been huge. First, since 1950 world output has increased six-fold, while world trade has increased over twenty-fold, meaning that the proportion of goods and services which are exported and consumed in countries other from that in which they originate has increased very markedly. Annual export growth across the world is now running at three to four times greater than the growth in world output. Second, we have seen unprecedented growth in levels of foreign direct investment (FDI) through which a corporation based in one country sets up operations overseas or acquires an existing overseas operation. FDI has grown even faster than international trade. This too is a long-term trend which saw great acceleration in the 1990s, since when FDI has grown annually at a faster rate than international trade and a much much faster rate than international output. Third, we are living through a period in which the amount of overseas travel, both for business and pleasure, has increased at unprecedented levels, making the travel industry by some margin the biggest and fastest-growing industry in the world. In 1954 the number of passengers going through UK airports was just 4 million. By 1974 it had reached 45 million, by 1984, 57 million and by 1994, 98 million. In 2015 the total number of passengers using UK airports was over 240 million (Civil Aviation Authority 2015). Internationally the rate of growth has been more spectacular still. The number of air passengers rose from just 9 million in 1945, to 88 million in 1972 and to 344 million in 1994. The International Air Transport Association reports that the figure topped 3.5 billion in 2015 and predicts that it will reach 7 billion by 2034 (IATA 2015).

Alongside increased international economic exchange, recent decades have also seen significant increases in migration across national boundaries. According to United Nations (UN) estimates, in 2015, there were 244 million people living long term in a country other than the one they were born in, compared to just 81.5 million in 1970. These figures probably represent a considerable underestimate because a great deal of cross-border migration is illegal in nature and so does not get recorded in the official statistics that governments collect, but they nonetheless demonstrate how much more likely people are now to move overseas than used to be the case, even when world population rises are taken into account (Goldin *et al.* 2011). The impact has been far greater in some regions than in others as migration is by no means spread evenly across the globe: 75% of all international migrants live in just 28 countries, over 20% of the total settling in the USA, while a further 30% live in the European Union countries. This means that organisations are much more likely to employ multicultural teams of staff in some areas than in others. For example, while over 12% of the population of Western Europe originates overseas, this is true of less than 2% of the Eastern European population. The biggest immigrant populations are found in the Gulf countries where people born overseas make up a majority of the total population in some cases (Bahrain 55%, Kuwait 70% and Qatar 74%). As a proportion of the workforce in these countries, migrants account for even larger shares. In the UAE, in 2013, 83.7% of the workforce was born overseas. Elsewhere immigration levels are very much lower. In Indonesia, Vietnam and China for example, only 0.1% of the population is made up by overseas immigrants, while in India it is just 0.4% (United Nations 2013).

GLOBALISATION AND THE UK

The UK has been affected by globalisation more than most countries for a range of reasons. First, thanks to its history as a major imperial and maritime power, the UK has long-established the habit of trading internationally and operating globally. UK industries have thus had to make less adjustment culturally in order to embrace some of the consequences of globalisation such as competing on an equal footing with overseas-based corporations. Second, the UK (along with the Republic of Ireland) has benefited greatly from being for the most part English-speaking at a time when English has firmly established itself as the language of international business, while also providing international investors with access to the European Single Market. This, combined with a relatively favourable tax regime, more limited business regulation and a preference for free trade arrangements has helped to attract a great deal of FDI. Over 20% of all FDI coming into the European Union from overseas now comes into the UK (Ernst and Young 2012). UK-based companies are also among the biggest foreign investors in the world. They invest more in the USA than those of any other country as well as being the second largest foreign investors globally after the USA. Overall, over 8.2% of world FDI is carried out by UK companies (UNCTAD 2012). The UK has also long been a destination which overseas migrants want to come to. Net inward migration has topped 200,000 in almost all of the past twenty years, making parts of the country very diverse in terms of the population's cultural background. The population of London is increasing by over 10,000 every month. Over 25% of the babies now born in England each year have mothers who were themselves born overseas, while the figure for London reached 56% in 2011 (ONS 2012).

The causes of globalisation

One of the major debates about globalisation concerns its origins. Why did we start thinking and acting globally in the second half of the twentieth century and not earlier, and why, in particular have we seen such an acceleration in the past two decades? While there is much disagreement about the significance of particular developments, it is generally agreed that different, interrelated factors have combined together to facilitate the change. Of these, two stand out as being particularly significant: technological developments and government policy.

Technology

There are two major areas of technological development which have made globalisation possible: transportation and information and communications technologies (ICTs), principally by bringing down very substantially both the costs associated with international communication and trade, and the time they take. Dicken (2015) notes that until the past 100 years, to all intents and purposes, communications and transportation technologies were one and the same. Their separation through telegraph, telephone, radio and now digital satellite thus represents one of the most extraordinary achievements of the twentieth century. Transportation was as slow 200 years ago as it was 2000 years ago. Since then a number of technological advances have transformed our ability to ship people, goods, raw materials and ideas around the world. The nineteenth century saw the arrival of steam power, enabling the development of trains and bigger, faster, ocean-going ships. These drove the development of international economic exchange in the years prior to the First World War. The early twentieth century then saw the development of the internal combustion engine, the arrival of the motor car and, in consequence, the speeding up of ships and trains. The late 1950s saw two major transport developments that have been major facilitators of globalisation:

1 The development of large commercial jet aircraft able to carry people and goods across the world at previously unimaginable speeds.

2 Containerisation (i.e. the use worldwide of standard-sized steel containers that can be easily and quickly shifted by crane from lorries, to trains and on to ships).

ICTs, by contrast, have transformed our ability to transmit information in the years since then. The big breakthroughs here have been the evolution of satellite communications technology since the 1960s, of fibre-optic cables since the 1970s, and of course the World Wide Web and internet technologies since the 1980s. Together these have given people, as well as organisations, the capacity to transmit very substantial quantities of information (now including video and sound as well as text) almost instantly to every corner of the world very affordably. Therefore, it is now not only possible for a consumer in the UK to find out about the existence of, say, a furniture manufacturer in Vietnam, but also to download detailed colour brochures, to order bespoke items and even to watch them being manufactured in real time. Moreover, the speed of container ships now permits delivery from Vietnam to the customer's home less than a month after the original order was placed.

Government action

Commentators often point to deregulation as being the other major driver of globalisation alongside technology. They are referring here to the liberalisation of the world trading and economic system over recent years. However, as Dicken (2015) argues strongly, it is important to understand that globalisation has also been accelerated by a good degree of additional regulation in the form of cross-national standardisation in different fields (40 ft containers for transportation, customs documentation, air traffic control conventions, accounting standards, insurance rules, global patents, etc.). Moreover, the establishment of international property rights across most countries has hugely helped to promote FDI.

Nonetheless, it is unquestionably true that a major impetus for increased international trade has been the abandonment or relaxation in recent years of foreign exchange controls and by reductions in the strength and size of tariff regimes aimed at stifling global free trade. We have also seen a strong trend across much of the world away from forms of socialist and communist governance towards forms of liberal democracy. As far as economic policy is concerned, the result has been a great deal less direct state intervention in business activity, a tendency to privatise and to deregulate markets, and a preference on the part of governments across the world actively to encourage competition between businesses while also encouraging entrepreneurship.

The impact of globalisation

It is no exaggeration to claim that globalisation processes of the kind we have described above have utterly transformed the environment in which the vast majority of business is conducted. Moreover, it is unquestionably the case that further transformation will occur in the future, not least in the world's established geo-political balance as economic power steadily transfers from west to east. We only have space here to discuss some of the more apparent, direct effects of these profound developments, concentrating in particular on those which have the greatest implications for the management of people.

Competition

It is notoriously difficult to measure the extent of competition in an industry in any objective or satisfactory manner, and hence impossible accurately to track growth or decline in competitiveness over time. This is because industries vary so much in terms of their competitive structures. You might think that the number of firms in competition would be a good measure on the basis that the more players there are in the competition, the tougher it is to do well. This is, however, over-simplistic as some of the most cut-throat markets in the world are dominated by just two or three companies. We thus have a situation in which all informed opinion agrees that trading conditions in most economies have become hugely more competitive in recent years, but there is no way of measuring whether the change has doubled, tripled or increased twenty-fold over the past few decades. Instead economists use a series of different measures which each act, some more satisfactorily than others, as proxies for measures of competitive intensity. Examples are as follows:

- reductions in the length of time leading firms are able to maintain dominance of a market;
- increases in the extent of churn in 'industry membership';
- increases in the incidence of financial instability (among both established and newer entrants to a market);
- increases in the length of time that episodes of financial instability last;
- increases in the extent to which a market is open to overseas competitors;
- increases in the number of small businesses/start-ups, and increases in their growth rates;
- increases in concentration ratios (i.e. the extent to which the top five or top ten companies in an industry contribute to its total output);
- increases in the extent of 'discounting' – i.e. price reductions;
- decreases in 'perceived ability to increase prices' as measured in surveys of executives.

Against all these measures, while the extent of change varies greatly, the majority of industries both in the UK and across the world can be judged to have become very substantially more competitively intensive over the past thirty years, much of the increase being experienced in the most recent years (McNamara *et al*. 2003).

There is no question that globalisation has played a major role in creating more competitive commercial conditions simply by increasing several-fold the number of potential competitors any one organisation faces. Established organisations that once dominated national markets now find themselves to be relative small-fry in an expanding and much less predictable global market. Indeed, in recent years a number of academics and consultants have advanced the view that the competitive environment in some industries is not just reaching a new level of intensity, but is developing in a qualitatively different direction than has been the case in the past. The term 'hyper-competition' is increasingly used in this context; another term that is sometimes used is 'high-velocity competition' (Adcroft *et al*. 2010, Chew and Osborne 2009). In conditions of hyper-competition, turbulence and unpredictability are the norm, so that firms which gain competitive advantage find that it is rapidly eroded by the changing business environment. Competitive advantage thus becomes transitory in nature, requiring organisations that wish to grow to continually 'reinvent the wheel' or 'ride the wave of innovation'.

Hyper-competitiveness conditions are most readily observed in the finance, manufacturing, IT and biotechnology industries. But more generally, all organisations with any kind of exposure to international competition are finding it harder either to gain or sustain any kind of competitive advantage or to maintain a high level of profitability. In many cases survival has also become increasingly hard to guarantee.

Organisations thus have to develop strategies to cope effectively. For example, they have to continually seek ways of increasing the efficiency with which they conduct their operations, keeping a lid on costs while ensuring sufficient investment in value-producing activities. There is also an increased requirement accurately to anticipate future environmental developments as well as customer tastes and preferences in order to stay ahead of their competitors. Additional competition also requires companies to drive technological advances themselves through appropriate research and development (R&D) activity, to enter and exit markets with greater frequency and to participate in more merger and acquisition activity in order to generate economies of scale.

A number of the more significant contemporary issues and developments in the HR field derive directly from increased competitive intensity in product markets. Examples are the following, all of which we return to discuss at length later in the text:

1 The need to run the HR function in as efficient a manner as possible. The growth of the shared-services model, as well as HR outsourcing, is a result. The increased emphasis on measuring HR outcomes and progress against quantitative targets is another.

2 A capacity to recruit, retain and motivate high performers becomes increasingly significant the more competitive an industry becomes. The firms which gain and maintain exclusive access to the best brains are best placed to survive and thrive.

3 Increased competition tends to dampen wage demands, but in any event, produces a situation in which the capacity to increase pay is increasingly limited. Positive motivation, as well as the attraction and retention of staff, thus has to be achieved through different means. This is leading to an increased focus on the relational aspects of the employment experience and a reduced focus on transactional aspects.

4 Growing competitiveness means that it is more necessary to maintain high standards of quality and of customer service. This means meeting customer expectations, if possible surpassing them, and treating them as individuals rather than as a mass. To achieve this it is necessary to treat employees in such a way as to elicit high levels of effort and performance. This requires more attention to be given to job satisfaction and to employee engagement so that employees feel both valued and committed.

Industrial restructuring

Over the past sixty years, the trend accelerating in more recent years, most economies in the world have restructured profoundly in response to globalisation. Put simply, agrarian economies have become industrial economies, while established industrial economies have largely become service-based and knowledge-based. This has rarely been a matter of choice. Instead, in order to maintain growth, economies have increasingly had to focus on industrial activities in which they have a particular competitive advantage of some kind. The UK is a good example of a country that has restructured profoundly in response to globalisation, experiencing what amounts to a second Industrial Revolution over the past three or four decades. The adjustment has often been very uncomfortable as our economy has moved in a generation from one which was largely based on manufacturing prowess to one which is now dominated by service industries.

The key long-term trends are shown in Figure 2.1. This shows how during the period known as 'the Industrial Revolution' the proportion of UK output devoted to agriculture fell hugely as farming became more efficient, the population grew and became urbanised. Until the 1960s the manufacturing sector continued to grow and accounted for a very substantial proportion of the economy. Since then growth has been focused on the service sector, which now accounts for over 80% of both output and jobs.

The UK's shift in balance from manufacturing to services is typical of all the major western industrialised countries, although the process has been notably faster, and has gone further, in the UK than in most other EU member states and in the USA. The trend is almost entirely explained by the globalisation of the world economy. Quite simply it has become far cheaper to manufacture most products overseas in low-wage economies and to ship them to the big consumer markets than it is to manufacture them close to the consumer. The same is true of mined goods and agricultural products. The manufacture

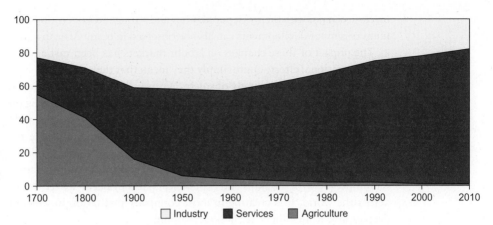

Figure 2.1
Proportion of the UK workforce employed in different sectors

of lower cost goods is no longer profitable in the UK because the sources of raw materials are distant and because labour costs are relatively high. It has also become cheaper for UK consumers to import much of our food from overseas rather than to grow it here.

In place of the mass production of manufactured goods, the UK economy like many others has had to adjust so that it specialises in the provision of services for which there is demand elsewhere in the world. Hence, in recent decades as traditional manufacturing and agriculture have become less significant, the following industries have grown:

- financial services
- business services
- creative and cultural industries
- higher education
- research/science
- tourism
- hi-tech manufacturing
- sports and leisure
- retailing
- restaurants/bars
- IT
- construction/engineering

Profound restructuring is also occurring across the developing world. Here we are seeing shifts of a similar nature to those experienced during the first Industrial Revolution in the UK. Agrarian economies in which most people work on the land producing food are becoming industrial economies, manufacturing goods which are sold all over the world. The key difference this time is in the speed with which developing economies are transforming themselves. They are also, in many cases, fast moving beyond the manufacture of cheaper manufactured goods into hi-tech, high value-added manufacturing and service provision. In the 1950s and 1960s Japan led the way, closely followed by other 'tiger economies' such as Hong Kong, South Korea, Singapore and Taiwan. These are now among the wealthiest nations in the world. We are currently seeing a similar transformation of the massive Chinese economy, which is truly now the centre of world manufacturing. Brazil, India and many other countries are following on close behind, with their vast populations and strong rates of economic growth. The beginnings of similar developments can also be observed in many African nations.

The impact of these changes on labour markets has been vast and continues to have a transformational effect. Quite simply they mean that the established stock of skills among a people becomes increasingly obsolete. We are all having to learn new ways of earning a living, and often having to relearn another set of skills later in life again. The process of industrial restructuring is thus a very painful one for many people, and indeed for whole communities. The skills that used to make people highly employable are increasingly not required. Established industries have less and less demand for people all the time as they decline and introduce labour-saving technologies, while newer industries often struggle to recruit people with the skills and experience that they need. We see this process happening across the world. It is creating in most countries a situation in which some skills are in over-supply, while others are in under-supply.

This has some deeply worrying social effects, as it leads inexorably to far greater levels of inequality. Goos and Manning (2007) and Goos et al. (2009) have argued in highly influential articles that labour markets in the UK and across Europe are increasingly assuming an hourglass shape as they become more polarised between higher and lower skills. In brief, they argue that the following is happening:

- Increasing numbers of people are being employed in relatively highly paid, secure, professional and managerial occupations in the finance, private services and some parts of the public sector.

- Jobs in manufacturing along with many clerical and administrative roles are being 'exported' to countries in Eastern Europe, to China, India and other developing economies where cheaper labour is readily available.

- At the same time, the growing number of higher paid people are using their disposable income to purchase services which cannot be provided from overseas. Hence the simultaneous and rapid growth in demand for hairdressers, beauticians, restaurant workers, and people to work in tourist and entertainment-oriented industries. These jobs tend to be lower paid.

The net impact is easy to appreciate. In the top half of the hourglass are people with skills that are in demand from the expanding industries. Here, over the long term, there are more jobs available than there are people who are appropriately qualified to fill them. The result is a relatively tight labour market in which skills shortages are relatively common, leading to upward pressure on wages and to desirable terms and conditions of employment. In short, employers have to pay well and to treat people well in order to attract and retain them. By contrast, in the bottom half of the hourglass things are very different. There are more people looking for jobs than there are jobs available. Wages are thus being pushed downwards, while employers get away with treating people poorly, employing them on terms which are undesirable. These trends can be traced back to the 1970s in the case of the UK and are clearly associated with the industrial restructuring that our economy has undergone in response to globalisation in the years since then. But the same processes are observable around the world as the new skills sought by economies are nearly always in shorter supply than those sought in the past. This is why, for example, there are major shortages of appropriately-qualified managerial staff in China (Cooke 2005: 175), skilled factory workers in South Africa (Wood 2011: 308, 317), academics in India (Thankachan et al. 2010) and medical staff in a great many developing countries (Koser 2007: 52).

SKILLS SHORTAGES IN THE UK

The Chartered Institute of Personnel and Development's (CIPD) annual surveys on recruitment report that throughout the past fifteen years a good majority of respondents work in organisations that are facing 'recruitment difficulties due to skills shortages':

2002:	77%	2007:	84%	2012:	82%
2003:	93%	2008:	86%	2013:	60%
2004:	85%	2009:	81%	2014:	78%
2005:	85%	2010:	68%	2015:	76%
2006:	82%	2011:	75%		

There is every reason to expect these to continue in the future, and if anything to worsen. This is for two main reasons:

1 The capacity of the UK's education and training system to furnish the workforce with the skills that the evolving economy requires is proving to be limited. All the growth as far as jobs are concerned is in the specialised, higher-level professional and managerial categories. Yet the UK still has a situation in which only a minority of young people go on to university courses after leaving school and in which vast numbers leave school either without any qualifications at all, or else with only very limited proficiency in science, maths and English. *The Leitch Report* (2006) characterised the UK's performance on skills development as 'mediocre' by international standards, while projecting a situation in which over 40% of jobs will require either a degree or a further degree by 2020.

2 In the past fifty years the supply of skills has kept pace with increasing demand thanks chiefly to three key developments in the UK labour market: the entry into the workforce of many more women (female participation has risen from 42% in 1950 to over 75% today), the presence in the workforce of the unusually large 'baby-boom generation' consisting of people born between 1945 and 1965, and substantial net inward migration from overseas. All three of these sources of labour supply are now beginning to dry up somewhat. Female participation levels are now almost as high in the UK as they are anywhere in the world, reducing the prospects for further expansion. The baby-boom generation, meanwhile, has begun to retire, requiring employers to source skills from the far smaller generation Y that is now being educated to provide them: 17.6 million people were born in the UK between 1945 and 1964, compared to just 14.8 million between 1985 and 2004. Finally of course we are seeing increasingly active attempts by government to curb the extent of net inward migration into the UK. The number of skilled and highly skilled entrants from outside the EU is already subject to a monthly cap, the aim being radically to reduce the numbers entering by tens of thousands each year. In due course, as a result of 'Brexit', reduced migration from the EU is also likely to occur.

The rise of multinational corporations

A multinational organisation is generally defined as one which is clearly based in a home country but which owns assets overseas. This is different from an organisation that operates internationally by exporting and importing products or services, but which does not own any overseas assets. Multinationals are also often distinguished from transnational corporations which operate internationally but are not run from or necessarily originate in any one country. There are plenty of multinational corporations (MNCs). Vodaphone is an example of a major British multinational. While based in the UK, the vast majority of its assets are overseas, as are its staff (85,000 of its 101,000 employees are based outside the UK).

As we explained above, FDI is the term that is used for a situation in which a company based in one country purchases assets in other countries. The United Nations Agency for Trade and Development (UNCTAD) publishes annual estimates of the total value of FDI across the world. They have been using the same methodology since 1980, allowing us to track the huge extent of its growth over the past thirty years, including a rapid acceleration in more recent years. Once inflation is taken into account, UNCTAD calculates the total value of FDI stock to have been worth just over $700 billion in 1980. By 1990 the figure had tripled to $2.1 trillion and by 2000 had reached $7.4 trillion. Their last published estimates in 2012 valued the total value of world FDI at $20.4 trillion, since when there have been further significant increases (UNCTAD 2012). The past thirty-five years have thus seen a thirty-fold increase in total FDI.

These figures illustrate the sheer scale of the rise of multinational organisations in recent years. Many now have combined assets that are worth more than the gross domestic products of small countries. The company with the largest amount of foreign assets in the world at present is BNP Paribas, the French banking corporation. Its total assets are estimated by UNCTAD to be worth nearly $2.9 trillion. It operates in 75 countries and employs over 180,000 people. Other banks are not far behind, including the UK's largest banking group HSBC Holdings PLC with its $2.7 trillion of worldwide assets, 48 million customers and 268,343 employees across 72 countries. *Forbes,* the American Business Journal, compiles a list of the biggest companies in the world as measured by an index which includes sales, profits, assets and overall market value. The top places are dominated by multinational banks and oil companies. But what is most interesting about the *Forbes* list is the way that it changes from year to year, allowing us to observe the key trends. In 2006, the top ten contained six American-owned companies, one Japanese company (Toyota), one from Germany (DaimlerChrysler), one from the UK (BP) and Dutch Shell. Of these none are still in the top ten today. Back then there were four car manufacturers in the top ten, there are now only four in the top 50. Another major recent trend is the rise up the list of the giant Chinese banking and oil corporations. They hardly featured in the upper echelons of the *Forbes* list ten years ago when there were only twelve listed in the top 500. There are now 53 Chinese companies in the top 500, including five of the top ten. In the same period the number of Indian companies in the top 500 has grown from one to eleven. In total, in 2006 out of the biggest 500, 430 were based in the USA, Europe or Japan. Ten years later 118 are based elsewhere in the world.

Giving these companies a single national designation is becoming less and less tenable over time as they expand internationally and are increasingly owned by shareholders based all over the globe. BP, for example, actively discourages the use of its full, original name (British Petroleum) on the grounds that it owns more assets in America than it does in the UK and employs as many people there too. DaimlerChrysler is labelled 'German' but was formed by the merging of two corporations, one German and the other American.

Firms internationalise their operations for a variety of reasons. For most the major motivation is growth and the wealth-generating possibilities that are associated with expansion into new markets. However in some cases there is another aim, namely the desire to reduce costs by locating operations where labour is cheaper or more productive and other resources are more readily available at a lower cost. Dicken (2015) distinguishes between these two approaches, naming the first a 'market orientation' approach to internationalisation, and the second, an 'asset orientation' approach. Other objectives are also mentioned in the books and articles on internationalisation are as follows:

1 To reduce risk associated with a domestic business cycle. When one country is in recession, another may be booming. It thus makes sense for a company to have a presence in several countries.

2 In response to foreign competition in the home market.

3 To reduce costs by producing close to customers and suppliers.

4 To avoid tariffs by serving foreign markets from within. This is a key reason that many US-based and Japanese-based corporations invest in the UK as it allows them to produce goods and services within the tariff wall operated by the EU.

Expansion into overseas markets tends to occur through two main mechanisms. One approach involves an organisation establishing subsidiaries in overseas countries, often with the help of intermediaries such as banks and consultants who are familiar with markets and how they operate in those countries. The second approach, which is becoming more common, involves merging with or taking over companies based in the target markets. One or two organisations, according to Dicken (2015), have been 'born global', in the sense that they start out as joint ventures between entrepreneurs who are based in different countries. He gives the example of the Momenta Corporation which was recently founded to exploit developments in 'pen-based computers'. Its founders come from four countries. Its initial operations were based in the USA, Germany and China, while its funding came from institutions based in several further countries.

In terms of its aims and objectives IHRM (i.e. HRM in an international or multinational organisation) is no different from HRM in an organisation based in one country. The purpose is to mobilise an appropriately qualified workforce, and subsequently to retain it, motivate it and develop it. IHRM, however, is more complex and necessarily has a rather different emphasis:

- IHRM involves working with an organisational structure that is more complex.

- There are a greater number of more diverse stakeholder groups to take account of.

- There is greater involvement in people's private/family lives because of the need to expatriate employees with their families.

- Diversity is necessary in terms of management style.

- There are greater numbers of external influences and risks to understand and manage.

IHRM is also generally harder to operationalise really well because of the communication difficulties that arise due to distance and language differences as well as cultural and institutional traditions and assumptions. This makes effective knowledge management and change management harder to achieve in particular. International HR managers thus need to have a somewhat different skill set from domestically focused HR managers and tend to develop careers exclusively in international organisations.

A particular issue of significance for international organisations concerns the design of internal structures and reporting lines. While these are complex issues at the best of times for large organisations, they are made a great deal more involved when geographically diverse workforces are included. Another significant way in which HR varies between nationally based and multinational organisations results from the presence of more multicultural teams, including senior management teams. While culturally diverse teams work well as generators of ideas and in their capacity to harness knowledge, they can operate in a dysfunctional fashion unless care is taken to manage them thoughtfully. Steers *et al.* (2010) set out what they describe as three 'coping strategies' to use and develop when managing culturally diverse teams:

- Avoiding cultural stereotypes (i.e. don't make assumptions about people based on a crude and limited understanding of their national cultures).
- See cultural differences in neutral terms (i.e. be fully aware of both the advantages and disadvantages that can come from the employment of diverse teams).
- Prepare for the unexpected (i.e. be aware of your own biases and cultural perspectives so that you can adapt quickly when dealing with those of others).

Volatility

The more competitive markets become, particularly as they internationalise, the more volatile and unpredictable the trading environment becomes for organisations. Economic stability of the kind that can exist and be promoted by government in a national market is much much harder to achieve internationally. Moreover, new technologies and applications are continually being developed all over the world and brought to market very rapidly. Insecurity, unpredictability and volatility are thus increasingly characterising many product markets, although the impact is far greater in some than it is in others. This inevitably makes it much harder than is the case in relatively stable business environments for organisations to be able to offer their staff long-term, stable employment of a traditional kind.

More intense competition and greater volatility also provide the pretext for organisations to change their structure more frequently. In some industries it has been observed that organisations are now engaged in 'permanent restructuring' as new opportunities present themselves and established businesses cease to generate the profits they once did.

Thanks in large part to globalisation we are thus faced with the evolution of a business environment which requires:

- more opportunistic approaches to business;
- maximum organisational agility;
- much more flexible working patterns;
- greater levels of functional flexibility;
- faster and more frequent change – both of a structural and cultural kind.

The result is a change in emphasis as far as HR is concerned. Different types of activity now top the HR agenda in organisations than used to in the past. There is, for example, a requirement to be much more actively involved in the promotion of effective change management. Organisations often handle the 'people side' of change very poorly. Decisions, even about major restructuring exercises, let alone mergers, acquisitions, downsizing and outsourcing initiatives, are frequently taken without consulting employees and, in many cases, without any genuine communication at all. This is partly due to poor management, partly due to wishes on the part of leaders to avoid conflict and resistance, and partly to the premium that must often be placed on commercial confidentiality in many situations (e.g. takeovers or sales of businesses).

Published research on the subject of change management is full of examples of situations in which change has been very poorly managed with negative consequences for organisations. Baxter and Macleod (2008), for example, undertook a major longitudinal research project involving change management episodes in twenty diverse organisations. The aim, in each case, was to increase efficiency or quality. In practice all failed to meet their initial expectations due to poor management. Communication exercises were typically inadequate, while managers failed to take proper account of 'employees' feelings of insecurity and anger'. What was worse though, according to this study, was that the senior managers who were responsible sometimes failed to accept that their initiatives had disappointed in practice. Great efforts were made to manipulate data so that the appearance of success could be proclaimed, even though the vast majority of employees knew this to be a fake. Further cynicism was then generated by the launch of newer initiatives aimed at achieving the same objectives, but with different names. According to Baxter and Macleod, it was only when employees were fully involved in planning and decision making that the same problems were subsequently avoided, making second attempts at introducing change more successful. This conclusion should come as no surprise. The well-known adage 'people support what they help to create' carries a great deal of truth, but is something that leaders in organisations often appear to ignore.

Conclusions

We can conclude this chapter by observing that globalisation is both deeply rooted and probably irreversible. Its impact on industry and the business context has been and continues to be transformational. As far as people management is concerned globalisation has not, however, changed the core purpose of the HRM function. This remains as it always has been: to recruit, retain, develop, motivate and engage employees more effectively than competitors are able to in order to sustain superior levels of performance. Instead the major impact has been to complicate HR practice and in important ways to make it harder to accomplish the core purpose effectively. Globalisation requires us increasingly to manage in culturally diverse settings and to manage teams of staff from a wider variety of backgrounds. It requires us to manage people through more complex organisational structures and often to do so in a state of near-perpetual change. Increased competitive intensity requires us both to work harder at recruiting, retaining and motivating good performers, while at the same time restricting the resources available to achieve these objectives as tighter cost control becomes increasingly necessary. We are tasked with making organisations much more flexible and responsive to change which inevitably reduces job security. Yet at the same time we are being urged to elicit loyalty and greater levels of discretionary effort from our staff. The need to keep a tight rein on costs is also creating a situation in which HR functions not only have to add value for their organisations, but also must be seen to be adding value, being required to justify their existence in raw financial terms. Above all, globalisation has brought much more uncertainty and unpredictability to our business environment. This makes longer-term human resource planning less and less viable, its place in HR strategy gradually being replaced by the need to build a capacity for flexibility and organisational agility so that unforeseen opportunities can be seized and exploited more rapidly and effectively than can be achieved by competitor organisations.

SUMMARY PROPOSITIONS

1.1. Globalisation is the most significant contemporary development in the business environment. It has largely been brought about as a result of technological developments and the choices made by governments around the world.

1.2. Globalisation has had a major impact on businesses and the management of people. This will continue for the foreseeable future.

1.3. The major changes brought about by globalisation have been increased volatility in product markets, increased competitive intensity, wholesale industrial restructuring and the rise to prominence of multinational corporations.

1.4. The impact on HRM has largely been to make it more challenging and complex to achieve core people management objectives.

GENERAL DISCUSSION TOPICS

1. Would it be either possible or desirable either to reverse the globalisation process or to slow it down considerably?

2. From a people management perspective who are the biggest winners and who are the biggest losers from globalisation?

3. Why are the developments discussed in this chapter affecting some industries more profoundly than others?

THEORY INTO PRACTICE

Dixon Ticonderoga

Until quite recently Dixon Ticonderoga was a dominant player in the American pencil market. Able to trace its origins back to the 1790s, throughout the twentieth century the company was a household name across the USA. For 100 years the company managed to maintain a highly profitable 30–40% share of a growing US pencil market, its iconic 'Number 2' yellow and green pencils being used across the country by millions of children when sitting school tests and exams. By 1990, 4 billion pencils were being sold each year in the USA, a good chunk of them manufactured by Dixon at its plants in Florida. At this time, four American manufacturers dominated the market, Dixon Ticonderoga being the second biggest, enjoying annual revenues of $90 to $95 million a year.

Things started to change rapidly after 1990 with the entry of Chinese manufactures into the American pencil market. By using cheaper labour and sourcing much cheaper raw materials of superior quality, Chinese pencils could be retailed at half the cost of those manufactured by Dixon. Moreover, in many consumers' eyes they not only looked the same, but functioned more effectively too. The result was a prolonged period in which pencils originating in Chinese factories steadily captured a greater share of the US market. In 1991 imported pencils accounted for just 16% of the total US pencil market, reaching 50% by the turn of the century. In 2004 imports accounted for 72% of the market and by 2010 for 87%. What is more, this level of penetration was achieved despite the US government applying big tariffs on imported pencils in order artificially to inflate their prices, $4 million being collected from Chinese pencil manufacturers in 2010.

Dixon Ticonderoga was slow to respond effectively to the challenge of overseas competition. Reluctant to downsize or close its US plants or to source materials from outside the USA, it held back from taking the radical strategic decisions necessary in order to secure its revenues and its future as an independent company. It was one of the companies that successfully lobbied for the imposition of tariffs on imported pencils in 1994.

Over time though, changes were made. Dixon started to ship wood from Indonesia, and rubber for erasers from Korea. The company also experimented by making pencils out of recycled paper cases. But they were still unable to compete effectively with their Chinese competitors. Eventually the difficult decision had to be taken to stop manufacturing standard, mass-market pencils in the USA, so in 2000 production was shifted to a plant in Mexico and to a wholly owned subsidiary in China.

Today the Dixon Ticonderoga brand remains in existence, but its market share is tiny compared to that which it enjoyed twenty or thirty years ago. It focuses increasingly on niche stationery products at the luxury end of the market, and no longer manufactures pencils in America or uses raw materials sourced in the USA. Since 2005 Dixon has been owned in its entirety by the Italian industrial conglomerate Fila-Fabricca Italiana.

Questions

1 How did Dixon Ticonderoga and the other US-based pencil manufacturers manage to hold on to such a dominant share of their market until 1990?

2 Why do you think managers at Dixon Ticonderoga were so slow to respond radically to the arrival of overseas competitors?

3 In retrospect, what steps should they have taken in the 1990s to secure their future?

4 What would have been the likely HRM consequences had they taken these steps?

Sources: www.fundinguniverse.com/company-histories/dixon-ticonderoga-company-history; www.bloomberg.com/news

FURTHER READING

The book entitled *Global Shift* by Peter Dicken (2015), now in its seventh edition, offers a superb introduction to all aspects of globalisation including detailed case studies of the impact on particular industrial sectors.

Global HR: Challenges Facing the Function by Peter Reilly and Tony Williams (2012) provides a very readable, well-informed and up-to-date survey of the various different ways in which mostly UK companies are adjusting their HRM practices in the face of globalisation.

In *Contemporary Issues in Human Resource Management*, Stephen Taylor (2011) develops a number of the points made in this chapter, particularly those relating to competition and skills shortages at greater length and in more detail.

REFERENCES

Adcroft, A., Teckman, J. and Willis, R. (2010) 'Is Higher Education in the UK becoming more competitive?', *International Journal of Public Sector Management*, Vol. 23, No. 6, pp. 578–88.

Baxter, L. and Macleod, A. (2008) *Managing Performance Improvement*. London: Routledge.

Chew, C. and Osborne, S.P. (2009) 'Exploring strategic positioning in the UK charitable sector: Emerging evidence from charitable organisations that provide public services', *British Journal of Management*, Vol. 20, No. 1, pp. 90–105.

Civil Aviation Authority (2015) *Aviation Trends*. www.caa.co.uk.

Cooke, F.L. (2005) *HRM, Work and Employment in China*. London: Routledge.

Dicken, P. (2015) *Global Shift: Mapping the changing contours of the world economy*, (7th edn.). London: Sage.

Ernst and Young (2012) *UK Attractiveness Survey 2012*. London: Ernst and Young.

Goldin, G., Cameron, G. and Balarajan, M. (2011) *Exceptional People: How Migration Shaped our World and will Define our Future*. Princeton: Princeton University Press.

Goos, M. and Manning, A. (2007) 'Lousy and Lovely Jobs: The rising polarization of work in Britain', *Review of Economics and Statistics*, Vol. 89, No. 1, pp. 118–33.

Goos, M., Manning, A. and Salomons, A. (2009) 'Job polarization in Europe', *American Economic Review*, Vol. 99, No. 2, pp. 58–63.

IATA (2015) Press release 55. www.iata.org.

Koser, K. (2007) *International Migration: A Very Short Introduction*. Oxford: Oxford University Press.

Leitch, S. (2006) 'Prosperity for all in the global economy – world class skills', *Final Report. The Leitch Review of Skills*. London: HM Treasury.

McNamara, G., Vaaler, P. and Devers, C. (2003) 'Same as it ever was: The search for evidence of increasing hypercompetition', *Strategic Management Journal*, Vol. 24, No. 1, pp. 261–78.

ONS (2012) *Births in England and Wales by Parents' Country of Birth, 2011*. Fareham, Hants: Office for National Statistics.

Reilly, P. and Williams, T. (2012) *Global HR: Challenges Facing the Function*. Farnham: Gower.

Scholte, J.A. (2005) *Globalisation: A Critical Introduction*, (2nd edn.). Basingstoke: Palgrave.

Steers, R., Sanchez-Rubde, C. and Nardon, L. (2010) *Management across Cultures: Challenges and Strategies*. Cambridge: Cambridge University Press.

Taylor, S. (2011) *Contemporary Issues in Human Resource Management*. London: CIPD.

Thankachan, T., Sharma, P.B. and Singh, R.K. (2010) 'Managing the shortage of teaching faculty for technical education in India', *International Journal of Continuing Engineering Education and Life Long Learning*, Vol. 20, Nos. 3–5, pp. 365–80.

UNCTAD (2012) *World Investment Report 2012*. New York: United Nations Conference on Trade and Development.

United Nations (2013) *Trends in International Migrant Stock: The 2013 Revision*. New York: United Nations.

Wes, M. (1996) *Globalisation: Winners and Losers*. London: Institute for Public Policy Research.

Wood, G. (2011) 'Employment Relations in South Africa and Mozambique', in M. Barry and A. Wilkinson (eds), *Research Handbook of Comparative Employment Relations*. Cheltenham: Edward Elgar.

CHAPTER 3

HRM AROUND THE WORLD

THE OBJECTIVES OF THIS CHAPTER ARE TO:

1 Set out the major ways in which HRM practice is similar from country to country

2 Recognise the major ways in which HRM practice varies from country to country

3 Identify models of HRM that are associated with particular countries

4 Explore the major dimensions of cultural difference between workplaces based in different countries

5 Assess how institutional differences help account for differences in HRM practice across national borders

It would be reasonable to assume that the globalisation of so much economic activity and the growth of multinational corporations would mean that HRM practice would also be thoroughly globalised. In fact, as has been demonstrated by many hundreds of comparative studies carried out in recent years, this is not the case at all. While some aspects of HRM activity are pretty standard across much of the world, there remains a great deal of diversity and this looks set to remain the case for the foreseeable future. That said, it is also true that much contemporary HR thinking and many theories concerning the effective management of people are now debated internationally and are thus inevitably having an influence across both industrialised and developing economies. It is also the case that models of HRM which have served particular countries very well over the years are widely studied internationally and that these have influenced practice well beyond the nations in which they originated. This is particularly true of the American and Japanese models, and also – at least within the context of Europe – of approaches associated with German HRM.

In this chapter we will introduce the field of comparative HRM, looking at the major ways in which HRM is carried out in a broadly similar way internationally and those in which we observe significant differences. We will also consider the evidence in support of greater convergence over time and that which points to continued divergence. We will go on to examine some of the major alternative models of HRM that are associated with different countries before discussing why, in an era of greater globalisation, HRM practice continues to retain such strong national characteristics.

Global HRM: similarities

In the published research on comparative HRM most of the attention is focused on the significant diversity of practice that we see across the world, but this should not obscure the fact that there are also very significant similarities too, particularly when it comes to fundamentals. We can state with some confidence, for example, that it is now usual to find a specialist function with responsibility for employment issues in organisations of any size everywhere in the world. This is true of the industrialised countries where such a function has been established in larger organisations for a century or more, and also of those in emerging economies where it is a much more recent innovation. Secondly, it is true to state that in the vast majority of countries the term 'human resource management' is commonly used to describe these activities and that this has replaced terms such as 'personnel administration' and 'personnel management' that were previously used very widely. It is also the case that across the world the core objectives of the HR function in organisations are broadly similar and very much along the lines that we set out in Chapter 1. Administrative objectives are more pronounced in some countries than others, but everywhere the administration of the employment relationship takes up a good portion of HR managers' time and is carried out along broadly similar lines (Lawler and Boudreau 2015: 17). It is thus reasonable to conclude that it is not what HR managers do that varies so considerably from country to country, but the way in which those core tasks are approached and the priority that is given to different types of activity.

In 2014, Bruce Kaufman published an edited text in which leading scholars based in seventeen diverse nations on all five continents discussed the historic development of HRM in their own countries. When reading these chapters one is struck as much by the similarities between their experiences as by the very different contexts in which contemporary HRM practice has evolved. Pretty well everywhere, for example, it is clear that the presence of specialised HR functions has become much more common in recent years and that HR management has grown in terms of its prestige and prominence within organisations. This has also been accompanied in most countries by the growth of some form of professional body to represent the interests of HR managers and of HRM courses being offered in business schools. This text also makes it clear that across the world there is a well-established interest in ideas about HRM strategy and the potential contribution that HRM can make to the achievement of organisational goals, including superior business performance. However, its authors also note that relatively slow progress has yet been made towards the realisation of such ideas in practice. In other words, while strategic thinking is in the ascendancy, the function remains essentially administrative in nature in the majority of organisations (Kaufman 2014).

Other researchers have argued that we are seeing a degree of convergence over time in terms of how HRM is carried out in different countries, although the evidence for this remains patchy and is the subject of considerable controversy. Lawler and Boudreau (2015), for example, in their study of multinational organisations based in seven countries, suggest that over time HRM functions are becoming increasingly sophisticated in the approaches they take, keener to adopt strategic thinking (if not practice) and also more likely to evaluate their contribution using analytical tools of one kind or another. Sparrow (2012: 285) cites International Labor Organisation (ILO) research which shows that 'new forms of employment have gained ground' all over the world in recent decades as organisations have adopted different forms of flexible working practices such as part-time working and variable hours. Others such as Briscoe *et al*. (2012: 403) note a tendency across most countries towards more of a 'performance-driven' approach to HRM, to which Brewster and Mayrhofer (2012: 9) add greater professionalisation and sophistication of HRM activity, more usage of contingent reward systems such as performance-related pay and much more focus on effective communication with employees.

However, these developments do not necessarily mean that we are heading towards a situation in which there is greater uniformity in the ways that HR managers approach their work across different countries. Most researchers working in this field make a distinction between what they call 'directional convergence', by which they mean the broad direction of travel that is observed in HRM across countries, and 'final convergence', which describes a situation in which a broadly similar approach to HRM is adopted across national boundaries. The consensus is that while we can identify a good deal of directional convergence, we are still a very long way from seeing much by way of final convergence. In other words, almost everywhere the same ideas are being adopted, influencing the way that HR management is carried out, but adoption and diffusion of these is occurring in countries which start from very different points. We can thus say that there is a tendency in most countries for better communication with employees (directional convergence) but that this still leaves a very big gap indeed between the nature and extent of that communication in, for example, the USA, where communication is already common and relatively sophisticated, and Russia, where communication has been very limited historically.

ACTIVITY 3.1

We introduced 'best practice' thinking in HRM (see Chapter 1), a commonly held point of view which holds that there is a bundle of HR practices that, when implemented, together provide a recipe for superior business performance. Importantly, supporters of this view argue that best practice HRM applies across all types of organisations, operating in all manner of industries.

What implications does the research on best practice HRM have for the debate about international convergence and divergence in approaches to HRM? What might it suggest will happen in the future?

Global HRM: differences

While it is, of course, true that HRM policies and practices vary very considerably within different countries, it is clear from decades of research that the differences between countries are considerably greater. In other words, we can usefully identify and make comparisons between the ways that people are typically managed in different countries and regions of the world. There is a distinct French approach which is different from the German approach, a distinct Russian approach, a distinct American approach and a range of different approaches used across Africa, South America, the Middle East and the Asia–Pacific countries.

The key differences are not always easy to summarise. This is because there is often a mismatch between formal HRM policies (which tend to be quite similar internationally) and the way things are actually done in practice by managers on a day-to-day basis. The following are some of the key variables that we can observe:

- The extent to which independent trade unions play a role in decision making and the manner in which managers and unions interact.
- The extent to which 'a rule of law' applies across an organisation, everyone complying with set policies regardless of rank or relationships.
- The level of sophistication of HR practices that are adopted and the extent to which HRM has a strategic character.
- The propensity of people to move from employer to employer when developing their careers.
- The extent to which labour law restricts management action and the costs associated with complying with the law, particularly when terminating contracts.
- The extent to which organisations are in the habit of planning for the long term when developing HR policies and practices.
- The level of individual employee involvement in decision making.
- The extent to which management decision making is evidence based and not informed by individual management 'hunches'.

We do not have the space here even to begin to summarise the different approaches that tend to be taken in each of these areas across the world, as every country differs in some respects from others. Instead, we will illustrate the extent of global diversity in HRM by

considering examples of national HRM models associated with some of the largest economies in the world: the American model, the Japanese model and the German model – each
of which has proved to be internationally influential over time.

The American model

Human Resource Management, as defined pejoratively (see Chapter 1) was largely
invented in the USA and is practised there – at least in larger organisations – with a good
degree of sophistication.

The presence of highly competitive, liberalised product markets and a strong trend
'towards a footloose capital without commitments to place or people' (Friedman 2013:
165) mean that organisations tend to focus on achieving relatively short-term financial
objectives and that employees are 'hired and fired' as required to help fulfil these objectives. Because of the widely held assumption in the USA that private sector companies
exist primarily in order to further their owners' financial interests, earnings per-quarter
per-share tend to be the most significant benchmark by which management teams are
judged. The short-termist outlook also apples to employees. It is not usual for people to
work in any one organisation for very lengthy periods and employees do not generally
enter employment with such expectations. It is more common for them to develop their
careers by moving from employer to employer every few years, resulting in relatively high
levels of staff turnover when compared with the norm in most other countries. In the USA
there is thus a very fluid and highly competitive labour market which obliges employers
to compete fiercely with each other to secure high-quality employees with the skills and
experience necessary to enable them to thrive as corporations.

It follows that the HRM activities in the USA are more central to an organisation's
ability to survive and compete effectively than is the case elsewhere. Strong performers
have to be treated well if they are to be recruited, retained, engaged and persuaded to
perform to high levels. This has led many US corporations to develop HR strategies which
mirror their organisational strategies, and to invest a good deal of money in sophisticated
selection, training and reward systems which help them to employ the best possible people.
Once hired, talented employees tend to be relatively well paid, but also to be rewarded
according to personal performance measured in financial terms. Poor performers, by contrast, tend to be dismissed without much ceremony. Trade unions have a peripheral role
in most US corporations, where they are present at all, and managers thus enjoy very
considerable freedom to shape HR practices according to the needs of their businesses.

Hampden-Turner and Trompenaars (1993) further observe that management (including HRM) in the USA has two characteristics that tend to differentiate it from common
practice elsewhere in the world:

1 A strong preference for evidence-based decision making and financial analysis. Everything
   is evaluated in financial terms and decisions made according to judgements about what will
   bring the best short-term financial returns.

2 A commitment to universalism. US managers like everything to be standardised across
   their operations. Rules-based decision making is thus the norm. Everyone is expected
   to conform to the same sets of rules and to apply them across the organisation.

HRM in the USA thus tends to be quite formal and rational in character, procedures being
developed at the corporate level which are then observed without exception across whole
organisation.

US-style HRM has been hugely influential globally, not least in the UK where broadly similar assumptions tend to underpin the way people are managed, at least in the private sector. The only fundamental differences between US and UK HRM arise from the much more restrictive legal environment in which UK-based organisations are obliged to operate. The US-model has also tended to be followed, albeit with significant local adaptations, by companies in other English-speaking countries, notably Canada, Australia, New Zealand and Ireland. Its influence, however, has proved to be far more widespread in recent years. As we noted above, the broad direction of travel for HRM internationally has been towards a more sophisticated, individualised, people-focused approach to the management of the employment relationship. Moreover, much global, contemporary thinking about HRM in a broad sense can be said to originate in large part in the USA. This is true, for example, of the idea that HRM managers should seek to develop a strategic approach to their work, looking to support the achievement of defined organisational objectives and adding value rather than simply carrying out administrative activities.

The German model

HRM in Germany differs from the US model in many respects. First and foremost management is less exclusively focused on serving shareholder interests. A 'stakeholder' approach underpins assumptions, recognising that a number of parties, including employees and the communities that they are drawn from, share with a company's owners a legitimate interest in its success and survival. The result is a longer-term orientation to decision making and a preference for management by consensus. The widespread presence of Works Councils ensures that employees participate formally in decision making and that their interests are taken into account. Moreover, industry-level collective bargaining serves to limit the extent to which HR managers are free to implement strategies which support the strategic objectives of their particular organisations (Zagelmeyer 2011: 322).

People are also much more likely in Germany to remain employed in the same enterprise for many years, and the commitment to investment in internal training systems reflects this. There are also strong internal labour markets and hence a focus on succession planning, career development and internal promotion.

Managers in Germany are also much more restricted than they are in the USA by legislation and by the continued presence of national-level collective bargaining whereby management representatives negotiate terms and conditions of employment with trade unions on behalf of a whole industry.

The result is a system of relatively generous holiday entitlement, limited working hours and high expenditure on training and development. Reward tends to be less heavily performance-based, more incentives being paid on a team rather than individual basis as in the US model. Differentials between high and low paid people are much less than in the USA. It is a great deal harder (and more costly) to fire people in Germany than in the US. This is partly because trade unions are much stronger, and partly due to legal restrictions.

Where the US and German models are similar is in their use of sophisticated HR practices that are universally applied. Hence recruitment and selection operates in a very similar way. General organisation rules are developed and applied to everyone in the same way too. The main difference is that in Germany staff participate to a far greater extent in the making of the rules.

Both the US and German models are associated with high levels of productivity, but this could be more to do with the strong work ethic that exists in both countries as much as the HR policies and practices which prevail. The German model has been influential across Europe, and is largely followed elsewhere with some significant variations. In Scandinavian countries such as Denmark and Sweden, a model that is similar to that of Germany is broadly followed, but here, because labour law is somewhat less restrictive than it is in Germany, managers have more freedom to hire and fire. However, because democratic approaches to management and trade union involvement are even more pronounced, workplace cultures tend to be less hierarchical and bureaucratic than they often are in Germany. In France and the southern EU counties (Italy, Spain, Portugal, etc.) unions are much weaker, but collective bargaining is still very common at industry level. Legal requirements are also stricter. Yet within businesses managers are less likely than they are in Germany to consult about decisions, being more autocratic and less rule-bound in their approaches. Legal restrictions limit what managers can do, but they interpret the rules unilaterally and expect to be deferred to. There is thus much less of a commitment to consensus decision making. This also appears to be true of the Eastern European countries as they have emerged from the communist era. They are adopting some elements of the German model, but also are heavily influenced by US-type HR thinking. Here, though, management is a lot less consensual, much more autocratic and less rule-bound than is the case in the USA (Morley *et al*. 2012: 567–8).

The Japanese model

The Japanese model of HRM, like the German model and the American model, has been widely studied and has been very influential globally over recent decades (Ahmadjian and Schaede 2015). In some respects, Japanese management practices are like those of Germany, only more extreme. The system of 'life-time employment', for example, ensures that there is relatively little competition for labour between companies and very strong internal labour market structures. Once employed by a company, the norm is for people to stay there for many years, showing very considerable levels of loyalty which are reciprocated by the employers. HR systems thus tend to be based heavily on consensus and a long-term orientation, with significant investment in training and development so that people can progress within their firms. The big differences are:

- much more flexibility on the part of Japanese workers to work in different parts of an organisation, retraining as required;
- far fewer formal rules and much more decision making influenced by personal relationships;
- unions are enterprise-based rather than industry-based;
- seniority-based payment systems that reward long service over individual performance.

Aspects of Japanese working practices have been copied all over the world, some more successfully than others. In the UK, for example, there have been strong moves in recent years towards team working and employee involvement, more flexible working practices and partnership agreements with trade unions including no-strike deals. The management philosophy known as 'total quality management' also originated in Japan and has proved highly influential internationally. This approach involves lighter-touch supervision and more team-working, teams taking responsibility for ensuring that they meet targets and achieve defined levels of quality when carrying out their work.

Accounts of the Japanese model nowadays always need to carry an important caveat. The long-term stagnation of the Japanese economy over the past two decades has tended to mean that aspects of the established model are being challenged in Japan, resulting in the adoption of new approaches which are less consensual in nature, more individually focused and more performance-driven (Woo 2014). While the core elements of the Japanese approach to HRM remain in place, there is a question mark over their longer-term survival.

HRM in industrialising countries

Across the world economies are industrialising at a rapid rate, developing large, educated, middle class populations while competing increasingly effectively in the global economy (see Chapter 2). This process involves people moving from agricultural employment into jobs in factories and offices that are mainly based in cities. In many cases it is also associated with the privatisation of state-owned enterprises and substantially increased competition between firms both for business and people. At the same time we see a more sophisticated approach to HRM evolving which resembles established practice in the industrialised countries. There is also a strong tendency, once a country begins to reach an advanced state of industrial development, for labour regulations to increase.

It is too early to tell whether a distinctive Chinese model or Indian model or South American model or African model will ultimately evolve which will be substantially different from the US, German or Japanese models discussed above. At present, in the main, we observe the adoption of these practices blended with local traditions. In China, for example, American-style HRM practices are mixed with the more traditional egalitarian and bureaucratic approaches that are associated with employment in state-owned organisations. Trade unions are weak and passive, but employees tend to be loyal and committed to their enterprises. By contrast, in India traditional and highly autocratic management styles are vying for dominance with the more democratic, involving thinking associated with more sophisticated, rules-based HR practices associated with western enterprises. Everywhere across the emerging economies multinational corporations play an important part in introducing more sophisticated HRM practices and strategic HR thinking as they seek to maximise their attractiveness as employers in order to recruit the most talented staff.

WINDOW ON PRACTICE

The success of the Chinese economy in recent decades and the country's emergence as one of the very biggest economies in the world has generated a great deal of interest among western researchers. This has led to much debate about the extent to which a distinctively Chinese approach to HRM is emerging which may, in time, prove to be as internationally influential as the US, Japanese and German models were in the past.

What might a Chinese model of HRM look like?

China shares its long-term orientation with Japan, but in China labour markets are much more competitive and open. Skills shortages prevail in many industries and people move from employer to employer much more readily than is the case in Japan. Trade unions exist in most larger Chinese enterprises, but they operate in a very different manner than that we are used to in western industrialised countries. They tend not to oppose management decisions and are, to all intents and purposes, part of an organisations' management. Labour law is developing quite rapidly, but because its enforcement is widely considered to be patchy, Chinese workers have little by way of formal employment regulation to protect them from unreasonable demands on the part of their managers. They remain productive in the large part because the strong collectivist traditions that are deeply embedded in Chinese culture ensure that managers take a reasonable approach, seeing it as their duty to look after the interests of their employees. The system retains discipline and integrity because of the importance in China of 'not losing face' and hence performing your duties effectively, as well as the presence of 'guanxi' which means that people feel a strong sense of obligation towards others in their personal social networks. Chinese HRM is also a lot less administratively sophisticated than it is in many other countries, companies being much less burdened with policy and bureaucracy of an HR-related kind (Lawler and Boudreau 2015: 159).

Things may change in China, but the model that appears to be emerging is decisively different from others in the world and may well prove globally influential in time. It is characterised by simplicity, and limited rules, combined with an autocratic management style which has a strongly paternalistic character. Decisions are taken with a long-term focus, steady evolution being preferred to more risky, revolutionary or transformative change of the kind so often favoured in western industrialised countries.

Explaining global diversity in HRM practice

Researchers who specialise in comparative HRM tend to disagree about which sets of factors are more or less important when it comes to explaining the reasons for the persistence of diversity between the various national models of HRM. There are two major schools of thought on this issue, one focusing largely on cultural factors, the other on institutional factors. The first group emphasises the significance of commonly held expectations on the part of employers and employees about the nature of their relationship, something that certainly varies quite considerably between national populations. The second group tends to downplay the significance of such cultural factors, preferring instead to explain differences in HRM practice with reference to regulations, government policy, business systems and the role played by bodies such as trade unions and employers' associations.

Cultural variations

In recent decades a number of extensive studies have been carried out among employees and managers working in different countries, the results subsequently being 'mapped'. The dominant features of business cultures across the globe have thus been categorised into readily understood types which demonstrate how they differ one from another. The best known contributions are those by:

- Kluckohn (1954).
- Strodtbeck (1961).
- Hofstede (1980, 1991 and 2004).

- Hall and Hall (1990).

- Lewis (1996).

- Trompenaars and Hampden-Turner (2006).

- House *et al.* (2004).

- Kirkman *et al.* (2006).

- Basanez (2016).

Inevitably this process oversimplifies matters to a considerable extent, downplaying the extent of cultural variation between organisations, generations and regions within countries, as well as changes over time, while emphasising cultural differences between countries. However, because the researchers have all, without exception, found that work cultures vary much more between countries than they do within national boundaries, these studies can claim to be both valid and useful.

Of all the work carried out by researchers working in this field, it is that of the Dutch scholar Geert Hofstede which has been by far the most influential. His work has been cited over 100,000 times in scholarly journals while his books have sold many hundreds of thousands of copies, making him one of the most widely read social scientists in the world (Ybema and Nyri 2015). Despite Hofstede's work now being rather dated, having mainly been carried out in the late 1960s and 1970s, it continues to be the starting point for anyone looking to understand the major ways in which managers and employees raised in different cultures tend to have distinct and disparate expectations when it comes to the world of work.

Hofstede's studies remain unrivalled in terms of their scale and scope, comprising the analysis of detailed questionnaires issued to 90,000 IBM employees in seventy different countries over a long period. The studies have led to the publication of several detailed books, including a number of editions of *Culture's Consequences: Software of the Mind* which was originally published in 1980 but has been updated on several occasions since. Hofstede's organisation also runs a most interesting website which explains his work and from which all manner of charts can be downloaded which show how different countries 'score' on all his dimensions (www.geert-hofstede.com).

Hofstede defines national culture as 'the collective mental programming which distinguishes one nation from another.' He originally identified four dimensions that allow different national characteristics to be classified or mapped. These are as follows:

Individualism is the extent to which people expect to look after themselves and their family only. The opposite is collectivism, which has a tight social framework and in which people expect to have a wider social responsibility to discharge because others in the group will support them. Those of a collectivist persuasion believe they owe absolute loyalty to their group.

Power distance measures the extent to which the less powerful members of the society accept the unequal distribution of power. In organisations this is the degree of centralisation of authority and the exercise of autocratic leadership.

Uncertainty avoidance. The future is always unknown, but some societies socialise their members to accept this and take risks, while members of other societies have been socialised to be made anxious about this and seek to compensate through the security of law, religion or technology.

Masculinity. The division of roles between the sexes varies from one society to another. Where men are assertive and have dominant roles these values permeate the whole of society and the organisations that make them up, so there is an emphasis on showing off, performing, making money and achieving something visible. Where there is a larger role for women, they are in more service oriented, caring roles, and the values move towards concern for the environment and the quality of life, putting the quality of relationships before the making of money.

Hofstede found some clear cultural differences between nationalities and from this he concluded that countries emphasising large power distance and strong uncertainty avoidance were likely to produce forms of organisation that relied heavily on hierarchy and clear orders from superiors: **a pyramid of people.** In countries where there is small power distance and strong uncertainty avoidance there would be an implicit form of organisation that relied on rules, procedures and clear structure: **a well-oiled machine.** The implicit model of organisation in countries with small power distance and weak uncertainty avoidance was a reliance on ad hoc solutions to problems as they arose, as many of the problems could be boiled down to human relations difficulties: **a village market.** The picture is completed by the fourth group of countries where there is large power distance and weak uncertainty avoidance, where problems are resolved by constantly referring to the boss who is like a father to an extended family, so there is concentration of authority without structuring of activities. The implicit model of organisation here is: **the family.** Table 3.1 shows which major countries are in the different segments.

Table 3.1

Pyramid of people	Well-oiled machine	Village market	Family
Arab speaking	Austria	Australia	East Africa
Argentina	Costa Rica	Britain	Hong Kong
Belgium	Finland	Canada	Indonesia
Brazil	Germany	Denmark	India
Chile	Israel	Ireland	Jamaica
Colombia	Switzerland	Netherlands	Malaysia
Ecuador		New Zealand	Philippines
France		Norway	Singapore
Greece		South Africa	West Africa
Guatemala		Sweden	
Iran		United States	
Italy			
Japan			
Korea			
Mexico			
Pakistan			
Panama			
Peru			
Portugal			
Spain			
Taiwan			
Thailand			
Turkey			
Uruguay			
Venezuela			

ACTIVITY 3.2

Identify your country and its type from those shown in Table 3.1. If it is not there, pick one with which you are familiar.

1 Do you agree with Hofstede's description of the type of organisation that is implicit?

2 Think of examples of how that implicit type of organisation affects HR activities.

The implicit form of organisation for the UK is a village market, for France it is a pyramid of people, for Germany it is a well-oiled machine and for Hong Kong it is a family. If we can understand the organisational realities and detail in those four countries, then this can provide clues about how to cope in Denmark, Ecuador, Austria or Indonesia because they each share the implicit organisational form and implicit organisational culture of one of the original four.

It is not quite as easy as that, because the clusters show only relative similarities and, inevitably, other studies do not entirely agree with Hofstede (for example, Ronen and Shenkar, 1985), but there is sufficient agreement for us to regard the four-way classification as useful, if not completely reliable.

Hofstede later produced a refinement of his model, citing two additional dimensions, the first of which he identified after surveying IBM staff in a further group of countries including China. This is 'Confucian dynamism', or long-term versus short-term orientation. Working with the Canadian Michael Bond, Hofstede used a Chinese value survey technique in a fresh study and uncovered the cultural variable of long-term orientation that none of the original, western, questions had reached. The highest scoring countries on this dimension were China, Hong Kong, Taiwan, Japan and South Korea. Singapore was placed ninth. Hofstede argues that countries in the west have derived their culture largely from the three religions of Judaism, Christianity or Islam, all of which are centred on assertion of truth that is accessible to true believers, whereas none of the religions of the east are based on the assertion that there is a truth that a human community can embrace. The 'Confucian' values found attached to this long-term orientation included perseverance, clearly maintained status differentials, thrift, and having a sense of shame. In many ways these values are valuable for business growth, as they put social value on entrepreneurial initiative, support the entrepreneur by the willing compliance of others seeking a place in the system, encourage saving and investment, and put pressure on those who do not meet obligations.

Hofstede's sixth dimension, labelled 'indulgence/restraint', is much more recent, having been added to his model in 2010 following the publication of data from the World Values Survey, a vast study that examines cultural difference outside as well as inside the workplace. Indulgent cultures are those, such as the UK's has now largely become, where the gratification of human desires is seen as desirable and where cultural norms have adapted to facilitate this. It is associated with freedom of expression, optimism, a preference for leisure over work, a live and let live attitude towards others, a strong commitment to personal freedom and a belief that attaining individual fulfilment is a basic right that all in society should be able to aspire to. By contrast, cultures that score highly on measures of 'restraint' are those where duty and social expectation are regarded as more important social aims than the pursuit of personal happiness or fulfilment. Here it is regarded as socially appropriate to keep personal emotions, ambitions and desires hidden and for people to accept the hand that life has dealt them. You may be lucky and be able to enjoy life to the full, but if not then this is a state you should accept. There tends to be a strong work ethic and, often, a more pessimistic view of the world than is found in more indulgent cultures. Countries that score relatively highly on measures of 'restraint' include those in Asia and North African countries. By contrast it is northern Europeans and northern Americans who score highest on measures of indulgence.

Hofstede's work is interesting in that it demonstrates that cultures (or collective mental programming) among a national people remain strikingly and persistently divergent despite convergence in areas such as technology and economic systems. Hence he found huge differences in culture between the OECD counties – i.e. the most industrially advanced countries, indicating that economic development does not have a major impact on culture. On uncertainty avoidance, for example, among OECD countries Greece is five times higher than Denmark. On the masculinity index Japan is 18 times higher than Sweden and Norway.

From a strategic perspective, cultural diversity has many implications for human resource management. Hodgetts and Luthans (2000: 36) selected some of these where the culture of a society can directly affect management approaches:

The centralisation of decision making. In some societies (especially the pyramid of people type) all important decisions are taken by a small number of managers in senior positions. In other societies (like the village markets) decision making is more decentralised. In a joint venture between two dissimilar societies, not only will these differences of approach need to be recognised, but management systems will have to enable members of the two cultures to understand each other and work together.

Rewards and competition. The level of financial rewards between countries can be a problem, when those in country A appear to receive much more money than those in country B for doing the same job; but a more subtle difference is the way in which rewards are disbursed. In some instances there is a culture favouring individual recognition, whilst elsewhere there is a convention of group rewards. Similarly some societies encourage competition rather than cooperation, and in others the reverse applies.

Risk. As Hofstede demonstrated in his first study, attitudes towards taking risks are a clear discriminator between cultures, with marked variations of uncertainty avoidance.

Formality. The well-oiled machine cultures place great emphasis on clear procedures and strict rules, while pyramid of people cultures emphasise clear hierarchies and observance of rank. This contrasts strongly with the village market type societies where relationships are more informal and ad hoc action more likely.

Organisational loyalty. In Japan there tends to be a strong sense of loyalty to one's employer, while in the UK and the US there is a growing sense of identification with one's occupational group, rather than with a particular employer. The longstanding importance of professional bodies and the declining long-term reliability of corporations to look after one's career development have increased this loyalty to one's occupation rather than to one's employer.

Short- or long-term orientation. Hofstede's identification of an eastern predilection to the long term is beginning to influence strategic decisions on where to locate those organisational activities for which long-term thinking is particularly appropriate.

Hofstede's work, along with that of the many other researchers who have been influenced by his approach, has always been the subject of a great deal of scepticism and outright criticism (see Ybema and Nyiri 2015). In particular critics are uncomfortable with aspects of his methodology (i.e. focusing on questionnaire responses from employees of a single multinational corporation) as well as the way that his models over-simplify a much more complex social reality. Not only, it is argued, is there much more cultural variation within countries than Hofstede acknowledges, but cultures also change over time. Things are not as monolithic and static as this stream of research tends to suggest. These criticisms are very compelling. Anyone who has lived in the UK for a long period of time will, for example, recognise the major cultural differences that exist, on the one hand, between London and the south-east of the country and, on the other, the northern and western regions. Most would also probably concur with the view that over the last few decades the UK has become more masculine (i.e. materialistic), more short-termist in outlook and a great deal more individualistic and indulgent. These are criticisms of detail which matter because they strongly suggest that management decision making should never be too closely rooted in a Hofstedian analysis of how people are likely to react. However, as a broad explanation as to why HRM practice varies from country to country, the work of Hofstede and his colleagues still has a great deal to offer. Their studies demonstrate that substantial variations exist between the workplace cultures in different countries, that these persist over time and that they are reflected in the prevalent approaches to people management that have evolved over time.

Institutional variations

The work of Hofstede and others who have carried out similar studies all emphasise cultural differences between countries, the implication being that different approaches to the management of people are required in each place if an organisation is to maximise its ability to recruit, retain, engage and motivate its staff. In recent years, however, studies have been published which question this point of view. There is general agreement that HR systems and policies do vary from country to country, but the extent to which this is due to cultural differences is disputed. Instead it is strongly argued that institutional differences offer a better explanation (Whitley 1999, Edwards and Rees 2006, Wright and De Voorde 2009). This conclusion has been reached from a reading of many studies looking at how HR practices vary across different locations within the same multinational company. A widely advanced view is that the following factors have a major influence on how HR is practised on a day-to-day basis:

- local laws;
- enforcement mechanisms/agencies;
- government and local government policies;
- collective bargaining structures;
- labour market institutions;
- corporate governance arrangements;
- national training systems;
- pension arrangements;
- social security systems;
- inter-firm relationships.

Moreover, it is further argued and that over time these become so well-embedded as to become management norms in the countries concerned:

'In the local context, the labour laws and regulations restrict the range of possible HRM practices, local managers have taken-for-granted views about good management practices that influence the policies and practices that they suggest for the subsidiary, strong professional norms may exist, and processes of institutionalization might also take place among MNCs in the focal country.'

Bjorkman (2006: 465)

While there is now a degree of international convergence as far as employment law is concerned thanks to the efforts of bodies such as the International Labour Organization and the European Union (EU), national systems remain very different from one another. Even within the EU where so many employment law principles apply in all member states, considerable differences persist. Dismissal law, for example, the most fundamental of all employment rights, is completely different depending on the country in which someone loses their job (see Chapter 22). In the UK many are excluded from bringing unfair dismissal cases at all, while those who can are unlikely to win much by way of damages unless they are older, with many years' service, and have difficulty finding alternative employment. In many other EU countries a suspected unfair dismissal can give rise to criminal proceedings, the case being brought not by the aggrieved employee, but by a local labour inspectorate. Damages are also far higher in many jurisdictions, fines also being levied by way of punishment. The presence in law of such different approaches to dismissal inevitably has a profound effect on the way that people are managed and their expectations about work. The Netherlands enforces some of the most restrictive dismissal laws in the world. Here it is considered unlawful to dismiss an employee until the employer has first secured the written permission of a local government official. By contrast, the USA mostly continues to adhere to a policy of 'employment at will', putting very few legal restrictions on the capacity of an employer to fire people. The impact of such legal differences on the balance of power in the employment relationship is profound and is a significant explanation for the presence of different approaches to HRM in these countries. Those who prefer institutional to cultural explanations might also point out that the Netherlands, the USA and the UK are all categorised as 'village markets' in Hofstede's model of cultural differences.

A further stream of thought concerns what have become known as 'varieties of capitalism', the idea here being that the whole institutional framework within which employers operate provides a meaningful and compelling explanation for the differences in HRM practice that we observe. In particular a distinction is made between 'liberal market economies' (LMEs) such as the USA and the UK and the 'coordinated market economies' (CMEs) found in Europe, the Middle East, Japan and much of Asia. These rival institutional frameworks are essentially the creation of successive governments responding in different ways to their evolving economic environments. In LMEs the assumption is that it is better for business and society if governments minimise the extent that they 'interfere' with the operation of free markets. By contrast, in CMEs the presence of a good degree of government-sponsored regulation of markets is the prevailing norm. Moreover, mechanisms that are not market-oriented, such as negotiating terms and conditions at industry level via employers' associations, play a major role in employment regulation. There is a practical knock-on effect for HRM in that CMEs tend to have much stronger trade unions with a legally mandated role and status than is the case in LMEs. In short, the extent to which an individual HR manager is free to develop an organisationally distinct approach is considerably higher in an LME than is the case in a CME. It also follows that organisations in CMEs tend to be less short-termist in their thinking, more committed to the welfare and prosperity of the individuals who work for them and more prepared to invest in their training and development.

WINDOW ON PRACTICE

Flexicurity in Denmark

Denmark provides a good example of the way that institutional structures help determine how a particular country's HR system evolves. Here it is the interplay of employment law and the welfare system which has had the biggest impact.

Denmark has the highest level of employee turnover in Europe (30% on average in recent years). It also has a very high level of job turnover, between 10% and 15% of its jobs disappearing each year and being replaced with new ones. Around a quarter of the Danish workforce finds itself unemployed for some portion of every year, while as many as 10% of the country's people are employed on fixed-term contracts. The proportion of small and medium-sized enterprises is also the highest in Europe. Economically, Denmark is a success story. Inflation has been low for decades, overall unemployment rates are well below those of other major EU economies and growth has been stronger.

The major reason for this appears to be the Danish social security system, which is very generous in comparison with those of other countries. It is relatively easy and inexpensive to dismiss people, but people who do find themselves out of work suffer a great deal less in financial terms than equivalents elsewhere. They are, however, obliged as a condition of receiving benefit to take part in government-sponsored retraining and educational programmes. It is this highly sophisticated and expensive unemployment benefit system that seems to have allowed Denmark to develop highly flexible labour markets. It means that people are more willing to take on insecure roles and that employers are less concerned than they are elsewhere to avoid redundancies at all costs.

The debate about which factors, cultural or institutional, best explain differences between the dominant approaches to HR practised across borders is of little practical relevance. Both play a part to a greater or lesser extent in different types of situation. De Cieri (2007: 519–20) demonstrates this by looking at recruitment and selection practices. These, she argues, in part vary from country to country because of cultural differences. In Anglo-Saxon cultures selection processes tend to be competitive and objective, the aim being to secure the services of the person who is likely to perform best in the job. Elsewhere in the world where personal networks and relationships play a stronger role in the business culture and where power distance (as defined by Hofstede) is great, it is the norm for employees to be appointed due to family or clan connections, on personal recommendation, or on occasion, because a bribe of some kind has been paid. These are cultural explanations for the differences. But there are also institutional explanations. In countries such as the UK and US discrimination law serves to deter employers from selection on anything other than objective grounds. De Cieri goes on to give other examples of HRM practices in which both institutional and cultural factors play a role in shaping international divergence, exploring performance appraisal and diversity management in particular.

In the end it therefore makes sense to acknowledge that both culture and institutions play an important part in helping to explain diversity of HRM practice. Moreover, it is also reasonable to argue that because culture helps to shape a nation's institutions, while institutions also play a role in shaping national workplace cultures, there is considerable interaction between these two central explanations.

ACTIVITY 3.3

Aside from those we have discussed in this chapter, what other examples of HR practices or established employment norms can you think of which differ from country to country? How far are these explained by cultural or by institutional differences, or is there some other explanation?

Is greater divergence a possibility?

Before we move on from the debate about diversity of HR practice around the world it is worth briefly considering whether we are in fact likely to see greater divergence across the world in the future. The assumption tends to be that thanks to globalisation, the sharing of ideas about how people are best managed, and the growing influence of multinational corporations, we will over time see greater convergence. Moreover, as we explained above, there is some evidence that this process is in fact occurring, albeit slowly.

There are, however, solid grounds for anticipating less similarity in HR practice rather than more in the future (Kaufman 2014: 12–13). This possibility arises from the trend towards greater industrial specialisation in response to globalisation (discussed in Chapter 2). Some commentators see this as highly significant, leading increasingly to a situation in which different countries largely earn a living in the world by trading in goods or services for the production of which they enjoy a comparative advantage. We are already seeing significant trends in this direction as China specialises in low-cost manufacturing, India in computer-based service provision and most western countries in hi-tech manufacturing, cultural, financial and business services. It follows that approaches to HRM will potentially increasingly develop in ways which suit the prevalent economic activities occurring locally. Hence, UK HRM will increasingly be tailored to meet the needs of knowledge workers and their employers, while Chinse HRM will be shaped largely by the requirement to meet the needs of large-scale manufacturing.

ACTIVITY 3.4

What is your view about the case for anticipating greater international divergence in HRM practice in the future? Can you spot any flaws in the arguments that are presented in its support?

SUMMARY PROPOSITIONS

3.1.   While there are important similarities between the approaches to HRM that are prevalent in different countries, there are also very significant differences and only limited evidence of any international convergence over time.

3.2. The largest economies in the world over recent decades – the USA, Japan and Germany – have each developed distinct models of HRM which have proved to be globally influential in different ways.

3.3. Academic opinion tends to be split between those who consider that cultural differences explain the ongoing differences between national approaches and those who favour institutional explanations.

3.4. It is possible that we will in the future see greater divergence in HRM practice around the world rather than convergence as organisations in particular countries increasingly specialise in defined forms of industrial endeavour.

GENERAL DISCUSSION TOPICS

1. Why might it be important for managers in a nationally based organisation that is about to expand internationally to be aware of the different ways that HRM is customarily carried out in different countries?

2. Some argue that the future will bring both increased convergence and increased divergence internationally as far as HRM practice is concerned. How is this possible?

3. To what extent do you find the models put forward by Geert Hofstede either compelling or practically useful?

THEORY INTO PRACTICE

You work in the HR department of a large corporation which operates a well-known chain of fashion stores (Large Co). Your company has outlets on the high streets of all the major UK cities and is steadily increasing its presence in out-of-town shopping complexes and airports. In addition, recent years have seen the start of what is intended to be a major expansion overseas with the opening of new flagship stores in a number of European cities. International online sales are also growing rapidly.

As part of its overseas expansion plans, a few weeks ago, your company took over another organisation (Small Co) which operates three high street fashion outlets in South East Asian cities and also supplies garments to a range of retailers in the UK from its factories. It employs around 400 people in India, Pakistan and Bangladesh.

You have been seconded for a year to work at Small Co which has not to date ever employed a professionally qualified HR manager.

Soon after your arrival at Small Co, you become aware of various management practices which you are uneasy about and which are very different indeed from what you are used to at Large Co.

Pay rates, for example, do not appear to be established using any rational system. Its staff are appointed at a variety of rates according to what they were able to negotiate when they start working for the company. There are also a good number of junior managerial staff who are working in excess of 60 hours each week. Trade union membership is actively discouraged, while training and development opportunities are minimal. There is no formal induction provided and no staff handbook. Health and safety procedures appear to be minimal. Staff turnover is running at 35%. You are even more concerned when you visit some of the stores and garment factories that Small Co operates in Asia. Here pay is very low and hours of work are long. The more senior posts all seem to be held by male relatives of top managers (all themselves men), while people seem to be hired and fired on a whim. While the managers you meet deny bullying their staff, this is not what the staff themselves say to you when you speak to them confidentially. Moreover, while it is denied that anyone under the age of 15 is employed, some staff look to you to be considerably younger. You are also concerned to observe that water contaminated with dyes and fixing agents appears to be being channelled directly into a river behind one of the factories you visit.

You are taken aback by what you observe in your first few weeks at Small Co. You are used to working in Large Co with its big HR division, range of 'good practice' employment policies and prominent corporate code of ethics. None of this exists at Small Co and there is no sign at all that any kind of ethical culture has been developed. It is, however, a very profitable business.

Questions

1 What are the main strands of the business case you could make in support of the introduction across Small Co's operations, as a matter of priority, an ethical culture alongside ethically sound HR policies and practices? What counter-arguments might you expect to have to answer?

2 To what extent might the differences in the way HR is practised in Large Co and Small Co operations be explained by cultural or institutional factors?

FURTHER READING

In recent years we have seen an explosion in interest in comparative HRM and the publication of numerous books and articles examining different aspects of the subject.

You might find it useful to start an exploration of this subject by reading Geert Hofstede's classic book pioneering thinking in the field. You can also visit his website and download short video presentations in which he explains different aspects of his theories. His most widely read book is: *Culture's Consequences: International Differences in Work-Related Values* (1980).

The text edited by Bruce Kaufman provides a useful historic perspective on these debates, his writers emphasising institutional rather than cultural factors when assessing the way HRM has developed in their respective countries: *The Development of Human Resource Management across Nations: Unity and Diversity* (2014).

A different approach which you may find serves to enhance the depth of your understanding might be to read Amelie Northomb's short autobiographical novel about the experiences of a young French woman working in a Japanese company. It is very entertaining and also revealing about how very wide cultural differences are when it comes to HRM practice: *Fear and Trembling* (2004).

REFERENCES

Ahmadjian, C. and Schaede, U. (2015) 'The impact of Japan on Western management', in N. Holden, S. Michailova and S. Tietze (eds), *The Routledge Companion to Cross-Cultural Management*. London: Routledge.

Basanez, M. (2016) *A World of Three Cultures: Honour, Achievement and Joy*. Oxford: Oxford University Press.

Bjorkman, I. (2006) 'International Human Resource Management research and institutional theory', in G. Stahl and I. Bjorkman (eds), *Handbook of Research in International Human Resource Management*. Cheltenham: Edward Elgar.

Brewster, C. and Mayrhofer, W. (2012) 'Comparative human resource management: An introduction', in C. Brewster and W. Mayrhofer (eds), *Handbook of Research on Comparative Human Resource Management*. Cheltenham: Edward Elgar.

Briscoe, D. Schuler, R. and Tarique, I. (2012) *International Human Resource Management: Policies and Practices for Multi-national Enterprises* (4th edn.). New York: Routledge.

De Cieri, H. (2007) 'Transnational firms and cultural diversity', in P. Boxall, J. Purcell and P. Wright (eds), *The Oxford Handbook of Human Resource Management*. Oxford: Oxford University Press.

Edwards, T. and Rees, C. (2006) *International Human Resource Management: Globalisation, National Systems and Multinational Companies*. London: FT/Pearson.

Friedman, G. (2013) 'The United States', in C. Frege and J. Kelly (eds), *Comparative Employment Relations in the Global Economy*. London: Routledge.

Hall, E. and Hall, M. (1990) *Understanding Cultural Differences*. Yarmouth: Intercultural Press.

Hampden-Turner, C. and Trompenaars, F. (1993) *The Seven Cultures of Capitalism*. Doubleday: New York.

Hofstede, G. (1980) *Culture's Consequences: Software of the mind*. Beverly Hills, California: Sage Publications.

Hofstede, G. (1991) *Cultures and Organizations: Software of the Mind*. London: McGraw Hill.

Hofstede, G. (2004) *Cultures and Organizations: Software of the Mind* (2nd edn.). London: McGraw Hill.

Hodgetts, R.M. and Luthans, F. (2000) *International Management*. New York: McGraw Hill.

House R., Hanges P., Javidan M., Dorfman P. and Gupta, V. (2004) *Culture, Leadership and Organisations: The GLOBE Study of 62 Societies*. Thousand Oaks, California: Sage.

Kaufman, B. (ed.) (2014) *The Development of Human Resource Management across Nations: Unity and Diversity*. Cheltenham: Edward Elgar.

Kaufman, B. (2014) 'The development of human resource management across nations: History and its lessons for international and comparative HRM', in B. Kaufman (ed.), *The Development of Human Resource Management across Nations: Unity and Diversity*. Cheltenham: Edward Elgar.

Kirkman, B.L., Lowe, K.B. and Gibson, C.B. (2006) 'A quarter century of *Culture's Consequences*: A review of empirical research incorporating Hofstede's cultural values framework', *Journal of International Business Studies*, Vol. 37, No. 3, pp. 285–320.

Kluckhohn, C. (1954) *Culture and Behaviour*. New York: Free Press.

Lawler, E. and Boudreau, J. (2015) *Global Trends in Human Resource Management: A Twenty Year Analysis*. California: Stanford University Press.

Lewis, R. D. (1996) *When Cultures Collide: Managing Successfully across Cultures*. London: Nicholas Brealey.

Morley, M.J., Minbaeva, D. and Michailova, S. (2012): 'The transition states of Central and Eastern Europe and the Former Soviet Union', in C. Brewster and W. Mayrhofer (eds), *Handbook of Research on Comparative Human Resource Management*. Cheltenham: Edward Elgar.

Ronen, S. and Shenkar, O. (1985) 'Clustering countries on attitudinal dimensions: A review and synthesis', *Academy of Management Review,* Vol. 10, No. 3, pp. 435–54,

Sparrow, P. (2012) 'Comparative analysis of employment contracts', in C. Brewster and W. Mayrhofer (eds), *Handbook of Research on Comparative Human Resource Management.* Cheltenham: Edward Elgar.

Strodtbeck, K. (1961) *Variations in Value Orientations.* Westport: Greenwood.

Trompenaars, F. and Hampden-Turner, C. (2006) *Riding the Waves of Culture: Understanding Diversity in Global Business.* Columbus: McGraw Hill.

Whitley, R. (1999) *Divergent Capitalisms: The Social Structuring and Change of National Business Systems.* Oxford: Oxford University Press.

Woo, J.-W. (2014) 'The evolution of human resource management in Japan: Continuity, change and enduring challenges', in B. Kaufman (ed), *The Development of Human Resource Management across Nations: Unity and Diversity.* Cheltenham: Edward Elgar.

Wright, P. and Van de Voorde, K. (2009) 'Multilevel issues in IHRM: Mean differences, explained variance and moderated relationships', in P. Sparrow (ed.), *Handbook of International Human Resource Management.* Chichester: Wiley.

Ybema, S. and Nyiri, P. (2015) 'The Hofstede factor: The consequences of *Culture's Consequences',* in N. Holden, S. Michailova and S. Tietze (eds), *The Routledge Companion to Cross-Cultural Management.* Abingdon: Routledge.

Zagelmeyer, S. (2011) 'Employment relations in France and Germany', in M. Barry and A. Wilkinson (eds), *Research Handbook of Comparative Employment Relations.* Cheltenham: Edward Elgar.

CHAPTER 4

STRATEGIC HUMAN RESOURCE MANAGEMENT

THE OBJECTIVES OF THIS CHAPTER ARE TO:

1 Clarify the nature of strategic HRM

2 Investigate the relationship between business strategy and HR strategy

3 Explain the universalist and the contingency or fit perspectives of HR strategy, each proposing a different means of identifying which HR practices will lead to high performance

4 Examine the resource-based view of HR strategy

5 Explain *how* HR strategy, and connected policies and practices, may result in higher performance

6 Evaluate all three theoretical perspectives on the nature of HR strategy, each expressing a different view on how the contribution of people to the organisation might be understood and enhanced

Human resources are increasingly viewed as a critical, if not *the* source of, competitive advantage for the business, rather than, say, access to capital or use of technology. Thus attention needs to be paid, at a strategic level, to the nature of this resource and its management, as this will impact on the performance of the organisation, however defined. Batt and Banerjee (2012) found that, in an analysis of strategic HR research articles in British and American journals, the link between human resources and performance remains the dominant theme. Indeed Boxall and Purcell (2015: 274) argue that:

> Human resource strategy is an essential element in business strategy, not some kind of dubious appendage to it, and plays a critical role in organizational viability and relative performance.

On a more practical level, in the 2004 Workplace Employment Relations Survey (WERS5) it was found that 87% of workplaces with a strategic plan included some issues relating to employment relations (broadly defined) (Kersley *et al*. 2006). Directly comparable results for WERS6 (2011) are not available, however the researchers report that the inclusion of both employee diversity issues and the forecasting of staffing requirements in formal strategic plans had increased from 2004 to 2011 (van Wanrooy *et al*., 2013). These increases were statistically significant.

Strategic HRM

Tyson's (1995) definition of HR strategy is a useful starting point, although somewhat limited:

> the intentions of the corporation both explicit and covert, towards the management of its employees, expressed through philosophies, policies and practices.

Thus HR strategy need not be written on a piece of paper, and published, and may not be explicit, but reflects the way that management sees employee relations in a particular workplace. The Cranet Survey of International Strategic HR found that 39% of UK companies did not have a written HR strategy (Guthridge and Lawson 2008).

Debates on HR strategy increasingly focus on the way that such philosophies, policies and practices can be designed to promote desired employee behaviour and attitudes which are judged to promote high performance and sustainable organisational success. Attention is also increasingly focused on *how* such practices result in high performance, requiring more exploration of strategy implementation and employee perceptions and choices.

ACTIVITY 4.1

Using an organisation with which you are familiar:

1 Identify the explicit intentions of the organisation towards the management of its people in terms of overall philosophy, policies and practices.

2 Assess the extent to which you consider these intentions to be implemented in practice, giving evidence to support your judgement.

3 How can you explain any mismatch between explicit intentions and actual practice?

A strategy may be a physical document but a strategic approach can also be seen as an incremental process, affected by political influences and generating learning. Strategies are often neither finished, nor complete, but rather incremental and piecemeal. Much strategic HR tends to be issue based rather than the formulation of a complete and integrated strategy. Strategic thinking, strategic decision making and a strategic orientation are sometimes more realistic expectations, although increasingly some organisations do achieve a superficially more complete approach by the use of scorecards and dashboards, which we look at in the following chapter. In any event HR strategies need to be flexible and adaptable as circumstances change.

WINDOW ON PRACTICE

Transport for London (TfL)

When Robert Jeffery interviewed Tricia Riley, HR Director at TfL, she explained that:

> We have strategic people priorities rather than an HR strategy because the people strategy is owned by the senior leadership team not by HR . . . We help pull it together, facilitate it and make sure it's aligned to the business strategy . . . We've come to realise you don't need the leading edge HR practice in the world because that may not be appropriate.

This quote usefully highlights the use of strategic priorities; the relationship between HR strategic issues and business strategy; ownership of the people strategy; and the strategic choice of using or not using leading edge HR policies/best practice. These are all issues which we explore further in this chapter and in chapter 30.

Source: Jeffery. R. (2015) 'You don't always have to be the best', *People Management*, April, pp. 18–20.

Much of the general strategy literature also views strategy as a process which is not necessarily rational and top down, but a political and evolutionary process. Mintzberg (1994), for example, argues that strategy is 'formed' rather than 'formulated' and that any intended strategy is changed by events, opportunities, the actions of employees and so on – so that the realised strategy is different from the initial vision. Strategy, Mintzberg argues, can only be identified in retrospect and is best seen in the ultimate behaviour of the organisation. Indeed strategy is not necessarily determined by top management alone but can be influenced 'bottom up', as ideas are tried and tested in one part of the organisation and gradually adopted in a wholesale manner if they are seen to be applicable and successful.

Strategy is inevitably a process of change, as the organisation attempts to change from the state it is in to a strategically identified future state. The literature draws out the need to sense changes in the environment, develop a resultant strategy and turn this strategy into action. While the HR function has often found itself excluded from the business strategy formation process, HR strategy has more often been seen in terms of the implementation of organisational strategies. However, implementation of HR strategy has, at best, been weak. Among the qualities of the most successful organisations is the ability to turn strategy into action quickly (Ulrich 1998), in other words to implement the chosen strategy, and this continues to be a challenge according to Kaplan and Norton (2005) who found that 95% of employees did not know or did not understand their company's strategy. A lack of attention to the implementation of HR strategy has been identified, and Guest (2011) points out how this focuses attention on the role of the line manager and HR effectiveness.

The Window on practice below shows how one organisation implemented business and HR strategy and how it used a set of desired values as focus.

WINDOW ON PRACTICE

Implementing strategy at Fujitsu

Fujitsu Services, which designs, builds and operates IT systems and services, was formed in 2002 when the Japanese IT group acquired ICL. Three years after this a need was identified to ensure all employees were working towards the same goal and communicating clearly. To meet this strategic need a programme called 'Reputation' was designed with the aim of aligning all employees (senior managers, on-call engineers, service desk teleworkers) operating out of more than twenty countries, to the same values and customer brand so that customers received a consistent experience.

The Reputation model was introduced into small group sessions cascading through the organisation with 'Reputation champions' initially leading the programme. These champions trained 2,000 managers to deliver the programme to their teams.

The values chosen to reflect the company brand were: realism, straight-talking and tenacious. These were important as historically Fujitsu had been known for overpromising and underperforming. Both the HR and marketing functions promoted the programme aiming to ensure the internal (staff) and external (customers) coherence of the brand.

Staff were helped to understand how their behaviour affected colleagues, customers and the business overall, and a shared vocabulary has been developed. All staff were encouraged to regard themselves as key players, and always 'put their best face forward'. The sessions were also designed to open lines of communication and engage staff in debates about the business in groups with a mix of staff level and from a range of departments. This was intended to help people recognise that their goals were the same. Employee contributions were viewed as key and the programme intended to be interactive, not top down.

Fujitsu aimed to embed its values across the business: for example, when HR policies are designed these are tested against the values, with the idea of ensuring a consistent experience. Cohesive working is the ultimate aim of the programme.

Source: Adapted from 'Build a better brand', *People Management*, Vol. 14, No. 15, pp. 24–5 (Chubb, L. (2008)), reproduced with the permission of the publisher, the Chartered Institute of Personnel and Development, London (www.cipd.co.uk).

The relationship between business strategy and HR strategy

The nature, desirability and feasibility of the link between business strategy and HR strategy is a consistent theme which runs through the strategy literature, although, as we shall discuss later, some theories suggest that implementing 'best practice' in HRM is even more important than this. Figure 4.1 is a simple model that is useful in visualising different ways in which this relationship may be played out and has relevance for the newer conceptions of strategy based on the resource-based view of the firm, as well as earlier conceptions.

In the *separation model* (A) there is no relationship at all, if indeed organisational and HR strategy *do* exist in an explicit form in the organisation. This is a typical picture of thirty years ago, but it still exists today, particularly in smaller organisations.

The *fit model* (B) represents a growing recognition of the importance of people in the achievement of organisational strategy. Employees are seen as key in the implementation of the declared organisational strategy, and HR strategy is designed to fit with this. Some of the early formal models of HR strategy, particularly that proposed by Fombrun *et al.*

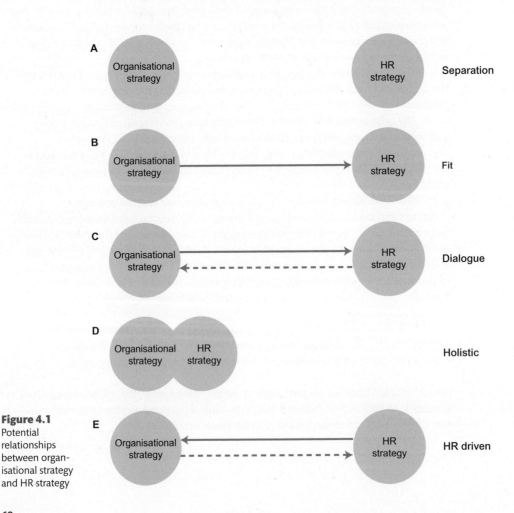

Figure 4.1
Potential relationships between organisational strategy and HR strategy

(1984), concentrate on how the HR strategy can be designed to ensure a close fit with business strategy. The main idea is that HR policies and practices can be designed to elicit the employee behaviour and attitudes which fit the business strategy.

This whole approach depends on a view of strategy formulation as a logical rational process, which remains a widely held view. The relationship in the fit model is exemplified by organisations which cascade their business objectives down from the senior management team through functions (including HR), through departments, through teams and so on, so that each can identify what they need to do to meet strategic organisational demands.

The *dialogue model* (C) takes the relationship one step further, as it recognises the need for two-way communication and some debate. What is demanded in the organisation's strategy may not be viewed as feasible and alternative possibilities need to be reviewed. The debate, however, is often limited, as shown in the example in the Window on practice which follows.

WINDOW ON PRACTICE

In one large multinational organisation an objectives-setting cascade was put in place. This cascade allowed for a dialogue between the planned organisational strategy and the response of each function. In the organisational strategy there was some emphasis on people growth and development and job fulfilment. The HR department's response included among other things an emphasis on line management involvement in these areas, which would be supported by consultancy help from the HR department.

The top management team replied to this by asking the HR department to add a strategic objective about employee welfare and support. The HR department strongly argued that this was a line management responsibility, along with coaching, development and so on. The HR function saw its customers as the managers of the organisation, not the employees. The result of the debate was that the HR function added the strategic objective about employee welfare.

Although the approach in this case appeared two-way, the stronger of the parties were the management team, and they were determined that their vision was the one that would be implemented!

The integrated/holistic model and the HR-driven model (D and E) show a much closer involvement between organisational and HR strategy.

The *integrated/holistic model* (D) represents the people of the organisation being recognised as the key to competitive advantage rather than just the way of implementing organisational strategy. In other words, HR strategy is not just the means for achieving business strategy (the ends), but an end in itself. HR strategy therefore becomes critical and, as Baird *et al.* (1983) argued, there can be no strategy without HR strategy. Boxall (1996) develops this idea in relation to the resource-based firm, and argues convincingly that business strategy can usefully be interpreted as broader than a competitive strategy (or positioning in the marketplace). In this case business strategy can encompass a variety of other strategies including HRM, and he describes these strategies as the pieces of a jigsaw. This suggests mutual development and some form of integration, rather than a slavish response to a predetermined business strategy, for example the integration of HR and marketing strategies so that the customer brand and the employer brand are aligned.

The *HR-driven model* (E) offers a more extreme form, which places HR strategy in prime position. The argument here is that if people are the key to competitive advantage, then we need to build on our people strengths. Logically, then, as the potential of our employees will undoubtedly affect the achievement of any planned strategy, it would be sensible to take account of this in developing our strategic direction. Butler (1988) identifies this model as a shift from HR as the implementers of strategy to HR as a driving force in the formulation of the strategy. Again this model is a reflection of a resource-based strategic HRM perspective, and sits well with the increasing attention being given to the notion of 'human capital' where it is the collective nature and quality of the people in the organisation which provide the potential for future competitive advantage (see e.g. Lengnick-Hall and Lengnick-Hall 2003).

ACTIVITY 4.2

1 Which of these approaches to HR strategy most closely fits your organisation? (If you are a full-time student read one or two relevant cases in *People Management* and interpret these as 'your organisation'.)

2 Why did you come to this conclusion?

3 What are the advantages and disadvantages of the approach used?

Theoretical perspectives of strategic HRM

Three theoretical approaches to strategic HRM can be identified. The first is founded on the concept that there is 'one best way' of managing human resources in order to improve business performance. The second focuses on the need to align employment policies and practice with the requirements of business strategy in order that the latter will be achieved and the business will be successful. This second approach is based on the assumption that different types of HR strategies will be suitable for different types of business strategies. The third approach is derived from the resource-based view of the firm, and the perceived value of human capital. This view focuses on the quality of the human resources available to the organisation and its ability to learn and adapt more quickly than its competitors. Supporters of this perspective challenge the need to secure a mechanistic fit with business strategy and focus instead on long-term sustainability and survival of the organisation via the pool of human capital.

Perspective 1: Universalist approach

The universalist approach is derived from the conception of HRM as 'best practice', as we discussed earlier (see Chapter 1). Researchers carried out large-scale statistical research projects to identify the HR practices which were linked to higher organisational performance. Attention was paid to sophisticated and innovative practices, and Huselid (1995), for example, evaluated the links between progressive HR practices and organisational performance using a sample of nearly 1,000 firms. His findings suggested clear statistical relationships between these practices and employee outcomes such as reduced labour turnover and productivity and long- and short-term firm measures of corporate financial performance. The focus was on identifying 'bundles' of practices, sometimes referred to as the configurational approach, which were mutually supporting in that the effect of combining a number of HR practices is greater than the effect of using them independently: combinations produce synergy, and this is known as the complementarity thesis (Boxall and Macky 2009).

It is also generally agreed that grouping HR practices into 'bundles' in what has become known as a high-performance work system (HPWS; Boxall and Macky 2009) is performance enhancing. Such practices generally devolve a degree of control to employees, through, for example, involvement programmes, team-based work, enhanced training and development, and incorporate progressive methods of reward such as gain sharing, all of which focus on motivation and development. Pfeffer (2005), another well-known advocate of the best practice perspective, identifies a bundle of thirteen HR practices which will result in higher performance, although Lepak and Shaw (2008) point out that Pfeffer's elaboration is based more on interpretation than solid empirical evidence.

The universalist approach is thus based on the premise that one model of labour management – a high-commitment model (sometimes referred to as a high-involvement or high-performance model) – is related to high organisational performance in all contexts, irrespective of the particular competitive strategy of the organisation.

However, there are problems with this approach. For example, the association between HRM and performance does not tell us that that HRM *causes* higher performance. In other words, a high-performing organisation may result in the use of innovative HR practices as it has the funds to do so.

There also remains some debate as to which particular bundle of HR practices will stimulate high commitment, as different researchers appear to have found different contradictory bundles. In addition there are problems with the reliability of how the HR practices were reported in the surveys – usually just one respondent at a higher level in the organisation – and no account is taken of line manager or employee views as to whether or how these practices were implemented. Yanadori and Van Jaarsveld (2014) have demonstrated that employees sometimes *choose* not to take part in high performance work practices. They also found that 'informal' high performance work practices influence performance, and of course a higher level manager may be unaware of these.

The universalist approach is also unitarist, being based on the assumption that all managers have to do is to apply a certain set of practices and higher performance will result as workers will comply with whatever is required of them without questioning whether it is to their advantage to do so. These models provide some clarity which is attractive, but this is where the problems also lie, as managing people is far more complex than suggested in the model, and in most studies little account appears to be taken of context; the need for an organisation to manage different sections of the workforce in different ways; and the potential for this approach to create work intensification. For example, Truss *et al.* (2012) point to the difficulty of applying these practices in different cultures and countries with different employment laws. Because the prescriptive approach brings with it a set of values, it suggests that there is only one best way and this is it.

ACTIVITY 4.3

1 To what extent could or should an organisation apply best practice to some groups of employees and not others?

2 Use an organisation which you know well and identify whether this is happening, and evaluate the benefits and disadvantages of this approach.

Perspective 2: Fit or contingency approach

The fit or contingency approach is based on two critical forms of fit. The first is external fit (sometimes referred to as vertical integration) – that HR strategy fits with the demands of business strategy. The second is internal fit (sometimes referred to as horizontal integration) – that all HR policies and activities fit together so that they make a coherent whole, are mutually reinforcing and are applied consistently. While external fit is most commonly interpreted as fit with business strategy, Lepak and Shaw (2008) remind us that HR strategy must also fit with, for example, the technology and industry sector, and they consider fit with workforce trends and worker values as emerging factors in respect of fit. Indeed fit with cultural characteristics is becoming more important as international companies increasingly recognise that HR policies and practices cannot be, simply, exported to other cultural contexts. For example, western practices which emphasise individual appraisal and reward will sit awkwardly in a collectivist culture such as Japan's.

One of the foundations of strategic HRM (see, for example, Kaufman 2015) and specifically of the fit approach is the work of Fombrun *et al.* (1984), who proposed a basic framework for strategic HRM, demonstrating, within the firm, how HR management and organisation structure (which interact) are derived from the firm's mission and strategy management, with all in turn being influenced by political, economic and cultural forces in the external context. This exemplifies how the *fit mode*l (B) is used (see Figure 4.1). Figure 4.2 shows how activities *within* HR management can be unified and designed in order to support the organisation's strategy.

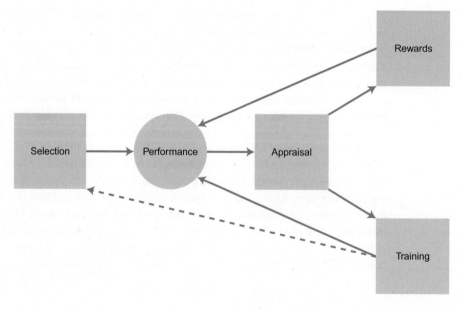

Figure 4.2
The HR cycle
Source: C. Fombrun, N.M. Tichy and M.A. Devanna (1984) *Strategic Human Resource Management.* p. 41. New York: John Wiley & Sons, Inc. © John Wiley & Sons, Inc. Reprinted with permission of John Wiley & Sons, Inc.

The strength of this model is that it provides a simple framework to show how selection, appraisal, development and reward can be mutually geared to produce the required type of employee performance. For example, if an organisation required cooperative team behaviour with mutual sharing of information and support, the broad implications for managing employees would be:

- **Selection:** successful experience of teamwork and sociable, cooperative personality; rather than an independent thinker who likes working alone.
- **Development:** group/team-based development emphasising communication and knowledge sharing rather than online modules individually experienced.
- **Appraisal:** based on contribution to the team, and support of others, rather than individual outstanding performance.
- **Reward:** based on team performance and contribution, rather than individual performance and individual effort.

Taking this model and the notion of fit one step further, HR strategy has been conceived in terms of generating specific employee behaviours. In the ideal form of this there would be analysis of the types of employee behaviour required to fulfil a predetermined business strategy, and then an identification of HR policies and practices which would bring about and reinforce this behaviour. In a step change from previous thinking, Schuler and Jackson (1987) produce an excellent example of this concept. They used the three generic business strategies defined by Porter (1980) and for each identified employee role behaviour and the HRM policies required. Their conclusions are shown in Table 4.1.

Table 4.1 Business strategies, and associated employee role behaviour and HRM policies

Strategy	Employee role behaviour	HRM policies
1 Innovation	A high degree of creative behaviour	Jobs that require close interaction and coordination among groups of individuals
	Longer-term focus	Performance appraisals that are more likely to reflect longer-term and group-based achievements
	A relatively high level of cooperative, interdependent behaviour	Jobs that allow employees to develop skills that can be used in other positions in the firm
		Compensation systems that emphasise internal equity rather than external or market-based equity
	A moderate degree of concern for quality	Pay rates that tend to be low, but that allow employees to be stockholders and have more freedom to choose the mix of components that make up their pay package
	A moderate concern for quantity; an equal degree of concern for process and results	Broad career paths to reinforce the development of a broad range of skills
	A greater degree of risk taking; a higher tolerance of ambiguity and unpredictability	
2 Quality enhancement	Relatively repetitive and predictable behaviours	Relatively fixed and explicit job descriptions
	A more long-term or intermediate focus	High levels of employee participation in decisions relevant to immediate work conditions and the job itself
	A moderate amount of cooperative, interdependent behaviour	A mix of individual and group criteria for performance appraisal that is mostly short term and results orientated
	A high concern for quality	A relatively egalitarian treatment of employees and some guarantees of employment security
	A modest concern for quantity of output	Extensive and continuous training and development of employees

Table 4.1

Strategy	Employee role behaviour	HRM policies
	High concern for process: low risk-taking activity; commitment to the goals of the organisation	
3 Cost reduction	Relatively repetitive and predictable behaviour	Relatively fixed and explicit job descriptions that allow little room for ambiguity
	A rather short-term focus	Narrowly designed jobs and narrowly defined career paths that encourage specialisation, expertise and efficiency
	Primarily autonomous or individual activity	Short-term results-orientated performance appraisals
	Moderate concern for quality	Close monitoring of market pay levels for use in making compensation decisions
	High concern for quantity of output	Minimal levels of employee training and development
	Primary concern for results; low risk-taking activity; relatively high degree of comfort with stability	

Source: R.S. Schuler and S.E. Jackson (1987) 'Linking competitive strategies with human resource management practices', *Academy of Management Executive,* Vol. 1, No. 3. Reproduced with permission of the Academy of Management.

Similar analyses can be found for other approaches to business strategy, for example in relation to the Boston matrix (Purcell 1992) and the developmental stage of the organisation (Kochan and Barocci 1985). Some HR strategies describe the behaviour of all employees, but others have concentrated on the behaviour of chief executives and senior managers; Miles and Snow (1984), for example, align appropriate managerial characteristics to three generic strategies of prospector, defender and analyser. The types of strategies described above are generic, and there is currently greater concentration on tailoring the approach more specifically to the strategic needs of the specific organisation via dashboards and scorecards (see Chapter 5).

WINDOW ON PRACTICE

The consequences of lack of fit

Samnani and Singh looked at both vertical and horizontal fit in ABC company, a premium educational provider who charged higher prices due to a record number of students successfully completing their courses (certification) and achieving high levels of subsequent employment. ABC employed approximately 70 employees (advisors). It was important for the company to have motivated and committed advisors in order to deliver the business strategy (achieving high levels of certification and employment). The researchers looked at four areas of HRM policy and practice:

Recruitment: A range of rigorous methods were used to ensure motivated and committed candidates were chosen who would remain with ABC. Candidates formed a positive impression of the company, thinking that it invested in its employees. There was clear fit with the business strategy.

Training and development: Once employed advisors found a lack of development opportunities and became dissatisfied that they were not provided with challenges that would help them grow or opportunities for promotion. They were consequently demotivated and many wanted to leave to get a more challenging job. This did not fit with the strategy or with recruitment practices.

Performance management: There were formal reviews and whilst high performers were identified they were not compensated accordingly or given career opportunities. The advisors saw performance management as a burden and not a development opportunity. This did not fit with the strategy. Internal fit appeared confusing.

Compensation: This was based on starting pay rather than performance and consequently high performers were often paid less than advisors who performed less well. There was a lack of vertical fit. Internal fit appeared confusing.

Insufficient vertical fit and inadequate internal fit sent confusing messages to employees, and they were consequently demotivated and put in minimum effort – the opposite of what was required by the business strategy.

Source: From Samnani, A. and Singh, P. (2013) 'Exploring the fit perspective', *Human Resource Management*, Vol. 52, No. 1, pp. 124–44.

Many HR strategies aim not just to target behaviour and attitudes, but through behaviour and attitude change to effect a movement in the culture of the organisation. The target is, therefore, to change the common view of 'the way we do things around here' and to attempt to manipulate the beliefs and values of employees. There is much debate as to whether this is achievable.

There is little doubt that this type of internal fit is valuable. However, questions have been raised over the model's simplistic response to organisational strategy. The question 'what if it is not possible to produce a human resource response that enables the required employee behaviour and performance?' is never addressed. So, for example, the distance between now and future performance requirements, the strengths, weaknesses and potential of the workforce, the motivation of the workforce and employee relations issues are not considered. This model has been criticised because of its dependence on a rational strategy formulation rather than on an emergent strategy formation approach. It has also been criticised due to its unitarist assumptions, as no recognition is made of employees' interests and their choice of whether or not to change their behaviour.

If fit can be seen as something that can be targeted, observed and measured and with an underlying assumption of stability, this is of little lasting value as most companies may have to change radically in response to the environment. Any degree of fit previously achieved will be disturbed. Thus fit is a theoretical ideal which can rarely be achieved in practice. The aim for consistency is also a challenge, as it has been shown that firms use different strategies for different sections of their workforce.

A further form of fit which we have not mentioned so far is cultural fit, and the Window on practice below demonstrates this aspect, and shows how fit has to go far beyond a simple fit with business strategy.

WINDOW ON PRACTICE

Cultural fit: The influence of national culture on HRM strategies

Fields and colleagues (2006) investigated whether, under similar conditions, organisations in different cultural contexts would strategically respond in a different manner. They compared US organisations with Hong Kong Chinese organisations and studied their strategic approach in conditions of uncertainty in the supply of qualified labour. They studied three aspects of HR relevant to this situation:

- training and development;
- monitoring and assessment of employee performance; and
- staffing through an internal labour market.

They found, as they expected, that in these conditions the Hong Kong Chinese companies increased their use of these three HRM strategies, but that the US companies decreased their use. They explain these different strategic approaches by reference to the cultural context.

Training and development (TD)

Fields *et al.* suggest that more TD would be positively viewed by the more collective Chinese culture as a symbol that the organisation is fulfilling its moral obligation to employees, as a way to increase the value of each individual to the collective organisation, and as a reward. Each of these would be valued by Chinese employees, and would encourage them to remain with the organisation. Alternatively, in the more individualistic US culture managers would be reluctant to invest in TD when labour supply is scarce as employees may take advantage of this and use it to find a better job elsewhere.

Emphasis on performance assessment (PA)

Fields *et al.* also suggest that in the Chinese culture, with greater power distance, greater PA may be viewed by employees as a positive symbol that managers are interested in them, and may act as a reminder of the employees' moral association with the organisation – thus encouraging employees to stay. Alternatively, in the US culture with lower power distance, more PA would be viewed negatively. It may be seen as emphasising the difference between managers and employees, and as a way of tightening up the employment relationship, both of which may lead employees to seek employment elsewhere.

Internal labour market (IL)

Greater use of the IL might be viewed in a collectivist culture by the Chinese employees as evidence that they are valued by the organisation and thus it may encourage retention. Alternatively, in an individualistic culture employees may view this unfavourably as evidence of a subjective rather than objective (based on merit) approach to promotion, and managers may view it as a means by which employees can barter for better rewards in a tight labour market.

Source: Adapted from Fields, D., Chan, A., Aktar, S. and Blum, T. (2006) 'Human resource management strategies under uncertainty', *Cross Cultural Management: An International Journal*, Vol. 13, No. 2, pp. 171–86.

Perspective 3: Resource-based approach

The resource-based view of the firm (Barney 1991) has prompted attempts to create a resource-based model of strategic HRM. The resource-based view of the firm is concerned with the relationships between internal resources (of which the human resource is one), strategy and firm performance. It focuses on the promotion of sustained competitive advantage through the development of human capital rather than merely aligning human resources to current strategic goals. Human resources can provide competitive advantage for the business, as long as they are unique and competing organisations cannot copy or substitute for them. The focus is not just on the behaviour and attitudes of the human resources (as with the fit approach), but on the skills, knowledge, deeper attitudes and competencies which underpin this, and which have a more sustained impact on long-term survival than current behaviour, although this is still regarded as important.

Barney (1991) states that in order for a resource to result in sustained competitive advantage it must meet four criteria, and Wright *et al.* (1994) demonstrate how human resources meet these. First, the resource must be *valuable*. Wright and his colleagues argue that this is the case where demand for labour is heterogeneous, and where the supply of labour is also heterogeneous, in other words where different firms require different competencies from each other and for different roles in the organisation, and where the supply of potential labour comprises individuals with different competencies. On this basis value is created by matching an individual's competencies with the requirements of the firm and/or the job, as individuals will make a variable contribution, and one cannot be substituted easily for another.

The second criterion, *rarity*, is related to the first. This assumes that the most important competence for employees is cognitive ability due to future needs for adaptability and flexibility. On the basis that cognitive ability is normally distributed in the population, those with high levels of this ability will be rare. The talent pool is not unlimited and many employers continue to have difficulty finding the talent that they require, even with relatively high levels of unemployment in many countries as this is written.

Third, resources need to be *inimitable*. Wright *et al.* argue that this quality applies to the human resource as competitors will find it difficult to identify the exact source of competitive advantage from within the firm's HR pool. Also competitors will not be able to duplicate exactly the resource in question, as they will be unable to copy the unique historical conditions of the first firm. This history is important as it will affect the behaviour of the HR pool via the development of unique norms and cultures. Thus even if a competing firm recruited a group of individuals from a competitor it would still not be able to produce the same outcomes in the new firm as the context would be different.

Finally, resources need to be *non-substitutable*. Wright and his co-authors argue that although in the short term it may be possible to substitute human resources with others, for example technological ones, in the long term the human resource is different as it does not become obsolete (like technology) and can be transferred across other products, markets and technologies.

Although sometimes human capital is interpreted as the leaders in the organisation, who are easily identifiable, or other employees with skills critical to competitive advantage, it may also be viewed as the totality of human resources in the organisation. This sits well with the view of strategy as evolutionary and strategy being influenced from the bottom up as well as from the top down. Human capital may be expressed as intellectual capital, that is the knowledge skills and attributes of employees, and sometimes social capital, meaning the networks that employees have both internally and externally.

Whereas the universalist and fit models focus on the means of competitive advantage (HR practices) the resource-based view focuses on the source (the human capital). Wright *et al.* argue that, although the practices are important, they are not the source of competitive advantage as they can be replicated elsewhere, and they will produce different results in different places because of the differential human capital in different places. The relationship between human capital, HR practices and competitive advantage is shown in Figure 4.3.

Boxall (1996) argues that this theoretical perspective provides a conceptual base for asserting that human resources are a source of competitive advantage, and as such valued as generating strategic capability. Thus there is a case for viewing HR strategy as something more than a reactive matching process. Indeed Wright *et al.* argue that it provides the case for HR to be involved in the formulation of strategy rather than just its implementation. They suggest that it provides a grounding for asserting that not every strategy is universally implementable, and that alternatives may have to be sought or the human capital pool developed further, via HR practices, where this is possible.

The importance of this perspective is underlined by an increase in the emphasis on a firm's intangible assets. Numerous studies have shown that a firm's market value, expressed by the sum of the value of the shares, is not fully explained by its current financial results (see e.g. Ulrich and Smallwood 2002) or by its tangible assets and the focus has moved to a firm's intangible assets such as intellectual capital and customer relationships – all of which are derived from human capital. In the early 2000s this emphasis resulted in more attention being paid to the evaluation of human capital through measuring, for example, the aggregate of knowledge, skills and abilities in the firm, reporting it in the annual report, say, and managing it. The perceived importance of people as an intangible asset is demonstrated in the action of Barclays Group, which on its Investor's Day was keen to demonstrate not only its financial results, but also its people strategies and improvements in staff satisfaction which it believed to have contributed to the results (Arkin and Allen 2002).

Such reporting was not made mandatory, however, and although encouraged where relevant, little progress has been made by companies overall. Currently the CIPD and other professional bodies are strongly promoting such external reporting, yet a research study in 2015 (CIPD), still found that investors' appetite for more information on human capital was variable. Yet the importance of human capital is frequently emphasised by academics and professional bodies.

This approach has great advantages from an HR point of view. People in the organisation become the focus, their contribution is monitored and made more explicit, the way people are managed can be seen to add value and money spent on people can be seen as an investment rather than a cost. Some firms are using the balanced scorecard to

Figure 4.3
A model of human resources as a source of sustained competitive advantage

Source: P. Wright, G. McMahon and A. McWilliams (1994) 'Human resources and sustained competitive advantage: A resource-based perspective', *International Journal of Human Resource Management*, Vol. 5, No. 2, p. 318. Reproduced with the permission of Taylor & Francis Ltd. See www.tandf.co.uk/journals.

demonstrate the contribution that human capital makes to firm performance, such as Aviva. However, there are inbuilt barriers in the language of the resource-based view. One is the reference to people as 'human capital', which some consider to be unnecessarily instrumental. Another is the focus on 'firms' and 'competitive advantage' which makes it harder to see the relevance of this perspective for organisations in the public sector. There is also the issue of what is being measured and who decides this. The risk is that too much time is spent measuring and that not everything that is measured is of critical value to the organisation. So far, such measures appear very varied, although different firms will, of course, need to measure different things. Measures often appear to be taken without a coherent framework and Ployhart and Moliterno (2011) warn us that more is not always better. To move things forward the CIPD (2014) propose four basic measures they suggest all companies produce and share: total cost of workforce employed; recruitment costs; total investment in training and development; and employee engagement survey scores.

Human capital is loaned: 'human capital is not owned by the organisation, but secured through the employment relationship' (Scarborough 2003: 2) and because this is so, the strategy for the management of people is also critical. It also means, as Wright and McMahan (2011) point out, that we should be concerned with how individuals themselves 'make choices regarding investments in their human capital, such as the choice to receive training, gain a college education or begin a physical workout regimen' (p. 94). Individuals may not choose to exploit their capital to the full, and of course they may leave the organisation.

Explaining the HRM practices–performance link

We noted above the importance of individual choice and increasingly researchers are going beyond identifying *which* HR practices best support high organisational performance, and seeking to explain *how* HR practices lead to enhanced performance. This has become known as unlocking the 'black box' of the HRM–performance link (Purcell *et al.* 2003). Picking up on the idea that HR practices improve performance through the influence they have upon employee attitudes, Purcell and colleagues have produced models showing how HR practices are at the beginning of a causal chain which seeks to influence attitudes, behaviour and then outcomes such as performance (Figure 4.4).

In academic terms, employee attitudes are described as being the mediating variables between HR practices and improved performance, and determine whether an employee will engage in discretionary behaviour (going above and beyond the minimum they are required to contribute) and consequently achieve higher performance. Clearly if attitudes are the crux of how to influence performance, it is important to understand which employee attitudes HR practices should seek to influence. Initial theorising focused on the concept of commitment, reflected in the widespread use of the terms 'high-commitment work practices' and 'high-commitment management' and their linkage with high performance. It was argued that such commitment from employees would lead to discretionary

Figure 4.4
The people management–performance causal chain
Source: Purcell and Hutchinson (2007: 7), Fig. 1.

behaviour, and thus improve performance, and would also reduce labour turnover and absence costs.

Other attitudes such as job satisfaction, motivation and trust have increasingly been recognised as also important in encouraging employees to engage in discretionary behaviour (Macky and Boxall 2007). In our own work, we have argued that employee attitudes such as happiness are also important in affecting behaviour and performance. Happiness has long been neglected in HR literature but has re-emerged, however, in the positive psychology movement, which refocuses the attention of psychologists on what makes people happy as opposed to the historical trend of investigating what makes people unhappy. Conceptualising happiness as well-being has led psychologists to argue once again for a link between this attitude and performance. Our own research (Atkinson and Hall 2011) certainly supports this line of argument and there is much work to be done in the area of employee attitudes and which HR practices influence them and to what extent.

Purcell *et al*. (2003) were early researchers in the field of opening and understanding the 'black box' which explains how HR practices impact on employee performance. Their model exemplifies the importance of how HR practices are applied in that they will impact on the Ability and skills of employees, the Motivation and incentive provided to them and the Opportunity to participate in discretionary behaviour (which is why this is often referred to as the AMO model). In turn AMO impacts on employee attitudes, which they suggest as commitment, motivation and job satisfaction, which promote discretionary behaviour and better performance outcomes. The model also highlights the importance of the organisation having a 'big idea' which provides an appropriate focus around which people can pull together.

Recent research continues to focus on the role of line managers and implementation; and also on the employee perspective in explaining the mechanisms mediating the HRM–performance link. This work recognises that intended strategy, policy and practices are not always implemented as designed, and this will of course interrupt or divert the link. Successful implementation depends on line managers understanding the purpose of each HR policy and what each HR practice is intended to achieve. It also requires 'buy in' from managers and their interpretation of the value of such practices. Training and support may play an important role here. This is often referred to as the 'implementation gap'.

Piening and colleagues (2014) report some fascinating research on the 'implementation gap' and also on the 'interpretation gap' which focuses on how employees perceive and experience implemented HR policies and practices, and Kinnie *et al*. (2005: 11) argue that:

> the fulcrum of the HRM–performance causal chain is the employees' reactions to HR practices as experienced by them.

So it is important to explore how employees understand the practices which are implemented; and part of this is the psychological processes by which employees attribute meaning to such practices. Put simply, do employees see the HR practices in their organisation as there to support their well-being or as exploitative? A useful introduction to the importance of 'the HRM process', as it is sometimes referred to, is Sanders and colleagues (2014). Employee expectations may have an influence here – for example if they have formed a view of the company as supportive they are more likely to interpret new HR practices as positive, and vice versa.

WINDOW ON PRACTICE

Have as many holidays as you like?

Some well-known companies have recently introduced the practice of allowing employees to take as much annual leave as they wish – there is no limit or entitlement given. How might employees interpret such a practice? It is entirely possible that employees in such progressive companies, with other practices supporting their well-being, interpret this policy as being supportive – allowing them flexibility; trusting and empowering them. In another company such a practice may be perceived as exploitative, raising questions such as: how will taking leave be perceived by the company?; will taking more leave than others brand the employee as not sufficiently committed to their job and damage their career prospects? Such employees may fear to take very much leave and feel exploited.

There may be other factors which affect employee perceptions, of course: their understanding of the HR practices they experience, their life experiences, personality, current life pressures, and so on. Clearly understanding these perceptions will help to explain the HRM practices–performance link.

Explaining the HR practices–performance link can best be understood using a multi-level perspective (Jiang *et al.* 2013). In summary, senior organisation members design HR philosophy, policy, systems and practices; line managers at team level implement these HR practices; and individual employees experience and perceive these practices.

Why does the theory matter?

It is tempting to think of the three underlying theories of strategic HRM (universalist; fit; human capital) as competing with each other. In other words, one is right and the others are wrong. If this were the case HR managers/directors and board members would need only to work out which is the 'right' theory and apply that. This is, of course, a gross oversimplification, as each theory can be interpreted and applied in different ways, and each has advantages and disadvantages. It could be argued that different theories apply in different sectors or competitive contexts. For example, Guest (2001) suggests that there is the possibility that a 'high-performance/high-commitment' approach might always be most appropriate in manufacturing, whereas strategic choice (which could be interpreted as choice to fit with business strategy) might be more realistic in the services sector. This could be taken one step further to suggest that different theories apply to different groups in the workforce. Indeed Storey (2007), on the basis of work in the public and private sector, suggests that there is value in HR directors crafting their strategy via four simultaneous pathways: best practice; best fit; building on and exploiting the people resource base (the three theoretical approaches we have discussed); and responding to an analysis of trends and demographics.

Consequently, these three theories do not necessarily represent simple alternatives. It is also likely that some board directors and even HR managers are not familiar with any of these theories. In spite of that, organisations, through their culture, and individuals within organisations operate on the basis of a set of assumptions, and these assumptions are often implicit. Assumptions about the nature and role of HR strategy, whether explicit or implicit, will have an influence on what organisations actually do. Assumptions will limit what are seen as legitimate choices.

Understanding these theories enables HR managers, board members, consultants and the like to interpret the current position of HR strategy in the organisation, confront current assumptions and challenge current thinking and potentially open up a new range of possibilities.

The international challenge

The strategic theories we have explored have all been developed in the west and while there is evidence that this body of knowledge is used internationally (see e.g. Sharma and Khandekar 2006), it must be acknowledged that they are limited by western cultures and mindsets. Turning the theories into practice internationally is even more of a challenge. We have mentioned that the universalist approach, identifying best practices which result in high performance, is dependent on the prevailing culture, institutions and legislation and therefore is most difficult to apply internationally. The fit approach presents the same challenge, unless fit with culture, institutions and legislation is included so that HR practices can be localised, but of course other aspects of fit are then lost. Perhaps it is easier to see how the resource-based perspective might be more easily translated into practice across the globe, but again actual practices adopted will inevitably be influenced by local circumstances.

Much literature on international HRM strategy is based on the multinational corporation (MNC), with an HQ in the originating country rolling out an HR strategy to international locations with the focus on applying it to expatriates, frequent international commuters, cross-cultural team members and specialists involved in international knowledge transfer (Sparrow and Braun 2007). Reilly and Williams (2012) note that western MNCs have a tendency to go for this 'one-company approach', yet suggest that a mix between global and local strategies may be more appropriate. They note that the Asian model is more decentralised, so more local than global practices. They recognise, however, that this is probably due to the fact that such Asian MNCs are holding companies for a diverse range of subsidiaries engaged in different activities, so meeting the needs of the specific business may be more important than commonality. Taking us forwards, Sparrow and Braun (2007) maintain that *global* strategic HRM is different from *international* strategic HRM in that it requires 'managing SIHRM activities through the application of global rule sets which carry meaning across cultures' (p. 186). This is a very different challenge.

SUMMARY PROPOSITIONS

4.1. Strategic HRM encourages us to consider strategy as a process, strategic thinking and strategic orientation, rather than limit ourselves to a 'strategy' which is written down and exists as a physical entity.

4.2. The nature of the link between business strategy and HR strategy is critical and can be played out in a variety of ways.

4.3. Three theoretical perspectives on strategic HR management can be identified: universalist/best practice; contingency/fit; and the resource-based/human capital view. Each has advantages and disadvantages.

4.4. The 'black box' research focuses on how HR practices impact on performance, and seeks to explain the mechanisms mediating the impact of HR practices on performance.

4.5. Globalisation presents more challenges for understanding and implementing HR strategy.

GENERAL DISCUSSION TOPICS

1. Is it feasible to link business strategy with the management of people in organisations?

2. HR strategies can be stimulating to produce and satisfying to display, but how can we make sure that they are implemented?

THEORY INTO PRACTICE

ARM Holdings

ARM Holdings according to its website is 'a truly global company with offices spread around the world'. It was founded in 1990 in Cambridge, UK, which remains its global headquarters; in addition it now has a regional headquarters in Shanghai covering Chinese, Indian, Japanese, Korean and Taiwanese offices, and another in San Jose covering US offices over five states from the east to the west coast.

The company designs chips for small low-powered devices, such as mobile phones and tablets (including i-Pods and i-Pads). ARM's business strategy is one of partnership, working with a wide range of other companies. It licenses production to manufacturing companies and carries out research and development on behalf of its customers. Also in its partnership collaboration are technology companies which write software or produce products using ARM-designed microprocessors. Sales growth is excellent, and ARM Holdings is the world's leading semiconductor IP company, winning a number of awards as top employer.

Interviewed for *People Management*, Graham Budd, Chief Operating Officer commented that: 'The value of the company is fundamentally in its people and in the network of relationships that those people have both inside the company and externally' (Arkin 2011: 37). Much HR activity is about connecting people across the global company sites and external partners – across cultures and time zones. The HR strategy is designed to develop an innovative, collaborative environment and focuses on social capital. Bill Parsons, the HR Director, says it is about 'the individual being less important than the network, the network being selfless individuals sharing knowledge to achieve a common vision' (Arkin 2011: 38).

ARM Holdings as an intellectual property company knows its biggest asset is its people and aims to recruit the best intelligent, leading-edge thinkers and release their talent within the company. The culture is collaborative and dynamic and the company has identified seven core values: delivery of results which benefit HRM; teamwork and selflessness; constructive pro-activity; partner and customer focus; responsiveness; innovation; and personal development.

Questions

1 How does HR strategy at ARM Holdings reflect the three theoretical perspectives on HR strategy which we have discussed in this chapter? Justify your answer.

2 How would you design and implement HR practices so that they supported the business and HR strategies? Give examples and justify for each HR practice – include recruitment/ selection, development and reward practices as a minimum, but add other relevant practices to these.

3 What special challenges does the global nature of ARM Holdings have in implementing your proposals?

Sources: Arkin, A. (2011) 'Cash in the chips', *People Management*, May, pp. 36–9; Cooper, R. and agencies (2012) 'ARM sales jump as outpaces peers' (accessed on January 2016), *Telegraph Media Group*, 25 July (accessed via the Internet at www.telegraph.co.uk); www.arm.com Sale of this UK firm to SoftBank, a Japanese telecoms company, was completed in September 2016.

FURTHER READING

Jiang, K., Takeuchi, R. and Lepak, D. (2013) 'Where do we go from here? New perspectives on the Black Box in strategic human resource management research', *Journal of Management Studies*, Vol. 50, No. 8, pp. 1448–80.

This article provides an excellent summary of the mechanisms mediating the HR–performance link. It provides an excellent review of all the literature in this area and proposes a multilevel model (organisational, team, individual) of how mediating mechanisms work.

Piening, E., Baluch, A. and Ridder, H. (2014) 'Mind the intended–implemented gap: Understanding employees' perceptions of HRM', *Human Resource Management*, Vol. 53, No. 4, pp. 545–67.

The authors report four case studies in German health and social services organisations and explore the links and potential gaps between intended, implemented and perceived HR practices. In particular they explore the importance of employee expectations.

Salaman, G., Storey, J. and Billsberry, J. (2005) *Strategic Human Resource Management: Theory and Practice. A Reader.* London: The Open University in association with Sage.

This is an excellent source book bringing together a variety of perspectives and divided into four sections: strategic HRM and knowledge; strategic HRM and business performance; the emergence of new organisational forms and relationships; and strategic HRM in practice. Each chapter is an article previously published, and is either produced in full or summarised. This means that some work is older than others, but the choice of chapters means that key and influential strategic works (e.g. Wright *et al.* mentioned in this chapter) are grouped together. No newer edition is available.

Truss, C., Mankin, D. and Kelliher, C. (2012) *Strategic Human Resource Management*. Oxford: Oxford University Press.

This is a very readable yet thorough and wide-ranging text of strategic HR. Chapters 5, 6 and 8 are particularly relevant for our chapter here.

WEB LINK

www.cranet.org

REFERENCES

Arkin, A. (2011) 'Cash in the chips', *People Management*, May, pp. 36–9.

Arkin, A. and Allen, R. (2002) 'Satisfaction guaranteed', *People Management*, Vol. 8, No. 21, pp. 40–2.

Atkinson, C. and Hall, L. (2011) 'Flexible working and happiness in the NHS', *Employee Relations*, Vol. 33, No. 2, pp. 88–105.

Baird, L., Meshoulam, I. and DeGive, G. (1983) 'Meshing human resources planning with strategic business planning: A model approach', *Personnel*, Vol. 60, Part 5, pp. 14–25.

Barney, J. (1991) 'Firm resources and sustained competitive advantage', *Journal of Management*, Vol. 17, No. 1, pp. 99–120.

Batt, R. and Banerjee, M. (2012) 'The scope and trajectory of strategic HR research: Evidence from American and British journals', *International Journal of Human Resource Management*, Vol. 23, No. 9, pp. 1739–62.

Boxall, P.F. (1996) 'The strategic HRM debate and the resource-based view of the firm', *Human Resource Management Journal*, Vol. 6, No. 3, pp. 59–75.

Boxall, P. and Macky, K. (2009) 'Research and theory on high-performance work systems: Progressing the high-involvement stream', *Human Resource Management Journal*, Vol. 19, No. 1, pp. 3–23.

Boxall, P. and Purcell, J. (2015) *Strategy and Human Resource Management*. Basingstoke: Palgrave Macmillan.

Butler, J. (1988) 'Human resource management as a driving force in business strategy', *Journal of General Management*, Vol. 13, No. 4, pp. 88–102.

Chubb, L. (2008) 'Build a better brand', *People Management*, Vol. 14, No. 15, pp. 24–5.

CIPD (2015) *Human Capital Reporting: Investing for Sustainable Growth*, Research Report. London: CIPD, January.

CIPD (2014) *Managing the Value of Your Talent: A New Framework for Human Capital Measurement. Key Findings and Conclusions*. London: CIPD, July.

Fields, D., Chan, A., Aktar, S. and Blum, T. (2006) 'Human resource management strategies under uncertainty', *Cross Cultural Management: An International Journal*, Vol. 13, No. 2, pp. 171–86.

Fombrun, C., Tichy, N.M. and Devanna, M.A. (1984) *Strategic Human Resource Management*. New York: Wiley.

Guest, D. (2001) 'Human resource management: When research confronts theory', *International Journal of Human Resource Management*, Vol. 12, No. 7, pp. 1092–106.

Guest, D. (2011) 'Human resource management and performance: Still searching for some answers', *Human Resource Management Journal,* Vol. 21, No. 1, pp. 3–13.

Guthridge, M. and Lawson, E. (2008) 'Divide and survive', *People Management,* Vol. 14, No. 19, pp. 40–4.

Huselid, M. (1995) 'The impact of human resource management practices on turnover, productivity and corporate financial performance', *Academy of Management Journal,* Vol. 38, No. 3, pp. 635–73.

Jeffery, R. (2015) 'You don't always have to be the best', *People Management,* April, pp. 18–20.

Jiang, K., Takeuchi, R. and Lepak, D. (2013) 'Where do we go from here? New perspectives on the Black Box in strategic human resource management research', *Journal of Management Studies,* Vol. 50, No. 8, pp. 1448–80.

Kaufman, B. (2015) 'Evolution of Strategic HRM as seen through two founding books: A 30th anniversary perspective of development in the field', *Human Resource Management,* Vol. 54, No. 3, pp. 389–407.

Kaplan, R. and Norton, D. (2005) 'The office of strategy management', *Harvard Business Review,* Vol. 83, No. 10, pp. 73–80.

Kersley, B., Alpin, C., Forth, J., Bryson, A., Bewley, H., Dix, G. and Oxenbridge, S. (2006) *Inside the Workplace: Findings from the 2004 Workplace Employment Relations Survey.* London: Routledge.

Kinnie, N., Hutchinson, S., Purcell, J., Rayton, B. and Swart, J. (2005) 'Satisfaction with HR practices and commitment to the organisation: Why one size does not fit all', *Human Resource Management Journal,* Vol. 15, No. 4, pp. 9–29.

Kochan, T.A. and Barocci, T.A. (1985) *Human Resource Management and Industrial Relations: Text, readings and cases.* Boston, MA: Little Brown.

Lengnick-Hall, M. and Lengnick-Hall, C. (2003) *Human Resource Management in the Knowledge Economy.* San Francisco, CA: Berrett-Koehler.

Lepak, D. and Shaw, J. (2008) 'Strategic HRM in North America: Looking to the future', *International Journal of Human Resource Management,* Vol. 19, No. 8, pp. 1486–99.

Macky, K. and Boxall, P. (2007) 'The relationship between "high performance work practices" and employee attitudes: An investigation of additive and interaction effects', *International Journal of Human Resource Management,* Vol. 18, No. 4, pp. 537–67.

Miles, R.E. and Snow, C.C. (1984) 'Organisation strategy, structure and process', *Academy of Management* Review, Vol. 2, pp. 546–62.

Mintzberg, H. (1994) 'The fall and rise of strategic planning', *Harvard Business Review,* January–February, pp. 107–14.

Pfeffer, J. (2005) 'Producing sustainable competitive advantage through the effective management of people', *Academy of Management Executive,* Vol. 19, No. 4, pp. 95–106.

Piening, E., Baluch, A. and Ridder, H. (2014) 'Mind the intended–implemented gap: Understanding employees' perceptions of HRM', *Human Resource Management,* Vol. 53, No. 4, pp. 545–67.

Ployhart, R.E. and Moliterno, T.P. (2011) 'Emergence of the human capital resource: A multilevel model', *Academy of Management Review,* Vol. 36, No. 1, pp. 127–50.

Porter, M. (1980) *Competitive Strategy.* New York: Free Press.

Purcell, J. (1992) 'The impact of corporate strategy on human resource management', in G. Salaman *et al.* (eds), *Human Resource Strategies.* London: Sage.

Purcell, J. and Hutchinson, S. (2007) 'Front-line managers as agents in the HRM performance causal chain: Theory, analysis and evidence', *Human Resource Management Journal,* Vol. 17, No. 1, pp. 3–20.

Purcell, J., Kinnie, N., Hutchinson, S., Rayton, B. and Swart, J. (2003) *Understanding the People Performance Link: Unlocking the Black Box,* Research Report. London: CIPD.

Reilly, P. and Williams, T. (2012) *Global HR: Challenges Facing the HR Function*. Aldershot: Gower.

Samnani, A. and Singh, P. (2013) 'Exploring the fit perspective', *Human Resource Management*, Vol. 52, No. 1, pp, 124–44.

Sanders, K., Shipton, H. and Gomes, J. (2014) 'Guest editors' introduction: Is the HRM process important? Past, current and future challenges', *Human Resource Management*, Vol. 53, No. 4, pp. 489–503.

Scarborough, H. (2003) *Human Capital: External Reporting Framework*. London: CIPD.

Scarborough, H. and Elias, J. (2002) *Evaluating Human Capital*, Research Report. London: CIPD.

Schuler, R.S. and Jackson, S.E. (1987) 'Linking competitive strategies with human resource management practices', *Academy of Management Executive*, Vol. 1, No. 3, pp. 207–19.

Sharma, A. and Khandekar, A. (2006) *Strategic Human Resource Management*. London: Sage.

Sparrow, P. and Braun, W. (2007) 'Human resource strategy in international context', in R. Schular and S. Jackson, *Strategic Human Resource Management*, 2nd edn. Malden, MA: Blackwell.

Storey, J. (2007) 'What is strategic HRM?', in J. Storey (ed.), *Human Resource Management: A Critical Text*. London: Thompson Learning.

Truss, C., Mankin, D. and Kelliher, C. (2012) *Strategic Human Resource Management*. Oxford: Oxford University Press.

Tyson, S. (1995) *Human Resource Strategy*. London: Pitman.

Ulrich, D. (1998) 'A new mandate for human resources', *Harvard Business Review*, January–February, pp. 125–34.

Ulrich, D. and Smallwood, N. (2002) 'Seven up', *People Management*, Vol. 8, No. 10, pp. 42–4.

van Wanrooy, B., Bewley, H., Bryson, A., Forth, J., Freeth, S., Stokes, L. and Wood, S. (2013) *Employment Relations in the Shadow of the Recession*. London: Palgrave Macmillan.

Wright, P. and McMahon, G. (2011) 'Exploring human capital: Putting human back into strategic human resource management', *Human Resource Management Journal*, Vol. 21, No. 2, pp. 93–104.

Wright, P., McMahon, G. and McWilliams, A. (1994) 'Human resources and sustained competitive advantage: A resource-based perspective', *International Journal of Human Resource Management*, Vol. 5, No. 2, pp. 301–26.

Yanadori, Y. and Van Jaarsveld, D. (2014) 'The relationship of informal high performance work practices to job satisfaction and workplace profitability', *Industrial Relations*, Vol. 53, No. 3, pp. 501–34.

CHAPTER 5

WORKFORCE PLANNING AND ANALYTICS

THE OBJECTIVES OF THIS CHAPTER ARE TO:

1 Discuss the contribution and feasibility of workforce planning
2 Explore the scope of workforce planning
3 Explain an integrated workforce planning framework
4 Investigate the contribution of workforce analytics and big data

Strategic workforce planning has experienced a resurgence of interest in our era of rapid and discontinuous change, and as Lavelle (2007) suggests it can help organisations tackle the two key challenges of competing for skills and talents and keeping payroll costs under control.

Rudge (2011: 12), Cabinet Minister for Equalities and Human Rights, Birmingham City Council, considers that:

> workforce planning and intelligence will be ever more important in order to avoid 'knee-jerk' reactions and falls in service standards

and the CIPD (2015) suggests that planning can assist sustainable performance by providing better information on which to base short- and long-terms decisions about people in our volatile and fast-changing economy. The resurgence of interest in planning is often connected to the disruption caused by the recession that started in 2008 and the need to upskill organisations. Workforce planning may specifically be prompted by revisions in service delivery, the need for increased efficiency and financial restraint, consolidation of operations in a single location, expansion and changing customer demand (IDS 2011), yet, paradoxically, planning is often unappreciated and underused.

The contribution and feasibility of workforce planning

A useful starting point is to consider the different contributions that strategy and planning make to the organisation. A common view has been that they are virtually one and the same – hence the term 'strategic planning'. Mintzberg (1994: 108) distinguished between *strategic thinking,* which is about synthesis, intuition and creativity to produce a not too precisely articulated vision of direction, and *strategic planning,* which is about collecting the relevant information to stimulate the visioning process and also programming the vision into what needs to be done to get there. It is helpful to look at workforce planning in the same way, and this is demonstrated in Figure 5.1. In more detail he suggests:

- **Planning as strategic programming:** planning cannot generate strategies, but it can make them operational by clarifying them, working out the consequences of them, and identifying what must be done to achieve each strategy.

- **Planning as tools to communicate and control:** planning can ensure coordination and encourage everyone to pull in the same direction; planners can assist in finding successful experimental strategies which may be operating in just a small part of the organisation.

- **Planners as analysts:** planners need to analyse hard data, both external and internal, which managers can then use in the strategy development process.

- **Planners as catalysts:** that is, raising difficult questions and challenging the conventional wisdom which may stimulate managers into thinking in more creative ways.

Figure 5.1 IHR strategic visioning and strategic planning
Source: After Mintzberg (1994).

Strategic planning
Providing HR data, ideas
Asking difficult questions

Strategic visioning
Defining a vision of the future (organisational and HR)

Strategic planning
Programme the vision –
HR objectives, targets, action plans

Planning is a basic building block of a more strategic approach, and there are four specific ways in which HR planning is critical to strategy, as it can identify:

- *capability gaps* – lack of sufficient skills, people or knowledge in the business which will prevent the strategy being implemented successfully;
- *capability surpluses* – providing scope for efficiencies and new opportunities to capitalise on the skills, people and knowledge, currently underused, in order to influence strategy;
- *poor workforce utilisation* – suggesting inappropriate HR practices that need to be altered;
- *talent pool development* – to ensure a ready internal supply of employees capable of promotion, and especially a leadership pipeline.

These four aspects are crucial to sustaining competitive advantage through making the most of human resources, reflecting the resource-based view we explained in the previous chapter.

Our environment of rapid and discontinuous change makes any planning difficult, and workforce planning is especially difficult as people have free will, unlike other resources, such as finance or technology. Both short- and longer-term planning are important and yet quarterly business reporting, as is common in the UK, encourages businesses to focus only on short-term planning. By contrast some other countries, like Japan, have a longer-term horizon for assessing business performance, reflecting cultural differences which we discussed more fully in Chapter 3. A survey by the Adecco Institute found acceptance of the need for long-term planning and yet the average planning horizon of HR specialists was 1.1 years (Chubb 2008).

WINDOW ON PRACTICE

The value of longer-term planning at National Grid (utility company in the UK)

National Grid's strategy focuses on a ten-year timeframe and is refreshed annually. A close watch is kept on core areas of the business and on job families which are critical to business success. Where likely future skills gaps are identified, plans can be put in place to address these before they become an issue.

Source: People Management (2014) 'Make workforce planning work', May, p. 36.

The example of National Grid highlights the timeframe that may be required to train and develop people to the level required for some roles.

The contribution and implementation of workforce planning is enhanced if:

- plans are viewed as flexible and reviewed regularly, rather than being seen as an end point;
- stakeholders, including all levels of manager and employee, are involved in the process through, for example, surveys, focus groups and line manager representatives on the HR planning team;

- planning is owned and driven by senior managers rather than HR specialists, who are facilitators;
- plans are linked to business and HR strategy;
- plans are user friendly and not overly complex;
- it is recognised that, while a comprehensive plan may be ideal, sometimes it may only be feasible to plan on an issue-by-issue basis, or by different workforce specialisms or segments (see Lavelle (2007) for a good example of segmentation).

The CIPD guide to workforce planning (2010) provides some very useful advice on implementation.

WINDOW ON PRACTICE

Workforce planning and the NHS in the UK

Workforce planning is considered to be a top priority for the NHS (National Health Service) as an appropriate and competent workforce is required to provide successful service delivery and quality, and to this end a rapid review of workforce planning was commissioned to identify the nature of workforce planning; to provide examples of best practice; and to identify the current effectiveness of UK health sector workforce planning. The work was carried out by the Institute for Employment Research at Warwick University.

    The review team found that:

- workforce planning is not a homogeneous activity and can be carried out at different levels, for example organisational or national;
- traditional healthcare workforce planning has focused on supply and demand for specific occupations – in other words, it is segmented;
- this approach can result in professional silos and an integrated approach, planning for the system as a whole, would add value, because covering all staff groups simultaneously is essential to address skill mix and substitution issues;
- data availability and lack of resources to build sophisticated models restrict planning activity;
- planning for internal labour markets, that is the movement between posts within the organisation, is also important;
- it is important to plan for demographic factors both in terms of healthcare need and in terms of workforce supply;
- given the importance of quality in a healthcare setting, productivity improvement can be expressed as higher quality from the same inputs (i.e. workforce);
- there is a general lack of published work on good practices in workforce planning, and no examples of fully integrated workforce planning models were found;
- workforce planning time horizons are generally longer in the public than the private sector and succession planning remains important in larger hierarchical public bodies;
- 'workforce planning requires accurate data, modelling, continuous and iterative planning, specialist skills, scenario building and stakeholder involvement' (p. 117);

- workforce planning is essential for the NHS as a long lead time is required for training; wage adjustments are influenced by market forces; patient needs must be met; and tax-payers' money should not be wasted by training too many staff.

Source: Curson, J., Dell, M., Wilson, R., Bosworth, D. and Baldauf, B. (2010) 'Who does workforce planning well? Workforce rapid review team summary', *International Journal of Health Care Quality Assurance*, Vol. 23, No. 1, pp. 110–19.

In spite of the above, the NHS was accused of poor workforce planning in 2015 and David Cameron (UK Prime Minister) stated that the NHS could be better at this. This comment was in the context of insufficient UK nurses causing reliance on overseas nurses, which was extremely costly in recruitment terms. Earlier in the year the exorbitant cost of using agency nurses to cover for insufficient permanent staff was exposed, and a cap has now been put on this cost. How did the NHS find itself in this situation of insufficient nurse supply? A major factor is the *Francis Report* (2013) which was an inquiry following serious nursing failures at North Staffordshire Hospital. A key recommendation of this report was a need for improved staffing levels of nurses on any shift. Hospitals responded by trying to recruit more nurses and from April 2014 NHS trusts had to publish employee numbers for every ward to assess whether the levels are sufficient and safe. None of this was anticipated so there were insufficient numbers of nurses in the training system (which takes four years). It was estimated that 21,000 more nurses were required than had been anticipated three years before (Cunningham 2015) and even covering this shortfall has been argued as insufficient as retirements were not adequately taken into account (Ham 2015). Better rostering systems have been proposed as a way of improving ward staffing levels, and Birmingham Hospital has had some success with this.

Source: Information taken from interviews on the BBC *Today* programme, Radio 4, on 31 May, 2 June, 28 July and 15 August 2015.

The scope of workforce planning

Originally workforce planning was concerned with balancing the projected demand for and supply of labour, in order to have the right number of the right employees in the right place at the right time. The demand for people is influenced by corporate strategies and objectives, the environment and the way that staff are utilised within the business. The supply of people is projected from current employees (via calculations about expected leavers, retirements, promotions, etc.) and from the potential availability of required employees and skills in the relevant labour market. Anticipated demand and supply are then reconciled by considering a range of options, and plans to achieve a feasible balance are designed.

Increasingly organisations now plan, not just for hard numbers, but for the *softer* issues of employee behaviour and organisational culture; organisation design and the make-up of individual jobs; and formal and informal systems. These aspects are all critical in terms of programming and achieving the vision or the strategic choice. Undoubtedly different

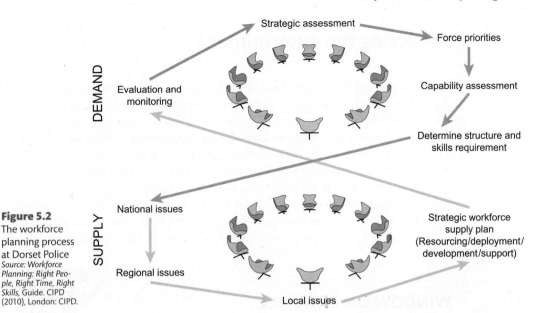

Figure 5.2
The workforce planning process at Dorset Police
Source: Workforce Planning: Right People, Right Time, Right Skills, Guide. CIPD (2010), London: CIPD.

organisations will place different emphases on each of these factors, and may well plan each separately or plan some and not others, but a good example is the workforce planning in the Dorset Police (CIPD 2010), shown in Figure 5.2.

The framework we shall use in this chapter attempts to bring *all* aspects of workforce planning together, incorporating the more traditional approach, but going beyond this to include behaviour, culture, systems and so on. Our framework identifies 'where we want to be', translated from responses to the strategic vision; 'where we are now'; and 'what we need to do to make the transition' – all operating within the organisation's environment. The framework is shown in diagrammatic form in Figure 5.3.

We shall now look in more depth at each of these four areas. The steps are presented in a logical sequence. In practice, however, they may run in parallel and/or in an informal fashion, and each area may well be revisited a number of times.

Figure 5.3
Integrated workforce planning framework

Analysing the environment

In this chapter we refer to the environment broadly as the context of the organisation, and this is clearly critical in the impact that it has on both organisational and HR strategy. Much strategy is based on a response to the environment – for example, what our customers now want or what competitors are now offering – or in anticipation of what customers will want or what they can be persuaded to want. In HR terms we need to identify, for example, how difficult or easy it will be to find employees with scarce skills and what these employees will expect from an employer so that we can attract them, and keep them. We shall be concerned with legislation which will limit or widen the conditions of employment that we offer, with what competitors are offering and with what training schemes are available, locally, nationally and internationally, depending on the nature of the organisation.

WINDOW ON PRACTICE

The global workforce challenge

Chinese wage increases

We have become accustomed to a world where global companies carry out their manufacturing in a low-wage country. However, some of these traditionally low-wage economies are now experiencing pressures for higher wages and better employment conditions. Jacob (2012) notes how 2012 has differed from previous years due to marked labour shortages in China. She highlights the case of David Liu, a handbag manufacturer who until recently would have queues of potential workers outside the factory gates, but now has to ask for help from employees to recruit new workers. There is a higher turnover of younger workers who switch jobs in search of better pay and conditions. She notes there have been double-digit wage increases over the past couple of years, and suggests that China is running out of workers.

Source: Jacob, R. (2012) 'Labour shortages: Double digit wage increases', www.ft.com, 11 December.

The impact on Japanese firms

Japanese businesses use Chinese operations for labour-intensive assembly, but have recently been moving to higher-value work requiring more skilled staff. At the same time the just-in-time production process leaves Japanese companies vulnerable to disruption. Decisions on pay are made centrally and not at plant level. This format has resulted in:

1 Higher pay in the Chinese plants (e.g. Honda upped wages by 24%).

2 Higher promotion levels for local managers (e.g. Komatsu aim to have Chinese managers leading all sixteen local subsidiaries).

3 More labour-intensive work is being moved to Vietnam, Thailand and Cambodia (e.g. Uniqlo is reducing the proportion of garments made in China from 90% to 65% between 2013 and 2015).

Source: The impact on Japan is adapted from Brewster, C., Sparrow, P., Vernon, G. and Houldsworth, E. (2011) *International Human Resource Management*. London: CIPD, pp. 391–2.

In summary we need to collect data on social trends; demographics; political legislative and regulatory changes; industrial and technological changes; and current/new competitors. We need to assess the impact these will have on our ability to recruit, develop and keep the required employees with appropriate knowledge, skills, attitudes and behaviours. Planners need to identify the challenges that the changes pose, and work out how to meet these in order that the organisation can achieve its declared strategies and goals.

WINDOW ON PRACTICE

Analysing the environment at Queensland University of Technology Library in Australia

Stokker and Hallam (2009) identify change as the main driver for the Library's engagement with workforce planning. They believed environmental scanning was a key part of the process to explore trends impacting on libraries, the context, and trends within libraries. The scanning was carried out over twelve months and involved reading relevant documents and inviting guest specialist speakers to address library staff. All library staff were involved in the scanning process and five key areas were investigated, each led by a member of the senior library team:

- Higher education sector/government policy
- Teaching and learning
- Client service
- Research
- Information resources and scholarly information.

Several trends emerged that would impact on the faculty liaison service, such as the university's desire to gain a higher research profile by increasing the number of researchers and research students. This led to the development of three workforce planning strategies for the faculty liaison service: methods to allow librarians to specialise in research support or academic skills support; a review of the job classification scheme allowing librarians to progress further in recognition of their specialist work; and the design of a development programme to allow liaison librarians to acquire new skills and knowledge.

In addition to staff involvement in environmental scanning they were also represented in the workforce planning party and planning strategies were built using consultation. These methods were used to encourage staff ownership and engagement.

Source: Stokker, J. and Hallam, G. (2009) 'The right person, in the right job, with the right skills at the right time: A workforce-planning model that goes beyond metrics', *Library Management*, Vol. 15, No. 89, pp. 561–71.

ACTIVITY 5.1

Consider the external environment, for any organisation in which you are involved, for three to five years ahead. Individually, or as a group, identify all the important environmental influences and select the six most important ones. Identify the challenges these present to the organisation in achieving its goals and how the organisation could respond. Write a summary (one side of A4) of what you think your organisation's priorities should be in the people area over the next three to five years.

Forecasting future HR needs

Organisation, behaviour and culture

There is little specific literature on the methods used to translate the strategic objectives of the organisation and environmental influences into qualitative or soft HR goals. In general terms, they can be summed up as the use of managerial judgement. Brainstorming, combined with the use of structured checklists or matrices, can encourage a more thorough analysis. Three simple techniques are an HR implications checklist (see Table 5.1), a strategic brainstorming exercise (Figure 5.4). The use of *scenarios* may also be helpful (see e.g. Boxall and Purcell 2015; Turner 2002) and such contingency planning can be used to prepare HR responses to alternative futures.

Table 5.1 The beginnings of an HR implications checklist

Corporate goal	HR implications	Methods of achieving this
	New tasks?	
	For whom?	
	What competencies needed? (knowledge, skills, attitudes, behaviours)	
	Relative importance of team/individual behaviour	
	Deleted tasks?	
	How will managers need to manage?	

Figure 5.4
Strategic brainstorming exercise

Managers write a corporate goal in the centre and brainstorm changes that need to take place in each of the four areas, one area at a time

Employee numbers and skills (demand forecasting)

There is far more literature in the more traditional area of forecasting employee number demand based on the organisation's strategic objectives. Both objective and subjective approaches can be employed. Objective methods include statistical and work-study approaches.

Statistical models generally relate employee number demand to specific organisational circumstances and activities. Models can take account of determining factors, such as production, sales, passenger miles, level of service, and other relevant factors such as employee utilisation, resulting from the introduction of new technology, or alternative organisational forms, such as high-performance teams.

The work-study method is based on a thorough analysis of the tasks to be done and the time each takes. From this the person-hours needed per unit of output can be calculated, and standards are developed for the numbers and levels of employees required. These are most useful in production work, but need to be checked regularly to make sure they are still appropriate. Work study is usually classified as an objective measure; however, it is often accepted that since the development of standards and the grouping of tasks is partly dependent on human judgement, it could be considered as a subjective method.

WINDOW ON PRACTICE

The postman's lot

Measuring workload has changed at Royal Mail. Roy Mayall, who has been a postman for many years, explains in his short book how volume of mail was previously measured by the weight of the grey boxes in which mail is delivered to the sorting offices. More recently he says it is done by averages, and it was agreed in consultation with the union that the average figure of letters in a box was estimated at 208. Subsequently Mayall (2009) reports that this estimate was changed to 150, and when a colleague did a one-man experiment counting the letters over a two-week period he found the average to be 267. Mayall recognises that this figure is neither representative nor scientific but the story does show how apparently objective figures can be subjective.

Source: Mayall, R. (2009) *Dear Granny Smith: A Letter from your Postman.* London: Short Books.

The most common subjective method of demand forecasting is managerial judgement and this can also include the judgements of other operational and technical staff and lower level managers. It relies on managers' estimates of workforce demand based on past experience. When this method is used it is difficult to cope with changes that are very different from past experiences.

The way that human resources are utilised will change the number of employees required and the necessary skills needed, and changes in utilisation are often prompted by the need to save money or the difficulty in recruiting. There are many ways to change how employees are used, and these are shown in Table 5.2. Some methods are interrelated or overlap and would therefore be used in combination.

Table 5.2 A range of methods to change employee utilisation

- Introducing new materials or equipment, particularly new technology
- Introducing changes in work organisation, such as:
  - quality circles
  - job rotation
  - job enlargement
  - job enrichment
  - participation
  - autonomous work groups
  - outsourcing
  - high-performance teams
  - changes in rostering
  - empowerment
- Organisation development
- Introducing changes in organisation structure, such as:
  - centralisation/decentralisation
  - new departmental boundaries
  - relocation of parts of the organisation
  - flexible project, matrix and network structures
- Introducing productivity schemes, bonus schemes or other incentive schemes
- Encouraging greater staff flexibility, multiskilling and work interchangeability
- Altering times and periods of work
- Training and appraisal of staff
- Developing managers and use of performance management

WINDOW ON PRACTICE

China's challenge

We introduced China's recruitment and higher-wages challenge above. Jacob (2012) quotes Sunny Tan, Executive Director of Luen Thai Holdings: 'We want to change our model and work differently in China.' There is an emphasis on the need to provide more training to younger workers and raise productivity or risk going out of business. In a survey of 750 executives, Neale O'Connor, from the University of Hong Kong, sought to find out how they were coping with the high-wage challenge. Rather than planning to introduce automation the emphasis was on changing the processes by which employees were managed, for example by introducing cross-functional teams and outsourcing some functions. Labour shortages were prompting efficiency improvements, more training and better people management.

Source: Jacob, R. (2012) 'Labour shortages: Double digit wage increases', www.ft.com, 11 December.

Analysing the current situation and projecting forward

Organisation, behaviour and culture

Possibilities here include the use of questionnaires to staff, interviews with staff and managerial judgement. Focus groups are an increasingly popular technique where, preferably, the chief executive meets with, say, twenty representative staff from each department to discuss their views of the strengths and weaknesses of the organisation, and what can be done to improve. These approaches can be used to provide information on, for example:

- Employee engagement.
- Motivation of employees.
- Job satisfaction.
- Organisational culture.
- The way that people are managed.
- Attitude to minority groups and equality of opportunity.
- Commitment to the organisation and reasons for this.
- Clarity of business objectives.
- Goal-focused and other behaviour.
- Organisational issues and problems.
- What can be done to improve.
- Organisational strengths to build on.

WINDOW ON PRACTICE

Jennifer Hadley is the Chief Executive of Dynamo Castings, a long-established organisation which had experienced rapid growth and healthy profits until the past five years. Around 800 staff were employed mostly in production, but significant numbers were also employed in marketing/sales and research/development. Poor performance over the last three years was largely the result of the competition who were able to deliver a quality product more quickly and at a competitive price. Dynamo retained the edge in developing new designs, but this consumed a high level of resources and was a lengthy process from research to eventual production. Most employees had been with the company for a large part of their working lives and the culture was still appropriate to the times of high profit where life had been fairly easy and laid back. Messages about difficult times, belt tightening and higher productivity with fewer people had been filtered down to employees, who did not change their behaviour but did feel threatened.

It was with some trepidation that Jennifer decided to meet personally with a cross-section of each department to talk through company and departmental issues. The first meeting was with research/development. As expected, the meeting began with a flood of concerns about job security. No promises could be given. However, the mid-point of the meeting was quite fruitful, and the following points, among others, became clear:

- Development time could be reduced from two years to one if some production staff were involved in the development process from the very beginning.
- Many development staff felt their career prospects were very limited and a number expressed the wish to be able to move into marketing. They felt this would also be an advantage when new products were marketed.

- Staff felt fairly paid and would be prepared to forgo salary rises for a year or two if this would mean job security; they liked working for Dynamo and did not want to move.
- Staff were aware of the difficult position the company was in but they really did not know what to do to make it any better.
- Development staff wanted to know why Dynamo did not collaborate with Castem Ltd on areas of mutual interest (Jennifer did not know the answer to this one).

The meeting gave Jennifer not only a better understanding of what employees felt, but also some good ideas to explore. Departmental staff knew their problems had not been wiped away, but did feel that Jennifer had at least taken the trouble to listen to them.

Turnover figures, absence data, performance data, recruitment and promotion trends and characteristics of employees may also shed some light on these issues.

Data relating to current formal and informal systems, together with data on the structure of the organisation, also need to be collected, and the effectiveness, efficiency and other implications of these need to be carefully considered. Most data will be collected from within the organisation, but data may also be collected from significant others, such as customers, who may be part of the environment.

Current and projected employee numbers and skills (employee supply)

Current employee supply can be analysed in both individual and overall statistical terms. To gain an overview of current supply the following factors may be analysed either singly or in combination: number of employees classified by function, department, occupation, job title, competencies, skills, qualifications, training, age, length of service, performance assessment results. This snapshot of the current workforce is essential when organisations face a sudden and/or major change, as it will allow them to respond more effectively.

Forecasting employee supply is concerned with predicting how the internal supply of employees will change, primarily how many will leave. Current levels of employee turnover are projected into the future to see what would happen if the same trends continued. Analyses can be segmented, for example by age group or job type or location. In countries where there is a legal pension age, this aspect of staff turnover can be predicted reasonably accurately. The impact of changing circumstances would also need to be taken into account when projecting turnover forward; for example, when job remits are substantially changed employee turnover often increases. Behavioural aspects are also important, such as investigating the reasons why employees leave. In larger and especially multinational organisations promotion and employee transfer trends may be analysed. Special attention is usually paid to the organisation's talent, however defined, and we discuss talent planning later (see Chapter 19).

Some sample statistics for projecting employee supply are included in the skills section.

ACTIVITY 5.2

1 Why do employees leave organisations?

2 What are the determinants of promotion in your organisation? Are they made explicit? Do staff understand what the determinants are?

3 What would be your criteria for promotion in your organisation?

Reconciliation, decisions and plans

We have already said that, in reality, there is a process of continuous feedback between the different stages of workforce planning activities, as they are all dynamic and interdependent. Key factors to take into account during reconciliation and deciding on action plans are the acceptability of the plans to both senior managers and other employees, the priority of each plan, key players who will need to be influenced and the factors that will encourage or be a barrier to successful implementation.

If the supply forecast is less than the demand forecast, the possibilities are to:

- alter the demand forecast by considering changes in the utilisation of employees (such as training, productivity deals, refocusing the performance management system, job redesign, organisational restructuring, multiskilling, high-performance teams and work intensification) by using different employees with higher skills, employing staff with insufficient skills and training them immediately, or outsourcing the work;

- alter the supply forecast through increasing retention by making the organisation a more attractive place to work (say, improving career and promotion prospects, proving more development opportunities, delaying retirement, increasing engagement, increasing rewards); recruitment campaigns demonstrating an improved 'employer brand', widening the supply pool to potential employees from other countries (depending on immigration rules), or using agency staff;

- change the company objectives, as lack of human resources will prevent them from being achieved in any case. Realistic objectives need to be based on the resources that are, and are forecast to be, available either internally or externally.

When the demand forecast is less than the internal supply forecast in some areas, the possibilities are to:

- consider and calculate the costs of overemployment over various timespans;

- consider the methods and cost of keeping staff but temporarily reducing their drain on company finances (e.g. by unpaid sabbaticals, reduced working hours), or not replacing staff who leave;

- consider changes in utilisation: work out the feasibility and costs of retraining, redeployment and so on;

- consider whether it is possible for the company objectives to be changed. Could the company diversify, move into new markets, etc.?

- if necessary prepare a process for downsizing. Further information on strategic and operational planning for downsizing can be found in Torrington *et al.* (2009).

Once all alternatives have been considered and feasible solutions decided, specific action plans can be designed covering all appropriate areas of HRM activity, as demonstrated by the examples above. Any changes would of course need to be accompanied by communications plans and employee relations plans.

WINDOW ON PRACTICE

Alternatives to downsizing

The last recession created a challenge in how to emerge in a healthy and strong position, unlike in the previous recession where unplanned and unthought-through downsizing meant that there was insufficient talent in many organisations to take advantage of the upturn. Evidence suggests that organisations have taken a more planful approach this time.

For example, the law firm Norton Rose has asked some of its graduate trainees who have been offered places but not yet started work if they would be prepared to defer their appointment until business picks up again. They were offered £10,000 if they accepted this option and used their time constructively such as doing voluntary work or learning a language. They are also using a redundancy avoidance plan in order to retain key workers by asking them to voluntarily change their terms and conditions for a year giving Norton Rose the chance to agree unpaid sabbaticals and reduced working hours. (Phillips 2009)

KPMG asked employees to voluntarily work a four-day week, if required, or take a sabbatical at 30 per cent pay for between four and twelve weeks. It is proposed that these temporary changes to employment contracts last 18 months, that the maximum salary loss in any year be limited to 20 per cent and full benefits be paid throughout. (*People Management* 2009)

Source: Phillips, L. (2009) "'Slash graduate recruitment at your peril'': firms advised to plan for the future', *People Management*, p. 8, 9 April; *People Management* (2009) 'KPMG asks staff to accept temporary flexible contracts if the need arises', *People Management*, Vol. 15, No. 3, p. 8, 29 January.

The way that planned changes are communicated to employees is critical. Plans need to include not only methods for informing employees about what managers expect of them, but also methods to enable employees to express their concerns and needs for successful implementation. Communications plans will also be important in generating greater employee commitment.

It is important that the plans are monitored to see if they are being achieved and if they are producing the expected results, pick up any unanticipated consequences and respond to changing circumstances.

Workforce analytics and big data

There are two broad ways in which analytics can be used to support the organisation, and we will explore these before moving on to big data. The first focuses on ensuring high-quality information to support business decisions. The emphasis is on 'what do we need to know about the workforce to run the company more effectively, and how can we turn that knowledge into action?' (Lesser 2010). To this end analytics can provide an in-depth picture of the current workforce and an expansion of the data that might be collected to assess current and future workforce supply and behaviour. So, for example, at a basic level, accidents, absence rates and so on may be measured in addition to turnover, and workforce profiles can be developed, for example against age, gender, skills and performance. With greater sophistication the measurement of attitudes and satisfaction can inform the development of people policies and potential antecedents to these can be tested, such as flexible working, coaching and mentoring to highlight and communicate the importance and effectiveness of these actions. In this process we are looking for a relationship or correlation between, say, engagement and a new mentoring programme. If we indeed find that engagement has increased in the very departments where the mentoring programme has been used more fully (as assessed by using the relevant statistical procedures, which are found in the skills section) we have some evidence that the mentoring programme *may* have improved engagement. We cannot say that the mentoring programme has caused improved engagement but the relationship does suggest that further investigation is worthwhile, perhaps seeking soft data to corroborate our suspicions.

Thus analytics needs interpretation from HR professionals who have a real and close understanding of the business, to develop insights. Such data can highlight the organisation's workforce challenges and enables the HR function to take a more proactive role in addressing them, for example the challenge of high absence levels in some departments, compared with others, or the characteristics of higher-performing managers. Analytics can be a means of identifying the most productive and/or the speediest/or most cost-effective recruitment channels, or whether new skills would be best delivered over a shorter or longer timeframe. Given this depth of information, better decisions can be made to address these challenges. So in this first approach to analytics the emphasis is on improving the effectiveness of the organisation's human capital and the processes by which it is managed, and having more facts to support longer-term business decisions, and decisions made in crises.

ACTIVITY 5.3

Thinking of an organisation you know well, address the following questions, including justifications:

1 What people measures are routinely collected?
2 Why are these collected?
3 To what extent are the reasons widely understood?
4 How are the measures used?
5 What changes would you recommend and why?

The second approach to analytics is more obviously strategic and integrated. Through the use of a strategic framework or model the organisation can identify what drives the performance of employees in relation to the organisation's strategy. These drivers can then be expressed as a range of measures with indicators, and targets can be set at about the levels that need to be achieved. These targets are often cascaded down to employee level, and form the base for the 'hard' metrics approach to performance management as opposed to the softer 'good management' approach to HRM which we discuss later (see Chapter 11).

There are a variety of models that can be used and considerable attention has been given to the use of scorecards, such as the balanced scorecard (Kaplan and Norton 1992) and, later, the HR scorecard (Becker *et al.* 2001), in linking people, strategy and performance. Such scorecards utilise a range of HR measures which are viewed as critical to the achievement of the business strategy. Kaplan and Norton widened the perspective on the measurement of business performance by measuring more than financial performance. Their premise is that other factors which lead to financial performance need to be measured to give a more rounded view of how well the organisation is performing. This means that measures of business performance are based on measures of strategy implementation in a range of areas. Kaplan and Norton identify three other areas for measurement in addition to financial measures: customer measures; internal business process measures; and learning and growth measures. Figure 5.5 provides an example of Norton and Kaplan's approach.

In each of these areas critical elements need to be identified and then measures devised to identify current levels and to measure progress. Some organisations implementing this scorecard have developed the learning and growth area to include a wider range of HR measures. The next Window on practice shows the Civil Aviation Authority's (CAA) tailor-made balanced scorecard approach.

Figure 5.5
Kaplan and Norton's approach using the 'learning and growth' quadrant of the balanced scorecard
Source: Adapted from Kaplan and Norton (1992).

'To achieve our vision/mission/strategic goals, how will we be able to sustain our ability to change and improve?'

What are the critical success factors?	What are the critical measurements?

WINDOW ON PRACTICE

Civil Aviation Authority's (CAA) approach to human capital measurement (HCM)

As 60% of the CAA's costs are people costs, the CAA began an HCM process hoping that this would allow it to quantify the value of its staff and explore the relationship between staff performance and business outcomes. The CAA also anticipated that it would help in quantifying its objectives of continuous improvement, improved efficiency and cost-effectiveness. The CAA developed a balanced scorecard approach to measuring human capital based on what constituted the 'bottom line', being a not-for-profit organisation. This bottom line comprised:

• External customer perception of CAA's performance

• Achievement of objectives

• Assessment of staff expertise.

What do we want to know?   How can we measure that?

In order to measure the value of their people, policies and practices, the CAA asked itself what it wanted to know about each of these in relation to the defined 'bottom line'. Having decided the questions, the CAA then worked out where that information might be found and how it could be measured. The questions and measures are shown in Figure 5.6.

Figure 5.6 How the CAA defined measures to answer its human capital questions
Source: Robinson, D. (2009) 'Human capital measurement: An approach that works', *Strategic HR Review,* Vol. 8, No. 6, pp. 5–11, Figure 1.

Success of our policies & practices

- Are staff engaged?
- Are we retaining key employees?
- Are we recruiting strong candidates?
- Do our new recruits stay with the CAA?
- Are we managing attendance levels?
- Are our reward levels competitive?
- Do our managers have the necessary skills to manage their staff?

Success of our policies & practices

- Engagement index
- Quality of leaver
- Quality of hire
- Recent recruit turnover
- Absence rates/costs
- Pay benchmarks
- Manager competency framework & performance management process

Value created by our people

- Are we continually raising the bar on performance?
- Are we developing our staff effectively?
- Are our 'customers' satisfied with our performance?

Value created by our people

- Performance management index
- Training evaluation
- External customer survey

The CAA then ordered its measures in a four-level hierarchy and worked up the hierarchy starting with the basic measures at the base:

Level 4: Performance measures: link between input/output data and measures of CAA strategic performance.

Level 3: Outcome measures: for example, absence rates and costs, engagement data.

Level 2: Operational data: for example, number of training days.

Level 1: Workforce data: for example, headcount, demographics, equal opportunities data.

The fourth level, not surprisingly, was the hardest to define and measure, so the CAA are looking at correlations between input measures such as absence, turnover, training and length of service and outputs such as employee engagement.

Source: Summarised from Robinson, D. (2009) 'Human capital measurement: An approach that works', *Strategic HR Review,* Vol. 8, No. 6, pp. 5–11.

Analytics of whatever type are often presented in the form of dashboards and use sophisticated software (see e.g. Asselman 2012). While the value of analytics may be acknowledged, many organisations face barriers in implementation.

Finally let us turn to big data. Whilst there is no agreed definition for this it seems to be a catch-all term for huge volumes of data which are unstructured and are continuous rather than static, with data being combined from different sources (see, for example,

Davenport 2014). Although it has been suggested that big data is a new word for analytics, there does appear to be a significant step change, although the boundary is of course fuzzy.

There is also an emphasis on predictive data which supermarkets have been using for some time, sending us offers on the products they think we are likely to buy based on analysis of previous buying behaviour. Netflix even had a prize for the best scientific method of optimising the company's movie recommendations to its customers.

WINDOW ON PRACTICE

Predicting employee behaviour

Preya Dewani, Head of People Strategy and Programmes at O2, the mobile phone company, refers to the 'employee performance life cycle' to predict when a drop in effectiveness might occur. She overlays data about length or service, age, engagement and performance to identify when intervention strategies could be implemented prior to a dip in effectiveness occurring.

At Oracle, Andy Campbell, Human Capital Management Director, notes how turnover can be predicted by using information from performance reviews and colleagues to identify dissatisfaction before someone leaves. Intervention strategies can then be targeted at the most disillusioned and most valued staff.

Source: Churchard, C. (2013) 'We love data', *People Management*, September, pp. 20–24.

Davenport suggests that it is sensor data which will most impact on the human resources function, gathering data from mobile phones (with permission) which provides location data, which can then be combined with other data.

WINDOW ON PRACTICE

Using sensors

The Bank of America were concerned about employee churn at some call centres, and called in consultants Sociometric Solutions. Employees agreed to wear a badge with sensors that collected information about individual location, tone of voice, volume and communication method. Analysis of this information suggested that employees needed more social time at work, and were encouraged to take their breaks with their friends. This solution was credited with reducing the turnover from 40% to 12%.

Source: Work (2014) 'How data analytics is revolutionising banking and hunting', *Work*, Winter, pp. 34–45.

SUMMARY PROPOSITIONS

5.1. Even in a context of rapid and discontinuous change, workforce planning still has a valuable contribution to make, but as HR planning deals with people, planners need to plan for what is acceptable as well as what is feasible.

5.2. The scope of workforce planning covers not only numbers of people and skills, but also structure, culture, systems and behaviour.

5.3. An integrated framework which attempts to cover all aspects of workforce planning involves:
- analysing the external environment and business strategy;
- analysing where we want to be (forecasting HR requirements);
- analysing where we are we now (defining the current HR position and projecting this forward);
- comparing the two and forming plans to bridge the gap.

5.4. Workforce planning is a continuous process rather than a one-off activity.

5.5. Analytics can assist in providing a clear picture of the current situation and can be used to monitor progress towards the desired state which will underpin the organisation's ability to achieve its goals.

5.6. Big data is a step change from previous workforce data in that it is unstructured, continuous, voluminous and combines data from different sources. It opens up new possibilities for improving HR and workforce effectiveness.

GENERAL DISCUSSION TOPICS

1. Discuss the proposition that traditional (numbers) workforce planning is only of interest to organisations in periods of growth when unemployment levels are low.

2. 'It is worthwhile planning even if you have no strategy.' For what reasons might you agree or disagree with this statement?

THEORY INTO PRACTICE

G4S and the London 2012 Olympics (August)

G4S, an international security firm, gained the contract to provide security at all Olympic locations. G4S contracted Wave, recruitment marketing specialists, to run the recruitment campaign. It was projected in 2010 that 2,000 security staff would be required, but by late 2011 this

➤

➤ had risen to 10,400. Wave appeared to run a very thorough recruitment campaign (see e.g. CIPD 2012) and in May 2012 it appeared that everything was on track for the increased number of guards. However, suddenly in mid-July G4S admitted that it could not fulfil the whole contract and 3,500 soldiers were drafted in to cover the shortfall. Nick Buckles of G4S, interviewed on BBC Radio 4, appeared to lack information about the detail of the recruitment/training/vetting processes, could not explain what had gone wrong and was unable even to confirm that all potential employees spoke fluent English.

G4S found there was a dropout of acceptable candidates when they realised the realities of the job, but even more importantly there was a shortage of licensed security guards and the company recognised that it would have to recruit inexperienced staff and train them in order to meet the new target. Such candidates had to provide a lot of data about themselves and be vetted and screened, then trained for four days in order to acquire the necessary skills, and then meet the criteria for a Security Industry Licence before they could begin their employment. The sheer scale of this task defeated the organisation, and it accepted that it had underestimated the challenge.

Questions

1 In what ways might contingency planning have helped G4S?

2 The chief executive of G4S only found out that it could not fulfil the contract in mid-July, which was very close to the start of the games. How might communication have been improved within G4S, and between G4S and Wave, and how might this have helped the planning process?

3 In a similar situation, if you were tasked with recruiting 8,000 similarly inexperienced staff, with less than a year to do this, how would you plan to ensure that all potential employees were vetted, screened, trained, licensed so they were qualified to begin work on time, and that the dropout rate was minimised?

Sources: Brockett, J. (2012) 'Olympian task', *People Management*, August, p. 9; Gabb, A. (2012) 'Safety in numbers', *PM Guide to Recruitment Marketing*, pp. 14–17; and general news media.

FURTHER READING

CIPD (2015) *Evolution of HR Analytics: A Middle East Perspective*. London: CIPD, and

CIPD (2015) *Evolution of HR Analytics: Perspectives from Singapore, Hong Kong and Malaysia*. London: CIPD.

These research reports provide an international perspective on the use of analytics. Each is based on a range of case study organisations so there are many examples of how analytics are used as well as overviews. The need for data scientist roles and analytics skills within the HR function is highlighted.

Day, G. and Schoemaker, P. (2005) 'Scanning the periphery', *Harvard Business Review*, November, pp. 135–48.

This article underlines the organisational importance of keeping a constant eye on peripheral features in an organisation's environment as well as its direct and close competitors. Examples are included of challenges that different organisations have faced and there are practical suggestions about how organisations could improve their scanning of the peripheral environment.

Davenport, T. (2014) *Big Data @ Work*. Boston: Harvard Business Publishing Corporation.

This is a very readable text which provides a thorough exploration of the nature of big data. It is a broadly focused book which does not concentrate on HR but does provide a perspective on the changing business world in which HR operates.

WEB LINKS

www.creatingpeopleadvantage.com

www.healthcareworkforce.nhs.uk

www.adeccoinstitute.com

REFERENCES

Asselman, S. (2012) 'Screen grabbers', *People Management,* June, pp. 43–6.

Becker, B., Huselid, M. and Ulrich, D. (2001) *The HR Scorecard: Linking People, Strategy and Performance*. Boston, MA: Harvard Business School Press.

Brewster, C., Sparrow, P., Vernon, G. and Houldsworth, E. (2011) *International Human Resource Management*. London: CIPD, pp. 391–2.

Boxall, P. and Purcell, J. (2015) *Strategy and Human Resource Management*. Basingstoke: Palgrave Macmillan.

Brockett, J. (2012) 'Olympian task', *People Management,* August, p. 9.

Chubb, L. (2008) 'Plan ahead to defuse the "demographic timebomb"', *People Management,* Vol. 14, No. 9, p. 7.

Churchard, C. (2013) 'We love data' *People Management,* September pp 20–24

CIPD (2010) *Workforce Planning: Right People, Right Time, Right Skills,* Guide. London: CIPD.

CIPD (2012) *Strategic Human Resource Planning Factsheet*. London: CIPD.

Cunningham, I. (2015) from a radio interview.

Curson, J., Dell, M., Wilson, R., Bosworth, D. and Baldauf, B. (2010) 'Who does workforce planning well? Workforce rapid review team summary', *International Journal of Health Care Quality Assurance,* Vol. 23, No. 1, pp. 110–19.

Davenport, T. (2014) *Big Data @ Work*. Boston: Harvard Business Publishing Corporation.

Francis, R. (2013) Report of the Mid Staffordshire NHS Foundation Trust Public Inquiry, London:TSO.

Gabb, A. (2012) 'Safety in numbers', *PM Guide to Recruitment Marketing,* pp. 14–17.

Ham, C. (2015) from an interview on the 'Today' programme. Chris Ham is Chief Executive of the King's Fund an independent charity seeking to improve healthcare in England.

IDS (2011) *HR Studies: Workforce Planning*. London: IDS.

Jacob, R. (2012) 'Labour shortages: Double digit wage increases', www.ft.com, 11 December.

Kaplan, R. and Norton, D. (1992) 'The balanced scorecard: Measures that drive performance', *Harvard Business Review,* January–February, pp. 71–9.

Lavelle, J. (2007) 'On workforce architecture, employment relationships and lifecycles: Expanding the purview of workforce planning and management', *Public Personnel Management,* Vol. 36, No. 4, pp. 371–84.

Lesser, E. (2010) 'Go figure', *People Management,* May, pp. 22–5.

Mayall, R. (2009) *Dear Granny Smith: A Letter from your Postman*. London: Short Books.

Mintzberg, H. (1994) 'The fall and rise of strategic planning', *Harvard Business Review,* January–February, pp. 107–14.

People Management (2009) 'KPMG asks staff to accept temporary flexible contracts if the need arises', Vol. 15, No. 3, p. 8.

People Management (2014) 'Make workforce planning work'. *People Management,* May, p. 36.

Phillips, L. (2009) '"Slash graduate recruitment at your peril": Firms advised to plan for the future', *People Management,* April, p. 8.

Robinson, D. (2009) 'Human capital measurement: An approach that works', *Strategic HR Review,* Vol. 8, No. 6, pp. 5–11.

Rudge, A. (2011) 'Workforce planning helps Birmingham to ride storms of change', *Human Resource Management International Digest,* Vol. 19, No. 1, pp. 12–14.

Stokker, J. and Hallam, G. (2009) 'The right person, in the right job, with the right skills at the right time: A workforce-planning model that goes beyond metrics', *Library Management,* Vol. 15, No. 89, pp. 561–71.

Torrington, D., Hall, L., Taylor, S. and Atkinson, C. (2009) *Fundamentals of Human Resource Management.* Harlow: Pearson Education.

Turner, P. (2002) 'How to do HR forecasting and planning', *People Management,* Vol. 8, No. 6, pp. 48–9.

Work (2014) 'How data analytics is revolutionising banking and hunting', *Work,* Winter, pp. 34–45.

CHAPTER 6
EMPLOYABILITY: THE BASIC SKILLS

THE OBJECTIVES OF THIS CHAPTER ARE TO:

1 Explain the importance for HR people of being effective with people and to explain appropriate methods

2 Discuss the value of analytics in quantifying issues in HR and then to set out various statistical methods that can be used

3 Describe how to make effective presentations to groups, a frequent task for HR people

4 Outline effective writing, an essential requirement. Although we all learned how to write in primary school, those skills need a more specialised focus for us at work

To close Part 1 we have four sections to set out the basic skills for being employable in HRM or a related role. We had to decide first, what could be identified as basic and second, what to place where in the text. We define a basic skill as something that is essential to HR work, the foundation of which can be grasped by someone without practical experience of HR itself. The four sections at the start all meet that criterion, but they are also widely applicable and will frequently be referred to later in the text.

6.a. Being Effective with People

HR people *must* work at this because people are our business. This is a skill that is at risk of being lost as a result of social media and the smartphone. A very interesting explanation of this is given by an American, Sherry Turkle, whose book is listed in Further Reading. She argues that smartphones take us away from reality in our relationships and effectiveness socially and at work. She quotes from one of her students:

> I spend my time online wanting to be seen as witty, involved, intelligent and having the right ironic distance from everything . . . I am giving up the responsibility for who I am to how other people see me. You get lost in your performance. (Turkle, p. 24)

That was a general comment; a later quotation is from a senior partner in a US law firm:

> My younger colleagues at the firm . . . are pilots in their cockpits. They assemble their multiple technologies – a laptop, two iPhones, an Ipad. And then they put in their earphones. Big ones, like pilots. They turn their desks into cockpits and they are isolated . . . It's not like it used to be when associates were available to be interrupted, but in a good way; you could talk to them. They were there to be worked, to be engaged and mentored.

Using text messages are fine for brief factual information at work, even if it is to a person in the same room, but any real engagement with another person or people, such as selection, appraisal, training, negotiation or joint problem-solving requires a degree of candour and openness that only comes from meeting face to face, even though there is still an element of performance, as Goffman (see Further Reading) demonstrates.

Effective people are likely to have some basic qualities. *Poise* enables a person to be at ease in a wide variety of social situations, often enjoying them, and being able to talk with different types of people in a relaxed and self-confident way, which comes partly from the feedback of willing responses constantly provided by other people. So work on winning good reactions.

Another element of poise is knowing what you are talking about; we are more poised in familiar situations than in strange circumstances, so brief yourself fully beforehand when approaching unfamiliar situations. You will be less apprehensive about appearing naive. Questions, and even criticism, are easier to deal with and are often wanted, so stimulating the interchange. Meeting a variety of people from differing backgrounds helps you to develop a rounded view of yourself without feeling too much anxiety about the possible adverse opinions of others.

A feature of poise is being *responsive* to the needs, feelings and level of understanding in other people, which prevents poise from becoming too egocentric. The teacher, for instance, looks for signs of misunderstanding in the student so that the message can be restated or clarified, and the market research interviewer will be looking for signals that the question has been accurately construed, or that it needs elaboration. Responsiveness can also include offering rewards, like friendliness, warmth, sympathy and helpfulness as features of general style.

All of these are done better by people who have *empathy,* which is the ability to see an issue from the other's point of view as well as your own. For some people empathy is instinctive; most of us try and develop it.

Certain general problems impair effective empathy. First, we tend to hear what we expect to hear rather than what we are being told.

The *frame of reference* is the standpoint from which a person views an issue, and understanding of the issue will be shaped by that view rather than any abstract 'reality'. The basic assumptions or standards framing our behaviour are through childhood conditioning, social background, education and through our affiliations. Differences in the frames of reference people hold can present inescapable problems. How, for instance, can those who manage and direct ever fully appreciate the point of view of those who are managed and directed?

The frame of reference on any particular matter is largely determined by opinions developed within a group with which we identify, as few of us alter our opinions alone. We both follow and help to shape opinion in our group, and most of us are in a number of such reference groups. This leads to complexities: some people can be vociferously anti-union as citizens and voters in general elections, yet support a union of which they are members at their workplace.

The *stereotype* is the standardised expectation we have of those who have certain dominant characteristics: typical stereotypes are that all Australians are brash, Scandinavians are tall and blond, women are more caring than men and men are more aggressive than women. The behaviour of some people in a category makes us expect all those in that category to behave in the same way. This is obviously invalid, but is a tendency to which we are prone. We have to listen to what people are actually saying to us rather than hearing what we think a person of that type *would say.*

Making use of stereotypes is necessary at the start of working relationships; it is not feasible to deal with every individual we meet as being a void until we have collected enough information to know how to treat them, so we always try to find a pigeon-hole in which to put someone. We begin conversations with a working stereotype, so that, for example, we stop someone in the street to ask directions only after we have selected a person who looks intelligent and sympathetic. If we are giving directions to a stranger we begin our explanation having made an assessment of their ability to understand quickly, or their need for a more detailed, painstaking explanation. The stereotype becomes a handicap when we remain insensitive to new information enabling us to develop a fuller, more rational appraisal of the other person. HR people must develop the skill of avoiding stereotyping.

Being aware of the dangers of stereotyping others can reduce how much you misunderstand them, but you still have the problem that they will put *you* into a stereotype and hear what you say in accordance with whatever their predetermined notion may be.

Cognitive dissonance is the difficulty we all have in coping with understanding or doing something that is not consistent with our beliefs. This makes us uncomfortable and we try to cope with the dissonance in various ways in order to reduce the discomfort. Either we persuade ourselves that we believe in what we are doing, or we avoid the necessary behaviour. We all interpret or decode words that we hear in order to make sense of them. If we decode the words we hear in a way that does not match what we believe, then we tend to reinterpret them in a way that we can believe.

Different types of face-to-face situation

Having considered some fundamentals, we now consider activities with which HR people engage as different types of situation require different approaches:

- *Enquiry* is where you need to find things out from someone else, with the selection interview being the classic example. What needs to be found out may be factual information, attitudes, feelings, levels of understanding or misunderstanding. The main skill is in types of questioning.

- *Expression* is almost the direct opposite. Instead of finding things out, you are trying to convey information, to develop in the other person a level of knowledge and understanding, acceptance of an argument or agreement with a proposition. Briefing a group is the obvious example. Some questioning is often an element but the main skill is in clear articulation, fluency, good organisation of material and effective illustration.

- *Joint problem solving* involves developing an exchange in which both parties work together to unravel a problem or understand a situation which neither fully understands beforehand. It is not one person transferring an 'answer' to another, but both trying to understand together something which they can only partly understand alone, as in coaching or performance review. The skills involve some questioning and explanation, but also careful listening and feedback. Joint problem solving assumes that both parties trust each other and see a common interest in helping the other.

- *Conflict resolution* begins without the mutual confidence above, as the parties have interests that inevitably conflict and they are not likely to trust each other fully. The skills here are, first, those of presentation and then of listening, questioning and feedback.

Setting the tone

Any meeting or interview begins by someone setting the tone of what is to follow. The HR specialist will set the tone of a selection interview, for instance, by explaining what is to happen and providing other contextual information that will enable the candidate to engage in the process constructively. This will also convey more subtle messages to say, 'I'm in charge; I know what I'm doing; you can trust me'. In other situations the way of setting the tone is different, but some features are common:

- Speak first.
- Smile, looking confident and relaxed (much easier said than done).
- Have *brief*, harmless exchanges that enable the parties to speak to each other without the answers mattering (weather, travel problems, etc.), but always react appropriately to answers.
- Explain your understanding of what is to happen.
- Check that that is understood and accepted.

The fundamentals of listening

Giving attention

Inclining the body towards the other person is a signal of attentiveness, so your posture should be inclined forward and facing the other squarely with an open posture: folded arms can be inhibiting.

Eye contact is a subtle art. You need to show interest and a desire to listen; look away occasionally but only briefly, not repeatedly looking away, staring or looking blank.

Physical responses can show attentiveness. Avoid distracting the other person by physical behaviour unrelated to what is being said; fiddling with a pen, playing with car keys, scrutinising finger nails, wringing hands, brushing specks of dust off our sleeves are a few typical behaviours that indicate inattention. Skilled listeners not only suppress these, they also develop minor gestures and posture variants that are directly responsive to what the other is saying.

Being silent helps you to listen by providing space for incoming messages, but it also provides opportunities to observe the other person and to think about what is being said. Most people are uncomfortable with silence and try to fill it with inconsequential chat, but this interferes with listening. Silence still has to be attentive and the longer the silence, the harder it is to be attentive.

The fundamentals of questioning

Closed questions seek precise, concise information and are useful when you want clear, straightforward data. Most interactions feature closed questioning at some point.

Open-ended questions avoid terse replies by inviting the other person to develop their opinions without prescribing what the answer should be. The question does little more than introduce a topic to talk about. The main purpose of such questions is to obtain the type of deeper information that the closed question misses, as the shape of the answer is not predetermined by the questioner. You are informed not simply by the content of the answers, but by what is selected and emphasised.

Indirect questions take an oblique approach on a difficult matter. A blunt 'Did you like that job?' almost suggests you didn't. Put indirectly as 'What gave you the most satisfaction in that job?' has the merit of concentrating on the work rather than the person.

The *probe* is a form of questioning to obtain information that the respondent is trying to conceal. When you realise that the other person is doing this you have to make an important, and perhaps difficult, decision: whether to respect their unwillingness and let the matter rest, or to persist with the enquiry. Reluctance is quite common, for instance, in selection interviews where a candidate may wish to gloss over an aspect of the recent employment history. The most common sequence for the probe takes the following form: (a) direct questions, replacing the more comfortable open-ended approach ('What were you doing in the first six months of 2015?'). Careful phrasing may avoid a defensive reply, but those skilled at avoiding unwelcome enquiries may still deflect the question, leading to (b) supplementaries, which reiterate the first question with different phrasing ('Yes, I understand about that period. It's the first part of 2015 that I'm trying to get clear: after you came back from Belgium and before you started with Amalgamated Widgets'). Eventually this should produce the information the questioner needs. (c) Closing. If the information has been wrenched out like a bad tooth and you look horrified or sit in stunned silence, then the candidate will feel badly put down. You have to make the divulged secret less awful than the candidate had feared, so that the interview can proceed with reasonable confidence ('Yes, well you must be glad to have that behind you'). You may feel able to develop the probe by developing the answer with a further question such as 'And how did that make you feel?' or 'And how did you react to that? It must have been a terrible blow.' It is only reasonable to do this if the resultant exchange adds something useful to the questioner's understanding of the client: simple nosiness is not appropriate.

WINDOW ON (MAL)PRACTICE

One dubious version of the probe is to offer an exaggerated explanation for something being avoided. In the imaginary situation described *above* the selector might do this:

Selector: Yes, I understand about that period. It's the first part of 2015 that I'm trying to get clear: after you came back from Belgium and before you started with Amalgamated Widgets. You weren't in prison or anything, were you?

Candidate: Oh no. I had a nervous breakdown.

The explanation offered by the selector is so appalling that the candidate rushes to offer a less appalling explanation. This is not recommended, but it is interesting to know about. It might happen to you one day.

The above assumes that the exchange is worth saving. If it is a killer response such as, 'Well I admit that I've not been completely candid with you. I had a spell in prison for embezzlement actually', however much you agree with aiming to rehabilitate offenders, you might feel that an abrupt ending to an interview of someone applying for a job in accounting would be best.

Some common lines of questioning should be avoided because they can produce an effect that is different from what is intended, as outlined below.

Leading questions ('Would you agree with me that . . . ?') will not necessarily produce an answer that is informative, but an answer in line with the lead that has been given.

Multiple questions give the other person too many inputs at one time ('Could you tell me something of what you did at university, not just the degree, but the social and sporting side as well, and why you chose to backpack your way round the world? You didn't travel on your own, did you?'). This sort of questioning is sometimes adopted by interviewers who are trying very hard to efface themselves and let the respondent get on with the talking. However helpful the interviewer intends to be, the effect is that the candidate will usually forget the later parts of the question, feel disconcerted and ask, 'What was the last part of the question?' By this time the interviewer has also forgotten, so they are both embarrassed.

Taboo questions are those that do not respect the reasonable personal privacy of the other person. Some questions have to be avoided, as they could be interpreted as biased. It is potentially discriminatory, for instance, to ask women how many children they have and what their husbands do for a living. Questions about religion or place of birth should also be avoided. Some questions may do no more than satisfy the idle curiosity of the questioner. If there is no point in asking them, they should not be put.

The fundamentals of feedback

As well as listening one has to provide feedback, indicating that you have received and understood what you are being told. There are six basic methods of providing feedback:

1 *In reflection,* the listener picks up and restates the content of what has just been said. In a difficult situation the listener picks out the emotional overtones of a statement and 'reflects' them back to the other without any attempt to evaluate them; neither approval nor disapproval, neither sympathy nor condemnation.

2 At a more prosaic level, there is *summary and rerun* to show you are listening and providing the opportunity for any misunderstanding to be pointed out. In appraisal, for instance, the appraisee will produce lots of information in an interview and you will be selecting that which is to be retained and understood. From time to time you interject a summary sentence or two with an interrogative inflection. This shows that you are listening, gives the respondent the chance to correct any false impressions and reinforces the key points that are being retained. It is also a useful way of making progress, as the interjection is easily followed by another open-ended question, 'Now perhaps we can turn to . . . '.

3 The standard method in both reflection and summary is *paraphrasing,* by which the listener states the essence of what has been said. This is done concisely, giving the other person a chance to review what has been said and, perhaps, to correct it.

4 We all respond positively when a listener shows *interest* in what is being said. If it is possible also to agree with what is being said, the reinforcement of the respondent will be greater.

5 The most common form of *affirmation* in feedback is the head nod, and many public speakers look for head nods (not to be confused with nodding off) as a way of judging the supportive mood of the audience. Other ways of affirming involve the use of the eyes. These are too subtle and individual to describe, but we each have a repertoire of signals to indicate such reactions as encouragement, surprise and understanding. When the eyes are part of a warm smile, there will be stronger reward to the talker. There are also words and phrases: 'Really?', 'Go on . . . ', 'Yes . . . ', 'Of course . . . ', 'My word . . . ', 'You were saying . . . '.

6 A variety of noises can be ways of feeding back to the other party. They are difficult to reproduce in words but are usually variations on a theme of 'Mmm . . . ' and they form a part of the exchanges that is inarticulate yet meaningful, keeping things going without interrupting.

SUMMARY PROPOSITIONS

6.a.1. Face-to-face skills are fundamental to all managerial work.

6.a.2. Effectiveness is aided by poise and being responsive to others, as well as by understanding the effects of the frame of reference, stereotyping and cognitive dissonance.

6.a.3. The basic types of interaction can be categorised as enquiry, expression and joint problem solving.

6.a.4. Listening skills include giving attention, eye contact, physical responses and being silent.

6.a.5. The main types of question are closed, open-ended, indirect and the probe. Inappropriate questions are leading, multiple and taboo.

GENERAL DISCUSSION TOPICS

6.a.1. Is the dependence of people on their phone for communication an irreversible change in human interaction or can a balance be found between this and face-to-face communication?

6.a.2. Which three forms of communication at work are best spoken and which three are best written?

6.a.3. We have decided that the skills chosen for this section are appropriate for the reasons we have stated at the beginning. Is our selection right?

PUTTING IT INTO PRACTICE

1 Watch two or three different television newsreaders reporting the same thing and compare their expressions, especially at the end of the report. Do their expressions draw you in to the news item or not? Did their expression and demeanour fit what they were reporting and the language they were using? Who was most effective and why? Especially watch eyes and the smile.

2 With a friend, separately spend two minutes preparing a statement about different controversial topics. Make your statement to your partner, who then restates it to you, reflecting and summarising as accurately as possible. You make corrections to show differences between what was said and what was understood. Now swap roles and repeat.

3 With a friend, separately prepare one or two open-ended questions about a similar topic, like where you each went on holiday. After one or two closed questions to get basic facts, you put an open-ended question about the topic, followed by supplementaries to develop your knowledge and understanding. Now swap roles and repeat. Discuss with each other what you feel you have learned from this exercise about your use of different types of questioning.

6.b. Using and Interpreting Basic Analytics

The objective of this section is to help you interpret the meaning and value of statistics presented in a report or article, and to guide you in choosing the appropriate statistics to use when presenting numerical data. We focus on basic statistics with most relevance for business and HRM, and we have been very selective.

Descriptive statistics are used to organise and summarise data in order to communicate them more clearly. They are used when we have data for the whole population we are aiming to describe, for example, all employees within an organisation. Some government statistics also cover the whole of the relevant population, such as unemployment statistics and the national census.

Descriptive statistics can also be used to describe the findings of a sample, for example a sample survey sent to HRM managers, each responding on behalf of a different multinational company (MNC), but it must be remembered that the results apply to the sample only. If we wish to say something about the total population from which the sample is drawn (i.e. all MNCs) we would need to use 'inferential statistics', which are more complex.

Our constant message throughout is one of caution. Statistics are factual pieces of information, designed to give the message that the producer of the statistics wants to put across. As Benjamin Disraeli, a British Prime Minister in the nineteenth century, said, 'There are lies, damned lies, and statistics'.

Frequency distributions

These distributions are often used in business generally and in HRM. For example we could break down the workforce by gender, or by highest qualification, or days of absence. Figure 6.1 shows how the workforce may be broken down by highest NVQ equivalent qualification displayed as a bar chart, and in table form it would look like Table 6.1. To present ages or salaries in a bar chart or frequency table it would be sensible to divide them into groups or bands, otherwise the figure or table would be far too big and fairly meaningless. Frequencies are often displayed as pie charts using the relevant percentages or frequencies, which are excellent for visual presentation. The most popular category is the **mode,** and in this case it is the NVQ Level 3. The mode is the **most frequently occurring,** or most numerous category. Frequency tables and the mode are particularly useful for categorical measures. Another example of the use of these measures is to analyse stated reasons for leaving an organisation.

Table 6.1 Frequency table of qualification levels

NVQ level	Number of employees who have this as their highest qualification	Percentage of employees who have this as their highest qualification
1	70	22
2	75	23
3	80	25
4	45	14
5	30	9
6	18	6
7	2	1

Employee total number = 320.

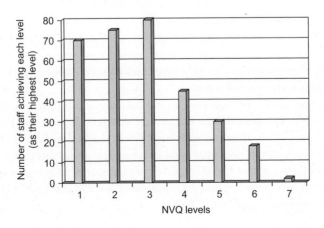

Figure 6.1
A bar chart of qualification levels

WINDOW ON PRACTICE

Some simple definitions

A categorical (sometimes called 'discrete') measure is just that, a category: such as gender, highest qualification, job type, reason for leaving. These measures are usually labelled by means of a word.

Some measures are ordinal measures such as in the NVQ example in that they are ranked numerically in order of difficulty; however, the rankings are not necessarily evenly spaced, and do not have a true zero. Therefore the numbers do not have any arithmetic relationship: so we cannot say that NVQ4 is twice as hard as NVQ2 or an NVQ1 plus an NVQ5 adds up to an NVQ6.

Continuous numeric measures, which have a true zero, such as length of service, salary and age all have arithmetic properties so a person with four years' service has twice as much service as a person with two years' service.

Measures of central tendency

If you are not familiar with statistics you may find the idea of 'central tendency' somewhat impenetrable but it is fairly straightforward if you think of the word 'average', and apply this to, say, the average annual salary in your organisation. You add up the salaries of everyone in the organisation and divide by the number of people receiving a salary. 'Average' is not strictly a statistical term; the correct term is the **arithmetic mean.** This is a useful measure of central tendency but it has limitations. For example, let us consider Entrepreneur Co, which employs ten people including the owner manager (who earns £80,000 p.a. – the accountant has not been very creative). A full list of all the salaries is:

£80,000 (owner manager)	£14,000
£29,000	£13,000
£17,000	£13,000
£15,000	£13,000
£14,000	£13,000

The mean salary would be £22,100, calculated by adding all salaries together and dividing by ten (number of employees). However, there is no indication here that eight employees earned less than the mean and only two employees were above, nor that one salary is at least £50,000 more than any other.

If, on the other hand, we took another measure of central tendency, the **median,** this would be £13,500, in Entrepreneur Co., a very different figure from the mean, as this represents the mid-point after everyone has been ranked according to their salary. The mid-point means that there are equal numbers of people above this salary and below it in the ranking. In Entrepreneur Co. there is an even number of employees so the median is calculated by taking the middle two measures which are £14,000 and £13,000, and taking the mid-point of these, which is £13,500.

WINDOW ON PRACTICE

The clipped mean

Sometimes the clipped, or cropped, mean is used to remove the effects of outliers, such as the £80,000 in the example above. This would be done by removing the top 5% and the bottom 5% of all salaries.

The same mean salary figure could have been reached in Co-operative Co., round the corner, where the salary list looks very different, and is based solely on length of service:

£22,850	£22,100
£22,850	£21,600
£22,600	£21,600
£22,600	£21,600
£22,100	£21,000

Someone comparing the wages paid in these two organisations on the basis of mean salary only would have no idea how different they were.

WINDOW ON PRACTICE

Some more about different types of measures

The mean can only be calculated for continuous measures like salary, age and years of post-qualification experience. If we try and work out a mean for discrete measures the answer just does not make sense. For example, we cannot find an average for gender of racial groups or area of functional expertise.

Using the example above you either have an NVQ3 or an NVQ2 not an NVQ2.85, which would be the mean if we calculated it! The mean is not appropriate as we are dealing with ordinal data with no evidence that the NVQ levels are equally spaced and no true zero.

However, if we worked out the mean age of the workforce in our company it might work out at 32.25 years. This makes sense because age moves continuously, and a specific person could be 32.25 years old. This works because we are dealing with continuous numeric data with a true zero.

This figure does distinguish the two organisations, as in Co-operative Co. the median salary would be £22,100 (again based on taking the two middle salary points, which in this case turn out to be exactly the same). However, while the median may differentiate Entrepreneur Co. from Co-operative Co. it is also a limited measure unless the end points of the range are disclosed. Tony Smith, on completing his degree and keen to pay off his student loan as fast as possible, might, on the basis of mean salaries, have no idea which was the best place to apply for a job. However, Tony gets more information from the median which suggests that he might receive a better starting salary from Co-operative Co. However, even this information is insufficient, as it doesn't tell Tony anything about the range of salaries. We know that they are tightly bunched in Co-operative Co. but salaries in another company could be spread more widely and still have the same median. We look at spread in the following section.

All this shows that it is unwise to take statistics at face value, and organisations can use statistics very cleverly and selectively in order to support their message. In looking at a statistic, three key questions to ask are:

1 What exactly can this statistic tell me?

2 What is it unable to tell me?

3 What more information do I need?

ACTIVITY 6.1

Gather some organisational HR statistics and look carefully at the information you are given. Absence statistics could be a good one to look at here, or turnover statistics. Ask yourself the above three questions. When you have answered them check out your understanding with someone else, preferably the person who produced the statistics.

Measures of dispersion

Dispersion explains how the measures are spread out, and there are two well-used measures of spread which can be used in addition to the mean and the median, and which give us more information. The **range** is determined from the highest and the lowest points. So in Entrepreneur Co. salaries go from £80,000 down to £13,000, giving a range of 67,000; while in Co-operative Co. it is from £22,850 down to £21,000, giving a range of 1,850. The range is useful and simple to identify, but its limitation is that it is very affected by 'outliers', measures at the extremes which are disconnected from the majority of measures. The owner manager's salary of £80,000 is an outlier at Entrepreneur Co. As another example we might say the age range in our organisation is from 18 to 66, but while there are many employees between 18 and 51 there is only one employee older than 51 and that person is 66. So while the range is a useful piece of information it only gives us limited knowledge about spread.

WINDOW ON PRACTICE

The interquartile range

As the range can be very affected by outliers, sometimes the interquartile range is used to counteract this effect. This uses the same principle as the median: if you remember, the median is the point at which half the results are above this point and half below. Imagine the results being divided into quarters rather than just halves. So the top point of the interquartile range is where one quarter of the results are above this point and three-quarters are below it. And the bottom point of the interquartile range is where three-quarters of the results are above this point and one quarter below it. Subtracting the lower point from the higher point gives the interquartile range.

The other well-used measure of spread is the **standard deviation** and this statistic expresses the average deviation from the mean. In other words, having worked out the mean we now work out how much each measure, such as salary in the example (above), differs from that mean, and then average all those differences. If everyone in an organisation earned exactly the same amount of money the standard deviation would be zero. It would not matter what that actual salary is, it could be £20,000 or £50,000, as long as everyone earns the same and there is no spread, the standard deviation is zero. The larger the standard deviation the larger the spread it represents, and we would expect that the standard deviation for Entrepreneur Co. would be greater than for Co-operative Co.

WINDOW ON PRACTICE

Let us compare the standard deviation at Entrepreneur Co. and Co-operative Co.
The standard deviation from the mean at Entrepreneur Co. is £20,934.
The standard deviation from the mean at Co-operative Co. is 631.
So you can see that they are quite different.

The standard deviation is affected by outliers just like the mean and the range, and so it is useful to accompany this statistic with the median and with the mean. In some calculations there is a method for removing outliers and it is worth asking if this has been done when you are given a standard deviation.

Describing relationships or association

There are many times when we would like to see how measures within our organisation are connected, and these often focus on performance measures of some kind or other. We might like to find out how days of absence are related to age, or how absence is related to length of service. One way we can look at relationships is to do this visually in a scatter plot, and a further method is to use a statistical technique called correlation.

Scatterplots

These are fairly simple to draw up and just require that for every person we have the two measures that we are investigating. For example, what is the relationship between the amount of work time devoted to test revision and the scores of trainees in the test? So we draw a plot with test scores on the vertical axis and hours of work time devoted to revision on the horizontal axis, and then plot each individual on that according to their score and the time they were allowed for revision by their manager. In the example in Figure 6.2 we can see how a greater number of work hours devoted to revising appears to be associated with higher test scores, which is generally what we would expect.

Correlation

Correlation is a more sophisticated approach, often applied when relating the selection scores of individuals to eventual performance levels in the organisation. The selection processes are generally intended to give us sufficient information to enable us to predict

Figure 6.2
A scatterplot: plotting revision time against test scores

who we think will perform best in our organisation. In our example we are going to relate the results that candidates achieved at an assessment centre to their performance two years later to see whether there is any relationship between them. To do this we rank the candidates who have been successful at the assessment centre and then rank their performance in two years' time. So, for example, we may be appointing 50 graduates to the company, all of whom have been through the assessment centre; we rank these from 1 to 50 according to their overall score at the centre. Two years later we look at the performance of each individual and again rank them from 1 to 50. Each individual will now have a rank from the assessment centre and a rank for their performance and it is these ranks that will be analysed in the correlation, and the sorts of results we might get are shown in the Window on practice.

WINDOW ON PRACTICE

There are different statistics that can be used for correlation based on the nature of the data, but the results of a correlation are always between 1 and -1 and are expressed as a correlation coefficient (r).

In our example, if the assessment centre ranks perfectly matched the performance ranks, this would mean that Joe, who was ranked sixth in the assessment centre, would also be ranked sixth for performance and Penny, who was ranked 49th in the assessment centre, would also be ranked 49th for performance, and so on for each graduate.

In this case of perfect correlation r = 1. If there were such an assessment tool it would be very popular!

If the relationship was completely random (imagine the scatterplot with dots all over the place and no pattern whatsoever) then r = 0. The assessment tool results do not appear to be able to relate to performance.

Somewhere nearer the middle, which is where most assessment tools are, would be something like r = 0.3, in which case the tool shows some relationship with performance but not a great deal. Occasionally higher associations have been found but they do not generally exceed r = 0.7.

If the relationship between assessment centre ranking and performance ranking produces a negative correlation, for example r = −0.6, then there is some evidence that higher assessment centre scores are related to lower performance scores and vice versa.

The statistic to use here would be a Spearman correlation coefficient as this is the appropriate one for ranked data.

One of the reasons that the results from selection tools do not appear to be highly related to performance measures may be that the performance measures are not well thought through. They could of course be anything, from scores on performance assessment reports to days of absence, level of promotion, assessment of potential and so on.

When any statistics are presented it is always wise to ask how the measures have been developed, before being impressed by the statistics that are produced.

Treating statistics with caution

We have indicated throughout this section how easy it is to misinterpret statistics and how important it is to question them. So here is a series of questions to ask when presented with statistics:

1 If you are given a statistic which you have not met before, ask 'What can this statistic tell me and what can it not tell?' This should prevent you from making any assumptions.

2 Ask for the number of people that percentages are based on, as percentages can sound impressive, but mean nothing if you do not know the numbers they are representing.

WINDOW ON PRACTICE

One of the authors was listening to student presentations on the psychological contract. One particular group contrasted the psychological contract in two organisations by comparing their answers to a range of questions. They produced wonderful histograms and pie charts and there were some impressive differences in the percentages, but they never mentioned how many responses the percentages were based on. It turned out that there were 20 responses from one organisation and six from the other! The students explained that all six were from one department and that had they gone to another department they think the answers to the questions might have been quite different!

3 Ask how the sample was chosen, as responses from employees in one department do not represent the organisation as a whole. Responses from managers do not represent responses from employees.

4 If you are presented with a measure which is ambiguous, such as 'Performance', ask how that measure has been compiled.

5 Survey results purport to reflect the responses of all members of the organisation. For example, if an employee engagement survey has been sent to all employees it is important to ask about response rate. Did all employees reply? If not, what percentage of employees did reply? Also, what patterns are there in relation to responses and non-responses?

6 When presented with the results of a questionnaire always ask for a copy of the questionnaire as the way in which questions are asked can prompt different sorts of responses.

7 Ask yourself what further data you require to understand fully the information you are looking at.

SUMMARY PROPOSITIONS

6.b.1. Each statistic describes data in a very specific way and it is important to be absolutely clear about what that statistic can and cannot tell you.

6.b.2. Statistics are often misused and misinterpreted and they need to be treated with caution.

GENERAL DISCUSSION TOPICS

1 HR practitioners need not develop skills in analytics, as there's always someone else who can be called upon to explain and interpret them. **2** Analytics are a step change in how organisations need to operate, not a passing fad.

PUTTING IT INTO PRACTICE

Have a look at the results of an organisational survey, for example an employee engagement survey or something similar. Go through the seven questions in the 'Treating statistics with Caution' section. Check out your interpretation with someone else, preferably the compiler of the survey.

6.c. Effective Writing

Most readers will be familiar with writing essays. Essays are hardly ever required in a work situation; a quite different approach is needed, as an essay is to show what you know, understand and can explain. It is to display your ability, but at work what you write has to be right for the recipient, especially if it requires action. What you write could be a positive result leading to action by the reader; it could be a negative result of 'covering your back' by demonstrating that a more senior person had received a report from you which justifies something you did that has turned sour; or it could be for the historical record. What you want to say is not as important as what the reader needs to know and then do. Response from the reader is the constant objective of the writer.

You may be asked to summarise a long article for your boss, or to prepare a briefing on a particular topic for a committee, or draft a letter for someone else to sign, to investigate a problem and prepare a report. All the following points are relevant to varied situations although the main focus is on report writing.

Generally what you write should be as brief and lucid as possible. Alfred Einstein once said that if you could not explain something in simple language you had not understood it well enough. Guidelines for prosecuting advocates includes that they should not expect a judge to appreciate 'arcane and obscure language'.

Typical things HR people write are notices, letters, briefing notes for a colleague who has to attend a crucial meeting for which some information is required, or reports. There follows a detailed suggestion of how to write an effective report.

Report writing

Content

Often the report has an appended *Executive Summary*. Although this short section is placed at the beginning of these notes on report writing, the summary is actually written last. Most readers do not really want to read your report at all; what they want is a quick summary of the main points. This may annoy you as you have spent sleepless hours perfecting your arguments and analysing your data, but the Executive Summary may lead the reader to refer to your main report for further explanation of recommendations or for the justification of a puzzling conclusion. It is, of course, a summary of the report that you have already written, not the other way round. The summary requires thorough analysis and succinct explanation and abbreviation, with clear references to the relevant sections and page numbers of the full report.

Appendices maybe used to remove detailed data from the report which are illustrative of points made in the report, but not essential to understanding. Reference to the extra information in an appendix may help to convince a reader of an argument that is presented in the report with enough evidence to convince most readers, but not enough to persuade the sceptical.

Some reports may require a note of *sources,* if some of the readers may need to refer to published material on which you have relied. You may not need full bibliographical details, but always sufficient information for the reader to locate the material you have used.

Writing procedure

Before the writing begins you need to *assemble and organise your material*. Dumping a pile of papers on the back seat of your car may be a form of assembling, but certainly not organising. A simple method is to divide the papers into several piles of different categories like raw data, interview responses, external comparisons, suggestions, implications and 'probably not needed'. Leaving out the 'probably not needed' for the time being, the next stage is to review the content of each pile for three reasons. First, you are recalling everything and beginning to see where you want to go. Second, you are probably moving some more material to that which is probably not needed. Third, as you begin to see where you want to go, you see what material you need to add: checks on the internet, visits to the library, telephone calls, finding *and marking* pages where you may need to refer to that book on the shelf behind you. With a clear idea of what you want to achieve, and able to see the logical way of getting there, you can proceed to the next stage.

Structure

You now need a *framework* to give a logical sequence to the writing and avoid the risk of duplication, as well as to ensure that you present material early in the report that will be needed to justify points made later. Ways of doing this vary. One popular writer of fiction, John Grisham, works out a comprehensive and detailed structure for each book before he starts writing. You have to employ the method that works for you. The framework comes from analysing the message that is to be sent in terms of the action expected and then subdividing the components of that message into logical groups. The framework may be modified during the writing until you are convinced that it is satisfactory.

You are likely to need a structure that has the following features:

- terms of reference;
- who commissioned the report;
- who has written it;
- sources/methods used;
- list of acronyms;
- Executive Summary at the front (as well as normal summary at the end);
- contents list;
- recommendations;
- date.

This is not necessarily the order in which the items should appear, as you will want to draw the reader into the body of the report as soon as possible. Another fiction writer, Lee Child, contends that you have to grab the reader in the first sentence. You will not be writing a novel, but you need to work out your structure in a way that catches the interest of the reader early.

The logical grouping of the material takes the form of *sections,* each dealing with a distinct aspect. This arrangement emphasises the logic of the way the material is grouped, but it is also part of the communication to the reader, because the sections have titles, like headlines in a newspaper, which sum up what the section contains. Titles should not tease or muddle the reader. 'Which way now?', for example, is an unhelpful title as it poses a question without giving any clue to the answer.

The *paragraph* is a unit of thought in the writing, dealing with a single topic or idea, and good paragraphing will ensure the material is read. It also reassures the reader that there will be occasional breathing spaces rather than a long, solid block of text to be ploughed through.

The appropriate length of paragraph varies with the material being written. Textbooks usually average 100–200 words, popular novels 60–75 and popular newspapers 30–40. Short paragraphs are easier for the reader, but reports will sometimes require detailed argument involving greater length. It is wise to keep the average under 120, if possible.

The *sentence* is the bit of writing between full stops, which makes sense and usually has a subject and a verb. The main difficulties in writing sentences are that either they are too long or they set up expectations that are not realised. Writing sentences that are too long comes through adding extra clauses and qualifications. Setting up expectations that are not realised comes from inferring what is to come in the sentence, but then changing tack or emphasis without returning to the original thought.

Punctuation is important in making your meaning clear. There are great subtleties of punctuation that can be deployed by pedants, but the basics are simple.

Punctuation

A *comma* makes a logical division within a sentence:

1 to separate the subject from descriptive words or phrases: 'Charles, Prince of Wales, plays polo'.

2 to separate clauses: 'if he scores, the crowd will cheer'.

3 to separate items on a list: 'her parents, husband and children came to watch'.

A *semi colon* links two sentences so closely related that a full stop would make too great a break: 'he didn't score; Jones did'.

A *colon* separates an announcement from what is announced, 'the order of play is as follows:'.

An *apostrophe* indicates either a possessive, 'the team's performance', or a missing syllable in abbreviations, 'it's time for tea'. There is so much uncertainty about the apostrophe that one often sees the quite unnecessary and misleading use of an apostrophe in a simple plural: on the side of a delivery van, 'Laptops and PC's'; in a newspaper, 'The 1960's were the best time ever for popular music'.

Inverted commas can be quite confusing. Basically they are to identify in a sentence something that is being quoted, as in the above examples. They are sometimes used to highlight the use of a phrase which you know is not quite right, but which you are too idle to express properly: the fans are 'not best pleased' with the manager's performance.

Emphasis can be shown in various ways, by means of *italics*, underlining, **emboldening,** CAPITAL LETTERS or !!!!!!!! The important thing is to use your chosen style for emphasis consistently and sparingly. Using styles for emphasis is quite different from using styles to differentiate headings, marking stages in the development of your argument and signalling what is coming next. In this text headings are given different weights, with emboldened capitals being for the biggest sections, followed by italics for sections within a bigger section and so on. For simple emphasis the best method is in the choice of words. In popular media there is a tendency to rely on extravagant language; in a reality TV programme a singer is described by successive judges as 'fantastic', 'absolutely fantastic' and 'truly amazing'. Much more effective are words and phrases which provide emphasis by describing what has happened accurately and meaningfully.

Table 6.1 provides a useful checklist for writers of reports.

Table 6.1a A checklist for report writers

1 Before writing
  a What action do you expect from this report?
  b Who will read it?
  c How short can it be?

2 Outline
  a What precisely is the topic of the report?
  b How many components are there?
  c How can those best be grouped?
  d How are the components brought into sections?
  e Do the titles inform the reader?
  f Will the report, as outlined, produce the action specified above?

3 Writing the report
  a Is the average paragraph length shorter than 100 words?
  b Have you used more words than are needed?
  c Have you used words that are precise and concrete rather than words that are vague and abstract?
  d Have you used any superfluous adverbs, adjectives and roundabout phrases?
  e Have you shown the source of any facts quoted?
  f Are any of the sentences too long?

4 Revising the report
  a Will the report, as written, produce the action specified above?
  b Is anything missing?
  c Are all calculations accurate?
  d Are the recommendations clear and justified?
  e Is the choice between alternatives clear?
  f Is any part of the report likely to cause offence to anyone? If so, can that be avoided?
  g What objections do you expect to the recommendations, and how will you deal with them?
  h Can any of the possible objections be prevented by rewriting part of the report?

5 Final presentation
  a Is the typing perfect and without spelling mistakes?
  b Are all the pages numbered?
  c Are abbreviations and symbols used consistently throughout?
  d Does the general appearance of the report encourage the reader to read it?
  e Is there a single page summary of proposals?
  f Is the report being distributed to all the appropriate people?
  g If the report is confidential, is that indicated on the report and ensured by the method of distribution?

SUMMARY PROPOSITIONS

6.c.1. Reports are written to be read and acted upon, not to show how clever the writer is.

6.c.2. A short Executive Summary is often added to the main report, both to summarise the main points and to guide the reader to particular sections for fuller explanation and evidence.

6.c.3. Appendices are often used to remove detailed evidence or illustration from the main report, while retaining it for reference by those who need it. One appendix might be necessary to give details of sources used.

6.c.4. Any report is planned with a framework, within which are sections so that the argument and recommendations can be written logically and appropriately for the reader.

6.c.5. Punctuation can alter the meaning of a phrase or sentence.

GENERAL DISCUSSION TOPICS

6.c.1. How important is punctuation? Is it sufficient that the words are accurate?

6.c.2. There is a small body of opinion that the apostrophe should be abolished as it is irrelevant. Do you agree or disagree?

PUTTING IT INTO PRACTICE

1 Identify a topic about which you feel strongly and on which you would like others to follow your lead and take action. Possibilities might be climate change, employment opportunities for adolescents, bankers' bonuses, healthy eating or something else. Then write a report for others to read which might galvanise them to action. Check that it is written in a way that will be likely to produce a positive reaction from your readership (which you may like to narrow to a specific group). Then write your Executive Summary. Give it to one or two of your friends and assess their reaction. Finally, rewrite it in the light of their responses.

2 Using the approach outlined here, rewrite a handout for people thinking about taking up a sport or pastime which you enjoy in order to encourage their interest.

6.d. Effective Presentation

The skill of presentation is required to inform and explain. HR people constantly have to present on such matters as explaining a change of policy, clarifying details of a new trade union agreement or setting out the implications in a change of employment legislation. There may be presentations on career prospects in the business at careers conventions, pitching to a senior management group for an improvement in the budget, 'selling' the advantages of a new performance-related pay scheme, or explaining to a small group of job applicants the details of the post for which they have applied.

Objectives

As with almost every aspect of management, the starting point is the objective. What are you aiming to achieve? What do you want the listeners to do, to think or to feel? Note that the question is not 'What do you want to say?' The objective is in the response of the listeners. That starting point begins the whole process, with a focus on results and payoff, turning attention away from ego. It also determines tone. If your objective is to inform, you will emphasise facts. If you aim to persuade, you will try to appeal to emotion as well as to reason.

One other preliminary point is the problem of the smartphone. In some situations it is sufficient to ask the audience to switch off their electronic devices, but that is not enough for a touch-screen age. One study of large American firms produced remarkable statistics of what people did during meetings: 65% do other work, 63% send email. If the accepted practice in your business is that people at presentations take their phones and tablets with them, then the form of presentation will need modification.

The material

What is to be said or, more accurately, what should members of the audience go away having understood and remembered?

> Organise your material with an introduction that previews, a body that develops, and a conclusion that reviews. When you organize the body of your presentation, start by sorting out the theme. The theme is a planning device that holds together the various ideas you want to discuss. If the theme of your presentation is informative, then the body should provide facts. If the theme is persuasive, the body should develop persuasive arguments. (Fandt 1994, p. 159)

In the introduction the speaker establishes rapport with the audience. Apart from gaining their attention, the speaker will include here an answer to the unspoken question: is it going to be worth our while listening? Is this person worth listening to? The person who is worth listening to is someone who looks at the audience and looks friendly, knowledgeable and, above all, enthusiastic. A useful format for the introduction is to explain what the members of the audience will know or be able to do at the end. It is also helpful to sketch out the framework of what is to come, so that people can follow it more readily. But stick to what you promise. If you say there are going to be five points, the audience will listen for five to make sure that they have not missed one.

Having secured the attention of the listeners, you now have them waiting not just for what you say next, but with a framework in their heads of what they will hear, so they will be able to locate their understanding within that framework. The main body of the presentation is the message that is to be conveyed, the development of the argument and the build-up of what it is that the audience should go away having understood and remembered.

The main body needs to be effectively organised. This will not only help members of the audience to maintain attention, but also discipline the speaker to avoid rambling, distracting irrelevance or forgetting. The most common methods are:

- **Chronological sequence,** dealing with issues by taking the audience through a series of events. A presentation to an employment tribunal often follows this pattern.

- **Known to unknown, or simple to complex.** The speaker starts with a brief review of what the audience already know or can easily understand and then develops to what they do not yet know or cannot yet understand. The logic of this method is to ground the audience in something they can handle so that they can make sense of the unfamiliar. This is the standard method of organising teaching sessions.

- **Problem to solution** is almost the exact opposite of simple to complex. A problem is presented and a solution follows. The understanding of the audience is again grounded, but this time grounded in an anxiety that the speaker is about to relieve.

- **Comparison** is a method of organisation which compares one account with another. Selling usually follows this path, as the new is compared with the old.

Whatever the method of organisation for the material, the main body of the presentation will always contain a number of key thoughts or ideas. This is what the speaker is trying to plant in the minds of the audience: not just facts, which are inert, but the ideas which facts may well illustrate and clarify. The idea that inflation is dangerously high is only illustrated by the fact that it is at a particular figure in a particular month.

The ideas in a presentation can be helpfully linked together by a device that will help audience members to remember them and to grasp their interdependence. One method of linkage is to enshrine the ideas in a story. If the story is recalled, the thoughts are recalled with it, as they are integral to the structure. Another method is to use key words to identify the points that are being made, especially if they have an alliterative or mnemonic feature, such as 'People Produce Prosperity'. In a lecture it is common to provide a framework for ideas by using a drawing or system model to show the interconnection of points.

Facts, by giving impact, keep together the framework of ideas that the speaker has assembled. They clarify and give a dimension to what is being said. The danger is to use too many, so that the audience are overwhelmed by facts and figures which begin to bemuse them. If the presentation is to be accompanied by a handout, facts may be usefully contained in that, so that they can be referred to later, without the audience having to remember them.

Humour is the most dangerous of all aids to the speaker. If the audience laugh at a funny story, the speaker will be encouraged and may feel under less tension, but how tempting to try again and end up 'playing for laughs'. Laughter is a most seductive human reaction, but too many laughs are even more dangerous than too many facts. What will the audience remember; the joke, or what the joke was intended to illustrate? Attempted humour is also dangerous for the ineffective comedian. If you tell what you think is a funny story and no one laughs, you have made a fool of yourself (at least in your own eyes) and risk floundering.

Very few people speak effectively without notes. Although there is a tendency to marvel at those who can, relying solely on memory risks missing something out, getting a fact wrong or drying up completely. Notes follow the pattern of organisation you have established, providing discipline and limiting the tendency to ramble. It is both irritating and unhelpful for members of an audience to cope with a speaker who wanders off down a blind alley. When an amusing anecdote pops up in your brain, it can be almost irresistible to share it.

There are two basic kinds of notes: headlines or a script. Headlines are probably the most common, with main points underlined and facts listed beneath. Sometimes there will also be a marginal note about an anecdote or other type of illustration. The alternative, the script, enables the speaker to try out the exact wording, phrases and pauses to achieve the greatest effect. The script will benefit from some marking or arrangement that will help you to find your place again as your eyes constantly flick from the page to the audience and back again. This marking can be underlining or using a highlighter. When using a script it is important not to make the reading too obvious. Head down, with no eye contact, and little light and shade is a sure-fire way of turning off the attention of the audience. Public figures increasingly use electronic prompters which project the script progressively through the presentation on to a glass screen some way in front of the speaker. By this means the script can be spoken with little break in eye contact with the audience. This will be too ambitious for most HR people, but the important thing is that the words should be *spoken* rather than *read*.

There are many variations of these basic methods of organising the material, so that one approach is to use varying line length, while another is to use rows of dots to indicate pause or emphasis. Some people like to have their notes on small cards, so that they are unobtrusive, but this is difficult if the notes are more than headlines. Standard A4 paper should present no problem, if the notes are not stapled, are well laid out and can be handled discreetly. Never forget to number the pages or cards, as the next time you speak they may fall to the floor moments before you are due to begin, and they may not land in the same order that they were on your lap.

Most presentations benefit from using visual aids. You may use a model, a sample or even a person ('Here is our trainee of the month'), but mostly you will use visual images. Blackboards still exist and white boards are fairly common. Flip charts and overhead projector acetates are widely used. The most rapidly-growing type of visual image in presentation is that from a computer, projected on a screen, usually using a PowerPoint package. PowerPoint is so good that it can be dangerous. One problem is its relative sophistication technically. It has to be operated by someone who knows what he or she is doing and has confidence in being able to manage the computer rather than being managed by it. Every reader will have had experience of a presenter being baffled by a technical glitch that held up the presentation and knocked the presenter's confidence sideways. If the computer is being managed by someone other than the presenter, there is the potential difficulty of presenter and operator not always being coordinated.

WINDOW ON PRACTICE

In 2006 a newly appointed vice chancellor of a British university was giving his first major address to a large audience, using a PowerPoint presentation which he controlled with a remote, although technical staff at the side of the hall had overall control. At one point he went back to a previous page, then went forward to the wrong page without realising it. Technical staff corrected the mistake at the same time as he noticed it. He then corrected it without realising they had spotted it. Confusion and uncertainty persisted for several minutes. At the subsequent lunch the muddle was discussed more extensively than the content of the address.

The rationale for visual aids is that we remember what we see for longer than we remember what we are told, and we can sometimes understand what we see better than we can understand what we hear. Too much displayed material can obscure rather than illuminate what is being said. Television news provides a good example of how much can be used. The dominant theme is always the talking head with frequently intercut pieces of film. Very seldom do words appear on the screen and then usually as extracts from a speech or report, where a short sentence or passage is regarded as being especially meaningful. The other situation in which words and numbers appear is when facts are needed to illustrate an idea, so that ideas such as football scores or a change in the value of the US dollar almost always have the figures shown on the screen to clarify and illustrate. Seldom, however, will more than two or three numbers be displayed at the same time. Speakers need to remember the size of what they are displaying as well as its complexity. Material has to be big enough for people to read and simple enough for them to follow. Material also has to be timed to coincide with what is being said.

PowerPoint is a most seductive toy for the presenter. The box of tricks is enormous and too many people give a show, with clever figures dancing across the screen and other distractions. We must always remember what the purpose of the presentation is; clever or spectacular forms of display can become what people remember rather than the message that is to be conveyed. Television news is again an illustration. Between programmes there may be all manner of clever visual entertainment in brief clips. Once the news report begins there are no such fancy tricks, although graphics are used to illustrate and highlight information.

SUMMARY PROPOSITIONS

6.d.1. Presentation is the main method used to convey information and understanding to a group of listeners.

6.d.2. Alternative methods of constructing a presentation are (a) chronological sequence, (b) known to unknown or simple to complex, (c) problem to solution, (d) comparison.

6.d.3. A presentation is spoken, not read. Visual aids illustrate but do not distract.

GENERAL DISCUSSION TOPICS

6.d.1. There is an old saying, 'What I hear I forget, what I see I can understand and what I do I know.' What is the relevance of this to presentation?

6.d.2. Why do students attend lectures where information is presented to them, rather than reading that information presented in a book?

PUTTING IT INTO PRACTICE

1 The next time you attend a lecture, a talk or a presentation, study the arrangement of the room and note the changes you would make if you were the speaker.

2 Prepare a five-minute talk on one of the following:
   a. Walking compared to cycling.
   b. Keeping fit.
   c. Your favourite sport or hobby.

   After careful preparation deliver the talk in an empty room whilst recording it. Play it back several times, making critical notes of voice, energy level etc., following the points in the chapter and then deliver it again. Listen to it and consider: how it was better, how not so good. What have you learned? How can you improve?

3 This may not work. Do the above in a different way; not alone but with a small group, with each person taking a turn at *standing up* and speaking with the critique coming from the listeners, not from a recording. The reason for saying 'It may not work' is because at least some people will be self-conscious to the point of giggling or hamming it up. Further, making constructive critical remarks has to be done so that it helps and does not demoralise.

FURTHER READING

Effectiveness with people

There has been little new work in this area, so it is best to look at two classics, which are still in print and constantly referred to:

Goffman. E. (1990) *The Presentation of Self in Everyday Life*. London: Penguin.

First published in 1959, Erving Goffman, a Canadian academic, examines the subject by comparing it with theatre. It is very readable and elegantly written. For those who do not have English as a first language, it has been extensively translated.

Argyle, M. (1994) *The Psychology of Interpersonal Behaviour*. London: Penguin.

The author is a British academic who is a contemporary of Goffman. He takes the discipline of psychology as his basis, rather than the sociology of Goffman, to produce an abundance of practical explanations.

It is well worth reading both these texts. For a contemporary but more narrowly focused read, try:

Bargiela-Chiappini, F. and Haugh, M. (2010) *Face, Communication and Social Interaction*. Sheffield, UK: Equinox Publishing.

Goffman and Argyle were both writing before the phenomenon of social media; for a learned and very readable analysis of living with the smartphone try:

Turkle, S. (2015) *Reclaiming Conversation: The Power of Talk in a Digital Age*. New York: Penguin Press.

Effective presentation

Fandt, P.M. (1994) *Management Skills: Practice and experience*. St Paul, Minn.: West Publishing.

Quinn, R.E. (1988) *Beyond Rational Management: Mastering the Paradoxes And Competing Demands Of High Performance*. San Francisco: Jossey-Bass.

Quinn, R.E., Faerman, S.R., Thompson, M.P. and McGrath, M.R. (2002) *Becoming a Master Manager*. New York: John Wiley.

Material on management skills is everywhere, but in this context the texts above are especially helpful.

Yate, M. and Sander, P. (2003) *The Ultimate Business Presentations Book*. London: Kogan Page.

Presentation is also preached very widely. This excellent recent import from the US covers the ground very thoroughly and readably.

Effective writing

Eats, Shoots and Leaves by Lynne Truss has sold three million copies worldwide since it was first published in 2003; the most recent edition was in 2009. It is a popular and helpful book. The original English edition as well as a special edition for Indian readers are published by Profile Books, London. Gotham Books of New York publish an American edition. For German readers there is a similar book: Stick, B. (2009) *Der Dativ ist dem Genitiv sein Tod*. Cologne: Kiepenhauer and Witsch.

For a full treatment of report writing, there is:

Bowden, J. (2008) *Writing a Report* (8th edn.). Oxford: How To Books.

So far we have said little about writing style. The classic guide is:

Burchfield, R.W. (2004) *Fowler's Modern English Usage* (revised 3rd edn.). Oxford: Oxford University Press.

This is an updated version of the original 1926 book by Henry Watson Fowler. Oxford University Press republished the original in 2009, with an introduction and notes by David Crystal. A more compact guide is:

Strunk, W. and White, E.B. (2000) *The Elements of Style* (4th edn.). Needham Heights, Mass.: Allyn and Bacon.

Written by two Americans, it was first published in 1959.

REFERENCES

Fandt, P.M. (1994) *Management Skills: Practice and Experience.* St Paul, Minn.: West Publishing.

Goffman. E. (1990) *The Presentation of Self in Everyday Life.* London: Penguin.

Turkle, S. (2015) *Reclaiming Conversation: The Power of Talk in a Digital Age.* New York: Penguin Press.

PART 2

RESOURCING: GETTING PEOPLE IN THE RIGHT PLACES TO DO THE RIGHT THINGS

CHAPTERS

In this section we deal with the resourcing aspects of HRM: how to design an organisation with a flexible workforce, how to get the right people in the right places and with the skills required to undertake all these activities.

The first major activity of the HR specialist is to facilitate an effective organisation design, one that is agile and offers flexibility to both worker and organisation (Chapter 7). Workers may be employed or may be consultants or sub-contractors; they may be temporary, full-time, part-time or occasional workers. Flexible arrangements may also cater for worker need via, for example, compressed working weeks.

Next Chapter deals with how to find and bring in the people that the business needs for its success. Recruitment activity, increasingly via social media, is central to this.

Selection follows, which nearly always involves a face-to-face meeting between the parties to agree terms before the relationship begins (Chapter 9). The process of 'coming to terms' is one of mutual assessment. Many prospective employees reject an employer by deciding not to apply for a post, or by discontinuing their application. Employers usually choose between many applicants, but often feel there are too few high-quality ones.

Employability, Chapter 10, deals with skills essential to resourcing: determining whether there is a vacancy to be filled and, if so, undertaking a job or competency analysis to construct job descriptions and person specifications.

The whole resourcing process is symbolised by the mutual assessment that takes place in the selection interview: 'Is this person right for us?' and 'Is this job and situation right for me?' The answers to those questions have major implications for both parties. The uncertainty about whether or not the right answers are found at the interview is why we have to examine resourcing so closely and selection interviewing skills are thus critical to effective appointment decisions. At the end of each chapter you will find a case study in Theory into Practice which will help you to put these ideas into context and explore them more thoroughly.

CHAPTER 7

ORGANISATIONAL AGILITY AND FLEXIBILITY

THE OBJECTIVES OF THIS CHAPTER ARE TO:

1 Explain the principles of organisation design and assess the need for organisational agility

2 Outline the most common types of organisation structure

3 Discuss the reasons for and types of workforce flexibility

4 Discuss forms of both employer and employee flexibility and the extent to which they are implemented in practice

Contemporary organisations are preoccupied with agility, that is, being able to deal with ongoing and substantial change in response to an external context that is described as 'VUCA' – volatile, uncertain, complex and ambiguous (Holbeche, 2015). This requires adoption of appropriate organisation design principles in order to create agile organisational structures. Organisation design is therefore central to a contemporary HR practitioner's role (CIPD, 2016). Underpinning organisational agility is workforce flexibility, that is, the capacity to adapt workforce size and skills in response to external pressures. This has often led employers to offer less secure jobs, using 'flexible' workers in order to keep costs down and to retain or increase market share. Developments in technology enable a greater control of workflow, requiring flexible working hours to extend capital utilisation. The change in the economic base whereby there are more service industries with an emphasis on knowledge and knowledge workers has also influenced flexibility, as jobs in a knowledge-based economy tend to be more flexible than industrial jobs, with more varied working hours. Allied to this has been a perceived need for '24/7' service availability, leading to a dramatic move away from the standard working time model of 9–5 Monday to Friday, and to employers demanding a far more flexible approach to work organisation.

The demand for flexibility, however, has not all been from employers. It has coincided with changes that have created a greater supply of labour at non-standard times. One of the primary drivers of this has been the increased labour force participation of women, particularly women in the childbearing years, which has led to a greater requirement for flexible working arrangements in order to accommodate childcare responsibilities. There has also been an increase in single-parent families and dual-career couples, meaning that a growing proportion of the workforce has to reconcile both work and non-work commitments. This augments the supply of labour at non-standard times, such as nights and weekends. A further demographic influence is the ageing population of western countries, with employees demanding flexibility to deal with both childcare and eldercare responsibilities. Pension concerns (see Chapter 27) may also force workers to remain in the workforce longer than previously anticipated and older workers frequently aspire to work flexibly in the later stages of their careers.

Workforce flexibility is thus a significant contemporary issue. In this chapter, we consider first organisation design and structures and the principles underpinning organisational agility. We then move on to consider workforce flexibility that delivers both employer and employee benefit.

Organisation design

Organisation design relates to the shaping of an organisation to ensure efficient delivery of its activity. Activities focus on:

> [ensuring] that the organisation is appropriately designed to deliver organisation objectives in the short and long-term and that structural change is effectively managed. (CIPD 2015)

Organisation design requires that choices made on a number of issues are consistent with contextual factors, such as the organisation's strategy and its environment (Burton and Obel 2004). Three key issues are **high** versus **low formality, differentiation** versus **integration,** and **decentralisation** versus **centralisation.**

High versus low formality refers to the design of organisational procedures. Typically small firms are relatively informal, low employee numbers meaning that face-to-face communication is usually possible in order to discuss and agree a way forward. As organisations grow procedures are normally established which guide action to ensure consistency across a range of situations and people. It is important to ensure that procedures support and enable action, rather than constraining and disempowering, as can happen when organisations become very large and develop lots of, often inflexible, procedures.

Differentiation requires specialisation of effort to ensure that an individual job or task is undertaken effectively, and integration is coordinating the output of the individual people so that the whole task is completed satisfactorily. Organising individual jobs varies according to the degree of predictability in what has to be done, so that organising manufacturing jobs or a call centre tends to emphasise strict obedience to the rules, clearly defined tasks and much specialisation. Jobs that have constantly fresh problems and unpredictable requirements, like marketing and social work, produce frequent redefinition of job boundaries, a tendency to flexible networks of working relationships rather than a clear hierarchy and a greater degree of individual autonomy. The integrating process will be influenced by the amount of differentiation. The greater the differentiation, the harder the task of coordination.

Centralisation/decentralisation refers to the extent to which certain aspects of authority and decision making are held at the centre of the organisation, as opposed to being devolved down to local level. Historically organisations have tended to favour centralisation, although the past couple of decades have seen greater decentralisation which is thought to make decision making and responding to local needs and customers easier and quicker to achieve. Worren (2012) presents a more detailed discussion of design principles than is possible here.

Using these three elements gives a range of design choices, often classified using systems metaphors (Eriksen 2005). Burns and Stalker (1961), for example, outline the classical distinction between organic and mechanistic designs. Organic systems are frequently described as loosely coupled systems where there is little formalisation, where complex integrating mechanisms are used, and decision making is delegated. In contrast, mechanistic organisations are highly formalised and centralised, and tend to use less complex integration mechanisms (Curado 2006). These design choices are presented in Table 7.1.

Table 7.1 Organisation design choices

Mechanistic design	High formalisation	Extensive use of written procedures High degree of task specialisation Strict performance control
	Low integration	Little use of liaison processes Little use of liaison structures
	High centralisation	Little delegation of decision-making authority
Organic design	Low formalisation	Little use of written procedures Low degree of task specialisation Relaxed performance control
	High integration	Extensive use of liaison processes Extensive use of liaison structures
	Low centralisation	Extensive delegation of decision-making authority

Source: Curado (2006: 38).

ACTIVITY 7.1

Thinking of an organisation with which you are familiar, how would you describe it in terms of the three key elements of organisation design:

1　To what extent are differentiation and integration evident?

2　Are procedures predominantly formal or informal?

3　What is the degree of centralisation versus decentralisation?

Different configurations of these design choices have prevailed at various times across the history of organisation design. The first attempts at organisation design were undertaken by F. W. Taylor and the scientific school of management. This approach was founded on the division of labour into simple jobs and rigid allocations of individuals to narrowly defined tasks. Concerns centred around efficiency, time and motion studies, for example, ensuring tasks were structured in a way that allowed workers to conduct them in the most efficient manner. This led to highly specialised jobs, workers at Ford's factories on assembly lines each carrying out, for example, very narrow specified elements of the construction of a motor car. Scientific management was premised upon the idea of 'man as machine': that is, rational, unemotional and focused upon economic concerns. Incentives, such as bonuses, were designed to meet the extrinsic motivations of employees. Jobs were, however, routine, repetitive and monotonous, leading to boredom and industrial unrest among workers.

Recognition that workers had needs beyond economic ones led, from the 1940s on, to worker motivation being a key concern within organisation design. Maslow (1954), for example, suggested that there was a hierarchy of needs within workers and that design should meet a range of needs, such as social ones, rather than simply focusing on economic concerns. In recent decades, organisation design focused on worker motivation has continued but preoccupation with organisational efficiency is also once again prominent. We see an emerging emphasis on job design, the flexible firm (see later in this chapter) and the role of strategic HRM within overall job design. We do not have space here to provide a comprehensive review of these varying approaches to organisation design and refer the reader to an organisational behaviour text for further information, for example, Huczynski and Buchanan (2013).

Organisation structures

There is no single ideal organisational form. Organisation structures reflect the decisions made by organisations about issues of formalisation, differentiation and centralisation (Table 7.1) and are based around hierarchy:

> The hierarchy is the chain of command, the pyramid of authority that narrows at the top . . . if we eliminate all the paraphernalia of rank and authority in large organisations, we don't really know what we would end up with. There are no clear examples of large human organisations that operate without a formal hierarchy . . . some form of hierarchy is necessary for organising a complex set of people and resources. (Leavitt *et al.* 1973: 31–2)

Hierarchy creates a predictable system of roles and jobs. It enables us to understand how to get things done and how matters will be handled. Hierarchy also distributes power, rations power and ensures that people accept the power of others in the system. Holders of specified roles or jobs are empowered to make certain decisions and to control the behaviour of other people. Traditionally, large organisations have had *tall* hierarchies (i.e. many levels in them) with *narrow* spans of control (each person being responsible for the supervision of only a small number of people). Since the 1980s, however, there has been a trend to much *flatter* hierarchies with much *wider* spans of control. This trend has been termed 'delayering' and is the process of taking out layers of management in the hierarchy in order to speed response times and make the operation more efficient.

WINDOW ON PRACTICE

Delayering in large organisations

From the mid-1980s onwards many organisations that had traditionally had tall hierarchies set about the process of delayering. This was common practice in financial services organisations such as large banks (see e.g. Atkinson 2002) and in some newly privatised companies. The logic behind this restructuring process was to make organisations more flexible and responsive to increasingly dynamic and competitive market conditions by devolving decision-making responsibilities to those closest to the customer. In removing layers of middle management which had come to be seen as blockages to change and responsiveness, organisations sought to improve the efficiency and effectiveness of their operations.

While the theory behind delayering was sound, its implementation was in many instances problematic. As is often the case with change programmes, senior management gave insufficient consideration to the people aspects of delayering. There is a large body of research from this period which identifies the negative impact on the morale and motivation of those remaining in delayered organisations. Those left behind were said to suffer from 'survivor syndrome', characterised by mourning for lost colleagues, fearing for their own future job security and suffering work intensification as they struggled to cope with often increased workloads with fewer staff. In the face of these conditions, the hoped-for efficiency gains were rarely achieved.

ACTIVITY 7.2

What experience have you, or someone you know, had of organisation restructuring? What happened? To what extent was agility improved by the restructuring?

Despite the problems identified in the Window on practice, the search for a responsive organisation structure continues, with a contemporary emphasis on agility (Holbeche, 2015). While a huge variety of organisation structures is possible, most can be categorised into one of three broad types: entrepreneurial, bureaucratic and matrix.

The entrepreneurial form

The entrepreneurial form relies on central power and can be described as primarily organic. It is like a spider's web, with one person or group so dominant that all power stems from the centre, all decisions are made by the centre and all behaviour reflects expectations of the centre. There are few collective decisions, much reliance on individuals, and with actions requiring the approval of key figures. This form is frequently found in businesses where decisions must be made quickly and with flair and judgement rather than careful deliberation. Newspaper editing has an entrepreneurial form of organisation and most of the performing arts have strong centralised direction.

This is the form of most small and growing businesses as they owe their existence to the expertise or initiative of one or two people, and it is only by reflecting accurately this originality that the business can survive. As the business expands, this type of structure can become unwieldy because too many peripheral decisions cannot be made without approval from the centre, which then becomes overloaded. It is also difficult to maintain if the spider leaves the centre of the web, as a successor may not have the same degree of dominance. In some instances the problem of increasing size has been dealt with by maintaining an entrepreneurial structure at the core of the enterprise and giving considerable independence to satellite organisations, provided that overall performance targets are met.

The bureaucratic form

The bureaucratic form emphasises the distribution rather than centralisation of power and responsibility: it has a more extended and complex hierarchy and is primarily mechanistic in structure. It has been the conventional means of enabling an organisation to grow beyond the entrepreneurial form to establish an existence that is not dependent on a single person or group of founders. Because the emphasis is on role, operational processes become more predictable and consistent, with procedure and committee replacing individual judgement and responsibility is devolved. Various choices exist as to how to structure the bureaucracy (CIPD, 2015) which include:

- Functional, for example, establishing sales, operations, finance and HR departments;
- Geographical, for example, having departments grouping operations in the north, south, east and west of a country;
- Product-line based, for example, certain parts of a technology organisation deal with computers, others with printers and so on;
- Customer/market based, for example, dividing the organisation into sections that deal with business customers, domestic customers, etc.

Bureaucracy is a method of organisation well suited to stable situations, making possible economies of scale and the benefits of specialisation. There is seldom the flexibility to deal with a volatile environment which can be problematic and procedures can become an end in themselves, rather than a means to an end. Bureaucracy has long been the standard form of structure for large organisations but has come under criticism because of its inflexibility in times of change and a tendency to frustrate personal initiative. 'Bureaucracy' is definitely a dirty word, so companies work hard at overcoming its drawbacks.

The matrix form

The matrix form combines hierarchical and functional approaches, usually with multiple reporting lines (CIPD 2015). It emphasises the coordination of expertise into project-orientated groups of people, usually specialists seconded from each functional area, with individual responsibility and a project manager exercises the degree of control necessary to make the responsibility effective. Authority can either remain with the functional hierarchy, while the project managers have a mainly coordinating, progress-chasing role as lone specialists, or power can be shifted towards the project managers, who then have their own teams of experts, with the functional areas being seen as a resource rather than the centre of action and decision. The matrix form is appealing because it is theoretically based on expertise and provides scope for people throughout the business to deploy their skills and carry responsibility.

This three-fold classification is a means of analysis rather than a description of three distinct types of organisation with any undertaking being clearly one of the three. Bureaucracies will typically have matrix features at some points and few entrepreneurial structures are quite as 'pure' as implied here. Most large organisations could have one form dominant in one section of the business and another form dominant elsewhere. Large banks, for example, are bureaucratic in their retailing operations as consistency is of paramount importance and any changes need to be put into operation simultaneously by a large number of people as well as being comprehensible to a large number of customers. The same banks will, however, tend towards an entrepreneurial emphasis in their merchant banking activities and in currency dealings.

Agile organisations

As we noted at the beginning of the chapter, agility is a preoccupation of contemporary organisations. Being agile means organisations can deal with and respond to fast-moving external environments dominated by changes in technology, consumer demand, competition and the wider economy (see Chapter 16 for more detailed discussion of organisational change). Agility allows organisations to be effective, make profits and outdo their competitors. Holbeche's (2015) latest book on the subject of agile organisations recommends managing organisations like projects, i.e. a matrix structure, to design in the required flexibility to deal with change.

The drive for agility challenges adoption of the more traditional hierarchical structures we describe above, although in practice many organisations still rely upon these to a greater or lesser extent. The achievement of workforce flexibility is, however, central to

WINDOW ON PRACTICE

How agile principles are used in holacracy

Online retailer Zappo has recently garnered a great deal of publicity from its decision to replace top-down hierarchical structures by self-organising teams. Designed to deliver agility, essential to the fast-moving and competitive online retail market, Zappo has removed job titles and traditional reporting lines in favour of distribution of power and decision making across the organisation. Some have termed this a 'holacracy' and suggested that this is a new form of organisational structure. Zappo's transition has been slower than anticipated, however, suggesting that adopting agile structures can be complex as existing powerholders resist its wider distribution. Despite this, Zappo claims to have improved its agility and ability to compete.

Source: Adapted from Weidner (2015) http://www.investopedia.com/articles/investing /070615/zapposcom-holacracy-will-it-work.asp and Nath 2015; http://www.investopedia .com/articles/professionals/081115/how-agile-principles-are-used-holacracy.asp.

most organisational efforts to increase agililty (CIPD 2015). We continue now to discuss both employer and employee forms of flexibility in the remainder of this chapter.

Workforce flexibility

A crucial aspect of organisation design is the extent to which it delivers agility. Workforce flexibility is central to this and has increased significantly since the mid-1980s. Initially this reflected employer need and resulted in many employees experiencing substantial change in their traditional working patterns. Terminology has changed rapidly and is inconsistent but practices for employer benefit are typically referred to as non-standard working arrangements (NSWAs, Stavrou *et al*. 2015) or flexible working arrangements (FWAs, Atkinson and Sandiford 2016). More recently there has been increased emphasis on forms of flexibility for employee benefit which were originally termed 'work–life balance' or 'family friendly' arrangements. Terminology has again developed over time and these are more typically also referred to as flexible working arrangements. This can cause confusion over whether flexibility is employer or employee-focused. Indeed, it is often argued that employer and employee needs are complementary and that the practices adopted have benefits for both parties. There are tensions, however, and practices presented as beneficial to employees are, in fact, often detrimental to them. For example, despite meeting the flexibility needs of some employees, part-time work is often insecure and low paid. Nevertheless, there can be a coincidence of needs when an employee has access to a contract of choice. We present first flexible working arrangements that are typically considered to be employer led, adopting Atkinson's (1984) model of the flexible firm. While this model is much criticised, it remains one of the most comprehensive treatments of organisational flexibility. We then present flexible working arrangements that are typically delivered for employee benefit.

ACTIVITY 7.3

Thinking of an organisation with which you are familiar, complete the agility test at http://www.agilefutureforum.co.uk/. To what extent does the organisation understand flexible working arrangements that support employees and agile working practices to support employer competitiveness?

Employer flexibility

Atkinson's (1984) model of the 'flexible firm' (Figure 7.1) is frequently adopted to describe how firms develop flexibility through numerical, temporal and functional means.

Numerical flexibility

Numerical flexibility allows the organisation to respond quickly to the environment in terms of the numbers of people employed. Some traditional full-time, permanent posts are replaced by short-term contract staff, staff with rolling contracts, outworkers and so on. This enables the organisation to reduce or expand the workforce quickly and cheaply.

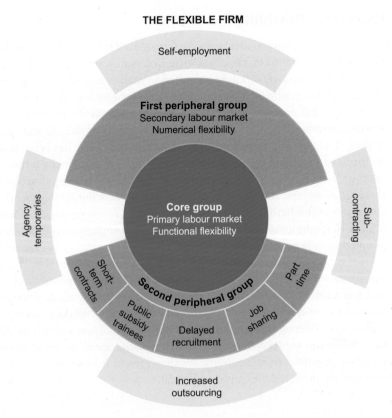

Figure 7.1
Atkinson's model of the flexible firm
Source: J. Atkinson (1984) 'Manpower strategies for flexible organisations', *Personnel Management*, August. Used with the permission of the author.

The flexible firm in this analysis has various ways of meeting its need for human resources. First, there are core employees, who form the primary labour market. They are highly regarded by the employer, well paid and involved in those activities that are unique to the firm or give it a distinctive character. These employees have improved career prospects and offer the type of flexibility to the employer that is so prized in the skilled professional with wide experience and adaptability.

There are then two peripheral groups: first, those who have skills that are needed but not specific to the particular firm, like typing and word processing. The strategy for these posts is to rely on the external labour market to a much greater extent, to specify a narrow range of tasks without career prospects, so that the employee has a job but not a career. Some employees may be able to transfer to core posts, but this is generally limited scope and likely to maintain a fairly high turnover, so that adjustments to the vagaries of the product market are eased.

The second peripheral group is made up of those enjoying even less security, as they have contracts of employment that are limited, either to a short-term or a part-time attachment. There may also be a few job sharers, although job sharing is not widely practised. An alternative or additional means towards this flexibility is to subcontract the work that has to be done, either by employing temporary personnel from agencies or by outsourcing the entire operation, adjusting the organisation boundary, redefining what is to be done in-house and what is to be subcontracted to various suppliers.

Temporal flexibility

Temporal flexibility concerns varying the pattern of hours worked in order to respond to business demands and employee needs. Moves away from the 9–5, five-day week include the use of annual hours contracts, increased use of part-time work, job sharing and flexible working hours. For example, an organisation subject to peaks and troughs of demand, such as an ice-cream manufacturer, could use annual hours contracts so that more employee hours are available at peak periods and fewer are used when business is slow. Flexible hours systems can benefit the employer by providing employee cover outside the 9–5 day and over lunchtimes, and can also provide employee benefits by allowing personal demands to be fitted more easily around work demands.

Research evidence suggests increasing use of temporal flexibility. Longer opening hours in retailing and the growth of the leisure sector mean that many more people now work in the evening and at night than used to be the case. The proportion of jobs that are part time also continues to rise, albeit at a slower rate than in the 1970s and 1980s, while the length of the working week for higher-paid full-time workers has increased substantially. There has also been some growth in the use of annual hours, but these arrangements have not become as widespread as was initially predicted and less than 10% of employers have chosen to adopt this approach (van Wanrooy et al. 2013).

Functional flexibility

The term 'functional flexibility' refers to a process in which employees gain the capacity to undertake a variety of tasks rather than specialising in just one area. Advocates of such approaches have been influenced by studies of Japanese employment practices as well as by criticisms of monotonous assembly-line work. Horizontal flexibility involves each individual employee becoming multiskilled so that he or she can be deployed as and where required at any time. Vertical flexibility entails gaining the capacity to undertake work previously carried out by colleagues higher up or lower down the organisational hierarchy.

The primary purpose of functional flexibility initiatives is to deploy human resources more efficiently. It should mean that employees are kept busy throughout their working day and that absence is more easily covered than in a workplace with rigidly defined demarcation between jobs. A further efficiency gain comes from employees being more stretched, fulfilled and thus productive than in a workplace with narrowly defined jobs. Despite its potential advantages, employers in the UK have been less successful than competitors elsewhere in Europe at developing functional flexibility, perhaps because of a reluctance to invest in the training necessary to support these new forms of working. Reilly (2001) also points to employee resistance and the increased likelihood of errors occurring when functional flexibility programmes are introduced. It could also simply be a reflection of increased specialisation as jobs become more technically complex, relying to a greater extent on specific expert knowledge.

Network organisations

As we noted above, Atkinson's model of the flexible firm is much criticised but has no clear successor. The network organisation (Powell 1990) has received increasing interest in the debate on organisational flexibility in recent years. Network organisations describe long-term contractual arrangements between supplier and client organisations which involve a co-production process, for example the outsourcing of cleaning or IT operations to an external supplier. In this way, an organisation can gain numerical and functional flexibility by establishing relationships with other organisations, rather than through its own labour management strategies, as advocated in Atkinson's model of the flexible firm. Functional flexibility is achieved through agreements with specialist suppliers or producers, while numerical flexibility is delivered through outsourcing and the use of temporary agency labour. These inter-organisational relationships are often referred to as strategic alliances, joint ventures, partnerships or subcontracting. They are ongoing relationships which can lead to the blurring of organisational boundaries such that it can be difficult for the worker to know who he or she is working for. CIPD's (2012b) report provides an interesting case study of Marks and Spencer's network arrangements, together with a detailed analysis of its advantages and drawbacks.

Debates about flexibility

The growth in flexible working arrangements combined with their promotion by governments since the 1990s has led to the development of robust debates about their desirability and usage in practice. There has been a continuing debate, for example, about whether Atkinson's model of core and periphery is a description of trends or a prescription for the future. Two streams of research have flowed from these interpretations. The first concerns the extent to which the model has been adopted in practice, the second focuses on the advantages and disadvantages of flexibility as a blueprint for the future organisation of work.

Evidence on the first of these questions is patchy. There is no question that rhetoric about flexibility and the language of flexibility is increasingly used. The flexible firm model appears to be something that managers aspire to, but the extent to which they have actually adopted it is questionable. Recent WERS data (van Wanrooy *et al.* 2013), for example, indicated an increased use of some non-standard working arrangements, but that many were still relatively unusual. Further, there was little increase in the UK between 2004 and 2011 in flexible working arrangements such as fixed-term and temporary contracts and the use of agency workers reduced in this period in response to recessionary financial constraints. Indeed, in many organisations the drive for economies of scale means that far from becoming more flexible, organisations are just as likely to introduce bureaucratic systems and standardised practices in response to competitive pressures. And yet we also have seen for a long period now increased use of part-time workers, consultants and sub-contractors. Legge's (1995) conclusion that flexibility is used in a pragmatic and opportunistic way rather than as a strategic HRM initiative thus seems to still hold true.

Turning to the second question, the desirability of flexibility is debatable. The theoretical advantage for organisations is that flexibility enables them to deploy employee time and effort more efficiently so that staff are only at work when they need to be and are focused on achieving organisational objectives throughout that time. However, the extent to which this is achieved in practice is not clear. Many writers equate the term 'flexibility' with 'insecurity' and argue that the consequences for organisations in terms of staff commitment and willingness to work beyond contract are damaging, staff turnover is likely to increase and recruiting talented people will be harder too. Ji *et al.* (2014) have recently found that in many cases of employment instability it is associated with reduced performance. It is questionable whether the flexible firm model, at least as far as the 'peripheral' workforce is concerned, is compatible with best practice approaches to HRM that seek to increase employee commitment. This is equally the case for the network organisation where terms and conditions for those providing numerical flexibility are still typically inferior to those providing functional flexibility. Another view, however, is that soft HRM adopting high-commitment HRM practices can adopt functional flexibility through practices such as flexible job design, cross-training, use of teams and work groups, and job rotation and enlargement. These all require strong employment relationships based on trust to deliver the required flexibility (Ji *et al.* 2014).

WINDOW ON PRACTICE

Flexible working is not 'inferior'

Churchard challenges the view that flexible jobs are insecure and undesirable, creating a lack of commitment on the part of both the employer and worker. She reports her survey of over 11,000 workers and claims that flexibility does not negatively impact on job satisfaction, particularly for fixed-term contracts (one of the most common types of flexible contract). While there is some evidence that male workers dislike temporary agency work and that there is lower satisfaction with job security, overall she argues that flexible jobs are not inferior to full-time, permanent roles.

This could be an important message for HR practitioners, who may struggle to fill flexible jobs if the negative messages around them persist. Indeed, highly qualified workers may prefer the variety and (frequently) higher pay that accompany flexible jobs.

Source: Adapted from Churchard (2012).

Nevertheless, flexibility is often viewed as creating precarious work (Standing 2011): that is, it is insecure and (usually) low paid and low skilled. A number of authors (Appelbaum 2012; Kalleberg 2012) have argued that precarious work has become a central feature of work in the USA and more widely. In Europe, a social partnership model of employment relations has led to a desire to address the problems associated with precarious work through 'flexicurity' which:

> provides employers with the flexibility to adjust employment to meet the requirements of changing market conditions or technology and provides workers with the income security, training opportunities, and job search support to successfully weather the lack of job security without a deterioration in earnings. (Appelbaum 2012: 315)

Flexicurity thus denotes an attempt to address the tensions between labour market flexibility for employers and secure work for employees. It comprises three main elements: workers are provided with economic security to address the consequences of precarious work; the right to collective representation and bargaining power is guaranteed; and (re)training to equip workers to thrive in the labour market is offered. In return, employers have the right to implement flexible working arrangements that enhance business efficiency. While flexicurity is attractive, high levels of unemployment can reduce its efficacy. Flexicurity policies have made it easy to dismiss workers but slack labour markets have rendered problematic transitions to alternative employment. There is a way to go yet to reconcile employer demands for flexibility with an acceptable deal for workers.

ACTIVITY 7.4

1 Do you agree with the view that flexible work is not inferior?

2 How effective do you think flexicurity is likely to be in reconciling employer and worker demands?

Employee flexibility

Now we consider employee flexibility and the mechanisms by which this might be achieved. Since 2014, UK legislation has offered most employees the right to request flexible working, though an employer may refuse the request in certain circumstances. A number of high-profile organisations have sought to position themselves as 'employers of choice' by offering flexible working arrangements beyond legislative requirements. Despite this, while provision of flexible working options grew in the UK for a number of years, this has now levelled off and the latest WERS survey (van Wanrooy *et al.* 2013) indicates no increase in provision between 2004 and 2011. While this may be because most organisations offer some form of flexible working (CIPD 2012a), an increasing number of managers in the WERS survey (76%) indicated that it is an individual's responsibility to manage domestic and work responsibilities. Further, the availability of practices says little about their uptake and we outline below the 'rhetoric versus reality' of flexible working for employee benefit in UK organisations.

There are three different types of flexibility: first, there is flexibility in terms of the number of hours worked; second, the exact timing of those hours; and, third, the location at which the work is carried out (see Atkinson and Sandiford 2016 for a detailed discussion of these). Some options may reflect all three types of flexibility. Not all are appropriate for all jobs or employees, and employers will need to be convinced of their business benefits. Flexitime and reduced hours are the most commonly used options (van Wanrooy *et al*. 2013) and usage of other flexibility options outlined in Table 7.2 is low (CIPD 2012a). Options which require reduction in hours, rather than rearrangement of hours, are generally taken up by women (Atkinson and Hall 2009) and it is important that these flexible working arrangements provide both adequate income and job security (Strachan and Burgess 1998). In addition, flexibility will mean different things to different people, depending on their age, life circumstances, values, interests, personality and so on. Our own research, for example, highlights the need for flexible working arrangements for older workers to sustain and extend their working lives (Atkinson and Sandiford 2016) and other research demonstrates their importance in supporting disabled workers (Baumgartner *et al*. 2015).

Table 7.2 Flexible working options

Part time	Term-time working	Unpaid leave
Flexitime	Job share	Unpaid sabbaticals
Compressed week	Self-rostering	Work from home
Annual hours	Shift swapping	Informal flexibility

Benefits of flexible working

As we note above, employees in the UK have only the legislative *right to request* flexible working. The government has further encouraged its offer via a 'business case' approach that suggests the organisational benefits that flow from adopting flexibility are greater than its associated costs. We consider in this section the benefits that are said to accrue from WLB practices flexibility that underpin this 'business case'.

Flexible working arrangements have been shown in some instances to raise morale and increase levels of job satisfaction (Atkinson and Hall 2011). CIPD (2012a) also suggests a positive impact on motivation and well-being and Whyman *et al*. (2015) found they were related to substantial reductions in absenteeism. Indeed, Beauregard and Henry (2009) and Avgar *et al*. (2011) link flexible working arrangements more generally to higher organisational performance. In our own research, we found that informal flexibility was highly valued and associated with employee discretionary effort in terms of supporting colleagues and being available and flexible to cover emergencies (Hall and Atkinson 2006).

Take-up of flexibility

Initially the demand for flexibility was much greater than its take-up, the 'take-up gap', although this has been narrowing in recent years. Nevertheless, the desire to work different or more flexible hours has been identified as a significant determinant of

WINDOW ON PRACTICE

Benefits and barriers to flexible working

Crush reports a 2015 survey that indicates most firms, particularly small and medium-sized enterprises (SMEs), believed that adopting flexible working had led to improved productivity. This was underpinned by improvements in technology which allowed employees to work remotely. Over half of firms also felt that offering flexible working had improved their reputation in the labour market.

Other research, however, shows that almost one fifth of organisations have not yet implemented a flexible working policy and concerns remained both that those working remotely would work less hard and that those employees not working flexibly would take the strain for those who did. Indeed, flexible working remains a thorny issue between colleagues with workers expressing concern over its detrimental impact on office culture and team spirit.

Source: Adapted from Crush, P. (2016).

employees moving jobs either within or between employers to achieve the flexibility they desire (Boheim and Taylor 2004). There are a number of reasons for this, which we discuss below.

Flexible working arrangements can be expensive, which limits the extent to which organisations offer it. Further, operational difficulties can prevent its uptake e.g. providing adequate cover, and this is the most common barrier (van Wanrooy *et al.* 2013). There is also evidence that some employers do not take a strategic approach to flexibility. While organisations can sometimes easily provide reduced hours of work for, say, administrative and sales staff, it is much more difficult to do this with professional staff. Anecdotal evidence suggests that many professionals moving from full- to part-time work find that they are really expected to do a full-time job in part-time hours and with part-time pay. There is also evidence that flexibility requests for childcare reasons are dealt with more favourably than other requests. The association that flexible working arrangements have with women bringing up children creates two problems. The first is that flexibility becomes a 'women's issue' (Atkinson and Hall 2009), as something done for women with children who are not interested in real careers. The second is that this causes alienation from the rest of the workforce who are not allowed these special privileges (van Wanrooy *et al.* 2013). In particular, working part time has been a popular option in combining work and other commitments, and yet there is considerable evidence that this limits career development (Smithson and Stokoe 2005). Miller (2013) presents an interesting example of a course that fathers can attend to learn how to work flexibly and still develop their careers in a sign that things are beginning, albeit very slowly, to change.

Managers also create a barrier to implementing flexible working arrangements (CIPD 2012a). While it is clear to those at a senior level in an organisation that flexibility can be of value, it is line managers who have the unenviable task of reconciling performance and flexibility, especially where flexible working for some may mean higher workloads for others. There is a pressure on line managers to be fair and their decisions about who

ACTIVITY 7.5

Discuss the following statement. To what extent do you agree or disagree with it, and why?

Employees should be equally entitled to flexibility options, as long as business needs are met. It doesn't matter whether the reason is childcare, the desire to engage in sports activities, do extra gardening, or just loll around on the sofa watching television.

can work flexibly and in what way are under scrutiny and may result in a backlash. Managing workers who are not visible (working at home, for example) is a particular concern for line managers. Felstead *et al.* (2003) report the fear that working at home is a 'slacker's charter', but they also found that home-workers themselves had fears about not being able easily to demonstrate their honesty, reliability and productivity. Some managed this by working more hours than they should in order to demonstrate greater output. Managers also felt that home-working represented a potential threat to the integration of teams and the acceptance of corporate culture, and that it impeded the transmission of tacit knowledge. Overall, managing flexible working arrangements is challenging and line managers are likely to need support and encouragement in order to do this effectively.

Employee role and flexibility

Many flexible options are not available to most employees. Swanberg *et al.* (2014) found that most low paid, full-time jobs have rigid working patterns and Felstead *et al.* (2002) argue that the option to work at home is usually the privilege of the highly educated and/or people at the top of the organisational hierarchy. People in these jobs, they suggest, have considerably more influence over the work processes they are engaged in. They also report that although more women than men work at home, there are more men who have the choice to work at home. Felstead *et al.* (2002) highlight an assumption in the flexibility literature, which portrays working at home as always a 'good thing'. They argue that what is important is the *option* to work at home, as some people work at home doing low-paid unsatisfying jobs with no choice of work location, such conditions not necessarily being conducive to flexibility.

Rhetoric or reality?

Although a number of blue-chip organisations actively publicise their flexible working arrangements, problems of implementation, line manager resistance and the restriction of such practices to certain groups mean that flexibility is still an aspiration rather than a reality for many employees. White *et al.* (2003), for example, argue that flexible working arrangements are enjoyed by only a small proportion of the workforce, and in any case only have a small effect. We suggest that work continues to be organised in a way that predominantly meets the needs of employers, the 'business case' for flexibility often failing to initiate sufficient action to offer genuine flexibility to the majority of employees.

SUMMARY PROPOSITIONS

7.1. Organisation design requires that choices are made in terms of formality, differentiation and centralisation of operations. Agility and flexibility are increasingly important to organisation design.

7.2. While an infinite range of organisation structures is possible, most can be described as entrepreneurial, bureaucratic or matrix in form. In practice, many organisations combine all three types of structure to varying degrees, although matrix is recommended as the most agile.

7.3. Organisations increasingly require employees to be flexible in their working patterns. Models such as Atkinson's flexible firm and Powell's network organisation attempt to describe/prescribe mechanisms of employer flexibility.

7.4. Tight labour markets in recent decades have required organisations to respond to employee demands for flexibility. A large number of flexible working arrangements now exist, although in reality many employees may not benefit from them.

GENERAL DISCUSSION TOPICS

1. Flatter organisation structures which decentralise decision making and empower employees will almost always be more efficient than highly centralised organisations with tall hierarchies. Discuss.

2. Flexibility in working time is nearly always for organisational benefit. In practice, few employees actually benefit from working time flexibility. Discuss.

THEORY INTO PRACTICE

Flex Co. is a large retail organisation that prides itself on its progressive approach to HRM. As a retailer, it recognises that its success depends on delivery of a 'fantastic' customer experience and invests heavily in the training and development of its store staff. Alongside this, it has a range of other progressive HR policies, including Work–Life Balance (WLB) options. The WLB policy allows for part-time working, term-time-only working, a compressed working week and shift swapping. For store employees, flexitime and working from home are not permissible, although these are offered to employees in head office and regional offices. A trial of self-rostering, where store workers pick their own shifts (within specified parameters), is also taking place within a small number of stores.

Flex Co. operates a decentralised structure in which each store is a profit centre and each store manager is responsible for the delivery of a certain level of sales and profits and for

➤ managing staff and other costs within the store. In common with many retail organisations, Flex Co. store managers use a range of employee contracts to ensure that high levels of staff are available at peak times, for example lunchtimes and weekends, but that a skeleton staff operate at quiet trading times. This means that, other than at store manager and assistant manager level, most contracts are part time and there is a high use of zero hours contracts. Managers argue that this is unproblematic as most employees are either women with childcare responsibilities or students. They are somewhat resistant to WLB policies that afford greater employee flexibility as this conflicts with their capacity to devise staff rosters that meet store requirements.

Flex Co. has just conducted a staff attitude survey and is disappointed with the results in relation to its WLB policy. Most store staff have indicated that the options within the policy are not readily available to them. Many wish to work term-time only for example but, as school holidays are typically busy trading periods, managers have been reluctant to agree these contracts. Those taking part in the self-rostering trial have also reported high levels of management interference in the determination of rosters and a sense that little autonomy has been gained. Finally, there is a sense of 'us and them' in respect of home-working and flexitime between those based in head and regional offices and those based in stores.

Questions

1 Flex Co. devises policies centrally at head office but devolves the responsibility for their implementation to store managers, whose priorities may conflict with the policy imperatives. To what extent will it ever be possible to ensure robust policy implementation in this organisation structure?

2 What tensions can you identify between flexibility that meets employer need and that which meets employee need? To what extent is it likely to be possible to reconcile these tensions? Which will take precedence?

3 What are the difficulties inherent in offering different flexibility options to different groups of employees? Is it better to have a 'one size fits all' approach?

FURTHER READING

Worren, N. (2012) *Organisation Design*. Harlow: Pearson Education.

Worren presents a detailed and insightful discussion into both traditional mechanisms of organisation design and more contemporary approaches to designing flexible and adaptive organisations.

Holbeche, L. (2015) *The Agile Organisation: How to Build an Innovative, Sustainable and Resilient Business,* London: Kogan Page.

The forces that drive the need for organisational agility, that is, technology, complexity and change, are discussed in detail. Effective mechanisms through which to respond to these are also considered, culminating in the recommendation that matrix approaches and the principles of project-based work are required to deliver agile working, even where the work is not project-based.

Atkinson, C. and Sandiford, P. (2016) 'An exploration of older worker flexible working arrangements in smaller firms', *Human Resource Management Journal*, Vol. 26, No. 1, pp. 12–28.

Here we explore flexible working arrangements (FWAs) for older workers to consider how far older workers need and value FWAs, the type of FWAs they need, and whether smaller firms can offer these FWAs. The adoption of FWA for this group of workers is demonstrated to be important in extending working lives.

REFERENCES

Appelbaum, E. (2012) 'Reducing inequality and insecurity', *Work and Occupations*, Vol. 39, pp. 311–20.

Atkinson, C. (2002) 'Career management and the changing psychological contract', *Career Development International*, Vol. 7, pp. 14–23.

Atkinson, C. and Hall, L. (2009) 'The role of gender in varying forms of flexible working', *Gender, Work and Organisation*, Vol. 16, pp. 650–66.

Atkinson, C. and Hall, L. (2011) 'Flexible working and happiness in the NHS', *Employee Relations*, Vol. 33, pp. 88–105.

Atkinson, C. and Sandiford, P. (2016). 'An exploration of older worker flexible working arrangements in smaller firms', *Human Resource Management Journal*, Vol. 26, pp. 12–28.

Atkinson, J. (1984) 'Manpower strategies for flexible organisations', *Personnel Management*, August, p. 19.

Avgar, A., Givan, R. and Lui, M. (2011) 'A balancing act: Work–life balance and multiple stakeholder outcomes in hospitals', *British Journal of Industrial Relations*, Vol. 49, pp. 717–41.

Baumgartner, M., Dwertmann, D., Boehm, S. and Bruch, H. (2015) 'Job satisfaction of employees with disabilities: The role of perceived structural flexibility', *Human Resource Management*, Vol. 54, pp. 323–43.

Beauregard, A. and Henry, L. (2009) 'Making the link between work–life balance practices and organisational performance', *Human Resource Management Review*, Vol. 19, pp. 9–22.

Boheim, R. and Taylor, M. (2004) 'Actual and preferred working hours', *British Journal of Industrial Relations*, Vol. 42, pp. 149–66.

Burns, T. and Stalker, G. 1961. *The Management of Innovation*. London: Tavistock.

Burton, R. and Obel, B. (2004) *Strategic Organisational Diagnosis and Design: The dynamics of fit*. Dordrecht: Kluwer Academic.

Churchard, C. (2012) 'Pay and flexible work deal saves thousands of jobs at Vauxhall', *People Management*, www.peoplemanagement.co.uk/pm/articles/2012÷05/pay-and-flexible-work-deal-saves-thousands-of-jobs-at-vauxhall.htm (accessed 29 May 2013).

CIPD (2012a) *Flexible Working: Provision and Uptake*. London: CIPD.

CIPD (2012b) *HR and its Role in Innovation*. London: CIPD.

CIPD (2015) *Organisation Design: Factsheet*, http://www.cipd.co.uk/hr-resources/factsheets/organisation-design.aspx (accessed 16 February 2016).

CIPD (2016) *CIPD Professional Map* [online]. London: CIPD (accessed 16 February 2016).

Crush, P. (2016) 'Flexible working boosts profits and productivity, say majority of employers' [online], http://www.cipd.co.uk/pm/peoplemanagement/b/weblog/archive/2016÷02÷09/flexible-working-boosts-profits-and-productivity-say-majority-of-employers.aspx?utm_medium=email&utm_source=cipd&utm_campaign=pm_daily&utm_term=678405&utm_content=pm_daily_090216-4871–5422--20160216135657-Flexible%20working%20boosts%20profits%20and%20productivity%2C%20say%20majority%20of%20employers.

Curado, C. (2006) 'Organisational learning and organisational design', *The Learning Organisation*, Vol. 13, pp. 25–48.

Eriksen, J. (2005) 'The influences of organisational design on strategy and performance: The case of exploration and exploitation', Workshop on Organisational Design EIASM, Brussels.

Felstead, A., Jewson, N., Phizacklea, A. and Walters, S. (2002) 'The option of working at home: Another privilege for the favoured few', *New Technology, Work and Employment*, Vol. 17, pp. 204–23.

Felstead, A., Jewson, N. and Walters, S. (2003) 'Managerial control of employees working at home', *British Journal of Industrial Relations*, Vol. 41, pp. 241–64.

Hall, L. and Atkinson, C. (2006) 'Improving working lives: Flexible working and the role of employee control', *Employee Relations*, Vol. 28, pp. 374–86.

Holbeche, L. (2015) *The Agile Organisation: How to Build an Innovative, Sustainable and Resilient Business*. London; Kogan Page.

Huczynski, A. and Buchanan, D. (2013) *Organisational Behaviour*. Harlow: Pearson Education.

Ji, Y.-Y., Guthrie, J. and Messersmith, J. (2014) 'The tortoise and the hare: The impact of employment instability on firm performance', *Human Resource Management Journal*, Vol. 24, 355–73.

Kalleberg, A. (2012) 'Job quality and precarious work', *Work and Occupations*, Vol. 39, No. 4, pp. 427–48.

Leavitt, H., Dill, W. and Eyrig, H. (1973) *The Organisational World*. New York: Harcourt Brace Jovanovich.

Legge, K. (1995) *Human Resource Management: Rhetoric and Realities*. Basingstoke: Macmillan.

Maslow, A. (1954) *Motivation and Personality*. New York: Harper & Row.

Miller, J. (2013) 'Can you teach dads how to work flexibly?', *People Management*, www.peoplemanagement.co.uk/pm/articles/2013/01/can-you-teach-dads-how-to-work-flexibly.htm.

Nath, (2015) http://www.investopedia.com/articles/professionals/081115/how-agile-principles-are-used-holacracy.asp.

Powell, W. (1990) 'Neither market nor hierarchy: Network forms of organisation', *Research in Organisational Behaviour*, Vol. 12, pp. 295–336.

Reilly, P. (2001) *Flexibility at Work*. Aldershot: Gower.

Smithson, J. and Stokoe, E. (2005) 'Discourses of work–life balance: Negotiating 'genderblind' terms in organisations', *Gender, Work and Organisation*, Vol. 12, pp. 147–68.

Standing, G. (2011) *The Precariat*. New York: Bloomsbury.

Stavrou, E., Parry, E. and Anderson, D. (2015) 'Nonstandard work arrangements and configurations of firm and societal systems', *International Journal of Human Resource Management*, Vol. 26, pp. 2412–33.

Strachan, G. and Burgess, J. (1998) 'The "family-friendly" workplace', *International Journal of Manpower*, Vol. 19, pp. 250–65.

Swanberg, J., Watson, E. and Eastman, M. (2014) 'Scheduling challenges among workers in low-wage hourly jobs: Similarities and differences among workers in standard- and nonstandard-hour jobs', *Community, Work and Family*, Vol. 17, pp. 409–35.

Van Wanrooy, B., Bewley, H., Bryson, A., Forth, J., Freeth, S., Stokes, L. and Wood, S. (2013) *The 2011 Workplace Employment Relations Study: First Findings*. London: BIS.

Weidner, (2015) http://www.investopedia.com/articles/investing/070615/zapposcom-holacracy-will-it-work.asp.

White, M., Hill, S., McGovern, P., Mills, C. and Smeaton, D. (2003) '"High performance" management practices, working hours and work–life balance', *British Journal of Industrial Relations*, Vol. 41, No. 2, June, pp. 175–95.

Whyman, P., Baimbridge, M., Buraimo, B. and Petrescu, A. (2015) 'Workplace flexibility practices and corporate performance: Evidence from the British private sector', *British Journal of Management*, Vol. 26, pp. 347–64.

Worren, N. (2012) *Organisation Design*. Harlow: Pearson Education.

CHAPTER 8
RECRUITMENT

THE OBJECTIVES OF THIS CHAPTER ARE TO:

1 Discuss how job and competency analysis support the determination of a vacancy's requirements

2 Explain the role played by job descriptions and person specifications in the recruitment process

3 Analyse rational and processual approaches to recruitment and discuss the role of employer branding

4 Compare and contrast the major alternative recruitment methods

While the terms 'recruitment' and 'selection' are often used interchangeably, they are in fact quite distinct activities. In this chapter, we consider recruitment which 'includes those practices and activities carried out by the organisation with the primary purpose of identifying and attracting potential employees' (Breaugh and Starke 2000: 45). Selection refers to the methods used to decide which applicant to appoint to a vacancy and we discuss this later (see Chapter 9). Formal, structured recruitment methods are part of a best practice set of HR practices that is argued to be strategic and improve organisational performance. They build upon job or competency analysis which determines the requirements of the vacant role and employ person specifications and job descriptions to identify suitable candidates. Historically this 'rational' approach has dominated discussions of recruitment but there is increasing recognition of the benefits of a more processual approach to recruitment, one which recognises the applicant's role, and interest in the concept of employer branding has grown accordingly. We discuss all these aspects of recruitment in this chapter, together with recruitment advertising, which is central to communicating the employer brand, and e-recruitment, which has seen substantial growth over a number of years. Finally we consider the evaluation of recruitment activity. In the Theory into practice section, we consider how many of these issues are increasingly applied in an international context.

WINDOW ON PRACTICE

Over 3 million people are recruited by employers in the UK each year. It can be a costly and difficult process, with estimates of average recruitment costs of £7,250 for senior managers and £2,000 for other staff (CIPD 2015c). As the UK emerges from a lengthy period of economic austerity, the CIPD (2015c) reports that over three-quarters of organisations in its survey have experienced recruitment difficulties. These were particularly severe for managerial, professional and technical staff.

In such circumstances the employer needs to 'sell' its jobs to potential employees so as to ensure that it can generate an adequate pool of applicants, but even then for some groups of staff it can be difficult to find people who are both willing and able to fill the vacancies that are available. That said, it is also important to avoid overselling a job in a bid to secure the services of talented applicants. Making out that the experience of working in a role is more interesting or exciting than it really is may be ultimately counter-productive because it raises unrealistic expectations which can damage the psychological contract established with the organisation. This can lead to demotivation and, perhaps, an early resignation. CIPD (2015c) reports that common approaches to tackling recruitment problems include sponsoring professional qualifications, developing existing employees and recruiting from different sectors or industries.

Determining requirements

There are four questions to answer in determining the requirements of a vacancy:

1 What does the job consist of?

2 In what way is it to be different from the job done by the previous incumbent?

3 What are the aspects of the job that specify the type of candidate?

4 What are the key aspects of the job that the ideal candidate wants to know before deciding to apply?

Job analysis is used to answer these questions. Job analysis comprises a series of techniques for collecting and analysing information about jobs. These include, among others, questionnaires, observations, interviews and critical incident techniques (Siddique 2004).

WINDOW ON PRACTICE

Searle (2004) outlines ten possible job analysis techniques:

1 Questionnaires and checklists: a structured questionnaire gathers information on a series of tasks.

2 Observation: information on tasks can be gathered by watching job holders undertake them.

3 Self-report by diaries and logs: role holders collect and log information about the tasks they undertake.

4 Participation: the analyst carries out the tasks him- or herself.

5 Hierarchical task analysis: a job is deconstructed into a series of tasks, sub-tasks and plans.

6 Interviews: job holders are questioned about the tasks they undertake.

7 Critical incident technique: job holders are asked to specify the most important tasks they undertake.

8 Repertory grid technique: an interview is used to elicit information on key aspects of the role using a grid construction technique.

9 Position analysis questionnaire: a verbal checklist of tasks is used to structure an interview.

10 Work-profiling system: an expert IT system is used to conduct structured job analysis.

The emphasis is on the work performed, not the person performing it. Job analysis is central to many HR activities and it is beyond the scope of this chapter to consider it beyond its influence on recruitment. Searle (2003) and Prien *et al.* (2009) provide a comprehensive coverage of job analysis techniques for those who require more detail.

In relation to recruitment, job analysis has traditionally sought to identify the key tasks and responsibilities which constitute a particular role and the knowledge, skills and abilities required to conduct those tasks and responsibilities. In more recent years, however, there has been a growth of interest in using job analysis to identify the competencies required to

Table 8.1 Traditional job analysis compared with competency-based approaches

Dimension	Traditional job analysis	Competency modelling
Purpose	Describe behaviour	Influence behaviour
View of the job	An external object to be described	A role to be enacted
Focus	Job	Organisation
Time orientation	Past	Future
Performance level	Typical	Maximum
Measurement approach	Latent trait	Clinical judgement

Source: After Sanchez and Levine (2009: 54).

undertake a particular role. We discuss competencies in detail later (see Chapter 18). In brief they describe the behaviours required to undertake the role successfully, for example the ability to communicate well or work effectively as a member of a team.

Sanchez and Levine (2009) undertake an interesting comparison of traditional job analysis and competency-based approaches. They argue that these differ against six key dimensions (see Table 8.1).

Their review of existing research finds that competency-based approaches seek to influence employee behaviour in the role undertaken, rather than simply describe it, and have a future orientation that encourages the maximisation of organisational performance. This contrasts with job analysis, which is backwards looking and reflects typical, rather than maximum, levels of performance. Siddique (2004) presents an interesting study of competency-based analysis in the United Arab Emirates which supports the argument that it serves to improve organisational performance. In practice, the distinction between traditional job analysis and competency-based analysis is often blurred. Indeed Sanchez and Levine (2009) argue for the merging of the two approaches for maximum benefit, drawing on traditional job analysis to describe and measure tasks and responsibilities and competency-based approaches to strategically influence employee behaviour.

Whichever type of analysis is adopted, it forms the basis of the next stage in the recruitment process, the drawing up of job descriptions and person specifications (CIPD 2015b). Job descriptions involve recording the component parts and principal accountabilities of a role. An example is provided in Figure 8.1. Methods of doing this are well established and good accounts are provided by Martin (2010), Brannick and Levine (2002) and IRS (2003).

A person specification listing the key attributes and/or competencies required of the person to undertake the role is then derived from the job description and used in recruiting the new person. You can see an example person specification at http://www.graduatejobsouth.co.uk/employers/sample-person-specification.aspx.

As you can see, this combines attributes derived from job analysis, such as qualifications, knowledge, skills and experience, with competencies such as time management and planning and organisation. Some attributes will be essential and others desirable. CIPD (2015b) recommends careful thought when specifying these. Too many essential criteria can both overly restrict applicant numbers and skew the applicant pool. For example, evidence shows that women apply for role when they have 100% of the essential criteria whereas men apply when they have 60%. While use of competencies is common, it has

Job title: SENIOR SALES ASSISTANT

Context
The job is in one of the 13 high-technology shops owned by 'Computext'
Location: Leeds
Supervised by, and reports directly to, the Shop Manager
Responsible for one direct subordinate: Sales Assistant

Job summary
To assist and advise customers in the selection of computer hardware and software, and to arrange delivery and finance where appropriate.
Objective is to sell as much as possible, and to ensure that customers and potential customers see 'Computext' staff as helpful and efficient.

Job content
Most frequent duties in order of importance
1 Advise customers about hardware and software.
2 Demonstrate the equipment and software.
3 Organise delivery of equipment by liaising with distribution department.
4 Answer all after-sales queries from customers.
5 Contact customers two weeks after delivery to see if they need help.
6 Advise customers about the variety of payment methods.
7 Develop and keep up to date a computerised stock control system.

Occasional duties in order of importance
1 Arrange for faulty equipment to be replaced.
2 Monitor performance of junior sales assistant as defined in job description.
3 Advise and guide, train and assess junior sales assistant where necessary.

Working conditions
Pleasant, 'business-like' environment in new purpose-built shop premises in the city centre. There are two other members of staff and regular contact is also required with the Delivery Department and Head Office. Salary is £18,000 p.a. plus a twice yearly bonus, depending on sales. Five weeks' holiday per year plus statutory holidays. A six-day week is worked.

Other information
There is the eventual possibility of promotion to shop manager in another location depending on performance and opportunities.

Performance standards
There are two critically important areas:
1 Sales volume. Minimum sales to the value of £700,000 over each six-month accounting period.
2 Relations with customers:
   – Customers' queries answered immediately.
   – Customers always given a demonstration when they request one.
   – Delivery times arranged to meet both customer's and delivery department's needs.
   – Complaints investigated immediately.
   – Customers assured that problem will be resolved as soon as possible.
   – Customers never blamed.
   – Problems that cannot be dealt with referred immediately to Manager.

Figure 8.1 Job description for a senior sales assistant

been criticised on the grounds that it tends to produce employees who are very similar to one another and who address problems with the same basic mindset (corporate clones, see e.g. Whiddett and Kandola 2000). This has also led to the suggestion that competency-based approaches can present a barrier to achieving an organisation's equality and diversity objectives (Kirton and Healy 2009). Where innovation and creativity are required, it is helpful to recruit people with more diverse characteristics, and the use of competencies may constrain this.

Job descriptions and person specifications underpin recruitment advertising, that is, the communication of employer requirements to potential applicants. They also form the basis of selection activity, which we consider later (see Chapter 9).

ACTIVITY 8.1

How useful are competencies in determining requirements for a vacancy? To what extent do you think they should be combined with traditional job analysis in drawing up job descriptions and person specifications?

Rational versus processual approaches to recruitment

The recruitment process as we have described it so far is known as the 'rational approach' to recruitment. That is, it is a one-way process in which the employer determines the vacancy's requirements and communicates these to potential candidates in order to generate a pool of applications to support the selection process. Job analysis, job descriptions and person specifications are central to this as the job is fixed and the emphasis is upon finding the applicant who best fits this job. A dominant role for management is presumed and candidates are seen to hold relatively little power. Criticisms of this rational approach can be made on various grounds. First, there is no recognition of the power and politics that run through organisational life and subvert these supposedly rational processes. Van den Brink *et al*. (2012) present a fascinating account of recruitment processes which demonstrates how line managers resist what they perceive to be HR's bureaucratic procedures so that the 'best' person is often not appointed to the vacancy. Second, those involved in the recruitment process often do not act rationally. CIPD's (2015a) recent report into behavioural science, which draws on organisational behaviour, psychology and economics, and recruitment evidences how we actually behave in the recruitment process and argues that recruitment may be more of an art than a science.

A further ground for criticism is that the rational approach ignores the role of the candidate. Increasingly recruitment is seen as a social process (Nickson *et al*. 2008) and there is recognition of the need to influence candidates to attract them to apply: a need to sell the organisation to potential employees. This is becoming increasingly important in an era of social media which facilitates employer/employee interaction (we explore the role of social media in recruitment later in this chapter). A processual approach often relies heavily upon competencies as the emphasis is upon identifying a candidate who fits well into the organisation, rather than a preoccupation with a restrictively defined role. Recruitment advertising is used to begin establishing the psychological contract, that is, the expectations that the employer and employee have of each other. It communicates to potential employees what the experience of working for the organisation will be like. The recruitment process thus becomes two-way, with candidates making decisions about prospective employers as well as vice versa, it being important to create a positive impression with potential employees. Person/organisation and person/job fit, that is, how well an employee's requirements match those of both the organisation and job, are well-established predictors of performance (CIPD, 2015c). A two-way recruitment process increases the prospect of achieving good fit. Indeed, increasingly organisations are engaging in job crafting, that is, designing jobs to suit individual needs (Bipp and Demerouti, 2015) and this has been shown to increase employee engagement (Bakker *et al.*, 2016).

The processual approach to recruitment has created considerable interest in employer branding, which advocates competing for staff by borrowing techniques long used in marketing goods and services to potential customers. In particular, many organisations have sought to position themselves as 'employers of choice' in their labour markets with a view to attracting stronger applications from potential employees. Those who have succeeded have often found that their recruitment costs fall as a result because they get so many more unsolicited applications. Central to this is the development over time of a positive 'brand image' of the organisation as an employer, so that potential employees come to regard working there as highly desirable. This approach has been used to positive effect by a number of public sector employers in the UK offering jobs that are presented as intrinsically rewarding rather than highly remunerated when recruiting, for example, teachers, social workers and police officers. It is also used in the voluntary sector to appeal to potential employees whose values match those of the organisation (Nickson *et al.* 2008). Developing a good brand image is an easier task for larger companies with household names than for those which are smaller or highly specialised, but the possibility of developing and sustaining a reputation as a good employer is something from which all organisations stand to benefit. As we discuss below, social media is increasingly providing a platform through which firms of all size can establish an employer brand. The two-way nature of this process does, however, reduce organisational control and requires careful thought. We consider below the potential for Glassdoor, a relatively recent social media platform, to help develop a positive employer brand.

WINDOW ON PRACTICE

Why you shouldn't ignore Glassdoor

Glassdoor is an online site that allows current and former employees to rate organisations as employers and share details such as salary – a bit like TripAdvisor for job seekers. It is developing quickly, being among the top 600 websites in the USA and growing in UK. It is highly trusted and users report relying on its information more than they rely on companies' brochures and websites. HR professionals need to understand the significance of this for building their employer brand. Glassdoor is used most at the early stages of recruitment and HR practitioners should engage with it to provide information that helps to create a realistic job preview and reduces candidate uncertainty. It is important to engage in a constructive way to influence the brand. Integrity is important and organisations should not fake positive reviews, as users argue they are easy to spot. Equally, an occasional poor review is not of especial concern, rather it is the overall picture that matters.

Source: Lakin (2015).

The key, as when branding consumer products, is to build on any aspect of the working experience that is different from that offered by other organisations competing in the same field, for example, flexible working, or a friendly and informal atmosphere, strong career development potential or job security. This is then developed as a 'unique selling proposition' and forms the basis of the employer branding exercise. The best way of finding out what is distinctive and positive about working in an organisation is to carry out some form of staff attitude survey or again engage with social media. Yammer, for example, is a fast-growing social media platform that many organisations use as an internal form of communication and can provide rich insights into the positives and negatives of working for an organisation. Employer branding exercises simply amount to a waste of time and money when they are not rooted in the actual lived experience of employees because people are attracted to the organisation on false premises. The employees attracted are not subsequently retained and resources are wasted recruiting people who resign quickly after starting.

Once a unique selling proposition has been identified, it can be used to inform all forms of communication that the organisation engages in with potential and actual applicants. The aim must be to repeat the message again and again in advertisements, in recruitment literature, on internet sites and at careers fairs. CIPD (2007) presents the 'candidate journey' in diagrammatic form (Figure 5, p. 16) demonstrating how the employer brand should underpin recruitment (and later selection) activity. It is also important that existing employees are made aware of their employer's brand proposition, both as it forms the basis of their own psychological contract with the organisation and because so much recruitment is carried out informally through word of mouth. Provided the message is accurate and provided it is communicated effectively over time, the result will be a 'leveraging of the brand' as more and more people in the labour market begin to associate the message with the employer.

In the Window on practice that follows we outline how small and medium-sized enterprises in India use social media to develop their employer brand.

WINDOW ON PRACTICE

Small and medium-sized enterprises (SMEs) form a huge proportion of the Indian economy and contribute substantially to employment generation. Attracting and retaining talented employees is essential to their success and they have been quick to recognise the opportunities offered by social media in creating an effective employer brand. Using a wide range of social media, SMEs were able to build brands based around both economic and social values that were highly attractive to both current and potential employees.

Source: Kaur *et al.* (2015).

Internal recruitment

Another important decision when filling a vacancy is whether to recruit internally or externally. Vacancies are often filled internally, creating what are referred to as 'internal labour markets'. Sometimes organisations advertise all vacancies publicly as a matter of course and consider internal candidates along with any external applicants. This approach is generally considered to constitute good practice, especially in respect of equality of opportunity and diversity, and is widely used in the UK public sector. However, many organisations prefer to invite applications from internal candidates *before* they look to external labour markets for new staff (Newell and Shackleton 2000; CIPD 2015a). There are considerable advantages for the employer: it is much less expensive with no need for job advertisements or recruitment agencies. Instead a message can simply be placed in a company newsletter or posted on its intranet or staff noticeboards. Further cost savings and efficiency gains can be made because internal recruits are typically able to take up new posts much more quickly than people being brought in. Even if they have to work some notice in their current positions, they are often able to take on some of their new responsibilities or undergo relevant training at the same time. The other advantage stems from the fact that internal candidates, as a rule, are more knowledgeable than new starters coming in from other organisations about what exactly the job involves. They are also more familiar with the organisation's culture, rules and geography, and so take less time to settle into their new jobs and to begin working at full capacity.

Giving preference to internal recruits, particularly for promotions, has the great advantage of providing existing employees with an incentive to work hard, demonstrate their commitment and stay with the organisation when they might otherwise consider looking for alternative employment. The practice sends a strong signal from management that existing employees are valued and that attractive career development opportunities are available to them. Failing to recruit internally may thus serve to put off good candidates with potential from applying for the more junior positions in an organisation. Bayo-Mariones and Ortin-Angel (2006) present an interesting study of the benefits of internal labour markets in Spain.

The main disadvantage of only advertising posts internally is that a limited field of candidates is considered. While it may mean that someone who 'fits in well' is recruited, it may also mean that the best available candidate is not even considered. Over the long term, the organisation can thus end up being less well served than it would have been had internal candidates been required to compete with outside people for their posts. For this reason, internal recruitment sits uneasily with a commitment to equal opportunities and to the creation of a diverse workforce. Talented candidates from under-represented groups are not appointed because they never get to know about vacancies in the organisation.

It is also important to note that the management of internal recruitment practices is difficult to carry out effectively. Research carried out by the Institute of Employment Research (2006) shows that serious problems often occur when internal candidates fail to be selected. This is because they tend to enter the selection process with higher expectations of being offered the position than external candidates. Bitterness, antipathy and low morale may thus follow. Moreover, failed internal candidates are considerably more likely to pursue claims of unfair discrimination following a selection process than external candidates. For these reasons it is essential that great care is taken when managing internal recruitment to ensure that the approach taken is both fair and seen to be fair. Giving honest, full, accurate and constructive feedback to non-appointed candidates is an essential part of the process.

External recruitment

Once an employer has decided that external recruitment is necessary, a cost-effective and appropriate method of recruitment must be selected. There are a number of distinct approaches to choose from, each of which is more or less appropriate in different

Table 8.2 Most effective recruitment methods

Corporate website	50%
Recruitment consultants	40%
Commercial job boards	25%
Professional networking (e.g. LinkedIn)	19%
Local newspaper advertisements	15%
Speculative applications	13%
Search consultants	13%
Specialist journals and trade press	11%
Job Centre Plus	8%
Professional referral scheme	8%
National newspaper advertising	8%
Social networking (e.g. Facebook)	6%
Apprenticeships	4%
Education liaison	4%
Secondments	4%
Alumni (former employees)	3%

Source: Table compiled from data in CIPD (2015c) *Resourcing and Talent Planning: Annual Survey Report 2012*. London: CIPD. Reproduced with the permission of the publisher, the Chartered Institute of Personnel and Development, London (www .cipd.co.uk).

circumstances. As a result most employers use a wide variety of different recruitment methods at different times. In many situations there is also a good case for using different methods in combination when looking to fill the same vacancy. Table 8.2 sets out the methods reported to be most effective by employers in a recent survey (CIPD 2015c).

A recruitment method must be chosen that will attract as many people as possible with the required skills and qualifications and reach people who are either actively looking for a new job or thinking about doing so. The need is therefore to place an advertisement where job seekers who are qualified to take on the role are most likely to look. All the various methods of recruitment have benefits and drawbacks and the choice of a method has to be made in relation to the particular vacancy and the type of labour market in which the job falls. As Table 8.1 shows, the most effective recruitment methods now include both traditional and electronic. This reflects the growth of e-recruitment, one of the most striking recent developments in the field over the past twenty years, although initial predictions that it would revolutionise the recruitment industry appear somewhat overstated (Parry and Tyson 2008). Indeed, most companies use traditional and electronic methods in combination, rather than one having replaced the other (CIPD 2015c). Despite this, e-recruitment is the second most-widely practised form of e-business (Simone and Esteves 2016).

E-recruitment draws on both corporate and commercial websites, the former being by far the more popular (50% and 25% respectively). Corporate websites refer to the employer's own website and advertise jobs alongside information about the products and services offered by the organisation. Larger organisations typically have part of their website dedicated to careers, or indeed even set up a website specifically for this purpose. Examples of this include the BBC, Coca-Cola, McDonald's, Google and Microsoft. This method is more suitable to large organisations with many visitors to their websites than smaller organisations which typically generate much less website traffic. Commercial websites, provided by cyber-agencies, combine the roles traditionally played by both newspapers and recruitment agents. They advertise the job and undertake shortlisting before they send on a selection of suitable CVs to the employer. The principal attraction of corporate and commercial websites is that they allow jobs to be advertised relatively inexpensively to a potential audience of millions. Simon and Esteves (2016) suggest that around three quarters of potential applicants view companies' corporate websites and that these are their most important source of information. Holm (2014) suggests that cost reductions of up to 90% can be made over traditional methods. Savings can also be made by dispensing with the need to print glossy recruitment brochures and other documents to send to potential candidates and online material can be amended quickly which offers flexibility. It is also a method that is easy for both candidates and employers to use. The other big advantage is speed. People can respond within seconds of reading about an opportunity by emailing their CV to the employer.

Corporate and commercial websites also have a number of disadvantages. A key drawback is that employers advertising jobs can be bombarded with hundreds of applications, many of which are unsuitable for the position advertised. This occurs because of the large number of people who read the advertisement and because it takes so little effort to email a copy of a CV to the employer. A further concern is the high number of applications received from candidates who do not have the necessary work permits. Additionally, these methods may not target passive job seekers or reach a diverse population of job seekers and thus may fail to generate applications from potentially suitable candidates. Goldberg and Allen (2008) outline the difference in responses to recruitment websites between black and white applicants and similar differences have been observed in groups such as older workers or women returners. While it is commonly used for graduates, knowledge workers and middle management jobs, it is often felt to be less appropriate for blue-collar and senior management jobs and for targeting groups such as older workers or women returners. Other problems concern fears about security and confidentiality and there have also been criticisms of poor ethical standards on the part of cyber-agencies. As with conventional employment agents, there are a number who employ poor practice such as posting fictional vacancies and falsely inflating advertised pay rates in order to build up a bank of CVs which can be circulated to employers on an unsolicited basis. Some cyber-agencies also copy CVs from competitors' sites and send them on to employers without authorisation. The pace of technological change can also be problematic: most job seekers now want to access corporate websites via mobile devices but most corporate websites are not yet sufficiently sophisticated to support this (Simon and Esteves 2016).

WINDOW ON PRACTICE

In 2000 an unemployed 53-year-old electronics manager called David Hall took part in a project commissioned by Wynnwith, an established recruitment company. He spent three months unsuccessfully looking for a job using the services of twelve well-known cyber-agencies. He registered with each, giving full details of his background and skills. At the end of the period he concluded that 'these sites appear to offer little more than pretty coloured graphics and empty promises about job opportunities'. He was offered one interview during the twelve weeks, for a role that was unsuitable given his experience. Of the hundreds of job opportunities emailed to him, he reckoned that only 5% matched his capabilities. Among his criticisms were the following:

- the same jobs were advertised week after week;
- very little information was provided about most vacancies;
- salary levels were inflated to make jobs more appealing;
- he received no feedback on applications that failed;
- he was concerned that his CV was being circulated without his consent;
- his emails were often not acknowledged.

Source: 'Online Recruitment Study' at www.wynnwith.com (accessed February 2013).

Recruitment consultants are cited as the second most effective method of recruitment by around 40% of organisations. This is a well-established recruitment method in which an organisation provides job descriptions and person specifications to an agent who both advertises the vacancy and trawls its own applicant databases to identify suitable candidates. In theory, this creates access to a large potential applicant pool which is suitably qualified and reduces the administrative burden on the employer. In practice, candidates are often a poor match for organisational requirements and, even where this is not the case, the service is provided at a high cost which can average around 30% of the appointed candidate's salary.

Another fast-emerging form of e-recruitment is social media. As shown in Table 8.1, professional sites, such as LinkedIn, are used by around a fifth of employers and social sites, such as Facebook, by around 6%. Although these figures are still relatively small, over 60% of organisations in a CIPD (2015c) survey indicated that they were soon planning to use social media for recruitment. A recent report by Broughton *et al.* (2013, on behalf of Acas) provides a detailed discussion of social media in recruitment and is recommended reading. LinkedIn is widely used for identifying and approaching potential candidates. Indeed, features have been developed on the site specifically for this purpose. Anecdotal reports indicate substantial growth in the use of LinkedIn, particularly in respect of professional-level jobs. Facebook is also popular, especially with younger age groups, and around half of all job seekers are now thought to use social media (Clements 2012).

As with other forms of e-recruitment discussed above, social media has both benefits and disadvantages. It offers speed, efficiency and the capacity to identify and target particular applicants or application groups (Broughton *et al.*, 2013). It is also a method that is easily available to SMEs and Faragher (2015) reports on how they use less popular sites, such as Snapchat, to create a more 'edgy' image. Social media allows for the provision of company information via videos, blogs and the chance to engage with existing employees and this can be more attractive to applicants than standard PDF brochures. Facebook, for example, has designed a recruitment campaign that runs on YouTube: www.youtube.com/watch?v=7Rp-JAFVwNs. Realistic job preview and self-selection are all improved via this type of information which can lead to more suitable applications. Longer term, organisations can use social media to develop permanent talent pools, rather than simply advertise vacancies in the short term.

Social media is not, however, without its drawbacks as a recruitment method. Holm (2014) evidences that it is not as cost-effective a form of recruitment as corporate and commercial websites. This results from the need to have HR practitioners engaging on a frequent basis on social media sites, which can be a time-consuming process. Speed of communication also means that inappropriate messages can be inadvertently posted. Broughton *et al.* (2013) report on a number of case study organisations and their approaches to managing this difficulty: many acknowledge that mistakes will be made and take a relaxed approach to this. Most, however, do not have a social media recruitment policy and this is advisable so that all parties are clear on what is acceptable. The method's effectiveness is also limited to applicants who can access social media and those who are likely to, again demographic differences existing across both age groups and ethnic categories. It may also be more appropriate for particular types of roles, e.g. managerial and professional, than for administrative roles (Gërxhani and Koster 2015). Issues around privacy and the extent to which it is appropriate to use information gathered from social networking sites in recruitment are particularly important (Broughton *et al.*, 2013). Information can be used in ways unintended by the applicant (Searle 2004) particularly on social networks such as Facebook. Again is it important to have a policy which specifies whether and how this information can be used (we discuss this further in Chapter 9, Selection). Curran *et al.* (2014) report that most students did not feel they provided information on their website pages that would be relevant to employers in making selection decisions. Employers in contrast believed that they could learn a great deal about the students in this way. This gap in perception demonstrates the care needed in using social media in recruitment processes.

While these recruitment methods may be at their relatively early stages, it is likely that we will see them continue to grow in adoption and influence in the coming years. The Window on practice below demonstrates innovative uses of social media for recruitment purposes.

WINDOW ON PRACTICE

Examples of innovative social media use abound. When Hard Rock opened a cafe in Italy, its recruitment campaign centred on using Facebook to target fans of particular rock groups. A well-designed social media site attracted huge interest and the campaign went 'viral'. In less than a week there were over 6,000 subscriptions to the site and around 4,000 applications in under a month. Unilever has also used Facebook to support its graduate recruitment campaigns and offers prizes to those who 'like' the page, thus drawing it to the attention of their peers, and who fill in surveys about their career aspirations, creating a valuable databank around which Unilever can develop its employment proposition.

Source: Adapted from Clements (2012).

Other once common recruitment methods, such as national and local newspapers and the specialist and trade press, have seen substantial falls in popularity given advances in e-recruitment. Another factor is the substantial cost of such advertising, which can run to several thousand pounds and is increasingly unattractive given the more modest cost of e-recruitment methods. Another noteworthy point is the effectiveness of informal methods of recruitment. Employee referral schemes, in which current employees recommend their contacts for employment in the organisation, have grown substantially in recent years. This is a low-cost method, as advertising costs are avoided, and those recommended are often suitable (as a current employee would not wish to recommend someone unsuitable) and a good organisational fit, as they know what to expect from their organisational contact. It does, however, limit the pool of candidates to those known by current employees and the best candidate for the job may never know that the vacancy exists. It can also create difficulties in relation to equality of opportunity and diversity in that recommendations are likely to perpetuate the make-up of the current workforce. Responding to speculative applications is also often an effective recruitment method. This supports reports of how people actually find their jobs in practice. These repeatedly show that informal methods (such as word of mouth and making unsolicited applications) are as, if not more, common than formal methods such as recruitment advertising, especially in sectors such as retail and hospitality (Warhurst and Nickson 2007). This is important to note and a point often overlooked in academic discussions of effective recruitment methods.

ACTIVITY 8.2

We have seen the significance of informal methods of recruitment whereby new employees come as a result of hearing about a vacancy from friends, or putting their names down for consideration when a vacancy occurs. What are the benefits and drawbacks of this type of arrangement? Why does it so often replace more sophisticated forms of recruitment?

Recruitment advertising

Effective recruitment advertisements are essential to an effective recruitment campaign (CIPD, 2015b). In order to assist in drafting advertisements and placing them in suitable media, many employers deal with a recruitment advertising agency. Such agencies provide expert advice on where to place advertisements and how they should be worded and will design them attractively to achieve maximum impact. This is important whether dealing with print copy or web-based advertisements. Large organisations often subcontract all their advertising work to an agency operating on the basis of a service-level agreement.

Recruitment advertising companies (as opposed to recruitment agencies) are often inexpensive because the agency derives much of its income from the commission paid by the journals on the value of the advertising space sold, the bigger agencies being able to negotiate substantial discounts because of the amount of business they place. A portion of this saving is then passed on to the employer so that it can easily be cheaper *and* a great deal more effective to work with an agent providing this kind of service. The important questions relate to the experience of the agency in dealing with recruitment, as compared with other types of advertising, the quality of the advice they can offer about media choice and the quality of response that their advertisements produce. Cyber-agencies now also play an important role in designing and placing website advertisements and we discuss this further below.

The decision on what to include in a recruitment advertisement is important because of the high cost of space, where using hard copy publications, and the need to attract attention, whether hard or e-copy. Where agencies are used they will be able to advise on this, as they will on the way the advertisement should be worded, but the following is a short checklist of items that must be included:

- Name and brief details of employing organisation.
- Job role and duties.
- Training to be provided.
- Key points of the personnel specification or competency profile.
- Salary and benefits.
- Employment status (e.g. permanent or fixed-term contract).
- Instructions about how to apply.

Uggersley *et al.*'s (2012) study demonstrates the importance of communicating the characteristics of the job, organisation and recruitment process in recruitment advertising. CIPD (2015c) also evidences that use of particular words attracts some applicants over others, again underlining the importance of advertisement design.

There are a number of other considerations when designing and placing a recruitment advertisement. For example, is the aim to deliver a high volume of applicants (graduate or call centre recruitment) or a smaller, highly selective group of applicants (senior manager recruitment, for example)? A balance also needs to be drawn between promoting the company and the job: one may be more attractive than the other, and this may reflect on whether the advertisement adopts a positive, selling approach or a more measured approach to what working in the organisation will be like. A final decision is how precise the information provided should be. A good example of this is in relation to salary. Many employers are reluctant to declare the salary that will accompany the advertised post. Sometimes this is reasonable as the salary scales are well known and inflexible. Elsewhere the reluctance is due either to the fact that the employer does not want to publicise the salary of a position to be filled for fear of dissatisfying holders of other posts, or to the fact that the employer does not know what to offer and is waiting to see 'what the mail brings'. All research evidence, however, suggests that a good indication of the salary is essential if the employer is to attract a useful number of appropriate replies. Recent research has also found that the use of photographs in recruitment advertising can increase the number of applications received. Crush (2012) reports on LV='s innovative approach using interactive recruitment posters featuring photographs of real staff.

WINDOW ON PRACTICE

Burt *et al.* (2010) report on three studies which investigated the use of photographs in recruitment advertisements in New Zealand. The first study demonstrated that around half of organisations used photographs of current employees as these were more positive in attracting applications than those not using photographs. The second study considered potential applicants' responses to the use of photographs in recruitment advertising. Applicants had more positive responses to photographs which showed teams of employees. The third study demonstrated that positive responses were higher when real teams of current *employees, rather than models, were used in recruitment advertisements.* The authors argue that more applicants are likely to be attracted by recruitment advertisements that use photographs and that the type of photograph used is important.

Source: Burt *et al.* (2010).

ACTIVITY 8.3

Table 8.3 contains phrases about the value in pay terms of twelve different jobs. Try putting them in rank order of actual cash value to the recipient. Then ask a friend to do the same thing and compare your lists.

Table 8.3 Phrases from a quality newspaper about salary

1	*c.*£60,000 + bonus + car + benefits
2	from *c.*£35k
3	£30,000 - £40,000 + substantial bonus + car
4	You will already be on a basic annual salary of not less than £40,000
5	Six-figure remuneration + profit share + benefits
6	*c.*£60,000 package
7	Attractive package
8	Substantial package
9	£50,000 OTE, plus car and substantial benefits
10	£ excellent + benefits
11	£ Neg.
12	*c.*£60k package + banking benefits

Evaluation of recruitment activity

The HR manager needs to monitor the effectiveness of recruitment methods, first, to ensure value for money and, second, to ensure that the pool of applicants produced by the various methods is suitable. As with many other HR activities, the evaluation of recruitment is typically poorly done by organisations and e-recruitment is no exception

(Allden and Harris, 2013). Breaugh and Starke (2000) outline a number of possible recruitment criteria against which recruitment activity can be measured and these include:

- the number, quality and diversity of applicants;
- cost per vacancy;
- speed of recruitment;
- number of vacancies filled;
- the ratio of offers to acceptances.

These are relatively short-term measures which are easy to quantify. For a deep understanding of recruitment effectiveness, Breaugh and Starke (2000) go on to argue that there should also be medium- to long-term measures of effectiveness such as job performance and retention rate and even softer measures such as staff attitudes. While an increasing number of organisations monitor short-term outcomes, attempts to link these to longer-term measures of success are much less common. This may result from a lack of robust processes for collecting relevant data. There is also a good case for monitoring effectiveness to ensure equality of opportunity is apparent across the recruitment process, in terms, for example, of gender, ethnic origin, reviewing those who are successful at each stage of the process and taking remedial action where an imbalance becomes apparent. Recent WERS data indicates that this is done by only a small minority of UK organisations (van Wanrooy *et al.*, 2013).

There also needs to be information to get to the more intangible questions, such as 'Did the best candidate not even apply?' The most important source of information about the quality of the recruitment process is the people involved in it. Do telephonists and receptionists know how to handle the tentative employment enquiry? What did they hear from applicants in the original enquiries that showed the nature of their reaction to the advertisement? Is it made simple for enquirers to check key points on websites or by telephone? Is there an unnecessary emphasis on written applications before anything at all can be done? Useful information can also be obtained from both successful and unsuccessful applicants. Social media is particularly effective for seeking this kind of feedback.

SUMMARY PROPOSITIONS

8.1. Job and competency analysis determine the requirements of a vacancy and support the drawing up of job descriptions and person specifications.

8.2. Rational approaches to recruitment have been increasingly criticised and a processual approach recognises a greater role for candidates and leads to an emphasis on employer branding. This involves actively selling the experience of working for an organisation by focusing on what makes the experience both positive and distinctive.

8.3. Effective recruitment methods are changing over time and traditional methods now combine with e-recruitment methods. Informal recruitment methods are also often highly effective.

8.4. Recruitment advertising draws on a range of methods to target suitable applicants. Well-designed advertisements are essential.

8.5. Evaluation of recruitment effectiveness is essential but often poorly done.

GENERAL DISCUSSION TOPICS

1. What are the advantages and disadvantages of e-recruitment from an employer's point of view?

2. How can organisations use social media to develop their employer brand?

3. What benefits are there to viewing recruitment as a social process as opposed to a rational process?

THEORY INTO PRACTICE

At one time, only HR practitioners responsible for recruiting and managing expatriates needed to consider the international dimension of recruitment. Globalisation now means that there are many types of staffing groups and international matters concern a great many recruiters. Examples of international staffing groups include workers on short-term overseas postings, international commuters, 'virtual' international workers on cross-country project teams, immigrants in national labour markets and workers based in one country but dealing with international customers and suppliers. The roles undertaken by these workers have also increased in variety and complexity and include: building new international markets, working on discrete projects, building social networks and facilitating knowledge exchange. Sparrow argues that this requires the internationalisation of all HR processes. In this adaptation of his paper, we concentrate on the internationalisation of recruitment. The recruitment processes of four UK-based case studies are discussed and include:

- South East London Strategic Health Authority: international recruitment focuses on the acquisition of skills for the domestic labour market to tackle labour shortages.
- BBC World Service: international recruitment focuses on the acquisition of specialist skills for the domestic labour market.
- Barclaycard International: international recruitment is focused on the setting up of operations in new countries as part of an expansion strategy.
- Save the Children: international recruitment is focused on the deployment of labour on overseas projects/operations.

The recruitment approaches adopted by these organisations are discussed in more detail below.

South East London Strategic Health Authority

South East London Strategic Health Authority (SHA) recruited in overseas markets to fill vacancies in specialist skill shortage areas, for example doctors and nurses. Global advertising campaigns were run using Web-based approaches which established and communicated a value proposition for international candidates. Part of this was the use of protocols to ensure that other (developing) countries were not damaged by recruitment of their specialist staff. The key matters to address included:

- Identifying professional expertise and technical support, for example HR networks and agencies.
- Balancing targeted recruitment campaigns with longer-term recruitment initiatives.
- Assessing the ethical and reputational issues linked to the campaigns.
- Developing an operational reputation as internationally competitive and attractive.

Three strategies flowed from this. First, active recruitment policies were established to target specific skills and countries. Arrangements with service providers were established and different media identified and tested. Second, passive recruitment policies simply tapped into the growing number of international employees in the domestic labour market. Finally, longer-term strategies ensured the continued attractiveness of the SHA in overseas markets.

BBC World Service

Here the emphasis was on the use of technology to recruit journalists/producers to work mainly in the UK but occasionally overseas. The BBC placed a heavy reliance on its employment brand in international recruitment and identified brand values including: international, trust-worthy, award winning, accessible, impartial, educational and online. These values were used to inform all recruitment materials such as brochures and there was a particular emphasis on their use in the commercial website which advertised vacancies. This activity was undertaken largely by external providers as the BBC outsourced its HR delivery.

Barclaycard International

Barclaycard used its multicultural workforce to support its ambitious internationalisation strategy. Internally, vacancies were advertised on intranets. An international HR business partner was appointed to negotiate preferred supplier arrangements with headhunters and other institutions. An employee value proposition and employment brand was developed across countries and global versus local processes were evaluated and adjusted. Many recruitment processes were adopted across the whole (international) operation, while others had to be more flexible. Recruitment was undertaken in target markets ahead of entering those markets and research was undertaken into a wide range of geographical labour markets.

Save the Children

Save the Children operated across six geographical regions and recruited three types of international labour: long-term overseas development posts, emergency overseas posts and locally appointed posts. To support this, it launched a new employment brand and proposition and recruitment was devolved to local line managers. There were four main activities:

- Regional HR managers worked to identify internal talent at local level, employ local advertising media and build candidate networks and databases.
- Global protocols were developed to identify sources of applicants and ways to advertise roles.
- Collaborative arrangements with other agencies and charities were entered into.
- Recruitment relied on the overall brand image which informed all advertising.

Online recruitment was heavily relied upon and sold the benefits of working in a particular programme, country or region.

Questions

1 Why do you think that all four case study organisations relied so heavily on employer branding in their recruitment activity?

2 Why is e-recruitment so effective in international recruitment?

3 To what extent should consistent global recruitment processes be adopted? How might more local tailored processes be more effective?

Source: Adapted from Sparrow, P. (2007) 'Globalisation of HR at function level: Four UK-based case studies of the international recruitment and selection process', *International Journal of Human Resource Management*, Vol. 18, No. 5, pp. 845–67.

FURTHER READING

Broughton, A., Foley, B., Leidermaier, S. and Cox, A. (2013) *The Use of Social Media in the Recruitment Process*. London: Acas.

Edwards, M. (2010) 'An integrative review of employer branding and OB theory', *Personnel Review*, Vol. 39, No. 1, pp. 5–23.

Parry, E. and Tyson, S. (2008) 'An analysis of the use and success of online recruitment methods in the UK', *Human Resource Management Journal*, Vol. 18, No. 3, pp. 257–74.

Searle, R. (2003) *Selection and Recruitment: A Critical Text*. Milton Keynes: The Open University.

Academic research on recruitment, as opposed to selection, processes is relatively undeveloped and there remain many central issues that have not been rigorously studied. Searle (2003) presents a detailed and critical text that begins to address some of these issues. E-recruitment has emerged as an influential recruitment method. Parry and Tyson (2008) present an in-depth review of its progress and limitations in recent years in the UK and Broughton *et al*. (2013) explore in detail the use of social media as a recruitment method. Edwards (2010) presents a synthesis of the rapidly increasing body of research on employer branding.

REFERENCES

Allden, N. and Harris, L. (2013) 'Building a positive candidate experience: Towards a networked model of e-recruitment', *Journal of Business Strategy*, Vol. 34, pp. 36–47.

Bakker, A., Rodríguez-Muñoz, A. and Vergel, A. (2016) 'Modelling job crafting behaviours: Implications for work engagement', *Human Relations*, Vol. 69, pp. 169–189.

Bayo-Mariones, A. and Ortin-Angel, P. (2006) 'Internal promotion versus external recruitment: Industrial plants in Spain', *Industrial and Labour Relations Review*, Vol. 59, No. 3, Article 7.

Bipp, T. and Demerouti, E. (2015) 'Which employees craft their jobs and how? Basic dimensions of personality and employees' job crafting behaviour', *Journal of Occupational and Organizational Psychology*, Vol. 88, pp. 631–55.

Brannick, M.T. and Levine, E.L. (2002) *Job Analysis: Methods, research and applications for human resource management in the new millennium*. Thousand Oaks, CA: Sage.

Breaugh, J. and Starke, M. (2000) 'Research on employee recruitment: So many studies, so many remaining questions', *Journal of Management*, Vol. 26, No. 3, pp. 405–34.

Broughton, A., Foley, B., Ledermaier, S. and Cox, A. (2013) 'The use of social media in the recruitment process', Research Paper, March. London: Acas.

Burt, C., Halloumis, S., McIntyre, S. and Blackmore, H. (2010) 'Using colleague and team photographs in recruitment advertisements', *Asia Pacific Journal of Human Resources*, Vol. 48, pp. 233–50.

CIPD (2007) *Employer Branding: A No-nonsense Approach*. London: CIPD.

CIPD (2015a) *A Head for Hiring: The Behavioural Science of Recruitment and Selection*. London: CIPD.

CIPD (2015b) *Recruitment: An Overview*. Factsheet. London: CIPD.

CIPD (2015c) *Resourcing and Talent Planning: Annual Survey Report 2015*. London: CIPD.

Clements, A. (2012) 'Social media and recruitment: Time for a coherent HR strategy?' [online] at http://www.hrmagazine.co.uk/article-details/social-media-and-recruitment-time-for-a-coherent-hr-strategy: HR Magazine. 2016.

Crush, P. (2012) 'Tough love', *People Management*, 26 November, pp. 40–2.

Curran, M., Draus, P., Schrager, M. and Zappala, S. (2014) 'College students and HR professionals: Conflicting views on information available on Facebook', *Human Resource Management Journal*, Vol. 24, pp. 442–58.

Faragher, J. (2015) 'How to find talent on a budget: Without cutting corners', *People Management*, pp. 44–47.

Gërxhani, K. and Koster, F. (2015) 'Making the right move. Investigating employers' recruitment strategies', *Personnel Review*, Vol. 44, pp. 781–800.

Goldberg, C. and Allen, D. (2008) 'Black white and read all over: Race differences in reactions to recruitment websites', *Human Resource Management*, Vol. 47, No. 2, pp. 217–36.

Holm, A. (2014) 'Institutional context and e-recruitment practices of Danish organizations', *Employee Relations*, Vol. 36, pp. 432–55.

Kaur, P., Shikha, S., Japneet, K. and Sharma, S. (2015) 'Using social media for employer branding and talent management: An experiential study', *Journal of Brand Management*, Vol. 12, pp. 7–20.

IRS (2003) 'Job descriptions and person specifications', *IRS Employment Review*, No. 776, 23 May.

Kirton, G. and Healy, G. (2009) 'Using competency-based assessment centres to select judges: Implications for equality and diversity', *Human Resource Management Journal*, Vol. 19, No. 3, pp. 302–18.

Lakin, T. (2015) 'Why you shouldn't ignore Glassdoor', *HR Magazine*, http://www.hrmagazine.co.uk/article-details/why-you-shouldnt-ignore-glassdoor.

Martin, C. (2010) *Perfect Phrases for Writing Job Descriptions*. New York: McGraw-Hill.

Newell, S. and Shackleton, V. (2000) 'Recruitment and selection', in S. Bach and K. Sisson (eds), *Personnel Management: A Comprehensive Guide to Theory and Practice*. Oxford: Blackwell.

Nickson, D., Warhurst, C., Dutton, E. and Hurrell, S. (2008) 'A job to believe in: Recruitment in the Scottish voluntary sector', *Human Resource Management Journal*, Vol. 18, No. 1, pp. 20–35.

Parry, E. and Tyson, S. (2008) 'An analysis of the use and success of online recruitment methods in the UK', *Human Resource Management Journal*, Vol. 18, No. 3, pp. 257–74.

Prien, E., Goodstein, L., Goodstein, J. and Gamble, L. (2009) *A Practical Guide to Job Analysis*. San Francisco, CA: Pfeiffer.

Sanchez, J. and Levine, E. (2009) 'What is (or should be) the difference between competency modelling and traditional job analysis?', *Human Resource Management Review*, Vol. 19, No. 1, pp. 53–63.

Searle, R. (2003) *Selection and Recruitment: A Critical Text*. Milton Keynes: The Open University.

Searle, R. (2004) 'New technology: The potential impact of surveillance techniques in recruitment practices', *Personnel Review*, Vol. 35, No. 3, pp. 336–51.

Siddique, C. (2004) 'Job analysis: A strategic human resource management practice', *International Journal of Human Resource Management*, Vol. 15, No. 1, pp. 219–44.

Simone, C. and Esteves, J. (2016) 'The limits of institutional isomorphism in the design of e-recruitment websites: A comparative analysis of the USA and Spain', *International Journal of Human Resource Management*, Vol. 27, pp. 23–44.

Sparrow, P. (2007) 'Globalisation of HR at function level: Four UK-based case studies of the international recruitment and selection process', *International Journal of Human Resource Management*, Vol. 18, No. 5, pp. 845–67.

Uggersley, K., Fassina, N. and Kraichy, D. (2012) 'Recruiting through the stages', *Personnel Psychology*, Vol. 65, pp. 597–660.

Van den Brink, M., Fruytier, B. and Thunnissen, M. (2012) 'Talent management in academia: Performance systems and HRM policies', *Human Resource Management Journal*, doi: 10.1111/j.1748–8583.2012.00196.x.

Van Wanrooy, B., Bewley, H., Bryson, A., Forth, J., Freeth, S., Stokes, L. and Wood, S. (2013) *The 2011 Workplace Employment Relations Study: First findings*. London: BIS.

Warhurst, C. and Nickson, D. (2007) 'Employee experience of aesthetic labour in retail and hospitality', *Work, Employment and Society*, Vol. 21, No. 103, pp. 103–20.

Whiddett, S. and Kandola, B. (2000) 'Fit for the job?', *People Management*, 25 May, pp. 30–4.

CHAPTER 9

SELECTION METHODS AND DECISIONS

THE OBJECTIVES OF THIS CHAPTER ARE TO:

1 Explain the importance of viewing selection as a two-way process

2 Examine the development and use of selection criteria

3 Review developments in e-selection, particularly the use of social network sites as a screening tool

4 Evaluate the range of selection methods that are available (interviewing will be dealt with in detail in Chapter 10, Employability: Skills in Resourcing) and consider the criteria for choosing different methods

5 Review approaches to selection decision making

6 Explain the importance of validating selection procedures

Selection is the process of choosing which applicant should be appointed to a vacancy. The costs of poor selection choices can be high and include poor performance, additional training, demotivation of others, high levels of absence and so on. Sophisticated selection processes thus form part of a strategic bundle of HR practices which contribute to improved organisational performance (see Chapter 4). However, effective selection is difficult to achieve in practice. HR and line managers use a variety of imperfect methods to predict which applicant will be most successful in meeting the demands of the job, and/or be the best fit with the work group and culture of the organisation. Attention is also required to the applicant's perspective and the increasingly international nature of selection. In addition, equal opportunities legislation has underlined the importance of using well-validated selection procedures, so that the selection process discriminates fairly, not unfairly, between applicants. Issues of equality of opportunity are dealt with later (see Chapter 23).

WINDOW ON PRACTICE

Pellizzari (2011) investigates the selection of unskilled workers in low-productivity jobs. While employers typically invest heavily in the selection of senior-level and/or skilled jobs, unskilled jobs comprise the bulk of vacancies in many countries. Pellizzari demonstrates that employers typically make limited investment in unskilled worker selection and that the resultant poor job/person matching leads to higher labour turnover with all its associated organisational costs, such as reduced productivity and worsening worker morale. More intensive selection leads to better matches that last longer and create higher employer satisfaction. This research suggests to us that organisations are well advised to adopt robust selection processes of the type discussed in this chapter.

Source: Summarised from Pellizzari, M. (2011) 'Employers' search and the efficiency of matching', *British Journal of Industrial Relations*, Vol. 49, pp. 29–53.

Rational versus processual approaches to selection

We discussed the role of candidate perceptions in the recruitment process in detail in the previous chapter. These perceptions are equally influential in selection processes, where the various stages provide information for decisions by both the employer and the potential employee. Applicants choose between organisations by evaluating the developing relationship between themselves and the prospective employer. This takes place via social media and correspondence from potential employers; in their experience of the selection methods used by the employer; and in the information they gain at interview. Applicants will decide not to pursue some applications. Either they will have accepted another offer, or they will find something in their dealings with the organisation that discourages them and they withdraw. When large numbers of candidates withdraw it may be because the information provided by the organisation was sufficiently detailed, accurate and realistic for them to be able to make an informed decision that they were not suited to the organisation. On the other hand, it might be that potentially suitable recruits were lost because of the way in which information was presented or a lack of (timely) information. The applicant's frame of reference is very different from that of the manager in the organisation and that difference is frequently forgotten. The majority of applicants vest a significant amount of time and energy in the submission of an application. The psychological contract of a potential employee begins to form at this stage and this should not be overlooked: timely responses are the first element of this process. Indeed CIPD (2015a) reports that up to one third of organisations lose candidates due to the length of the recruitment and selection process.

Some of the points that seem to be useful about interacting with the candidate are:

1 Reply, meaningfully and quickly. Use of social network sites can facilitate this but other forms of communication also need to be effective.

2 Conduct correspondence in terms of what the applicants want to know. How long will they have to wait for an answer? If you ask them in for interview or to an assessment centre, how long will it take, what will it involve, do you defray expenses, can they park their car, how do they find you, etc.?

3 Interviewers should be trained to ensure that they have not only full knowledge of the relevant information, but also the skills to manage the interaction effectively.

Selection criteria

Selection criteria need to be explicitly defined in order to choose the most appropriate selection methods, make credible selection decisions and validate the selection process (Searle 2003). Selection criteria are typically presented in the form of a person specification or competency profile representing the ideal candidate (see the previous chapter for further detail). Three perspectives can be used to determine selection criteria: job fit, team/functional fit and organisational fit (CIPD, 2015b). Job fit emphasises the requirements of the person specification and identifies a candidate who can conduct that job, essentially selecting a 'square peg to fit a square hole'. Team and organisational fit approaches are less concerned with the job requirements and more concerned with how well a candidate will slot in. There has recently been an increasing emphasis on team and organisational fit, which has been supported by greater use of competencies in selection (Branine 2008). Competency profiles, often expressed in terms of personality, attitudes, flexibility, commitment and goals, are adopted as a means of setting the criteria against which to select, rather than the ability to do the specific job for which the person is being recruited. In many organisations, for example call centres, such selection approaches have led to a much greater emphasis on these competencies than on the education or experience typically demanded by the use of person specifications. Such organisational criteria are also important where jobs are ill defined and constantly changing. There is growing interest in how to select to ensure a good team fit, see for example Burch and Anderson's (2008) New Zealand study of a Team Selection Inventory. Whiddett and Hollyforde (2003) also provide a useful practical source of information on how to use competencies in the selection process.

The aim of compentencies is to promote objective selection criteria which are explicit and transparent, although Kirton and Healey (2009) warn that these still require human interpretations so may be less objective than suggested. Other critiques of selection based on competency have also included the danger of 'cloning', that is, selecting very similar types of people for an organisation and thus limiting diversity, and that competencies are backward looking, focusing on what has previously made the organisation successful rather than the competencies that it may need for future success. Use of both person specifications and competency profiles to inform selection criteria is criticised and the search continues for criteria that will improve the process of selecting potential employees.

ACTIVITY 9.1

Write a person specification for your job (or one with which you are familiar). Now write a list of the competencies required to undertake the same role. Which do you think will be more helpful in the selection process and why?

Shortlisting

Robust selection criteria are essential to the whole selection process. Traditionally, they have been used in the first stage, shortlisting, to assess formal applications and select those who are suitable for the later stages such as tests and interviews. Increasingly, however, there is a less formal stage that precedes this, namely screening via social network sites (SNS). Roth *et al.* (2016) found that nearly half of recruiters in their survey reported searching for candidate information on SNS and around one third did not shortlist at least one candidate based on that information. Broughton *et al.* (2013) provide a detailed discussion of screening via SNS which we recommend reading. We outline the key points here and discuss both the benefits and concerns that surround this practice. Organisations increasingly view potential employees' SNS, for example, Facebook, to inform decision making as they can quickly and easily gain information which is often greater than that provided in a formal application. It also allows information in the formal application to be confirmed and a view to be formed as to the applicant's likely fit into the organisation. Yet few organisations have policies on the use of SNS for screening purposes, which could be problematic both in terms of invasion of privacy and basing selection decisions on irrelevant matters that are not outlined in the selection criteria. Davison *et al.* (2012) found that most SNS content is not relevant to formal selection criteria, for example, inappropriate information on social activity or unfavourable comment on previous employers. There is also a risk of (possibly inadvertent) discrimination where issues such as gender, race or religion influence selection decisions. One important issue discussed by Broughton *et al.* (2013) is whether organisations should disclose their use of SNS screening to applicants and, currently, the majority do not. We outline Hamilton *et al.*'s recommendations on screening using SNS in the following Window on practice.

WINDOW ON PRACTICE

Using SNSs to screen applicants

If organisations intend to screen using SNS, there are five important steps they can take to ensure the process is robust:

1   Devise and publish a policy to guide appropriate screening behaviour.

2   Ensure that screening is based on the formal selection criteria and not irrelevant material.

3   Evaluate the benefits of this approach and ensure that they outweigh the risks.

4   Ensure that there is a standard screening process conducted by a few people that leads to broadly similar selection decisions.

5   Check that the information used from SNS is accurate.

Source: Summarised from Davison *et al.* (2012).

A more traditional approach to shortlisting involves consideration of the selection criteria against application forms or curriculum vitae (CVs) to produce a shortlist of the best candidates to move forward to the next stage. Shortlisting of candidates can be difficult in some instances because of small numbers of applicants and in other instances because of extremely large numbers of applicants. Such difficulties can arise unintentionally when there is inadequate specification of the criteria required or intentionally in large-scale recruitment exercises such as those associated with an annual intake of graduates. A fair and objective shortlisting system is essential to avoid bias inherent in the process, as, for example, most people recruit people similar to themselves (CIPD 2015b). This can be achieved in one of three basic ways, which can be used separately or in combination. The first involves using a panel to undertake shortlisting, reducing the likelihood that individual prejudices will influence the process. A number of distinct stages can be identified:

Stage 1: Panel members agree essential criteria for those to be placed on the shortlist.

Stage 2: Using those criteria, selectors individually produce personal lists of, say, ten candidates. An operating principle throughout is to concentrate on who can be included rather than who can be excluded, so that the process is positive, looking for strengths rather than shortcomings.

Stage 3: Selectors reveal their lists and find their consensus. If stages 1 and 2 have been done properly the degree of consensus should be quite high and probably sufficient to constitute a shortlist for interview. If it is still not clear, they continue to the next stage.

Stage 4: Discuss those candidates preferred by some but not all in order to clarify and reduce the areas of disagreement. A possible tactic is to classify candidates as 'strong', 'possible' or 'not suitable'.

Stage 5: Selectors produce a final shortlist by discussion.

The second approach involves employing a scoring system. As with the panel method, the key shortlisting criteria are defined at the start of the process (e.g. a degree in a certain discipline, certain types of job experience, evidence of particular competencies, etc.). The shortlister then scores each CV or application form received against these criteria, awarding an A grade (or high mark) where clear evidence is provided that the candidate matches the criteria, a B grade where there is some evidence or where the candidate partially meets the criteria and a C grade where no convincing evidence is provided. Where a structured application form has been completed by the candidates, this process can be undertaken quickly (two or three minutes per application) because a candidate can be screened out whenever, for example, more than one C grade has been awarded.

The third approach involves making use of the e-systems which shortlist candidates electronically. While widely available, these technologies are subject to much criticism and are not widely used outside of high volume recruitment. Some search for key words and inevitably have a 'hit and miss' character and can be criticised for being inherently unfair. Stone *et al.* (2015) explain that good candidates may be rejected simply because they did not use a particular word or phrase. The same doubt exists about online application systems which include a handful of 'killer' questions designed to sift out unsuitable candidates at a very early stage. People with an unconventional career background may be automatically disregarded and concerns about equality of opportunity and discrimination have been noted. Caution is thus required. Despite these problems, such systems can be useful where the criteria are very clearly and tightly defined, and where an online application form is completed which makes use of multiple choice answers. Such forms can be scored speedily and objectively, the candidates being given feedback on whether or not they have been successful. Only those who make the 'right' choices when completing the online questionnaire are then invited to participate in the next stage of the selection process which may comprise various selection methods.

Selection methods

We present below recent CIPD (2015a) research that outlines the most frequently used selection methods (Table 9.1) and discuss these in detail. In the survey, interviews following an application form or CV have replaced competency-based interviews as the most frequently used selection method, although both are popular. Other common methods include various types of tests and around a third of respondents use assessment centres. Typically, a combination of two or more of these methods is used, and the choice of these is dependent upon a number of factors:

1 **Selection criteria for the post to be filled.** For example, group selection methods and assessment centre activities would be most useful for certain types of jobs, such as managerial, professional, supervisory.

2 **Acceptability and appropriateness of the methods.** These are for the candidates involved, or likely to be involved, in the selection. The use, for example, of intelligence tests may be seen as insulting to applicants already occupying senior posts.

3 **Abilities of the staff involved in the selection process.** This applies particularly in the use of tests and assessment centres. Only those staff who are appropriately qualified by academic qualification and/or attendance on a recognised course may administer psychological tests.

Table 9.1 Methods used to select applicants (%)

Interviews following contents of a CV/application form	83
Competency-based interviews	77
Tests for specific job-related skills	52
General ability tests	47
Literacy and/or numeracy tests	45
Assessment centres	38
Personality/aptitude questionnaires/psychometric tests	36
Group exercises (e.g. role playing)	27
Online tests (new method in this survey)	22
References	22
Base: 505	

Source: From Chartered Institute of Personnel and Development (2015a) *Resourcing and Talent Planning: Annual Survey Report 2015*, Table 7. With the permission of the publisher, the Chartered Institute of Personnel and Development, London (www.cipd.co.uk).

4 **Administrative ease.** For administrative purposes it may be much simpler, say, to arrange one or two individual interviews for a prospective candidate than to organise a panel consisting of four members, all needing to make themselves available at the same time. Online testing may save much administrative time, particularly when there are large numbers of candidates.

5 **Time factors.** Sometimes a position needs to be filled very quickly, and time may be saved by using telephone or video-based interviews, or organising individual interviews rather than group selection methods, which would mean waiting for a day when all candidates are available.

6 **Cost.** Tests may cost a lot to set up but once the initial outlay has been made they are reasonably cheap to administer. Assessment centres involve an even greater outlay and continue to be fairly expensive to administer. Interviews, on the other hand, cost only a moderate amount to set up in terms of interviewer training and are fairly cheap to administer. For the costlier methods great care needs to be taken in deciding whether the improvement in selection decision making justifies such costs.

7 **Accuracy.** In selection, this is usually referred to as validity and is the extent to which a selection method predicts subsequent job performance. If selection decisions relate highly to future performance, however defined, then the method is a good predictor. Validity is usually expressed as a correlation coefficient (r): if $r = 1$, then the selection method perfectly predicts performance; if $r = 0$, then there is no relationship between the selection method and performance. In practice, r will fall between 0 and 1, with different methods having varying levels of validity. A range of studies (see e.g. Schmidt and Hunter 1998) have shown that assessment centres have a correlation coefficient of around 0.6, structured interviews 0.5, work sampling 0.4, personality tests 0.3, unstructured interviews 0.1 and references 0. Validity in selection generally increases in relation to the number of appropriate selection methods used (see e.g. IRS 2002).

Choice of selection method is determined by all these factors. For example, while assessment centres may have the highest levels of validity, they are also expensive, time consuming and difficult to administer. This explains why they are used only by around one third of organisations (CIPD 2015a), despite their capacity to predict job performance relatively effectively.

It is interesting to note that online selection tests appeared for the first time in the CIPD (2015a) survey and are used by 22% of organisations. This reflects the fact that technology plays an increasing role in selection, often to support rather than replace existing methods. E-selection can help manage increasingly large applicant pools. Google, for example, receives over one million applications each year (Johnson and Guetal 2013). Stone *et al.* (2015) present a detailed review of e-selection systems and show that they can speed up screening processes, reduce the workload involved in assessment, support interviews using web-based methods and improve effective storage of applicant data. All these lead to reductions in both time and cost. They also, however, outline a number of disadvantages which include potential discrimination, possible lack of privacy and the capacity of applicants to cheat (particularly in online tests). Johnson and Guetal (2013) also warn that applicants must not feel disadvantaged by the use of e-selection systems and that technology and/or training must be provided if required. It is also important to be aware that there are differences in the uptake and acceptance of e-selection systems across applicant characteristics such as age, gender and race (Stone *et al.*, 2015).

The 'classic trio', namely application forms, interviews and references, are traditional methods of selection. We consider these first, other than for face-to-face interviews which we consider in depth later (see Chapter 10). We then move on to consider more advanced methods of selection, such as testing, group methods and assessment centres.

The classic trio

Application forms

Application forms are generally used as a straightforward way of giving a standardised synopsis of the applicant's history. This helps applicants present their case by providing them with a predetermined structure, it speeds the sifting of applications either by hand or electronically and it guides the interviewers, with each piece of information on the form being taken and developed in the interview, as well as providing the starting point for employee records. While there is heavy use of CVs for managerial and professional posts, many organisations, especially in the public sector, require both for reasons of equality of opportunity. While this maybe off-putting to the applicant, it is helpful to the organisation in eliciting comparable data from all applicants.

Application forms can also be used to collect biodata which describes personal information collected about a candidate (Breaugh 2009). Biodata is perhaps of most use for large organisations filling fairly large numbers of posts for which they receive substantial numbers of applications. This method is an attempt to relate the characteristics of applicants to the characteristics of a large sample of successful job holders. The obvious drawbacks of this procedure are, first, the time that is involved and the size of sample needed, so that it is only feasible where there are many job holders in a particular type of position. Second, it lacks face validity for applicants who might find it difficult to believe that success in a position correlates with being, for example, the first born in one's family. Despite this, Breaugh (2009) presents a review of biodata research and suggests that, as a selection method, it is one of the best predictors of employee performance and turnover and argues for its increased usage.

Despite the widespread adoption of application forms and CVs, there remain concerns about their reliability. There are also concerns about inherent bias related to, for example, assumptions about an applicant's name which leads CIPD (2015b) to recommend that all forms presented to those shortlisting should be anonymous.

Telephone interviewing

All forms of interview have low predictive validity, that is, they are not especially effective at selecting those who will perform well in the job (CIPD 2015b). They are nevertheless widely used, although telephone interviews have dropped out of the most recent CIPD (2015a) survey as a popular selection method. This is perhaps because these interviews are commonly used as part of a group of selection methods. Johnson and Guetal (2013) report, for example that candidates might have a telephone interview, followed by an online video interview and finally a face-to-face interview. In the early stage, telephone interviews are quick to arrange and overcome geographical barriers. They also have an important role when selecting for jobs in which telephone manner is critical, such as call centre staff. There may be problems such as lack of non-verbal information, and difficulties getting hold of the applicant. However, positive aspects have been reported, such as concentration on content rather than the person. From an applicant perspective telephone interviews can be daunting, if applicants have no experience of them, and Murphy (2005) refers to and replicates checklists for organisations and candidates in the most effective use of such interviews. It is also worth remembering that candidates are generally more positive about and more likely to accept a job offer after face-to-face interviews so telephone interviews should not be over-relied upon (Johnson and Guetal 2013).

References

One way of informing the judgement of managers who have to make employment offers to selected individuals is the use of references. Nearly a quarter of organisations use this selection method (CIPD 2015a). Candidates provide the names of previous employers or others with appropriate credentials and then prospective employers ask them to provide information. There are two types: the factual check and the character reference. The factual check is fairly straightforward as it is no more than a confirmation of facts that the candidate has presented. It will normally follow the employment interview and decision to offer a post. The character reference is a very different matter. Here the prospective employer asks for an opinion about the candidate before the interview so that the information gained can be used in the decision-making phases. The logic of this strategy is sound: who knows the working performance of the candidate better than the previous employer? It may not, however, be particularly effective, as it depends on the writers of references being good judges of working performance, strong communicators and – most difficult of all – disinterested. Employers are increasingly nervous about providing character references, particularly where the comments to be made are not wholly positive. We outline some of the concerns employers face in providing references in the Window on practice below.

WINDOW ON PRACTICE

References: what employers should do and what they should avoid

May (2012) discusses the frequent concern among employers that providing a poor reference may lead to their being sued and cites a case where a former employer sued for libel over a statement contained in a reference. Although the case did not succeed, as employers are protected against libel claims providing that any inaccurate statements have not been made maliciously, it does serve to reinforce employer concerns. May provides the following checklist for employers to follow when providing references:

- Ensure there is an organisational policy on who can provide references, in what format and what its contents should be.
- Ensure that the policy is consistently applied to all current and former employees.
- Retain written notes of verbal references.
- If references confirm only employment dates and roles held, then this should be explicit.
- Ensure that genuine reasons for dismissal are provided.
- Ensure that refusal to provide a reference is not discriminatory and that disability is not a factor in any judgements made on performance or attendance.
- All statements should be clear and accurate.
- Ensure that the employee is aware of any concerns referred to in the reference.
- The reference does not need to be detailed: exercise caution when commenting on suitability for the new post.
- Mark the reference 'Private and Confidential' and for the attention of the addressee only.

Source: Summarised from May (2012).

Advanced methods of selection

We now consider more advanced methods of selection and issues surrounding their usage. Advanced methods comprise various forms of testing (including aptitude, attainment, personality and work sampling tests), group methods and assessment centres.

Testing

The use of tests in selection is surrounded by strong feelings for and against. Those in favour of testing in general point to the unreliability of the interview as a predictor of performance and the greater potential accuracy and objectivity of test data. Tests can be seen as giving credibility to selection decisions. Those against them either dislike the objectivity that testing implies or have difficulty in incorporating test evidence into the rest of the evidence that is collected. Questions have been raised as to the relevance of the tests to the job applied for and the possibility of unfair discrimination and bias. Also, some candidates feel that they can improve their prospects by a good interview performance and that the degree to which they are in control of their own destiny is being reduced by a dispassionate routine. CIPD (2015a) found that there is an increasing reliance on tests, with 47% of organisations using general ability tests, 45% using literacy/numeracy tests and 36% using personality tests. The survey also shows a steep climb in the popularity of tests for specific job-related skills (used by 52% of organisations) which may be associated with the increased use of online testing (used by 22%). Once confined to management, professional and graduate jobs, online testing means tests are now more likely to be used for a wider range of jobs.

Types of test

Aptitude tests

People differ in their performance of tasks, and tests of aptitude (or ability) measure an individual's potential to develop in either specific or general terms. This is in contrast to attainment tests, which measure the skills an individual has already acquired. When considering the results from aptitude tests it is important to remember that a simple relationship does not exist between a high level of aptitude and a high level of job performance, as other factors, such as motivation, also contribute to job performance.

Aptitude tests can be grouped into two categories: those measuring general mental ability or general intelligence and those measuring specific abilities or aptitudes.

General intelligence tests

Intelligence tests, sometimes called mental ability tests, are designed to give an indication of overall mental capacity. A variety of questions are included in such tests, including vocabulary, analogies, similarities, opposites, arithmetic, number extension and general information. Ability to score highly on such tests correlates with the capacity to retain new knowledge, to pass examinations and to succeed at work. However, the intelligence test used would still need to be carefully validated in terms of the job for which the candidate was applying. Examples of general intelligence tests are found in IDS (2004).

Special aptitude tests

There are special tests that measure specific abilities or aptitudes, such as spatial abilities, perceptual abilities, verbal ability, numerical ability, motor ability (manual dexterity) and so on. An example of a special abilities test is the Critical Reasoning Test developed by Smith and Whetton (see IDS 2004).

Attainment tests

Whereas aptitude tests measure an individual's potential, attainment or achievement tests measure skills that have already been acquired, for example keyboard skills or the ability to use Word, PowerPoint or Excel software. There is much less resistance to such tests of skills as candidates are sufficiently confident of their skills to welcome the opportunity to display them and are in control, whereas they feel that the tester is in control of intelligence and personality tests as the candidates do not understand the evaluation rationale. Attainment tests are often devised by the employer.

Personality tests

Debate rages about the importance of personality for success in some jobs and organisations. The need for personality assessment may be high but there is even more resistance to tests of personality than to tests of aptitude, partly because of the reluctance to see personality as in any way measurable. There is much evidence to suggest that personality is also context dependent and may change over time.

Theories of human personality vary as much as theories of human intelligence. Jung, Eysenck and Cattell, among others, have all proposed different sets of factors/traits which can be assessed to describe personality. Robertson (2001) argues that it is now possible to state that there are five basic building blocks of personality: extroversion/introversion; emotional stability; agreeableness; conscientiousness; and openness to new experiences and many tests are based around these traits. However, it is dangerous to assume that there is a standard profile of 'the ideal employee' (although this may fit nicely with theories of culture change) or the ideal personality for a particular job, as the same objectives may be satisfactorily achieved in different ways by different people. Another problem with the use of personality tests is that they rely on an individual's willingness to be honest, as the socially acceptable answer or the one best in terms of the job can be easy to spot. Ipsative tests (as opposed to normative tests)[1] seek to avoid the social desirability problem by using a different test structure – but other problems arise from this approach. Heggestad *et al.* (2006) suggest that in their pure form ipsative tests are inappropriate for selection and that in their partial form they might be just as susceptible to faking as normative tests. Dalen *et al.* (2001) show that tests are indeed manipulable but not sufficiently for the candidate to match an ideal profile, and that such manipulation would be exposed by detection measures within the test. There is a further problem that some traits measured by the test will not be relevant in terms of performance on the job.

Work sampling tests

Work sampling of potential candidates for permanent jobs can take place by assessing candidates' work in temporary posts or on government training schemes in the same organisation. For some jobs, such as photographers and artists, a sample of work in the form of a portfolio is expected to be presented at the time of interview. It has been suggested that managers and professionals should also be developing portfolios of their work experiences and achievements as one way of enhancing their employability. Increasingly candidates are required to undertake work experience as part of the selection process, for example, spending a day working in a shop or restaurant so that their suitability can be assessed.

Online testing

Many of the tests described above were traditionally undertaken using 'paper and pencil' but are increasingly being conducted online. Johnson and Guetal (2013) present an interesting discussion of this transition and caution that organisations should not assume that these are superior to, or indeed as good as, traditional tests. For example, candidates may read more slowly from a computer screen and internet connection problems may reduce test performance. Discrimination concerns may also arise; for example, younger people have been demonstrated to perform better in online tests and differences such as these are not apparent in traditional tests. Candidates from lower socio-economic and particular ethnic minority groups have also been found to be less frequent users of computers and the internet, creating a disadvantage for them. Cheating is also possible as the person taking the test may not be the candidate. Nevertheless, organisations continue to develop increasingly sophisticated online tests as we outline in the following Window on practice.

---

[1] Ipsative tests require the candidate to make a *choice*, usually between two statements or adjectives, rather than allowing the candidate to answer, for example, 'true' or 'false' or give a rating of 'to what extent' they agree an item applies to themselves, as in a normative test.

WINDOW ON PRACTICE

Online tests

Surveys continue to show an increased use of online testing, with around three quarters of firms indicating its adoption in 2013. Tests can take many forms. Hays, for example, asks applicants to select the best candidates for a particular role based on a client brief. Another method, used by CERN, involves a-synchronous interviews. Applicants are sent a link asking them to record a video interview that can be seen by those involved in selection at a time convenient to them. While applicants can practise, once they have started the recording, they cannot then stop it, which reflects face-to-face interview conditions. CERN then invites only four applicants per vacancy to face-to-face interview and an assessment centre.

Source: Adapted from Syedain, H. (2013) *The New Rules of Recruitment*, http://www.cipd .co.uk/pm/peoplemanagement/b/weblog/archive/2013÷06÷23/the-new-rules-of-recruitment.aspx.

Critical features of test use

Validity

Tests are chosen on the basis that test scores relate to, or correlate with, subsequent job performance, so that a high test score would predict high job performance and a low test score would predict low job performance (see above on choice of selection methods). The use of tests may vary by type of role. Lockyer and Scholarios (2004), for example, suggest that ability tests and work sample tests have high predictive validity for manual workers.

Reliability

The reliability of a test is the degree to which the test measures consistently whatever it measures. If a test is highly reliable, then it is possible to put greater weight on the scores that individuals receive on the test. However, a highly reliable test is of no value in the employment situation unless it also has high validity.

Use and interpretation

Tests need to be used and interpreted by trained or qualified testers. Test results, especially personality tests, require very careful interpretation as some aspects of personality will be measured that are irrelevant to the job. The British Psychological Society (BPS) provides a certificate of competence for occupational testing at levels A and B. Both the BPS and CIPD have produced codes of practice for occupational test use. It is recommended that tests are not used in a judgemental, final way, but to stimulate discussion with the candidate based on the test results and that feedback is given to candidates. In addition it is recommended that test data alone should not be used to make a selection decision (which could contravene the 1998 Data Protection Act), but should always be used as part of a wider process where inferences from test results can be backed up by information from other sources.

Problems with using tests

A number of problems can be incurred when using tests:

1 A correlation coefficient of $r = 0.4$ is comparatively good in the testing world and this level of relationship between test scores and performance is generally seen as acceptable. Tests are, therefore, not outstanding predictors of future performance.

2 Validation procedures are very time consuming, but are essential to the effective use of tests. There are concerns that with the growth of online testing, new types of tests, such as emotional intelligence tests, are being developed without sufficient validation (Johnson and Guetal 2013).

3 The criteria that are used to define good job performance in developing the test are often inadequate. They are subjective and may account to some extent for the mediocre correlations between test results and job performance.

4 Tests are often job specific. If the job for which the test is used changes, then the test can no longer be assumed to relate to job performance in the same way. Also, personality tests only measure how individuals see themselves at a certain time and cannot therefore be reliably reused at a later time.

5 Tests may not be fair as there may be a social, sexual or racial bias in the questions and scoring system. People from some cultures may, for example, be unused to 'working against the clock'. Tests also require a high facility with the language in which they are constructed. With many countries experiencing increasing levels of migrant workers, this may be problematic. In the Theory into practice section, we consider alternative types of test which may address this problem.

ACTIVITY 9.2

In what ways could you measure job performance for the following?

- A data input clerk.
- A mobile plumber.
- A call centre operator.
- A supervisor.

Group selection methods and assessment centres

Group methods

The use of group tasks is to provide evidence about the candidates' ability to:

- get on with others;
- influence others and the way they do this;
- express themselves verbally;
- think clearly and logically;
- argue from past experience and apply themselves to a new problem;
- identify the type of role they play in group situations.

These features are difficult on the whole to identify using other selection methods and one of the particular advantages of group selection methods is that they provide the selector with examples of behaviour on which to select. When future job performance is being considered it is behaviour in the job that is critical, and so selection using group methods can provide direct information on which to select rather than indirect verbal information or test results. The use of competencies and behavioural indicators, as a way to specify selection criteria, ties in well with the use of group methods.

There is a range of group exercises that can be used including informal discussion of a given topic, role plays and groups who must organise themselves to solve a problem within time limits which may take the form of a competitive business game, case study or physical activity.

Group selection methods are most suitable for management, graduate and sometimes supervisory posts. One of the difficulties with group selection methods is that it can be difficult to assess an individual's contribution, and some people may be unwilling to take part.

ACTIVITY 9.3

To what extent does a person's behaviour on these group selection tasks accurately reflect behaviour on the job? Why?

Assessment centres

Assessment centres incorporate multiple selection techniques, and the group selection methods outlined above form a major element, together with other work-simulation exercises such as in-basket tasks, psychological tests, a variety of interviews and presentations. Assessment centres are used to assess, in depth, a group of broadly similar applicants, using a set of competencies required for the post on offer and a series of behavioural statements which indicate how these competencies are played out in practice. Even assuming that the competencies for the job in question have already been identified, assessment centres require a lengthy design process to select the appropriate activities so that every competency will be measured via more than one task. Assessment centres have been proven to be one of the most effective ways of selecting candidates. This is probably due, as Suff (2005) notes, to the use of multiple measures, multiple assessors and predetermined assessment criteria. Thornton and Gibbons (2009) present a detailed evaluation of the validity of assessment centres in selection.

A matrix is usually developed to show how the required competencies and the activities link together. In terms of running the centre, sufficient well-trained assessors will be needed, usually based on the ratio of one assessor for two candidates to ensure that the assessor can observe each candidate sufficiently carefully. Lists of competencies and associated behaviours will need to be drawn up as checklists and a careful plan will need to be made of how each candidate will move around the different activities – an example of which is given in Table 9.2. Clearly candidates will need to be very well briefed both before and at the start of the assessment at the centre.

Table 9.2 An example of the scheduling of events based on an assessment centre for a professional post (central government)

Day 1 Times	Activity	Who is involved
9.30–10.00	Introduction to centre	All
10.00–10.45	General discussion – given topics	All
10.45–11.15	Coffee	
11.15–12.00	General intelligence test	All
12.00–12.30	One-to-one interviews (30 min each)	Candidates A, B, C
12.30–1.30	Lunch	
1.30–2.00	One-to-one interviews (30 min each)	Candidates B, E, C
2.00–2.45	Spatial reasoning test	All
2.45–3.15	Coffee	
3.15–4.00	Personality test	All
4.00–4.30	One-to-one interviews (30 min each)	Candidates C, F, D

Day 2 Times	Activity	Who is involved
9.30–10.15	Verbal reasoning test	All
10.15–10.45	One-to-one interviews (30 min each)	Candidates D, A, F
10.45–11.15	Coffee	
11.15–12.00	Critical thinking test	All
12.00–12.30	One-to-one interviews (30 min each)	Candidates E, B, A
12.30–1.30	Lunch	
1.30–3.00	In-tray exercise	All
3.00–3.30	Coffee	
3.30–4.00	One-to-one interviews (30 min each)	Candidates F, D, E

Note: Based on six candidates (A, B, C, D, E, F) and three assessors.

At the end of the procedure the assessors have to come to an agreement on a cumulative rating for each individual, related to job requirements, taking into account all the selection activities. The procedure as a whole can then be validated against job performance rather than each separate activity. The predictive validities from such procedures are not very consistent, but there is a high 'face validity' – a feeling that this is a fairer way of selecting people. Reliability can also be improved by the quality of assessor training, careful briefing of assessors and a predetermined structured approach to marking. The chief disadvantage of these selection methods is that they are a costly and time-consuming procedure, for both the organisation and the candidates. The time commitment is extended by the need to give some feedback to candidates who have been through such a long procedure which involves psychological assessment – although feedback is still not always provided for candidates. Despite this, there is evidence of increasing use of assessment centres. A helpful text relating competency profiles and assessment centre activities is Woodruffe (2000), and IDS (2005) provides examples of different company experiences. Spray (2010) outlines 'how to run an assessment centre'.

As with all other aspects of selection, technology can now play a larger role in assessment centres, as we demonstrate in the Window on practice below.

WINDOW ON PRACTICE

'Hi-tech' assessment centres

KPMG has launched what it describes as a 'hi-tech' assessment centre for graduate recruitment. It contains a one-hour 'virtual office' exercise which is designed to simulate closely the working environment in which candidates complete an assigned task while dealing with emails and telephone calls. This is combined with more traditional selection methods such as interviews, role plays and report writing. Group exercises have, however, been removed from the process as KPMG believes that they do not accurately represent how candidates really behave. The interactive technological experience is designed to generate greater insight into candidate behaviour and reduce the number of candidates who are rejected at a late stage in the selection process.

Source: Summarised from Brockett (2011).

Final selection decision making

The selection decision involves measuring the candidates individually against the selection criteria defined, often in the person or competency specification, and not against each other. A useful tool to achieve this is the matrix in Table 9.3. This is a good method of ensuring that every candidate is assessed against each selection criterion and in each box in the matrix the key details can be completed. The box can be used whether a single selection method was used or multiple methods. If multiple methods were used and contradictory information is found against any criterion, this can be noted in the decision-making process.

When more than one selector is involved there is some debate about how to gather and use the information and about the judgement of each selector. One way is for each selector to assess the information collected separately, and then for all selectors to meet to discuss assessments. When this approach is used, there may be some very different assessments, especially if the interview was the only selection method used. Much heated and time-consuming debate can be generated, but the most useful aspect of this process is sharing the information in everyone's matrix to understand how judgements have been formed. This approach is also helpful in training interviewers.

Table 9.3

Selection criteria	Candidate 1	Candidate 2	Candidate 3	Candidate 4
Criterion a				
Criterion b				
Criterion c				
Criterion d				
Criterion e				
General comments				

An alternative approach is to fill in only one matrix, with all selectors contributing. This may be quicker, but the drawback is that the quietest member may be the one who has all the critical pieces of information. There is a risk that not all the information available may be contributed to the debate in progress.

Validation of selection procedures

We have already indicated that test scores may be validated against eventual job performance for each individual in order to discover whether the test score is a good predictor of success in the job. In this way we can decide whether the test should be used as part of the selection procedure in future. The same idea can be applied to the use of other individual or combined selection methods. Yet, despite the cost involved in selecting potential employees, few firms formally evaluate the success of their selection methods (CIPD, 2015b). Clifford (2008) presents a detailed methodology for evaluating selection methods and many organisations would benefit from its use.

SUMMARY PROPOSITIONS

9.1. Selection is a two-way process. The potential employer and the potential employee both make selection decisions.

9.2. Selection criteria are derived from person specifications and competency profiles and are essential to a structured and effective shortlisting process. Technology is increasingly used in shortlisting but can be problematic.

9.3. A combination of selection methods is usually chosen, based upon the job, appropriateness, acceptability, time, administrative ease, cost, accuracy and the abilities of the selection staff.

9.4. The most well-used selection methods are application forms, interviews (including those conducted by video and telephone), tests, group selection procedures, assessment centres and references. Online testing continues to increase.

9.5. A procedure for selection decision making needs to be agreed which can integrate all the selection information available.

9.6. Selection methods should be evaluated for their effectiveness.

GENERAL DISCUSSION TOPICS

1. It could be argued that the selection process identifies candidates who are competent in the selection process rather than candidates who are most competent to perform the job on offer. Discuss this in relation to all forms of selection.

2. 'It is unethical and bad for business to make candidates undergo appraisal at a selection assessment centre without providing detailed feedback and support.' Discuss.

THEORY INTO PRACTICE

Pearson and Daff (2011) report on a fascinating study of selection methods that are not reliant upon work experience or high levels of formal education, particularly in relation to tests requiring a high facility with a country's dominant language. They argue for a particular type of personality test that is not language dependent to support the employment of Australian Indigenous people in Australia.

The Discovery Session is a selection test designed to be free of cultural bias that has been used in Australia, New Zealand and other countries in the region. It uses coloured beads, tiles and shapes and requires the candidate to construct forms or recall patterns. This does not require the candidate to have English-language competence and can be delivered in any language. Across six activities, it tests eighteen types of aptitude which have been identified as predictive of good job performance. One activity, for example, involves a computer screen which displays seven lily pads and six frogs. The objective is to change the position of the frogs, as per a defined set of instructions. The activity requires seventeen precise moves and a total of three minutes is allowed to complete it. Assessment of the aptitudes of motivation, coordination and knowledge building is undertaken.

The test is easy to administer, cannot be distributed to other candidates and has the potential to predict high job performance. Most candidates have also responded positively to its use and found the exercises demanding but enjoyable. The authors argue that its popularity relates to its lack of invasiveness, a difficulty often experienced by non-English-language speakers in other tests. As a selection method, it has wider application to societies experiencing problems with drawing marginalised populations into the mainstream workforce. Often these workers are disadvantaged as they lack competency in the dominant language and are typically screened out during a selection process. Administration of the Discovery Session is oral and is acultural, allowing candidates to demonstrate their capacity to learn and potential job performance. Research is at an early stage but it may have a substantial contribution to make to effective selection.

Questions

1 This research is based in Australia. To what extent can its findings be applied to other countries where substantial numbers of prospective employees, often migrant or poorly educated workers, do not have the language in which selection tests are constructed as a first language? What are the implications of this?

2 How applicable are these selection techniques across a wide range of jobs?

3 What difficulties might you face in using these selection techniques?

Source: Adapted from Pearson, C. and Daff, S. (2011) 'Extending boundaries of human resource concepts and practices: An innovative recruitment method for Indigenous Australians in remote regions', *Asia Pacific Journal of Human Resources*, Vol. 49, No. 3, pp. 325–43.

FURTHER READING

CIPD (2015) *A Head for Hiring: The Behavioural Science of Recruitment and Selection*. London: CIPD.

This report discusses the application of behavioural science (a combination of behavioural economics and cognitive and occupational psychology) to the recruitment and selection process. It extends the traditional boundaries of factors that are considered relevant to these activities and creates interesting new insights into candidate behaviour.

Stone, D., Lukaszewski, K., Stone-Romero, E. and Johnson, T. (2012) 'Factors affecting the effectiveness and acceptance of electronic selection systems', *Human Resource Management Review,* Vol. 23, pp. 50–70.

The authors argue that e-selection systems are now in widespread use and investigate the factors that influence their effectiveness and acceptance by candidates. Six stages of the selection process are considered: job analysis, job applications, pre-employment testing, interviews, selection decision making and validation of selection decisions. The authors also discuss potential adverse impacts in respect of applicant privacy and make recommendations in respect of system design and implementation.

Murphy, N. (2006) 'Voyages of discovery: Carrying out checks on job applicants', *IRS Employment Review,* No. 850, 7 July, pp. 42–8.

This article reports the results of a survey into employer practices to check the background details of applicants, and is much broader than seeking references from previous employers. It covers the type of information that is checked on, together with the mechanisms used.

Noon, M. (2012) 'Simply the best? The case for using threshold selection in hiring decisions', *Human Resource Management Journal,* Vol. 22, pp. 76–88.

This article argues for the use of 'threshold selection', a progressive approach to diversity and inclusion incorporating positive discrimination, in the selection process. It is interesting for this reason but it is also a very useful article as, in arguing for threshold selection, it presents an insightful critique of selection processes and the influence of expediency, politics and professionalisation on these.

REFERENCES

Branine, M. (2008) 'Graduate recruitment and selection in the UK', *Career Development International,* Vol. 13, pp. 497–513.

Breaugh, J. (2009) 'The use of biodata for employee selection: Past research and future directions', *Human Resource Management Review,* Vol. 19, pp. 219–31.

Brockett, J. (2011) 'KPMG launches "immersive" graduate assessment centre', *People Management,* www.peoplemanagement.co.uk/pm/articles/2011/10/kpmg-launches-immersive-graduate-assessment-centre.htm (accessed 29 May 2013).

Broughton, A., Foley, B., Ledermaier, S. and Cox, A. (2013) 'The use of social media in the recruitment process', Research Paper, March. London: Acas.

Burch, G. and Anderson, N. (2008) 'The team selection inventory: Empirical data from a New Zealand sample', *Asia Pacific Journal of Human Resources,* Vol. 46, pp. 241–52.

CIPD (2015a) *Resourcing and Talent Planning: Annual survey report.* London: CIPD.

CIPD (2015b) *A Head for Hiring.* London: CIPD.

Clifford, B. (2008) 'How to . . . evaluate your selection process', *People Management,* www.peoplemanagement.co.uk/pm/articles/2008÷01/howtoevaluateyourselectionprocess.htm (accessed 29 May 2013).

Dalen, L., Stanton, N. and Roberts, A. (2001) 'Faking personality questionnaires in selection', *Journal of Management Development,* Vol. 20, pp. 729–41.

Davison, H., Maraist, C., Hamilton, R. and Bing, M. (2012) 'To screen or not to screen? Using the internet for selection decisions', *Employee Rights and Responsibilities Journal,* Vol. 24, pp. 1–21.

Heggestad, E., Morrison, M., Reeve, C. and McCloy, R. (2006) 'Forced-choice assessments of personality for selection: Evaluating issues of normative assessment and faking resistance', *Journal of Applied Psychology*, Vol. 91, pp. 9–24.

IDS (2004) 'IDS Study Plus: Psychological tests', *IDS Study 770*. London: IDS.

IDS (2005) 'Assessment centres', *IDS Study 800*. London: IDS.

IRS (2002) 'Psychometrics: The next generation', *Employment Review*. London: IRS.

Johnson, R. and Guetal, H. (2013) 'Research-based tips for increasing the effectiveness of e-selection: Part I', *Workforce Solutions Review*, October/November, pp. 4–7.

Kirton, G. and Healey, G. (2009) 'Using competency-based assessment centres to select judges: Implications for diversity and equality', *Human Resource Management Journal*, Vol. 19, pp. 302–18.

Lockyer, C. and Scholarios, D. (2004) 'Selecting hotel staff: Why best practice does not always work', *International Journal of Contemporary Hospitality Management*, Vol. 16, pp. 125–35.

May, L. (2012) 'References', *People Management*, www.peoplemanagement.co.uk/pm/articles/2012/07/references.htm (accessed 29 May 2013).

Murphy, N. (2005) 'Got your number: Using telephone interviewing', *IRS Employment Review*, Vol. 832, pp. 43–5.

Pearson, C. and Daff, S. (2011) 'Extending boundaries of human resource concepts and practices: An innovative recruitment method for Indigenous Australians in remote regions', *Asia Pacific Journal of Human Resources*, Vol. 49, No. 3, pp. 325–43.

Pellizzari, M. (2011) 'Employers' search and the efficiency of matching', *British Journal of Industrial Relations*, Vol. 49, pp. 29–53.

Robertson, I. (2001) 'Undue diligence', *People Management*, Vol. 7, pp. 42–3.

Roth, P., Bobko, P., Iddekinge, C. and Thatcher, J. (2016) 'Social media in employee-selection-related decisions: A research agenda for uncharted territory', *Journal of Management*, Vol. 42, pp. 269–98.

Schmidt, F. and Hunter, J. (1998) 'The validity and utility of selection methods in personnel psychology: Practical and theoretical implications of 85 years of research findings', *Psychological Bulletin*, Vol. 124, pp. 262–74.

Searle, R. (2003) *Selection and Recruitment: A Critical Text*. Milton Keynes: The Open University.

Spray, J. (2010) 'How to . . . run an assessment centre', *People Management*, www.peoplemanagement.co.uk/pm/articles/2010/01/how-to-run-an-assessment-centre.htm (accessed 29 May 2013).

Stone, D., Deadrick, D., Lukaszewski, K. and Johnson, R. (2015), 'The influence of technology on the future of human resource management', *Human Resource Management Review*, Vol. 25, pp. 216–31.

Suff, R. (2005) *Centres of Attention*. London: IRS Employment Review.

Syedain, H. (2013) *The New Rules of Recruitment*, http://www.cipd.co.uk/pm/peoplemanagement/b/weblog/archive/2013÷06÷23/the-new-rules-of-recruitment.aspx

Thornton, G. and Gibbons, A. (2009) 'Validity of assessment centres for personnel selection', *Human Resource Management Review*, Vol. 19, pp. 169–87.

Whiddett, S. and Hollyforde, S. (2003) *The Practical Guide to Competencies*. London: CIPD.

Woodruffe, C. (2000) *Development and Assessment Centres: Identifying and Assessing Competence*. London: Institute of Personnel and Development.

CHAPTER 10
EMPLOYABILITY: SKILLS IN RESOURCING

THE OBJECTIVES OF THIS CHAPTER ARE TO:

1 Explain the skills of determining a vacancy

2 Explore job and competency analysis skills, all as preliminaries to the recruitment process, and

3 Explore selection interview skills

10.a. Determining the Vacancy

Recruitment begins with a vacancy. It may be through someone resigning and leaving a gap to be filled. A typical situation is when a section head rings the HR person and says, 'Mabel Richards has announced she's leaving, which presents me with a real problem. Can you get an ad in straight away?'; a knee-jerk reaction. This is where the HR person questions the assumptions behind the request. Is there an alternative? This could be an opportunity:

- to reorganise the work in the section so that what has to be done is rethought and redistributed. This could lead to simple improvements in efficiency, making a replacement for Mabel unnecessary.

- to use some overtime or stagger the hours of the remaining people perhaps?

- Do the remaining people have any suggestions? They certainly have an interest and will probably know the reality of what actually happens in the section better than the head does.

WINDOW ON PRACTICE

A company making flight simulators for airlines had production pods designing and making the electronics in line with the requirements of individual airlines. Each pod was staffed by a team of very well qualified experts, typically with PhDs in physics or electronic engineering, and they usually had two or three orders to run at the same time. They reported to two people, a technical expert who was as up-to-date as the rest of them, whom they held in high regard, and a manager, who used to be highly skilled but now spent his time in his office 'looking after the money side of things'.

One member of the team, Alice, took maternity leave, fully intending to return after her full leave entitlement. The manager assumed they would recruit a replacement straight away and that they would 'have to deal with Alice's return-to-work rights when the time comes. She may not want to come back anyway'. The technical expert was not sure: 'I'm certain she will come back. She's very keen and she runs rings round the rest of them. Let's see what they think.' The team members talked it through over coffee and decided that they could cover for Alice while she was away, although they were not pleased about the 'runs rings round' comment. It would help to have a newish graduate on six- to twelve-months' work experience to do some of the simpler stuff.

After twelve months Alice had returned, and the manager had left and was not replaced after it was realised that his 'job' was simply collecting information from the team, which he then displayed in charts on the wall of his office. Two members had already guessed this and developed a simple method of creating sets of figures that could be submitted as required and without any adverse effects that they could discover. Two electronics students took six months' work experience placements before the final year of their four-year masters' degrees and subsequently were recruited to jobs elsewhere in the company.

The section head may dismiss all the tentative suggestions on how to proceed as ridiculous, but the process of determining the vacancy has begun. Job analysis is the next step.

Vacancies also occur when a business is expanding: more business = more jobs and vacancies to be filled. To a great extent the determination of the vacancy is the same as with the Mabel Richards resignation. The business is the same, with the same policies and procedures; an HGV driver working from Birmingham will have a job similar to one working from a branch in Newcastle.

A different situation is when there is an organisational change requiring adaptation to a shaken-up workplace; jobs are now different and require retraining of employees. If some of the new jobs require new skills that cannot come by retraining, these create no more than a prima facie case for recruitment. Recruiting a new employee may be the most obvious tactic but it is not necessarily the most appropriate; there may be other ways of filling the gap, such as subcontracting the work. If your decision is that you are going to recruit, there are three questions to answer in determining the vacancy:

1 What does the job consist of? Here the next step is job analysis, which will also be necessary for subcontracting.

2 In what way is it to be different from the job done previously? Looking at the job analysis, what are the aspects of the job that specify the type of candidate? This is the first necessity for any advertisement for the post(s). Here is where the job specification starts.

3 What are the key aspects of the job that the ideal candidate wants to know before deciding to apply? This takes the job specification and develops the further particulars that are provided for those expressing an interest.

SUMMARY PROPOSITIONS

10.a.1. When a vacancy occurs it should not be filled until the nature of the job opening has been identified. It might be left unfilled, or only filled after reorganising the work of other post holders.

10.a.2. The post might need to be rethought because of a change in circumstances requiring different skills to those of the previous incumbent.

10.a.3 If a vacancy is to be filled the next questions are:
   a. What does the job consist of and how is it different from the job done previously?
   b. How does the nature of the job specify the appropriate type of candidate?
   c. What are the features of the job that will appeal to appropriate candidates?

GENERAL DISCUSSION TOPICS

10.a.1. In what circumstances might a manager automatically recruit when a vacancy arises and in what circumstances might a manager be keen to avoid immediately replacing the leaver?

10.a.2. Why may managers be tempted to automatically recruit in the likeness of the person leaving?

PUTTING IT INTO PRACTICE

1 Download or clip from a newspaper, magazine or similar medium three or four advertisements for similar jobs. Compare the clarity and effectiveness of each in describing the job and the candidate specification to potential candidates.

2 Using no more than the average number of words in the pieces you have read, draft an advertisement for your own job (or one you have had in the past). How clear and effective have you been in appealing to potential candidates?

10.b. Job Analysis

Job analysis collects and analyses information about the tasks, responsibilities and context of jobs, and then collates them into some form of job description. We place this area of skill in the same part of the text as recruitment and selection, but it can also be applied in other areas such as performance, development and reward.

The information to be collected

While the exact data will be affected by the specific purpose of job analysis, in general the following data needs to be collected:

1 **Job identification data.** Job title and location; department; division; company name.

2 **Purpose of job.** Overall purpose such as to 'ensure an effective marketing package is up and running as soon as product is licensed or delivered'.

3 **Job content/tasks.** Actual tasks or duties such as level of responsibility for tasks; importance of tasks; and how often they are performed.

4 **Performance standards/objectives.** These can be either for the job as a whole or specific tasks. They can be expressed in quantitative terms such as amount of output or sales, budgets or time limits to meet; or in qualitative terms such as maintaining group cohesiveness.

5 **Relationships with others.** This includes reporting relationships, supervisory relationships, liaison with others and coordinating relationships.

6 **Working conditions.** This includes the physical environment, such as heat, noise, light, accident and health risks, hours of work and any unusual times of work; pay and benefits; opportunity for flexibility in working hours or place of work; whether working in a group or alone.

7 **Human requirements.** The physical and psychological characteristics of the individual who could fulfil the demands of the job, for example (potential) strength and stamina requirements for a physical job such as greenkeeper, builder's labourer or walk leader. Psychological requirements may be tolerance of tight deadlines; calmness and confidence in a constantly busy environment or in the face of angry customers, such as in an airport.

Methods of collecting the data

There is a wide range of methods that may be used, and it is often a good idea to use more than one as a cross-check. Here are two methods in more detail.

Work diaries

This method requires the job participant to fill in a structured log of his or her daily activities over a period, the period being determined by the nature of the job. It would be no good asking a shop assistant to log the tasks for Monday to Wednesday if deliveries take place only on Thursdays and Saturdays. Similarly, asking an administrative assistant to make a log for a two-week period at the beginning of the month is of no use when there are end-of-month tasks that this does not cover. Asking a greenkeeper to log tasks for a month over the summer, when winter tasks are completely different, will be of little help. Professional jobs are usually even more varied and unpredictable. So some assessment of the nature of the job needs to take place before deciding whether work diaries will be a good method to analyse a job. Table 10.1 shows a structure that might be used for a work diary.

This structure is useful as it allows the job holder to note everything done at the time, rather than trying to remember it all, probably badly, at the end of the day. It is like an eating diary, if a person wants to lose weight, so that when it is analysed at the end of the week a picture will emerge that the person is probably not aware of, as they are so immersed in the day-to-day or minute-to-minute nature of their lives and eating. Thus trends and patterns emerge that the individual is not aware of. For example, 'I can see that in the mornings I eat a healthy breakfast and snack on fruit; I usually eat a healthy lunch and nothing in the afternoon; in the evening I eat crisps/nuts before my meal and will often eat two or three puddings and maybe more crisps.' Or, in another case, 'I can see that I spend half my time in meetings with employees from other departments and my role is usually to persuade others of the type of marketing strategy I think appropriate; and I spend 20% of my time on the phone answering queries about marketing material.' In other words, the job holders could not have expressed the nature of their job as accurately without this attention to detail over a particular period.

Table 10.1 An example of the structure of a work diary

Start time	End time	Task purpose	Task actions	Who else is involved	Means of communicating with others involved	Importance of task rate 1 to 10	Urgency of task rate 1 to 10	Who is responsible for decisions made	Other information
9.30	10.40	Agree structure of new induction programme for research staff	Act as chair of meeting + take notes	2 staff who report to me in the dept. + rep from HR	Face to face	7	10	I sign it off	

ACTIVITY 10.1

Try to keep a work diary for a week using the format suggested, or adapt this to better meet your needs.

1 What have you learnt about your job?

2 What other questions do you wish you had included in the work diary format?

3 Explain your experience of filling out a work diary. Would you recommend it as a method of job analysis? Justify your view.

However, this mass of information requires vast amounts of time to be analysed, and time costs money. Another problem with this approach is that the individuals completing the diaries may get bored and adopt a slapdash approach. Or they may become fretful that yet another task has been added to their already overloaded day.

Individual interviews

These are a fast and holistic means of collecting job data, and can be conducted with job holders, supervisors and perhaps peers and subordinates. Semi-structured interviews are probably most useful, so that a range of topics and questions can be designed in advance, but there is still the opportunity to probe for details and follow up on unexpected information. An HR specialist is usually the most appropriate person to do this. The disadvantage with interviews is that processed data rather than raw data is collected as with work diaries. In other words, we find out what the job holders *think* they do rather than what they actually do. Some sample interview questions are given in the Window on practice below. You would need to adapt these questions so that they are relevant to the level and type of job which you are analysing.

WINDOW ON PRACTICE

Some basic questions for the job holder:

1 What is your job title and location in the organisation structure?

2 Where physically do you work? What/who determines this?

3 What hours of work do you do and what/who determines this?

4 Who do you report to directly, and who reports directly to you?

5 What is the overall purpose of your job?

6 How do you know when this purpose is achieved; and/or what standards are applied to the achievement of this purpose?

7 What tasks do you have to carry out to achieve this?

8 How frequently do these tasks need to be carried out?

9 Which are the most important/critical tasks, and what makes them so important?

10 Who do you have to liaise or work with to achieve your job tasks and purpose?

11 For what tasks do you have decision-making authority?

12 What tasks do you carry out which do not relate to the achievement of your purpose?

13 What do these tasks achieve, and what would happen if you did not do them?

14 What other things about your job have we not covered?

Competency analysis

This is not another way of describing jobs, but a way of describing the capacities or competencies that people need to bring with them if they are going to be able to do the job; it is a preliminary to the personnel specification. It has other uses, mainly in training and development, but here we are placing it in recruitment and selection. Some competencies are widely applicable across a number of jobs as a result of general education and experience, such as self-confidence. Others are much narrower and more specific, such as competence with Excel, PowerPoint and Web publishing.

There is no 'official' list of core competencies that are widely applicable, but some of the most common are:

- Interpersonal skills (we prefer the term 'being effective with people').
- Planning and organisation.
- Team working.
- Group leadership.
- Accepting responsibility for the work of others.
- Critical thinking.
- Commercial awareness.
- Strategic awareness.

These are mainly simply starting points for refining to suit the situation of the business and its objectives. There will be other specific competencies relating to the working situation of the prospective recruit, for instance working overseas.

WINDOW ON PRACTICE

An international London-based bank decided to create the post of HR Director, Middle East. The following is an adapted version of a confidential memorandum circulated to certain categories of senior staff:

> We have decided to create the post of HR Director, Middle East. The person appointed will be based in one of the region's capital cities, although the final decision will be made only after widespread consultation. The general experience and competencies needed

are those of all recipients of this memorandum because of the position they already hold. The main objective is to ensure that the Bank's overall strategy is implemented in the region by all our expatriate and local employees and subcontractors. It is important that all the Bank's policies on employment should be followed, taking due account of cultural and political differences. If the Director believes that specific variations are needed, these should be discussed with London's HR Director before implementation.

The appointment will be made in the first instance for three years. The usual arrangements will be offered to spouses and other family members for whom the Director is expected to offer reasonable and appropriate care. London will offer orientation on matters like living in a very different physical, social and cultural environment. The Director will need to work at a diplomatic level of regional governments. A family member who was willing to assist with some of the social events, and whose assistance would be welcome, could be a great help to the Bank, but there is no obligation on anyone to help in this way.

The Director needs to work with a full appreciation of local social conventions and political differences. Although English is the working language of politics, diplomacy, banking and business in the region, some facility with Arabic would be useful. Our consultants on such matters say they could provide the necessary intensive tuition to produce an acceptable level in four to six weeks. Any recipient of this memorandum having a potential interest in this post should speak to Mrs . . . , PA to the Managing Director, so she can arrange a private and confidential meeting away from the office for him to discuss things further with the enquirer.

A set of competencies for a prospective appointment will feed in to the advertisement and the job description.

SUMMARY PROPOSITIONS

10.b.1. Job redefinition is followed by job analysis, which is a systematic method of detailed analysis of what the job is.

10.b.2. Competencies describe the qualities needed to do the job. Together with job analysis, it feeds into the job specification, the advertisement and further particulars for applicants.

GENERAL DISCUSSION TOPICS

On what occasions might a thorough job analysis be critical, and what reasons support your choice?

PUTTING IT INTO PRACTICE

Consider a well-known person who interests you, such as sporting or music celebrity, and produce a definition of their job, using the ideas above.

Re-read the Window on practice about the banking vacancy and write out a set of competencies needed for the post

Locate in a magazine, or on the internet, a job advertisement for a post that might interest you and for which you feel adequately qualified. How well defined is it? How effective do you think it will be in appealing to people like you? Will you apply? If not, what are the crucial bits of information that you think would be helpful to you, and reasonable for the recruiters, to include?

10.c. The Selection Interview

In the selection interview the interviewer is trying to obtain information from an applicant in order to form a judgement about that person for a particular job or position in an organisation, working with a particular group of working colleagues. At the same time those being interviewed are presenting information to influence that decision and collecting information that will help them decide whether they want the job or not. This fact of *exchange* has led personnel/HR texts to describe the interview as 'a two-way conversation with a purpose'. This comfortable axiom is largely accurate but misses an important element, that the interviewer is in charge, setting the agenda, controlling the development, deciding when to close and making the key judgement: yes or no. Candidates may decide not to take the job; even if it is offered, they would still like to have the ego boost of refusing. The interviewer needs to set the agenda and lead the interview.

Varieties of selection interview

There are working situations where the amount of discussion between the parties is limited to perfunctory exchanges about trade union membership, hours of work and rates of pay; labourers on building sites and extras on film sets being two examples. As interviews move up the organisational hierarchy there is growing equilibrium, with the interviewer becoming more courteous and responsive to questions from the applicant, who will probably be described as a 'candidate' or someone who 'might be interested in the position'. For the most senior positions it is less likely that people will be invited to respond to vacancies advertised in the press, although equality legislation is leading to more senior positions being openly advertised. Likely candidates may be approached, either directly or through consultants, and there will be an elaborate ritual in which each party tries to persuade the other to declare an interest first.

The purpose of the interview is threefold:

- to collect information in order to predict how well the applicants would perform in the job for which they have applied, by measuring them against predetermined criteria;

- to provide candidates with full details of the job and organisation to facilitate their decision making;

- to conduct the interview in such a way that candidates feel that they have been given a fair hearing.

Handling this most crucial of encounters is a key skill for HR people as the interview has a number of important advantages which cannot be provided by any other means. It cannot be bettered as a means of exchanging information and meeting the human and ritual aspects of the employment process.

Human and ritual aspects

An interview enables the parties to assess matters that cannot be approached in any other way, such as the potential compatibility of two people who will have to work together. Both parties need to meet before the contract begins, to 'tune in' to each other and begin the process of induction. The interview is valuable in that way to both potential employee and potential employer. It gives applicants the feeling that they matter, as another person is devoting time to them and they are not being considered by a computer. Also, giving applicants a chance to ask questions underlines their decision-making role, making them feel less helpless in the hands of the all-powerful interviewer. Selection interviewing has important ritual elements, as the applicants are seeking either to enter, or to rise within, a social system. This means that they defer to the interviewer more than they would in other situations.

At the same time those who are already inside and above display their superiority and security, even unconsciously, in contrast with the behaviour of someone so obviously anxious to share the same privileged position. Reason tells us that this is inappropriate in the twenty-first century as the books are full of advice to interviewers not to brandish their social superiority, but to put applicants at their ease and to reduce the status differentials. This, however, still acknowledges their superiority as they are the ones who take the initiative; applicants are not expected to help the interviewer relax and feel less apprehensive. Also the reality of the situation is usually that of applicants anxious to get in and selectors choosing among several. Status differentials cannot simply be set aside. The selection interview is at least partly an initiation rite, not as elaborate as entry to commissioned rank in the armed forces, nor as whimsical as finding one's way into the Brownie ring, but still a process of going through hoops and being found worthy in a process where other people make all the rules.

ACTIVITY 10.2

For a selection interview in which you recently participated, either as selector or as applicant, consider the following:

1 What were the ritual features?

2 Were any useful ritual features missing?

3 Could ritual have been, in any way, *helpfully* reduced?

The approach to selection interviewing varies considerably from the amiable chat in a bar to the highly organised, multi-person panel.

Interview strategy

By far the most common strategy has been described as *frank and friendly*. Here the interviewer is concerned to establish and maintain a constructive tone for the exchanges; English has no better descriptor of this than the French *rapport*. This approach is taken in the belief that if applicants do not feel threatened, and are relaxed, they will be more forthcoming in the information that they offer. It is straightforward for both interviewer and interviewee and has the potential advantage that applicants will leave with a favourable impression of the business.

A variation is the *problem-solving approach*. The interviewer presents the candidate with a hypothetical problem and evaluates the answer. The questions asked are derived from the job description. Candidates are required to imagine themselves as the job holder and describe what they would do in a variety of hypothetical situations. This method is most applicable to testing elementary knowledge, such as the colour coding of wires in electric cables or maximum dosages of specified drugs. It is less effective for testing understanding and ability.

There is no guarantee that the candidate would actually behave in the way suggested. The quick thinker will score at the expense of those who can take action more effectively than they can answer riddles.

The *biographical* method focuses on the candidate's past behaviour and performance, which is a more reliable way of predicting future performance than asking interviewees what they would do in a certain situation. Candidates are asked to describe the background to a situation and explain what they did and why; what their options were; how they decided what to do; and the anticipated and real results of their action. The success of this method depends on in-depth job analysis, and preferably competency analysis, in order to frame the best questions. We have already seen that the focus on competencies is growing, as it deals first with the applicant's record and other evidence like test results and then moves to consider the work that needs to be done. For both the biographical approach is an excellent method.

Number of interviews and interviewers

There are two broad traditions governing the number of interviewers. One says that effective, frank discussion can only take place on a one-to-one basis, so candidates meet one interviewer, or several interviewers one at a time. The other tradition is that fair play must be demonstrated and nepotism prevented, so the interview must be carried out, and the decision made, by a panel of interviewers.

The individual interview

The individual interview gives the greatest chance of establishing rapport, developing mutual trust and is the most efficient deployment of time in the face-to-face encounter, as each participant has to compete with only one other speaker. It is usually also the most satisfactory method for the candidate, who has to tune in to only one other person instead of needing constantly to adjust to different interviewers. The candidate can more readily ask questions and it is the least formal method. The disadvantages lie in the reliance placed on the judgement of one person, although this can be mitigated by a series of individual interviews. A sole interview with the line manager is very popular in the selection of people for manual work, being used in a third of all interviews. It is less popular for administrative and management posts.

Sequential interviews

Sequential interviews are a series of one-to-one interviews. The most frequent combination is an interview with the line manager and one with a representative of the HR department. For managerial posts this will be extended to interviews with other departmental managers, top managers and significant prospective colleagues. Sequential interviews can give the employer a broader picture of the candidate and they also allow the applicant to have contact with a greater number of potential colleagues. However, for the advantages of sequential interviews to be realised there is a need for effective organisation and for all interviews to be held on the same day. All interviewers meet beforehand to agree on the requirements of the post and to decide how each will contribute to the overall theme. Immediately after the interviews candidates can be jointly evaluated at a further meeting. One disadvantage is the organisation and time that it takes from both the employer's and the candidate's point of view. It requires considerable commitment from the candidate, who may have to keep repeating similar information and whose performance may deteriorate throughout the course of the interviews due to fatigue.

Panel interviews

The panel interview method has the specious appeal of sharing judgement and may appear to be a way of saving time in interviewing as all panel members are operating at once. It is also possible to legitimise a quick decision, always popular with candidates, and there can be no doubt about the ritual requirements being satisfied. Personal bias is reduced, particularly in guarding against possible infringements of legal requirements.

Panel interviews can also ensure the candidate is acceptable to the whole organisation, and allow the candidate to get a good feel for the business and its culture. The drawbacks lie in the tribunal nature of the panel. They are not having a conversation with the candidates; they are sitting in judgement upon them and assessing the evidence they are able to present in response to the panel's requests. There is little prospect of building rapport and developing discussion, and there is likely to be as much interplay between members of the panel as there is between the panel and the candidate.

Panel interviews tend towards over-rigidity and give ironic point to the phrase 'it is only a formality'. They are ritualistically superb, but dubious as a useful preliminary to employment. However, the benefits of the panel interview can be increased, and the disadvantages reduced, if the interviewers are properly trained and the interview well organised, thoroughly planned and made part of a structured selection process.

ACTIVITY 10.3

In your organisation how many interviews and interviewers are used? How effective is this approach and why? In what ways could it be improved?

The selection interview sequence

Preparation

The preliminaries of job analysis, recruitment and shortlisting are complete and the interview is now to take place. The first step is for the interviewers to brief themselves by checking the job description or similar details of the post to be filled, the candidate specification or statement of required competencies, and the application forms or curricula vitae of the candidates.

If there are several people to be interviewed the interview timetable needs greater planning than it usually receives. The time required for each interview can be determined beforehand only approximately. A rigid timetable will weigh heavily on both parties, who will feel frustrated if the interview is closed arbitrarily at a predetermined time. If an interview that has 'finished' is drawn out to complete its allotted time span it becomes increasingly artificial and exasperating. However, the disadvantages of keeping people waiting are considerable and underrated.

Most candidates will have competing calls on their time, as they will have taken time off to attend and have earmarked the anticipated interview time to fit into a busy schedule. Some may have other interviews to go to. An open-ended waiting period can be worrying, enervating and a poor preliminary to an interview. If the dentist keeps you waiting you may get distressed, but when the waiting is over you are simply a passive participant and the dentist does not have the success of the operation jeopardised. The interview candidate has, in a real sense, to perform when the period of waiting is over and the success of the interaction could well be jeopardised.

The best timetable is the one that guarantees a break after all but the most voluble candidates. If candidates are asked to attend at hourly intervals, for example, this would be consistent with interviews lasting between forty and sixty minutes. This would mean that each interview begins at the scheduled time and that the interviewers have the opportunity to review and update their notes in the intervals. The whole plan can still go wrong if one or more candidates fail to turn up.

Reception

Candidates arrive on the premises of their prospective employer on the lookout for every scrap of evidence they can obtain about the business and its people. A candidate is likely to meet at least one and possibly two people before meeting the interviewer. First will be the receptionist. There is frequently also an emissary from the HR department to shepherd them from the front door to the waiting room. Both are valuable sources of information, and interviewers may wish to prime such people so that they can see their role in the employment process and can be cheerful, informative and helpful.

The candidate will most want to meet the interviewer, the unknown but powerful figure on whom so much depends. Interviewers easily forget that they know much more about the candidates than the candidates know about them, because the candidates have provided a personal profile in the application form. Interviewers do not reciprocate. To bridge this gap it can be useful to introduce themselves to the candidate in the waiting room, so that contact is made quickly, unexpectedly and on neutral territory. This makes the opening of the interview itself rather easier.

Candidates wait to be interviewed. Although there are snags about extended, open-ended waiting periods, some extra time is inevitable and necessary to enable candidates to compose themselves and visit the toilet. It is a useful time to deal with travelling expenses and provide some relevant background reading about the employing organisation.

Setting

The setting for an interview has to be right for the ritual and right from the point of view of enabling a full and frank exchange of information. It is difficult to combine the two. Many of the interview horror stories relate to the setting in which it took place. A candidate for a senior local authority post was interviewed on a stage while the panel of seventeen sat in the front row of the stalls, and a candidate for a head teacher post came in to meet the interview panel and actually moved the chair on which he was to sit. He only moved it two or three inches because the sun was in his eyes, but there was an audible frisson and sharp intake of breath from the members of the panel.

Remaining with our model of the individual interviewer, here are some simple suggestions about the setting:

- The room should be suitable for a private conversation.
- If the interview takes place across a desk, as is common, the interviewer may wish to reduce the extent to which the desk acts as a barrier, inhibiting free flow of communication.
- All visitors and telephone calls should be avoided, as they do not simply interrupt: they intrude and impede the likelihood of frankness.
- It should be clear to the candidates where they are to sit.

Interview structure

There are several important reasons why the employment interview should be structured, making use of the application or CV:

- The candidate expects the proceedings to be decided and controlled by the interviewer and will anticipate a structure within which to operate.
- It helps the interviewer to make sure that all relevant areas are covered and irrelevancies avoided.
- Structure can be used to guide the interview and ensure that it makes sense.
- It assists the interviewer in using the time available in the most effective way.
- The application form can be used as a memory aid by the interviewer when making notes directly after the interview or during it.
- It makes it easier to compare candidates.

The interview

There are several different ways to structure the interview. We recommend the form set out in Table 10.2; this divides activities and objectives into three interview stages: opening, middle and closing.

While there are few, if any, alternative satisfactory ways for conducting the beginning and the end of the interview, the middle can be approached from a number of different angles, depending on the circumstances. The interviewer needs to work systematically

Table 10.2 Interview structure: a recommended pattern

Stage	Objectives	Activities
Opening	To put the candidate at ease, develop rapport and set the scene	Greet candidate by name Introduce yourself Explain interview purpose Outline how purpose will be achieved Obtain candidate's assent to outline
Middle	To collect and provide information	Ask questions within a structure that makes sense to the candidate, such as biographical areas of the application form, or competencies identified for the job Listen Answer questions Summarise interview
Closing	To close the interview and confirm future action	Check candidate has no more questions Indicate what happens next and when

through the structure that has been planned, but not too rigidly, abandoning his or her own route whenever the candidate chooses one that seems more promising.

The opening of the interview is the time for mutual preliminary assessment and tuning in to each other. A useful method is for the interviewer to sketch out the plan or procedure for the interview and how it fits into the total employment decision process. The application form may provide an easy, non-controversial topic for these opening behaviours.

One objective is for the two parties to exchange words so that they can feel reasonably comfortable with each other. Interviewers who can do this can then further develop a relationship in which candidates trust the interviewer's ability and motives so that they speak openly and fully. The interviewer's effectiveness will greatly depend on being skilled at this process.

We are working on the assumption that candidates will behave in a reasonably genuine way, provided the interviewer can convince them that the process is fair. Some candidates do not and such people have been labelled as 'white-collar psychopaths', although it has to be said that they are rare. They are very good at presenting themselves as being exactly what the interviewer is looking for. Not only are they manufacturing the truth about their experience, but also the trait (or psychopathic tendency) that drives them causes them to wreak havoc once they are appointed. A New York psychologist cites the example of 'Ron' who was appointed to a sales post in a pharmaceuticals company:

> Ron fiddled his sales figures, charged call girls to the company and nearly succeeded in using his charm to get his new boss fired when he was questioned about his behaviour. Psychopaths are motivated by three things: thrill-seeking, game-playing and hurting people. Once inside the organisation they build networks of influence that make it very difficult to get rid of them and can help them join the management fast track. (Paul Babiak, quoted in Butcher 2004)

For the middle of the interview the biographical approach is the simplest. It works on the basis that candidates at the time of the interview are the product of everything in their lives that has gone before. To understand the candidate the interviewer must understand the past and will talk to the candidate about the episodes of his or her earlier life, education and previous employment.

The advantage of this is that the objectives are clear to both interviewer and interviewee; there is no deviousness or 'magic'. Furthermore, the development can be logical and so aid the candidate's recall of events. Candidates who reply to enquiries about their choice of A-level subjects will be subconsciously triggering their recollection of contemporaneous events, such as the university course they took; questions about choice of university subject are likely to come next in the interview. The biographical approach is the simplest for the inexperienced interviewer to use as discussion can develop from the information provided by the candidate on the application form. Some version of sequential categories, such as employment, education and training, seems the most generally useful, but it will need the addition of at least two other categories: the work offered and the organisational context in which it is to be done. The middle of the interview can be structured by systematically working through items of the job description or the person specification. Increasingly, where competencies have been identified for the job, these are used as the basis of the structure.

In the preparatory stage of briefing, the interviewer will also prepare notes on two elements to incorporate in the plan: key issues and checkpoints. Key issues will be the two or three main issues that stand out from the application form for clarification or elaboration. This might be the nature of the responsibilities carried in a particular earlier post, the content of a training course, the reaction to a period of employment in a significant industry, or whatever else strikes the interviewer as being productive of useful additional evidence. Checkpoints are matters of detail that require further information: grades in an examination, dates of an appointment, rates of pay and so forth.

At the close of the interview the explanation of the next step needs especial attention. The result of the interview is of great importance to the candidates and they will await the outcome with anxiety. Even if they do not want the position they will probably hope to have it offered. The great merit of convention in the public sector is that the chosen candidate is usually told before the contenders disperse: the great demerit is that they are asked to say yes or no to the offer at once.

In the private sector it is unusual for an employment offer to be made at the time of the interview, so there is a delay during which the candidates will chafe. Their frustration will be greater if the delay is longer than expected and they may start to tell themselves that they are not going to receive an offer, in which case they will also start convincing themselves that they did not want the job either! It is important for the interviewer to say as precisely as possible when the decision will be made, but ensuring that the candidates hear earlier rather than later than they expect, if there is to be any deviation.

The interviewer will need to call into play certain key aspects of method:

1 Some data can be collected by simple observation of the candidate. Notes can be made about dress, appearance, voice, height and weight, if these are going to be relevant (and not unlawfully discriminatory), and the interviewer can also gauge the candidate's mood and the appropriate response to it by the non-verbal cues that are provided.

2 The remainder of the evidence will come from listening to what is said, so the interviewer has to be very attentive throughout, not only listening to the answers to questions, but also listening for changes in inflection and pace, nuances and overtones that provide clues on what to pursue further. The amount of time that the two spend talking is important, as an imbalance in one direction or the other will mean that either the candidate or the interviewer is not having enough opportunity to hear information. Being silent and deliberately leaving verbal lulls in face-to-face situations provide the opportunity for the other person to say more, perhaps more than was intended. Silence still has to be attentive and the longer it lasts, the harder it is to achieve this.

3 In order to have something to hear, the interviewer will have to direct the candidate by questioning, encouraging and enabling the candidate to talk, so that the interviewer can learn. The art of doing this depends on the personality and style of the interviewer, who will develop a personal technique through a sensitive awareness of what is taking place in the interviews.

The selection interviewer needs to distinguish between different types of question. In our introduction to face-to-face and communication skills we explained the difference in nature and usage of various questioning methods.

4 The best place for the interviewer to make notes is on the application form or CV. In this way they can be joined to information that the candidate has already provided and the peculiar shorthand that interviewers use when making notes during interviews can be deciphered by reference to the form and the data that the note is embellishing. It also means that the review of evidence after the interview has as much information as possible available on one piece of paper. An alternative is to record notes on the interview plan where the structure is based on job description, person specification or competencies. Interviewers are strangely inhibited about note taking, feeling that it in some way impairs the smoothness of the interaction. This apprehension seems ill-founded as candidates are looking for a serious, businesslike discussion, no matter how informal, and note taking offers no barrier, provided that it is done carefully in the form of jottings during the discussion, rather than pointedly writing down particular comments by the candidate which makes the interviewer seem like a police officer taking a statement.

5 Data exchange marks a change of gear in the interview. Establishing rapport is necessarily rather rambling and aimless, but data exchange is purposeful, with the interviewer controlling both the direction and the pace of the exchanges. Candidates will respond throughout to the interviewer's control, and the better the rapport, the more responsive they will be. Skilled interviewers close off areas of discussion and open fresh ones. They head off irrelevant reminiscences and probe where matters have been glossed over. They never abandon control. Even when the time has come for the candidates to raise all their queries, they will do this at the behest of the interviewer and will constantly look for a renewal of the mandate to enquire by using conversational prefixes such as, 'Can I ask you another question?', 'If it's not taking up your time, perhaps I could ask . . .?', 'I seem to be asking a lot of questions, but there was just one thing . . .'.

6 Closing the interview can be as skilful as opening it. Most of the suggestions so far have been to encourage a response, but it is easy to nod and smile your way into a situation of such cosy relaxation that the respondent talks on and on . . . and on. A surprising number of interviewers have great difficulty closing. These methods can help:

Braking slows the rate of talking by the candidate by working through a series of steps. You will seldom need to go beyond the first two or three, but five are described in case you have to deal with a really tough case.

a One or two closed questions to clarify specific points may stem the tide.

b Our facial expression changes with the brow furrowed to indicate mild disagreement, lack of understanding or professional anxiety. The reassuring nods stop and the generally encouraging, supportive behaviours of reward are withdrawn.

c Abstraction is when the eyes glaze over, showing that they belong to a person whose attention has now shifted away from the respondent and towards lunch.

d To look at one's watch during a conversation is a very strong signal indeed, as it clearly indicates that time is running out. Other, milder ways of looking away are: looking for your glasses, looking at your notes or looking at the aircraft making a noise outside the window. A rather brutal variant is to allow your attention to be caught by something the respondent is wearing, a lapel badge, a tie, a ring or piece of jewellery, maybe. Putting on your glasses to see it more clearly is really going too far!

e If all else fails, you simply have to interrupt.

Closing requires the interview to end smoothly. Future action is either clarified or confirmed. Also, candidates take a collection of attitudes away with them, and these can be influenced by the way the interview is closed. There is a simple procedure.

a First signal, verbal plus papers. The interviewer uses a phrase to indicate that the interview is nearing its end ('Well now, I think we have covered the ground, don't you? There isn't anything more I need to ask you. There's nothing further you want from me?'). In this way the interviewer signals the impending close at the same time as obtaining the candidate's confirmation. There is additional emphasis provided by some paper play. A small collection of notes can be gathered together and stacked neatly, or a notebook can be closed.

b Second signal, the interviewer confirms what will happen next ('There are still one or two people to see, but we will write to you no later than the end of the week').

c The final signal is to stand up: the decisive act to make the close. By standing up the interviewer forces the candidate to stand as well and there remain only the odds and ends of handshakes and parting smiles.

SUMMARY PROPOSITIONS

10.c.1. Despite criticisms and shortcomings, the selection interview remains a central feature of the recruitment and selection process.

10.c.2. Typical interview strategies are frank and friendly, problem solving and biographical.

10.c.3. Aspects of interview preparation are timetabling, reception and deciding the right setting.

10.c.4. Features of the interview itself are the opening for preliminary mutual assessment; data gathering involving a logical sequence, key issues and checkpoints; and the closure, which prepares candidates for the next step in the process.

GENERAL DISCUSSION TOPICS

10.c.1. This analysis of the selection interview assumes that the candidate is seeking to become an employee. How would the interview be different if the candidate were being interviewed with a view to becoming a freelance consultant doing work for the organisation rather than being an employee in it?

10.c.2. 'HR are constantly wanting to "involve me" in their recruitment and selection of staff. I'm too busy to spend time doing that. I want HR to do their job properly and send the people through to me when everything is sorted out and a new recruit is ready to start.' How do you react to that comment from an operations manager in an airline?

PUTTING IT INTO PRACTICE

For this exercise you need a cooperative, interested relative, or a very close friend, who would welcome interview practice.

1 Follow the sequence suggested in Table 10.2. to give your partner practice in being interviewed for a job, and giving yourself practice in interviewing and note taking.

2 After the interview, discuss your mutual feelings about the process around questions such as:

Selector	Did you ever feel you were being misled? When? Why?
Friend	Did you feel the interview got out of your control? When? Why?
	How could you have avoided the problem?
	How was your note taking?
Selector	What, if anything, made you bored or cross?
Both	What did you find most difficult?
	How comprehensive is the data you have collected?
Friend	Were you put at your ease?
	Were you at any time inhibited by the selector?
	Did you ever mislead the selector? When? How?
	Did the selector ever fail to follow up important points? When? Which?
	Were you in any way disconcerted by the note taking?
	Has the selector got a comprehensive set of data about you, so that you could feel any decision made about you would be soundly based?
Both	What did you think of the interview experience?

3 Now swap roles.

FURTHER READING

Job and competency analysis

Whiddett, S. and Hollyforde, S. (2003) *A Practical Guide to Competencies*. London: CIPD.
The title speaks for itself!

The selection interview

Anderson, N. and Shackleton, V. (1993) *Successful Selection Interviewing*. Oxford: Blackwell.
There short work deals with the conduct of the interview itself. This is still available and a very sound and practical read.

McDaniel, M.A., Whetzel, D.A., Schmidt, F.L. and Maurer, S.D. (1994) 'The validity of the employment interviews', *Journal of Applied Psychology*, Vol. 79, No. 19, pp. 599–616.
Provides research findings on interview validity.

Arthur, D. (2012) *Recruiting, Interviewing, Selecting and Orienting New Employees*. New York: Amacom.
Covers much more than the interview and an American approach; has been through five editions since 1986.

Chamorro-Premuzik, T. and Furnham, A. (2010) *The Psychology of Personnel Selection*. Cambridge: Cambridge University Press.

Williamson, L.G. *et al.* (1996) 'Employment interview on trial: Linking interview structure with litigation outcomes', *Journal of Applied Psychology*, Vol. 82, No. 6, pp. 900–12.
Not strictly relevant to selection, but an interesting piece of research.

REFERENCE

Babiak, P. (2004) quoted in Butcher, S., 'When the ideal applicant is too good to be true', *Financial Times*, 12 January 2004, p. 12.

PART 3

PERFORMANCE: SUCCESS THROUGH INDIVIDUAL AND COLLECTIVE ACHIEVEMENT

CHAPTERS

It is no good having all the right people all in the right places if they are not delivering the performance needed. This part of the text starts with consideration of how to manage individual employee performance. It has been suggested that there has been a general change of emphasis in attitude to the contract between the parties, away from a contract *of employment* towards a contract *for performance*. We all have to perform effectively. Performance management (Chapter 11) is an idea that has been developed to coordinate several features, especially targets, training, appraisal and payment, in order to deliver effectiveness.

A large part of achieving effective performance is getting the individual processes right, but within the organisational framework there are the teams, groups and individuals who do the work. Also within that framework we have to understand what it is that motivates people to perform and deploy leadership skills that match those motivations (Chapter 12). A key feature of this is the nature of leadership and how it is carried out effectively.

Engagement and retention (Chapter 13) are also critical to performance as an engaged workforce is more motivated to perform. People can be retained within the business by a series of strategies that sustains their interest and motivation as well as keeping the focus of their activities within an evolving organisation and a changing business context.

Also included, in Chapter 14, is the management of absence or of attendance. What is needed by organisations is not just managing processes which encourage people to attend, but also dealing with the problem of people being absent. These are separate issues, not simply alternative ways of wording the problem.

Employability, Chapter 15, deals with skills essential to the management of performance: conducting an appraisal interview, designing questionnaires (for engagement surveys, for example) and measuring labour turnover to inform retention activities. At the end of each chapter, you will find a case study in Putting it into practice which will help you to put these ideas into context and explore them more thoroughly.

CHAPTER 11

EMPLOYEE PERFORMANCE MANAGEMENT

THE OBJECTIVES OF THIS CHAPTER ARE TO:

1 Clarify the nature and purpose of performance management and performance appraisal

2 Outline the characteristics of performance management systems

3 Explain the stages of a typical performance management system

4 Evaluate the impact of varying national contexts on performance management

5 Evaluate the effectiveness of performance management systems in improving individual and organisational performance

Managing individual performance in organisations has traditionally centred on assessing performance and allocating reward, with effective performance seen as the result of the interaction between individual ability and motivation. Increasingly, it is recognised that planning and enabling performance have a critical effect on individual performance, with performance goals and standards, appropriate resources, guidance and support from the individual's manager all being central. The words 'performance management' are sometimes used to imply organisational targets, frameworks like the balanced scorecard, measurements and metrics, with individual measures derived from these. Here, however, we focus on softer developmental and motivational approaches to aligning the individual and the organisation that equate to good management practice. We begin by comparing and contrasting performance appraisal and performance management systems, before outlining the characteristics of a typical performance management system. We then consider in detail the component parts of performance management, drawing out their likely effectiveness in a range of national contexts. Finally, we evaluate the effectiveness of performance management systems in improving individual and thus organisational performance.

Performance management or performance appraisal?

Performance appraisal systems have operated in many organisations since the 1950s and are distinct from performance management systems, which have changed (and broadened) the nature of performance appraisal (Aguinis *et al.*, 2011). Here we compare and contrast performance management and performance appraisal. Detailed definitions of each can be found in Aguinis (2013) and Decramer *et al.* (2012).

Performance appraisal

Traditionally performance appraisal systems have provided a formalised process to review employee performance. They are centrally designed, usually by the HR function, and require each line manager to appraise the performance of staff, often in just one performance review meeting a year. Elaborate forms are completed as a record of the process, but these are not living documents. They are generally stored in the archives of the HR department, and the issue of performance is often then neglected until the next round of performance review meetings. But while performance appraisal has gradually been applied to wider groups of employees, beyond managers and professionals, there are concerns that appraisal systems are treated as an administrative exercise, are ineffective and do little to improve the future performance of employees. Aguinis *et al.* (2011) present a detailed discussion of the problems of performance appraisal.

Performance management systems

While many appraisal systems are still in existence and continue to be updated, performance management systems are recommended as a better way to manage employee performance. An appraisal/review process is incorporated into this but is distinct from a traditional appraisal system. We consider the performance appraisal interview later in the context of either an appraisal or a performance management system (see Chapter 15).

Aguinis and Pierce (2008: 139) provide a useful definition of performance management, stating that its essence is:

> a continuous process of identifying, measuring, and developing the performance of individuals and teams and aligning performance with the strategic goals of the organisation.

A strategic approach is thus adopted in which there is an attempt to ensure that employee efforts are directed to the achievement of organisational goals. Attention is paid to both task *and* contextual performance. Contextual performance is often addressed via the use of competencies (Hutchinson 2013) so that *how* something is achieved is as important as the results themselves. In this way, organisations seek to ensure long-term sustainable performance rather than quick wins which may damage ongoing business relationships. Employee development also becomes recognised as a key element of performance management and the emphasis is on an ongoing cycle of performance development. The system is line manager driven although, as Biron *et al.* (2011) note, senior management have an important role is setting strategic direction.

Many organisations now claim to operate performance management systems and Biron *et al.* (2011) present a detailed review of their uptake and application. Originally a private-sector phenomenon, performance management has now spread to the public sector in many countries (Tuytens and Devos 2012; Decramer *et al.* 2012) in support of neo-liberal agendas which seek to operate sectors such as health and education using business principles. It is also a global phenomenon. Aguinis and Pierce (2008), for example, suggest that over 90% of the multinational companies surveyed across fifteen countries implemented a performance management system and that this figure also reflects practice in Australian companies. Emerging economies, such as India (Gupta and Kumar 2013), are also recognising its importance. Almost all research into performance management emanates, however, from a western context (Briscoe and Claus 2008) and there is limited understanding of how effective these systems might be in other national contexts. We consider the implications of this throughout the chapter.

It is important to distinguish, as we have done here, between performance appraisal and performance management systems. There has been much hype since 2015 about many large firms 'abandoning' performance management. We present discussion of this in the following Window on practice and suggest that it is in fact performance appraisal that is being abandoned and that most firms will continue to operate systems of performance management.

WINDOW ON PRACTICE

Appraisals are finished: what next?

Kirton reports on an increasing trend to do away with performance appraisals. She cites Accenture, Google, Facebook and Netflix as examples of firms that no longer conduct annual performance reviews. This does not mean that these firms are not interested in managing employee performance. Quite the opposite; many of them are moving towards more frequent and less formal systems of discussing performance on the basis that these are likely to be more effective in improving performance. The emphasis is on coaching and developing a feedback culture. As we discuss throughout this chapter, it is these dynamic processes that are fundamental to effective performance management rather than a static performance appraisal. The death of performance management appears to be somewhat exaggerated.

Source: Adapted from http://www.cipd.co.uk/pm/peoplemanagement/b/weblog/archive/2015/08/20/appraisals-are-finished-what-next.aspx.

Characteristics of performance management systems

A view is emerging of performance management that centres on 'dialogue', 'shared under-standing', 'agreement' and 'mutual commitment', rather than rating for pay purposes. To this end organisations are increasingly suggesting that employees take more ownership of performance management (see Scott (2006) for a good example) and become involved in collecting self-assessment evidence throughout the year (Trosten-Bloom *et al.* 2014). Many organisations do, however, try to achieve both development and reward outcomes, which may undermine the motivational outcomes of development-focused approaches that encourage time spent with the line manager and two-way communication. Alterna-tively, where there is a measurement focus, performance management is seen as judge-mental, a chance to assess and get rid of employees, emphasises control and getting more out of staff, raises false expectations and is a way to manage the salaries bill. Krats and Brown (2013) have found that employees are generally more supportive of performance management systems when they are used for developmental rather than judgmental purposes.

We summarise the characteristics of performance management systems discussed in this section in Table 11.1.

Table 11.1 Characteristics of performance management systems

- Top-down link between business objectives and individual objectives (compared with performance appraisal where there may be no objectives, or objectives not explicitly linked to business objectives)
- Line manager driven and owned (rather than being owned by the HR function, as typically with performance appraisal)
- A living document where performance and development plans, support and ongoing review are documented as work progresses, and prior to annual review (rather than an archived document retrieved at appraisal time to compare achievement with intentions) .
- Performance is rewarded and reinforced

ACTIVITY 11.1

Think of the performance appraisal or performance management system at your place of work.

1 To what extent does it focus on development and to what extent does it focus on reward?

2 How, and how well, are each of these purposes achieved? Explain why this is.

3 What would you do to improve the system, and what impacts would these actions have?

In summary, performance management, as opposed to performance appraisal, provides strategic links to organisational objectives, provides ongoing feedback to improve performance and is a continuous process driven by management, rather than an annual event owned by HR (Aguinis and Pierce 2008). In this chapter, we discuss performance management systems. We use the term 'performance appraisal' to denote the review of performance comprised within these systems, *not* to describe traditional performance appraisal systems.

Theoretical bases of performance management

The conceptual foundation of performance management relies on a view that performance is more than ability and motivation. It is argued that clarity of goals is key in enabling the employee to understand what is expected and the order of priorities. In addition, goals themselves are seen to provide motivation. This is based on goal-setting theory (Locke and Latham 2006). Research to date suggests that for goals to be motivating they must be sufficiently specific, challenging but not impossible, and set participatively. Also the person appraised needs feedback on future progress.

Expectancy theory provides a second theoretical base for performance management as individuals will be motivated to act provided they expect to be able to achieve the goals set, believe that achieving the goals will lead to other rewards and believe that the rewards on offer are valued (Vroom 1964). Some performance management systems are development driven and some are reward driven, although Hendry *et al.* (2000) use expectancy theory to demonstrate the difficulties of reward-based systems. Linking performance management to reward was at one stage very common, but has decreased in popularity in recent years.

A final theoretical perspective that is emerging strongly in relation to performance management and appraisal is that of organisational justice. In recent years there has been a stream of papers that reinforce this (see e.g. Byrne *et al.* 2012; Dewettinck and van Dijk 2012; Gupta and Kumar 2013; Sharma *et al.* 2016). The three facets of organisational justice can be clearly linked to performance management:

- **Procedural justice:** this relates to the extent to which procedures are perceived to be fair and requires performance management procedures to be transparent and robust.

- **Distributive justice:** this relates to the perceived fairness of the allocation of outcomes. This is particularly important where performance management is linked to pay but is also relevant in relation to training, promotion and other similar outcomes of a performance management system.

- **Interactional justice:** this relates to the perceived quality of interpersonal treatment received and relates to performance appraisal but also to other interactions such as coaching and feedback.

The growing weight of evidence is persuasive that these forms of justice need to be demonstrated in order for performance management systems to achieve their potential in improving performance at both individual and organisational levels.

Performance management across national contexts

As we noted above, almost all research into performance management has been conducted in a western context and the implications for its effectiveness in other national contexts are not well understood (Briscoe and Claus 2008). Hofstede's work on the dimensions of national culture has informed early attempts to explore these issues (see e.g. Fletcher and Perry 2001; Milliman *et al.* 2002; Mendonca and Kanungo 1996) but there is little or no exploration of matters such as religion on performance management systems. We have written elsewhere, for example, about the tensions between Buddhist beliefs and providing negative feedback. It seems to be widely accepted, however, that national context will influence the operation of all aspects of these systems from the content or aim of the appraisal through objective setting to the review/appraisal stage, as well as influencing who provides the feedback and the process or style used. We consider this in more detail in each of the stages of the performance management process outlined below, providing an early indication of contextual implications for performance review in the next Window on practice.

WINDOW ON PRACTICE

Applicability of review/appraisal in different cultural settings

The way that an appraisal process is used may be affected by the cultural context in which it takes place. For example, Varma *et al.* (2005) compare the use of performance appraisal in manufacturing organisations in the USA and India using statistical analysis. They found that interpersonal affect (the like–dislike relationship between supervisor and subordinate) appeared to have no impact in performance appraisal rating given in the USA, but that in India supervisors inflated the rating of low performers. Varma *et al.* suggest that this may be due to local cultural norms and a collectivist Indian culture as opposed to an individualistic US culture, and a greater concern in India for positive relationships.

Another example is an event experienced by one of this text's authors when running a course on performance appraisal in the Czech Republic sometime after the Velvet Revolution. Managers on the course said that the use of performance appraisal would be entirely unacceptable at that time as workers would associate it with what had gone before under the communist regime. Apparently every year a list of workers was published in order of the highest to the lowest performer. Although this list was claimed to represent work performance, the managers said that in reality it represented degrees of allegiance to the Communist Party and was nothing to do with work performance.

Stages in a performance management system

Figure 11.1 shows a typical performance management system. The system is cyclical: it starts by defining the organisation/work group objectives and then moves to translate these into individual-level objectives and to specify the development required to achieve these. Performance is then delivered by the individual and monitored by the manager: this is the most important stage of the continuous cycle of performance management in which coaching may take place and ongoing feedback is provided. Finally there is an assessment of performance and (where appropriate) a link to reward before the cycle begins again. The main stages of the cycle are discussed in more detail below.

Business mission, values, objectives and competencies

There is an assumption that before it is able to plan and manage individual performance, the organisation will have made significant steps in identifying the performance required of the organisation as a whole. In most cases this will involve a mission statement so that performance is seen within the context of an overriding theme. In addition many organisations will identify the strategic business objectives that are required within the current business context to be competitive and that align with the organisation's mission statement. The efforts of senior management here are crucial to an effective performance management system that underpins organisational strategy (Biron *et al.* 2011).

Many organisations will also identify core values of the business and the key competencies required. Each of these has a potential role in managing individual performance. Organisational objectives are particularly important, as it is common for such objectives to be cascaded down the organisation in order to ensure that individual objectives contribute to their achievement (for an example of an objective-setting cascade, see Figure 11.2).

The cascade of strategic objectives is often, however, weak (Decramer *et al.* 2012). This may relate in part to the emergent, rather than rational, nature of organisational strategy.

Planning performance: a shared view of expected performance

Individual objectives derived from team objectives and an agreed job description can be jointly devised by manager and employee. These objectives are outcome/results orientated rather than task orientated, are tightly defined and include measures to be assessed. The

Figure 11.1
Stages of a typical performance management system

Key

Direction of objectives cascading down
the organisation.

Direction of feedback going up the organisation
in the process of agreeing objectives.

Figure 11.2
An objective-
setting cascade

objectives are designed to stretch the individual, and offer potential development as well as meeting business needs. It is helpful to both the organisation and the individual if objectives are prioritised. Many organisations use the 'SMART' acronym for describing individual objectives or targets:

- Specific
- Measurable
- Appropriate
- Relevant
- Timebound.

It is clearly easier for some parts of the organisation than others to set targets. There is often a tendency for those in technical jobs, such as computer systems development, to identify purely technical targets, reflecting the heavy task emphasis they see in their jobs. Moving staff to a different view of how their personal objectives contribute to team and organisational objectives is an important part of the performance management process. An objective for a team leader in systems development could be:

> To complete development interviews with all team members by end of July 2017 (written March 2017).

Clearly, the timescale for each objective will need to reflect the content of the objective and not timescales set into the performance management system. As objectives are met, managers and their staff need to have a brief review meeting to look at progress in all objectives and decide what other objectives should be added, changed or deleted. Five or six ongoing objectives are generally sufficient for one individual to work on at any time. A mix of objectives about new developments and changes as well as routine aspects of the job is generally considered to be appropriate.

Difficulties have, however, been experienced with purely results-focused objectives (the 'what') as there may be appropriate and inappropriate ways of achieving an objective. For example, a manager with an objective to ensure that another department agrees to a plan of action could achieve this in different ways. The manager may pressure the other department and force agreement through. This may alienate that department and damage future good relations. For this reason, it is recommended that organisations also set behavioural objectives, usually in the form of competencies, as to 'how' results are to be achieved (Hutchinson 2013). The requirement to display teamwork in achieving results might, for example, prevent the inappropriate behaviour described in the previous example. The use of competencies also supports a softer, developmental approach to performance management as opposed to a harder, target-driven approach. Further, it allows employees to achieve goals, even where they have relatively little influence over results (Williams 2002) and emphasising these developmental aspects has been shown to be effective in improving employee performance (Tuytens and Devos 2012). However, CIPD (2005) research demonstrating that only around a third of organisations actually use competencies in their performance management systems might suggest that many systems are not as developmentally focused as claimed. Dewettinck and van Dijk (2012) also argue that results are typically emphasised over development.

WINDOW ON PRACTICE

Leadership competencies in performance management

People managers at Microsoft are scored in a 'leadership league' to underline the drive for performance management, according to one of the company's HR business partners. As the software industry has become more complex and competitive, the company decided to develop its culture, and leadership competency is a very important part of the evolved culture. A spokesperson said:

> If a manager does not achieve excellence goals and good employee feedback, even if their business results are exceptional, they will not receive 'execution excellence'. This is part of Microsoft's performance review and is tied to salary increases and bonuses, so it's a real driver.

The league rating is partly based on the employee survey, which asked staff to rate how their manager interacted with the rest of business. League scores are based on the competencies in Microsoft's People Scorecard, which gives a performance snapshot and includes the employee feedback.

Source: People Management, 18 November 2009, http://www.cipd.co.uk/pm/ peoplemanagement/b/weblog/archive/2013/01/29/microsoft-uses-leadership-league- table-to-rate-managers-2009-11.aspx.

Objectives may also be set at the team rather than individual level (Aguinis and Pierce 2008). However, despite the claimed importance of teamworking, only 6% of organisations operate a team system (CIPD 2005). Supporting team and individual performance is a critical balancing act as there can be conflicts built into performance management activity causing employees' pursuit of individual objectives to damage the performance of the team they are in, and vice versa. Team objectives, however, might experience difficulties in the form of peer pressure and social loafing (see e.g. Clark 2005). Peer pressure can be experienced by an individual, such as, for example, the pressure not to take time off work when feeling ill, as this may damage the achievement of objectives; or pressure to work faster, make fewer mistakes and so on. Social loafing occurs in a situation where one or more team members rely on the others to put in extra effort to achieve objectives, to cover for their own lack of effort. It works when some members are known to be conscientious or competitive or to care deeply about the rewards available, and there are others who are likely to be less concerned and who know the conscientious team members will make sure by their own efforts that the objectives are achieved. Van Vijfeijken *et al.* (2006) provide a helpful discussion of managing the performance of teams.

Whether at team or individual level, establishing a *shared* view of performance is essential: handing out a job description or list of objectives/competencies to the employee is not adequate. Performance expectations need to be understood and, where possible, to involve a contribution from the employee. For example, although key accountabilities may be fixed by the manager, they will need to be discussed and the competencies required to achieve them identified. Planning the support, development (usually in the form of a personal development plan) and resources necessary for employees to achieve their objectives is imperative. A key benefit of performance management is that it directs training and development resources efficiently (Aguinis and Pierce 2008). Without this support it is unlikely that even the most determined employees will achieve the performance required.

Objective setting is not, however, a straightforward process. SMART targets can be problematic if they are not constantly reviewed and updated, although this is a time-consuming process. Pre-set objectives can be a constraining factor in such a rapidly changing business context, and they remind us of the trap of setting measurable targets, precisely because they are measurable and satisfy the system, rather than because they are most important to the organisation. A further concern with SMART targets is that they inevitably have a short-term focus, yet what is most important to the organisation is developments which are complex and longer term, which are very difficult to pin down to short-term targets. In this context systems which also focus on the development of competencies will add greater value in the longer term. There is, however, a long way to go to describe performance adequately and define what is really required for organisational success.

National context may also create challenges for the use of objectives and competencies. For example, we have argued that objective setting should be a joint activity between supervisor and employee. This notion of participation is, however, a western concept that does not translate well into countries where supervisors are expected to direct employees what to do and to assign them goals (Fenwick 2004). This respect for hierarchy is typically found in China where goals have to be both assigned and easily attainable, to avoid loss of face if not achieved (Lindholm *et al.* 1999). Chinese firms have also been shown to evaluate moral and ideological behaviour, rather than task achievement (Shen 2004), and in Indian workplaces personalised relationships are often privileged over the accomplishment of job objectives (Mendonca and Kanungo 1996). Much fuller understanding of the implications of these contexts for performance management is required.

Delivering and monitoring performance

While the employee is working to achieve the performance agreed, the manager retains a key enabling role. Organising the resources and off-job training is clearly essential. So too is being accessible. There may well be unforeseen barriers to the agreed performance that the manager needs to deal with, and sometimes the situation will demand that the expected performance needs to be revised. The employee may want to sound out possible courses of action with the manager before proceeding, or may require further information. Sharing 'inside' information that will affect the employee's performance is often a key need, although it is also something that managers find difficult, especially with sensitive information. Managers can identify information sources and other people who may be helpful.

Ongoing **coaching** during the task is especially important as managers guide employees through discussion and by constructive feedback. Managers can refer to practical job experiences to develop the critical skills and competencies that the employee needs, and can provide job-related opportunities for practice. Managers can identify potential role models to employees, help to explain how high achievers perform so well, and oil the organisational wheels. Coaching is an opportunity to both seek and deliver feedback – essential as feedback has been demonstrated to improve job performance, increase job satisfaction and discretionary behaviour and reduce intention to quit (Krasman 2013).

ACTIVITY 11.2

Think of any organisation in which you have had some involvement:

1 How has individual performance been supported?

2 How effective was/is this?

3 How would you improve the way in which performance was/is supported?

Employees carry out ongoing reviews to plan their work and priorities and also to advise the manager well in advance if the agreed performance will not be delivered by the agreed dates. Joint employee/manager review ensures that information is shared. For example, a manager needs to be kept up to date on employee progress, while the employee needs to be kept up to date on organisation changes that have an impact on the agreed objectives. Both need to share perceptions of how the other is doing in their role, and what they could do that would be more helpful.

These reviews are normally informal, although a few notes may be taken of progress made and actions agreed. They need not be part of any formal system and therefore can take place when the job or the individuals involved demand, and not according to a pre-set schedule. The review is to facilitate future employee performance, providing an opportunity for the manager to confirm that the employee is 'on the right track', redirecting him or her if necessary. The review thus provides a forum for employee reward in terms of recognition of progress. A 'well done' or an objective signed off as completed can enhance the motivation to perform well in the future. During this period evidence collection is also important to support ongoing assessment. Employees are expected to build up a portfolio of evidence of their performance over the period to increase the objectivity of reviews and to provide an audit trail to back up any assessment ratings. It is also during this part of the cycle that employees in many organisations can collect 360-degree feedback to be used developmentally and as part of an evidence base. This developmental approach may be problematic, however, in some national contexts. In countries such as China and Russia, for example, development through feedback may not be successful as managers are more likely to be reluctant to engage in two-way communication and the offer of direct feedback is not culturally acceptable (Fletcher and Perry 2001).

Formal performance review/appraisal

Regular formal reviews (perhaps once or twice each year) are required. A well-designed system will measure the extent to which set (ideally agreed) objectives have been met. When a competency profile has been identified for a particular job, it is also possible to use this in the appraisal of performance. Many systems combine competency assessment with assessment against objectives or job accountabilities. IRS (2005) reports that 89% of its respondents that used appraisals measured employees against objectives or goals, with 56% measuring against competencies and 53% measuring against pre-set performance standards, as might be used in a harder approach to performance improvement. In many organisations, employees are invited to assess their own performance and prepare an initial draft of their achievements. Performance measures may be either quantitative or qualitative. Qualitative appraisal is often an unstructured narrative on the general performance of the appraisee, although some guidance might be given about the areas on which the appraiser should comment. The problem with qualitative appraisals is that they may leave important areas unappraised, and that they are not suitable for comparison purposes. When using quantitative measures, it is common to use a Likert scale to rate performance with either numbers or letters. Some organisations continue to have overall assessment ratings which have to conform to a forced distribution, requiring each team/department to have, say, 10% of employees on the top point, 20% on the next point, and so on, so that each individual is assessed relative to others rather than being given an absolute rating. These systems are not popular: Chattopadhayay and Ghosh (2012) present a detailed review of their problems, suggesting that they create employee dissatisfaction and lead to high labour turnover. These authors propose using an employee's relative position within his or her work group to improve the effectiveness of forced distribution systems. Other approaches include behaviourally anchored rating scales (BARS) and behavioural observation scales (BOS), which are specific methods of linking ratings with behaviour at work, although evidence suggests that these are not widely used (Williams 2002). An increasing trend in the UK is to what is known as 'rank and yank', where the bottom (say) 10% of performers in any year are exited from the organisation. This creates many difficulties for the employment relationship, not least with employee perceptions of the fairness of the performance management system. We consider an example of this in the Window on practice.

WINDOW ON PRACTICE

Tax officials to strike over HMRC 'must improve' employee appraisals

HMRC staff have taken industrial action over proposals for a new performance management system which forces managers to identify 10% of staff as underperforming. Managers who fail to do this will themselves be marked as underperforming.

Initially, this group will be supported to improve performance but there are concerns that these ratings could affect pay rises and ultimately lead to job losses. There will be no appeals process, leading to concerns over the fairness of the system and lack of recourse to support if an employee feels wrongly rated.

Source: Summarised from http://www.theguardian.com/politics/2014/feb/04/senior-tax-officials-strike-hmrc-employee-appraisals.

Performance may also be appraised by collecting primary data via various forms of electronic surveillance system. There are increasing examples of how activity rates of computer operators can be recorded and analysed, and how the calls made by telephone sales staff can be overheard and analysed. On another level some companies test the performance of their sales staff by sending in assessors acting in the role of customer, often termed 'mystery shoppers'. Other organisations encourage employees to give upwards feedback to their managers at this point in the cycle. Further details of this stage in the process will be presented later (see Chapter 15).

One particular form of review/appraisal is 360-degree feedback, which is a very specific term used to refer to multi-rater feedback. It is increasingly being used within performance management systems and as a separate development activity. This approach to feedback refers to the use of the whole range of sources from which feedback can be collected about any individual. Thus feedback is collected from every angle on the way that the individual carries out his or her job: from immediate line manager, peers, subordinates, more senior managers, internal customers, external customers and from individuals themselves. It is argued that this breadth provides better feedback than relying on the line manager alone, who will only be able to observe the individual in a limited range of situations. It also provides a better way to capture the complexities of performance and individuals will find feedback from peers and subordinates compelling and more valid (Atwater *et al.* 2002). Space here precludes a detailed discussion of 360-degree feedback and you can find this in Torrington *et al.* (2008).

Performance review/appraisal attracts perhaps most criticism of any aspect of a performance management system. Its effectiveness hinges on a range of different factors. Research by the Institute for Employment Studies (IRS 2001) found that review was only seen as fair if the targets set were seen as reasonable, managers were seen to be objective and judgements were consistent across the organisation. Longenecker (1997) identified the three most common reasons for failure of an appraisal system as: unclear performance criteria or an ineffective rating instrument (83%); poor working relationships with the boss (79%); and that the appraiser lacked information on the manager's actual performance (75%). Other problems were a lack of ongoing performance feedback (67%) and a lack of focus on management development/improvement (50%). Smaller numbers identified problems with the process, such as lack of appraisal skills (33%) and the review process lacking structure or substance (29%). See also Davis (2011) for common problems with appraisal. Aguinis and Pierce (2008) have also found that many employees are dissatisfied with the level of feedback and frequency of performance review. Informal reviews that are more frequent may thus be more effective (Dewettinck and van Dijk 2012). Fairness and trust in supervisors are thus essential to an effective appraisal (Byrne *et al.* 2012) and to fostering employee participation (Dewettinck and van Dijk 2012). Subjectivity is, however, hard to avoid and may explain managers' reluctance to undertake appraisals (Neu Moren 2013).

Research has started to take an interest in neuroscience and explore how HR practice affects the brain and subsequent behaviour. Recent research, as we discuss in the following Window in practice, has suggested that performance review might even damage performance.

WINDOW ON PRACTICE

The corporate kabuki of performance reviews

McGregor reports research that suggests performance reviews negatively affect the brain. Neuroscience, that is, research into how the brain works, demonstrates that it operates less effectively when a person feels under threat. Given a typical employee's response to their performance review, we might expect the perceived threat to reduce both the ability to process data and to be creative. Hardly the desired outcome of a performance review. McGregor also considers numerous other performance review difficulties, which makes this article an interesting read.

Source: Summarised from https://www.washingtonpost.com/business/on-leadership/the-corporate-kabuki-of-performance-reviews/2013÷02÷14÷59b60e86–7624–11e2-aa12-e6cf1d31106b_story.html.

National context also has substantial implications for performance review. The emphasis on relationships in India, for example, leads managers to rate all employees at a similar standard and direct criticism is unacceptable in cultures such as China where importance is attached to saving face (Lindholm *et al*. 1999). Milliman *et al*.'s (2002) study of performance appraisal in ten countries across the Pacific Rim found that cultural difference impacted on its purpose. Some used it primarily for development while others emphasised its judgmental/reward functions. Shen (2004) supports this, arguing that Chinese firms use performance review to drive pay, whereas Western firms tend to focus on its developmental aspects.

ACTIVITY 11.3

Think of any organisation in which you have had some involvement:

1   How has individual performance been measured and rated?

2   What impact has this had?

3   Would you recommend qualitative or quantitative descriptions of performance?

Reward

Performance management systems, and performance review/appraisal in particular, can be used to allocate reward. This can be both financial and non-financial reward, although much of the debate centres around financial reward. It is not difficult to understand why.

Performance management systems are effective and relatively uncontentious in supporting non-financial rewards such as training and development, quality of working life and strong supervisor/employee relationships. The allocation of financial reward is much more contentious (Aguinis and Pierce 2008). Many performance management systems still include a link with pay, although this is reducing in popularity and staff almost universally dislike the link. Many authors, for example Trosten-Bloom *et al*. (2014), recommend linking performance to team or organisation reward to avoid many of the difficulties of linking it to individual reward. Clark (2005) provides a good discussion of the problems with the pay link and we include a detailed discussion of performance-related pay later (see Chapter 25).

National cultures again impact on the performance management/reward link, particularly in relation to pay. Milliman *et al*. (2002) argue that performance/pay links are common in individualistic countries such as the USA, Canada and Australia but less common in cultures which place a high value on harmony, face and teamwork. Here importance is placed on not disturbing group harmony through differentiation of employees in performance review. In contrast, Snape *et al*. (1998) argue that monetary rewards are emerging as being of prime importance to workers in Hong Kong as Asian cultures are more materialistic than their western counterparts. Again further research is needed to develop better understanding of these issues.

Performance management: does it improve performance?

Although the practitioner literature somewhat uncritically accepts that effective performance management systems improve individual and organisational performance (e.g. CIPD 2009), the findings of academic research have been more mixed. This might, in part, derive from the failure of many organisations to evaluate their performance management systems (Armstrong and Baron 2005). For example, Houldsworth and Jirasinghe (2006) report that the majority of organisations rated their performance management effectiveness as excellent, yet it is not clear how effectiveness was measured. Similarly, research on the HR/performance link (see e.g. Purcell *et al*. 2003, West *et al*. 2002) has included performance management in the bundle of HR practices that are associated with improved organisational performance. Some studies on performance management itself have been similarly promising. For example, it has been demonstrated that over half of organisations with formal performance management systems have better financial outcomes than those without and over 40% have better outcomes in respect of customer satisfaction and employee retention (Aguinis and Pierce 2008). Decramer *et al*. (2013) have also reported positive outcomes within higher education systems. Yet other research has been much more pessimistic. Haines and St-Onge (2012) found no improvement in performance in 80–90% of cases and Pulakos *et al*. (2008) found similar results for around a third of organisations in their study. Further research is clearly needed but to achieve potential benefits, robust systems that are well implemented are essential. We consider below some of the key requirements, together with some of the criticisms of performance management systems.

Performance management must have credibility with employees, particularly in terms of fairness and accuracy, to be effective (Sharma *et al*. 2016). It must also be line rather than HR driven. The incorporation of line managers alongside HR managers in a working party to develop the system is important as it not only takes account of the needs of the line in the system design, but also demonstrates that the system is line led. CIPD (2005) reports that 75% of managers suggest that they own and operate the performance management process. Training in the introduction and use of the system is also ideally line led. However, some researchers have found that line managers are the weak link in the system (Tuytens and Devos 2012) and training is rarely provided (Biron *et al.*, 2011). Difficulties can arise in many forms. Redman *et al.* (2000) found incomplete take-up of performance management, with some aspects being adopted and not others. They noted that there was a general lack of integration of activities. This is rather unfortunate as one of the key advantages of performance management is the capacity for integration of activities concerned with the management of individual performance. There remains confusion both over the nature of performance management and what an integrated approach means. Ownership of the system is also important. If it is designed and imposed by the HR function, there may be little ownership of the system by line managers. Similarly, if paperwork has to be returned to the HR function it may well be seen as a form-filling exercise for someone else's benefit and with no practical value to performance within the job. Performance management also seems to suffer from the same problems as traditional appraisal systems. Armstrong and Baron (2005) report, for example, that employees feel that managers give their best ratings to people that they like and many managers feel they do not receive sufficient training in performance management processes. A further problem with performance management systems is the lack of clarity of purpose and they may be expected to deliver in too many areas. Systems may focus on development, identifying future potential, reward, identifying poor performers, or motivation. Many systems try to encompass both developmental and judgemental approaches; for example, in the IRS survey (IRS 2005) 92% of companies used appraisal to determine training and development needs (mainly formally), and 65% used the system either formally or informally to determine pay, with 43% using it formally or informally to determine bonuses. However, as these approaches conflict, the results are typically unsatisfactory. Although it is recommended that a primarily developmental approach is adopted, many managers still predominantly perceive the primary purpose of the performance management process to be performance evaluation and control (Dewettinck and van Dijk 2012). An emerging issue given demographic changes in many countries is managing performance across different generations within the workforce. A recent report for example has claimed that a younger generation of workers, the so-called 'generation Y', needs a very different type of approach to performance management than their older colleagues (Churchard 2012). More research is required into these intergenerational differences and, as we note at various points above, the impact of national context on performance management processes.

More fundamentally some argue that the problems are not simply related to poor design or implementation of performance management systems, but rooted deeply in the basic reaction of organisational members to performance management. In the critical literature, debates on the role and theory of appraisal centre on the underlying reasons for appraisal (see e.g. Townley 1993; Newton and Findlay 1996). These are radical critiques which posit that performance management systems are an abuse of power and create exploitation and work intensification. These are powerful criticisms which have been recently built upon by Neu Moren (2013) in her challenge to the basis of performance appraisal and the need to view it as a social practice.

SUMMARY PROPOSITIONS

11.1. Employee performance management systems incorporate appraisal activity, but include other aspects such as a link to organisational objectives and competency frameworks, an emphasis on ongoing review, motivation, coaching and support, and reinforcement/reward for performance achieved.

11.2. There is a conflict in many appraisal and performance management systems as managers frequently have a dual role as assessor and developer.

11.3. Current trends in sophisticated performance management activity include greater employee ownership, emphasis on the 'how' as well as the 'what', emphasis on evidence collection from both manager and employee, and upwards feedback to the line manager as well as downwards feedback to the employee.

11.4. Most employee performance management systems focus on the individual, but there is a need to ensure that team contributions are not neglected and more importantly that team and individual goals do not conflict.

11.5. Performance management systems are generally believed to improve performance but research evidence is mixed.

11.6. The impact of national context on performance management processes is poorly understood and further research is required.

GENERAL DISCUSSION TOPICS

1. In what ways is the concept of performance management different from the way in which appraisal has been traditionally practised? What are the advantages and disadvantages for employees and employers?

2. Critics argue that, rather than being focused on development and improvement, performance management systems are a form of employee control that create work intensification. How would you respond to this criticism?

THEORY INTO PRACTICE

Steel Co. is a small manufacturing company, run by an owner manager and employing around sixty-five people, mainly male, full-time, permanent, unskilled or semi-skilled workers. The firm has been established for approximately thirty years, many of the employees having long periods of service, and has, in this time, had mixed performance. In recent years, however, in the face of increased competition and difficult trading conditions, financial performance has been poor and little profit has been made. This situation has meant that the owner manager has imposed a pay freeze for the last three years. Employees have expressed discontent with the pay freeze and suggest that, in general, the firm is a poor employer.

The firm is divided into two main sections, the sales team ('Sales'), which comprises around eight employees, and the manufacturing operation (the 'Works'), which comprises the remainder of the employees, other than for a small number of employees who work in administrative or quality assurance roles. Historically, the owner manager has managed the whole firm, but about twelve months ago, appointed a Divisional Director who is now responsible for managing the Works. In line with his autocratic approach, the owner manager has always adopted a command and control style of management, viewing employees as a cost to the business and investing little in them. This is evident in his management of the sales team, who have sales targets to hit and are closely monitored by the owner manager in respect of achieving these targets but receive little other support from him. The Divisional Director, however, has a more participative style of management and understands the need to view employees as assets through which the firm can develop and sustain high performance.

The historical management style meant that, on his arrival, the Divisional Director was faced with a group of employees who lacked commitment to the firm and were focused purely on working their shift and earning their pay, making the minimum possible contribution to the firm. The Divisional Director has thus undertaken a number of initiatives in order to improve both individual and firm performance, including the implementation of a performance management system. The system revolves around production targets which have been devised by the Divisional Director, based on the firm's overall requirements, and are posted on the noticeboard at the beginning of each week, together with a report indicating performance against the previous week's targets. Production data is available at both the team and individual level and the Works Manager regularly discusses poor performance with individuals where appropriate. It is common for those employees regularly not meeting their targets to be disciplined. An annual performance review is held for employees at which their performance is rated unsatisfactory, satisfactory or good.

In an attempt to overcome the dissatisfaction created by the pay freeze, the Divisional Director then introduced a bonus scheme where payment is triggered by individual and team achievement of production targets. Employees support management's disciplinary approach as they perceive that those who are underperforming are likely to prevent payment of team bonuses. Team leaders are nominally responsible for coordinating team efforts, although the role is a new one, which has not been formally defined, and the employees appointed to these roles have been given no training and do not understand their responsibilities. Indeed, little training, other than on health and safety issues, takes place at any level in the Works.

A year after implementing the changes, the Divisional Director undertook a review of performance and was disappointed to discover that neither productivity nor quality have improved in the Works. In discussions with the Works Manager, the Divisional Director has formed the view that the attitude of the employees has changed little and motivation is still weak, despite most earning bonuses in seven of the twelve months.

Questions

Advise on why this might be the case with particular reference to:

1 The methods used to set targets/objectives.

2 The failure to manage behaviours or competencies.

3 A discipline- rather than a development-focused approach to managing performance.

4 The linking of financial reward to performance.

FURTHER READING

Hutchinson, S. (2013) *Performance Management: Theory and Practice*. London: CIPD.

This is a well-balanced textbook that effectively combines discussion of theory and practice across the whole performance management process.

Kang, H. and Shen, J. (2016) 'International performance appraisal practices and approaches of South Korean MNEs in China', *International Journal of Human Resource Management*, Vol. 27, No. 3, pp. 291–310.

The authors present an interesting study into how practices designed in a western context are adapted for South Korean organisations.

Kuvaas, B. (2006) 'Performance appraisal satisfaction and employee outcomes: Mediating and moderating roles of work motivation', *International Journal of Human Resource Management*, Vol. 17, No. 3, pp. 504–22.

This article reflects a stream of research looking at the outcomes of appraisal from the employee perspective, in particular focusing on job satisfaction, intention to quit and commitment.

Byrne, Z. *et al.* (2012). 'Trusting the fair supervisor: The role of supervisory support in performance appraisals', *Human Resource Management Journal*, Vol. 22, pp. 129–47.

This article is part of the fast-increasing literature which emphasises the vital role of organisational justice in effective performance management systems.

REFERENCES

Aguinis, H. (2013) *Performance Management* (3rd edn.). Harlow: Pearson.

Aguinis, H., Joo, R. and Gottfredson, H. (2011) 'Why we hate performance management – and why we should love it', *Business Horizons*, Vol. 54, pp. 503–7.

Aguinis, H. and Pierce, C. (2008) 'Enhancing the relevance of organisational behaviour by embracing performance management research', *Journal of Organisational Behaviour*, Vol. 29, pp. 139–45.

Armstrong, M. and Baron, A. (2005) *Managing Performance: Performance Management in Action*. London: CIPD.

Atwater, L., Waldman, D. and Brett, J. (2002) 'Understanding and optimising multi-source feedback', *Human Resource Management*, Vol. 41, pp. 193–208.

Biron, M., Farndale, E. and Paauwe, J. (2011) 'Performance management effectiveness: Lessons from world-leading firms, *International Journal of Human Resource Management*, Vol. 22, pp. 1294–311.

Briscoe, D. and Claus, L. (2008) 'Employee performance management: Policies and practices in multinational enterprises', in P. Budwar and A. Denisi (eds), *Performance Management Systems: A Global Perspective*. Abingdon: Routledge.

Byrne, Z., Pitts, V., Wilson, C. and Steiner, Z. (2012) 'Trusting the fair supervisor: The role of supervisory support in performance appraisals', *Human Resource Management Journal*, Vol. 22, pp. 129–47.

Chattopadhayay, R. and Ghosh, A. (2012) 'Performance appraisal based on a forced distribution system: Its drawbacks and remedies', *International Journal of Productivity and Performance Management*, Vol. 61, pp. 881–96.

Churchard, C. (2012) 'Gen Y "demands improved performance management" ', *People Management,* www.peoplemanagement.co.uk/pm/articles/2012/05/gen-y-demands-improved-performance-management.htm.

CIPD (2005) *Performance Management.* London: CIPD.

CIPD (2009) *Performance Management: Discussion Paper.* London: CIPD.

CIPD (2012) *Performance Management,* Factsheet [Online]. London: CIPD.

Clark, G. (2005) 'Performance management strategies', in G. Salaman *et al.* (eds), *Strategic Human Resource Management: Theory and Practice.* London: The Open University/Sage.

Davis, P. (2011) 'Seven biggest problems with performance appraisals: And seven development approaches to rectify them', *Development and Learning in Organisations,* Vol. 26, pp. 11–14.

Decramer, A., Smoulders, C., Vanderstraeten, A., Christiaens, J. and Desmidt, S. (2012) 'External pressures affecting the adoption of employee performance management in higher education institutions', *Personnel Review,* Vol. 41, pp. 686–704.

Decramer, A., Smoulders, C. and Vanderstraeten, A. (2013) 'Employee performance management culture and system features in higher education: Relationship with employee performance management satisfaction', *International Journal of Human Resource Management,* Vol. 24, pp. 352–71.

Dewettinck, K. and van Dijk, H. (2012) 'Linking Belgian employee performance management system characteristics with performance management system effectiveness: Exploring the mediating role of fairness', *International Journal of Human Resource Management,* Vol. 24, pp. 806–25.

Fenwick, M. (2004) 'International compensation and performance management', in A. Harzing and J. Ruysseveldt (eds), *International Human Resource Management* (2nd edn.). London: Sage.

Fletcher, C. and Perry, E. (2001) 'Performance appraisal and feedback: A consideration of national culture and a review of contemporary and future trends', in N. Anderson *et al.* (eds), *International Handbook of Industrial, Work and Organizational Psychology.* Beverley Hills, CA: Sage.

Gupta, V. and Kumar, S. (2013) 'Impact of performance appraisal justice on employee engagement: A study of Indian professionals', *Employee Relations,* Vol. 35, pp. 61–78.

Haines, V. and St-Onge, S. (2012) 'Performance management effectiveness: Practices or context?' *International Journal of Human Resource Management,* Vol. 23, pp. 1158–75.

Hendry, C., Woodward, S., Bradley, P. and Perkins, S. (2000) 'Performance and rewards: Cleaning out the stables', *Human Resource Management Journal,* Vol. 10, pp. 42–62.

Houldsworth, E. and Jirasinghe, D. (2006) *Managing and Measuring Employee Performance.* London: Kogan-Page.

Hutchinson, S. (2013) *Performance Management: Theory and Practice.* London: CIPD.

IRS (2001) 'Performance appraisal must try harder', *IRS Employment Trends.* London: IRS.

IRS (2005) 'Appraisals (2): Learning from practice and experience', *IRS Employment Review.* London: IRS.

Krasman, J. (2013) 'Putting feedback-seeking into "context": Job characteristics and feedback-seeking behaviour', *Personnel Review,* Vol. 42, pp. 50–66.

Krats, P. and Brown, T. (2013) 'Unionised employee's reactions to the introduction of a goal-based performance appraisal system', *Human Resource Management Journal,* Vol. 23, pp. 396–412.

Lindholm, N., Tahvanainen, M. and Borkman, I. (1999) 'Performance appraisal of host country employees: Western MNE's in China', in C. Brewster and H. Harris (eds), *International HRM: Contemporary Issues in Europe.* London: Routledge.

Locke, E. and Latham, G. (2006) 'New directions in goal setting theory', *Association for Psychological Science,* Vol. 15, pp. 265–8.

Longenecker, C. (1997) 'Why managerial performance appraisals are ineffective: Causes and lessons', *Career Development International,* Vol. 2, pp. 212–18.

Mendonca, M. and Kanungo, R. (1996) 'Impact of culture on performance management in developing countries', *International Journal of Manpower,* Vol. 17, pp. 65–75.

Milliman, J., Nason, S., Zhu, C. and de Ciere, H. (2002) 'An exploratory assessment of the purposes of performance appraisals in North and Central America and the Pacific Rim', *Human Resource Management,* Vol. 41, pp. 87–102.

Neu Moren, E. (2013) 'The negotiated character of performance appraisal: How interrelations between managers matters', *International Journal of Human Resource Management,* Vol. 24, pp. 853–70.

Newton, T. and Findlay, P. (1996) 'Playing God? The performance of appraisal', *Human Resource Management Journal,* Vol. 6, pp. 42–58.

Pulakos, E., Mueller-Hanson, R. and O'Leary, R. (2008) 'Performance management in the United States', in Varma, A., Budhwar, P. and Denisi, A. (eds.), *Performance Management Systems: A global perspective.* Abingdon: Routledge.

Purcell, J., Kinnie, N., Hutchinson, S., Rayton, B. and Swart, J. (2003) *Understanding the People Performance Link: Unlocking the Black Box.* London: CIPD.

Redman, T., Snape, E., Thompson, D. and Ka-Ching Yan, F. (2000) 'Performance appraisal in the National Health Service: A Trust Hospital study', *Human Resource Management Journal,* Vol. 10, pp. 1–16.

Scott, A. (2006) 'Intensive care', *People Management,* Vol. 12, pp. 14–15.

Sharma, N., Sharma, T. and Agarwal, M. (2016) 'Measuring employee perception of performance management system effectiveness', *Employee Relations,* Vol. 38, pp. 224 – 47.

Shen, J. (2004) 'International performance appraisals: Policies, practices and determinants in the case of Chinese multinational companies', *International Journal of Manpower,* Vol. 25, pp. 547–63.

Snape, E., Thompson, D., Ka-Ching Yan, F. and Redman, T. (1998) 'Performance appraisal and culture: Practice and attitudes in Hong Kong and Great Britain', *International Journal of Human Resource Management,* Vol. 9, pp. 841–61.

Torrington, D., Hall, L., Taylor, S. and Atkinson, C. (2008) *Fundamentals of Human Resource Management.* Harlow: Pearson Education.

Townley, B. (1993) 'Performance appraisal and the emergence of management', *Journal of Management Studies,* Vol. 30, pp. 27–44.

Trosten-Bloom, A., Deines, T. and Carsten, T. (2014) 'Positive performance management: Bold experiments, provocative possibilities', *Performance Improvement,* Vol. 53, pp. 26–37.

Tuytens, M. and Devos, G. (2012) 'Importance of system and leadership in appraisal', *Personnel Review,* Vol. 41, pp. 756–66.

Van Vijfeijken, H., Kleingeld, A., Van Tuijl, H. and Algera, J. (2006) 'Interdependence and fit in team performance management', *Personnel Review,* Vol. 35, pp. 98–117.

Varma, A., Pichler, S. and Srinivas, E. (2005) 'The role of interpersonal affect in performance appraisal: Evidence from two samples – the US and India', *International Journal of Human Resource Management,* Vol. 16, pp. 2029–44.

Vroom, V. (1964) *Work and Motivation.* Chichester: Wiley.

West, M., Borrill, C., Dawson, J., Carter, M. and Waring, J. (2002) 'The link between the management of employees and patient mortality in acute hospitals', *International Journal of Human Resource Management,* Vol. 13, pp. 1299–310.

Williams, R. (2002) *Managing Employee Performance.* London: Thomson Learning.

CHAPTER 12
LEADERSHIP

THE OBJECTIVES OF THIS CHAPTER ARE TO:

1 Introduce a working definition which reflects the general nature of leadership

2 Examine the trait approach to leadership

3 Examine the style (behavioural) and contingency approaches to leadership

4 Explore the nature of heroic and post-heroic leadership

5 Examine the concept of followership

Leadership is a loaded and sometimes misunderstood word in management. Some individual managers are seduced by concepts of leadership that show them to be knights in shining armour with superhuman qualities and (this is the really dangerous bit) adoring followers. The followers rarely have that view of their managers. There is sometimes a need for individual leaders with outstanding qualities who achieve extraordinary change in their business, but there are more roles which call for different, more subtle and modest leadership skills, which can be learnt and which are equally important, even if they lack 'heroism'. We should never underestimate the importance and variety of effective leadership.

Understanding of leadership developed greatly in the second half of the twentieth century and leadership research has increased enormously even in the past ten years (see Ford and Harding 2015). Recent major developments have included: an appreciation of the impact of the changing circumstances of contemporary business; the role of women in leadership; the neglect of followers in leadership theory; and the need to recognise the influence of national context. All of the twentieth-century studies and theories were based on two complementary assumptions: first, the business norm was of large, stable organisations steadily getting bigger; second, management was almost exclusively a male activity, with male norms conducted in a western (predominantly American) context. This led to explanations and suggestions based on those two givens. We now see a weakening of these assumptions. Effective businesses are not necessarily large, growing organisations and there are many more women in the workforce and in management positions within it. Although charismatic leaders (a predominantly male concept) are still needed in some situations, empowering leaders are increasingly required. The applicability of American leadership theory to a variety of contexts has also been subject to increasing scrutiny and we have seen an increasing interest in the concept of followership and its impact on leadership effectiveness. We chart the development of leadership theories and their implications throughout this chapter.

WINDOW ON PRACTICE

Much of the leadership research considered in this chapter has emerged from the USA and has been unproblematically applied across the world. In their internationally recognised GLOBE study, however, House *et al.* (2004) demonstrate how effective leadership is influenced by national context. Differences are apparent even in the western context. Tavanti (2012), for example, demonstrates how cultural dimensions in Italy affect approaches to leadership. In non-western contexts, stark differences are beginning to emerge as understanding of leadership develops. Yooyanyong and Muenjohn (2010) demonstrate these differences in Japan and Bolden and Kirk (2009) introduce the idea of an 'African renaissance' and call for a re-engagement with indigenous knowledge and practices. This is part of a stream of research that explores the notion of Ubuntu (a social philosophy that highlights good social and familial relations, and encourages collectivism and kinship among indigenous peoples) and its role in African leadership. Eyong (2012), for example, presents one typology of African leadership based upon Ubuntu that is premised on the promotion of respect and dignity of followers, teamwork and group solidarity, service to others, and valuing harmony and interdependence. Religion may also have a role to play in understanding leadership; for example, El Garah *et al.* (2012) explore Islam and leadership.

Leadership and management

Northouse (2006) presents four components that characterise leadership: leadership is a process; it involves influence; it occurs within a group context; and it involves goal attainment. This corresponds with Shackleton's (1995: 2) definition, which we shall use as a working definition for the remainder of the chapter:

> leadership is the process in which an individual influences other group members towards the attainment of group or organisational goals.

This definition is useful as it leaves open the question of whether leadership is exercised in a commanding or a facilitative manner. It does suggest, however, that the leader in some way motivates others to act in such a way as to achieve group goals.

The definition also makes no assumptions about who the leader is; it may or may not be the nominal head of the group. Managers may or may not be leaders, and leaders may or may not be managers. Some authors distinguish very clearly between the nature of management and the nature of leadership. Bennis and Nanus (1985), for example, suggest that leadership is path finding while management is path following, and that leadership is about doing the right thing whereas management is about doing things right. Kotter (1990) identifies leaders as establishing a direction (whereas managers plan and budget); leaders align people with the vision (whereas managers organise things); leaders motivate and inspire (whereas managers control and solve problems); and leaders encourage change (whereas managers encourage order and predictability). This draws on a particular perspective, that of the transformational leader, which is a school of thought that concentrates on the one leader at the top of the organisation. This is very different from organisations and individuals who use the terms 'manager' and 'leader' interchangeably with nothing more than a vague notion that managers should be leaders. Indeed, any individual may act as a manager one day and a leader the next, depending on the situation, and we should not assume that leadership is always a downwards process, as sometimes employees and managers lead upwards (Hollington 2006). Recently Bresnen *et al.* (2015) have suggested that the term 'leader' is increasingly used in certain contexts, for example healthcare, as 'manager' has become a somewhat pejorative term. Clearly, this says little about the actual nature of the role.

The flow of articles on leadership continues unabated, but it would be a mistake to think that there is an ultimate truth to be discovered; rather, there is a range of perspectives from which we can try to make sense of leadership and motivation. Grint (1997: 3) comments insightfully that:

> What counts as leadership appears to change quite radically across time and space.

In the following sections, we look at three questions which underlie virtually all the work on leadership. First, what are the traits of a leader, or an effective leader? Second, what is the 'best' leadership style or behaviour? Third, if different styles are appropriate at different times, what factors influence the desired style?

What are the traits of (effective) leaders?

Trait approaches were the earliest to be employed and sought to identify the traits of leaders; in other words, what characterises leaders as opposed to those who are not leaders. These approaches rest on the assumption that some people are born to lead due to their personal qualities, while others are not. It suggests that leadership is only available to the chosen few. These approaches have been discredited for this reason and because there has been little consistency in the lists of traits that research has uncovered. However, this perspective is frequently resurrected (see e.g. Fache 2009) and we discuss it here as, implicitly, it underpins many contemporary understandings of leadership.

While long-debated, leadership traits are generally supposed to include: drive to achieve; the motivation to lead; honesty and integrity; self-confidence, including the ability to withstand setbacks, standing firm and being emotionally resilient; cognitive ability; and knowledge of the business. Northouse (2006) provides a useful historical comparison of the lists of traits uncovered in numerous studies. Perhaps the most well-known expression of the trait approach is the work relating to charismatic leadership. House (1976), for example, describes charismatic leaders as being dominant, having a strong desire to influence, being self-confident and having a strong sense of their own moral values.

In a slightly different vein, Goleman (1998) has argued that leadership competencies comprise technical, cognitive and emotional competencies, and that emotional competencies 'proved to be twice as important as the others'. He goes on to describe five components of what he terms 'emotional intelligence':

- **Self-awareness:** this he defines as a deep understanding of one's strengths, weaknesses, needs, values and goals. Self-aware managers are aware of their own limitations.
- **Self-regulation:** the control of feelings, the ability to channel them in constructive ways; the ability to feel comfortable with ambiguity and not panic.
- **Motivation:** the desire to achieve beyond expectations, being driven by internal rather than external factors, and to be involved in a continuous striving for improvement.
- **Empathy:** considering employees' feelings alongside other factors when making decisions.
- **Social skill:** friendliness with a purpose, being good at finding common ground and building rapport. Individuals with this competency are good persuaders, collaborative managers and natural networkers.

As we explain in the following Window in practice, the concept of emotional intelligence is very influential in contemporary organisations.

WINDOW ON PRACTICE

Empathy is a top leadership skill

Sky CEO, Jeremy Darroch, claims that empathy, an essential element of emotional intelligence, is now more important in leadership than command and control. All of Sky's senior management team are receiving training in emotional intelligence that emphasises softer leadership skills. Darroch argues that his emotional intelligence impacts those around him and that developing self-awareness creates better leadership. Couching this in business terms is, however, essential to gaining acceptance of it within the business community.

Source: Adapted from http://www.cipd.co.uk/pm/peoplemanagement/b/weblog/archive/2015/03/23/empathy-is-the-top-leadership-skill-says-sky-ceo.aspx.

Goleman refers to competencies which include a combination of traits *and* abilities. He maintains that the five aspects of emotional intelligence can be learnt, although we feel that this is still a matter for debate, and as many of the terms used by Goleman are similar to those of the previous trait models of leadership, we have categorised his model as an extension of the trait perspective. To some extent his work sits between the trait approach and the style approach (which follows below). It is interesting that a number of researchers and writers are recognising that there is value in considering a mix of personality characteristics and behaviours, and in particular Higgs (2003) links this approach to emotional intelligence.

What is the 'best way to lead'? Leadership styles and behaviours

Dissatisfaction with research that saw leadership as a set of permanent personal characteristics led to further studies that emphasised the nature of the leadership process, the interaction between leader and follower, aiming to understand how the leaders *behave* rather than what they *are*. The first such studies sought to find the 'best' leadership style; from this perspective leadership comprises an ideal set of behaviours that can be learnt. Fullop *et al.* (1999) suggest that McGregor's (1960) work, *The Human Side of Enterprise*, can be understood from this perspective. McGregor argued that American corporations managed their employees as if they were work-shy, and needed constant direction, monitoring and control (theory 'x'), rather than as if they were responsible individuals who were willing and able to take on responsibility and organise their own work (theory 'y'). The underlying assumptions of the manager determined the way he or she managed the employees and this in turn determined how the employees would react. Thus if employees were managed as if they operated on theory 'x' then they would act in a theory 'x' manner; conversely, if employees were managed as if they operated on theory 'y' then they would respond as theory 'y' employees would respond. The message was that management style should reinforce theory 'y' and then employees would take on responsibility, be motivated by what they were doing and work hard. Although the original book was written nearly sixty years ago, this approach has been revisited in more recent years (see e.g. Heil *et al.* 2000) and it fits well with the empowering or post-heroic approach to leadership that we discuss later.

Another style approach is reflected in Blake and Mouton's (1964) famous 'Managerial Grid'. The grid is based on two aspects of leadership behaviour: concern for production, that is task-orientated behaviours such as clarifying roles, scheduling work, measuring outputs; and concern for people, that is people-centred behaviour such as building trust, camaraderie, a friendly atmosphere. These two dimensions are at the heart of many models of leadership and have been more recently explored by Cowsgill and Grint (2008) who develop the task/relationship dichotomy by suggesting that senior managers who seek to satisfy the demands of both their superiors and subordinates will be the most successful leaders.

Blake and Mouton proposed that individual leaders could be measured on a nine-point scale in each of these two aspects, and by combining them in grid form they identified the four leadership styles presented in Table 12.1.

These studies suggest that leadership is accessible for all people and is a matter of learning leadership behaviour. Many leadership development courses have therefore been based around this model and Herd *et al.* (2016) explain how assessment centres can be used to identify and develop leaders and leadership competencies. However, as Northouse (2006) argues, there is an assumption in the model that the team management style (high concern for people and high concern for production; sometimes termed 9,9 management) is the ideal style, yet this claim is not substantiated by the research. This approach also fails to take account of the characteristics of the situation and the nature of the followers. Much of the recent work on the notion of transformational/heroic leadership, and post-heroic leadership, similarly assumes that what is being discussed is the one best way for a leader to lead, and we return later to this leadership debate.

ACTIVITY 12.1

Think of different leaders you have encountered – in particular those that were especially effective or ineffective:

1 What differences can you identify in terms of their traits (personal characteristics)?

2 What differences can you identify in terms of their behaviour?

3 Are the trait and behaviour lists connected in any way? If so, how?

4 Which of these two approaches – trait or behaviour – do you find more useful in helping you to understand the nature of effective leadership?

Table 12.1 Blake and Mouton's four leadership styles

High concern for people	High concern for people
Low concern for production	High concern for production
Country Club management	**Team management**
Low concern for people	Low concern for people
Low concern for production	High concern for production
Impoverished management	**Authority-compliance management**

Source: Adapted from R.R. Blake and J.S. Mouton (1964) *The Managerial Grid.* Houston, TX: Gulf Publishing.

WINDOW ON PRACTICE

Goffee and Jones (2006) highlight the situational nature of leadership by using examples of key figures. They identify how Winston Churchill was an inspirational wartime leader but when this time and place were gone his 'bulldog' style was not well suited to leading the reconstruction of post-war Britain. As an alternative they name Nelson Mandela as someone who could offer leadership across a wide range of contexts, adjusting from leading while in a prison cell on Robben Island to leading from Union House in Pretoria when he was released and was elected President of South Africa.

Source: Goffee, R. and Jones, G. (2006) 'The Lizard Kings', *People Management,* Vol. 12, No. 2, 26 January, pp. 32–4.

Do leaders need different styles for different situations?

A variety of models, sometimes termed contingency models, have been developed to address the importance of context in the leadership process. While this stream of research began many years ago, the role of context continues to be emphasised in contemporary research (see, for example, Bresnan *et al.* 2015). Contingency models are complex and many retain the concepts of production-centred and people-centred behaviour but use them in a different way. Hersey and Blanchard (1988) developed the Situational Leadership® model which identified that the appropriate leadership style in a situation should be dependent on the model's diagnosis of the follower's 'readiness' to perform a task. The model works on the premise that leaders can 'adapt their leadership style to meet the demands of their environment' (Hersey and Blanchard 1988: 169). Readiness of followers is defined in terms of ability and willingness. Level of ability includes the experience, knowledge and skills that an individual possesses in relation to the particular task at hand; and level of willingness encompasses the extent to which the individual has the motivation and commitment, or the self-confidence, to carry out the task. Having diagnosed the Performance Readiness® level of the followers, Hersey and Blanchard suggest that the leader then adapts his or her behaviour to fit. They identify two dimensions of leader behaviour: task behaviour, which is sometimes termed 'directive'; and relationship behaviour, which is sometimes termed 'supportive'. Task behaviour refers to the extent to which leaders spell out what has to be done. On the other hand, relationship behaviour is defined by the extent to which the leader engages in two-way or multi-way communication. The behaviours include listening, facilitating and supporting behaviours. The extent to which the leader emphasises each of these two types of behaviour results in the usual two-by-two matrix. The four resulting styles are identified as shown in Table 12.2.

Other well-known contingency models include Fiedler's (1967) contingency model where leadership behaviour is matched to three factors in the situation: the nature of the

Table 12.2 Hersey and Blanchard's four styles of leadership

High relationship behaviour	High relationship behaviour
Low task behaviour	High task behaviour
Followers are able, but unwilling or insecure	Followers are unable, but willing or confident
Supportive (participating) style (3)	**Coaching (selling) style (2)**
Low relationship behaviour	Low relationship behaviour
Low task behaviour	High task behaviour
Followers are both able and willing or confident	Followers are unable and unwilling or insecure
Delegation style (4)	**Directing (telling) style (1)**

Source: Adapted from P. Hersey and K.H. Blanchard (1988*) Management of Organizational Behavior: Utilizing human resources,* 5th edn. Englewood Cliffs, NJ: Prentice Hall International. © Copyright material, adapted and reprinted with the permission of Center for Leadership Studies, Escondido, CA 92025.

Table 12.3 Six leadership styles reported by Goleman

Coercive style	Leader demands immediate compliance
Authoritative style	Leader mobilises people towards a vision
Affiliative style	Leader creates emotional bonds and harmony
Democratic style	Leader uses participation to build consensus
Pacesetting style	Leader expects excellence and self-direction from followers
Coaching style	Leader develops people for the future

Source: Reprinted by permission of *Harvard Business Review.* Adapted from 'Leadership that gets results', by D. Goleman, March–April, pp. 80 and 82–3. Copyright © 2000 by the Harvard Business School Publishing Corporation; all rights reserved.

relationship between the leader and members; the extent to which tasks are highly structured; and the position power of the leader. The appropriate leader behaviour (i.e. whether it should be task orientated or relationship orientated) depends on the combination of these three aspects in any situation. Fielder's model is considered to be well supported by the evidence. The research was based on the relationship between style and performance in existing organisations in different contexts. For a very useful comparison of contingency models see Fullop *et al.* (1999).

Goleman (2000) makes a further contribution to the leadership debate in identifying six leadership styles, which are shown in Table 12.3, and argues that 'leaders with the best results do not rely on only one leadership style' (p. 78). Goleman goes on to consider the appropriate context and impact of each style, and argues that the more styles the leader uses, the better. We have already reported Goleman's work on emotional intelligence, and he links this with the six styles by suggesting that leaders need to understand how the styles relate back to the different competencies of emotional intelligence so that they can identify where they need to focus their leadership development.

ACTIVITY 12.2

For each of Goleman's six styles think of a leader with whom you have worked, or who you know. For each of these individuals write a list of the behaviours that they use. Then consider the impact that these behaviours have on followers.

Do the behaviours have the same impact on all followers? If not, why not?

In a less mechanistic vein Goffee and Jones (2006) suggest that what works for one leader will not necessarily work for another. While adaptability of styles to suit different contexts is key, aspiring leaders need to discover what it is about themselves that they can mobilise in a leadership situation. Given this perspective, leadership appears very personal and is influenced by psychosocial perspectives and our sense of self (see Ford (2010) for an interesting discussion of this).

One of the differences between the contingency models we have just discussed and the 'best' style models is the implications for development. The Blake and Mouton model suggests leaders can be developed to lead in the one best way. The Hersey and Blanchard model, and most other contingency models, stress the flexibility of the leader – to learn to lead differently with different employees depending on their needs; hence, leaders should learn many styles and learn to diagnose the needs of their employees. Fielder's model, however, emphasises matching the leader to the context (a selection decision), rather than developing leaders in the context. An interesting contribution comes from Hannah *et al.* (2009) who acknowledge a high degree of complexity and present an overarching model which seeks to integrate a substantial number of the factors discussed above.

Transformational leadership: do we really need heroes?

A popular approach to understanding leadership is transformational (or heroic) leadership, which focuses on the leader's role at a strategic level, so there is a concentration on the one leader at the top of the organisation. There is a wide range of literature in this vein, most of it written in the 1980s. Since that time the academic literature may have moved on but the image of the transformational leader still remains widely attractive. Transformational leadership shows elements of the trait approach, as leaders are seen to 'have' charisma, which sets them apart as extraordinary and exceptional, and they are also seen to use a set of 'ideal' behaviours, with the assumption in many studies that this is the 'best' approach. A relatively recent analysis of leadership advertisements demonstrates the extent to which notions of transformational leadership now dominate conceptualisations of leadership (den Hartog *et al.*, 2007) and research continues to explore the approach. Jin *et al.* (2016), for example, have recently suggested that happy leaders are better transformational leaders.

Leaders are usually characterised as heroes with adoring followers (see for example, Ford and Harding 2015). They appear to know exactly what they are doing and how to 'save' the organisation from its present predicament (and consequently such leadership is found more often when organisations are in trouble). Leaders involve followers by generating a high level of commitment, partly due to such leaders focusing on the needs of followers and expressing their vision in such a way that it satisfies these needs. They communicate high expectations to followers and also the firm belief that followers will be able to achieve these goals. In this way the leaders promote self-confidence in the followers and they are motivated to achieve more than they ordinarily expect to achieve. In terms of behaviours, perhaps the most important is the vision of the future that the leaders offer and that they communicate this to the followers. Such leaders are able to help the followers make sense of what is going on and what needs to be done in the future as well as why. The approach does have a great strength in taking followers' needs into account and seeking to promote their self-confidence and potential, and the idea of the knight in shining armour is very attractive and potentially exciting. However, in spite of the emphasis on process there is also an emphasis on leadership characteristics which harks back to the trait approach to leadership, which has been characterised as elitist. Further, Fullop *et al.* (1999) argue that in a rapidly changing turbulent environment, driven by globalisation and changing technology, the appropriateness of concentrating on the one leader at the top of the organisation is questionable. Change is seen as a responsibility of all levels of the organisation, not just the top. They also note a dissatisfaction with corporate failures, identify few transformational leaders as positive role models, suggest that such a model of male authoritarian leadership is less relevant, and in particular that the macho leader with all the answers does not necessarily fit well with the encouragement of creativity and innovation. In addition they suggest that increasing teamwork and an increasing emphasis on knowledge workers mean that employees will be less responsive now to a transformational leader. Collinson (2012) has also termed this approach 'prozac leadership' in that the all-powerful leader is persuaded to believe in his or her own rhetoric and success and followers are unable to raise problems or acknowledge mistakes. Transformational leadership is flawed in its reliance on romanticised leadership behaviours (Spector 2014).

Maybe we should ask whether organisations really require such leaders or, indeed, whether such transcendental, all-powerful leaders can really exist (Ford 2010). Different conceptions of leadership, encompassed in the term 'post-heroic leadership', are now offered as alternatives, partly a reaction to the previous approach and partly a response to a changing environment. While much debate surrounds these, heroic leadership remains a pervasive notion.

Post-heroic leadership

The focus in leadership research has moved away from understanding the traits and style of the one leader at the top of the organisation who knows how to solve all the organisation's problems, to how post-heroic leaders can facilitate many members of the organisation in taking on leadership roles. In this context Appelbaum *et al.* (2003) comment that female leadership styles may be more effective in today's team-based, consensually driven organisations. Many commentators speak of leaders with integrity and humility, the ability to select good people and to remove barriers so they can fulfil their potential and perform (see e.g. Alimo-Metcalfe and Alban-Metcalfe 2002). There are a number of streams within post-heroic leadership research including distributed leadership, servant-leadership, authentic, ethical and respectful leadership (Ford and Harding 2015) and we discuss each in what follows.

Distributed leadership presents a challenge to heroic models in that, rather than reliance on a single figure, many people can contribute to motivation towards collective goals through collaborative modes of working (Mailhot *et al.*, 2016). It is not just the *what* of leadership, but the *how* and *why*, and encourages a focus on leadership practice rather than roles (Spillane 2006). Distributed leadership can emerge anywhere and is growing in importance as a result of increasingly virtual or distributed teams (Hill and Bartol 2016). Mailhot *et al.* (2016), for example, demonstrate its effectiveness in a collaborative research environment. As might be expected, however, there are also criticisms of distributed leadership and Jones (2014) argues that it is less effective in other higher education contexts with greater formality of structure. Ford and Harding (2015) provide a detailed discussion of these criticisms.

According to **servant-leadership** theory, the leader becomes a developer who can help others identify problems as opportunities for learning, and who can harness the collective intelligence of the organisation. Leaders should *design* the organisation in terms of vision, purpose, core values and the structures by which these ideas can be translated into business decisions and involve people at all levels in this design task. It is the role of the leader not to identify the right strategy, but to encourage strategic thinking in the organisation, and to design effective learning processes to make this happen. The leader should coach, guide and facilitate, and act as a servant in taking responsibility for the impact of his or her leadership on others, and in the sense that he or she overrides his or her own self-interest by personal commitment to the organisation's larger mission. This involves actively seeking others' views, experimenting, encouraging enquiry and distinguishing 'the way things are done' from 'the way we think things are done'.

WINDOW ON PRACTICE

'Servant-leadership' was first proposed by the American management development guru Robert Greenleaf and was based on a much older tradition of service and promotes leadership that is not motivated by self-interest and the pursuit of power. Great leaders are motivated by the desire to serve others and the best test of the servant-leader is whether those who are served grow as people. Do they, while being served, become healthier, wiser, freer, more autonomous, more likely themselves to become servants? There are ten characteristics of a servant leader:

1 Listening: seeks to identify the will of a group and helps to clarify that will.

2 Empathy: strives to understand and empathise with others.

3 Healing: has the potential for healing, or helping to 'make whole', oneself and others.

4 Awareness: understands issues involving ethics and values; can view most situations from a more integrated, holistic position.

5 Persuasion: seeks to convince others, rather than to coerce compliance. This aspect offers one of the clearest distinctions between the traditional authoritarian model and that of servant-leadership.

6 Conceptualisation: demonstrates the ability to look at a problem (or an organisation) from a conceptualising perspective, meaning that he or she must think beyond day-to-day realities.

7 Foresight: displays the ability to predict the likely outcome of a situation.

8 Stewardship: Greenleaf's view of all institutions was one in which chief executives, staff and trustees all played significant roles in holding their institutions in trust for the greater good of society.

9 Commitment to the growth of people: is deeply committed to the growth of each individual within his or her institution.

10 Building community: seeks to identify some means for building a community among those who work within a given institution.

Arkin (2009) argues that leaders adopting these characteristics might be what is required to lead organisations out of troubled times.

Source: Adapted from: Arkin, A. (2009) 'Back seat drivers', *People Management*, 7 May, p. 26.

Servant-leadership is an interesting development and has been linked to improved organisational citizenship behaviour and task performance (Chiniara and Bentein 2016). It has nevertheless attracted criticism on a number of grounds. Collinson and Tourish

(2015), for example, identify over forty characteristics that research suggests are essential to servant-leadership and question whether any leader can realistically demonstrate all of these. It may be over-simplistic (Ford and Harding 2015) and again ignores the importance of national context (on servant-leadership in Italy see e.g. Bobbio *et al.* 2012).

There is also an increasing interest in **authentic leadership.** Wong and Cummings (2009) argue that authentic leadership is at the heart of effective leadership because of its emphasis on honesty, integrity and high ethical standards. Other conceptions focus on self-awareness and being true to oneself, which may have some resonance with trait theory and an emphasis on personal charisma (Lawler and Ashman 2012). Authentic leadership focuses on relationship building with followers and in this way raises the profile of followership, an emergent theme with leadership theory that we discuss below. This focus on authenticity is perhaps an outcome of a long period of economic uncertainties in which trust in those leading in government and institutions has been severely damaged:

> Upheavals in society have energised a tremendous demand for authentic leadership. The destruction on 9/11, corporate scandals at companies like WorldCom and Enron and massive failures in the banking industry have all created fear and uncertainty. People feel apprehensive and insecure . . . they long for bona fide leadership they can trust and for leaders who are honest and good. People's demand for leadership makes the study of authentic leadership timely and worthwhile
>
> (Northouse 2010: 205, cited in Lawler and Ashman 2012).

Authenticity certainly became a widely used term in the late 2000s to describe the behaviour required of politicians and leaders: followers want leaders who mean what they say and live what they believe (Deegan 2009). As noted in the following Window on practice, authentic leadership is not without its critics.

WINDOW ON PRACTICE

Authenticity is overrated

Jeffery (2015) reports research that argues principles such as authenticity are questionable and should be disregarded. Instead, leaders should focus on three things.

1 Redefining the role: ensure that there is a high-level focus and that operational matters are delegated, something leaders often do poorly.

2 Networking: often this does not come naturally to leaders and they need support in developing networks beneficial to themselves and the organisation.

3 Developing an appropriate sense of self: authenticity demands that leaders be 'themselves' but it is acceptable to copy the style of successful leaders and adopt a 'fake it 'til you make it' approach to leadership. Authenticity might be about what a leadership aspires to become, rather than what they currently are.

Source: Adapted from Jeffery (2015), http://www.cipd.co.uk/pm/peoplemanagement/b/weblog/archive/2015/11/06/authenticity-is-overrated-says-herminia-ibarra.aspx.

Aligned to authentic leadership, the notion of **ethical leadership** is also becoming popular. Neubert *et al.* (2009) suggest that leaders can become 'agents of virtue', positively influencing the ethical climate within an organisation. This creates space for employee voice and a climate for creativity (Chen and Hou 2016) which can have positive outcomes such as increased job satisfaction and improved organisational commitment. In this way, positive ethical leadership behaviours can have desirable impacts on organisational performance. Ethical leadership also makes prominent the role of followers and **respectful leadership** follows in this vein (Quaquebeke and Eckloff 2010). Claudel and Casse (2012) outline two aspects to ethical leadership. The first is business leadership, which considers which stakeholder interests should be privileged, for example whether to pay or avoid corporation tax, an issue prominent in the UK in recent years. The second is team leadership, the key elements of which they outline as:

- reinforcing the team's purpose and mission
- not taking personal credit for the team's success
- encouraging team spirit and co-operation
- aligning individual and team interests
- treating all team members objectively, equally and fairly
- not abusing authority for personal advantage.

(p. 34)

Ethical leadership also provides increasing recognition of the influence of religion on leadership. Ben-Hur and Jonsen (2012) explore Judaism and the role of Moses' teachings in respect of the visionary, teacher, servant, shepherd in leadership. Similarly Beekun (2012) considers leadership from an Islamic perspective.

Both authentic and ethical leaders allow employees to identify and solve problems themselves and learn to take responsibility. The role of the leader is to develop collective self-confidence. As Grint (1997: 13) puts it, 'the apparent devolvement (or desertion – depending on your perspective) of responsibility has become the new standard in contemporary models of leadership'.

These visions of leadership are very attractive but they do require a dramatic change in thinking for both leaders and followers. For leaders there is the risk of giving away power, learning to trust employees, developing new skills, developing a different perspective of their role and overriding self-interest. Followers have the challenge of taking responsibility, which some may welcome, but others shun. Yet, if sustained competitive advantage is based on human capital and collective intelligence, these perspectives would seem to have much to offer.

Although empowering/authentic/ethical leaders have been shown to fit with the current climate, we may sometimes need heroic leaders. Kets de Vries (2003) makes the point that heroic leadership will never die as change makes people anxious and we need heroic leaders to calm them down, but since no one can live up to the expectations of heroic leaders, they will eventually become a disappointment. We conclude with the thought that there is no one best way: different leaders and different leader behaviours are needed at different times.

Followership

Much of the research on leadership takes a rather managerialist approach: that is, it assumes that leadership is a 'good thing' if only the right way of doing it can be found. Increasingly, however, more critical perspectives on leadership can be found which question the whole premise of leadership (for an example of this trend see Ford *et al.* 2008). One aspect of critical perspectives is to suggest that followers are important, but largely neglected, in treatments of leadership. Followers are clearly critical if leaders are to lead, but little thought has been given to them other than as a recipient of the leader's actions. Indeed, while leaders are typically celebrated as resilient, flexible and innovative, followers are demonised as passive and resistant to change (Ford and Harding 2015). There are a number of studies that develop thinking in terms of followership, for example Rigio *et al.* (2008) have presented an edited collection of conference papers on followership. Jackson and Parry's (2008) work suggests ways of thinking that will support the examination of followers, for example social identity theories. Further, Smothers *et al.* (2012) argue that followers want equity rather than personalised treatment. These are early days for the study of followers but those who are engaging in this research have gone so far as to suggest that including the study of followers in leadership theory may call into question much of the existing theory. We give an example of this in the Window on practice that follows, which explores followership using a metaphor from Greek mythology – that of Odysseus leading his followers home from war.

WINDOW ON (MYTHICAL) PRACTICE

The story starts at the end of the Trojan War, when Odysseus sets out to return to his home in Ithaca. He leads several ships of soldiers who, we may presume, are similarly keen to return home. They are not to know that it is only Odysseus who will set foot once again on Ithaca, for the many adventures they will meet along the way will result in their decimation. For example, many men are lost in a battle at their first port of call, the island of the Cicones, and more are eaten by Polyphemus, a one-eyed giant, on the island of the Cyclops. And so it continues along the journey. Homer tells us of Odysseus's cleverness, in saving himself and (some of) his crew in many dangerous situations yet his crew are denied the pleasures of food and wine enjoyed by Odysseus and, ultimately, all perish.

Leadership contains, in this earliest recounting, a promise to followers of only horror, failure, betrayal, disappointment and denial. We are told that followers are incapable of agency unless organised by a leader, but is it not the case that without his crew Odysseus literally could not have sailed between the Greek islands? Without his crew Odysseus is revealed to be incapable. We can imagine one of his crew telling his story:

> The crew had waited interminably for Odysseus to continue the journey home to Ithaca, but Odysseus was bewitched on this enchanted island until one day we saw our chance. Circe was away. The lads begged me to go to Odysseus and to tempt him with thoughts of his home, his wife and son, so that he would agree we could leave that fated island and return to Ithaca. He eventually gave in, but blow me down if he did not find another reason for delay, and another, and another. And all along the way he was enjoying himself, while our number of men dwindled until only a few of us now remain. I have a foreboding about the future. I fear none of us will return to Ithaca.

Source: Adapted from Ford, J. and Harding, N. (2009) 'Telling an untold story: On being a follower rather than a leader', EGOS Colloquium, Barcelona.

This alternative telling of Odysseus's tale presents a very different perspective from the heroic one that has been perpetuated across the centuries. This may have resonance for many workers who question the effectiveness of leadership in their own organisations. It may now be that the time is right for a more detailed examination of the flipside of leadership: followership.

ACTIVITY 12.3

Thinking of your own experiences of being led (at work, school or other settings), what consideration was there of the role of followers? How could including their perspective have changed events?

SUMMARY PROPOSITIONS

12.1. Leadership is a process where one person influences a group of others to achieve group or organisational goals – leadership is thus about motivation.

12.2. The trait model of leadership, although often discredited, continues to play a part in our understanding of leadership.

12.3. Behavioural models are more helpful than earlier models as they concentrate on what leaders do rather than on what they are.

12.4. Some behavioural models offer a 'one best way' of leadership, but more sophisticated models take account of contingency factors such as maturity of followers and the nature of the task.

12.5. Models of transformational leadership treat the leader as a hero who can (single-handedly) turn the organisation around and deliver it from a crisis, whereas empowering and post-heroic leadership models conceptualise the leader as teacher and facilitator, who involves many in the leadership task.

12.6. There is an increasing interest in distributed, servant, authentic, ethical and respectful leadership as an appropriate response to leading in turbulent economic times.

12.7. Critical perspectives on leadership argue for the surfacing of the role of followers and suggest that this may call into question much current leadership theory.

GENERAL DISCUSSION TOPICS

1. Do we need leaders at all? Discuss what alternatives there might be.

2. How likely is it that post-heroic forms of leadership will replace heroic leadership approaches?

3. In what way do you think that including the perspective of followers in the study of leadership will contribute to theory?

THEORY INTO PRACTICE

We have argued in this chapter that leadership models developed from American research may not be effective in other contexts, even other western contexts such as Europe, and certainly not in Asia and Africa. Here we go further to consider whether integration of leadership concepts from elsewhere may in fact improve current leadership models. We draw on Bertsch's (2012) work on the African philosophy of Ubuntu and his application of this to American leadership models to explore this in some detail.

Our (widely adopted) definition of leadership centred on influencing people towards organisational ends. Globalisation and growing international operations have increased both the need to lead and influence across national and cultural boundaries and the recognition that what works in one country may not work in another. Yet multinational corporations have been slow to recognise this despite a substantial evidence base of the role of national context on leadership. Bertsch illustrates this through comparing the African philosophy of Ubuntu with heroic leadership models. Despite much criticism, these models of heroic leadership, centred on influencing, motivating and empowering, dominate American leadership thinking and Bertsch demonstrates that Americans tend to prefer charismatic and participative leadership styles. Ubuntu, however, is a philosophy of humaneness that rejects this notion of influence.

Bertsch defines Ubuntu as humaneness and explains it thus: 'a person is a person because of other persons [and requires] the capacity to express compassion, reciprocity, dignity, humanity, and mutuality in the interest of building and maintaining communities with justice and mutual caring' (p. 83). A person can only then function effectively as a human (and leader) when they acknowledge and appreciate the roles played by others. The five key elements of this philosophy comprise: survival; solidarity with others (missing in individual-centric American approaches); compassion; respect; and dignity. Bertsch argues that words such as harmony, connectedness, compassion, respect, human dignity and unity describe Ubuntu.

Ubuntu is thus at odds with American heroic leadership styles: it emphasises participation and agreement in decision making and presents a mechanism to ensure that decisions are ethical and that colleagues treat each other in appropriate ways. This arises from the fact that individuals are interconnected and must respect each other. Indeed, within this philosophy the ego and self-centredness often associated with heroic leaders is detrimental to good leadership. Leaders should be available and supportive of subordinates: a leadership position can only be retained if leaders act with civility, trust and respect and put the team's interests above their own. Self-awareness and self-assurance are essential. Leaders must promote the work and contribution of the team, which is again contrary to heroic leaders who seek recognition and glory.

Bertsch uses his analysis to argue that traits such as self-sacrificial, sincere, trustworthy, honest, group-focused and non-elitist are missing in contemporary American leadership practices. Further, that a move towards encouragement, compassion, solidarity would substantially alter these leadership practices and could address the ethical dilemmas facing many American-based corporations.

Questions

1 Do you agree that many of the aspects associated with Ubuntu are missing from heroic leadership models?

2 What similarities can you see between Ubuntu and emerging leadership models such as servant-leadership and authentic and ethical leadership models?

3 To what extent do you agree that the Ubuntu philosophy could improve American leadership models?

FURTHER READING

Crossman, B. and Crossman, J. (2011) 'Conceptualising followership: A review of the literature', *Leadership* 7(4): 481–97.

The authors review the followership literature to establish a definition of followership. They seek to develop understanding of followership so that it can inform improved leadership training and support higher organisational performance.

Avolio, B.J. and Gardner, W.L. (2005) 'Authentic leadership development: Getting to the root of positive forms of leadership', *Leadership Quarterly*, Vol. 16, pp. 315–38.

This editorial introduces a special issue on authentic leadership. It considers the environmental and organisational forces that have created interest in authentic leadership and the emerging questions and concerns that relate to it. Authentic leadership is also compared with other forms of leadership such as transformational and servant.

Gardner, W. *et al.* (2010) 'Scholarly leadership of the study of leadership: A review of The Leadership Quarterly's second decade, 2000–2009', *Leadership Quarterly*, Vol. 21, pp. 922–58.

This article presents a detailed analysis of published leadership research and how trends are developing. It demonstrates increased focus on post-heroic leadership research, but also that transformational leadership is still prominent.

REFERENCES

Alimo-Metcalfe, B. and Alban-Metcalfe, J. (2002) 'The great and the good', *People Management*, Vol. 8, pp. 32–4.

Appelbaum, S., Audet, L. and Miller, J. (2003) 'Gender and leadership? Leadership and gender? A journey through the landscape of theories', *Leadership and Organisation*, Vol. 24, pp. 43–51.

Arkin, A. (2009) 'Back seat drivers', *People Management*, 7 May, p. 26.

Beekun, R. (2012) 'Character centred leadership: Muhammad (p) as an ethical role model for CEOs', *Journal of Management Development*, Vol. 31, pp. 1003–20.

Ben-Hur, S. and Jonsen, K. (2012) 'Ethical leadership: Lessons from Moses', *Journal of Management Development*, Vol. 31, pp. 962–73.

Bennis, W. and Nanus, B. (1985) *Leaders: The strategies for taking charge.* New York: Harper & Row.

Bertsch, A. (2012) 'Updating American leadership practices by exploring the African philosophy of Ubuntu', *Journal of Leadership, Accountability and Ethics*, Vol. 9, pp. 81–97.

Blake, R. and Mouton, J. (1964) *The Managerial Grid.* Houston, TX: Gulf Publishing.

Bobbio, A., Van Dierendonck, D. and Manganelli, A. (2012) 'Servant leadership in Italy and its relation to organisational variables', *Leadership*, Vol. 8, pp. 229–43.

Bolden, R. and Kirk, P. (2009) 'African leadership: Surfacing new understandings through leadership development', *International Journal of Cross Cultural Management*, Vol. 9, pp. 69–86.

Bresnen, M., Hyde, P., Hodgson, D., Bailey, S. and Hassard, J. (2015) 'Leadership talk: From managerialism to leaderism in health care after the crash', *Leadership*, Vol. 11, pp. 451–70.

Chen, A. and Hou, Y. (2016) 'The effects of ethical leadership, voice behavior and climates for innovation on creativity: A moderated mediation examination', *Leadership Quarterly*, Vol. 27, pp. 1–13.

Chiniara, M. and Bentein, K. (2016) 'Linking servant leadership to individual performance: Differentiating the mediating role of autonomy, competence and relatedness need satisfaction', *Leadership Quarterly*, Vol. 27, pp. 124–41.

Claudel, P. and Casse, P. (2012) 'The ethical leader', www.trainingjournal.com, August, pp. 32–5.

Collinson, D. (2012) 'Prozac leadership and the limits of positive thinking', *Leadership,* Vol. 8, pp. 87–107.

Collinson, D. and Tourish, D. (2015) 'Teaching leadership critically: New directions for leadership pedagogy', *Academy of Management Learning and Education,* doi: 10.5465/amle.2014.0079.

Cowsgill, R. and Grint, K. (2008) 'Leadership, task and relationship: Orpheus, Prometheus and Janus', *Human Resource Management Journal,* Vol. 18, pp. 188–95.

Deegan, D. (2009) 'The changing face of leadership: Past, present and future', www.trainingjournal. com, December.

Den Hartog, D., Caley, C. and Dewe, P. (2007) 'Recruiting leaders: An analysis of leadership advertisements', *Human Resource Management Journal,* Vol. 17, pp. 58–75.

El Garah, W., Beekun, R., Habisch, A., Lenssen, G. and Adaui, C. (2012) 'Practical wisdom for management from the Islamic tradition', *Journal of Management Development,* Vol. 31, pp. 991–1000.

Eyong, J. (2012) 'Leadership re-construction in sub-Sahara Africa (SSA): Interpretation from an ancient indigenous organisation', The EKPE 4th Developing Leadership Capacity Conference, University of Exeter.

Fache, D. (2009) 'Are great leaders born or are they made?', *Frontiers of Health Service Management,* Vol. 26, pp. 27–30.

Fiedler, F. (1967) *A Theory of Leadership Effectiveness.* New York: McGraw-Hill.

Ford, J. (2010) 'Studying leadership critically: A psychosocial lens on leadership identities', *Leadership,* Vol. 6, pp. 1–19.

Ford, J. and Harding, N. (2009) 'Telling an untold story: On being a follower rather than a leader', EGOS Colloquium, Barcelona.

Ford, J. and Harding, N. (2015) 'Followers in leadership theory: Fiction, fantasy and illusion', *Leadership,* DOI: 10.1177/1742715015621372.

Ford, J., Harding, N. and Learmonth, M. (2008) *Leadership as Identity: Constructions and deconstructions.* London: Palgrave Macmillan.

Fullop, L., Linstead, S. and Dunford, R. (1999) 'Leading and managing', in L. Fullop and S. Linstead (eds), *Management: A critical text.* South Yarra: Macmillan.

Goffee, R. and Jones, G. (2006) 'The Lizard Kings', *People Management,* Vol. 12, pp. 32–4.

Goleman, D. (1998) 'What makes . . . a leader?', *Harvard Business Review,* November–December, pp. 93–102.

Goleman, D. (2000) 'Leadership that gets results', *Harvard Business Review,* March–April, pp. 78–90.

Grint, K. (1997) *Leadership.* Oxford: Oxford University Press.

Hannah, S., Woodfolk, R. and Lord, R. (2009) 'Leadership self-structure: A framework for positive leadership', *Journal of Organisational Behaviour,* Vol. 30, pp. 269–90.

Heil, G., Bennis, W. and Stephens, D. (2000) Douglas McGregor, Revisited: Managing the human side of the enterprise. New York: Wiley.

Herd, A., Alagaraja, M. and Cumberland (2016) 'Assessing global leadership competencies: The critical role of assessment centre methodology', *Human Resource Development International,* Vol. 19, pp. 27–43.

Hersey, P. and Blanchard, K. (1988) *Management of Organizational Behavior: Utilizing human resources,* 5th edn. Englewood Cliffs, NJ: Prentice Hall International.

Higgs, M. (2003) 'How can we make sense of leadership in the 21st century?', *Leadership and Organisational Development Journal,* Vol. 24, pp. 273–84.

Hill, M. and Bartol, K. (2016) 'Empowering leadership and effective collaboration in geographically dispersed teams', *Personnel Psychology,* Vol. 69, pp. 159–98.

Hollington, S. (2006) 'How to lead your boss', *People Management,* Vol. 12, pp. 44–5.

House, R. (1976) 'A 1976 theory of charismatic leadership', in L. Hunt and L. Larson (eds), *Leadership: The Cutting Edge.* Carbondale: Southern Illinois University Press.

House, R., Hanges, P., Javidan, M., Dorfman, P. and Gupta, V. (2004) *Culture, Leadership and Organisations: The GLOBE study of 62 societies.* Thousand Oaks, CA: Sage.

Jackson, B. and Parry, K. (2008) *A Very Short, Fairly Interesting and Reasonably Cheap Book about Studying Leadership.* London: Sage.

Jin, S., Seo, M. and Shapiro, D. (2016) 'Do happy leaders lead better? Affective and attitudinal antecedents of transformational leadership', *Leadership Quarterly,* Vol. 27, pp. 64–84.

Jones, S. (2014) 'Distributed leadership: A critical analysis', *Leadership,* Vol. 10, pp. 129–41.

Kets De Vries, M. (2003) 'The dark side of leadership', *Business Strategy Review,* Vol. 14, pp. 25–8.

Kotter, J. (1990) A Force for Change: How leadership differs from management. New York: Free Press.

Lawler, J. and Ashman, I. (2012) 'Theorising leadership authenticity: A Sartrean perspective', *Leadership,* Vol. 8, pp. 327–44.

Mailhot, C., Gagnon, S., Langley, A. and Binette, L. (2016) 'Distributing leadership across people and objects in a collaborative research project', *Leadership,* Vol. 12, pp. 53–85.

McGregor, D. (1960) *The Human Side of the Enterprise.* New York: McGraw-Hill.

Neubert, N., Carlson, D., Kacmar, K., Roberts, J. and Chonko, L. (2009) 'The virtuous influence of ethical leadership behaviour: Evidence from the field', *Journal of Business Ethics,* Vol. 90, pp. 157–70.

Northouse, P. (2006) *Leadership: Theory and practice.* Thousand Oaks, CA: Sage.

Quaquebeke, N. and Eckloff, T. (2010) 'Defining respectful leadership: What it is, how it can be measured, and another glimpse at what it is related to', *Journal of Business Ethics,* Vol. 91, pp. 343–58.

Rigio, R., Chaleff, I. and Lipman-Blumen, J. (2008) *The Art of Followership: How great followers create great leaders and organisations.* San Francisco, CA: Jossey-Bass.

Shackleton, V. (1995) *Business Leadership.* London: Routledge.

Smothers, J., Absher, K. and White, D. (2012) 'In the eye of the beholder: A configurational analysis of followers' conceptualizations of the ideal academic department leader at private universities', *Leadership,* Vol. 8, pp. 397–419.

Spector, B. (2014) 'Flawed from the "Get-Go": Lee Iacocca and the origins of transformational leadership', *Leadership,* Vol. 10, pp. 361–79.

Spillane, J. (2006) *Distributed Leadership.* San Francisco, CA: Jossey-Bass.

Tavanti, M. (2012) 'The cultural dimensions of Italian leadership: Power distance, uncertainty avoidance and masculinity from an American perspective', *Leadership,* Vol. 8, pp. 287–301.

Wong, C. and Cummings, G. (2009) 'The influence of authentic leadership behaviours on trust and work outcomes of health care staff', *Journal of Leadership Studies,* Vol. 3, pp. 6–23.

Yooyanyong, P. and Muenjohn, N. (2010) 'Leadership styles of expatriate managers: A comparison between American and Japanese expatriates', *Journal of American Academy of Business,* Vol. 15, pp. 161–7.

CHAPTER 13

ENGAGEMENT AND RETENTION

THE OBJECTIVES OF THIS CHAPTER ARE TO:

1 Debate the meaning of the term 'engagement' in the context of work and employment

2 Discuss the benefits associated with engaging people

3 Identify concerns about engagement

4 Outline the main reasons for voluntary resignations

5 Assess the arguments for and against investing resources in labour turnover reduction programmes

6 Explore approaches that can improve engagement and retention

While the search for an agreed definition of 'engagement' in the context of work and employment continues, there is a widely held view that an engaged workforce is more likely to deliver higher performance than one that is disengaged. In the introduction to a recent special issue on the *International Journal of Human Resource Management* (2013), Truss *et al.* weigh the evidence and generally support this view, although they acknowledge that better understanding of the engagement/performance relationship is needed. Nevertheless, the increased emphasis on this relationship has led us, in this latest edition, to move engagement from the section dealing with resourcing (with a focus on employee retention) to this section, which deals with performance. We retain discussion of employee retention, positioning it as a key performance outcome of engagement. Both engagement and retention are critical issues for HR practitioners and line managers seeking to effectively manage the workforce.

Engagement and retention are closely linked in a number of ways. First, it is clear from published research that relatively high levels of engagement tend to correlate quite strongly with relatively high employee retention rates. In other words, engaged employees are a good deal less likely to resign and seek alternative employment than disengaged employees. Indeed it is often disengagement that leads to resignations. Second, it is apparent from research into both areas that there is a good deal of similarity between the types of HR intervention that are commonly associated with high levels of engagement and low levels of unwanted turnover. It follows that implementing the same broad suite of initiatives is likely to have a positive effect on both turnover rates and the extent to which people in an organisation are positively engaged. We discuss these initiatives in more detail later.

Defining engagement

The term 'employee engagement' has become very widely used in recent years. This is because 'engagement' seems to capture concepts that other commonly used terms such as 'motivation', 'satisfaction' and 'commitment' do not quite manage to so well. Credit for inventing the term 'employee engagement' is often given to the American psychologist W.A. Kahn (1990) who conceived of its being made up of two distinct elements:

- **emotional engagement:** a situation in which employees have strong emotional ties to their managers, feel their opinions count and feel that their managers have an interest in their development;

- **cognitive engagement:** a situation in which employees know what is expected of them, understand their purpose or mission, are given opportunities to excel and grow, and are given information about how to improve their progress.

Subsequent researchers have taken up these ideas and have carried out many significant studies, refining their definitions of the term along the way and a recent CIPD Factsheet (2015) presents a helpful comparison of several well-recognised definitions. It remains the case, however, that we lack any kind of clear, precise, concise and widely agreed definition (see Purcell, 2014, for a more detailed discussion).

Part of the problem is the sheer number of different ways in which the verb 'to engage' is defined in dictionaries and commonly used in everyday speech:

- we like people who are engaging company;

- in the context of war, we talk about engaging the enemy;

- we make engagements to meet with other people;

- we talk about engaging on a mission or a journey or a programme of study;
- we use the term to signify a betrothal leading to marriage.

The term 'employee engagement' does not seem to equate well to any of these usages. Instead it draws on another use of the term 'engage', namely the act of 'engaging' someone's interest in an idea or organisational goal. However, just as employees can become engaged, they can also become disengaged. The lack of an agreed definition is problematic for researchers trying to reach a better understanding of how employee engagement can be measured, for example, or improved through management interventions. As matters stand, nearly every study that is published starts with its own definitions, some of which are more complex than others. Here are some examples:

> Work engagement is a positive, fulfilling, affective-motivational state of work-related well-being that can be seen as the antipode of job burnout. Engaged employees have high levels of energy and are enthusiastically involved in their work. Leiter and Bakker (2010: 1–2)
>
> The extent to which employees thrive at work, are committed to their employer, and are motivated to do their best for the benefit of themselves and their organisation. Stairs and Gilpin (2010: 158)
>
> A combination of commitment to the organisation and its values and a willingness to help out colleagues (organisational citizenship). It goes beyond job satisfaction and is not simply motivation. Engagement is something the employee has to offer; it cannot be 'required' as part of the employment contract. Daniels (2010)

Peccei (2013) points out that, as yet, when it comes to defining 'employee engagement' we do not really even have agreement on the fundamentals. For example, he asks, when we use the term are we referring to engagement with our work or to engagement with our organisations? Purcell (2014) develops this to argue that, for HR purposes, work engagement should be disregarded and it is behavioural ('employee') engagement that is the focus of our interest. Further debate continues as to whether 'engagement' is a long-term state, some being more engaged than others, or a state that we can move in and out of depending on our mood or the tasks we are working on at a particular time. More fundamentally, Peccei (2013) asks, is employee engagement properly conceived of as a state at all? Guest (2014) is blunter still in his assessment, expressing confusion about whether 'employee engagement' is an attitude, a behaviour, an outcome or a combination of the three, going on to argue that we should abandon the term altogether unless these very basic definitional questions can be answered.

As matters stand, however, we are far from abandoning the term. Instead its usage continues to grow, as demonstrated by Purcell (2014) who cites research showing the many thousands of publications on the topic in recent years. In truth, engagement is now seen as one of the key aims of HRM and people management more generally in organisations. The absence of a clear definition is not perhaps perceived as being problematic because, as several interviewees who contributed to the government-commissioned Macleod Report (Macleod and Clarke 2009) said, an 'engaged workforce is something that you know when you see it'.

ACTIVITY 13.1

What is your understanding of employee engagement? Which of the definitions in the CIPD *Factsheet* have most resonance for you and why? How important is an agreed definition?

Despite problems of definition, there is a sufficient degree of common ground between them to make the concept of 'employee engagement' useful from a practical management point of view. There is, for example, a shared understanding that 'engagement' represents a step beyond 'job satisfaction' and 'commitment' or even 'motivation'. Engaged employees have an emotional attachment to their work and/or their organisations which leads them to expend greater energy. There is thus a link to other widely used terms in HRM such as 'organisational citizenship', 'going the extra mile', 'working beyond contract' and 'discretionary effort'. Second, there is general agreement that being a positively engaged employee is beneficial both to the organisation and to the individual concerned. Engaged staff do not demonstrate enthusiasm and effort because they are forced to, but because they want to. Finally, it is abundantly clear that 'employee engagement' can only be usefully defined as a multidimensional concept that encompasses a variety of different elements. Indeed, it is quite likely that the antecedents of employee engagement vary from person to person, let alone workplace to workplace and country to country. In the following Window on practice, we report Gallup's recent work on variations in engagement levels across 142 countries.

WINDOW ON PRACTICE

Global engagement levels

We have so far discussed the importance of employee engagement but that should not be taken to mean that engagement levels are high. Indeed, in a 2013 survey Gallup (Gallup 2013), an organisation recognised as leading the field in employee engagement research, found that only 13% of employees worldwide were highly engaged, while 63% were not engaged and 24% were actively disengaged. Gallup research confirms engagement/performance relationships showing, for example, that organisations with highly engaged employees outperform other organisations in terms of productivity, profitability, customer satisfaction and employee retention. This provides a clear opportunity for HR professionals to improve engagement and thus increase performance.

Marked variations in engagement by country are evident, however, and interventions to improve it are likely to vary by context. In China (and East Asia more widely), only 6% of employees are highly engaged as compared to 24% in Australia and New Zealand. The Middle East and North Africa also evidenced high levels of disengagement of around 50% as compared to the Philippines where 29% are highly engaged. While much further research is required to understand these patterns, Gallup suggests that economic performance and employment levels might be strong influences. We also argue that cultural context will have a substantial role to play.

The benefits of employee engagement

The Gallup surveys we refer to above draw on data collected internationally over many years and are, to date, by far the biggest and most cited research studies on employee engagement and its impact, taking in several thousand organisations and hundreds of thousands of employees. The survey uses a simple twelve-question instrument comprising statements such as:

I know what is expected of me at work.
In the last seven days, I have received recognition or praise for doing good work.

Respondents are asked to indicate the extent of their agreement with statements and scores are generated for a business unit's level of engagement (Harter *et al*. 2002). The sheer size of this dataset gives the analysis a strong credibility. Furthermore, it enables statistically significant correlations to be sought between the extent of employees' emotional and cognitive engagement and other variables such as profitability, productivity, customer satisfaction and, importantly for our purposes in this chapter, employee retention. Some of the key findings are as follows:

1 There is greater variation in terms of the level of employee engagement between different business units within the same organisation than there is between organisations. This is significant because it implies that the variability in levels is not related to the type of industry or characteristics of employees – it is in most cases due to the quality of management.

2 Impressive correlations were found to exist between relative levels of employee engagement in a business unit and the success of business units. Business units with the highest rates of employee engagement are twice as successful as those with the lowest when measured against indicators such as productivity, customer responses and profitability.

3 A particularly strong relationship was found between levels of employee involvement and retention, that is, rates of labour turnover. The size of the dataset allows separate analysis of high-turnover industries and low-turnover industries. In high-turnover business units (above 60% turnover rate), labour turnover was, on average, 29% lower in units which scored in the upper quartile for employee engagement than in the lower one. The variation, however, ranged between 14 and 51 percentage points. In low-turnover units the average difference was 10% (ranging from 4 to 19 percentage points) between upper and lower quartiles.

Other key headline findings from the Gallup studies demonstrate the potential advantages of employee engagement from the perspective of employees:

- 86% of engaged employees 'very often feel happy at work' compared with only 11% who are disengaged;
- 45% of engaged employees 'get a great deal of their life happiness from work' compared with only 8% of people who are disengaged;
- 54% of actively disengaged staff state that 'work stress has caused them to behave poorly with friends or family in the past three months' compared with only 17% of engaged staff;
- 54% of actively disengaged staff report that their work lives 'are having a negative effect on their physical health' compared with just 12% of engaged staff.

The CIPD has also published research evidence (Truss *et al*. 2006) suggesting that people who are cognitively engaged with their work are three times as likely to exhibit 'six key positive emotions' at work – enthusiasm, cheerfulness, optimism, contentment, feeling calm and relaxed – than they are to experience negative emotions such as depression, gloominess and tension.

This research, like that of other researchers (e.g. Seligman 2003; Waddell and Burton 2006; Black 2008; Stairs and Gilpin 2010; Truss *et al.* 2013), links engagement to employee well-being and hence to better heath and lower absence rates. Another significant study that provides evidence of the positive business benefits associated with improving levels of employee engagement was that carried out by Towers Perrin–ISR (2006). Like the Gallup Studies this research was global in its scale, the data being gathered from question-naires completed by 664,000 people working for fifty different corporations. Here too statistically significant links were found to exist between the level of engagement among a workforce and measures of business success, notably rises in operating income, net income and earnings per share. The highest-performing companies in terms of measures of employee engagement saw an average improvement in their operating income during the twelve-month period prior to the study of 19.2%. This compared with average falls of 32.7% in the operating income of companies with low levels of employee engagement. Furthermore, average net income was found to have grown by 13.7% in the companies with high employee engagement scores, but to have declined by an average of 3.8% in those with low levels of engagement.

WINDOW ON PRACTICE

Macleod and Clarke (2009: 37–59) summarise the results of several smaller-scale studies looking for evidence linking relatively high levels of employee engagement with superior business performance. Because they tend to define the term 'employee engagement' rather differently and measure 'business success' in a variety of ways, we must be cautious in reaching general conclusions, but all provide at least some evidence to suggest strong links between high levels of engagement and positive business outcomes.

The most interesting and compelling evidence is found in studies that compare different business units in the same company, each of which provides the same range of services using the same operational procedures. Boots, the Standard Chartered Bank and the Nationwide Building Society all carried out research of this kind, and in all three cases found good evidence of business outcomes being positively associated with high levels of engagement. Nationwide found that its 'high-engagement' branches achieved 14% higher sales of banking products and 34% higher sales of insurance than branches with low-engagement scores. There were similar findings on measures of customer service, labour turnover and absence. Standard Chartered and Boots also identified significant differences between high- and low-engagement branches on measures of profitability.

In this section, we have presented extensive evidence of the benefits of employee engagement. It should also be noted that engagement has a number of criticisms. We have already discussed the lack of an agreed definition and Guest (2014) develops this to argue that engagement is essentially a meaningless term and a management fad. Purcell (2014) also argues that engagement can lead to work intensification and can be problem-atic. Employees are encouraged to engage and 'go the extra mile' to the extent that they may become stressed and burnout. The extra performance delivered via their engagement is not then sustainable. With less than one third of UK employees, in any event, being engaged (Gallup 2013) it appears that much further research is required to address both the desirability and feasibility of achieving employee engagement.

Employee retention

As we note above, employment engagement has a number of important performance outcomes. Retention is one of these outcomes and we discuss it in some depth in the remainder of the chapter. Retention is typically measured by labour turnover rates which, in their simplest form, measure employee departures from an organisation's employment (for information on calculating labour turnover rates, see Chapter 15c). Within this wide definition, however, turnover can take many forms. For example, employees may resign, retire, be dismissed or be made redundant. It is important to understand the reasons behind turnover in order to reduce it: labour turnover is extremely costly and most organisations work to reduce turnover levels to minimise these costs. The focus is typically upon labour turnover that is not employer-initiated and is avoidable, mainly employee resignations.

The impact of labour turnover

There is some debate about the level at which labour turnover becomes problematic. The answer varies from organisation to organisation. In some industries it is possible to sustain highly successful businesses with turnover rates that would make it impossible to function in other sectors. Some chains of fast food restaurants, for example, are widely reported as managing with turnover rates in excess of 300%, which means that the average tenure for each employee is only four months. Yet the companies concerned are some of the most successful in the world. By contrast, in a professional services organisation, where the personal relationships established between employees and clients are central to ongoing success, a turnover rate in excess of 10% is likely to cause damage to the business.

There are sound arguments that can be made in favour of a certain amount of labour turnover. First, it is fair to say that organisations need to be rejuvenated with 'fresh blood' from time to time if they are to avoid becoming stale and stunted. This is particularly true at senior levels, where new leadership is often required periodically to drive change forward. More generally, however, new faces bring new ideas and experiences which help make organisations more dynamic. Second, it is possible to argue that a degree of turnover helps managers to keep firmer control over labour costs than would otherwise be the case. This is particularly true of organisations that are subject to regular and unpredictable changes in business levels. When income falls, it is possible to hold back from replacing leavers until such time as it begins to pick up again. In this way organisations are able to minimise staffing budgets while maintaining profit levels during leaner periods. Redundancy bills are also lower in organisations with relatively high labour turnover because they are able to use natural wastage as the main means of reducing their workforce before compulsory lay-offs are needed. Third, it can be plausibly argued that some employee turnover is 'functional', that is, it benefits the organisation, rather than 'dysfunctional' because it results in the loss of poor performers and their replacement with more effective employees.

The arguments against labour turnover are equally persuasive. First, there are the sheer costs associated with replacing people who have left, ranging from the cost of placing a recruitment advertisement, through the time spent administering and conducting the selection process, to expenses required in inducting and training new employees. On top of these there are less easily measurable losses sustained as a result of poorer performance on the part of less experienced employees. For larger organisations employing specialist recruiters, these costs can add up to millions of pounds a year, with substantial dividends to be claimed from a reduction in labour turnover levels by a few percentage points. The second major argument in favour of improving staff retention results from a straightforward recognition that people who leave represent a lost resource in whom the organisation has invested time and money. The damage is all the greater when good people, trained and developed at the organisation's expense, subsequently choose to work for competitors. Finally, it is argued that high turnover rates are symptomatic of a poorly managed organisation. They suggest that people are dissatisfied with their jobs or with their employer and would prefer to work elsewhere. It thus sends a negative message to customers and helps create a poor image in the labour market, making it progressively harder to recruit good performers in the future.

We may thus conclude that the case for seeking to reduce labour turnover varies from organisation to organisation. Where replacement employees are in plentiful supply, where new starters can be trained quickly and where business levels are subject to regular fluctuation it is possible to manage effectively with a relatively high level of turnover. Indeed, it may make good business sense to do so if the expenditure required to increase employee retention is greater than the savings that would be gained as a result. In other situations, the case for taking action on turnover rates is persuasive, particularly where substantial investment in training is required before new starters are able to operate at maximum effectiveness. Companies that achieve turnover rates below their industry average are thus likely to enjoy greater competitive advantage than those whose rates are relatively high.

WINDOW ON PRACTICE

The length of time that employees remain in their jobs, or at least with the same employers, varies considerably from country to country. Auer *et al.* (2004) analysed the proportion of staff who had less than a year's service in the OECD countries and the proportion who had completed more than ten years' service. The country with the most shorter-term employees is the USA, where 24.5% have less than a year's service, while only 26.2% have been with their employers for more than ten years. At the other end of the scale is Greece, where only 9.8% have less than a year's service and as many as 52% have over ten years' service. High rates of job stability are also common in Italy, Belgium and Portugal. By contrast relatively low stability rates are found in the UK, Denmark and Ireland.

ACTIVITY 13.2

Why do you think labour turnover rates are so much higher in some industries than others? Make a list of the different factors that you consider may account for variations.

Analysing labour turnover

There is little that an organisation can do to manage turnover unless there is an understanding of the reasons for it. Information about these reasons is notoriously difficult to collect. Most commentators recommend exit interviews (i.e. interviews with leavers about their reasons for resigning), but the problem here is whether the individual will feel able to tell the truth, and this will depend on the culture of the organisation, the specific reasons for leaving and support that the individual will need from the organisation in the future in the form of references. Despite their disadvantages, exit interviews may be helpful if handled sensitively and confidentially, perhaps by the HR department rather than the line manager. In addition, analyses of turnover rates between different departments and different job groups may well shed some light on causes of turnover. Attitude surveys can also provide relevant information.

People leave jobs for a variety of different reasons, many of which are wholly outside the power of the organisation to influence. One very common reason for leaving, for example, is retirement. It can be brought forward or pushed back for a few years, but ultimately it affects everyone. In many cases, people leave for a mixture of reasons, certain factors weighing more highly in their minds than others. Below we outline one approach to categorising the main reasons that people have for voluntarily leaving a job, each requiring a different kind of response from the organisation. While functional turnover benefits the organisation, all other categories can be detrimental and organisations typically work to reduce turnover in these categories.

Functional turnover

Functional turnover includes all resignations which are welcomed by both employer and employee alike. The major examples are those which stem from an individual's poor work performance or failure to fit in comfortably with an organisational or departmental culture. While such resignations are less damaging than others from an organisation's point of view, they should still be regarded as lost opportunities and as an unnecessary cost. The main solution to the reduction of functional turnover lies in improving recruitment and selection procedures so that fewer people in the category are appointed in the first place. However, some poorly engineered change-management schemes are also sometimes to blame, especially where they result in new work pressures.

Outside factors

Outside factors relate to situations in which someone leaves for reasons that are largely unrelated to their work. The most common instances involve people moving away when a spouse or partner is relocated. Others include the wish to fulfil a long-term ambition to travel, pressures associated with juggling the needs of work and family and illness. To an extent such turnover is unavoidable, although it is possible to reduce it somewhat through the provision of career breaks, forms of flexible working and/or childcare facilities.

Push factors

With push factors, the problem is dissatisfaction with work or the organisation, leading to unwanted turnover. A wide range of issues can explain such resignations. Insufficient development opportunities, boredom, ineffective supervision, poor levels of employee involvement and straightforward personality clashes are the most common precipitating factors. Organisations can readily address all of these issues. The main reason that so many fail to do so is the absence of mechanisms for picking up signs of dissatisfaction. If there is no opportunity to voice concerns, employees who are unhappy will inevitably start looking elsewhere.

Pull factors

The opposite side of the coin is the attraction of rival employers. Salary levels are often a factor here, employees leaving in order to improve their living standards. In addition, there are broader notions of career development, the wish to move into new areas of work for which there are better opportunities elsewhere, the chance to work with particular people, and more practical questions such as commuting time. For the employer losing people as a result of such factors, there are two main lines of attack. First, there is a need to be aware of what other employers are offering and to ensure that as far as possible this is matched – or at least that a broadly comparable package of pay and opportunities is offered. The second requirement involves trying to ensure that employees appreciate what they are currently being given. The emphasis here is on effective communication of any 'unique selling points' and of the extent to which opportunities comparable with those offered elsewhere are given. Refer to Chapter 8 where we discuss establishing an effective employer brand.

What are the most common reasons for labour turnover?

UK-based studies focusing on people's reasons for leaving organisations are few and far between, but those that have been published tend to emphasise that a mix of different factors applies and that these vary from industry to industry (e.g. DiPietro *et al.* 2007; Carroll *et al.* 2008). Taylor and his colleagues (2002) interviewed 200 people who had changed employers about why they left their last jobs. They found a mix of factors at work in most cases but concluded that push factors were a great deal more prevalent than pull factors as causes of voluntary resignations. Very few people appear to leave jobs in which they are broadly happy in search of something even better. Instead the picture is overwhelmingly one in which dissatisfied employees seek alternatives because they no longer enjoy working for their current employer.

Interestingly this study found relatively few examples of people leaving for financial reasons. Indeed more of the interviewees took pay cuts in order to move from one job to another than said that a pay rise was their principal reason for switching employers.

Other factors played a much bigger role:

- Dissatisfaction with the conditions of work, especially hours.
- A perception that they were not being given sufficient career development opportunities.
- A bad relationship with their immediate supervisor.

This third factor was by far the one most commonly mentioned in the interviews, lending support to the often stated point that people leave their managers and not their organisations.

Branham (2005), drawing on research undertaken by the Saratoga Institute, reached similar conclusions. His seven 'hidden reasons employees leave' are as follows:

- the job or workplace not living up to expectations;
- a mismatch between the person and the job;
- too little coaching and feedback;
- too few growth and advancement opportunities;
- feeling devalued and unrecognised;
- stress from overwork and work–life imbalance;
- loss of trust and confidence in senior leaders.

Samuel and Chipunza (2009) looked at why long-serving staff had remained in their jobs, rather than focusing on why leavers had left. Their study took place in four large South African organisations: two in the private sector and two in the public sector.

They found that the four key factors that served to retain staff were:

- training and development;
- challenging and interesting work;
- freedom for innovative thinking;
- job security.

A recent study in the Philippines has also identified mismatch between employee and organisation values as a key reason for labour turnover (Presbitero *et al.* 2016). It would follow logically that organisations must address these issues to reduce labour turnover.

ACTIVITY 13.3

Think about jobs that you or members of your family have left in recent years. What were the key factors that led to the decision to leave? Was there one major factor or did several act together in combination?

Engagement and retention strategies

Engagement has been linked with improved performance in a number of areas, not least improved retention (Truss *et al.* 2014). A number of researchers, including Alfes *et al.* (2013) and Eldor and Harpaz (2016), have demonstrated that engagement mediates between HR practice and retention. Here we discuss a number of HR practices identified by Presbitero *et al.* (2016) as important to improving engagement and thus retention. These HR practices should provide them with a better deal, in the broadest sense, than they perceive they could get by working for alternative employers. This will also help to engage them. It is much more than a question of getting the terms and conditions of employment right. There is also a need to provide jobs which are genuinely satisfying, along with career development opportunities, as much autonomy and involvement as is practicable and, above all, competent line management. Indeed, it can be argued that most of the practices of effective HRM described in this text can play a part in enhancing engagement and reducing labour turnover. Below we look at five interventions that can be shown to have a positive effect.

Managing expectations

For some years, research evidence has strongly suggested that employers benefit from ensuring potential employees gain a 'realistic job preview' before they take up a job offer (see Chapter 8 for further information). Its purpose is to make sure that new staff enter an organisation with their eyes wide open and do not find that the job fails to meet their expectations. A major cause of job dissatisfaction, and hence of high labour turnover and low levels of employee engagement, is the experience of having one's high hopes of new employment dashed by the realisation that it is not going to be as enjoyable or stimulating as anticipated.

We also know from extensive research carried out into the nature of 'psychological contracts' that failing to meet expectations, and hence managing them effectively, can have serious de-motivational effects. The establishment of the concept of the 'psychological contract' is one of the most significant recent developments in the study of HRM (see Rousseau 1989; Conway and Briner 2005). The core idea is that employers and employees have a relationship that is much more complex and sophisticated than is set out in formal contracts of employment. The legal contract sets out the expectations and obligations each side has towards the other in respect of pay and terms and conditions of employment, but the reality of the relationship consists of much more than this. The 'psychological contract' can thus be defined as comprising expectations and obligations that the two sides have of one another and their relationship above and beyond what is formally agreed in any legal contract.

When an employer breaches the legal contract of employment there are legal consequences. For example, if pay is cut or the work location changed without contractual authorisation the employees who are affected can go to court to get injunctions or to sue for damages. If an employee breaches the legal contract (e.g. by going on strike), the employer responds by cutting wages. By contrast, when the psychological contract is breached the consequences are psychological – reduced commitment and loyalty, lower levels of motivation and reduced levels of trust both individually and collectively. The result is reduced employee engagement and higher levels of unwanted labour turnover.

Pay

There is some debate in the literature about the extent to which raising pay levels either reduces labour turnover or improves job satisfaction to any significant degree. On the one hand, there is evidence to show that, on average, employers who offer the most attractive reward packages have lower attrition rates than those who pay poorly (Gerhart 2009: 215–16), an assumption which leads many organisations to use pay rates as their prime weapon in retaining staff (White 2009: 35–9). On the other, there is evidence which suggests that pay is a good deal less important than other factors in a decision to quit one's job (Taylor 2002). The consensus among researchers is that pay has a role to play as a satisfier, but that it will not usually have an effect when other factors are pushing an individual towards quitting. Raising pay levels may thus result in greater job satisfaction, and hence employee engagement, where people are already happy with their work, but it will neither deter unhappy employees from leaving, nor re-engage many disengaged employees. Sturges and Guest (1999), in their study of leaving decisions in the field of graduate employment, summed up their findings as follows:

> As far as they are concerned, while challenging work will compensate for pay, pay will never compensate for having to do boring, unstimulating work. (Sturges and Guest 1999: 19)

Recent research findings thus appear to confirm the views expressed by Herzberg (1966) that pay is a 'hygiene factor' rather than a motivator. This means that it can be a cause of dissatisfaction at work, but not of positive job satisfaction. An employer who pays badly or is perceived to pay people inequitably will be unlikely to benefit from a highly engaged workforce. But higher pay will not generally lift levels of engagement if other factors such as the quality of the work or the management are poor. Similarly, people may be motivated to leave an employer who is perceived as paying badly, but once they are satisfied with their pay, additional increases tend to have little effect on turnover intentions.

While pay rates and benefit packages may play a relatively marginal role in the engagement and retention of good people, reward in the broader sense plays a more significant role. If employees do not find their work to be 'rewarding' in the broadest sense of the word, they will be much more likely to start looking for alternative jobs. This is a good deal harder for managers to achieve because different people find different aspects of their work to be rewarding. There is thus a need to understand what makes people tick and to manage them as individuals accordingly. It is far harder for would-be competitors to imitate the effective motivation of an individual than it is for them to increase the salary that a person is paid.

ACTIVITY 13.4

The case for arguing that pay rates have a relatively minor role to play in explaining individual resignations rests partly on the assumption that other elements of the employment relationship are more important. It is argued that people will 'trade in' high pay in order to secure other perceived benefits and that consequently low-paying employers can retain staff effectively.

1 What other factors do you think employees consider to be more important than pay?

2 What role can the HRM function play in helping to develop these?

Training and development

Both induction and ongoing training and development can influence engagement and reduce turnover. Induction processes play an important role in establishing expectations at the start of the employment relationship. It is very easy to overlook the importance of induction in the rush to get people into key posts quickly and it is often carried out badly. But it is essential, particularly if avoidable early turnover is to be kept to a minimum. Gregg and Wadsworth (1999: 111) show in their analysis of 870,000 workers starting new jobs in 1992 that as many as 17% had left within three months and 42% within twelve months. No doubt a good number of these departures were due either to poorly managed expectations or to ineffective inductions.

Induction has a number of distinct purposes, all of which are concerned with preparing new employees to work as effectively as possible and as soon as is possible in their new jobs. First, it plays an important part in helping new starters to adjust emotionally to the new workplace. Second, induction provides a forum in which basic information about the organisation can be transmitted. This may include material about the organisation's purpose, its mission statement and the key issues it faces. Third, induction processes can be used to convey to new starters important cultural messages about what the organisation expects and what employees can expect in return. It thus potentially forms an important stage in the establishment of the psychological contract, leaving new employees clear about what they need to do to advance their own prospects in the organisation. All these matters will be picked up by new starters anyway in their first months of employment, but incorporating them into a formal induction programme ensures that they are brought up to speed a good deal quicker, and that they are less likely to leave at an early date.

Ongoing training is also a key issue. There are two widely expressed, but wholly opposed, perspectives on the link between training interventions and employee turnover. On the one hand, there is the argument that training opportunities enhance commitment to an employer on the part of individual employees, making them less likely to leave voluntarily than they would if no training were offered. The alternative view holds that training makes people more employable and hence more likely to leave in order to develop their careers elsewhere. The view is thus put that money spent on training is money wasted because it ultimately benefits other employers. Green *et al.* (2000: 267–72) report research on perceptions of 1,539 employees on different kinds of training. The authors found that the overall effect is neutral, 19% of employees saying that training was 'more likely to make them actively look for another job' and 18% saying it was less likely to do so. However, they also found the type of training and the source of sponsorship to be a significant variable. Training which is paid for by the employer is a good deal less likely to raise job mobility than that paid for by the employee or the government. Firm-specific training is also shown in the study to be associated with lower turnover than training which leads to the acquisition of transferable skills. The point is made, however, that whatever the form of training, an employer can develop a workforce which is both 'capable and committed' by combining training interventions with other forms of retention initiative.

The evidence linking training and career development opportunities to employee engagement is much less unambiguous. Meta-analyses investigating the antecedents of relatively high levels of employee engagement place 'opportunities for development' close to the top of the list of factors that have a positive influence (Peccei 2013: 348). This is unsurprising because, in financing courses and training events, employers are sending a very clear signal to the employees concerned that their contribution is valued sufficiently for money to be invested in their personal development and potential career advancement.

WINDOW ON PRACTICE

Jenkins and Delbridge (2014) compare and contrast soft and hard approaches to employee engagement in two case study organisations, the softer approaches drawing on many of the type of retention initiatives we are discussing here. Voicetel's soft approach focused on provision of good workplace conditions and positive manager/employee relationships with no direct focus on improved productivity. By contrast, EnergyServ's explicit focus was on increasing engagement to improve performance outcomes. The softer approach saw positive employee engagement whereas the harder approach resulted in high levels of employee disengagement. The authors suggest that both organisational context and the underlying premise of engagement initiatives are central to the outcomes achieved.

Flexible working arrangements

Family or personal reasons are key triggers of labour turnover, particularly amongst women. UK employers believe that 21% of their leavers resign 'to have children or look after them', a further 7% leaving to look after other family members (CIPD 2009: 31). Official statistics also show that average job tenure among women with children in the UK is over a year shorter than that of women without children and almost two years shorter than that of men. Taken together these statistics suggest that one of the more significant reasons for voluntary resignations from jobs is the inability to juggle the demands of a job with those of the family. They indicate that there is a good business case, particularly where staff retention is high on the agenda, for considering ways in which employment can be made more flexible. Research into the antecedents of employee engagement also strongly suggests that the ability of people successfully to combine work and home responsibilities is one of the most significant factors in explaining high levels of engagement (Peccei 2013: 346–9).

Providing flexible working arrangements of these kinds is a very good way of retaining and engaging staff, particularly when organisations do more than their competitors. This is because juggling family and work responsibilities is a big issue in many employees' lives and because evidence suggests that it is thus hugely appreciated by them (DiPietro *et al.* 2007). We discuss types for flexible working arrangements in more detail in Chapter 7.

Improving the quality of line management

If it is the case that many, if not most, voluntary resignations are explained by dissatisfaction on the part of employees with their supervisors, it follows that the most effective means of reducing labour turnover in organisations is to improve the performance of line managers. Investing in improving the quality of line management can also be shown to improve the chances that staff will be more engaged with their work, 'leader–member exchange' being a significant factor in determining how engaged any individual employee is likely to be (Peccei 2013: 348).

Too often, it appears, people are promoted into supervisory positions without adequate experience or training. Organisations seem to assume that their managers are capable supervisors, without recognising that the role is difficult and does not usually come naturally to people. Hence it is common to find managers who are 'quick to criticise but slow to praise', who are too tied up in their own work to show an interest in their subordinates and who prefer to impose their own solutions without first taking account of their staff's views. The solution is to take action on various fronts to improve the effectiveness of supervisors to:

- select people for line management roles following an assessment of their supervisory capabilities;

- ensure that all newly appointed line managers are trained in the art of effective supervision;

- regularly appraise line managers on their supervisory skills.

This really amounts to little more than common sense, but such approaches are the exception to the rule in most UK organisations.

Of particular importance in promoting both employee retention and engagement is the need for line managers to involve people in decision making, and particularly, to allow them as much autonomy as possible in terms of how they perform their own role. Line managers thus need to be encouraged to stand back as much as possible to avoid supervising people more closely than is necessary. It is also important for line managers to ensure, at least as far as is possible given operational constraints, that working life is as interesting and varied as can be achieved.

SUMMARY PROPOSITIONS

13.1. Despite the lack of a clear and generally accepted definition, the term 'employee engagement' is increasingly used, while the concept is increasingly perceived as being important to improving organisational performance.

13.2. An engaged employee is someone who willingly works with greater enthusiasm and effort than is strictly required under the terms of his or her contract.

13.3. Considerable research evidence is now being amassed which links high levels of employee engagement to superior business performance.

13.4. Although modest levels of labour turnover can be beneficial, it is generally agreed that too high a rate is damaging for an organisation.

13.5. In planning retention initiatives it is important to analyse the causes of turnover among different groups of employees.

13.6. HR initiatives which lead to improved employee engagement and retention include the effective management of expectations, fair pay, sound induction and training opportunities, flexible working arrangements and the improvement of line management in organisations.

GENERAL DISCUSSION TOPICS

1. Labour turnover is generally low during recessions, but it increases substantially in firms which get into financial difficulty. What factors account for this phenomenon?

2. Why has interest in employee engagement as an idea increased so much in recent years?

THEORY INTO PRACTICE

McDonald's UK

During the 1990s negative impressions about employment at the McDonald's restaurant chain were fuelled in the UK, as elsewhere, by the growth in usage of the term 'McJob' as a generic label for low-status occupations. The term first appeared in 1991 in the bestselling novel *Generation X* written by the Canadian writer Douglas Coupland, where it is defined as 'a low-pay, low-dignity, low-benefit, no-future job in the service sector'. In 2003, much to the irritation of the company, the term 'McJob' appeared in the *Oxford English Dictionary* for the first time, defined as 'an unstimulating, low-paid job with few prospects, especially one created by the expansion of the service sector'.

The McDonald's UK operation tended to suffer from negative connotations about its employment practices more than was the case in most of the other countries where the company operates. This is partly because food service work in general tends to be accorded less prestige in the UK than is the case elsewhere in the world and partly because of the extraordinary growth that McDonald's enjoyed in the country during the 1980s and 1990s when the company opened between 50 and 100 new restaurants each year. This mass expansion was accompanied by limited central direction as far as employment practices were concerned. Local managers and franchisees were given responsibility for staffing up their restaurants, leading to the adoption of inconsistent approaches. They often struggled to recruit and retain effective employees, and were not always particularly choosey when deciding who to hire. This led to the development of the widely held view that anybody could get a job 'flipping burgers' at their local McDonald's just by turning up and asking for a job.

McDonald's UK responded by carrying out a staff attitude survey which found that the popular characterisation of its jobs was by no means accurate. In 2004, 74% of the company's employees reported being satisfied with their jobs and happy to 'recommend working at McDonald's to a friend', 77% stated that they were committed to their work, while 86% were happy with the training and skills development opportunities they were given. Staff were particularly positive about the flexibility that their jobs gave them to juggle work and home responsibilities, the career paths that were provided for them to follow and the enjoyment they got from working as a member of a team. The definition accorded to the term 'McJob' was not therefore a fair or correct reflection of the lived reality for a good majority of people working in the company's 1,200 UK restaurants.

However, the survey also revealed that staff were generally dissatisfied with their pay and that only 60% agreed with the statement 'I am proud to work at McDonald's'. Labour turnover was also running at very high levels in 2004. The annual rate had reached over 80%, while the ninety-day turnover rate (i.e. the proportion of new starters leaving before they have completed three months' service) was running at 24.5%. It appeared that poor hiring decisions were being made too often and that the company was not effectively managing the expectations of new starters about exactly what their jobs would involve on a day-to-day basis. The 2004 staff attitude survey thus showed that, although the company had plenty of scope to improve its HR operations, its poor reputation as an employer in the UK was by no means at all justified. The definition of the term 'McJob' was a thoroughly unfair characterisation of the experience of working in the company's UK outlets.

The company addressed these issues in a variety of ways, investing substantial sums in initiatives that were designed to improve retention and engagement, while also radically altering the company's reputation as an employer:

- A state-of-the art corporate development centre was established offering highly flexible training programmes and the opportunity for staff to gain a range of qualifications up to degree level. Management development was the major priority.

- A discount scheme was set up which could save employees many hundreds of pounds on a range of retailed products, on holidays and driving lessons.

- More flexible working initiatives were launched including family and friends contracts which allowed groups of people to decide for themselves who would work which shift.

- A range of employee involvement initiatives was introduced enabling, for example, staff to play a role in determining uniform styles.

- Additional investment was put into the organisation of social events for staff, often revolving around raising money for charities.

Managers at McDonald's in the UK are generally very happy with the impact that their initiatives have had. Between 2004 and 2010 the percentage of staff stating in surveys that they were committed to the company increased from 77% to 88%, while the percentage of those stating that they are proud to work for McDonald's went up from 60% to 84%. Increased staff satisfaction was also reflected in the figures for employee turnover. The crude annual rate for staff working in McDonald's restaurants declined from 80.2% in 2004 to 37.9% in 2010. The ninety-day turnover rate, a measure of the number of new staff leaving within the first three months, stood at 24.5% in 2004, reflecting the tendency for people to have false expectations about what their jobs would involve and the number of unsuitable people that managers were hiring. By 2010 this had fallen to just 2.4%.

Questions

1 What other factors, aside from the introduction of these HR initiatives, might explain the striking reduction in labour turnover levels that McDonald's achieved between 2004 and 2010?

2 What other sorts of initiative might the company consider introducing in the future to further increase levels of employee engagement and retention?

3 What wider business advantages might accrue to the company as a result of its success in improving its reputation as an employer?

FURTHER READING

Truss, C., Delbridge, R., Alfes, K., Shantz, A. and Soanne, E. (2014) *Employee Engagement in Theory and Practice.* Abingdon: Routledge.

Truss *et al.* provide detailed discussion of both practical and critical perspectives on employee engagement. The book contains numerous detailed case studies that demonstrate the application of recent research in contemporary business environments, written by both academics and practitioners.

Purcell, J. (2014) 'Disengaging from engagement', *Human Resource Management Journal,* Vol. 24, pp. 241–54.

Purcell discusses both work and behavioural engagement, with a focus on the latter, which he argues reflects current understanding of 'employee' engagement. He provides a detailed discussion of debates in employee engagement, including issues of its definition, measurement and connection to financial performance. He also presents an NHS case study to demonstrate how engagement can be effective in particular contexts.

Taylor, S. (2014) *Resourcing and Talent Management* (2nd ed.). London: CIPD.

Taylor's book contains two chapters covering the practicalities of managing turnover and retention. There are detailed sections on measurement, costing, analysing the reasons for turnover and on the major steps that employers can take to reduce turnover levels. Key debates in the field are also covered.

REFERENCES

Alfes, K., Shantz, A., Truss, C. and Soane, E. (2013) 'The link between perceived human resource management practices, engagement and employee behaviour: A moderated mediation model', *International Journal of Human Resource Management,* Vol. 24, pp. 330–51.

Auer, P., Berg, J. and Coulibaly, I. (2004) *Is a Stable Workforce Good for the Economy? Insights into the Tenure–Productivity–Employment Relationship.* Geneva: International Labour Organization.

Black, C. (2008) *Working for a Healthier Tomorrow: Review of the Health of Britain's Working Age Population.* London: The Stationery Office.

Branham, L. (2005) *The Seven Hidden Reasons Employees Leave.* New York: The American Management Association.

Carroll, M., Smith, M., Oliver, G. and Sung, S. (2008) 'Recruitment and retention in front-line services: The case of childcare', *Human Resource Management Journal,* Vol. 19, No. 1, pp. 59–74.

CIPD (2009) *Recruitment, Retention and Turnover: Annual Survey Report 2009.* London: Chartered Institute of Personnel and Development.

CIPD (2015) 'Employee engagement', in *Factsheet* (ed.). London: CIPD.

Conway, N. and Briner, R. (2005) *Understanding Psychological Contracts at Work: A Critical Evaluation of Theory and Research.* Oxford: Oxford University Press.

Daniels, K. (2010) 'Employee engagement', *CIPD Factsheet,* www.cipd.co.uk.

DiPietro, R., Thozhur, S. and Milman, A. (2007) 'Hourly employee retention factors in the United Kingdom quick service restaurant industry', *Journal of Foodservice Business Research,* Vol. 10, No. 4, pp. 39–61.

Eldor, L. and Harpaz, I. (2016) 'A process model of employee engagement: The learning climate and its relationship with extra-role performance behaviors', *Journal of Organizational Behavior,* Vol. 37, pp. 213–35.

Gallup (2013) *State of the Global Workforce,* http://www.gallup.com/services/178517/state-global-workplace.aspx [accessed 26 July 2016].

Gerhart, B. (2009) 'Compensation', in A. Wilkinson *et al.* (eds), *The Sage Handbook of Human Resource Management*. London: Sage.

Green, F., Felstead, A., Mayhew, K. and Pick, A. (2000) 'The impact of training on labour mobility: Individual and firm-level evidence from Britain', *British Journal of Industrial Relations,* Vol. 38, No. 2, pp. 261–75.

Gregg, P. and Wadsworth, J. (1999) 'Job tenure, 1975–98', in P. Gregg and J. Wadsworth (eds), *The State of Working Britain*. Manchester: Manchester University Press.

Guest, D. (2014) 'Employee engagement: fashionable fad or long-term fixture?', in Truss, C., Delbridge, R., Alfes, K., Shantz, A. and Soanne, E. (eds.), *Employee Engagement in Theory and Practice*. Abingdon: Routledge.

Harter, J., Schmitdt, F.L. and Hayes, T.L. (2002) 'Business-unit-level relationship between employee satisfaction, employee engagement and business outcomes: A meta-analysis', *Journal of Applied Psychology,* Vol. 87, No. 2, pp. 268–79.

Herzberg, F. (1966) *Work and the Nature of Man*. Cleveland, OH: World Publishing.

Jenkins, S. and Delbridge, R. (2014) 'Context matters: Examining "soft" and "hard" approaches to employee engagement in two workplaces, *International Journal of Human Resource Management,* Vol. 24, pp. 2670–91.

Kahn, W. (1990) 'Psychological conditions of personal engagement and disengagement at work', *Academy of Management Journal,* Vol. 33, pp. 692–724.

Leiter, M. and Bakker, A. (2010) 'Work engagement: Introduction', in A. Bakker and M. Leiter (eds), *Work Engagement: A Handbook of Essential Theory and Research*. New York: The Psychology Press.

MacLeod, D. and Clarke, N. (2009) *Engaging for Success: Enhancing Performance through Employee Engagement. A Report to Government*. London: Department for Business, Innovation and Skills.

Peccei, R. (2013) 'Employee engagement: An evidence-based review', in S. Bach and M. Edwards (eds), *Managing Human Resources* (5th edn.). Chichester: John Wiley.

Presbitero, A., Roxas, B. and Chadee, D. (2016) 'Looking beyond HRM practices in enhancing employee retention in BPOs: Focus on employee–organisation value fit', *International Journal of Human Resource Management,* Vol. 27, pp. 635–52.

Purcell, J. (2014) 'Disengaging from engagement', *Human Resource Management Journal,* Vol. 24, pp. 241–54.

Rousseau, D.M. (1989) 'Psychological and implied contracts in organizations', *Employee Responsibility and Rights Journal,* Vol. 2, pp. 121–39.

Samuel, M. and Chipunza, C. (2009) 'Employee retention and turnover: Using motivational variables as a panacea', *African Journal of Business and Management,* Vol. 3, No. 8, pp. 410–15.

Seligman, M. (2003) *Authentic Happiness: Using the New Positive Psychology to Realise your Potential for Lasting Fulfilment*. London: Nicholas Brealey.

Stairs, M. and Gilpin, M. (2010) 'Positive Engagement: From employee engagement to workplace happiness', in A. Linley *et al., Oxford Handbook of Positive Psychology and Work*. Oxford: Oxford University Press.

Sturges, J. and Guest, D. (1999) *Shall I Stay or Should I Go?* Warwick: Association of Graduate Recruiters.

Taylor, S. (2002) *The Employee Retention Handbook*. London: CIPD.

Towers Perrin–ISR (2006) *The ISR Employee Engagement Report*. London: Towers Perrin.

Truss, C., Delbridge, R., Alfes, K., Shantz, A. and Soanne, E. (2014) *Employee Engagement in Theory and Practice*. Abingdon: Routledge.

Truss, C., Shantz, A., Soane, E., Alfes, K. and Delbridge, R. (2013) 'Employee engagement, organisational performance and individual well-being: Exploring the evidence, developing the theory', *International Journal of Human Resource Management*, Vol. 24, pp. 2657–69.

Truss, C., Soane, E., Edwards, C., Wisdom, K., Croll, A. and Burnett, J. (2006) *Working Life: Employee Attitudes and Engagement 2006*. London: CIPD.

Waddell, G. and Burton, A. (2006) *Is Work Good for Your Health and Well Being?* London: The Stationery Office.

White, G. (2009) 'Determining pay', in G. White and J. Druker (eds), *Reward Management: A Critical Text* (2nd edn.). London: Routledge.

CHAPTER 14

MANAGING ATTENDANCE AND ABSENCE

THE OBJECTIVES OF THIS CHAPTER ARE TO:

1 Review the national context of employee absence

2 Identify the impact of absence on the business

3 Explore the process and causes of absence

4 Discuss methods to minimise long- and short-term absence.

Our understanding of the importance of attendance at the workplace and the problem of absence is linked to the changes in working practices over the past 200 years:

> industrial revolutions which transformed the economies of nations that had hitherto known only agriculture and handicrafts, aided by simple machines, brought new dangers and difficulties into society. (Neal and Robertson 1968: 9)

Note the phrase 'dangers and difficulties into society': the social impact was considerable and much quicker than any previous such change. Instead of fields and individual workshops, the standard workplace became the factory, with the central discipline of machinery powered from a single source, first water and later other forms of energy, and for reasons connected to supply of fuel, raw materials and transport. The underlying principle was that work had to be centralised to be efficient, and that principle has continued, regardless of the nature of the work being done. The modern 'factory' may be a bank in London, a restaurant in Paris, an automobile plant in Chicago, a hospital in Cape Town, or a hotel in Bangkok, but the workers have to be there, usually in large numbers. There may be moves towards home-working, decentralisation and subcontracting, but the traditional reasons of power, raw materials and transport have been replaced by specialisation and the concomitant need for intense communication, social interaction and proximity to the supply chain, facilities and resources. If employees need to be brought together for these newer reasons, they obviously need to be present at roughly the same time. People have to attend work in a specific place and at a specified time for a specified period. Attendance is key; absence is a problem.

The previous paragraph is exactly as it was in the last edition of this text; things are now changing, but not much. The rapid development of social networking and IT gadgets produces a change in the notion of the factory. Employees are still gathered to some central point to meet many of the terms of their contract. There is an erosion of the boundary element of the factory in that those in certain roles find that they do not have a clear distinction between being at work and being away from work. Emails continue to arrive and – for the obsessives – there is the need 'just to check up on what is happening'. One of the peculiarities of travel on cruise ships is when a person excuses themselves from the breakfast table to go where the reception is better, leaving a spouse with a look of weary resignation to continue alone with the toast and marmalade.

Attendance *by employees* is key; absence is a problem, although increasing flexibility of employments patterns, as described in Chapter 7, means that many people doing the work of the business are not employees but freelancers, sub-contractors or those on zero hours contracts, for whom the contract with the employer is different, as explained in Chapter 33.

The national context

Now we need to introduce the concepts of absenteeism/presenteeism. 'Absenteeism' is defined in the dictionary as regularly staying away from work without good reason, but is scarcely used in this text. It is included here simply to highlight its antonym, 'presenteeism', a term recently coined to describe the practice of people coming to work when they should not, as when unwell, for instance. Some people feel they may lose their job or a promotion opportunity if they are away. The management concern is that if they return too soon they may either aggravate their symptoms and ultimately be absent longer or they may jeopardise the health and safety of themselves or their colleagues by making mistakes or spreading germs.

Absence may be short-term or long-term, authorised or unauthorised, due to sickness, holiday, maternity/paternity, parenting, the performance of public duty, company business, public holiday and so on. The CIPD carries out an annual survey of the level of absence, omitting holidays and company business. In 2015 it found an average of 6.9 days absence per employee per year (CIPD 2015), down from 8.0 in 2009 (CIPD 2009) and 7.4 in 2008 (CIPD 2012). The average level of absence varies according to employment sector, being highest in the public sector and lowest in manufacturing and production and private-sector services. The CIPD is not the only organisation conducting such surveys, yet the results reported are broadly similar. Research by the Work Foundation (Silcox 2006) concluded that absence has remained broadly at the same level for the past thirty years, with small fluctuations due to unemployment and the wider economic cycle. This general conclusion confirmed earlier work by Hill and Halliday (2003).

One possible exception is in sickness absence. A nationwide analysis by the British Office for National Statistics was published in 2014 (ONS 2014) which showed a 27% decline in the number of days lost to sickness absence from 178 million in 1993 to 131 in 2013. This is attributed to various causes, particularly public attitudes and general health improvement for the working population at large.

WINDOW ON PRACTICE

Comparative absence figures

Lokke and her colleagues (2007) used data from the European Employee Index. The data was collected from employees, randomly selected, in 2004. Days absence per employee in 2004 were as follows: Denmark 2.8; Norway 3.5; Sweden 3.9; Finland 4.6. In each country absence in the public sector was higher than in the private sector, except for Sweden where there were no differences.

It is interesting to compare these figures with UK data for the same year where the CBI reports 6.8 working days lost per employee (CBI/AXA 2005) and the CIPD reports 8.4 (CIPD 2005). The differences might be explained by the choice of respondents, as the UK surveys collect data from managers about their employees, rather than directly from employees themselves. The TUC (2005) reported European comparisons based on figures produced by the University of Surrey. These indicate that short-term absence in the UK is lower than in any other country, apart from Denmark, and that long-term absence is lower than others except for Ireland, Austria and Germany.

Comparative figures are difficult to rely on as so much depends on sources and methods.

Sources: Lokke, A., Eskildsen, J. and Jensen, T. (2007) 'Absenteeism in the Nordic countries', *Employee Relations*, Vol. 29, No. 1, pp. 16–29; TUC (2005) *Countering an Urban Legend: Sicknote Britain?* TUC: London; CBI/AXA (2005) *Who Cares Wins: Absence and Labour Turnover 2005.* CBI/AXA: London; CIPD (2005) *Absence Management: A Survey of Policy and Practice.* CIPD: London.

The general conclusions from all survey data are that:

- absence is higher in larger organisations than in small ones;
- public-sector absence is higher than in the private sector;
- absence rates are higher for women, full-time workers and those under 30;
- managers, professionals and administrative professionals have lower levels of absence than other occupational groups (although this may be because they tend to have more flexibility in their working arrangements);
- absence is higher among manual workers.

The CBI reports that absence costs the UK economy around £13 billion per year and it constantly asserts that around 13% of all absence is not genuine or absenteeism, while unions point to the efforts that workers often make to attend work even when ill – presenteeism (e.g. TUC 2005). Big sporting events, such as the World Cup, often attract attention in terms of their impact on absence levels, but organisations can use these events to their advantage, given some thought. Smethurst (2006) reports on how Prudential and Egg responded to the World Cup by offering more flexible working over the period, with incentive schemes and themed competitions to incorporate interest in the event.

At a national level the cost of sickness absence is considerable to employers and to the taxpayer. Despite the decline since 1993 mentioned above, in 2013 in the UK, for instance, over 2.6 million people claimed long-term sickness and disability benefit, considerably more than those claiming unemployment benefit. More recently there have been major changes to the rules about claiming benefit and data from the initial trials of the new arrangements showed a net reduction in eligibility of 30% after appeals were taken in to account.

The organisational context

Attendance and absence are relatively easy to monitor in the sense of a common culture and rules, deviation from which is obvious and manageable. Absence has always been a problem for employers for the obvious reasons of dislocation in the production and administrative processes of the business, and methods for reducing it have frequently focused on disciplinary or punitive measures. Recently absence has been framed in a more constructive way by shifting the focus to what can be done to promote attendance, as well as the rehabilitation of employees with long-term absence.

The CIPD (2006) found that over 90% of organisations in its survey considered absence to be a significant cost to the organisation, but less than half monitored this cost. The average cost was reported to be £598 per year per employee, which had risen to £673 in 2011 (CIPD 2012). Several studies (e.g. Barham and Leonard 2002; Bevan 2002) show that estimating the costs of absence is complicated, and that the estimate needs to include not only direct costs (i.e. paying salary and benefits for a worker who is not there), but also indirect costs such as replacement staff, overall reductions in productivity and administrative costs. Most employers underestimate the true costs of sickness absence, particularly long-term sickness; even the most sophisticated companies are not well equipped to calculate such costs.

Traditionally employers have concentrated on managing short-term absence, and while long-term absence accounts for only around 20% of absence incidents, it can represent more than 40% of total working time lost.

Process and causes of absence

The most frequently stated causes of absence are minor illness for short-term absence: back pain and minor illness (for manual workers) and stress and minor illness (for non-manual workers). For long-term illness the most frequent causes for manual workers are back pain and musculoskeletal injuries; and for non-manual workers stress remains the greatest, and an increasing, cause. The increase in stress as a cause may well partly be due to the fact that this is now a more legitimate reason for non-attendance than previously. Cynics will point out that lower back pain and stress are both very difficult for anyone other than the sufferer to corroborate.

It is important to realise that much of employee absence is either at the behest of the employer, like training or visiting customers, or it is unavoidable, like holidays, maternity/paternity leave or on compassionate grounds. Despite this employer preoccupation is typically with what is often described as 'illegitimate' absence, such as young single men missing on Monday mornings. It is this that produces the focus on trying to reduce avoidable absence. This is shown in a model of absence (Rhodes and Steers (1990) that we still regard as the most useful (Figure 14.1).

The emphasis is completely on individual employee motivation to attend. However sensible this is, there may be need for an additional requirement for a strategic approach to managing the *inefficiencies* that absence causes, involving staffing levels, increasing skill diversity, effective procedures for inducting temporary staff and so on.

The causes of absence are complex and interrelated and a process approach is generally agreed to be the most useful way of understanding absence behaviour, although there are criticisms that such models are not supported by the evidence. One of the most widely

Figure 14.1
The Rhodes and Steers process model of attendance
Source: Rhodes, S. and Steers, R. (1990) *Managing Employee Absenteeism.* Reading, MA: Addison-Wesley.

quoted models is from Rhodes and Steers (1990) and in our view this is the most useful of the process models.

The Rhodes and Steers model (see Figure 14.1) focuses on attendance motivation and the ability to attend in terms of resulting attendance behaviour. They suggest that *attendance motivation* is directly affected by two factors: *satisfaction with the job* and *pressure to attend*. Pressure to attend may result from such factors as market conditions. Examples include the likelihood that there will be redundancies at the individual's workplace and how easy it would be to get another job; incentives to attend, such as attendance bonuses; work group norms on what is acceptable in the work group and the effects of absence on other group members; personal work ethic producing internal pressure to attend based on beliefs about what is right; and commitment to the beliefs and values of organisation and an intention to remain with it. On this basis threat of redundancies, attendance bonuses, team structures where team members have to cover the workload of an absent member, a personal ethic about the need to attend work wherever possible, and feelings of loyalty to the business all promote the motivation to attend. All of these factors contribute to the current phenomenon of 'presenteeism', which is explored in the Glossary at the end of the book.

WINDOW ON PRACTICE

In the Preface we mentioned disaggregation of the workforce, including people working at home. Here is a story about a move that is towards recentralisation.

The huge business Yahoo had run into major problems of competitiveness threatening its survival. In 2012 the newly appointed CEO, 37-year-old Marissa Mayer, decreed that working from home would be discontinued, causing outcry from Yahoo's workers from home who were stay-at-home mothers and many others who bombarded social networking sites with hostile reactions to this 'attack on workers' rights'.

One of the reactions was from the CEO of a different company who pointed out that the needs for corporate survival override the issue of employee expectation. When a company is in difficulty, needing a culture change, you need to have your people physically together if it is going to work.

Rhodes and Steers suggest that satisfaction with the job is determined by the *job situation* and moderated by *employee values and job expectations*. Factors in the job situation are identified as job scope and level of responsibility and decision making; role stress such as work overload, underload, difficult working conditions or hours; work group size; leadership style of an individual's immediate manager, particularly the openness of the relationship and how easy it is to discuss and solve problems jointly; strength of relationships with co-workers; and the opportunity for promotion. On this basis higher levels of responsibility and the opportunity to make decisions in relation to job demands, balanced workload and good working conditions, small work group size, an open relationship with the immediate manager, good relationships with colleagues and the opportunity for promotion should all improve attendance motivation.

However, job satisfaction is moderated by the values and expectations of the employee. Such values and expectations are shaped by personality, personal characteristics and life experiences, but can also change during the course of one's life. A close match between one's job situation expectations and values is more likely to lead to satisfaction than a mismatch.

Managing for attendance

Long-term and short-term absence require different management approaches. Causes may be identified by examining patterns of absence and then helping people to be open about why they are not at work. Measures range from proactive methods intended to reduce the risk of ill health, to measures intended to reduce spells of absence and those intended to reduce the length of absence. Typically there is a mix of processes both to discourage absence and positively encourage attendance, but these work differently with those on long- and short-term sickness absence.

Whatever approach is chosen, consistency is essential in devising and implementing absence management policies and procedures to ensure fairness and to support any disciplinary action taken, but also to provide employees with clear expectations about how absence will be tackled, and promoting an attendance culture. While different approaches may be needed in different sectors and with different types of staff, the policies themselves need to be consistent, encouraging employee acceptance and line manager support. Dunn and Wilkinson (2002) illustrated this by reporting the difficulties of a line manager in a production company because manufacturing staff were subject to more stringent absence procedures than other staff in the company.

Inconsistent implementation weakens any policy and procedures. The role of the line manager is key and there is much emphasis on giving the line manager ownership of absence and attendance issues, with support from the HR department. Whatever policies and procedures are set up, the line manager must have ownership of these, while sticking within the overall policy framework. James and his colleagues (2002) found that two-thirds of their interviewees in a long-term absence management study had problems in the way that line managers carried out their responsibilities. Managers frequently did not follow the guidelines in matters such as ongoing contact with absent employees, and consequently the HR department did not know what was happening and often had to step in and manage cases. James and his colleagues found that managers' behaviour resulted from time pressures, lack of awareness of what the procedure was and lack of training.

WINDOW ON PRACTICE

Managing absence at HBOS

McFadzean (2003) reports on a pilot project at HBOS which encouraged the HR department to look at absence from a different perspective. The project was intended to test two theories: first, that much absence had non-medical causes and therefore could be tackled by the HR department; and, second, that absence could be reduced without buying in any extra resources.

To introduce the project workshops were held with HR members and best practice guidelines were made available, HR advisers were then encouraged to go out and talk to managers about absence. The best practice model included an emphasis on finding the underlying cause of absence in terms of social or work-related issues, based on the belief that such issues are the root cause of much absence, and if not dealt with they will gradually produce medical symptoms. The skill was therefore in getting beyond the symptoms on the medical note to understand the underlying cause of absence. Once the underlying cause was understood then temporary or permanent changes could be made to help, such as reducing targets, hours and responsibilities or changing work patterns.

HBOS promoted an absence champion network in its first-tier approach which would adopt the best practice principles provided by the HR department, and would receive up-to-date information on absence and target cases for intervention (over twenty days' absence for long-term absence and four periods in a year for short-term absence). The HR department received consistent management information, and progress was monitored in all cases. A health provider network was also set up, as a second-tier approach (for long-term absence), to target high-risk areas and the top two causes of absence. Individuals were referred after ten days' absence in these cases, and the health provider network included a psychologist and a physiotherapist. Treatment was considered justified if there was deemed to be an 80% chance of return to work. HBOS feels that rehabilitation back into work needs to become part of the business culture.

The project was only carried out in some areas and performance was measured against control groups. HBOS saved 21,000 days over the six-month period (6,000 headcount) and £880,000. Short-term absence was reduced by 35%, but there was no impact on long-term absence, which continued to creep up.

Source: After McFazdean, M. (2003) 'Managing absence', Paper presented at the CIPD National Conference, Harrogate, 22–24 October.

Some measures intended to manage absence actually increase it, so monitoring any new policies and procedures is critical. A long-standing and well-used approach to implementing a new absence strategy is the simple ALIEDIM process of Huczynski and Fitzpatrick (1989). The process has seven stages:

- Assess the absence problem.
- Locate the absence problem.
- Identify and prioritise absence causes.
- Evaluate the current absence control methods.
- Design the absence control programme.
- Implement the absence control programme.
- Monitor the effectiveness of the absence control programme.

The important thing is to follow the logic. Some people believe they can start at the third stage because 'everyone knows what the problem is: they take a couple of days off when they don't feel like it and say they've got a bad back', but careful consideration at the earlier stages begins the process of eventually getting the right answers which are appropriate to the specific situation. What works elsewhere may not be appropriate.

Some of the most frequently used approaches to managing absence follow. Some work better for short-term absence, others are better suited to long-term absence, and some meet the needs of both.

Accurate records

Managing absence is almost impossible without an accurate picture of current absence levels and patterns, which requires identification of areas of high absence and the most common reasons for absence in the organisation. However, such data collection is more often reported in the public sector and in the manufacturing industry than in the rest of the private sector. The Health and Safety Executive (HSE) (Silcox 2005a), in a bid to aid employers, has produced a computerised absence recording and management tool, SART, which encourages employers to record such data in a more consistent manner.

Absence reports are frequently produced by the HR department and sent to line managers – and such reports will often include details of employees where trigger points have been hit and where intervention is required by the line manager. However, Dunn and Wilkinson (2002) found that the attention line managers gave to these reports varied, and some managers never even looked at the reports, because they did not agree that this was the best way to manage staff. As one manager commented, 'I know my staff well enough not to need these reports . . . at the end of the day it all comes down to good management and knowing your staff.' Some managers argued that the reports were of little use because the employees they managed often worked long hours (beyond contract) and came in at weekends. It was felt that to punish such employees, who were clearly committed to the company, because they had reached certain absence levels was unreasonable, and would be counter-productive.

Absence review and trigger points

One way to pick out people with less than satisfactory absence records is to identify trigger points in either the number of absence spells in a period or their length, or their frequency. If you identify a trigger point for those three aspects, the absence recording system will signal to the appropriate manager when any individual employee's trigger point is reached. CIPD (2006) reported that 67% of organisations reporting a decrease in absence levels attributed this to tightened policies for reviewing absence.

There is a risk of such trigger points becoming well known to employees, however, and Connex (IDS 2001) found that some employees were able to manipulate the system and regularly have absence levels just below the trigger point. Dunn and Wilkinson (2002) found organisations where the trigger system was avoided because it was felt that it would encourage employees to take time off until they were just under the trigger limit.

Some organisations have absence review groups, such as the absence champion network at HBOS, and the safety, health and absence unit at HM Customs and Excise (IDS 2001). While the role of these groups varies, they are frequently used to review all absences and identify those who have hit trigger points, which will then require intervention, such as an absence review meeting with the employee.

Absence targets and benchmarking

Some businesses have absence targets phrased in terms of a reduction on current absence levels or a lower absence level to attain. However, the CIPD (2006) found that although 80% of the organisations it surveyed believed that absence levels could be reduced, less than half of these had set targets for this, and only around 37% benchmarked their absence levels against other organisations. An alternative approach, used by some organisations, is to give managers absence targets for their group, and tie this into their performance review and performance payments. This is the approach used in Connex (IDS 2001). Such overall and local targets need to be carefully used, however, so as not to give the impression to employees that absence is not allowed. This is the sort of dilemma at the core of all HR. Implementation of policy should be fair, as that is a basis for action throughout civilised society, but there must be flexibility to avoid silly mistakes. Exercising flexibility in managerial action will be seen as unfair by some.

ACTIVITY 14.1

We have noted that some organisations link improvements in absence levels in their departments to managers' performance assessments and performance-related pay.

1 What are the potential advantages of this approach?

2 What are the potential problems?

3 How else might managers be encouraged to treat absence levels as a key priority?

Training and support for line managers

If line managers play a key role in making absence procedures work and in reducing absence levels, training will be needed when a new absence system is introduced. Connex (IDS 2001) introduced a creative form of training. The company takes managers to an employment tribunal to view an absence-related case so that managers will understand the consequences of not dealing fairly and consistently with employees when they have to deal with similar situations at work. HM Customs and Excise (IDS 2001) uses training videos showing role plays of return to work interviews (see below). These demonstrate that such a meeting is not about accusation or recrimination. The idea is that managers watch the video with their team of supervisory staff and then discuss the issues that arise.

However, both James *et al.* (2002) and Dunn and Wilkinson (2002) found managers who could not understand how 'sickness' could be managed, were scared of dealing with the situation and were embarrassed about asking personal questions about an employee's state of health. This requires specialised training and not everyone will be able to do it.

Absence notification procedures

Many organisations specify that when employees phone in as absent they must phone themselves, rather than asking another person to phone on their behalf. Many also specify that the employees must speak to their direct line manager or nominated representative.

This means that such a telephone conversation can be the first stage of the absence management process. The conversation is welfare-based and the intention is that the manager is able to ask about the nature of the problem and the anticipated date of return to work. An alternative to this method is to re-route the call either to a member of HR or to an external agency employing a trained nurse to answer and give professional advice on treating the ailment (see IDS 2005b), making no reference to a possible date to return to work. The call is, however, recorded and the appropriate line manager informed. Often the employee will volunteer expected return-to-work date, for example, ". . . tell Charlie I should be back in a couple of days'. Appropriate follow-up is then decided on a case-by-case basis. Managers appreciate the removal of the immediate burden and concentrate their attention on any employees whose absence level has reached a trigger point.

Some organisations, such as First Direct (IDS 2001), make every effort to offer alternative work. For example, a telephone operator who cannot do telephone work with a sore throat may be able to do other work, and managers are asked to bear this in mind when employees phone in sick and to try to encourage the employees to come in, where appropriate, to carry out other tasks. This telephone conversation is also seen as an important tool in reducing the length of the absence. This encourages people who want to come in to work, but it may backfire if the returnee is not really fit enough, spreads germs to colleagues and causes more problems than being absent.

Better understanding of the causes of absence

Understanding absence requires sound data. Three measures are commonly used. The *absence rate* is the number of days of absence, when attendance would be expected, of all employees. The *absence percentage rate* is the absence rate divided by the total number of actual working days for all employees over the year, multiplied by 100. This simple percentage is widely used to compare absence level with national data and with data of other organisations in the same sector.

The *absence frequency rate* is the number of spells of absence over the period, usually a year. Comparing this and the absence percentage rate gives a key snapshot of the absence situation in the organisation. As well as making external comparisons, the same types of analysis can be used to compare departments, work groups, occupations, grades and so on.

Analysis of absence data may help employers develop absence management methods relevant to the most frequent causes. However, as we have said, the reasons employees give for absence will be those that the organisation considers legitimate, and further investigation may be necessary.

Organisations can encourage individuals to be open about the real cause for their absence; for example, a minor illness may be used as an excuse to cover for caring responsibilities, a stressful working environment or alcohol or drug problems. However, this is easier said than done. The London Borough of Brent (IRS 2002a) decided that the next stage in its efforts to tackle long-term absence was to try to unpick its causes. This employer had a feeling that the explanation may be partly related to issues of stress and the nature and organisation of the work. Helping employees to feel that they can trust the employer sufficiently to admit the real cause of absence means that absence can then effectively be tackled by providing the appropriate form of support. Another key tool is risk assessment, for example assessing the risk of back pain or stress and then training to meet identified needs. The CIPD (2006) found that organisations used risk assessments, training, staff surveys, policy development, flexible working, employee assistance programmes, focus groups and changes in work organisation as methods to identify and reduce stress. The HSE encourages the use of focus groups for stress identification and management; more details and examples can be found in Silcox (2005b).

WINDOW ON PRACTICE

Risk assessments for stress

Stress accounts for a large proportion of sickness absence in the NHS, so researchers from the Institute of Work, Health and Organisations at Nottingham University studied five groups of hospital staff working under pressure: nurses, healthcare assistants, technical and professional staff, catering staff and clerical/reception staff to measure and tackle stress at work. The intervention began with risk assessment, and a well-being questionnaire was used to gather employee feelings about tiredness and exhaustion. Employees were asked to identify not only causes of stress, but also changes to management practice which would provide a solution. One of the examples provided is the catering team, who identified causes as peak-time high workloads, poorly maintained equipment and inadequate training. Resultant interventions included regular equipment maintenance, additional peak-time staff and regular team briefings.

Source: Summarised from HSE (2002a) *Interventions to Control Stress at Work in Hospital Staff,* HSE Contract Research Paper No. 435. London: HSE.

Ongoing contact during absence

Maintaining contact during absence can be a way of reducing the length of absence, providing that it demonstrates continuing interest in the employee's welfare and not just checking up. This maintains employee motivation. In some cases it is the line manager who will keep in touch, and in others alternative personnel take on this role. A useful summary of methods of keeping in touch with employees who are off sick is given in Silcox (2005c). The Employers Organisation for Local Government (EO) (HSE 2002b) suggests that more effort should be made to keep in touch with employees after operations, partly to keep them up to date, but also to see if it is possible for them to come back to work on light duties or on a part-time basis. This constructive approach avoids the risk of people returning to work too early.

Return to work interviews and formal absence reviews

Return to work interviews are used increasingly as a key part of attendance procedures. The CIPD (2006) reports that these were used by 81% of organisations in 2006 compared with 57% in 2000. These interviews are regarded as the most effective way of managing short-term absence. They are mandatory in some businesses, even following a single day's absence, but there is frequently some flexibility about the nature of the interview depending on the circumstances. The general purpose is to welcome people back and update them on recent events; to check that the employee is well enough to resume normal duties; and to determine whether any further support is needed. This reinforces the fact that the employee has been missed and that attendance is a high priority in the organisation. Dunn and Wilkinson (2002) found managers in their research who said that there was not time to concentrate on return to work interviews, as the practicalities of getting the job done were more critical. They also found a view among line managers that they were just so glad to get the employee back that they did not want to 'rock the boat'. Where formal absence reviews are held these need to be handled with sensitivity and tact, and care needs to be taken so that the interview does not become recriminatory or accusatory.

Use of disciplinary procedures

If someone is genuinely ill and unable to work, disciplinary action whether threatened or real is unlikely to bring about a return to work. There are, however, situations in which people who are too ill to work have to be dismissed. Never a pleasant task, it often falls to the HR manager to carry it out. The key is to make sure that the dismissal is carried out in a legally sound manner. Briefly the main points are:

1 Dismissing someone who is unable to work because of ill health is potentially fair under unfair dismissal law.

2 It is necessary to warn the individual concerned that he or she may be dismissed if he or she does not return to work and to consult with them ahead of time to establish whether a return in the foreseeable future is feasible.

3 It is necessary to act on whatever medical advice is available.

4 In larger organisations, except where a person's job is very specialised or senior, it is normally considered reasonable to refrain from dismissing a sick employee for at least six months.

5 In any case no dismissal should occur if the employee falls under the definition of 'disabled' as set out in the Disability Discrimination Act 1995. In these cases an employee should only be dismissed once the employer is wholly satisfied that no reasonable adjustments could be made to accommodate the needs of the sick employee so as to allow them to return to work.

Where someone is persistently absent for short periods of time, the course of action taken will depend on whether there is a genuine underlying medical condition which explains most of the absences. If there is, the matter should be handled in the same way as cases of long-term absence due to ill health outlined above. If not, then it is feasible for the employer to take a tougher line and to threaten disciplinary action at an earlier stage. It is quite acceptable in law to dismiss someone whose absence record is unacceptably high, provided the individual has been warned ahead of time and given a fair opportunity to improve his or her attendance. It is also necessary to treat different employees in a consistent fashion. Taking disciplinary action in the form of issuing a formal warning is therefore credible and likely to be successful.

Absence levels and performance assessments

Some organisations include the review of attendance levels as one of the factors in any performance assessment. Dunn and Wilkinson (2002) found that in the three retail companies in their case sample, employees were assessed via a separate rating category on their absence levels. Employees with unacceptable absence levels would not be put forward for transfers or promotion. At HBOS (IDS 2005a) line managers had a key performance objective relating to employee absence, reflecting their enhanced roles in managing absence.

Attendance bonus and rewards

Some organisations pay bonuses direct to employees on the basis of their attendance records. For example, in Richmondshire District Council (Silcox 2005d) staff receive an additional day's leave for 100% attendance in the previous year. When this bonus and other absence management measures were employed, absence was reduced from ten days to eight days in the first year. The council argues not only that this is a cost saving, but that an anticipated day's holiday is much easier to manage than an unanticipated day's sickness absence. Connex (IDS 2001) were paying a quarterly attendance bonus of £155 at the end of each thirteen-week period for full attendance and an additional lump sum of £515 if an employee has had no sickness absence during a full calendar year. In addition Connex sends out letters commending employees for improving their absence record. The company considers that its absence scheme is a success as 80% of eligible employees now qualify for payments. However, some managers do not support attendance bonuses as they feel that employees are already paid to turn up, and they are effectively being paid twice. Connex also found managers who felt that attendance bonuses were a signal to employees that managers cannot control the work environment themselves and that they have relinquished all responsibility for managing absence. On the other hand, Dunn and Wilkinson (2002) found that managers felt attendance bonuses were unfair as they penalised those employees who were genuinely ill. A further problem is that such rewards may encourage employees to come into work when they are genuinely ill, which is not good for either the individual or the organisation. Such rewards therefore remain controversial.

ACTIVITY 14.2

In your own organisation consider the approaches by which sickness absence is minimised in terms of proactive ill-health prevention methods, discouragement of sickness absence and encouragement of attendance:

1   Where is the emphasis in terms of approach?
2   Why do you think this is?
3   Is this the most appropriate approach? Why?
4   To what extent are different employee groups treated differently?
5   Why do you think this is?
6   Is this the most appropriate approach? Why?

Occupational health support, health promotion and well-being

Some organisations carry out pre-employment screening to identify any potential health problems at this stage. Others screen employees for general fitness and for potential job hazards, such as working with radiation, or VDUs. General screening may involve heart checks, blood tests, eye tests, well-woman/man clinics, ergonomics and physiotherapy, and discussions about weight and lifestyle, such as smoking, drinking and fitness levels. The value of such screening is that problems can be identified at an early stage so that the impact on sickness absence will be minimised. In some situations encouragement will be given to employees to follow healthy lifestyles, such as healthy eating, giving up smoking, taking up exercise routines. Increasing numbers of employers offer exercise classes and/or an on-site gym, or alternatively pay for gym membership. Healthier canteen menus are appearing, as well as healthier snacks in some vending machines. However, the CIPD (2006) found that barriers to such well-being initiatives were lack of resources, lack of senior management buy-in, and lack of employee buy-in, especially in manufacturing and production. The government has provided some funding, together with other organisations, for nine health promotion projects in England, and a good example of one of these is the 'Be Active 4 Life' programme at Exeter City Council which was evaluated by a team from Loughborough University. Details of this project and the eight others are provided by Silcox (2005e).

For long-term absence the CIPD (2006) reported that the involvement of occupational health professionals was the most effective management tool, although HSE (2002c) shows that only one in seven workers has the benefit of comprehensive occupational health support. However, such support does not have to be in-house and can be purchased; this is the course followed by the London Borough of Brent (IRS 2002a).

Physiotherapists, counsellors and psychologists are often employed, and the occupational health role may include remedial fitness training and exercise therapy for those recovering from an illness. Stress counselling as part of an employee assistance programme can reduce the liability in stress-related personal injury cases. Also training in stress management may be offered.

James and his colleagues (2002) found that the role of occupational health workers was ambiguous and problematic. Their respondents suggested that while occupational health professionals worked on behalf of the employer, their professional codes of practice require them to put the best interests of the individual employee's well-being first. Despite this James found that employees were very sceptical about visiting occupational health workers as they saw it as the first step in termination of their employment.

Changes to work and work organisation

Many employers appear to offer flexible working hours, part-time work and working from home. Employers also sometimes consider offering light duties or redeployment. However, operational factors often limit what can be done. James and his colleagues (2002) found in the three manufacturing organisations they visited it was not always feasible to offer light duties or make adjustments to the workplace. They also found that other departments were reluctant to accept someone who was being redeployed after sickness, partly because they felt the employee might have lost the work habit, and also because there might be problems with pay if the levels of the old and new job differed. They also noted that there might be no budget to pay for adaptations to equipment or to purchase further equipment.

WINDOW ON PRACTICE

Flexible working cuts sickness absence

People Management reports that the London Borough of Merton halved its sickness absence rate and improved productivity by introducing flexible working as part of a work–life balance pilot project. The flexible patterns of work involved a compressed working week, working from home, career breaks, job sharing and special leave including compassionate leave. Keith Davis, the Assistant Chief Executive, explained that the management style had to change from managing attendance to managing output, and significant training was required. The council planned to roll out the scheme over the entire council.

Source: Summarised from *People Management* (2002) 'Flexible working cuts sickness absence', Vol. 8, No. 1, 10 January, p. 13.

Practical support

There are many ways in which the employer can provide practical support to minimise sickness absence. Organisations experiencing frustrations while employees are on waiting lists for diagnostic procedures and operations may be prepared to pay the medical costs for employees where there is a financial case to do this, for example the Corporation of London (Silcox 2005f). Training in areas such as stress management and time management may help employees minimise feelings of stress, childcare support may simplify childcare arrangements, and phased return to work after a long-term absence is also a useful strategy. For more details on phased return to work and some examples see Silcox (2005g).

SUMMARY PROPOSITIONS

14.1. Employee absence continues to be a major problem for both the country and business in terms of direct costs and lost performance.

14.2. The most often reported cause of short-term absence is minor illness; however, back pain for manual workers and stress for non-manual workers are the leading causes of long-term absence.

14.3. It is important to understand the true nature of the causation of absence, as remedies can only be developed with this knowledge. Absence can result from a complex interrelationship of factors.

14.4. Typical attendance management policies include absence monitoring and reporting, absence review and trigger points, training and support for line managers, absence notification procedures, better understanding of the causes of absence, risk assessments, ongoing contact during absence, return to work interviews and absence review interviews, use of disciplinary procedure, absence-influenced performance assessments, absence bonus and rewards, occupational health support, changes to work and work organisation, and practical support. The mix of policies and processes used needs to be tailored to the needs of the organisation.

GENERAL DISCUSSION TOPICS

1.   In the Window on practice about Marissa Mayer we included a comment from an anonymous tweeter about needs for corporate survival overriding employment preferences. Do you agree or disagree?

2.   To what extent do you consider that absence statistics underestimate the extent of absence in the UK, and why?

3.   It could be argued that encouraging employees to engage in exercise and keeping fit will improve their work motivation and sense of well-being, and that this would reduce absence. To what extent do you agree with this notion?

THEORY INTO PRACTICE

Until recently Arthur and John worked as service engineers in a business that supplied deep cleaning equipment to the catering industry to service the company's equipment on customers' premises. Because of growing public concern about hygiene in industrial kitchens, the company is expanding rapidly and demand for equipment servicing is increasing even more rapidly because the equipment, once installed, is rarely properly maintained. By agreement with their employer, Arthur and John have set up a separate company offering a regular maintenance service for the range of equipment from their erstwhile employer, as well as that of rival suppliers, with the additional option of an annual deep clean of the entire kitchen. Some of their previous colleagues have joined them as engineers and other people have been employed to do some of the deep clean work. The new company is very successful, but the product offered has two attendance/absence problems: the work often exposes its employees to infection risk because of what they have to clean; and the hours are erratic because the customer needs to keep its business running. A work shift could be 12–14 hours, with a lot of weekends.

Question

Arthur and John are finding that absence is increasing. They would like some advice on what to do. What do you suggest?

FURTHER READING

Evans, A. and Walters, M. (2003) *From Absence to Attendance* (2nd edn.). London: CIPD.

A thorough text which covers absence measuring and monitoring; understanding the causes of absence; absence management policies; the disciplinary and legal framework of absence management; and developing and implementing absence management strategies.

James, P., Cunningham, I. and Dibben, P. (2006) 'Job retention and return to work of ill and injured workers: Towards an understanding of the organisational dynamics', *Employee Relations,* Vol. 28, No. 3, pp. 290–303.

This paper proposes a conceptual framework of policies and practices appropriate to the effective management of long-term ill and injured workers and makes some assessment of UK current practice in relation to this framework.

Robson, F. (2006) 'How to manage absence effectively', *People Management,* Vol. 12, No. 17, pp. 44–5.

This is a brief and well-focused summary of how to improve absence management.

Silcox, S. (2005) 'Absence essentials: The why and wherefores of sick notes', *IRS Employment Review,* No. 850, pp. 18–21.

This interesting article explains the current sickness certification system and explores the role of the GP in this. The GP perspective is outlined and the tensions between this and the government's recent welfare reforms aimed at reducing long-term absence from work and the numbers receiving invalidity benefit.

Smith, G. (2013) *Absence Management: A Real World Approach*. Create Space Independent Publishing Platform.

Very little has been published in book form recently, but this text is useful in having a clever model and by its focus on sickness absence. Published through Amazon, it is available in both print and e-book form.

REFERENCES

Barham, C. and Leonard, J. (2002) 'Trends and sources of data on sickness absence', *Labour Market Trends,* April. London: ONS, pp. 177–85.

Bevan, S. (2002) 'Counting the cost of absence', *IRS Employment Review,* No. 739, pp. 46–7.

CBI/AXA (2005) *Who Cares Wins: Absence and Labour Turnover 2005*. London: CBI/AXA.

CBI/AXA (2006) *Absence Minded: Absence and Labour Turnover in 2006. The Lost Billions: Addressing the Cost of Absence*. London: CBI.

CIPD (2005) *Absence Management: A Survey of Policy and Practice*. London: CIPD.

CIPD (2006) *Employee Absence 2006*. London: CIPD.

CIPD (2009) *Absence Management Survey Report*. London: CIPD.

CIPD (2012) *Absence Management Survey Report*. London: CIPD.

CIPD (2015) *Absence Management Survey Report*. London: CIPD.

Dunn, C. and Wilkinson, A. (2002) 'Wish you were here: Managing absence', *Personnel Review,* Vol. 31, No. 2, pp. 228–46.

HSE (2002a) *Interventions to Control Stress at Work in Hospital Staff,* HSE Contract Research Paper No. 435. London: HSE.

HSE (2002b) *Initiative Evaluation Report: Back in Work,* HSE Research Report No. 441. London: HSE.

HSE (2002c) *Survey of the Use of Occupational Health Support,* HSE Research Report No. 445. London: HSE.

Hill, D and Halliday, S. (2003) *A Review of Current Research into Absence Management* Brighton: Institute of Employment Studies.

Huczynski, A.A. and Fitzpatrick, M.J. (1989) *Managing Employee Absence for a Competitive Edge.* London: Pitman.

IDS (2001) *Absence Management,* No. 702, January. London: IDS.

IDS (2005a) *Absence Management,* No. 810, November. London: IDS.

IDS (2005b) 'Brakes', *Absence Management,* No. 801, November. London: IDS.

IRS (2002a) 'Tackling long-term absence (2): London Borough of Brent', *IRS Employment Review,* No. 763, 11 November, pp. 44–6.

IRS (2002b) 'Tackling long-term absence in local government (1): Bracknell Forest Borough Council', *IRS Employment Review,* No. 762, 21 October, pp. 42–6.

James, P., Cunningham, I. and Dibben, P. (2002) 'Absence management and the issues of job retention and return to work', *Human Resource Management Journal,* Vol. 12, No. 2, pp. 82–94.

Lokke, A., Eskildsen, J. and Jensen, T. (2007) 'Absenteeism in the Nordic countries', *Employee Relations,* Vol. 29, No. 1, pp. 16–29.

McFadzean, M. (2003) 'Managing absence', paper presented at the CIPD National Conference, Harrogate, 22–24 October.

Neal, L.F. and Robertson, A. (1968) *The Manager's Guide to Industrial Relations.* London: George Allen & Unwin.

Office for National Statistics (2014) *Sickness Absence in the Labour Market, February 2014.* London: The Stationery Office.

People Management (2002) 'Flexible working cuts sickness absence', Vol. 8, No. 1, p. 13.

Rhodes, S. and Steers, R. (1990) *Managing Employee Absenteeism.* Reading, MA: Addison-Wesley.

Silcox, S. (2005a) 'Making progress towards an absence-recording standard', *IRS Employment Review,* No. 820, pp. 18–19.

Silcox, S. (2005b) 'Absence essentials: Using focus groups in stress management', *IRS Employment Review,* No. 832, pp. 21–4.

Silcox, S. (2005c) 'Absence essentials: Maintaining contact', *IRS Employment Review,* No. 818, pp. 23–4.

Silcox, S. (2005d) 'Attendance incentives are on the HR agenda once again', *IRS Employment Review,* No. 832, pp. 18–20.

Silcox, S. (2005e) 'Exeter City Council wants its employees to "Be Active 4 Life"', *IRS Employment Review,* No. 836, pp. 19–21.

Silcox, S. (2005f) 'Corporation of London tackles long-term absence', *IRS Employment Review,* No. 834, pp. 19–21.

Silcox, S. (2005g) 'Absence essentials: Phased return to work', *IRS Employment Review,* No. 828, pp. 18–21.

Silcox, S. (2006) 'The CBI and EEF agree that absence is falling', *IRS Employment Review,* No. 850, pp. 22–3.

Smethurst, S. (2006) 'Sporting chance', *People Management,* Vol. 12, no. 13, pp. 32–4.

TUC (2005) *Countering an Urban Legend: Sicknote Britain?* London: TUC.

CHAPTER 15

EMPLOYABILITY: SKILLS IN PERFORMANCE

THE OBJECTIVES OF THIS CHAPTER ARE TO:

1 Explain the skills of the appraisal interview, a key element in performance management

2 Explore the design of questionnaires, often used in assessing engagement

3 Illustrate different methods of measuring labour turnover

15.a. The Appraisal Interview

This skill is unequivocally about a crucial act of micro-management: appraising performance *face to face*. It is linked to our previous thorough discussion of performance management (see Chapter 11). Face-to-face appraisal is crucial in the whole process of achieving effective, focused performance by individuals. It may be undertaken in conversations with our colleagues, our bosses and perhaps our customers or clients, both by assessing how things are going and by providing a basis for future development. We move forward in our understanding of how we are doing and how we are going to be where we need to be. Usually it is an erratic sequence of a word here, an observation there, a complaint, an argument, an explanation of why something failed or was brilliantly successful. As we build up our understanding of who we are, where we want to be, what we want to do and how we can make progress towards whatever our goals may be, we piece together the products of dozens of such inputs. Occasional landmark conversations crystallise our thinking. These are most likely to be appraisal interviews, and they are landmarks because of their relative formality, their official nature and because they are dedicated solely to bringing our personal performance up to an even higher level than it is already.

The novelist, the textbook writer, the popular vocalist, the newspaper editor, the sculptor or painter, the athlete or the owner of a corner shop all have in common the fact that their performance is measurable in an absolute way by numbers. When Adele releases an album, she can see the effectiveness of her performance in the irrefutable logic of the numbers sold. When Mo Farah races, that performance is measured by the time taken. These measurements can then be compared with those of competitors. There are no mitigating circumstances. The writer may feel that the publisher should have done a better job (not often!) or that the reviewers were incompetent (usually), but that has no weight compared with the inescapable fact of the numbers. The shop owner may grumble about local authority planners or about unfair competition from the local hypermarket, but that explanation will not stop customers from drifting away.

Few working people have that same absolute measure for their own personal performance, which is all part of an integrated corporate endeavour. Individual effectiveness is rarely measurable by a market indicator, as so many other people contribute to the effectiveness or ineffectiveness of any individual's activity. The inexorable logic of the marketplace or other external arena has to be replaced by internal measures, mediated by managerial judgement. This is tricky.

Appraising performance is not a precise measurement but a subjective assessment based on hard evidence about the performance, and that evidence has to be put together and assessed. The assessment has a long history of being damned for its ineffectiveness at the same time as being anxiously sought by people wanting to know how they are doing. It is difficult to do, it is frequently done badly with quite serious results, but on the rare occasions when it is done well it can be invaluable for the business, and literally life transforming for the appraisee. It is probably the most demanding and skilful activity for any manager to undertake and is dreaded by both appraisers and appraisees. Recent research about appraising the performance of UK school teachers found that the appraisal itself was often accompanied by long periods of sickness absence due to stress. To a great extent this centred on the difficulty of appropriate criteria for judgement, particularly where head teachers link capability to personal qualities such as 'open-minded and prepared to adapt and take on new skills' or 'attitude' or where generalised descriptions such as 'unable to do the job properly' or 'not meeting standards' are offered. Measurement is also inevitably imprecise when it is subjective, making the judgement difficult to substantiate and prone to challenge. This leads to the risk that the yardsticks of acceptable performance chosen are those that can best be justified rather than those that are most important (Torrington *et al*. 2003).

We all seek approval and confirmation that we are doing the right thing, and we could all do better. There is widespread management frustration about the working of appraisal, as explained in Chapter 11. Despite the problems, the potential advantages of appraisal are so great that organisations continue with them and appraisal can produce stunning results. Here is an extract from a CIPD examination answer:

> I have had [an] annual appraisal for three years. Each time it has been a searching discussion of my objectives and my results. Each interview has set me new challenges and opened up fresh opportunities. Appraisal has given me a sense of achievement and purpose that I had never previously experienced in my working life. (from an insurance company)

We have to try and reduce the tendency for qualitative appraisal to be unstructured, avoiding awkwardness and being unsuitable for comparison. There are two difficulties: the first is the potential lack of the *systematic* reporting that is looked for in attempts at management control of, and information about, the process; second, qualitative appraisal interviewing is not easy and requires a high level of *mutual trust* between appraiser and appraisee. How many appraisees are appraised by a paragon in whom they can trust?

Frances Storr described an approach to performance appraisal that sought to take out almost all the formality. It included the appraisees choosing their own appraisers and usually the feedback is face to face, with virtually no form filling:

> its purpose is stated clearly: to improve performance and enable people to learn and grow. We emphasise that appraisal is as much about celebrating people's achievements, as it is about helping them to identify areas in which they can improve. Within that framework it is up to individuals to decide how they will carry out their own 360 degree appraisal. In more than 90 per cent of cases, feedback is given face to face, with people talking to their appraisers as a group. Any written material . . . belongs to the appraisee, with the result that the appraisal has become a dialogue rather than a survey. (Storr 2000: 39)

ACTIVITY 15.1

A managerial approach to appraisal is to *control* performance. Those being appraised are interested in *developing* their performance. Can the benefits of both approaches be achieved in a single scheme?

Who does the appraisal?

Individuals are appraised by a variety of people, including their immediate superior, their superior's superior, a member of the HR department, themselves, their peers or their subordinates.

Some of the problems for appraisers are:

- **Prejudice**: some appraisers may be prejudiced against the appraisee, or be over-anxious not to be prejudiced; either could distort their judgement.

- **Insufficient knowledge of the appraisee**: appraisers often carry out appraisals because of their position in the hierarchy rather than because they have a good understanding of what the appraisee is doing.

- **The 'halo effect'**: the general likeability, or the opposite, of an appraisee can influence the assessment of the work that the appraisee is doing.

- **The problem of context**: it is difficult to distinguish the work of appraisees from the context in which they work, especially when there is an element of comparison with other appraisees.

- **The paperwork**: documentation soon gets very cumbersome in the attempts made by scheme designers to ensure consistent reporting.

- **The formality**: although appraisers are likely to try to avoid stiff formality, both participants in the interview realise that the encounter is relatively formal, with much hanging on it.

ACTIVITY 15.2

Think of jobs where it is difficult to disentangle the performance of the individual from the context of the work. How would you focus on the individual's performance in these situations?

Other common problems, which often cause appraisal schemes to fail, are:

- **Outcomes are ignored:** follow-up action for management to take, although agreed in the interview, does not happen.

- **Everyone is 'just above average':** most appraisees are looking for reassurance that all is well, and the easiest way for appraisers to deal with this is by stating or inferring that the appraisee is doing at least as well as most others, and better than a good many. It is much harder to deal with the situation of presenting someone with the opinion that they are average; who wants to be average?

- **Appraising the wrong features:** sometimes issues other than real work are evaluated, such as time-keeping, looking busy and being pleasant, because they are easier to see.

The appraisal interview style

The different styles of appraisal interview were succinctly described over fifty years ago by the American psychologist Norman Maier (1958). His three-fold classification remains the most widely adopted means of identifying the way to tackle the interview. The *problem-solving* style can be summarised as an opening in which the appraiser encourages appraisees to review their performance, evaluate it and identify any problems. The appraiser then takes a more active role by sharing in reviewing the problems that the appraisee has first identified and jointly discussing possible solutions. Any evaluation comes as a result of the discussion rather than being a unilateral judgement by the appraiser.

This is certainly the most effective style provided that both the appraiser and appraisee have the skill and ability to handle it, but it is not the only style. Maier's alternatives included, first, *tell and sell,* where the appraiser acts as judge, using the interview to tell the appraisee the result of the appraisal and how to improve. This 'ski instructor' approach can be right for appraisees who have little experience and who lack the self-confidence to analyse their own performance. *Tell and listen,* the second alternative, still casts the appraiser in the role of judge, passing on the outcome of an appraisal that has already been completed and listening to reactions. Both of these approaches could sometimes change the assessment, as well as enabling the two people to have a reasonably frank exchange.

It is tempting to identify the problem-solving approach as 'the best', because it appears to be the most civilised and searching, but not all appraisal situations call for this style, not all appraisees are ready for it.

The appraisal interview sequence

Certain aspects of the appraisal interview are the same as for selection. The appraiser determines the framework of the encounter, there is a need to open in a way that develops mutual confidence as far as possible and there is the use of closed and open-ended questions, reflection and summarising. It is also a difficult meeting for the two parties to handle.

The appraiser needs a degree of confidence and personal authority that few managers have in their relationship with all those whom they have to appraise. The most contentious aspect of many appraisal schemes is that appraisees have no part in deciding who the appraiser should be.

For the appraisee there are concerns about career progress, job security, the ongoing working relationship with the appraiser and the basic anxieties relating to self-esteem and dealing with criticism.

The fundamental difference between selection and appraisal is that the objective is to reach an understanding that will have some impact on the future performance of the appraisee: it is not simply to formulate a judgement by collecting information, as in selection. A medical metaphor may help. A surgeon carrying out hip replacements will select patients for surgery on the basis of enquiring about their symptoms and careful consideration of the evidence. The surgeon asks the questions, makes the decision and implements that decision. A physician examining a patient who is overweight and short of breath may rapidly make the decision that the patient needs to lose weight and take more exercise. It is, however, not the physician but the patient who has to implement that decision. The physician can help with diet sheets, regular check-ups and terrifying advice about the alternative; the real challenge is how to get the patient to respond. The easy part of appraisal is sorting out the facts; bringing about a change in performance is the difficult bit. The interview, like the discussion in the physician's consulting rooms, is crucial in getting a change of attitude, fresh understanding and commitment to action.

Preparation

The appraiser should brief the appraisee on the form of the interview, possibly asking for a self-appraisal form to be completed in advance. To some extent this is setting the tone, making the opening of the eventual interview easier.

Asking for the self-appraisal form to be completed will only be appropriate if the scheme requires this. As we have seen, self-appraisal gives the appraisee some initiative, ensures that the discussion will be about matters which the appraisee can handle and on 'real stuff'. The appraiser has to collect and review all the available evidence on the appraisee's performance, including reports, records or other material regarding the period under review. Most important will be the previous appraisal and its outcomes.

Most of the points made about preparing for the selection interview also apply to appraisal, especially the setting. Several research studies (e.g. Anderson and Barnett 1987) have shown the extremely positive response of appraisees who felt that the appraiser had taken time and trouble to ensure that the setting and supportive nature of the discussion were considerate of the appraisee's needs.

Interview structure

A recommended structure for a performance appraisal interview is shown in Table 15.1. Alternative frameworks can be found in Anderson (1993: 112–13).

Rapport or setting the tone is unusual because it attempts to smooth the interaction between two people who probably have an easy social relationship, but now find themselves ill at ease. They are not used to having this sort of conversation together, so they have to find new ground-rules. The appraisal interview itself may be easier to introduce and handle if, as generally recommended, there are mini-reviews throughout the year. This should ensure that there are no surprises, and the two people concerned get used to having performance-focused meetings, however informal. There is still the problem of appraisee reaction to the tentative presentation of things the appraisees are not doing properly. A minority will misconstrue comments to focus on the good at the expense of the not so good, while a different minority will do the exact opposite: demoralised collapse at facing a suspended sentence. The majority will react sensibly and most appraisees will have the simple guts to face up to issues that are problematic.

The opening of the interview itself still needs care. The mood needs to be light, but not trivial, as the appraisee has to be encouraged towards candour rather than gamesmanship and the appraiser needs to concentrate on the basis of feedback, which we considered in introducing face-to-face skills.

Table 15.1 Structure for a performance appraisal interview

1 Purpose and rapport or setting the tone	Agree purpose with appraisee Agree structure for meeting Check that pre-work is done
2 Factual review	Review of known facts about performance in previous period Appraiser reinforcement
3 Appraisee views	Appraisee asked to comment on performance since the last appraisal: what has gone well and what has gone less well; what could be improved; what they liked; what they disliked; possible new objectives
4 Appraiser views	Appraiser adds own perspective, asks questions and disagrees, as appropriate, with what appraisee has said
5 Problem solving	Discussion of any differences and how they can be resolved
6 Objective setting	Agreeing what action should be taken, and by whom

ACTIVITY 15.3

What do you think of the following openings to appraisal interviews heard recently?

1 'Well, here we are again. I'm sure you don't like this business any more than I do, so let's get on with it.'

2 'Now, there's nothing to worry about. It's quite painless and could be useful. So just relax and let me put a few questions to you.'

3 'I will be straight with you if you will be straight with me. All right?'

4 'Right. Let battle commence!'

Factual review is reviewing aspects of the previous year's work that are unproblematic. The appraiser begins by reviewing the main facts about the performance, without expressing opinions about them but merely summarising them as a mutual reminder, perhaps reviewing previous objectives set and including the outcome of the previous appraisal. This will help to key in any later discussion by confirming such matters as how long the appraisee has been in the job, any personnel changes in the period, turnover figures, training undertaken and so forth.

The appraiser will still be doing most, but not all, of the talking, and can isolate those aspects of performance that have been disclosed which are clearly satisfactory, mention them and comment favourably. This will develop rapport and provide the basic reassurance that the appraisee needs in order to avoid being defensive. The favourable aspects of performance will to some extent be *discovered* by the factual review process. It is important that 'the facts speak for themselves' rather than appraiser judgement being offered. Not, for instance:

> Well, I think you are getting on very well. I'm very pleased with how things are going generally.

That sort of comment made at this stage would have the appraisee waiting for 'but . . .' as the defences have not yet been dismantled. A different approach might be:

> Those figures look very good. How do they compare with . . . ? That's X per cent up on the quarter and Y per cent on the year. . . . That's one of the best results in the group. You must be pleased with that. . . . How on earth did you do it?

This has the advantage of the evidence, including that collected throughout the year **as we suggested earlier,** being there before the eyes of both parties, with the appraiser pointing out and emphasising. It is also specific rather than general, precise rather than vague. This type of approach invariably raises the question from appraisers about what to do in a situation of poor performance. Appraising stars is easy; what about the duds? The answer is that all appraises have some aspects of their performance on which favourable comment can be made, and the appraisal process actually identifies strengths that might have been previously obscured by the general impression of someone who is not very good – the opposite of the halo effect. The appraiser may discover something on which to build, having previously thought the case was hopeless. If there is not some feature of the performance that can be isolated in this way, then the appraiser probably has a management or disciplinary problem that should have been tackled earlier. If the system is one in which appraisees complete a self-report beforehand, then much of the factual review could be centred on this.

The appraiser then asks for the *appraisee's views* on things that are not as good as they might be in the performance, areas of possible improvement and how these might be addressed. These will only be offered by the appraisee if there has been effective positive reinforcement in the previous stages of the interview. People can only acknowledge short-comings about performance when they are reasonably sure of their ground. Now the appraisee is examining areas of dissatisfaction by the process of discussing them with the appraiser, with whom it is worth having the discussion, because of the appraiser's exper-tise, information and 'helicopter view'. There are three likely results of debating these matters:

- some will be talked out as baseless;
- some will be shown to be less worrying than they seemed when viewed only from the single perspective of the appraisee, and ways of dealing with them become apparent;
- some will be confirmed as matters needing attention.

This stage in the interview is fraught with difficulties for the manager, and is one of the reasons why an alternative style is sometimes preferred. Some people prefer to be told on the basis that the appraiser is the one whose judgement matters and they do not like hav-ing to make the running, perhaps exposing themselves to criticism before they have been able to work out what the appraiser's position is.

Appraiser views can now be used in adding to the list of areas for improvement. In many instances there will be no additions to make, but usually there are improvement needs that the appraisee cannot, or will not, see. If they are put at this point in the inter-view, there is the best chance that they will be understood, accepted and acted upon. It is not possible to guarantee success. Demoralised collapse or bitter resentment is always a possibility, but this is the time to try, as the appraisee has developed a basis of reassurance and has come to terms with some shortcomings that he or she had not already recognised. The appraiser has to judge whether any further issues can be raised and, if so, how many. None of us can cope with confronting all our shortcomings, all at the same time, and the appraiser's underlying management responsibility is to ensure that the appraisee is not made less competent by the appraisal interview. There is also a fundamental moral respon-sibility not to use a position of organisational power to damage the self-esteem and adjust-ment of another human being.

Problem solving is the process of talking out the areas for improvement that have been identified, so that the appraisee can cope with them. Underlying causes are uncovered through further discussion. Gradually huge problems come into clearer and less forbid-ding perspective, perhaps through being analysed and broken up into different compo-nents. Possibilities for action, by both appraiser and appraisee, become clear.

These central stages of the interview, namely factual exchange, appraisee views, appraiser views and problem solving, need to move in that sequence. Some may be brief, but none should be omitted and the sequence should not alter.

The final stage of the encounter is to agree what is to be done: *objective setting*. Actions need to be agreed and nailed down, so that they actually take place. One of the biggest causes of appraisal failure is with action not being taken, so the objectives set must be not only mutually acceptable, but also deliverable. It is likely that some action will be needed from the appraiser as well as some from the appraisee.

Making appraisal interviewing work

Appraisers need training in how to appraise and how to conduct appraisal interviews. Appraisees will also need some training if they have any significant involvement in the process. An excellent performance appraisal system is of no use at all if managers do not know how to use the system to best effect.

In all appraisal situations where the style is problem solving or tell and listen, rather than tell and sell, the interview must be given appropriate salience in the whole process: it must fit and other features must fit with it. If the outcome of the overall appraisal is predetermined then tell and sell is better. This can often be the emphasis where appraisal is directly linked to pay rather than to development or improvement.

SUMMARY PROPOSITIONS

15.a.1. Performance appraisal has a poor track record, but it has considerable potential, when done well.

15.a.2. Among the problems of appraisal are prejudice, insufficient knowledge by the appraiser of the appraisee, the halo effect, the problem of context, the paperwork, the ignoring of outcomes, appraising the wrong features and the tendency for everyone to be appraised as just above average.

15.a.3. Three alternative approaches to the appraisal interview are problem solving, tell and sell, and tell and listen.

15.a.4. Features of the interview itself are the opening for preliminary mutual assessment; factual review; appraisee views on performance; appraiser views, to add perspective; problem solving; and objective setting.

15.a.5. Appraisers must follow up on interviews, making sure that all agreed action (especially that by the management) takes place.

15.a.6. Training in appraisal is essential for appraisers and for appraisees.

GENERAL DISCUSSION TOPICS

15.a.1. 'What right does he have to ask me questions about my motivation and objectives? I come here to do a job of work and then go home. What I want to do with my life is my business.' How would you react to that comment by someone who had just emerged from an appraisal interview?

15.a.2. In what situations have you seen outstanding individuals depress the performance of a team where the other people were demoralised by the dominance of that individual? How do you cope with this?

PUTTING IT INTO PRACTICE

For this you need a fellow learner who is to practise appraising and being appraised. You need to be in similar work so that you can understand what the other person is talking about, but without any hierarchical relationship with each other. You also have to trust each other to be ultra-discreet about what you hear.

A interviews B about what B did at work last week, what went well, what less well, problems and disappointments (15 minutes).

B interviews A about what A did at work last week, what went well, what less well, problems and disappointments (15 minutes).

This is to obtain information, not to discuss except for clarification. You both now separately review what you have learnt and identify two or three issues that the other seems to have difficulty with.

A and B then take it in turns to lead the other in a discussion about possible ways forward with the difficult issues, following the suggested sequence for the appraisal interview.

15.b. Designing Questionnaires

The appraisal interview deals with the performance of individuals, but collective performance is in many situations more important in affecting the overall effectiveness of the business. The work of all employees interacts with that of colleagues, sometimes so closely that they cannot even start until they are all ready and working together, like mechanics in Formula 1 changing wheels on a racing car. Here the questionnaire can be used to test the level of engagement that people have with the business.

In HR, questionnaires are used in different ways, often to test attitudes among employees towards some draft policy initiative, although some organisations use them instead of exit interviews to establish reasons for leaving. Other examples are post-course assessments, views on aspects of current working practice, checking understanding of a new payment scheme, or testing the value of a house newspaper.

The questionnaire is a method of finding out, but very different from the finding out that is deployed in the selection interview that we considered earlier: it is more like the finding out that is used in application forms. The source of information, however, is not a sole individual where there is the need to shape the enquiry to the respondent as the interview proceeds. The questionnaire is intended to produce aggregate information from a group of people. Precise questions have to be prepared in advance with great care so that all respondents will understand them in the same way and provide an inflexible pattern of focused responses. In other words, the questionnaire must be designed to elicit responses that are answers to exactly the question presented and not to a similar but different question that the questionnaire has not asked.

One of the preconditions for accurate responses is that the respondent should feel confident in the neutrality of the inquiry and in his or her anonymity, so that answers will

ACTIVITY 15.4

For which of the following would an attitude survey questionnaire be an appropriate method of finding out the information required?

1 The most popular dates for a company close-down at Christmas.

2 Whether employees are in favour of a proposed merger with another company.

3 Suggestions for improving company management.

4 The value of team briefing in a company.

5 Identifying prospective volunteers for voluntary redundancy.

be truthful and informative, rather than answers sounding right but being misleading. We discovered one survey in XYZ Ltd, a light engineering company, where every sixth question was, 'Is XYZ a great place to work?', so it was hardly neutral.

Preparing a questionnaire

In deciding what the survey is to discover, we begin by considering what this form of inquiry can discover. There are two basic requirements:

1 Respondents must have sufficient common vocabulary for it to be possible to formulate questions which will have the same meaning to all respondents.

2 The questions must be unambiguous, so that all respondents understand what information is sought.

Careful pilot investigations, development and pre-testing will provide a final schedule of questions that meets these requirements. For the inquiry to succeed the respondents must, therefore, be a population with sufficient in common to fulfil the expectations. Also, the information sought must be of the type that can be reduced to precise units of response to standard questions. Here is a checklist:

1 What will be the reaction of respondents to the subject of the survey? Responses to questions about payment arrangements are likely to be more guarded than responses on the (slightly) less sensitive topic of catering facilities.

2 How can the subject be presented to respondents to achieve a high degree of useful responses? In-company investigations are less likely to have problems with response rate than those conducted among the public at large, as the respondents are almost a captive population, but the requirement of anonymity makes it possible that you will get some blank or spoiled responses if the initial reaction to the survey is not positive. The presentation of the questionnaire needs not only to make clear its subject and purpose, but also to explain what is expected from the respondent and what will be done with the aggregated information being collected.

3 What is the best order in which to introduce topics? The early questions need to be easy for respondents to understand and reply to accurately, as well as getting them 'on the wavelength' of the inquiry before proceeding to more complex questions.

4 What wording of questions will produce precise data? Spend as much time as possible on writing them out, improving them and trying them out on people. Here you need to take into account vocabulary and semantics; you need to use words that are unequivocal, where the meaning is not likely to 'drift' with the respondent. Another consideration is the distinction between questions to obtain facts and questions to seek opinion. There is more on this topic later.

5 How long will the questionnaire take to complete? The need to know has to be balanced with the ability and willingness of the respondent to reply. Some respondents will have difficulty in maintaining concentration and others will have much more to say than the questionnaire provides for. It is not much use if the questionnaire is completed fully only by the conscientious and enthusiastic. Some people will be fed up after 10–15 minutes, others will still be happily answering after 30.

6 What is the best layout of the survey forms? To some extent this depends on the make-up of the respondent population, but the layout must be clear and easy to follow, with a short explanatory introduction answering the questions, 'What is it for?' 'Why me?' 'Is it in my interests to respond?' 'How long will it take?' 'What do I have to do?' Each section of the form needs to have a short introduction indicating what the respondent is to expect, using phrases such as, 'Now we turn to . . .', 'Now we have a slightly different type of question . . .'.

Types of question

In the skills section, Chapter 6, at the end of Part 1 on face-to-face situations, we made a distinction between closed and open-ended questions. It is similar in a questionnaire. There will be some *closed questions,* which ask for specific, factual information, like length of service. If the need of the questionnaire is for a precise number of years, it is best done with a box in which the four digits of a year can be written, but if a more general distribution will suffice, there could be a set of choices with a box to tick. For example:

How long have you been with the company? Please tick the appropriate box:
Less than one year ☐
1-5 years ☐
6-10 years ☐
More than 10 years ☐

This is easy and more anonymous, giving you the sort of general indication that you need.

Opinion-seeking questions are harder. Face to face you can ask a question like, 'What do you think about . . .', and gradually shape and focus answers to clarify what the person means. In a questionnaire you have only one chance, so one method is the *forced choice* approach by asking respondents to pick which one of several statements most closely reflects their personal opinion. For example:

1 I understand the new pay arrangements and believe they represent a good way forward.

2 I don't yet fully understand the new pay arrangements, but they seem all right.

3 I don't understand the new pay arrangements and do not see the need to change.

4 I understand the new pay arrangements, but think they need improvement.

5 I understand the new pay arrangements and don't like them at all.

6 I will go along with whatever is suggested.

A different type of forced choice question is where the respondent is asked to rank a series of statements by writing a digit between 1 and 5, 1 and 9 or whatever number of statements is presented, with 1 being closest to the respondent's personal view and so on. There is a need to point out that each digit is used only once.

An alternative type of question is one that asks, 'To what extent do you agree with . . . ?', with a scale of 1–5, 1–7, 1–10, or even 1–3 being provided for the respondent to tick the appropriate box. The end points of such a scale may be labelled 'Disagree completely' or 'Agree completely' or other more appropriate wording. Some questions may be of the simple Yes/No variety. They are closed because there are only two options, but the options must be precise and clear cut.

Questions such as these save the respondent from needing to find a suitable form of words to express an opinion and to make the process easy. The difficulty is to find a range of statements that reflects reliably the attitudes that are likely to prevail among the people completing the questionnaire. Devising these statements begins the process of classifying the answers.

Another method of seeking opinions is simply to ask respondents to put in writing their opinion on a question, but this is difficult. Some will not have an opinion at all, some will have a vague idea only, some people write clearly and succinctly while others express themselves poorly on paper. Classifying the answers is a nightmare. A modification is to provide after a forced choice question a box in which the respondent may add further comments. By now you have forced a focus on their thinking, so *you may* get some additional useful ideas, but don't count on it, and don't be seduced into thinking that one interesting statement is representative of all respondents.

Data analysis

When all the forms are complete and gathered together, analysis of the data begins. This is basically counting the numbers in each category in each section and making sense of those numbers. This will first be done by compiling simple totals of answers, e.g. those saying 'Yes' and those saying 'No' or whatever the question asked. There may then be a stage of collating the numbers for different groups and perhaps deploying some of the statistical interpretations, such as moving averages or the standard deviation, described earlier in Part 1, Chapter 10. Whatever is done is for the sole purpose of answering the classic question, 'So what?' Analysis is not just for fun, nor to show how clever you are, but to provide a justification for some form of action to be taken, abandoned or changed.

SUMMARY PROPOSITIONS

15.b.1. Questionnaires require very careful design and piloting to ensure that the questions are clear and consistently interpreted.

15.b.2. A variety of different question types may be used, aligned closely with the purpose of the questionnaire.

GENERAL DISCUSSION TOPICS

15.b.1. What is your usual response when asked to complete a questionnaire? What is it about questionnaires that provoke this response?

15.b.2. Questionnaires take a lot of money and time to design and administer. In what circumstances is this justifiable, and why?

PUTTING IT INTO PRACTICE

Visit https://yougov.co.uk/ and find the section on opinion polls. This is sponsored by the British government to measure public opinion on a variety of matters of public interest and to demonstrate expertise in polling. Navigate to *Five recommendations to improve employee satisfaction surveys*. Read the suggestions and then:

15.b.1. Take one of the open opinion surveys on any subject that interests you and work out, in the light of our suggestions above, how good the questionnaire is and whether it could be improved.

15.b.2. Devise a questionnaire of your own on any topic, try it out on a few friends or relatives and then see how you could improve it.

15.c. Analyses of Staff Leaving the Organisation

We discussed the advantages to the organisation of some level of turnover (Chapter 13) but concluded that it is in the interests of most organisations to keep that turnover reasonably low. In this section we look at different ways to analyse the extent and nature of turnover, as this gives us an accurate picture of the situation and helps provide some clues to the causes, thus helping us to focus our efforts on turnover reduction. A fuller discussion on the reasons for turnover is in Chapter 13.

Annual labour turnover index

The annual labour turnover index is sometimes called the percentage wastage rate, or the conventional turnover index. This is the simplest formula for wastage and looks at the number of staff leaving during the year as a percentage of the total number employed who could have left.

$$\frac{\text{Leavers in year}}{\text{Average number of staff in post during year}} \times 100 = \text{percentage wastage rate}$$

This measure has been criticised because it gives only a limited amount of information. If, for example, there were 25 leavers over the year, it would not be possible to determine whether 25 different jobs had been left by 25 different people, or whether 25 different people had tried and left the same job. Length of service is not taken into account with this measure, yet precisely that has been shown to have a considerable influence on leaving patterns, such as the high number of leavers at the time of induction.

So, for example, if 8 out of 70 staff left during the preceding year, then the calculation would be:

$$\frac{8}{70} \times 100 = 11\% \text{ wastage rate}$$

Stability index

The stability index is based on the number of staff who could have stayed throughout the period. Usually, staff with a full year's service is expressed as a percentage of staff in post one year ago.

$$\frac{\text{Number of staff with one year's service at date}}{\text{Number of staff employed exactly one year before}} \times 100 = \text{per cent stability}$$

So using the example as in the turnover calculation, the stability calculation would be:

$$\frac{62}{70} \times 100 = 89\% \text{ stability rate}$$

However, if 3 of the 8 leavers left the same job shortly after being recruited then the stability rate would be:

$$\frac{64}{72} \times 100 = 91\% \text{ stability rate}$$

This index, though, ignores joiners throughout the year and takes little account of length of service.

ACTIVITY 15.5

In an organisation with 250 employees exactly one year ago and an average of 150 employees over the year:

1   What would be the wastage rate and stability index if 18 employees left, each leaving different jobs?

2   If 15 people left, and 2 of these both left the same job, what would be the wastage rate and the stability index?

Cohort analysis

A cohort is defined as a homogeneous group of people. Cohort analysis tracks what happens as some people leave a group of people with very similar characteristics who all joined the organisation at the same time. Graduates are an appropriate group for this type of analysis. A graph showing what happens to the group can be in the form of a survival curve or a log-normal wastage curve, which can be plotted as a straight line and can be used to make predictions. The disadvantage of this method of analysis is that it cannot be used for groups other than the specific group for which it was originally prepared. The information has also to be collected over a long time period, which produces problems of availability and reliability of data.

Half-life

The half-life is a figure expressing the time taken for half the cohort to leave the organisation. The figure does not give as much information as a survival curve, but it is useful as a summary and as a method of comparing different groups.

Census method

The census method is an analysis of leavers over a reasonably short period of time – often over a year. The length of completed service of leavers is summarised by using a histogram, as shown in Figure 15.1.

Retention profile

Staff retained, that is those who remain with the organisation, are allocated to groups depending on the year they joined. The number in each year group is translated into a percentage of the total number of individuals who joined during that year.

Age and retirement profile

Analyses by staff group, whether by seniority or specialism, of potential retirements over the next three to five years can provide an age and retirement profile. This is more useful in countries where there is a mandatory retirement age. In the UK where there is no mandatory retirement age the calculation can still be useful in indicating the size of the potential *risk* of staff loss.

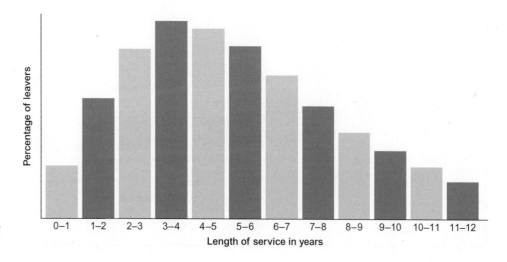

Figure 15.1
Census analysis: percentage of leavers with differing lengths of service

SUMMARY PROPOSITIONS

15.c.1. There is a wide range of analyses that can be used to measure staff leaving the organisation. These range from calculations of turnover or stability rate to cohort analysis and profiles of retention and age and potential retirement.

15.c.2. These analyses can give some clues about the reasons for staff leaving the organisation, but would need to be supplemented by other data such as interviews with employees and managers.

GENERAL DISCUSSION TOPICS

15.c.1. Under what conditions would it be inappropriate to put time and effort into calculating labour turnover? What is your justification for this?

15.c.2. What categories of employee most warrant the calculation of labour turnover, and why is this the case?

PUTTING IT INTO PRACTICE

Cohort analysis at City Hotel

Refer to Figure 15.2 regarding staff at City Hotel to answer the questions below.

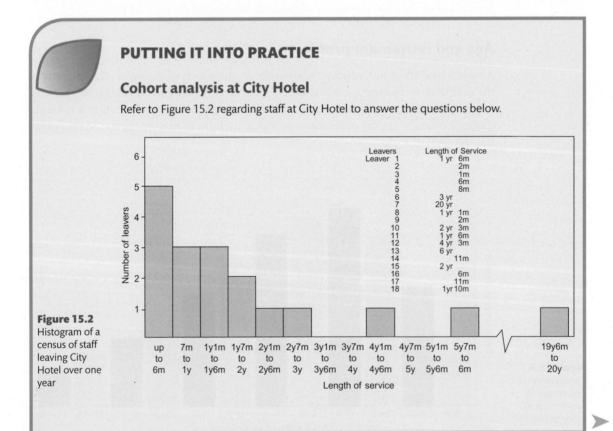

Figure 15.2 Histogram of a census of staff leaving City Hotel over one year

> ## Questions

15.c.1   What are the main conclusions that you draw from the histogram?

15.c.2   What other analyses might you want to carry out to give a fuller picture of staff leaving?

15.c.3   What supplementary data would you look for to help explain this pattern of staff leaving?

15.c.4   What potential solutions might there be to reduce turnover in this hotel?

FURTHER READING

Appraisal interview

Fletcher, C. (1999) *Appraisal: Routes to Improved Performance*. London: CIPD.

Fear, R.A. and Chiron, R.J. (2002) *The Evaluation Interview* (5th edn.). London: McGraw Hill.
This American classic ranges widely over evaluation in different situations, including performance appraisal.

Milliman, J., Nason, S., Zhu, C. and De Ciere, H. (2002) 'An exploratory assessment of the purposes of performance appraisals in North and Central America and the Pacific Rim', *Human Resource Management*, Vol. 41, pp. 87–102.
This is an interesting piece of work comparing the way in which performance appraisal is carried out in contrasting cultures.

Ling Sing Chee (1994) 'Singapore Airlines: Strategic human resource initiatives', in D. Torrington, *International Human Resource Management*. London: Prentice Hall, pp. 143–60.
Dr Ling Sing Chee's chapter includes an account of how the Thai office had difficulty in writing negative comments because of Buddhist beliefs about reincarnation, and the office needed to adapt various aspects of its embryonic performance management system to accommodate cultural differences.

Designing questionnaires

Elinci, Y. (2015) *Designing Research Questionnaires for Business*. London: Sage.

Blair, J. and Czaja, R.F. (2013) *Designing Surveys*. London: Sage.
Two similar books from the same publisher; both sound and practical.

REFERENCES

Anderson, G.C. (1993) *Managing Performance Appraisal Systems*. Oxford: Blackwell.

Anderson, G.C. and Barnett, J.G. (1987) 'The characteristics of effective appraisal interviews', *Personnel Review*, Vol. 16, No. 4, pp. 18–25.

Maier, N.R.F. (1958) *The Appraisal Interview: Objectives, Methods and Skills*. New York: John Wiley.

Storr, F. (2000) 'This is not a circular', *People Management*, May, pp. 38–40.

Torrington, D.P., Earnshaw, J.M., Marchington, L. and Ritchie, M.D. (2003) *Tackling Underperformance in Teachers*. London: Routledge Falmer.

PART 4

DEVELOPMENT

CHAPTERS

Having set up appropriate methods of organisation and systems to ensure performance, we now have to consider in more detail the ways in which the organisation itself can be developed and how people acquire skill, knowledge and effectiveness in their capacity to perform.

In our fast-changing world, organisations need to be both proactive and responsive to change, and Chapter 16 focuses on how such change can be most effectively implemented, taking account of the natural difficulties which people experience when change is thrust upon them.

A key feature of development is the national qualifications and credit framework (NQF) within which vocational skills can be acquired (Chapter 17). Here the individual employer relies on, and attempts to influence, the provision of the education and training system and the arrangements of professional and other bodies, which specify the appropriate standards for vocational competence.

In Chapters 18 and 19 we consider how individuals are developed further within the business, especially in management development, where the skills and knowledge needed tend to be much more specific to the organisation within which they are employed, where the methods of development are geared to the ongoing processes of the business.

Talented people are key to organisational success and they require focused development in planning and supporting their career development as well as their current performance (Chapter 20). At the end of each chapter you will find a Theory into Practice case study which will help you to put these ideas into context and explore them more thoroughly.

CHAPTER 16

ORGANISATIONAL CHANGE AND DEVELOPMENT

THE OBJECTIVES OF THIS CHAPTER ARE TO:

1 Review the nature of change, the traditional model of planned change and the limitations of this model

2 Explain how organisations may be designed to be more responsive to change

3 Explore the employee experience of change and the impact this may have on the success of change

4 Examine the nature of change when the organisation is conceptualised as a human living system

5 Explore organisational development (OD) as a specific approach to change in organisations, describe its evolution and consider its future

6 Summarise the role of HR professionals in change

We are all now familiar with change as a constant in our world and that its pace is ever increasing. In the latest WERS survey almost half the organisations experienced technological change over the previous two years and over a third experienced changes in each of the following areas: work techniques, work organisation and product/service innovation (van Wanrooy *et al.* 2013). Inevitably, therefore, leaders find themselves leading, promoting, encouraging and stimulating change, with a belief that they can 'manage' change.

All change, no matter how small, presents a challenge for everyone in the organisation. For leaders there is the challenge of making the required changes happen, and for everyone else there is the challenge of coping with changes over which they often have no control and for which they have potentially no desire. Such changes invariably involve them in engaging in new activities, behaviours and thinking, and the even more difficult task of letting go and unlearning old activities, behaviours and thinking.

It is therefore unsurprising that it is frequently reported that upwards of 70% of change programmes fail (see, for example, Balogun *et al.* 2014). Soltani and colleagues (2007: 153) found that:

> very few change programmes produce an improvement in bottom-line, exceed the company's cost of capital, or even improve service delivery

while Beer and Nohria (2000: 133) recognise that the consequences of such programmes

> exert a heavy toll both human and economic.

However, change is considered to be a necessity in our complex world, for example changing the culture of financial institutions after the 2008 global financial crisis, and change in response to public spending cuts in many parts of Europe. Stephen Moir, Deputy Chief Executive of the Yorkshire Ambulance Service, notes that the HR function has the opportunity and responsibility to 'help to encourage and facilitate radical long-term thinking and embed the cultural changes we all need' (Maclachlan 2012: 14).

In this chapter we explore the ways in which organisations approach change; explore some of the reasons why change may be unsuccessful; and review current approaches to improving that success rate. We consider OD as a specific approach to change which may bring added benefits and conclude with a summary of the HR role in change.

The nature of change and the role of planned change

There are many reasons why a business has to change, such as competitor behaviour, customer expectations, development of technology and communications, response to a crisis, or a need to maximise shareholder value and for a thorough analysis of the causes of change see, for example, Myers and colleagues (2012).

Sometimes change is an initiative to seize an advantage and make something happen (proactive); on other occasions it is an attempt to catch up with what is already happening (reactive). Other distinctions are made, for example whether the push for change comes externally or internally. The change may be revolutionary, sudden and dramatic, or incremental; it may be planned or evolutionary. However, underlying all of this is the fundamental reason for change, which is to enable organisations to survive and thrive in our complex global world.

Table 16.1 Aspects of change

Structure, size and shape	Formal and informal systems
	Processes and procedures
Culture, values and beliefs	People and behaviours at all levels

The nature of change has also been hotly debated and the emphasis has increasingly been on transformational change. Transformational change is sometimes equated with revolutionary change, but evolutionary change can equally be transformational. Change may involve movements in organisational shape, size, structure which are technically termed 'hard' aspects, and which are very visible and perhaps more straightforward to implement, requiring less persuasion. Change may also involve 'softer' aspects such as rewards, values, beliefs, systems, procedures, roles, responsibilities, culture, tasks and behaviour, which are potentially more difficult to manage. In Table 16.1 we have summarised the different aspects of the organisation which change might affect.

While transformational change may involve all of the aspects shown in Table 16.1, transformational change is more than this and involves fundamentally new ways of understanding what the organisation is for and is doing, requiring a re-examination of its mission and a vision of a different future state of the organisation. Transformational change is about the change in mental models of what the organisation is about, sometimes referred to as change in the organisational paradigm, a completely different way of looking at things.

ACTIVITY 16.1

Think of a major change which you have experienced at work, university, school or in any other organisation. (You may even consider your family to be an organisation.)

Consider all of the different aspects of that change and then draw a table similar to Table 16.1 and allocate the different aspects of the change to each box.

It has been assumed that leaders can plan and manage change given the right processes and tools to use. There is a variety of models in the literature, and used by consultants, with most focusing on such stages as:

- identify the need for change;
- define the current state;
- envisage the future desired state;
- identify the gap;
- diagnose capacity for change including barriers and how they can be overcome;
- plan actions and behaviours needed to close the gap;
- implement required actions;
- manage the transition;
- constantly reinforce changes, sustain momentum and measure progress.

For more examples and details on such processes see, for example, Cameron and Green (2015), Balogun *et al.* (2014; 2015) and Al-Haddad and Kotnour (2015). Such models make this top-down change process sound very straightforward with a logical approach to what needs to happen, and may well involve a good degree of training to prepare people for what will happen and what they will need to do. However, as we highlighted in our introduction to this chapter, change is often both painful and unsuccessful.

In beginning to understand the great difficulties of achieving change it is helpful to address the limitations of the planned change model. On a practical level we have little time for such lengthy processes in our world of constant change and there is little opportunity to reinforce and embed a change as another change may be following closely on its heels and indeed may be happening at the same time. Organisations need to become more responsive to the need for change as well as proactive where possible.

A second difficulty with the planned approach to change is its underlying assumptions. It can be seen as allied to the metaphor of the organisation as a machine which emphasises rationality and ignores emotion (see e.g. Lewis *et al.* 2008; Morgan 2006). The machine develops a problem: the owners of the machine work out how to fix it: they put the plan into action and repair the machine. It is based on a scientific logical approach to problem solving in organisations, which may be appropriate for some problems, but is often inappropriate as it neglects the important fact that the organisational machine is made up of human beings who have a will of their own. Binney and Williams (2005) suggest that this approach deals inadequately with the unintended consequences of change, its messiness, the gap in perceptions between leaders and followers, the fact that visions often do not inspire. They also point out that it is based on the assumption that change is something which is done to organisations (and hence the people that make them up), rather like the assumption that leadership is done to followers rather than with them. The machine metaphor also focuses change on the observable, in other words behaviour, and does not allow for employee thinking processes, and fails to consider the employee experience of change and employees' potential contribution to change.

In the next three sections we address the above limitations of the planned change model.

How can organisations be responsive to change?

On a very practical level one way of trying to enable organisations to be more responsive to change is to *design* them so that they can change more easily. Designing the structure and processes of the organisation so they can be quickly responsive to change and constantly adaptive (see, for example, Zheltoukhova 2014), is critical and together, with flexibility of labour which we focused on in Chapter 7, such approaches underpin an agile organisation. Lawler and Worley (2009) suggest that, given the increasing pace of change, organisations need to anticipate change and constantly reconfigure, and hence require a built-in capacity to change continuously. To do this Lawler and Worley suggest that organisations need to design themselves so that they can 'adjust their strategic intents, structures and human deployments as a matter of routine' (p. 28), and need to develop the ability to think creatively about the future to achieve sustained success.

WINDOW ON PRACTICE

Built-to-change

Lawler and Warley (2009) use the example of Capital One Financial Services to demonstrate a built-to-change approach.

1 **Strategising**: At Capital One change is a continuous forward-looking activity rather than an annual or biannual one and there is a 'test and learn' approach to drive growth. To do this Capital One identifies services, products and other elements that will, under a range of conditions, create high performance. These become strategic imperatives where capabilities must be developed.

2 **Structure**: The organisation is designed flexibly, ensuring that no one is more than one or two steps away from the external environment to ensure connection with the marketplace, regulators and so on.

3 **Information production and sharing**: Capital One employs processes to share internal and external information such as financial performance, market conditions, competitor performance, on the basis that people are more likely to accept change if they understand what needs to happen for the business to succeed.

4 **Job design**: New entrants to Capital One are rotated round the business so that they can contribute in any area. This ensures flexibility and responsiveness to changing demands.

5 **Selecting the right people**: Capital One selects employees who enjoy change, are quick to learn and actively seek professional growth.

6 **Employment contract based on employee willingness to accept change**: Employees are expected to learn new skills and deliver high performance. Capital One cannot promise always to offer the training and support that employees need and if an individual's skills are outdated that person may no longer have a place in the organisation if the skills are readily available in the external labour market.

7 **Performance management and development**: This is a flexible, dynamic and interactive process with goals regarding performance and the development experiences that individuals will need to contribute to the business in the future. Appraisals focus on both performance achievement and the acquisition and application of skills and knowledge required for the future.

8 **Leadership**: Lawler and Worley propose that, given the complexity of change today, leadership needs to shift from a small group of people at the top of the organisation to all levels, where managers are urged to grasp leadership opportunities as soon as they arise.

Source: Adapted from Lawler, E. and Worley, C. (2009) 'The rebirth of change', *People Management*, Vol. 15, No. 3, 29 January, pp. 28–30.

ACTIVITY 16.2

How would you assess the advantages and disadvantages of working for the type of organisation described in the previous Window on practice?

This approach goes some way to address the needs of organisations in a constantly changing environment, but it does not address other fundamental problems with the planned change model.

Addressing the employee experience of change

There has been increasing recognition of the value of understanding the employee experience of HRM, which we noted in Chapter 4, and this is central to HRM research and practice. Oreg *et al.* (2013) note the critical importance of, yet lack of attention to, the employee perspective on change, and there remains a 'dearth of evidence on employee reactions to change' (Conway and Monks 2008: 73). Reactions are likely to be affected by the context of the change, for example whether the company is shrinking and fighting for survival or is expanding. The planned change model pays insufficient attention to employee perceptions of and reactions to change.

When our jobs and their context change significantly the psychological contract can be damaged and unable to support the employee. Particularly where change involves mergers and acquisitions it is possible that employees end up doing a job for which they did not apply, in a company for which they do not want to work, so it is not surprising that employees are likely to experience a breach of the psychological contract (CIPD 2009) as the deal for which they signed up appears to have been broken. When the psychological contract is breached employees may display behavioural symptoms such as holding back information, may make more errors or leave the organisation, and may express feelings such as frustration, anger and distrust.

Although the planned change model inevitably focuses on employee behaviour, as this is an essential part of the change being successful, it neglects other types of employee responses such as the emotions referred to above. If behaviour does not change in the required manner, there is a tendency for change agents and leaders to ascribe this to the fact that the planned change model was not applied rigorously enough (Lewis *et al.* 2008). Within this view there is an assumption that employee resistance to change is a characteristic of the individual psyche that, ultimately, has to be overcome, rather than that resistance stems from legitimate reasons and is partly a result of the way that change is conceived and led in the organisation.

Employee response to change is typically couched in terms of 'resistance' to change, a most unhelpful word, suggesting an illegitimate reaction, hence we use the term 'response', a neutral word, implying that this can be understood and developed. Table 16.2 shows the combination of individual responses to change.

As human beings our reactions to change are a mix of all four areas, which are bound up together and difficult to separate. A cognitive response to change may be to reevaluate the advantages and disadvantages of working for a current employer or gaining alternative employment. When an organisation moves out of town, employees with marketable skills may not want the longer journey, higher costs and lack of lunchtime shopping. So a cognitive assessment results in the behaviour of leaving the organisation.

Table 16.2 Individual response to change

Behavioural responses	Cognitive responses
Emotional responses	Physical responses

WINDOW ON PRACTICE

It depends on your perspective

How many times have you heard it said that the old system was more efficient than the new one? As a change is implemented it is almost inevitable that efficiency suffers as new procedures are being learnt, flaws in new procedures are identified and fixed, and sometimes old and new systems are run in parallel. So lack of efficiency is often a temporary matter. But not always. For example, the centralisation of administrative officers and systems in an organisation (usually associated with a reduction in staff numbers) may well permanently, or for a period of years, result in records being more difficult to access and amend, lengthier and more time-consuming processes, loss of accuracy of data and a loss of local knowledge. No matter how great the goodwill of all parties, the new system is less efficient than the old, and the frustrated and demoralised administrative staff and their contacts may feel they could have contributed to designing a more efficient system. Organisational leaders may, however, be very satisfied with the change as savings have been made, budgets are looking healthier and the share price has gone up.

Cognitive and emotional responses often go together. For example in a restructuring/downsizing environment or merger/acquisition which involves the removal or amalgamation of work units, employees may lose their role identity. In other words, they are unclear about where they fit in the new structure, cease to feel confident and may construe this loss of role identity as a threat to their self-esteem and work validation. The following Window on practice presents an alternative example of role identity being under threat.

In trying to understand employees' emotional reactions to change, managers have used models from other parts of the social sciences. An example is the Kubler-Ross (1997) change curve which tracks the stages an individual generally experiences when coping with loss, a model that was developed in the context of bereavement. This model suggests that individuals move through the stages of shock, denial, fear, anger, bargaining, depression, understanding and acceptance before moving on. Although the theoretical base for this is weak, it does have an intuitive appeal. Kanter (1983) identifies change as exhilarating when done by us and disturbing when done to us. Truss and colleague (2012: 283) provide a useful set of people management strategies that can be used to help employees move through a similar transition curve.

WINDOW ON PRACTICE

Resisting change in an Australian credit union

Cutcher (2009) explains how the credit union Coast implemented changes affecting front-line staff in its branches in rural communities in New South Wales, and how staff resisted such changes.

In the context of the deregulation of financial services, management introduced a new sales strategy emulating that employed by the large retail banks. This shift from service to sales appeared to be accepted in the northern and central regions of the union which were more urban areas but resisted in the southern, poorer, rural region branches, labelled as problem branches by the general manager.

Coast's new strategy places a requirement on members to be profitable customers, with front-line staff focusing on increasing sales of new financial products in competition with each other. Employee performance was measured by level of sales against sales performance targets which had an influence on pay increases. Overall, 25% of Coast's employees left when the new strategy was introduced, and the remaining employees reported higher levels of stress.

Management blamed the problems in the southern region on the intransigence of staff but failed to recognise the contradictions within the new sales strategy and the complexity of the employee response to the changes.

Front-line staff continued to refer to members, rather than customers, two years after management changed the language. They also continued to refer to themselves as Member Service Officers rather than Sales Consultants (their new job title). Staff disliked the idea of targeting individuals in the queue and the competition to get to them first, knowing there was a possible sale of an insurance policy to be had. They cared more about knowing the people who used the union, whom they had known over many years, and who were satisfied with the service they received. They enjoyed being welcoming and friendly and valued going out of their way to help people. This was the basis of their work identity and they refused to accept the new discourse of 'enterprise'.

Staff explained that they did not want to compete against each other as they were all local women who had grown up together. Some described the branch as like a family – including staff and members. They did not want targets coming between them and entered the daily sales figures to show that the sales were shared equally between themselves irrespective of who had actually made the sales. They saw their work as a team effort, and were concerned to ensure that branch performance was good.

Their resistance to change was based on protecting their friendships both within the union and with members of their community. Managers had failed to take account of this.

Source: Adapted from Cutcher, L. (2009) 'Resisting change from within and without the organisation', *Journal of Organisational Change Management*, Vol. 22, No. 3, pp. 275–89.

Emotions have a powerful impact on our behaviour and are very personal to the individual, and we cannot assume that all employees will react in the same way. Steigenberger (2015) found that an individual's emotional state before a change affected their perceptions of that change and hence their sensemaking of it, and in turn this impacted on their resulting emotions and behaviours. In addition, we should not assume that emotions can be managed in line with organisational strategy. Individuals themselves have

WINDOW ON PRACTICE

Mergers and acquisitions: emotional reactions

Bansal (2015) investigated five mergers/acquisitions and found a range of negative emotional reactions from employees: confusion, anger, worry, depression, insecurity, frustration, misunderstanding, and tension. In addition, shock was experienced by employees in four of the five companies. Some positive emotions were expressed: happiness and pride. Bansal found that where organisations had made efforts to foster human integration, in addition to task integration, the negative emotions were less prevalent, but, importantly, not absent. The company in which employees felt most satisfaction was one in which human integration processes were seen as core and substantial consideration was given to joint organisational activities (such as cultural seminars and training programmes), informal joint activities (such as sports clubs), and other informal opportunities for integration at work (such as shared common rooms and office premises).

Source: Bansal, A. (2015) 'Understanding the integration mechanisms practiced during organizational change', *Journal of Organizational Change Management*, Vol. 28, No. 6, pp. 929–47.

enough trouble managing their emotions, but it is known that suppressing them is not a healthy approach. In times of change it is important therefore for individuals to accept and address their emotions, and for change leaders to recognise that such emotions may be negative, and to be prepared to try and understand them and accept them, responding where possible, rather than trying to manipulate them. The role of emotions helps to explain why change leaders have such different perceptions about the success of change compared with employees. Loss of choice and uncertainty for employees can trigger a wide variety of emotional responses.

Middle managers in particular may experience difficulties in coping with the contradictions and tensions of top-down change and bottom-up pressures from change agents (see e.g. Conway and Monks 2011). In a health service context, Kelliher and Parry (2015) found that the impact of implementing new public management principles (as in private sector organisations) was positively associated with work outcomes such as expanding responsibilities, the need to constantly meet deadlines, longer hours, difficulties of managing workload and work–life balance. In turn these outcomes were positively related to increased stress.

Change can cause a wide range of physical reactions. Worrall and Cooper (2006) found that absence levels were significantly higher in those organisations with cost-cutting programmes, and larger proportions of managers reported insomnia, persistent headaches, appetite problems, muscular tension, constant tiredness and other symptoms; the researchers suggest that such levels of change are literally making managers ill. Such problems interestingly did not apply to the same extent to directors, who felt much more positively about the changes taking place, reporting lower levels of stressors.

Recognising the different feelings, physical reactions and perceptions that employees may have is the first step in helping change become more successful. There is a range of measures that may help. Communication is the first in helping to address the uncertainty associated with change. When First Choice and Tui Travel merged, Jacky Simmonds, Tui Travel's HR Director, was surprised at the emotions the merger stirred up, even with senior staff, and recognised how difficult some people find it to cope with uncertainty. She explained that 'people want to be updated even if there isn't anything specific to say' (Syedain 2009).

ACTIVITY 16.3

Consider a change which you instigated either at work or in your personal life. Then consider a change that was forced upon you in your work or personal life.

    For each of these situations identify the emotions that you experienced and how you dealt with them.

Other measures that may help change leaders include involving different levels of employee in shaping some of the details of the change and allowing them some feelings of control. Discussing and, where possible, addressing concerns of staff and monitoring levels of engagement may also keep change leaders in touch with employees.

In helping employees through change and recognising their needs, Conway and Monks (2008) distinguish between management-centred and employee-centred HR practices and argue that employee-centred HR practices might be more important in encouraging employee commitment to change. In their research they found that basic HR practices such as communication, sufficient staffing and appropriate reward were important influences and explain how each is particularly relevant in a period of change. They also

WINDOW ON PRACTICE

Changing culture in the HEY (Hull and East Yorkshire) Hospitals NHS Trust: communication and engagement

HEY Trust were bottom (number 168) of the league table for mortality rates in a Keogh Review and were in danger of becoming a failing trust.

    Jayne Adamson, Chief of Workforce and OD, explains how the Trust re-examined its culture by first asking staff, through a number of meetings, what kinds of behaviour they thought would make a difference to patient care. These were summarised and staff were then asked to vote on what they thought were the most important ones.

    Adamson also recognised that messages from senior management were not being heard on the front-line and to address this a 'Link Listeners' scheme was created so that staff volunteers could call senior managers at any time and put questions to them. For example, they could ask questions about rumours that were circulating or ask for clarification of proposed changes.

Adamson's department also facilitated conversations between staff in different roles. Whilst she notes there was some staff cynicism, engagement scores did double to 80% and mortality rates fell, so the Trust moved up to number 39 on the mortality rates league table.

Source: Churchard, C. (2013) 'Can the NHS talk its way back to health?', *People Management*, October, pp. 10–11.

suggest that a positive employment relationship is an important factor measured by the industrial relations climate or the psychological contract.

Understanding the employee perceptions of and reactions to change takes us further towards a different approach to change whereby employees are viewed as human beings rather than cogs in a machine, and this is a step towards dealing with change in an alternative manner.

Reconceptualising change

In response to concerns about the leadership of change, Binney and Williams (2005), among others, suggest alternative ways in which change can be led by reconceptualising change, based on the metaphor of the organisation as a living system rather than a machine. They suggest that this perspective helps us see organisations as adaptive (as behaviour and thinking shift of their own accord in response to the pressure of events), as self-organising (to achieve an equilibrium), as interdependent with their environment (interacting in complex ways), and as dynamic. This is different to planned change models where there is a danger of assuming a static environment and constant environmental scanning may be neglected.

They propose that this perspective suggests change is natural, if painful, and that the challenge is to release the potential for change rather than drive it. In addition they identify the need for some stability as well as change. They suggest that this perspective encourages the view that managers cannot control change, and that the problem with a vision for the future is that it denigrates the present and the past of the organisation. This thinking fits well with the increasing attention being paid to the importance of continuity alongside change (see e.g. Saboohi and Saboohi 2011), and the idea of recognising current strengths and not destroying everything.

The living organism approach also suggests that trying to copy excellence elsewhere is a fruitless task, as is a change consultant or chief executive telling people to change; changes, Binney and Williams suggest, emerge and the key is seeing the new pattern, drawing attention to it and reinforcing it. An acceptance that the future is unknowable

WINDOW ON PRACTICE

An unnamed company

In a longitudinal study of a merger which was cancelled, one of the organisations was unable to return to its pre-merger strategy. Mantrere *et al.* (2012) trace this failure to a lack of attention to continuity in making changes and question the view that managers need to destroy current organisational meaning in order to facilitate change.

Source: Mantrere, S., Schildt, H. and Sillince, J. (2012) 'Reversal of strategic change', *Academy of Management Journal*, Vol. 55, No. 1, pp. 172–96.

and unpredictable is important, as is the need for leaders to recognise that they are also part of the problem, and to acknowledge that people are not rational and that feelings and emotion are legitimate. Binney and Williams characterise this approach to change as a learning approach rather than a leading approach, but recognise that both perspectives add value in a change situation; in order to reflect this they propose the concept of 'leaning into the future'.

If you look back to the characteristics of empowering leadership (see Chapter 12) you will be able to see the commonality between this and the learning approach to change suggested by Binney and Williams. This analysis reminds us that there is a broad spectrum of leadership styles that may be employed in promoting change, and it is important that the balance of styles used matches the nature of the change and the context.

WINDOW ON PRACTICE

Leadership and change

Hope (2006) explains how Lady Marie Stubbs turned round an inner London school after its previous Head, Philip Lawrence, was murdered. Stubbs set out to make the children feel valued, first by physically transforming the building and, second, by welcoming them back to the school individually. Another way she approached this was to break down the division between teachers and pupils. For example, instead of locking the pupils out and the staff in at break times, she opened the school and created an atrium that students could use, with staff presence, and played music that the pupils would relate to. In the same vein she secured the part time use of games pitches at Harrow Public School. She consulted the pupils on changes and gave them responsibility, such as handling reception for school visitors, focused on their aspirations and believed in them.

Sources: Hope, K. (2006) 'Lessons learnt', *People Management*, Vol. 12, No. 6, 23 March, pp. 30–1.

Organisational development as a specific approach to change

Organisational development (OD) is a specific approach to change, also based on the concept of the organisation as a living system, which we have discussed above. However, it is not only this systemic approach which distinguishes OD, but more importantly its legacy of humanistic values (see e.g. Garrow *et al.* 2009). These humanistic values, derived primarily from the work of Rogers (1961), underpin the work of an OD specialist. Humanistic values comprise:

- a respect for and the valuing of individuality;
- a belief that people are basically 'good' and do the best they can in the circumstances in which they find themselves;
- a belief that every individual is a set of potentials that can be realised;
- a belief that individuals have the capacity to strive for growth, dignity and self-determination in being all that they can (akin to achieving Maslow's self-actualisation).

There is also some resonance here with McGregor's theory 'y' of motivation, which has a similar positive view of workers wanting to do their best, being trustworthy, reliable and responsible, and that as long as managers treat them in this way, then this is what they are able to be. From an OD point of view individuals need to be given the environment and opportunity in the workplace which facilitates their striving to be themselves and realise their potential. Allied with humanistic values, OD work aims to make the organisation a better workplace for the benefit of both employees and the wider public that the organisation serves.

Alongside this respect for humanity, and with equal weight, OD specialists also focus on the efficient and effective running of the organisation. Such effectiveness is often expressed in terms of the alignment of the organisation with its environment so that it is responsive to it and interacts effectively with it. It is not surprising therefore that much current OD work is expressed strategically, as the organisation needs to review its mission and values and implement strategic interventions so that it is successful in a constantly changing world. Such interventions may include, for example, organisational learning, knowledge management and organisational design. Cheung-Judge and Holbeche (2015) provide an excellent theoretical and practical guide to OD diagnosis, interventions and evaluation.

Internal alignment is also considered key so that all parts of the organisation interact effectively together. This may involve teambuilding and working on interpersonal and intergroup conflict. OD employs a systemic approach where work on any part of the organisation (such as a particular department) is never isolated but encompasses the impact of this on the rest of the organisation and its relationship with the environment.

WINDOW ON PRACTICE

School parking system

A high school asked parents not to park in the road near the front of the school when picking up their children. The school explained that this was causing hold-ups in the road for residents and other passing traffic and was a danger. The willing group of parents realised the next best place to wait was near the side entrance to the school which led into the next-door leisure centre car park. They therefore waited in the leisure centre car park, resulting in serious car park chaos for users of the leisure centre who found it difficult to get either in or out of the car park, causing them to be late for the leisure centre sessions they had booked. The school's best efforts at reducing chaos in one area resulted in the unanticipated consequence of chaos developing in another area! The school had neglected to consider the whole car parking system and just looked at one aspect of it in isolation.

ACTIVITY 16.4

1 If you work, or have worked, in an organisation, think of two or three organisation changes and identify both the intended and unintended impacts of these on different parts of the organisational system.

2 Alternatively think of two or three changes in school, university, sports teams, family or other membership groups to which you belong. Identify both the intended and unintended consequences of this on different parts of the whole system.

A key part of the OD approach is that in order to solve organisational problems and improve the organisation data need to be collected which enable members of the organisation to understand the nature of the problem or current state and upon which solutions may be built. Given OD's humanistic approach it is unsurprising that members of the organisation collect this information for and from themselves with the guidance of the OD specialist. This is the first step of the whole OD process which moves from data collection to diagnosis to action to evaluation, very much as in action research.

Finally OD specialists emphasise a processual approach where the focus of investigation and diagnosis is on the process of what is happening rather than on the content. For example, in a meeting we could summarise the content of what is discussed and agreed but from a processual approach we would be more interested in how the meeting was controlled, how different members contributed, how decisions were made and so on.

OD work is based on a broad base of behavioural science knowledge including social science, psychology and therapeutic psychology, and uses an eclectic mix of tools and techniques, for example CIPD (2015). OD practice is contextual (Garrow *et al.* 2009), meaning that how it is carried out depends very much on the context, so it is difficult to paint a clear picture of what it is as it is played out in many different ways in different organisations. It also depends very much on the practitioners themselves, and in a study of Dutch OD experts the authors concluded OD to be 'a loosely coupled community of practice, linking very diverse members' (Korten *et al.* 2010: 393). This reflects the many varied definitions of OD, but for the purpose of this chapter we suggest the following one identifying what OD work aims to achieve:

> a pragmatic improvement of organisational capabilities – enhancing intra-organisational efficiency and performance, including those capabilities relating to individual health and psychological well-being at work. (King and Anderson 2002)

So OD has twin foci: a humanistic approach to enabling people to become all that they can within the organisation; and a business imperative to help the organisation become effective and successful in its environment. The aim is sometimes expressed as achieving the best fit between organisational and individual goals. This is no mean task!

The evolution and future of OD

OD has been used in organisations for over fifty years, and just like HRM it has evolved. It reached some level of popularity in and around the 1960s and early 1970s but this tailed off and it is only recently that OD has regained a high profile, perhaps because of a stronger business focus. Francis and colleagues (2012) provide a good summary of how OD has developed over time. Interestingly Marshak and Grant (2008) make some helpful comparisons between classical earlier OD and newer approaches since the 1980s onwards. They characterise classical OD as having a positivist perspective, assuming that there is one objective reality, that the one truth can be uncovered using rational processes, that collecting data and using objective problem solving leads to change which can be planned and managed with the emphasis on changing behaviour. In contrast to this, newer approaches are based on a post-modernist perspective, where truth emerges and there are many socially constructed realities (in that we all perceive our world differently – see Chapter 17). In these approaches, creating new mindsets, possibly through negotiation, can lead to change which is continuous.

The contrast between these two approaches is very much in line with the traditional planned view of change and the alternative approach, characterised by Binney and Williams' (2005) learning approach to change. Some of the newer approaches to OD include appreciative inquiry (AI), which put simply includes the use of conversation to highlight, reinforce and encourage the spread of the positive aspects of what people currently do, rather than focusing on the negative ones. An excellent text on this growing approach is Lewis *et al*. (2008).

A key challenge for OD going into the future is whether the more traditional humanistic values of OD are still relevant or whether more weight should be given to pragmatic business considerations (Marshak and Grant 2008). For example, David Stephenson, Group Head of OD at Royal Mail, explained that the 2008 recession enabled OD specialists to engage with changes that would not have been possible otherwise, but he warned that both HR and OD professionals may be pressured by short-term demands to 'collude and command' (*People Management* 2009: 11) and that both sets of specialists are facing a challenge in 'keeping true to their values' (*People Management* 2009: 11). In this context of HR having to prove its value in terms of the maximisation of human capital, Nirenberg (2012) notes the worrying trend that many of the tools of OD have become integrated into mainstream management practice, but not for their original purpose.

OD is not a discipline but a field of practice and hence does not have an organisational home (see e.g. Garrow *et al.* 2009) when OD specialists are employed in-house. Indeed it does not have a professional and regulatory body, unless the OD specialist is a member of the British Psychological Society (BPS: OD Division). There have been moves of late to combine OD more closely with HRM and in the current set of ten professional standards from the CIPD (www.cipd.co.uk/cipd-hr-profession/profession-map) a whole standard is devoted to OD. Job advertisements increasingly combine HR and OD. Indeed OD has been termed a 'strategic **HR tool**' (*HR Magazine* 2007), and OD has been similarly combined with learning and development functions. One of the challenges of combining is that HR is derived from different roots, which may form pressure to dilute the humanistic values characteristic of OD, and does not provide the OD specialist with sufficient distance from the organisation.

WINDOW ON PRACTICE

Recent literature questions whether 'western'-derived OD is appropriate or effective in global companies and whether OD values will be compromised. Working in different social, economic, political and cultural contexts presents a challenge to OD as there is likely to be a clash of values.

McKnight proposes a potential solution. She suggests that the individual OD specialist demonstrates OD values by being respectful of other cultures, being knowledgeable about them and prepared to learn continuously, and remaining authentic and demonstrating integrity. Through this demonstration and through encouragement and empowerment she suggests that OD values and work may be more easily assimilated.

Source: McKnight, L. (2012) 'Global consulting: The use of self to transfer OD values into national cultures', *Organisation Development Journal*, Vol. 30, No. 2, Summer. pp. 67–77.

Summary of the HR role in change

The discourse of strategic involvement suggests that in some organisations HR specialists may have a role in determining the need for change and the content of that change. In other organisations the HR role may be more limited to facilitating change and proposing, providing or supporting change processes, for example communication and training. HR specialists have a unique role in raising awareness of how employees and other stakeholders might respond to the intended changes; propose/provide/support processes for participation where this is appropriate; and propose other ways of engaging employees with the intended changes. Maheshwari and Vohra (2015) provide a good summary of the literature on HR practices and HR roles which impact on employee perceptions and commitment in change situations.

SUMMARY PROPOSITIONS

16.1. Change is constantly increasing and leaders use the planned change model in an attempt to manage change, but it has limitations.

16.2. It may be possible to design organisations to be more responsive to change.

16.3. It is important to take the employee experience into account and consider all four forms of response: behavioural; emotional; cognitive; physical.

16.4. Communication and involvement are important aspects of successful change management as are basic aspects of HRM such as sufficient staffing and appropriate reward.

16.5. An alternative approach to change is based on reconceptualising the organisation as a human living system rather than a machine.

16.6. OD is a specific approach to change and the key characteristics of OD are that it is based on humanistic values, aiming to get the best fit between both individual and organisational goals, and has a systemic and processual approach.

16.7. OD has received more attention of late and recent trends in OD encompass social constructivist principles and appreciative inquiry (AI). OD is increasingly paired with HRM.

16.8. In some organisations HR specialists may have a hands-on role in determining the need for and content of change, while in others they may be restricted to facilitating change.

GENERAL DISCUSSION TOPICS

1. 'Change has to be planned and dictated from the top otherwise the organisation would be out of control.' Discuss reasons for agreeing or disagreeing with this statement.

2. 'Organisation Development loses its unique contribution to the organisation if its humanistic values base is diluted; and this unique contribution is too important to lose.' Discuss reasons for agreeing or disagreeing with this statement.

THEORY INTO PRACTICE

Implementing change in the Norwegian civil aviation industry

'Avinor' was created as a government-owned private company from the government-administered civil aviation authority (Luftfartsverket) in response to economic challenges in the whole of the aviation industry. A major change initiative 'Take-off 05' was implemented to promote the survival of the business. The plan was to make some structural–technical changes such as reorganisation of administration and management structures and systems, reorganisation of some service areas and downsizing, and in addition to make changes to air traffic control which also involved downsizing and the closure of some operations. The context was one of predicted decrease in air passengers.

This initiative had broad support from employees including the air traffic controllers and the air traffic control union, who understood the dire situation that the organisation was in. They appreciated that this service was overweight, poorly structured and increasingly bureaucratic. The change process began as participative in terms of identifying the changes needed, and there was much cooperation and communication with staff and unions, producing a good level of engagement. Many cost savings were identified.

However, this consensus did not last because, when senior management unveiled the implementation plan, employees were shocked at the magnitude, speed and depth of change with 25% of employees being lost in the first two years, and more air traffic control centres to be closed than in the original plan. None of this matched expectations. Trust was breached and employee representatives who had participated felt undermined. The change had now become top-down driven and was no longer participative.

One part of the organisation – the air traffic controllers – had more power and had a history of resisting change; the union first asked for a delay to investigate and discuss matters, but senior management ignored this and pressed on. This led to resistance, yet the senior management became increasingly committed to the change in the face of this. Feeling overwhelmed the air traffic controllers said they no longer felt capable of operating safely and air traffic control over most of Norway ceased, stopping air traffic. At this point passenger numbers were actually increasing rather than decreasing as predicted, and this put increasing strain on the system which was being slimmed down. However, senior management had the support of the government and continued to push ahead with the changes. The only communication between the parties was through the media.

The situation changed dramatically when a new government was elected and ordered an independent investigation. The project collapsed in respect of the changes to air traffic control, although many of the other changes had been implemented successfully in a top-down manner (around 80% it is claimed with revenue savings). The director of air navigation services resigned and the CEO of Avinor was forced out.

Questions

1 Analyse the way that implementation was carried out and identify what caused the problems.

2 What recommendations would you make for the way that further changes should be implemented in Avinor?

Source: Lofquist, E. (2011) 'Doomed to fail: A case study of change implementation collapse in the Norwegian aviation industry', *Journal of Change Management*, Vol. 11, No. 2, pp. 223–43.

FURTHER READING

Cheung-Judge, M. and Holbeche, L. (2015) *Organisation Development: A Practitioner's Guide to OD and HR*. London: Kogan Page.

This a comprehensive handbook for senior leaders, OD and HR professionals involved in change. It combines theory and practice very well.

Cameron, E. and Green, M. (2015) *Making Sense of Change Management* (4th edn.). London: Kogan Page.

A very accessible text which combines theories, models, and practical tools and techniques of change. This is a book which is easy to dip into and out of at any point.

Dasborough, M., Lamb, P. and Suseno, Y. (2015) 'Understanding emotions in higher education change management', *Journal of Organisational Change,* Vol.28, No. 4, pp. 579–90.

The authors report a phenomenological study of the merger of departments. They demonstrate how employee perceptions shape emotional responses to change. They suggest that responses are collective, with different groups of employees experiencing different emotions.

Garden, A. (2015) *The Roles of Organisation Development.* Franham, Surrey: Gower.

A fascinating book based on the author's growing experience in this field. Garden identifies four key principles which guide her work and seven generally implicit roles of OD specialists (Seer, Translator, Cultivator, Catalyst, Navigator, Teacher and Guardian).

REFERENCES

Al-Haddad, S. and Kotnour, T. (2015) 'Integrating the organizational change literature: A model for successful change', *Journal of Organizational Change Management*, Vol. 28, No. 2, pp. 234–62.

Balogun, J., Hope Hailey, V. and Stuart, R. (2014) *Landing Transformational Change,* Research Report. London: CIPD.

Balogun, J., Hope Hailey, V., Cleaver, I., and Stuart, R. (2015) *Landing Transformational Change: Closing the Gap Between Theory and Practice,* Research Report. London: CIPD.

Bansal, A. (2015) 'Understanding the integration mechanisms practiced during organizational change', *Journal of Organizational Change Management,* Vol. 28, No. 6, pp. 929–47.

Beer, M. and Nohria, N. (2000) 'Cracking the code of change', *Harvard Business Review,* Vol. 78, May–June, pp. 133–41.

Binney, G. and Williams, C. (2005) 'The myth of managing change', in G. Salaman *et al.* (eds), *Strategic Human Resource Management: Theory and Practice. A Reader.* London: Sage.

Cameron, E. and Green, M. (2015) *Making Sense of Change Management* (4th edn.). London: Kogan Page.

Churchard, C. (2013) 'Can the NHS talk its way back to health?', *People Management,* October, pp. 10–11.

CIPD (2009) *The Impact of Mergers and Acquisitions.* London: CIPD.

CIPD (2012) *Organisation Development,* Factsheet. London: CIPD, June.

CIPD (2015) *Organisation Development,* Factsheet. London: CIPD, June.

Cheung-Judge, M. and Holbeche, L. (2015) *Organisation Development: A Practitioner's Guide for OD and HR.* London: Kogan Page.

Conway, E. and Monks, K. (2008) 'HR practices and commitment to change: An employee-level analysis', *Human Resource Management Journal,* Vol. 18, No. 1, pp. 72–89.

Conway, E. and Monks, K. (2011) 'Change from below: The role of middle managers in mediating paradoxical change', *Human Resource Management Journal,* Vol. 21, No. 2, pp. 190–203.

Cutcher, L. (2009) 'Resisting change from within and without the organization', *Journal of Organizational Change Management,* Vol. 22, No. 3, pp. 275–89.

Francis, H., Holbeche, L. and Reddington, M. (2012) *People and Organisational Development: A New Agenda for Organisational Effectiveness.* London: CIPD.

Garrow, V., Varney, S. and Lloyd, C. (2009) *Fish or Bird? Perspectives on Organisational Development.* Brighton: Institute of Employment Studies.

Hope, K. (2006) 'Lessons learnt', *People Management,* Vol. 12, No. 6, pp. 30–1.

HR Magazine (2007) 'Organisation development: A strategic HR tool', Vol. 52, No. 9, pp. 1–9.

Kanter, R.M. (1983) *The Change Masters.* New York: Simon & Schuster.

Kelliher, C. and Parry, E. (2015) 'Change in healthcare: The impact on NHS managers', *Journal of Organizational Change Management,* Vol. 28 No. 4, pp. 591–602.

King, N. and Anderson, N. (2002) *Managing Innovation and Change: A Critical Guide for Organizations.* London: Thompson.

Korten, F., De Caluwe, L. and Geurts, J. (2010) 'The future of organisation development: A Delphi study among Dutch experts', *Journal of Change Management,* Vol. 10, No. 4, pp. 393–405.

Kubler-Ross, E. (1997) *On Death and Dying.* Washington, DC: Touchstone.

Lawler, E. and Worley, C. (2009) 'The rebirth of change', *People Management,* Vol. 15, No. 3, pp. 28–30.

Lewis, S., Passmore, J. and Cantore, S. (2008) *Appreciative Inquiry for Change Management: Using AI to Facilitate Organisational Development.* London: Kogan Page.

Lofquist, E. (2011) 'Doomed to fail: A case study of change implementation collapse in the Norwegian aviation industry', *Journal of Change Management,* Vol. 11, No. 2, pp. 223–43.

Maclachlan, R. (2012) 'Public sector: A clear distinction is needed between HR and people management for transformation programmes to succeed', *People Management,* April, p. 14.

Maheshwari, S. and Vohra, V. (2015) 'Identifying critical HR practices impacting on employee perception and commitment during organizational change', *Journal of Organizational Change Management,* Vol. 28, No. 5, pp. 872–94.

Mantrere, S., Schildt, H. and Sillince, J. (2012) 'Reversal of strategic change', *Academy of Management Journal,* Vol. 55, No. 1, pp. 172–96.

Marshak, R. and Grant, D. (2008) 'Organisational discourse and new organisational development practices', *British Journal of Management,* Vol. 19, pp. S7–17.

McKnight, L. (2012) 'Global consulting: The use of self to transfer OD values into national cultures', *Organisation Development Journal,* Vol. 30, No. 2, pp. 67–77.

Morgan, G. (2006) *Images of Organisation.* Thousand Oaks, CA: Sage.

Myers, P., Hulks, S. and Wiggins, L. (2012) *Organisational Change.* Oxford: Oxford University Press.

Nirenberg, J. (2012) 'Two roads to the bottom line: HR and OD', *Organisation Development Journal,* Vol. 30, No. 1, Spring, pp. 9–18.

Oreg, S., Michel, A. and By, R. (eds) (2013) *The Psychology of Organisational Change: Viewing Change from the Employee's Perspective.* Cambridge: Cambridge University Press.

People Management (2009) 'Recession benefits ODs who stay true to their values', 8 October, p. 11.

Rogers, C. (1961) *On Becoming a Person: A Therapist's View of Psychotherapy.* London: Constable.

Saboohi, N. and Saboohi, S. (2011) 'Revisiting organisational change: Exploring the paradox of managing continuity and change', *Journal of Change Management,* Vol. 11, No. 2, pp. 185–206.

Soltani, E., Lai, P. and Mahmoudi, V. (2007) 'Managing change initiatives: Fantasy or reality? The case of public sector organisations', *Total Quality Management,* Vol. 18, No. 1–2, pp. 153–79.

Steigenberger, N. (2015) 'Emotions in sensemaking: A change management perspective', *Journal of Organizational Change Management,* Vol. 28, No. 3, pp. 432–51.

Syedain, H. (2009) 'A smooth landing', *People Management*, 29 March, pp. 18–22.

Truss, C., Mankin, D. and Kelliher, C. (2012) *Strategic Human Resource Management*. Oxford: Oxford University Press.

Van Wanrooy, B., Bewley, H., Bryson, A., Forth, J., Freeth, S., Stokes, L. and Wood, S. (2013) *The 2011 Workplace Employee Relations Survey: First Findings*. London: Department for Business, Innovation and Skills.

Worrall, L. and Cooper, C. (2006) 'Short changed', *People Management*, Vol. 12, No. 13, pp. 36–8.

Zheltoukhova, K. (2014) *Getting Smart about Agile Working*, Research Report. London: CIPD.

CHAPTER 17

THE CONTEXT OF EMPLOYEE LEARNING AND DEVELOPMENT

THE OBJECTIVES OF THIS CHAPTER ARE TO:

1 Review the national UK picture of skills, training and development, and make some international comparisons

2 Explain the UK's skills aspirations and training framework, the role of UKCES, Investors in People, apprenticeships, vocational qualifications and the QCF

3 Explore the learning context in terms of behavioural competencies

4 Explore the learning context in terms of theories of learning and the process of learning from experience

Development, training and skills are at the heart of government policy as they impact on business and economic performance, unemployment levels, employability and social inclusion. Yet, the UK ranked eleventh for its high-level, twenty-fifth for its intermediate-level and twentieth for its low-level skills base out of thirty-two OECD countries (UKCES 2015a). UKCES project that by 2020 we will move up the league table for higher skills; move down the league table for intermediate skills; and that we will remain where we are for low level skills. In addition there has been long-term concern with the management skills base. Successive governments have constantly changed and developed the national framework to encourage skills development and training by employers and reduce the skills gap between what employers need and what employees can offer. The skills gap, however, remains large. CIPD (2015a) reported that over 75% of respondents to its 2015 Resourcing and Talent Planning Survey said they were still experiencing recruitment difficulties, mainly due to the lack of specialist and technical skills, and overall the hardest posts to fill were managers, professional and technical staff.

WINDOW ON PRACTICE

UK skills shortages

- The UK is investing in the offshore wind industry as a key part of meeting the 2020 EU targets for increasing the proportion of energy produced from renewable sources. However, the skills shortage in this area is a major barrier. Carol Frost, HR Director at Centrica Energy, claims we are capable of growing them but questions whether this can be done quickly enough (Smedley 2011).

- There was a significant shortage of trained and licensed security staff for the 2012 Olympics and the army had to be recruited in their stead (Brockett 2012).

- Stephen Ball (2015), CEO of Lockheed Martin, notes the predicted shortfall of 400,000 engineers in the UK until at least 2020.

- UKCES (2016) identifies growing skills shortages in a large-scale survey, with the Electricity, Gas and Water and Construction sectors having the highest densities of skill shortage vacancies. This represents a shift from 2013 when skill-shortage vacancy density was highest in Manufacturing, Business Services and Agriculture.

While everyone agrees that training and development is a good thing it is difficult to demonstrate a causal link between training and development and organisational and economic performance, partly because such terms are difficult to define precisely, and partly because the pay-off from development may not be seen in the short term. However, there is a clear employee demand for training and qualifications and unions are beginning to engage in bargaining for development.

The first part of this chapter focuses on the governmental framework of training in the UK and makes some international comparisons. The second part of the chapter looks at the nature and specification of learning as the other part of the context of learning and development in organisations.

The UK national picture and strategy

Employee development has traditionally been seen as a cost rather than an investment in the UK, although this is certainly changing in some organisations. For over thirty years UK organisations have given less support to training and development than our European partners. So, for example, in the Cranet international survey (2011, the most recent at the time of going to press) the UK spent 3.02% of payroll costs on training compared with an EU average of 3.72%, with only Austria, the Czech Republic, Denmark and France spending less than the UK. This lack of investment in training and development has been identified as a major factor in the UK's economic performance, and it has been argued that without such investment the UK will be trapped in a low-wage, low-skills economy (Wright *et al*. 2010), with the emphasis on competing on price rather than quality. Our national training framework is voluntarist, with the government's role limited to *encouraging* training rather than intervening, as in many other countries, although some change is happening in this area which we look at later in this section. In Table 17.1 the Cranet (2011) survey shows that the UK has the least average training days (3.88 days) of all seventeen EU countries, and there was only one country in the full survey of twenty-nine countries that had a lower average than the UK. This was Switzerland with an average of 3.77 days.

Alternatively it has been argued that it is not a lack of investment in training that is the problem but the way such investment is distributed: who it is spent on and the content of the training. Training spend is unevenly distributed with people at the lower end of the hierarchy and part-timers missing out on training. This imbalance of training days is true for many countries, as shown in Table 17.1, based on the Cranet survey (2011).

Hoque (2008) labels this very aptly as the 'training apartheid' and the 2011 WERS survey found that those with most qualifications receive most training, although increase in training since the previous survey in 2004 was concentrated on those with low skills (Van Wanrooy *et al*. 2013). Finegold and his co-researchers (2005) investigated the access to training of temporary workers in the US. They found that fewer than 25% of these workers took part in training and that educated and experienced individuals were more likely to be offered training. Lower-skilled individuals were, however, more likely to accept training when offered it.

In the aerospace and pharmaceuticals businesses, defined as high-skills sectors, Lloyd (2002) found a conflict of interests between employees' desire for training and development and managerial short-term aims, lack of accreditation of skills, structured

Table 17.1 The distribution of training days across different employee types (selected countries)

Country	Manual	Clerical	Professional/technical	Management	Average
EU average	4.14	4.71	7.88	7.20	5.98
UK	2.8	3.07	5.23	4.44	3.88
Estonia	5.11	6.78	13.10	12.66	9.41
Europe Non-EU average	4.35	5.49	8.43	9.16	6.86
Non-European average	6.36	7.17	9.23	9.04	7.95

Note: The non-European countries surveyed were Israel, Japan, Philippines, USA, Australia, Taiwan and South Africa.
Source: Cranet (2011).

development focused on key employees, access to training being dependent on individual initiative, senior managers viewing training as a minor issue to be dealt with by lower-level managers and insufficient resources. She suggests that there was underinvestment and lack of support for flexibility and employability. Much training is related to induction and particularly health and safety, as demonstrated in the WERS survey (van Wanrooy *et al*. 2013), which does nothing to drive the development of a knowledge-based economy. Employees in small organisations are at a disadvantage in terms of access to training, and evidence from the WERS survey suggests that the highest levels of training are in the public sector and larger organisations, particularly those with high levels of professional employees.

ACTIVITY 17.1

1 In your own organisation how is training/development shared out between employees?

2 Is there an explicit rationale for this? And if so, what is it?

3 How would you explain the spread of training?

4 If you are not currently in employment choose five consecutive editions of *People Management* and analyse all articles and news items identifying the type of training/development being discussed and those for whom the training is provided.

The solution to this problem may be to increase state intervention, as voluntarism has had a limited effect. One option is a levy system, to be introduced in 2017 for apprenticeships, and other options may be statutory rights for paid study leave and employer tax credits. Also, funding mechanisms to create a demand-led system could be introduced.

WINDOW ON PRACTICE

The apprenticeship levy

The Chancellor announced in his 2015 Autumn Statement that an apprenticeship levy will be introduced in the UK in April 2017 (Faragher 2016a). Employers with a wage bill of over £3 million will pay 0.5% of the pay bill to the government and the money raised will be used to fund high-quality apprenticeships. All employers will receive a £15,000 allowance, paid to them in vouchers. These vouchers can be used to purchase training for apprentices. There is little detail of the exact mechanisms that will be used as we go to press. The reaction from employers is mixed, with some suggesting that their investment in other areas of workforce training will be reduced to compensate for this.

Source: Faragher, J. (2016a) 'Spot the apprentice', *People Management*, January, p. 9.

The *Leitch Review* (Leitch 2006) provides a useful starting point in differentiating between a supply-led and a demand-led training system. The review characterises the supply-driven approach as being based on ineffectively articulated collective employer views of training needed and a central system of provision planned by the government to meet these needs, and predict future needs. The review suggests that employers and individuals find it difficult to articulate their needs partly because they are asked to provide input to a profusion of bodies, and because this approach results in too little investment by employers, too little responsibility being taken by individuals for their own training and a qualifications system divorced from the needs of the workplace. In contrast the review suggests a demand-led system directly responding to demand rather than planning supply. To achieve this, suppliers (such as colleges of further education) only receive funding as they attract customers (rather than being given block funding in advance, based on estimated demand), driving them to respond flexibly and immediately to employer demand, thus providing training provision which is more relevant, reflects the needs of customers and is likely to produce higher completion rates and better value for money. However, to date these ideas have proved impossible to implement effectively, partly because of simultaneous efforts to hit nationally imposed skills targets designed to take us up the OECD league table (see for example, CIPD 2015b).

Even if demand-led mechanisms are effectively introduced and training supply is much more reactive to the real needs of employers, the limitations of this approach are that it focuses on current and short-term needs at the expense of anticipating and preparing for future needs, and does not address the structure of jobs in this country.

A subtly different school of thought in relation to the supply/demand debate suggests the problem lies with the demand side of the equation rather than the supply side. In other words, the problem is not with government initiatives and measures to encourage training, development and learning, but with the way that skills are used and jobs are constructed, hence the employers' demand for training, development and learning. Whilst the UK has maintained a reasonably high level of employment since the 2008 recession it appears that this has been at the expense of business investment in more productive working environments, such as investments in technology, requiring jobs with higher skills and progression routes (see, for example, Cheese 2015). There is considerable evidence of underutilisation of skills in the UK labour market (CIPD 2014b) alongside recruitment difficulties for higher skilled jobs, and UKCES (2015b) found that over a third of employees in a large-scale survey had qualifications higher than those necessary to be hired for their current job. Stern (2014) rightly suggests that we need to address both supply side and demand side issues when it comes to skills.

This implies that training and development needs to be considered at a strategic level in the business but also, and perhaps more challenging, that employers need to change their business strategies to focus on quality rather than cost.

WINDOW ON PRACTICE

Global skills shortages

The UK is not the only country experiencing skills shortages, and some countries are experiencing specific difficulties.

- In Singapore there is a shortage of finance managers, lawyers, inventory managers and sales administrators, according to Hays consultancy company. This reflects the rapid and continuing growth of the economy in Singapore.
- China is still experiencing a lack of democratic leadership skills needed for global growth as historically leadership has been autocratic.
- Japan is losing key skill sets mainly due to an ageing population.
- Malaysia has been experiencing high levels of talent migration, around double the world average.

Source: Stern, S. (2014) 'Making the grade', *Work*, Autumn, pp. 52–9.

UK skills policy and framework

The UK training framework is complex, based on a number of reports and papers, and comprises implementing bodies and a range of specific initiatives. The framework constantly evolves, sometimes dramatically but most often in smaller changes as, for example, individual initiatives or bodies are introduced, changed or abandoned. We have chosen to discuss just some key government initiatives, rather than attempting to be comprehensive, as our system is complex:

> A labyrinth, a maze and even a dog's breakfast. All three terms have been used by employers to describe the UK's skills landscape as it stands now . . . (Phillips 2009: 21)

> In the UK there has been a long, and not always happy, history of government interventions in the training market, and a rather confusing cocktail of different qualifications and intermediate institutions. (Stern, 2014: 56)

Skills policy in the UK includes the aims of upskilling the adult workforce and encouraging private investment in this; simplifying and improving the vocational training framework; stimulating the demand for skills and their better use; and improving management and leadership capability (CIPD 2012).

The UK Commission for Education and Skills (UKCES)

UKCES is a publicly funded, industry-led organisation that offers guidance on skills and employment issues in the UK, sponsored by the Department for Business, Innovation and Skills. It is a social partnership and its commissioners are CEOs from large and small businesses, employment advisers and trade union representatives from across the UK. It is responsible for:

- giving businesses and people advice on the labour market so they can make informed decisions;
- carrying out employment and skills policies to develop a workforce that can compete internationally;
- helping more employers invest in their employees' skills, www.gov.uk/government/organisations/uk-commission-for-employment-and-skills/about.

Objectives for 2015–16 include leading the debate with industry to drive better outcomes for skills, jobs and growth; working with others to push forward employer ownership of skills; testing methods of addressing barriers to growth through people; and helping businesses realise the potential of their people through Investors in People.

'Employer ownership' of skills could be seen as a revitalisation of demand-led education and training which recognises that nationally imposed skills targets are not in themselves helpful to the skills needs of business. The focus becomes more about empowering employers in the training and education system. 'Employer ownership' is a vaguely specified concept and is sometimes referred to as 'demand-led solutions'. CIPD (2015b) found mixed understanding and mixed feelings from employers in their survey on this topic, yet UKCES have been promoting this concept since 2011. It explains that currently employers are unable to get what they want from publicly-funded vocational training (as this is dominated by government-driven targets, rather than being employer driven); and that publicly-funded and employer-funded training need to merge rather than being two separate training markets. As part of this process, UKCES is carrying out pilot studies and apprenticeships are being reformed (the *Richard Review* 2012) as are vocational qualifications (the *Whitehead Review* (UKCES 2013) and others). We return to both these topics after the following section on Investors in People.

Investors in People (IiP)

From 2010 UKCES became the champion and guardian of IiP. Compared with many government initiatives it has had a long-lasting impact since being introduced in 1991, although since then there have been several major revisions. More recent versions are increasingly less prescriptive and have more emphasis on outcomes rather than the process by which the business achieves IiP recognition. In addition, attempts have been made to simplify the framework and make it more user-friendly. The current 2015 standard is referred to as the sixth generation standard, and IiP say:

> the standard defines what it takes to lead, support and manage people well for sustainable growth. www.investorsinpeople.com.

The IiP framework underpins the standard and nine key indicators express what an employer needs to demonstrate and be assessed on to meet the standard. The idea is that the employer does some baseline assessment of their performance and with support works on areas where improvement is required. Assessors finally look at hard evidence and verbal evidence by interviewing a range of employees in relation to the standard. There has been increasing emphasis in IiP on continuous improvement and there are now four levels against which employers can be assessed and accredited, as shown in the Window on Practice.

WINDOW ON PRACTICE

Four levels of IiP accreditation

Developed

The principles and practice are in place, communicated, and understood. Everyone in the organisation knows what is expected of them.

Established

Employees are actively engaged in ensuring that principles and practices are applied consistently. These ways of thinking and behaving become second-nature within the organisation.

Advanced

Employees actively drive positive outcomes, taking ownership of the principles and practices, and applying their knowledge to solve new problems.

High performing

The principles and practices are fully integrated with wider activities. Employees take responsibility for delivering consistently positive results, always with an eye on future improvement.

Source: www.investorsinpeople.com/iip-standard.

A commitment to IiP requires significant time and effort, and the benefits from gaining recognition of IiP status have been debated. Some studies have found that an increase in commitment to HR development, a belief in the value of the process and perceived performance gains and that such firms are more likely to achieve organisational goals (Bourne 2008). Hoque (2008), reporting on WERS survey data, found that training incidence and duration are higher in workplaces with the IiP standard and employees were more likely to agree with the statement 'Managers here encourage people to develop their skills'. However, the author found no evidence to suggest greater equality in the distribution of development opportunities and in fact IiP workplaces demonstrated less equality than non-IiP workplaces. In addition, Hoque found that those workplaces with the standard were no better than others in respect of 'training apartheid' where the unskilled and those with no academic qualifications are provided with fewer training opportunities.

There is considerable evidence that the standard is sought for its 'stamp of approval' rather than because of a genuine commitment to improving training and it is often those organisations that have most to gain from pursuing the standard that are least likely to attempt to do this. Rayton and Georgiadia (2012: 1455) in a statistical study of WERS data found that 'high-training workplaces self-select into' IiP and they questioned the value of the standard for promoting training.

ACTIVITY 17.2

Using an IiP-accredited organisation with which you, or someone you know, is familiar, consider the following:

1 How did the process of gaining accreditation impact on employees and managers?

2 What type of changes were experienced as a result of IiP accreditation?

3 Analyse the overall benefits and disadvantages of IiP accreditation.

Apprenticeships

Apprenticeships are continuing to grow and are strongly supported by the government, as suggested by the new apprenticeship levy which we have already discussed. They are available in more than 170 industries and range in grade to higher and degree level apprenticeships (www.gov.uk/government/publications/key-facts-about-apprenticeships/), so they are very different from the traditional manufacturing and trades apprenticeships of the past. Apprenticeships are partly funded by the government and partly the employer. Apprentices generally work alongside a skilled member of staff while undertaking an appropriate college course for one or two days a week.

WINDOW ON PRACTICE

Levels of apprenticeships

- **Traineeship/pre-employment schemes:** aimed at preparing young people for apprenticeships.
- **Intermediate apprenticeships:** most employers require a good range and standard of GCSEs to be eligible.
- **Advanced apprenticeships:** most employers require an intermediate apprenticeship or five good GCSE passes to be eligible.
- **Higher apprenticeships:** equivalent to foundation degree, bachelor's degree and master's degree levels.

Source: Faragher, J. (2016b) 'Apprenticeships: make them work for you', *People Management*, January, pp. 42–4.

Schemes vary by sector and employer but can take up to five years and are partly funded by the government. They are therefore a long-term training commitment and most often used by larger employers, the most well known being BT and British Gas. Traditionally these schemes have been used in manufacturing but have now been developed in a wider range of occupations such as retail, clerical and professional.

Currently the National Apprenticeship Service (run by the Skills Funding Agency)

supports, funds and co-ordinates the delivery of apprenticeships and traineeships throughout England and provides a dedicated, responsive service for both employers and learners, www.gov.uk/government/organisations/skills-funding-agency/about.

As we write, however, the apprenticeship system is undergoing major change, and in April 2017 when the apprenticeship levy is introduced, the government will set up the Institute for Apprenticeships where employers can submit standards and assessment plans. This is in response to the recommendations of the *Richard Review* (2012) which proposed new standards of what the apprentice should be able to do at the end of their training and greater involvement of employers in design and assessment of the standards and in directly accessing funding for apprentices. The Institute for Apprenticeships will also oversee the quality of apprenticeships which will need to last at least twelve months and have 20% minimum off-job training (Faragher 2016a). Funding for old apprenticeships will gradually be withdrawn as the new standards are approved and used.

Apprenticeships are not without criticism in terms of their quality. In a *Panorama* TV programme on 3 April 2013 examples were given of apprenticeships where there was no real job at the end or where the training was almost all college based or very limited, or where the apprenticeship was very short. The programme identified that the funding available for offering apprenticeships was attracting subcontractors whose work is not inspected and who cream off profits from the scheme. The new apprenticeship system may help resolve these problems, however there are concerns that the new system will discourage SMEs from taking on apprentices due to greater administration and upfront payments being required (Crush 2014).

WINDOW ON PRACTICE

German apprenticeships

The German apprenticeship system is highly valued and combines school-based learning with a greater amount, usually, of firm-based practical training. Employers train apprentices for the whole economy, beyond their specific needs, and to standards set by national committees. A wide range of firms contribute in this way to national skills development, not just the largest ones. Any in-house training may be monitored and supervised to ensure the national standards and being met. There is some state support but also a heavy reliance on private-sector sponsorship. There has of late been a decline in firm-based training due to the requirement for a different skills mix involving broader skills and more theoretical underpinning. Some of this is associated with the decline of the manufacturing sector. Fewer apprenticeships have been available, and there has been greater emphasis on school-based vocational training. The state and individuals themselves are taking on more financial responsibility for training thus easing the burden on employers.

Sources: Adapted from Thelen, K. (2007) 'Contemporary challenges to the German vocational training system', *Regulation and Governance*, No. 1, pp. 247–60; Brewster, C., Sparrow, P., Vernon, G. and Houldsworth, E. (2011) *International Human Resource Management.* London: CIPD.

National occupational standards, vocational qualifications and the QCF (Qualifications and credit framework)

Vocational qualifications are described in terms of national occupational standards, and are directed at developing the ability of trainees to perform specific tasks directly related to the job they hold or for which they are preparing, expressed in terms of performance outcomes. The design of the standards is somewhat complex, although they have been simplified from earlier versions. The management standards were last updated in 2008 and we show a small section of these below:

WINDOW ON PRACTICE

Example: Management and Leadership Standards 2008

The standards divide into six key areas:

Managing self and personal skills (3 units)

Providing direction (12 units)

Facilitating change (6 units)

Working with people (17 units)

Using resources (17 units)

Achieving results (19 units)

Different combinations of units are relevant for different awards.

Inside one unit, for example **D7 'Provide Learning Opportunities for Colleagues'**, you will find:

List of relevant skills: for example, coaching, mentoring, providing feedback.

Outcomes of effective performance: for example, 'give colleagues fair and regular feedback on their work performance, discussing and agreeing how they can improve'.

Behaviour which underpins effective performance: for example, 'You recognise the achievements and success of others'.

Knowledge and understanding:

General: for example, 'how/where to identify and obtain information on different learning activities'.

Industry sector specific: for example, 'working culture and practices in the industry/ sector'.

Context specific: for example, 'the current knowledge, skills and understanding of colleagues'.

Source: www.management-standards.org/standards/full-list-2008-national-occupational-standards, accessed 16 March 2016.

The standards to be achieved are determined by designated standards-setting bodies some of which are Sector Skills Councils (SSCs), which involve or consult employers, practitioners and professional bodies, so that vocational standards are decided by those in charge of the workplace instead of by those in charge of the classroom. This variety in the setting of standards is a concern which is addressed by the *Whitehead Review* (UKCES 2013) as we discuss below. The standards-setting body for the management and leadership standards is the Management Standards Centre at **www.management-standards.org/**.

ACTIVITY 17.3

Try an experiment:

On the Internet search and locate the full set of health and social care standards and identify the name of the standards-setting body.

1 How easy was it to complete this task?

2 What difficulties did you experience with this task?

3 What recommendations would you make for improving access to the standards?

Vocational qualifications (initially called NVQs, national vocational qualifications) have an emphasis on being able to do rather than to know and the standards are designed so that the vast majority of work can be done 'on the job' with maybe small inputs from educational providers. This introduces greater flexibility into the learning process, so that career aspirants are not restrained by the elitist exclusiveness of either educational institutions or professional associations, and there are no artificial barriers to training, such that it is available only to people who have certain previous qualifications. Flexibility is further supported as candidates can stop and start their work towards the standard as it suits their personal or work needs, and they can complete the units in any order. This means that standards can be worked on in line with business demands, and completed when the candidates can provide a portfolio of evidence demonstrating their competence, which can then be assessed.

There is evidence that some organisations adopting the management standards have been able to identify gaps in competence, identify competence development targets, develop a coherent structure for training and development, and identify clearer criteria for HR planning and career progression. In our own studies, again in relation to the management standards, it was found that participants developed self-confidence in their managerial role, became better organised and were motivated to focus on improvement and that following the standards was a rite of passage for those who were new to the managerial world. However, the standards are criticised as being reductionist. In other words, because the standards try to spell out the detail of what management entails, the complexity of management gets lost as it is difficult to specify this in the structure and language of the standards.

There are a large number of awarding bodies for vocational qualifications, and concerns have been expressed about the laborious nature of assessment, and in particular the difficulty of ensuring high-quality assessments, where so much depends on a large number of individual assessors. Many standards now have both mandatory and optional units at each level so that the qualification itself gives only a partial indication of areas of competence. It has also been argued that following the standards rubber-stamps the level of competence already achieved, rather than stimulating further development.

The *Whitehead Review* identifies many of the problems we have noted above and also highlights insufficient emphasis on economically valuable skills in the system. Whitehead proposes a simplification of the current system which includes a set of design principles which should apply to all vocational qualifications, giving them a clearer identity, and greater employee ownership with a view to creating a better match between supply and demand for skills. He asserts that vocational qualifications should be rigorous, relevant and recognised and that the skills landscape should be decluttered and simplified. This, he recognises, is a journey.

ACTIVITY 17.4

Interview at least three people who have followed the national/vocational qualification standards. They may be employees of your organisation, but this is not essential, so friends and family can be included. Ask your interviewees:

1 What were the most positive aspects of following the standards, and why?

2 What were the problematic aspects of following the standards, and why?

3 How might these negative aspects be overcome?

The original NVQ framework attempted to simplify UK qualifications by putting in place nine levels of NVQ (0–8) reflecting increased difficulty from 0, being basic numeracy and literacy, to 8, being high-level specialist skills. An individual could gain the award by completing an NVQ directly and by gaining an alternative national qualification. This framework enabled all other qualifications to be expressed as NVQ equivalents so that it is clear for employers and individuals what the value of every qualification is. Even higher education is expressed in terms of the framework, with the first year of a degree course being level 4 and a PhD being 8.

QCF (the qualifications and credit framework) has now taken over from the NVQ framework, over a transition period, but the levels 0–8 are still included in the model (see www.accreditedqualifications.org.uk/qualifications-and-credit-framework-qcf-html), although the names have changed from NVQ level 1 or 2 and so on, to awards, certificates and diplomas. Each requires a certain number of credits and learning hours. The advantage of the system is that individuals have greater flexibility as they complete units which give them credits and which finally add up to a qualification. The credits remain even if the qualification itself is not completed and there is greater flexibility to move been different awarding bodies and qualifications, as credits can be transferred. However, the system is being changed yet again, and it has been announced that the QCF will be withdrawn, as a number of the rules within it were causing problems, such as limitations on how the qualifications are designed (Ofqual 2015). New rules and guidance are being implemented.

Behavioural competencies

While national occupational standards are output-based competencies (i.e. expressed in terms of job performance), behavioural competencies describe the behaviours which underpin performance (sometimes described as 'input' competencies).

Boyatzis (2008) in a development of his previous work defines a competency as an ability or capability expressed in a range of related behaviours attached to 'intent'. He uses the example of a range of listening and questioning behaviours which may be attached to the underlying intent of genuinely being interested in the other person's views. This competency might be described as 'understanding the other person'. Boyatzis maintains his position that a competency is 'an underlying characteristic of a person which results in effective and/or superior performance in a job' (Boyatzis 1982: 21), and in 2008 identifies three major groups of competencies relating to emotional intelligence, social intelligence and cognitive intelligence.

Boyatzis originally developed a common competency framework for managers but subsequently tailor-made competency frameworks have come thick and fast from the training and development specialists, and most large companies have produced such a framework. Most frameworks have clusters of competencies, like the Boyatzis model, and to each of the competencies within the cluster a list of behavioural indicators is usually attached. Some frameworks include level definitions encapsulating the simplicity or sophistication of the way that the competency is displayed, while others include positive and negative behaviours in relation to a competency, as shown in the following two Windows on practice.

WINDOW ON PRACTICE

OECD (Organisation for Economic Co-operation and Development) competency framework

The OECD framework identifies 15 core competencies grouped into three clusters: Delivery-related (achieving results); Interpersonal (building relationships); and Strategic (planning for the future). For each competency there are behavioural indicators at 5 levels appropriate to a range of different job levels. Below we use the example of the 'client focus' competency and provide a sample of behavioural indicators at each job level.

Level 1 (typically associated with jobs such as assistants, secretaries and operators)

- Responds to and anticipates client needs in a timely, professional, helpful and courteous manner, regardless of client attitude.
- Clearly shows clients that their perspectives are valued.
- Strives to consistently meet service standards.

Level 2 (typically associated with jobs such as statisticians, corporate management and administration assistants/officers, logistics officers and documentalists)

- Follows-up with clients during and after the delivery of services to ensure that their needs have been met.
- Keeps clients up-to-date on the progress of the service they are receiving and changes that affect them.
- Ensures service is provided to clients during critical periods.
- Prioritises clients' issues and address them accordingly.

Level 3 (typically associated with economists/policy analysts, IT analysts and HR advisors)

- Brings together aspects of a trend or policy into a clear picture for others to understand.
- Looks for ways to add value beyond clients' immediate requests and acts on them.

- Anticipates clients' upcoming needs and concerns.
- Explores and addresses long-term client needs.

Level 4 (typically associated with such jobs as senior economists/policy analysts or managers)

- Acts as a seasoned adviser, providing independent opinions on complex client problems and novel initiatives, and assists with handling priority issues.
- Gives the client constructive feedback about issues/problems encountered.
- Advocates on behalf of clients to senior management, identifying approaches that meet the clients' needs as well as those of the organisation.

Level 5 (typically associated with jobs such as head of division, counsellors, deputy directors and directors)

- Builds client's confidence using own personal reputation in the international community and expertise.
- Knows when it is appropriate to push clients to consider difficult issues and acts accordingly.
- Determines strategic direction and long-term opportunities to best meet clients' evolving needs.
- Monitors, evaluates and, as needed, renews the client service model and service standards.

Source: Extracts from *Competency Framework*, http://www.oecd.org/careers/competency_framework_en.pdf, accessed 16 March 2016.

WINDOW ON PRACTICE

A sample competency from the police force

Respect for race and diversity – A
Behaviour category

Considers and shows respect for the opinions, circumstances and feelings of colleagues and members of the public, no matter what their race, religion, position, background, circumstances, status or appearance.

Understands other people's views and takes them into account. Is tactful and diplomatic when dealing with people, treating them with dignity and respect at all times. Understands and is sensitive to social, cultural and racial differences.

Positive indicators

- Sees issues from other people's viewpoints.
- Is polite and patient when dealing with people, treating them with respect and dignity.
- Shows understanding and sensitivity to people's problems, vulnerabilities and needs.
- Listens to and values others' views and opinions.
- Understands what offends and adapts own actions accordingly.
- Respects and maintains confidentiality wherever appropriate.

[This is a selection from a full list of 14.]

Negative indicators

- Does not consider other people's feelings.
- Does not encourage people to talk about personal issues.
- Makes situations worse with inappropriate remarks, language or behaviour.
- Is thoughtless and tactless when dealing with people.
- Is dismissive and impatient with people.
- Does not respect confidentiality.

[This is a selection from a full list of 8.]

Source: www.cambs.police.uk/recruitment/docs *(however, these are national competencies),* accessed 16 March 2016.

Behavioural competencies are often seen as a means of expressing what is valued by the organisation as well as what characteristics have been seen to result in superior performance. In addition, they are seen to provide a critical mechanism for the integration of HR practices which is considered essential to a strategic HR approach. Thus, once a competency framework has been researched and designed it can be used in recruitment, selection, training, performance management and reward (see e.g. IDS 2008). In this way employees are given consistent messages about what is valued and what is expected of them, and because not all competencies are equally developable it gives good direction as to which competencies need to be selected for in new employees. Westminster City Council, for example, has introduced a competency framework (CIPD 2006) which Tony Reynolds, Organisation Development Manager, describes as 'a golden thread running through the people management process' (p. 12); he also says that 'they are the behaviours we want to recruit, develop, manage and reward' (p. 12). However, in practice this link is often weak, with the competencies being used for some processes but not others. A further advantage of competency frameworks is that, because they can be expressed as behaviours, they are more easily measurable, and thus can be used explicitly in all HR processes. This means, for example, that in a development centre, assessors can be trained in how to observe a long list of behaviours.

Criticisms of the approach have been focused around the complex process required to research the appropriate competencies for the organisation, and, perhaps more importantly, the fact that such competencies, due to the research process itself, will be inevitably backward looking rather than future orientated. Hayes *et al.* (2000) also note that a competency framework may not include every aspect that is critical to superior performance, and also that while one set of competencies may result in high performance this does not necessarily mean that such performance may not be achieved via a different set of competencies. Whiddett and Kandola (2000) similarly argue that processes *solely* based on competencies are flawed and that a wider perspective needs to be taken. Without the wider perspective the scope for encouraging and using diversity may be diminished. We also need to remember that a person's behaviour is not necessarily consistent, and may be affected by the environment and the situation. Boyatzis (2009) does suggest that it is important to identify the 'tipping point' which identifies how often the relevant behaviours need to be displayed. Salaman and Taylor (2002) suggest that there are five inherent weaknesses where organisations limit themselves to a behavioural competency approach for managers including: marginalisation of the cultural, social and organisational context; the fact that such frameworks emphasise a narrow set of behaviours and attitudes with a lack of emphasis on the long-term processes of management development; and that competencies are founded on the questionable assumption that managers behave rationally and are achievement driven. In spite of these concerns behavioural competency frameworks have now become part of the fabric of employee development.

ACTIVITY 17.5

Research the use of behavioural competencies in your own organisation (if they are used), or one with which you are familiar.

1 What are the advantages of their use?

2 What are the disadvantages?

3 Compare views, if you can, from members of the HR function, line managers elsewhere, other professionals and employees.

The nature of learning: theories

For the purpose of this text we consider the result of learning to be changed or new behaviour resulting from new or reinterpreted knowledge that has been derived from an external or internal experience. There are broadly four theoretical approaches or perspectives to understanding the nature of learning, and the training and development that organisations carry out reflects the explicit or implicit acceptance of one or more perspectives. We will look at each perspective in the evolutionary order in which they became important. There is no right or wrong theory – each has strengths and weaknesses.

The **behaviourist** perspective is the earliest, which, reflecting the label, concentrates on changes in observable behaviour. Experiments with animals formed the foundation of this theory, for example the work of Skinner, Watson and Pavlov. Researchers sought to associate rewards with certain behaviours in order to increase the display of that behaviour. The relevance of this for organisations today may be seen for example in telesales training where employees are taught to follow a script and calls are listened to, to ensure that the script is followed. Reward or punishment follows depending on behaviour. Trainers are not interested in what is going on in the heads of employees, they merely want them to follow the routine to be learnt. This approach has also been used for a range of interpersonal skills training. One American company, for example, plays video sequences to trainees portraying the 'correct' way to carry out, say, a return to work interview. Trainees then practise copying what they have seen and are given cue cards to use when carrying out that particular interpersonal event. The problems with the perspective are that it is overtly manipulative, simplistic and limited. It may produce only temporary changes in behaviour and increase cynicism.

Cognitive approaches are based on an information-processing perspective and are more concerned with what goes on in the learner's head. This is a more technical perspective and maps out the stages of learning, such as: expectancy to learn (motivation); attention and perception required; experience is coded (meaning is derived); meaning is stored in long-term memory; meaning is retrieved when needed; learning is applied; feedback is received (which may supply reinforcement). The strengths of this perspective are that it stresses the importance of learner motivation and individual needs, it recognises that the individual has some control over what is learnt and it identifies feedback as an important aspect of learning. The weaknesses are that it assumes learning is neutral and unproblematic and it is a purely rational approach that ignores emotion. From this perspective useful development activities would be seen as formal courses offering models and ideas with lots of back-up paperwork. Activities to improve learning motivation are also important, for example helping employees to recognise their own development needs and providing rewards for skills development. Mechanisms for providing feedback to employees are also key.

The third perspective is based on **social learning theory**: in other words, learning is a social activity and this is based on our needs as humans to fit in with others. In organisations this happens to some extent naturally as we learn to fit in with things such as dress codes, behaviour in meetings and so on. Fitting in means that we can be accepted as successful in the organisation, but it is not necessary that we internalise and believe in these codes. Organisations often use role models, mentors and peer support, and 'buddies', to intensify our natural will to fit in. The disadvantages of this perspective are that it ignores the role of choice for the individual and it is based, to some extent, on a masquerade.

The **constructivist** perspective is a development of the information-processing perspective, but does not regard learning as a neutral process: it is our perception of our experiences that counts; there is no 'objective' view. This perspective accepts that in our dealings with the world we create 'meaning structures' in our heads and these are based on our past experiences and personality. New information and potential learning need to fit with these meaning structures in some way, which means that a similar new experience will be understood differently by different people. We tend to pay attention to things which fit with our meaning structures and ignore or avoid things that do not fit. As humans we are also capable of constructing and reconstructing our meaning structures without any new experiences. These meaning structures are mainly unconscious and therefore we are not aware of the structures which constrain our learning. We are generally unaware of how valid our meaning sets are, and they are deeply held and difficult to change. Making these structures explicit enables us to challenge them and to start to change them. This perspective recognises that learning is a very personal and potentially threatening process. We develop mechanisms to protect ourselves from this threat, and thus protect ourselves from learning. The implication of this is that learning support needs to encourage introspection and reflection, and providing the perspectives of others (e.g. as in 360-degree feedback, outdoor courses or relocations) may assist in this process.

In the skills chapter, Chapter 20, at the end of this part of the text, you will see that we use another framework for learning – the CRAMP framework. This focuses on the practical aspects of what has to be learned and implicitly uses one or more of the learning theories identified above.

The nature of learning: learning from experience

A significant amount of work has been done which helps us understand how managers, and others, learn from their experiences. Kolb *et al.* (1984) argue that it is useful to combine the characteristics of learning, which is usually regarded as passive, with those of problem solving, which is usually regarded as active. From this combination Kolb *et al.* developed a four-stage learning cycle, which was further developed by Honey and Mumford (1989).

The four stages, based on the work of both groups of researchers, are shown in Figure 17.1.

Each of these four stages of the learning cycle is critical to effective learning, but few people are strong at each stage and it is helpful to understand where our strengths and weaknesses lie. Honey and Mumford designed a questionnaire to achieve this which identified individuals' learning styles as 'activist', 'reflector', 'theorist' and 'pragmatist', and explain that:

- **Activists** learn best from 'having a go', and trying something out without necessarily preparing. They would be enthusiastic about role-play exercises and keen to take risks in the real environment.

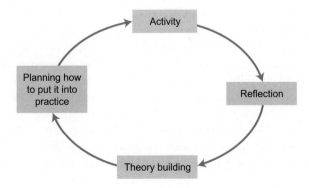

Figure 17.1
The learning cycle

- **Reflectors** are much better at listening and observing. They are effective at reflecting on their own and others' experiences and good at analysing what happened and why.
- **Theorists'** strengths are in building a concept or a theory on the basis of their analysis. They are good at integrating different pieces of information, and building models of the way things operate. They may choose to start their learning by reading around a topic.
- **Pragmatists** are keen to use whatever they learn and will always work out how they can apply it in a real situation. They will plan how to put it into practice. They will value information/ideas they are given only if they can see how to relate them to practical tasks they need to do.

Understanding how individuals learn from experience underpins all learning, but is particularly relevant in encouraging self-development activities. Understanding our strengths and weaknesses enables us to choose learning activities which suit our style, and gives us the opportunity to decide to strengthen a particularly weak learning stage of our learning cycle. Although Honey and Mumford adopt this dual approach, Kolb firmly maintains that learners *must* become deeply competent at all stages of the cycle. There has been considerable attention on the issue of matching and mismatching styles with development activities and the matching and mismatching of trainer learning style with learner learning style.

The nature of learning: insights from neuroscience

Another perspective on learning is the emerging information coming from neuroscience, a complex and interdisciplinary area of science. The integration of learning and neuroscience is very recent and there are generally low levels of awareness about how progress in neuroscience, such as brain imaging, can impact on our understanding of the learning process (CIPD 2014a). In such a new field there is the danger of reading too much into the research (it is just one perspective that can be used alongside others) or accepting research findings which are not robust, and Collins (2015) provides some good questions to use to check whether the research is sound.

Paine (2015) identifies five ways in which neuroscience research can inform learning design: learning is more effective when learners are emotionally engaged, committed and enthusiastic; exercise is useful in between learning sessions; stimulating online and physical environments are conducive to learning; we can learn at any stage in our life (our brains still enjoy challenges); and the brain needs time to reflect to embed learning. In addition, in relation to change, there is evidence that when the brain reacts to fear it is likely to freeze. When people's routines are forced to change this can elicit a fear response as our routines and habits keep us safe (see, for example, CIPD 2014c).

From some of the ideas above you can see that neuroscience is not revolutionary but evolutionary, and generally reinforces what we would anyway describe as good learning design. However, it is reassuring to have a growing evidence base for this.

SUMMARY PROPOSITIONS

17.1. There is currently a voluntarist approach to training and development in the UK, which means that employers make their own choices about the extent to which they train. The government attempts to influence what organisations do by a range of supply-side initiatives. However, the apprenticeship levy is the first government intervention for many years.

17.2. UKCES has a responsibility in encouraging skills improvements in the UK, aided by a complex and constantly changing skills framework. Vocational qualifications (output competences), apprenticeships and IiP are a part of this framework alongside many other bodies and initiatives. The vocational qualifications system and Apprenticeship system are undergoing significant changes at present.

17.3. Behavioural competencies (input competencies) outline the behaviours which underpin job performance.

17.4. There are four learning theories, namely behaviourist, cognitive, social learning and constructivist, which provide different explanations of how people learn, and in addition there are models of how we learn from experience.

17.5. The national context, behavioural competencies, learning theories and neuroscience all underpin practical employee development in organisations, which we look at in the following chapter.

GENERAL DISCUSSION TOPICS

1. 'Both the UK as a whole and organisations themselves would benefit if the government adopted a more interventionist approach to training.'

- Do you agree or disagree? Why?
- How might this intervention be shaped?

2. Should apprenticeships be restricted to the under 25s? List your arguments for and against and justify your conclusion.

THEORY INTO PRACTICE

The CIPD have produced a guide for employers illustrating how to create successful apprenticeships. As part of this they give two short case studies of individuals who have completed apprenticeships at Rolls-Royce. Below there is a short summary of each individual's perspective of what they gained from their experiences.

> Gurjit Johal felt that her manufacturing/mechanical apprenticeship helped her develop both personally and professionally. She felt her life skills were enhanced, giving an example of teamworking: Gurjit and another apprentice were tasked with updating and collating new manufacturing instructions, which involved significant co-ordination with different departments to gain approval. She is proud that 15 years later these instructions are still being used and that she and her colleague moved these instructions from a manual to an electronic version for the first time.
>
> Gurjit also appreciated the training available to her to strengthen her weaker skills, such as maths, and recognised that this improved her confidence. The can-do culture also struck Gurjit and made her feel that anything's possible, and her increased belief in herself and her abilities enabled her to complete two very different placements following the completion of her apprenticeship.
>
> In retrospect, Gurjit, now a nuclear plant design engineer, is delighted that she has gained qualifications to degree level whilst working and being paid. Rolls-Royce are continuing to support her development in this new project management role. She feels her apprenticeship was special due to the support she received to gain the ability, skills and experience which provided a great start to her career.
>
> Neeraj Sunger is currently a manufacturing engineering apprentice who feels that initially becoming a Young Apprentice at Rolls-Royce was the best decision he has ever made. He achieved a 'highly commended' in the Young Apprentice of the Year awards in 2009, of which he is very proud, and is not surprised that the scheme has been assessed as outstanding by Ofsted. In his current apprenticeship role he is studying for an NVQ3 in engineering maintenance and has one day a week off work to study for a foundation degree.
>
> Neeraj wants to stay with Rolls-Royce (as 98% of apprentices do) and hopes that they will sponsor him to do a full engineering degree. He very much appreciates the guidance, support and knowledge he has gained so far, and feels that the apprenticeship is 'the opportunity of a lifetime'.

Questions

1 For what reasons are Gurgit and Neeraj satisfied by their apprenticeship experiences?

2 What issues do Rolls-Royce and other employers need to consider so that their apprenticeships are well resourced and successful?

3 Design an apprenticeship scheme for a specified job in your own organisation, or one with which you are familiar.

Source: CIPD (2012) *Apprenticeships that Work: A Guide for Employers.* London: CIPD.

FURTHER READING

IDS (2012) *HR Studies: Competency Frameworks.* London: IDS.
Interesting up-to-date examples of competency frameworks in use with different employers.

Smith, A. and Collins, L. (2007) 'How does IIP deliver the lifelong learning agenda to SMEs?', *Education and Training*, Vol. 49, No. 8–9, pp. 720–31.

This paper, based on a case study, demonstrates the difficulties in matching IiP requirements with the individual requirements of SMEs. Business Link Advisers, acting as consultants to SMEs, find themselves in a difficult position trying to hit government-set targets for IiP and delivering a useful consultancy service at the same time, which might not lead to IiP recognition. http://feweek.co.uk/2013/11/08/whiteheads-bonfire-of-the-quals/

This is an excellent and very readable summary of the changes proposed by the *Whitehead Review.*

REFERENCES

Ball, S. (2015) 'We need greater acceptance of average', *Work,* Winter, pp. 56–9.

Bourne, A. (2008) *The Impact of Investors in People Standard on People Management Practices and Firm Performance.* Cranfield: Cranfield University.

Boyatzis, R. (1982) *The Competent Manager.* New York: Wiley.

Boyatzis, R. (2008) 'Guest editorial: Competencies in the 21st century', *Journal of Management Development,* Vol. 27, No. 1, pp. 5–12.

Boyatzis, R. (2009) 'Guest editorial: Competencies as a behavioural approach to emotional intelligence', *Journal of Management Development,* Vol. 28, No. 9, pp. 749–70.

Brewster, C., Sparrow, P., Vernon, G. and Houldsworth, E. (2011) *International Human Resource Management.* London: CIPD.

Brockett, J. (2012) 'Olympian task', *People Management,* August, p. 9.

Cheese, P. (2015) 'The productivity puzzle', *People Management,* July, p. 5.

CIPD (2006) 'Competency work pays off for Council', *People Management,* Vol. 12, No. 13, p. 12.

CIPD (2012a) *Factsheet: Skills Policy in the UK.* London: CIPD.

CIPD (2012b) *Apprenticeships that Work: A Guide for Employers.* London: CIPD.

CIPD (2015a) *Recruitment and Talent Planning Survey 2015.* London: CIPD.

CIPD (2015b) *Unlocking Workplace Skills: What is the Role for Employers?* Policy Report, London: CIPD.

CIPD (2014a) *Fresh Thinking in Learning and Development, Part 1 of 3: Neuroscience and Learning.* London: CIPD.

CIPD (2014b) *Industrial Strategy and the Future of Skills Policy: The High Road to Sustainable Growth, Research Insight,* February.

CIPD (2014c) *Neuroscience in Action: Applying Insight to L & D Practice.* London: CIPD.

Collins, S. (2015) 'Neuroscience under scrutiny', *Training Journal,* June, pp. 29–32.

Cranet (2011) *Cranet Survey on Comparative Human Resource Management.* Cranfield: Cranfield University.

Crush, P. (2014) 'Apprenticeships: Now it's HR's job', *People Management,* January, pp. 8–9.

Faragher, J. (2016a) 'Spot the apprentice', *People Management,* January, p. 9.

Faragher, J. (2016b) 'Apprenticeships: Make them work for you', *People Management,* January, pp. 42–4.

Finegold, D., Levenson, A. and Van Buren, M. (2005) 'Access to training and its impact on temporary workers', *Human Resource Management Journal,* Vol. 15, No. 2, pp. 66–85.

Hayes, J., Rose-Quirie, A. and Allinson, C. (2000) 'Senior managers' perceptions of the competencies they require for effective performance: Implications for training and development', *Personnel Review,* Vol. 29, No. 1, pp. 92–105.

Honey, P. and Mumford, A. (1989) *A Manual of Learning Opportunities.* Maidenhead: Peter Honey.

Hoque, K. (2008) 'The impact of Investors in People on employer-provided training, the equality of training provision and the "training apartheid" phenomenon', *Industrial Relations Journal,* Vol. 39, No. 1, pp. 43–62.

IDS (2008) *Competency Frameworks,* HR Study No. 865, March.

Kolb, D.A., Rubin, I.M. and McIntyre, J.M. (1984) *Organisation Psychology* (4th edn.). Englewood Cliffs, NJ: Prentice Hall.

Leitch, S. (2006) *Leitch Review of Skills: Prosperity for all in the global economy – final report,* December. London: The Stationery Office.

Lloyd, C. (2002) 'Training and development deficiencies in "high-skill" sectors', *Human Resource Management Journal,* Vol. 12, No. 2, pp. 64–81.

Ofqual (2015) *After the QCF: A New Qualifications Framework.* London: Crown copyright.

Paine, N. (2015) 'Game changers for learning', *Training Journal,* May, pp. 5–8.

Phillips, L. (2009) 'The skills maze', *People Management,* 7 May, pp. 21–4.

Rayton, B. and Georgiadis, K. (2012) 'Workplace self-selection into Investors in People', *Applied Economics Letters,* Vol. 19, pp. 1455–8.

Richard, D. (2012) *The Richard Review of Apprenticeships.* London: Department for Business, Innovation and Skills, November.

Salaman, G. and Taylor, S. (2002) 'Competency's consequences: Changing the character of managerial work', Paper presented at the ESRC Critical Management Studies Seminar: Managerial Work, The Judge Institute of Management, Cambridge.

Smedley, T. (2011) 'Generating jobs', *People Management,* December, pp. 24–8.

Stern, S. (2014) 'Making the grade', *Work,* Autumn, pp. 52–9.

Thelen, K. (2007) 'Contemporary challenges to the German vocational training system', *Regulation and Governance,* No. 1, pp. 247–60.

UKCES (2015a) *UK Skills levels and International Competitiveness,* Report 96. London: UKCES.

UKCES (2015b) *Growth Through People.* London: UKCES.

UKCES (2016) *Employer Skill Survey 2015: UK Results.* London: UKCES.

UKCES (2013) *Review of Adult Vocational Qualifications in England,* led by Nigel Whitehead. London:.UKCES.

van Wanrooy, B., Bewley, H., Bryson, A., Forth, J., Freeth, S., Stokes, L. and Wood, S. (2013) *The 2011 Workplace Employee Relations Survey: First Findings.* London: Department for Business, Innovation and Skills.

Whiddett, S. and Kandola, B. (2000) 'Fit for the job?', *People Management,* 25 May, pp. 30–4.

Wright, J., Brinkley, I. and Clayton, N. (2010) *Employability and Skills in the UK: Redefining the Debate,* a report prepared by the London Chamber of Commerce and Industry Commercial Education Trust. London: The Work Foundation.

CHAPTER 18

LEARNING AND DEVELOPMENT

THE OBJECTIVES OF THIS CHAPTER ARE TO:

1 Describe different ways in which learning needs can be identified and expressed

2 Explain the various methods of addressing learning and development needs

3 Investigate the nature of evaluation in this context

There has been a considerable shift in the way that individual development is understood and characterised. We have moved from identifying training needs to identifying learning needs, the implication being that development is owned by the learner with the need rather than by the trainer seeking to satisfy that need. This also has implications for who identifies the needs and the way that those needs are met. Current thinking suggests that needs are best developed by a partnership between the individual and the organisation, and that the methods of meeting these needs are not limited to formal courses, but to a wide range of on-the-job development methods and approaches involving technology. While a partnership approach is considered ideal, the phrase 'self-development' is key in our development lexicon, indicating that individuals increasingly own and take responsibility for their own development. There has also been a shift in the type of skills that are the focus of development activity: from technical skills to the development of personal skills, self-management and attitudes. Lastly, while the focus on development for the current job remains high, there is greater pressure for development to be future orientated. These shifts reflect the changes which we have already discussed in terms of global competition: fast and continuous change, and the need for individuals to develop their employability in an increasingly uncertain world.

In the UK the three *most effective* development methods are on-job training (47%), coaching by line managers (40%) and in-house development courses (34%), as identified in the CIPD 2015 *Learning and Talent Development Survey* (CIPD 2015c). In the same survey the *most used* methods were the same three as the most effective, in the following order: on-job training (48%), in-house programmes (46%) and coaching (32%). Table 18.1 shows the most used learning methods in the Asia Pacific region according to the Cegos 2012 survey (Blain 2013).

Cegos compared these figures with its pan-European survey and note that classroom methods are used in 90% of organisations in Europe and online methods used in 43%.

Whilst in this chapter we focus on development for employees we note that development is increasingly being offered to non-employees such as volunteers, clients, students, contractors, consultants and suppliers (CIPD 2015c).

Table 18.1 Methods of learning in the Asia Pacific region

Learning method	Percentage using this
Classroom	79
Online	58
Individual mentoring	42
Group mentoring	34
On the job	54
Blended	39

Source: Blain, J. (2013) *Major Learning Trends and Indicators for 2013 and Beyond within the Asia Pacific Region.* Singapore: Cegos.

Identifying learning and development needs

Learning needs may be identified by the individual, by the organisation or in partnership. There are various approaches to analysing needs, a more traditional one being matching the individual's competency profile with that for the job that person is filling. The profile comparison approach takes a broad view and is perhaps most useful when an individual, or group of individuals, are new to a job, using information from the selection or promotion process, including development centres which we discuss in the following chapter. This approach is also useful because strategic priorities change and new skills are required of employees, and the nature of their job may change substantially, even though they are still officially in the same role with the same job title. This approach is useful when there is time to plan.

An alternative, problem-centred approach focuses on any performance problems or difficulties, or small job changes and explores whether these are due to a lack of skills or knowledge or inappropriate attitudes and, if so, which ones. This is a much more flexible approach and action can be taken immediately the need is identified, as speed is often critical.

When a gap has been identified, by whatever method, the development required needs to be phrased in terms of a learning objective, so that an appropriate learning experience can be chosen/designed. For example, when a gap or need has been identified around team leadership, appropriate learning objectives may be that learners, by the end of the development, **will be able** 'to ask appropriate questions at the outset of a team activity to ascertain relevant skills and experience', and 'to check understanding of the task' or 'to review a team activity by involving all members in that review'. So you can see that learning objectives are phrased in terms of an activity that the learner will be able to perform once learning has been completed – hence they always begin with a verb.

ACTIVITY 18.1

Write learning objectives for the following individuals who are experiencing problems in their performance:

1 Tina, who always dominates meetings, and neglects the contribution of others.

2 Brian, who has never carried out a selection interview before, and is very unsure of how to go about this.

3 Mark, who feels he has lots of contributions to make at meetings, but never actually says anything.

4 Sara, who can never get to meetings on time.

The planning and design of learning will be influenced by the learning objectives and also by the HR development strategy, which for example may contain a vision of who should be involved in training and development activities, and the emphasis on approaches such as self-development and use of technology.

WINDOW ON PRACTICE

A strategic approach to L&D at John Lewis Partnership

John Lewis is a UK department store where all employees are partners of the business in the sense that they each own a share of it. Product knowledge is important and a focus on technology means that learning can be agile and partners can update quickly.

Many partners are given tablets so they can update whilst on the shop floor. There is heavy investment in a self-service L&D website where partners can access training on demand using any device and at any time. This was not a cost-saving measure. Also available online is a mentoring database that all can access as well as online courses provided by Ashridge Business School. The focus is on equipping all partners so they can deliver excellent customer service. John Lewis is passionate about lifelong learning and is committed to developing the whole person. This includes subsidised leisure learning where partners can claim up to 50% off the cost of any course outside work, whatever the topic, from cookery to yoga. They believe that this approach results in people who are more well-rounded and fulfilled and that it encourages partners to 'bring their whole selves' to work.

Source: Adapted from Newbery, C. (2015a) 'No matter where you're learning, we're there', *People Management*, June, pp. 20–21.

Once development activities begin it is helpful that they are monitored so that they can be adapted if required, and that they are finally evaluated at an appropriate time in the future to assess how behaviour and performance have changed

Methods of learning and development

Below we look at a range of development methods and, although we look at each separately, most organisations and individuals use a combination of methods at any one time, as is demonstrated by the examples that we use.

Off-job methods: education and training courses

Educational courses undertaken during a career are frequently done on a part-time basis leading to a diploma, degree or professional qualification. Masters' degrees in management and MBAs are considered to provide value for both the employer and the participant; for debates around these and their advantages see for example *People Management* (2012) and Smedley (2012). This is an alternative approach to the QCF route which we discussed in the previous chapter, which is more closely tied to on-the-job experiences and not concerned with 'education'.

In addition there are external consultancy courses, varying from a half-day to several weeks in length, and run by consultants or professional bodies for all comers. They have the advantage that they bring together people from varying company and occupational backgrounds providing new perspectives. They are relatively expensive and may be superficial but are good for swapping experiences among course members, and future networking. The most valuable courses of this type are those that concentrate on specific skills or knowledge, such as developing time management or interviewing skills, or being introduced to topical issues such as a new national initiative, or legislation where interpretation and sharing views is important.

In-house courses are often similar in nature to consultancy courses, and are sometimes run with the benefit of some external expertise. In-house courses can be particularly useful if the training needs relate to specific organisational procedures and structures, forthcoming organisational changes and ways of encouraging employees to work more effectively together. The drawbacks of in-house courses are that they suffer from 'organisational groupthink'.

Alternatively, there are outdoor-type courses, sometimes known as Outward Bound, after the organisation that pioneered them. Outdoor courses attempt to develop skills involved in working with and through others, and aim to increase self-awareness and self-confidence through a variety of experiences, including outdoor physical challenges. Their differential value is assumed to hinge on their separation from the political, organisational environment. A different environment is assumed to encourage individuals to forsake political strategising, act as their raw selves and be more open to new ideas, but this is perhaps more hope than reality. Learning experiences based on drama are increasingly popular; in these participants are engaged in improvisation through role play and exercises. For example, London Underground has a mock tube station, 'West Ashfield', where underground staff can practise before going live, and fire, ambulance and police services can prepare for emergency situations such as mass evacuations and people falling under trains (Stevens 2010). We explore other forms of off-job simulation and experiential learning in a later section on the use of technology in learning.

WINDOW ON PRACTICE

Hazardous training

To make the most of an overnight closure of the M56 motorway, five fire crews from across Cheshire Warrington and Halton played out a scenario involving a multi-vehicle collision where a tanker containing hazardous chemicals had crashed into the central reservation. Actors and volunteers played the parts of casualties and the fire crews did not know what to expect when they attended the scene. It was felt that such realistic training experiences would be the best preparation for a real incident.

Source: Cheshire Fire and Rescue Service (2012) *Cheshire East Annual Report 2011–12*. Cheshire East.

One of the major concerns with these different types of off-job courses and activities is the difficulty of ensuring transfer of learning back to the workplace. One of the most helpful ideas is to review the materials immediately after the programme and develop goals/plans for implementing new skills. Reviewing the material with others can also be very helpful, especially their line manager who can include development goals in performance reviews. Insights from neuroscience suggest that learning experiences which are emotionally involving are more likely to be transferred to the workplace.

WINDOW ON PRACTICE

Experiential activities: role reversal

Phillips (2006) provides an example of BUPA care staff in a retirement home. As part of a 'Personal Best' programme aimed at improving customer service, staff took the role of residents so as to see life through their customers' eyes. So, for example, they were fed puréed food and were hoisted in a mechanical sling from a chair into a bed. As a result staff behaviour towards residents has changed, for example explaining the hoisting procedure to residents and doing it more slowly.

Source: Phillips, L. (2006) 'BUPA stars', *People Management*, Vol. 12, No. 22, 9 November, pp. 30–32.

Learning on the job

Natural learning and self-development

To some extent self-development may be seen as a conscious effort to gain the most from natural learning in a job, and to use the learning cycle, which was explained in the previous chapter, as a framework. Learners may start by understanding their own strengths and weaknesses in the learning cycle as this will inform their choice of development method and perhaps development goals.

ACTIVITY 18.2

1 If you have not already done so, obtain the Honey and Mumford questionnaire and work out your learning style(s).

2 Select your weakest style and try to identify two different learning activities which fit with this style, but that you would normally avoid.

3 Seek opportunities for trying out these learning activities. If you practise these activities on a regular basis this should help you strengthen the style you are working on.

4 Log your experiences and in particular what you have learnt about these 'new' learning activities.

The emphasis in self-development is that each individual is responsible for, and can plan, his or her own development, although he or she may need to seek help when working on some issues. Self-development can be focused in specific skills development, but often extends to attitude development and personal growth. It involves individuals in analysing their strengths, weaknesses and the way in which they learn, primarily by means of questionnaires and feedback from others. This analysis may initially begin on a self-development course, or with the help of a facilitator, but would then be continued by the individual back on the job. From this analysis individuals, perhaps with some help at first, plan their development goals and the way in which they will achieve them, primarily through development opportunities within the job. When individuals consciously work on and sometimes plan self-development they use the learning cycle in a more explicit way than in natural learning. They are also in a better position to seek appropriate opportunities and help, in their learning, from their manager. The following Window on practice gives an example.

WINDOW ON PRACTICE

Gwen is a management trainer in a large organisation running a number of in-house management courses. She has just moved into this position from her role as section leader in the research department; the move was seen as a career development activity in order to strengthen her managerial skills.

Gwen is working with her manager to learn from her experiences. Here is an extract from her learning diary based on the learning cycle:

Activity – I've had a go at running three sessions on my own now, doing the input and handling the questions.

Reflection – I find the input much easier than handling questions. When I'm asked a question and answer it I have the feeling that they're not convinced by my reply and I feel awkward that we seem to finish the session hanging in mid-air. I would like to be able to encourage more open discussion.

Theory building – If I give an answer to a question it closes off debate by the fact that I have 'pronounced' what is 'right'. If I want them to discuss I have to avoid giving my views at first.

Planning practice – When I am asked a question rather than answering it I will say to the group: 'What does anyone think about that?' or 'What do you think?' (to the individual who asked) or 'What are the possibilities here?' I will keep encouraging them to respond to each other and reinforce where necessary, or help them change tack by asking another question.

David Megginson characterises learners by the extent to which they plan the direction of their learning and implement this, namely planned learning; and the extent to which they are able to learn from opportunistic learning experiences, namely emergent learning. Warriors are those who are strong at planning what they want to learn and how, but are less strong at learning from experiences they had not anticipated. They have a clear focus on what they want to learn and pursue this persistently. On the other hand, Adventurers respond to and learn from opportunities that come along unexpectedly; they are curious and flexible. However, they tend not to plan and create opportunities for themselves. Sages are strong on both characteristics, and Sleepers display little of either characteristic at present. To be most effective in self-development activities learners need to make maximum use of both planned and emergent learning. For a further explanation of this model also see Megginson and Whitaker (2007).

Many of the activities included in self-development are based on observation, collecting further feedback about the way the individual operates, experimenting with different approaches and in particular reviewing what has happened, why and what the individual has learnt. Self-development, however, is not a quick fix and attention needs to be paid to how the self-development process is to be supported. Extensive induction into the process is important as is an explanation of the theoretical underpinning, appropriate skill development, preparation for peer feedback, and further support in tracking progress.

Learning logs can be used as a mechanism for learning retrospectively as they encourage a disciplined approach to learning from opportunistic events. The log may be focused around one particular activity and is usually designed to encourage the writer to explain what happened, how he or she has reflected on this, what conclusions he or she has made and what future learning actions he or she wishes to make. Alternatively logs can be used in the form of a daily or weekly diary.

ACTIVITY 18.3

Identify a management skills area that you need to develop. (You may find it particularly helpful to choose an interpersonal area, for example assertiveness, influencing others, presentation, being more sociable, contributing to meetings, helping others.)

Keep a learning diary over the next few weeks, logging anything that is relevant to your development area. Use the framework which Gwen used in the previous Window on practice box.

At the end of the period review what you have learnt in your development area and also what you have learnt about the learning cycle.

Social learning

Social learning is a label frequently used as if it is something new, but looking back at the learning theories in Chapter 17 you will see that it has been around for a long time. What is new is the emphasis on *collaborative* social learning, *immediacy, flexibility,* and the *integration of technology* into the social learning process. Traditional social learning processes include job shadowing, job swaps and secondments, all of which allow an individual to experience a different job/different part of the organisation, make new contacts and understand alternative perspectives.

Individual supportive peer relationships are a more flexible form of social learning and are accessible to all. Peer relationships can vary in depth, which can be expressed on a continuum. Some peer relationships consist of sharing information and skills; some may provide job-related feedback and friendship, and share career planning; others may focus on emotional support, personal feedback, friendship and confirmation. Most of us benefit from one or a number of peer relationships at work but often we do not readily appreciate their contribution towards our development. Peer relationships most often develop on an informal basis and provide mutual support. Some organisations, however, formally appoint an existing employee to provide such support to a new member of staff through the first 12–18 months in the organisation. These relationships may, of course, continue beyond the initial period. The name for the appointed employee will vary from organisation to organisation, and sometimes the word 'buddy', 'coach' or 'mentor' is used – which can be confusing! The skills and qualities sought in peer providers are likely to include accessibility, empathy, organisational experience and proven task skills.

A more collaborative, but structured, form of traditional social learning is self-development groups, which usually involve a series of meetings of peers where they jointly discuss their personal development, organisational issues and/or individual work problems. Groups may begin operating with a leader, but the group itself is the primary source of information and may operate without outside help as its members' process skills develop. The content and timings of the meetings can be very flexible, although meetings will require a significant level of energy and commitment if they are to operate well. Action learning groups are similar and we refer to some action learning case studies in the Further Reading section at the end of the chapter.

Immediate and flexible collaboration with internal and external networks often involves the use of technology but equally some of this immediate collaboration may be face to face, as in the Window on practice below, focusing on helping teams learn together as they work, and applying learning immediately.

WINDOW ON PRACTICE

Social learning in A&E

Anita Esser, head of wider healthcare teams education at Southampton University Hospitals NHS Trust, explains a very productive form of social learning used by one of the A&E consultants. Regular 30-minute 'huddles' take place with the entire clinical team. They talk openly about difficult or unusual cases and what could have been done better. The aim is to capture and share all learnings.

Source: Jeffery, R. (2015) 'What apple pie can teach you about social learning', *People Management*, July, pp. 36–40.

Other forms of collaboration are technology based and may include 'communities of practice' between groups of professionals, online discussion forums which extend networking and learning for those who have been on a course together, and platforms for uploading video, text and podcasts. So, just as we may turn to YouTube to find an instructional video on how to use a new appliance or complete a DIY task, learners can use contributions from all comers to help them complete an unfamiliar task at work. Much of this is based upon the natural desire of most people to share knowledge, boosting their self-worth, and this is aligned to the natural inclination for sharing in our world of social media. Social enterprise networks may also be used, for example Yammer and Jive, which provide a platform for staff across an organisation to chat and share ideas at work.

WINDOW ON PRACTICE

Selling tips in video clips

Dixon Retail developed 'The Edge', which was deliberately designed on the lines of BBC iPlayer. Salespeople were asked to share tips for selling laptops and 520 video clips were received in a month.

Source: Crush, P. (2013) 'The technologies that will transform learning', *People Management*, April, pp. 38–9.

Manager coaching and other internal and external coaching

The line manager's role in learning and development has increased with the devolution of HR tasks. Coaching is an informal approach to individual development based on a close relationship between the individual and one other person, either internal or external to the organisation. The coach is often the immediate manager, who is experienced in the task, but there is increasing use of external coaches, especially for more senior managers, or specially trained internal coaches. The CIPD (2012a) found that 43% of organisations used coaching to improve poor performance and 47% used it to build on good performance.

The line manager as coach helps trainees to develop by giving them the opportunity to perform an increasing range of tasks, and by helping them to learn from their experiences. Managers work to improve the trainee's performance by asking searching questions, actively listening, discussion, exhortation, encouragement, understanding, counselling and providing information and honest feedback. The manager coach is usually in a position to create development opportunities for the trainee when this is appropriate. For example, a line manager can delegate attendance at a meeting, or allow a trainee to deputise, where this is appropriate to the individual's development needs. Alternatively a line manager can create the opportunity for a trainee to join a working party or can arrange a brief secondment to another department. Coaches can share 'inside' information with the individual being coached to help him or her understand the political context in which the individual is working. For example, they are able to explain who will have most influence on a decision that will be made, or future plans for restructuring within a department.

Skilled coaches can adapt their style to suit the individual they are coaching, from highly directive at one end of the scale to non-directive at the other. The needed style may change over time, as the trainee gains more confidence and experience. IDS (2009) found that a good coach is one who had a genuine interest in the trainees; believes that everyone is capable of more and focuses on potential rather than past performance; knows that the coach does not have all the answers; believes a person's past is no indication of his or her future; understands that an open, supportive and mutual relationship is required for effective coaching; understands that results may be short or long term; and believes they should build awareness, responsibility and self-belief. A variety of barriers to coaching have been identified including performance pressures and a feeling that the role was not valued, but Anderson (2009) found that time pressures, lack of confidence to deal with difficult people and organisational culture were key. The emphasis in coaching on honest self-reflection suggests that there will be barriers in organisations where the culture is not one of openness and honesty.

There has been an increasing trend to broaden the concept of coaching in terms of both content and who carries out the coaching. Some organisations are now providing or arranging intensive training for designated internal coaches who operate broadly in the organisation, just in a coaching role. This is quite different from the basic training line managers are likely to receive. External executive coaching is often provided by consultancies and specialist coaching organisations. Various forms of coaching may include career coaching, performance coaching, skills coaching, business coaching and life coaching. Sometimes roles may be reversed and slightly more junior managers give feedback to more senior managers on the impact of their behaviour, or more junior staff may coach more senior ones in technical skills such as IT. Many organisations aim to develop a coaching culture where coaching is part of the way that everyone works.

WINDOW ON PRACTICE

Coaching the coaches

The Guildhall School of Music and Drama is one of the world's most famous conservatoires but staff had little experience of coaching. To encourage this Professor Helena Gaunt, vice principal and director of academic affairs, worked with Jane Cook, an experienced education coach. They developed a nine-month pilot scheme for 15 members of staff. This began with an intensive skills development day followed by three half-day workshops and three personal coaching sessions. Between the formal sessions delegates were expected to coach each other to embed their growing skills. There was initial scepticism as coaching, getting students to work out solutions for themselves, was in some ways opposed to traditional teaching, and it was experienced as a culture shock. However the benefits of student confidence and performance were enough to encourage many more staff to voluntarily go through the programme and some staff are supported to do coaching diplomas. They also found that these skills promoted more supportive staff relationships and meetings are now run in a more collaborative way.

Source: Newbery, C. (2016) 'Coaching was a culture shock', *People Management*, February, p. 27.

Group coaching is sometimes used; for example Sue Miller, head of global talent management at Hilton Worldwide, reports on the use of group coaching for new graduates which has sparked 'healthy' competition. She acknowledges that this new scheme has resulted in two graduates leaving but felt it was discouraging people from staying in the wrong role (*People Management* 2014). The use of such an approach needs to be carefully thought through and very much depends on the purpose of the coaching as, of course, there will be no individual confidentiality.

Given the increasing professionalisation of coaching it is not surprising that the quality of the coaching experience is receiving attention. Supervision of practice is increasingly being used in a way that is similar to supervision for counsellors, which involves regular meetings with a more experienced practitioner to explore their client relationships and reflect on practice. Such individual supervision is carried out with a mind to client confidentiality; however, the use of group supervision of coaches and the desire of organisations to collect common coaching themes to inform organisational thinking puts client confidentiality at greater risk.

Mentoring

Mentoring offers a wide range of advantages for the development of the mentee or protégé, coaching as described above being just one of the possible benefits of the relationship. The mentor may occasionally be the individual's immediate manager, but usually it is a more senior manager in the same or a different function. The CIPD (2015a) identifies the purposes of mentors as sharing their greater understanding of the workplace to support the development of a junior/inexperienced member of staff. We would add that it is often used informally to enhance career advancement (such as increasing exposure and visibility, and sponsorship), and building confidence.

WINDOW ON PRACTICE

Mentoring at MBNA

MBNA takes a speed dating approach to mentoring where mentees and mentors get together in a room and potential mentees take five minutes to explain to each potential mentor what they are looking for from mentoring. At the end the mentees make a choice of who can best support them. Prior to this potential mentors attend a workshop to identify their own strengths and what they can bring to a mentoring relationship. They then work through an app which guides them through the mentoring relationship, and which is built on a *Treasure Island* theme. It is designed to capture their imagination and be engaging. They work through this app whilst completing training workshops and mentoring meetings. The app has four chapters: an introduction to mentoring; mentoring skills; listening skills; and the do's and don'ts of mentoring. Completing each chapter enables them to unlock the relevant diamond, which is the object of their quest.

Source: Marshall, D. (2015) 'Smart coaching', *Training Journal*, April, pp. 29–31.

Fowler and O'Gorman (2005), on the basis of research with both mentors and proteges, describe eight individual mentoring functions which are: personal and emotional guidance; coaching; advocacy; career development facilitation; role modelling; strategies and systems advice; learning facilitation; and friendship. There is evidence that mentoring does benefit both parties, and mentors can gain through recognition from peers, increased job satisfaction, rejuvenation, admiration and self-satisfaction. Indeed reciprocity is expected in a mentoring relationship and there is evidence both mentor and mentee can make claims on each other (Oglensky 2008).

ACTIVITY 18.4

Listen to the BBC Radio 4's *The Bottom Line* episode entitled 'Lonely at the Top?' first broadcast on 17 March 2016.
  A podcast can be downloaded from BBC.co.uk/bottomline.

1 How are the terms 'mentor' and 'coach' differentiated and what other labels are used for this relationship?

2 In what ways did this relationship aid these very senior managers?

3 What potential problems were identified?

The drawbacks to mentoring include the risk of overreliance, the danger of picking up bad habits, the fact that the protégé may be alienated from other sources of expertise and the sense of loss experienced when the mentoring relationship ends. Some may find it difficult to deal with conflicting views in such an unequal relationship. There is a danger of assuming that mentoring is unquestionably good and Oglensky (2008) notes that mentoring can be a source of stress, conflict and dysfunction.

Managers are also seen as responsible for developing talent, and although a mentor/protégé relationship might not naturally occur, mentorship may be encouraged or formalised. For example, there are systems where all new graduates are attached to a mentor as soon as they join the organisation. The difficulties of establishing a formal programme include the potential mismatch of individuals, unreal expectations on both sides and the time and effort involved.

Using learning technologies

Learning technologies can be defined as:

> the broad range of communication and information technologies that can be used to support learning (CIPD 2015c, p. 15)

Often still referred to as e-learning, such technologies include e-learning courses, collaborative and social learning technologies, MOOCs (massive open online courses), mobile device based learning, virtual worlds and gamefied learning, virtual classrooms and webinars, and user generated content. Increasingly such technologies are integrated with other learning methods as we have demonstrated earlier in the chapter.

Learning with technology, which began as an electronic form of distance learning, provides the opportunity for learners to study flexibly in terms of time and topics which match up with immediate job demands. Learning can be done opportunistically and need not be in work time, and learners can progress at their own pace. E-learning courses also come into their own when training has to be delivered to a large number of people in a short space of time, such as a new product launch – giving speed and cost-effectiveness. Also where training must be consistent yet regularly updated, such as health and safety training, e-learning has much to offer. Despite these advantages Ruth Stuart suggests e-learning courses are often just copies of what would have been delivered face to face with few animations and are limited in their scope (Faragher 2014).

MOOCs are in some ways a technologically updated version of this e-learning. They are online courses developed by universities, employers, professional bodies and others.

For example, the CIPD brought out their first MOOC, 'Working digitally: social media and HR', which is free. Being completely open, and usually free, the hope was that MOOCs would attract those who would not normally have the opportunity for such development, although the take-up currently appears to be from well-qualified professionals wanting to develop their career (see, for example, Little 2015; de Coutre 2014). MOOCs can provide high-quality continuous development and incorporate collaborative learning and user-generated content so they can be informal and engaging, but with minimal accreditation. Concerns have been raised about massive dropout rates with few completing the courses, but de Coutre argues that this is a means of self-selection, and Crush (2014) suggests that dropout rates do not mean that people have not benefited from the experience – they just dip in to use the things they are interested in. University College London (*People Management* 2014) warns that cheating is rampant among MOOCs and that vigilance is required.

Interactive Web 2.0 technology, cloud computing and mobile devices have presented much greater opportunities for the use of learning technologies, and these are used in MOOCs as well as other settings such as other programmes developed by employers. For example, synchronous learning can be used where all participants log on at the same time, with a tutor or facilitator being available online. Individuals can progress through material alone or network with others to complete a task and use chatrooms and have a dialogue with the tutor. Videoconferencing can also be used to bring participants together at the same time, with some academic and employer courses being delivered via videoconferencing rather than classroom-based teaching, and webinars (seminars delivered via the Web) are popular. Virtual reality can be used (as in gaming) and this is especially helpful in situations where it would be dangerous to learn solely on the job. In virtual reality games an individual creates a virtual persona, called an avatar, and engages with other avatars. Organisations may create their office, store or campus so that learners experience a virtual world which mirrors their real one.

Virtual worlds can be used to give individuals experience of trying out new skills, learning new ideas and making mistakes. There is the potential for individuals to 'meet' and engage with others in ways that would be difficult in the real world. One way that the virtual worlds can be used for people development is for there to be a 'scripted' approach. This means that some of the avatars are controlled to create situations which can then be discussed afterwards. 'Open access' (i.e. not scripted) learning may also be used, for example for team exercises where teams address a challenge and are given feedback, just as on an 'outdoor' team training event. In using gaming for learning there are a number of important considerations to bear in mind such as the type of audience, the appropriateness of competitiveness, and the nature of the topic, and therefore it needs to be used selectively (see, for example, Churchard 2015).

Increasingly learning designers are focusing on developing systems which enable content to be used on all types of devices, from desk/laptop to tablet to smartphone, so that there is no loss of data when moving from one device to another and the material and systems retain complete integrity (Paine 2015). The focus is increasingly on using mobile technology and, while this is progressing slowly in the west, in many Asia Pacific countries employees are leapfrogging traditional IT hardware to embrace tablets and mobile learning. India in particular is ahead on this. Use of mobile technologies fits in with the expectations of the changing workforce and, for example, many university lecturers often ask students to look up material on the Web as an integral part of a class.

WINDOW ON PRACTICE

Mobile learning for Save the Children staff

Together with Skill Pill, Save the Children have produced a mobile app for developing management skills. This is available for most countries they cover including the Yemen, Nepal and Ethiopia. Use of mobile technology was most appropriate as smartphones are commonplace in these countries.

When the app was designed it was important that there was the ability to download the material as well as accessing it directly from the Web as wi-fi signals in these countries can vary enormously.

The content was designed to be informal, with a coaching and collaborative tone to help overcome any resistance from users to being told what to do by western authorities. They felt it also suited the sensitivity of the subject matter.

The content was designed with simple colours, text appropriate to small screen size and chunks of content are rarely more than three minutes long. It was designed to be engaging and interactive.

The app was integrated into a programme using Webinars, a four-day course, and a series of shared events. There was built-in feedback to encourage people to discuss the app.

Just under 10% of staff used it as last-minute preparation for a particular task; around 20% used it to provide an introduction to a new topic; around 50% used it to help them teach or coach others; and around 70% used it to revise or top up existing knowledge.

Source: Adapted from *Training Journal* (2015) 'Mobile learning in action', December, pp. 32–5.

The use of social media platforms, such as Facebook, Linkedin, Instagram and Twitter, are also being integrated into learning and development. Such tools provide learners with a further means to be contributors as well as receivers of knowledge, and allow multiway discussion and interpretation of content. This also allows communities to form around a topic, and enables learners to collaborate whatever their geographical location. Blogs and wikis can be used as well as social networking sites and some companies do develop their own sites.

Progress with technology in learning has been mixed, despite high expectations. Early on it was realised that e-learning courses can be a solitary activity and are often very dependent on individual self-discipline, and there are some learners who will simply find that an interactive Web-based learning unit does not compare with the conviviality and action associated with attending a course. Thus motivation dwindles unless there is other support to encourage learners to complete the units they need. Also, using more sophisticated packages involving synchronous learning and joint learner tasks, bulletin boards and group/tutor dialogues can be very difficult at first for many employees, even though they may have good everyday computer skills, and they will need time to learn how particular packages work and how to use the facilities. If the right preparation and support are not made available employees can easily be put off by one difficult experience in which they found they could not keep up with the rest of the synchronous learning group.

The integration of learning technology with other learning methods appears to have much greater success, as is shown in the examples we have provided. At a very basic level e-learning can be very effectively used before a face-to-face course to do pre-work so that, for example, all attendees are starting from a roughly similar knowledge base. In this case those employees who have the knowledge base already can be exempt, while learning via technology enables the others to get up to speed before the course begins. Similarly, technology can be used effectively for course briefings and general preparation, such as the completion and analysis of pre-course questionnaires and other pre-work which saves time at the beginning of the event itself. At the end of a course technology can be used for refreshers, for self-checking of understanding, and planning how to apply the learning gained on the course. In the same way, technology can be used in combination with manager coaching, and we have used examples to show how technology can be integrated with other development methods.

WINDOW ON PRACTICE

Going global

Increasingly, global organisations are faced with the challenge of translating a successful L&D programme from one country to a host of different ones. The challenge is for designers to determine which skills translate across national borders, what delivery methods are appropriate in other cultures, and the balance between central provision and local flexible provision.

Ruth Stuart, CIPD research advisor for L&D, notes that most international organisations have adopted varieties of e-learning such as pre-recorded videos, peer-to-peer video calling, and other interactive elements. But care needs to be taken with translation and a choice needs to be made as to whether to use subtitling or dubbing. There are cultural considerations too, for example showing ankles would be seen as inappropriate in some cultures, according to Matt Fletcher of Atticmedia.

Jacky King, head of learning and development at the charity VSO, opted for global programmes as volunteers were spread over the world and it was impossible to gather them together in any one place at the appropriate time. However, VSO are keen to encourage volunteers to connect with each and so they join a cohort that starts on a specific day with a webinar to enable them to build a support network. Self-study follows this.

Armi Stephanie Trenas, founder of consultancy Performance Partners Inc., says that understanding local working culture is key in deciding what elements should be consistent globally and what elements need to remain local. There is the risk of losing engagement if the training package does not suit the audience. She gives an example of a US programme which was brought to Asia. The design of the programme involved significant use of personal reflection and dialogue from the outset and this caused problems as the Asian learners needed more time before they were ready to be involved in personal disclosure. She notes that the hierarchical/egalitarian balance in a culture also needs to be taken into consideration in design, affecting how collaborative learning is used, and that age groups have an influence, for example younger age groups like using mobile devices in the classroom. Even among Asians, she notes, while there is much in common there are key differences in learning preferences:

- Indian participants thrive on individual competition;
- Those from south-east Asia prefer team-based competition;
- Filipino learners respond well to the integration of music; and
- Malaysians enjoy role-play scenarios.

Source: Newbery, C. (2015b) 'The international verdict on your L&D programme . . . ?', *People Management*, April, pp. 44–9.

Evaluation of training and development

One of the most nebulous and unsatisfactory aspects of the training job is evaluating its effectiveness, yet it is becoming more necessary to demonstrate value for money. However we remain unsure whether training breeds success or success breeds training. Evaluation is straightforward when the output of the training is clear to see, such as reducing the number of dispatch errors in a warehouse or increasing someone's typing speed. It is more difficult to evaluate the success of a management training course or a programme of social skills development, but the fact that it is difficult is not enough to prevent its being done.

A familiar method of evaluation is the post-course questionnaire, which course members complete on the final day by answering vague questions that require them to assess aspects of the course using only such general terms as 'good', 'very good' or 'outstanding'. The drawbacks with such questionnaires are, first, that there is a powerful halo effect, as the course will have been, at the very least, a welcome break from routine and there will probably have been some attractive fringe benefits such as staying in a comfortable hotel and enjoying rich food. Second, the questionnaire tends to evaluate the course and not the learning, so that the person attending the course is assessing the quality of the tutors and the visual aids, instead of being directed to examine what has been learnt.

Hamblin (1974), in a much-quoted work, identified five levels of evaluation: (1) evaluating the training, as in the post-course questionnaire above; (2) evaluating the learning, in terms of how the trainee now behaves; (3) evaluating changes in job performance; (4) evaluating changes in organisational performance; and (5) evaluating changes in the wider contribution that the organisation now makes. Perhaps the most well-referenced approach to evaluation is Kirkpatrick (1959) who suggested four levels of evaluation, somewhat similar to Hamblin: (1) reaction level; (2) learning level (have the learning objectives been met?); (3) behaviour (how has the individual's behaviour changed after returning to the job?); and (4) results and impact on the bottom line (what is the impact of training on performance?).

CIPD (2015c) report that whilst most organisations evaluate L&D in some way, only a small minority, 7%, of respondents to their 2015 L&D survey evaluated the impact on business and society (Hamblin level 4–5). And only 22% assess behaviour change by assessing the transfer of learning to the workplace (Hamblin level 3), with 21% evaluating the change in knowledge and skills of participants (Hamblin level 2). Meanwhile 37% assess the satisfaction of participants in L&D processes (Hamblin level1). In terms of methods used for this evaluation, 80% used learner reflection and feedback and 52% used manager reflection and feedback. Interestingly 39%, the third most-used method, used general HR metrics such as absence, sickness, retention, engagement. This latter measure may or may not provide an evaluation of a specific L&D intervention, but it can also be useful as a general measure of the value and perceived value of L&D overall, particularly if L&D was being used, for example, to increase retention.

WINDOW ON PRACTICE

The focus of L&D at Jamie Oliver's flagship Italian restaurant

Stacy O'Hagan, head of people development of the Jamie Oliver group, explains how she aims to innovate and in addition to offering the opportunity to study for a CMI qualification to the 400 most senior staff she is aware that not everyone wants such a formal offering. There are experiential opportunities such as 'destressing your mind', 'foodspiration' days on preparation other than Italian food, live Skype presentations from Oliver and hotlines where experts make themselves available for three or four hours for phoned-in questions. O'Hagan is keen to offer development that doesn't involve moving to a new role or site as the chain is now stabilising rather than growing. They aim to offer everyone some L&D and use this to win loyalty as they fight to keep hard-to-recruit staff.

In this case evaluating retention, and probably engagement, would be key.

Source: Jeffery, R. (2015) 'Every week there's someone new after our staff', *People Management*, February, pp. 16–18.

Such metrics draw our attention to the importance of a baseline when evaluating L&D – whether it be current retention figures or current assessments of an individual's performance/ behaviour via, say, 360-degree appraisal. In the former, change in retention rates can be easily measured, and in the latter a further 360-degree appraisal can also be compared with an earlier one made prior to the L&D intervention. Elsewhere performance objectives set for a learning experience can be more woolly and measures taken of the extent to which these have been achieved – client, customer and peer feedback – can be very useful here. Measuring performance effectiveness after a learning intervention involves identifying changes in behaviour, knowledge, skills and attitudes, and it is important that the criteria for evaluation are built into development activities from the very beginning, not tagged on at the end.

ROI (return on investment) of any learning activity can be helpful in demonstrating its value. It requires that the full cost of the activity, for example design costs, time away-from-the-job costs, location costs and so on are calculated, and a helpful guide to this is CIPD Factsheet on costing development (2015b). These costs need to be set against the benefits of the activity. These benefits need to line up with organisational objectives and the reason for the development activity, and are demonstrated using the types of evaluation we have discussed in this section.

SUMMARY PROPOSITIONS

18.1. The emphasis has moved from training to learning, with individuals taking owner-ship of identifying and addressing their own learning needs, or at least contributing to this. To be effective learners we need to understand the nature of learning and our own strengths and weaknesses.

18.2. The emphasis on formal development programmes is declining in favour of greater interest in approaches to on-the-job development, such as coaching, mentoring, peer relationships, self-development and technology based learning. However, in-house courses remain popular and effective.

18.3. The interest in learning via technology continues; however, the extent to which employees take advantage of such opportunities will be affected by the context and the support available. The use of technology is increasingly being integrated with other forms of learning.

18.4. Evaluation of development is critical but difficult. It is most effective when built into the design of the development activity rather than tagged on at the end.

GENERAL DISCUSSION TOPICS

1. If learning is an individual process, why is so much training done in groups? What are the implications of moving towards more individualised learning?

2. Discuss the view that the role of the trainer/facilitator is critically important in the effectiveness of a training programme.

THEORY INTO PRACTICE

Micropower

Micropower is a rapidly growing computer software firm, specialising in tailor-made solutions for business. Increasingly, training for other businesses in its own and other software packages has occupied the time of the consultants. Micropower sees this as a profitable route for the future and such training is now actively sold to clients. Consultants both sell and carry out the training. As an interim measure, to cope with increasing demand, the firm is now recruiting some specialist trainers, but the selling of the training is considered to be an integral part of the consultant's role.

Micropower has just issued a mission statement which accentuates 'the supply of and support for sophisticated computer solutions', based on a real understanding of business needs. The firm considers that it needs to be flexible in achieving this and has decided that multiskilling is the way forward.

All consultants need to sell solutions and training at all levels, and be excellent analysts, designers and trainers. Some 200 consultants are now employed. Most have a degree in IT and most joined the firm initially because of their wish to specialise in the technical aspects of software development, and spent some years almost entirely in an office-based position before moving into a customer contact role. A smaller proportion were keen to concentrate on systems analysis, and were involved in customer contact from the start.

In addition there are 300 software designers and programmers who are primarily office based and rarely have any customer contact. It is from this group that new consultants are appointed. Programmers are promoted to two levels of designer and those in the top level of designer may then, if their performance level is high enough, be promoted to consultant. There is some discontent among designers that promotion means having to move into a customer contact role, and there are a growing number who seek more challenges, higher pay and status, but who wish to avoid customer contact. Another repercussion of the promotion framework is that around a quarter of the current consultants are not happy in their role. They are consultants because they valued promotion more than doing work that they enjoyed. Some have found the intense customer contact very stressful, feel they lack the appropriate skills, are not particularly comfortable with their training role and are unhappy about the increasing need to 'sell'.

Questions

1 What immediate steps could Micropower take to help the consultants, particularly those who feel very unhappy, perform well and feel more comfortable in their new roles?

2 In the longer term how can Micropower reconcile its declared aim of multiskilling with a career structure which meets both organisational and employee needs?

3 What other aspects of HR strategy would support and integrate with the development strategy of multiskilling?

4 Micropower wishes to develop a competency profile for the consultant role. How would you recommend that the firm progress this, and how might the profile be used in the widest possible manner in the organisation?

FURTHER READING

Harvey, M. (2012) *Interactional Coaching*. Abingdon: Routledge

A practical, accessible and business-focused book which includes the debate between directive and non-directive coaching, and also acknowledges the client's choice of whether to implement its learning in the workplace. Harvey focuses on three types of interactions in order to understand a situation: our relationship with time and how the past and future impact on the present; our interaction with our self, for example in terms of our values, beliefs and strengths; and our interactions with others.

Cosgrove, E. (2015) 'Action learning unplugged', *Training Journal*, February, pp. 38–41.

Cosgove explains an action learning programme developed for operational managers at Mencap (a charity supporting people with a learning disability) that was focused on increasing engagement. Some good practical examples of what was done are included.

Robertson, D. and Aylott, B. (2015) *Training Journal*, November, pp. 30–3.

This case is from *Guide Dogs for the Blind* and as well as practical descriptions of what was carried out, the authors look at the barriers and benefits that were experienced.

London, M. and Hall, M. (2011) 'Perspectives: Web 2.0 support for individual, group and organisational learning', *Human Resource Development International*, Vol. 14, No. 1, pp. 103–13; 'Unlocking the value of Web 2.0 technologies for training and development: The shift from instructor-controlled adaptive learning to learner-driven, generative learning', *Human Resource Management*, Vol. 50, No. 6, pp. 757–75.

Using each stage of Kolb's learning cycle, these articles demonstrate the ways in which Web 2.0 interactive learning can support generative learning, comparing this with more traditional training methods. The articles provide lots of practical learning methods that can be used for each approach.

Crush, P. (2015) 'Video has the power to transform your L&D efforts – but first you need to decide how and why you're using it', *People Management*, September, pp. 46–50.

A great example of how Travis Perkins made videos, using staff to front them, for L&D to create learning that involves emotion. Also some tips on making videos.

REFERENCES

Anderson, V. (2009) 'Research: Line manager as coach', *People Management*, 21 May, p. 42.

Blain, J. (2013) *Major Learning Trends and Indicators for 2013 and Beyond within the Asia Pacific Region*. Singapore: Cegos.

Cheshire Fire and Rescue Service (2012) *Cheshire East Annual Report 2011–12*. Cheshire East.

CIPD (2012a) *Sustainable Organisation Performance: Research Report: Coaching – the Evidence Base*. London: CIPD.

CIPD (2012b) *Research Insight: From E-learning to 'Gameful' Employment*. London: CIPD.

CIPD (2015a) *Coaching and Mentoring*, Factsheet. London: CIPD.

CIPD (2015b) *Costing and Benchmarking Learning and Development*, Factsheet. London: CIPD.

CIPD (2015c) *Learning and Talent Development: Annual Survey 2015*. London: CIPD.

Churchard, C. (2015) 'Become an L&D master', *People Management*, March, pp. 32–9.

Crush, P. (2013) 'The technologies that will transform learning', *People Management*, April, pp. 38–9.

Crush, P. (2014) 'Could a MOOC help you learn smarter?', *People Management*, July, pp. 28–9.

De Coutre, B. (2015) 'To MOOC or not to MOOC?', *Training Journal*, January, pp. 18–22.

Faragher, J. (2014) 'Face to face "most effective"', *People Management*, May, pp. 8–9.

Fowler, J. and O'Gorman, J. (2005) 'Mentoring functions: A contemporary view of the perceptions of mentees and mentors', *British Journal of Management*, Vol. 16, pp. 51–7.

Hamblin, A.C. (1974) *Evaluation and Control of Training*. Maidenhead: McGraw-Hill.

IDS (2009) *Coaching and Mentoring*, HR Study No. 897, July. London: IDS.

Jeffery, R. (2015) 'Every week there's someone new after our staff', *People Management*, February, pp. 16–18.

Kirkpatrick, D. (1959) 'Techniques for evaluating training programs', *Journal of the American Society of Training Directors*, Vol. 13, pp. 3–26.

Little, B. (2015) 'What's new in on-line learning?', *Training Journal,* August, pp. 16–20.

Marshall, D. (2015) 'Smart coaching', *Training Journal,* April, pp. 29–31.

Megginson, D. and Whitaker, V. (2007) *Cultivating Self-development.* London: IPD.

Newbery, C. (2015a) 'No matter where you're learning, we're there', *People Management,* June, pp. 20–21.

Newbery, C. (2015b) 'The international verdict on your L&D programme . . . ?', *People Management,* April, pp. 44–9.

Newberry, C. (2016) 'Coaching was a culture shock', *People Management,* February, p. 27.

Oglensky, B. (2008) 'The ambivalent dynamics of loyalty in mentorship', *Development and Learning in Organisations,* Vol. 61, No. 3, pp. 419–49.

People Management (2012) 'First person: Career clinic: Should I pursue an MBA?', August, p. 66.

People Management (2014) 'What you learned at the L&D show', *People Management,* June, p. 11.

Paine, N. (2015) 'Game changers for learning', *Training Journal,* July, pp. 14–17.

Phillips, L. (2006) 'BUPA stars', *People Management,* Vol. 12, No. 22, pp. 30–2.

Smedley, T. (2012) 'Fast masters', *People Management,* February, pp. 49–52.

Stevens, M. (2010) 'Fake station offers real training', *People Management,* 28 January, p. 12.

Training Journal (2015) 'Mobile learning in action', December, pp. 32–5.

CHAPTER 19

TALENT AND CAREER DEVELOPMENT

THE OBJECTIVES OF THIS CHAPTER ARE TO:

1 Clarify various definitions of talent

2 Explore ways in which talent can be identified

3 Review a strategic approach to talent and career development, and succession planning

4 Examine different talent and career development activities including managing talent in a developmental way, international development and the perspective of those labelled as 'talented'

5 Explain how organisations evaluate the practice of talent management

Alistair Cox from Hays plc says:

> Everything comes back to talent management. Financial performance is driven by talent, as it drives momentum within the business (PA Consulting 2015:1)

and since the 2008–9 economic downturn organisations in the UK have fought to protect and keep their talented employees, and the practice of talent 'hoarding' has become familiar in preparation for the upturn. This reflects the difficulty and cost of finding talent. Indeed some organisations saw the downturn as an opportunity to pick up talent from competitors. This is very different from the previous downturn when many organisations let go of their talented employees and consequently did not have the talent resources to take advantage of the upturn when it came.

As the west is experiencing the retirement of the post-war baby-boomer generation and developing countries continue to grow, albeit at a slower rate, there is a shortage of talent, with this being particularly severe in Asia. As talent is so important in driving organisational competitiveness, transformation and long-term success it is key that organisations develop a pool of talent and also secure a long-term leadership pipeline.

Whilst during the downturn organisations focused on retaining and developing talent, now growth is gradually picking up and organisations are increasingly looking for talent externally. In a 2015 survey (CIPD 2015a) three-quarters of organisations were recruiting key talent, with the percentage of organisations focusing on talent retention and development remaining stable.

What is talent?

Definitions of talent are varied, and different organisations will use a definition appropriate to their needs. Michaels *et al.* (2001) were employees of McKinsey, and coined the term 'war for talent'. They initially limited talent to a small number of individuals with high potential to reach the top jobs in the organisation. This is an elitist definition which focuses on a few employees.

However, this approach may miss those who are most critical to business success and it is important to link talent to the organisation's strategy, so identifying the talent in the organisation that, when improved, would be pivotal to the organisation's achievements. This gives room for a slightly different way of identifying which talent to focus on and Scott Snell (Pickard 2007) uses Ryanair as an example, arguing that its value is created by turnaround speed and therefore the most valuable, but not the highest paid or trained, jobs are ground staff. These jobs are critical to the competitive advantage of the organisation. However, in a recent survey PA Consulting found that while 63% of CEOs aspire to a talent management approach that is fully aligned with business strategy and drives high performance in the organisation, only 15% believe they are anywhere close to this (PA Consulting 2015).

Both the above perspectives are selective and hence cut across equal opportunities. Focusing on talent development for the few can lead to greater individual competition rather than teamwork, and can be alienating for the remainder of employees. It can also mean that latent talent is never identified as these individuals are not offered the development they need, which would enable them to demonstrate and exploit their talent for the benefit of themselves and their organisation.

An alternative view is that *all* employees possess latent talent. This inclusive approach is about enabling everyone in the organisation to be their best by unlocking the talent that they have.

WINDOW ON PRACTICE

Aviva

Aviva has a clear statement which reads 'If you work for Aviva you're talented', which John Ainsley, Group HR Director of Aviva, contrasts with star development programmes. He says that 'Everyone in Aviva has the same conversation about their development, so all our colleagues, wherever they are in the world, are covered by the same process.' He claims that this has increased employee engagement scores and that employees say they feel recognised. He says that Aviva provides strong encouragement for people to have honest and authentic conversations about their development.

Source: Smedley, T. (2012a) 'On my agenda', *People Management*, March, pp. 51–3.

In the PA Consulting survey only 34% of organisations said that most or all employees are defined as talent, although 66% expect that in the future this will be the case. This more restricted view is echoed by the CIPD's (2015b: 1) definition of talent:

Talent consists of those individuals who can make a difference to organisational performance either through their immediate contribution or, in the longer-term, by demonstrating the highest levels of potential.

WINDOW ON PRACTICE

Talent development philosophy

Kirst Scott, head of talent and development at Jaguar Land Rover, says that one of their fundamental principles is that everyone has potential to develop and that their aim is to create tailored development plans for all 30,000 employees globally. However, she acknowledges that this is a five-year plan, and that high-potential managers are being targeted first with a two-year intensive development programme designed to fit with their strengths and ambitions.

Source: Newbery, C. (2015) 'Talent development isn't a process it's a philosophy', *People Management*, March, pp. 18–20.

A more flexible approach to defining talent, sometimes called blended, has been for organisations to identify different talent groups and provide different types of development and career planning for each. Hills (2012) provides an interesting model of four talent groups representing different ways in which organisations define talent, but which also demonstrates how they could potentially group different parts of the workforce. The four groups are listed below and indicate the focus of talent development:

- leadership and senior roles;
- high potentials;

- talent pools;
- all employees.

You will have identified how each group becomes broader. The PA report (2015) proposed a fluid approach where different groups (defined according to the business context) come into and out of focus at different times as circumstances continually change.

In this chapter we generally focus on senior managers and leaders, high-potential employees and graduates, because we looked at the development of broader talent in Chapter 18.

ACTIVITY 19.1

1 How does your organisation define talent? (If you are a full-time student read one or two relevant cases in *People Management* and interpret these as 'your organisation'.)

2 Is this definition explicit or implicit?

3 What are the advantages and disadvantages of the approach taken?

4 Provide evidence to support your conclusions.

Identification of talent

The recruitment and selection process is one way to identify and then buy in talent, but too much emphasis on this can make other employees feel undervalued and can be unhelpful in the development of organisational culture. Lack of career development opportunities may encourage employees with potential to move elsewhere and may be a disincentive to be proactive and give of their best (see e.g. Crawshaw *et al*. 2012). A balance between external and internal talent is usually most appropriate and can be matched to the needs of the organisation.

WINDOW ON PRACTICE

Virtusa's approach to talent management

Recognising that millennials seek out the prospect of continuous development and 'high-flying' careers, Sundararajan Narayanan, global head of HR, explains how the business has introduced a set of highly visible values and a talent management programme to make it clear to employees that the business expects 70% of its talent to be developed internally. He says they are constantly on the lookout for people who can be fast-tracked. They also seek employee views on what they are looking for from the company.

Source: Crush, P. (2015) 'If you're good enough we'll find you', *People Management*, May, p. 25.

For current employees, appraisal and potential ratings from the manager, 360-degree feedback and the evaluation of previous development experiences will be of value in the identification of talent. Assessment and development centres are commonly used to identify talent by means of psychometric tests, interviews, role play, business games and direct experiences of work tasks at higher or different grades. We have discussed these centres in some detail earlier (see Chapter 8), and when used internally they usually assess candidates against a set of competencies required or desired at higher job grades.

However, putting too much emphasis on assessing sets of competencies can be problematic. For example, Rob Goffe and Gareth Jones (Chubb and Phillips 2008) warn against assessing people against a rigid set of competencies as this provides a limited view of employees and minimises diversity within the organisation; and Cunningham (2007a) suggests that organisations go astray when they expect a total talent package from one individual, insisting that a person displays talent across a wide range of competencies in order to justify being labelled as talented. He goes on to suggest that people may have an enormous talent in one area but be weak in others, so jobs need to be designed around their talents to maximise them.

Also some may not display talent in their current junior role but they might in a higher-level role, or a different role. Alternatively someone displaying talent in a current role, such as a professional or technical role, may not have the talent for a managerial role. In addition talent needs to be identified for future needs and possibilities rather than just current needs. So a clear distinction needs to be made between current performance and potential future performance in a different role.

Psychologist Adrian Furnham (Jeffery 2015) stresses the importance of looking beyond those who fit the organisational mould and looking out for the mavericks who don't easily fit any box but are hardworking and productive almost to an obsession, combined with having imaginative creativity and vision. PA Consulting found that many CEOs identified compatibility (natural fit between the organisation's culture and individual values); comfort with ambiguity (able to operate effectively and adapt in ambiguous environments); and courage (be willing to take key strategic decisions even when time is limited) as important characteristics in the identification of talent.

Cunningham (2007b) identifies two strategic approaches to talent management, first aligning roles with people (in other words, fitting talented people to current job roles) and, second, aligning people with roles (in other words, designing jobs to fit the talented people in the organisation). He suggests that both these strategies are critical and there needs to be a dynamic interaction between these two approaches.

ACTIVITY 19.2

1 In your own organisation what is the balance between growing and buying in talent? (If you are a student choose a case organisation from *People Management* magazine or elsewhere.)

2 How well does this balance work? Provide evidence for your conclusion.

3 What might be the disadvantages of an over-reliance on growing talent?

Before responding to this activity you might find it helpful to read the article by Hills (2009) in *Industrial and Commercial Training* as detailed in the References.

There is a debate as to whether individuals who are identified as talented should be informed of this. One school of thought is that it is best to be open as this will provide motivation for the individual and encourage retention. Bjorkman and colleagues (2013) in a statistical survey found a positive effect on those openly identified as 'talent' in terms of encouraging commitment to increased performance, the building of relevant competencies supporting the organisation's strategy and lower turnover intention. They additionally found that there were no negative effects on those not identified as long as processes were transparent and fair and they had the opportunity to be identified as talent at another point in time.

The alternative view is that those identified as talent may become arrogant and demanding (see, for example, Furnham (quoted in Jeffery 2015)). Additionally if people know their value and their expectations are not met this could lead to retention problems.

Strategic talent and career development

Since the acquisition, development and retention of talent is key to success, organisations are constantly advised to manage all aspects of talent in a strategic and integrated manner; however, they often fall short. Such a strategic approach, similar to the strategic criteria we discussed earlier (see Chapter 4), requires that:

- The approach needs to be embedded in the organisation and therefore requires senior management sponsorship rather than being led by the HR department.
- Talent development activities need to be integrated with each other and with other talent activities, and to be consistent.
- The approach needs to support the strategic objectives for the organisation. Garrow and Hirsh (2008) propose three questions that need to be answered in terms of focus on strategic objectives. The first is which job roles need to be managed in this way (e.g. senior leadership, IT specialists, airport ground staff, or all roles)? The second is where does the talent come from for these roles (e.g. from outside the organisation or is there potential to be developed within)? The third is what are the development outcomes required for individuals who have the potential to fill the specified job roles?
- The approach to talent needs to fit more generally with the organisation, its values and other activities. Garrow and Hirsh (2008) say there needs to be a fit with culture, the psychological contract in the organisation, other HR policies and practices, and the skills of the managers who will be implementing talent management. Powell and Lubitsh (2007) suggest talent activities need to be congruent with the aspirations of the organisation, its underlying systems and processes and core beliefs, and warn that a mismatch will cause confusion and cynicism.

Strategic talent development is most often expressed as a system incorporating a structured approach to job development and planned moves and there may be centralised monitoring of talent. Such a structured approach may work in some contexts and situations but in others a more flexible approach may be required. A structured approach focusing on integrating talent management and development activities is exemplified by the example in the Window on practice below.

WINDOW ON PRACTICE

Talent management at ChemCo

Although ChemCo is a public organisation it is run by a management company who aim to change the culture from civil service style to a more commercial one. The programmes are:

> 'aimed to expand leadership and scientific capability by identifying, developing, deploying and retaining high-potential employees and as such create and sustain a flow of high potentials throughout the organisation.' (p.117)

Each talent programme runs for two years and recruits, internally, 20–30 candidates and there are three talent pools:

1 Emerging talent (early career talent who have shown management or technical potential and have expressed a desire for fast-tracking to a more senior position).

2 Scientific (seen as technical leaders in their discipline or have shown ability to manage teams undertaking complex technical work. They have the potential to be acknowledged by their peers as global experts).

3 Leadership group (those who have the potential to undertake 'business critical' leadership roles in the future).

Selection for each pool was highly structured and a detailed framework outlines competencies required, target population, nomination processes, entry and exit criteria and so on. Entry criteria involved placement on a grid which characterised levels of performance and promotability.

    The first stage involved the individual in a Performance Management Agreement which was geared around a set of values and behavioural competencies. The line manager reviewed this using a set of guidelines for talent identification. If individuals get through this they are considered by an Employee Development Group for entry into one of the talent pools, using all available information. The emerging group and the scientific group also had an interview before membership of the talent pool was confirmed, and the leadership group went through an even more rigorous process via a development centre.

    Development plans were produced for each talent pool member and highly-structured development programmes were implemented, including master classes by members of the executive enabling networking with other members of the talent pool, conferences, career mentoring, 360-degree appraisal, exposure to organisation-wide projects and Myers Briggs assessment and leadership diagnostics.

Source: Adapted from Swailes, S. and Blackburn, H. (2016) 'Employee reactions to talent pool membership', *Employee Relations*, Vol. 38, No. 1, pp. 112–28.

The highly structured approach at ChemCo can be contrasted with companies whose rigorous recruitment results in all employees being seen as having high potential. Google, for example, has no talent programmes but does allow every employee formal thinking time and time for their own projects within a carefully crafted job description. An interesting, relatively informal, approach is adopted by Kingfisher in the Window on practice below, alongside other approaches.

WINDOW ON PRACTICE

International talent marketplace at Kingfisher

Kingfisher identified a pool of high-potentials and wanted to make intelligent connections to showcase this talent and match it with problem solving in the business. HR created a book with its cadre of 200 'wanted leaders' and hosted an event where all CEOs from different parts of the business visited each HR director to discuss the 'wanted leaders' in their part of the business. The CEOs also bring their problems to the event and hopefully find the expertise they are looking for to help solve them. Whilst this concept was first used for the top 200 it was soon being used for other levels of international moves – and this included commercial and retail staff, such as buyers and store managers. Each HR director sets up a stall displaying staff with high levels of skill and regional managers worldwide wander round to find a match for a problem they need to solve. This could result in a job, more or short-term consultation.

Source: Adapted from Churchard, C. (2014) 'Foreign object', *People Management*, February, pp. 42–43.

In implementing a strategic approach to talent management, line managers have a significant role to play. Wendy Hirsh (2015), principal associate at the Institute for Employment Studies (IES), identified four key roles for line managers in strategic talent management. The first is 'talent spotter' which involves managers really getting to know their people and what motivates them, observing what they're good at and enjoy, and noticing when they have started to outgrow their job. The second is opening up career conversations with their people, surfacing aspirations and identifying what could be done to match these with the needs of the organisation. Thirdly, line managers need to facilitate development, helping the individual access required work experiences and nominating them for formal opportunities. And finally, they need to act as a collaborator with other managers to help create a rounded view of each individual and collectively spot career opportunities. PA Consulting (2015) underline the importance of line managers having honest, meaningful and productive conversations with staff and wonder whether we are asking too much of line managers. In their survey, 75% of HR managers said that upskilling their line managers to give feedback to top talent was a management priority. Hirsh suggests that line managers often find this area confusing and frustrating.

Promotion and succession planning

Focused succession planning can only accommodate a limited number of roles and individuals as it can be a time-consuming process – so it is usually reserved for top jobs and for individuals of high potential. A major strength of growing talent is the building of talent pipelines, which is a key aspect of the CIPD's Shaping the Future research, so that a depth of talent is available if a key employee leaves unexpectedly. This is important as it avoids long gaps between an employee leaving and a new recruit beginning, thus protecting service and production levels. Such a pipeline may involve both company-suggested lateral and upwards moves and applications for promotions from those on the talent track. Building flexible pools of talent ready to fill a wide range of roles within the business is different from older approaches to succession planning where specific individuals were groomed and developed to fill a specific job, or at best a very narrow range of jobs, when they became available in the future. Secondments, lateral moves and international experience often figure in development for succession planning based on the range of company experience that top jobs require. Mobility through a range of roles provides the individual with a more rounded view of the organisation.

Those identified on the talent track may move quickly through a number of job roles. This may be very stimulating for the individual, but there is a danger of becoming derailed later in career, despite earlier successes. As individuals only stay a short time in any position they may not have the experience of setbacks and recovering from them, and they may not be there long enough to experience the impact of any changes they make. In addition high flyers may alienate others on their way up and may not stay in any one place long enough to form a development and support network. To compensate for this it is critical that high flyers receive high levels of developmental feedback as they progress.

ACTIVITY 19.3

We noted above the difficulty that high flyers may experience later in their career. What other developmental activities would you recommend for such employees? Explain why they would aid long-term career success.

Succession planning can assist retention if plans are shared with individuals, and especially if there is some form of consultation. This raises the issue of transparency, which would need to be carefully handled to avoid expectations which might not be fulfilled, as the pool of individuals covered by succession planning will inevitably be larger than the number of key roles to be filled. It is also difficult to plan with any certainty as frequent mergers and acquisitions change the nature of the organisation, different competencies become important, and the available talent pool changes.

WINDOW ON PRACTICE

A long-term approach to succession planning

As the economy improves, at the time of writing, there is evidence that some organisations are taking a longer-term and more strategic view of succession, and many employers are connecting with potential employees up to two years before the right position opens up for them to be recruited. A sensitive and responsive process is required, says John Gardener, chief executive of NBI Consulting, which involves identifying future talent and engaging with them informally to understand their career drivers, aspirations and suitability for the organisation. He suggests this type of pipeline shortens the time to hire when a suitable vacancy arises and provides more certainty in succession planning.

Source: Kirton, H. (2015) 'You're hired. Can you start in five years?', *People Management*, April, pp. 8–9.

Developing talent and careers

We have already discussed a broad range of developmental activities in the previous chapter, some of which are considered to be particularly valuable for career and talent development, although different surveys produce slightly different views. The CIPD survey (2015b) found that the most used developmental activities for high potential people were in-house schemes (42%), coaching (40%), mentoring (33%) and 360-degree appraisal (29%). These were also identified as the four most effective approaches, in the same order. Other common career development activities are project teamwork, special tasks/projects, cross-organisation and interdisciplinary tasks. The theme here appears to be gaining the broadest possible organisational understanding and networking.

In addition to the usual development activities we would add another three methods which are particularly relevant to developing talent and careers: managing people in a developmental way; international experience; and working with employee perspectives of their careers.

Managing talent in a developmental way

Employers not only need to understand what people's capabilities are, but also need to give them scope to use and develop them. Charles Handy suggested that organisations should take more risks and allow talented people more power to make decisions. The way that talented people are managed will not only affect their performance and development, but also determine whether they wish to stay with the organisation.

Talented people generally want to display their talents and give of their best but can be alienated by a lack of empowerment within their job and by formal organisational procedures and processes. Managers need to engage talented employees by providing appropriate scope and decision-making capacity and manage them lightly on a day-to-day basis – you may wish to refer to our discussion on organisation design and flexibility at this point (see Chapter 7). Managers also need to be prepared to manage talented employees' careers in a joint and flexible manner. As high flyers move through an organisation quickly there is evidence that they experience difficulties and therefore support needs to be available to them.

High performers may deliver results but can be very challenging and demanding to manage and sometimes, especially in the field of science/technology/creative jobs, whilst brilliant in their area of expertise may not have comparable communication skills. Powell and Lubitsh, for example (2007), propose that talented people know their worth to the organisation and have their own views on the direction of their career. They will often fail to respond to traditional management approaches and may respond unpredictably, not valuing hierarchy and avoiding being controlled.

Goffee and Jones (2009) also recognise that while talented people may add most value to the organisation, they are often the hardest to manage. Some of the authors' recommendations for those who manage bright people are that they should: recognise their knowledge, accepting their independence and difference; try and align the goals of the individual with those of the organisation; win resources for them but allow them space to get on with things alone; encourage them to achieve external recognition; protect them from administrative matters which they may see as a distraction; and provide as few rules as possible.

Michael Brook (Smedley 2014), UK lead, learning and development at BNP Paribas, suggests top traders are a demanding audience; development activities need to be carefully chosen and they are likely to avoid something which appears too straightforward. He brings in external speakers from the military, medicine or the performing arts to provide more intellectual challenge. Additionally, allowing thinking space can be very important, something provided at Google. Allowing people to fail and learn from their mistakes is valuable and requires that the reward system takes this into account.

International development

International experience has become a critical part of leadership preparation. This can be provided in a number of developmental ways such as frequent international travel, virtual international teams, short-term assignments/visits (say a few weeks) and international commuting. However, in spite of the costs, longer-term international assignments of two or more years remain well used.

WINDOW ON PRACTICE

International experience at Adidas

David Enser, head of mobility at Adidas Group, explains the different ways in which they use international experience. First they avoid use of the term 'expatriate' as they want to get away from the idea that international experience is just for the over-privileged westerner who receives generous relocation allowances and benefits, school fees and so on. He says younger people are moving abroad without these expectations, and going on to local contracts (similar rewards and benefits as local employees). He is using more and more short-term overseas assignments and international commuters. This provides greater flexibility and international experience brings career benefits to a more diverse group of people.

Source: Chynoweth, C. (2015) 'Global mobility is "the biggest HR role of 2015"', *People Management*, August, pp. 8–9.

From the organisation's point of view, international assignments provide not only vital management development, but also the opportunity for skills and knowledge transfer and a means of control of subsidiaries.

Careful preparation is critical and will often involve some language and cultural training as well as role-relevant preparation. A clear remit, support (such as a local manager, but also a mentor from the home country), development goals and performance expectations need to be agreed and set down before the assignment begins. Repatriation also needs to be carefully handled as repatriates will be partial outsiders on their return and need to be reintegrated as quickly as possible. It is also critical to match them on their return with a job which uses their newly acquired experience and skills. Some useful practical information on international assignments can be found in the CIPD factsheet (2013).

WINDOW ON PRACTICE

Compelled to go abroad?

Pinto and her colleagues carried out an interview survey of Portuguese expatriates and repatriates and overall these employees found international experience to be valuable. However, around half of those interviewed felt themselves compelled to accept an international assignment, this being the third most popular motive for agreeing the assignment, after the opportunity for challenge and improvement of career prospects. They felt subtle pressure from the company indicating that their career prospects would be damaged if they did not accept, and that other opportunities would not be made available to them. Turning down an assignment indicated some sort of failure. The effects of feeling compelled had an impact on the assignment. These individuals experienced a longer and more difficult adjustment to their new location and were generally less satisfied with the assignment. The authors conclude by questioning the appropriateness of organisational pressure as they suggest it may also affect the long-term commitment of these employees to the company.

Source: Pinto, L., Cabral-Cardoso, C. and Werther, W. (2012) 'Compelled to go abroad? Motives and outcomes of international assignments', *International Journal of Human Resource Management*, Vol. 23, No. 11, pp. 2295–314.

Valuing employees' perspective and meeting their needs

The Window on practice above indicates the potential different perspectives on career progression between employers and employees, and this is an area where more research is really needed. We have already mentioned the importance of having a thorough and rounded knowledge of all talented people and, in addition, Jones (2015) suggests that 'stay' interviews with high performers helps not only to uncover their motivation, but also provides ongoing opportunities to identify and address the risk of losing them.

Earlier on in this chapter we discussed the attitude and performance enhancements that can come from being identified as someone with talent. One downside of this is the impact that this can have on the rest of the workforce who have not been selected. Swailes and Blackburn (2016) compared the talent pool group with a control group in ChemCo. While the talent group felt they had positive views of line manager and career mentoring support, the control group overwhelmingly felt they did not have line manager support and that access to development was unfair. They felt abandoned, with no career development discussions, opportunities to grow or help in identifying their development needs. The organisation was unaware of these negative effects and did not realise that they were missing opportunities to develop the careers of many other employees who had potential.

This piece of research demonstrates that it would be a mistake for organisations to ignore career support for all employees, who too have potential and career aspirations. Toolkits for all employees can provide career support, helping them to work through the questions: where am I now; where do I want to be; and how do I get there? Aviva, one of our early examples in this chapter show how such an approach can improve engagement.

Job role design and flexibility can also be important in retaining talent. We noted before that for the high-potential few, designing jobs which make the most of their strengths and contribution is worth consideration. In addition, flexible working may retain older people who are talented but who may not wish to continue to work full time as the only alternative to retiring. Offering part-time and flexible hours is a way to hold on to the knowledge of talented people. At the other end of the spectrum many younger employees, 'generation Y', often expect a better balance between work and home life.

Flexible working may also help attract talent back after career breaks. It is important to engage people in discussions about their careers as their views may be surprisingly different from what senior managers may suppose. For example, work–life balance, the meaningfulness of a job, the interest in a job, travel opportunities and speed of promotion will all be valued differently by different individuals.

How organisations evaluate talent management

Measuring the outcomes of HR practices has a long history and has always been beset by difficulties, and talent management is no different. Internal HR measures are often used as these are easier to collect (such as internal promotions and retention rates) and these can be of great value if there is an identified problem around these issues. It is much easier to measure processes and activities rather than outcomes. For example, an organisation may measure the numbers of people who have a development plan, but this does not tell us whether the development plan is actually used, whether intended development has been achieved or whether this has impacted on the individual's performance. At the other end of the scale there are external measures such as profit, share price and sales. As with any case of measurement, there is the hurdle of proving that the results obtained, such as increased retention or a higher share price, are indeed caused by the talent management activity that has been undertaken.

Talent management can be evaluated as a whole or different activities of talent management may be evaluated separately, for example the use of expatriate assignments. The most critical thing is to lay down the strategic objectives of the activity or activities, and only then can some evaluation be made of the extent to which these have been achieved. On a simple level the objective of using expatriates might be to retain talent, or develop international networks, or boost the performance of a subsidiary, or prepare rounded talent for top jobs on repatriation. The list is endless, but it is all about the strategic needs of the organisation. However, it is also important to stay open-minded as outcomes from an activity may arise which the organisation did not set out to achieve but which can be very beneficial.

It is surprising how many organisations use very informal and imprecise methods of evaluation. For example, McNulty De Cieri (2016) carried out some research in multinational companies to find out the ROI (return on investment) of using expatriates. The mobility managers had no formal processes of evaluation but gauged success from one-off bits of data, intuition, observations and conversations, and these were seldom aligned to global strategy.

In the CIPD's international study (2011) the most popular methods of evaluation were feedback from employees covered by talent management initiatives and their managers and retention. Less than one-quarter in each country had clear success criteria at the outset, and only around 20% in each country considered the implementation of formal succession plans in evaluation. Around 10% admitted to no evaluation. All of these studies revealed little in terms of external measures such as business performance, revenue, margins and shareholder value. Yapp (2009), in her research with an unspecified number of global organisations, found that the measures used were internal HR measures such as retention, engagement, promotion, succession and diversity.

WINDOW ON PRACTICE

Maynardleigh Associates (2009) found that only one company of the twenty they researched calculated the return on investment (ROI) of talent management activities in a formal way. This company used a comparative approach and calculated the value of graduate trainees by identifying the profit on revenue-generating projects they were involved in multiplied by the number of graduates. The company did a similar calculation with a non-graduate control group. The graduate group contributed more revenue and the company found that for every £1 of money spent on talent management (with the graduates) it received multiple returns in respect of extra sales.

Yapp (2009) describes a similar approach which she calls a micro ROI approach in npower. This company invested heavily in identifying and developing leaders and future leaders who could successfully drive culture change in the organisation by inspiring, promoting pride in the company, providing opportunities for personal growth and helping employees understand their role in the company. The leadership project was evaluated in terms of sales revenue and employee perceptions. In the first division to experience this initiative sales were up by 54% and productivity almost 5% and customer service complaints down by 14%. Employees' pride in working for npower increased by 14 points, and their willingness to recommend npower as an employer increased by 11 points. Staff retention also increased by 33%. Comparison figures with other divisions are, however, not provided.

Sources: Maynardleigh Associates (2009) *Talent Management at the Crossroads: How 20 of the UK's Best Employers are Rising to Meet the Challenge of Turbulent Times.* London: Maynardleigh Associates; Yapp, M. (2009) 'Measuring the ROI of talent management', *Strategic HR Review*, Vol. 8, No. 4, pp. 5–10.

SUMMARY PROPOSITIONS

19.1. Talent is sometimes defined exclusively as possessed by the high-potential few and sometimes inclusively as something that everyone has. Some organisations now identify different types of talent groups with different defined offerings for each one.

19.2. Talent may be bought in or home-grown and the organisation needs to decide the most appropriate balance between the two. Methods of identifying potential include assessment/development centres, 360-degree feedback, line manager views and appraisal results.

19.3. Organisations are more likely to gain from a strategic and integrated approach to talent management and development which fits with organisational needs. A traditional approach will be structured and planful, and may include succession planning for key roles, whereas some organisations use a more flexible approach.

19.4. Key activities for talent and career development include: managing talent in a developmental way; providing international experience; and understanding employee perspectives on careers.

19.5. Few organisations formally evaluate talent management and development, and those who do use internal HR measures to a greater extent than external outcomes.

GENERAL DISCUSSION TOPICS

1. 'Talent development programmes targeted on the high-potential few are very divisive. Recognising the different talents of each employee and enabling everyone in the organisation to do their best is a much healthier approach and more likely to result in employee engagement and the long-term success of the organisation.' Discuss the value and limitations of this perspective.

2. How would you evaluate the success of international assignments? Give reasons for your approach.

THEORY INTO PRACTICE

Careers at Ernst & Young

Ernst & Young provide a thorough range of global career development activities for graduates, and there are three key aspects to provision: learning; job experiences; and coaching.

Learning focuses on building general business skills and acumen, constantly refreshing and enhancing technical skills across service lines to promote improved service and better client relationships. Building relationships and leading people are seen as key aspects of learning and career development.

In terms of job experiences, secondments are offered, as well as cross-border and cross-service line placements, on both a short- and long-term basis. Some are domestic and some international, but all will involve connecting with people from around the world and provide challenging and stimulating assignments. These are intended to help graduates develop an inclusive mindset and thrive in an increasingly global market while matching clients' needs. Graduates are also encouraged to use their professional skills to give back to the community, benefiting others but also enhancing their career and life – through development of leadership, communication or project management skills.

Graduates work closely with a coach who will put time and effort into becoming an expert in the individual and his or her career development. Coaches encourage learning and development, and help graduates to consider new ideas and challenges to ensure a stimulating and evolving career. High-quality feedback and support is offered to help graduates progress quickly. Mentoring provides support, insights and practical advice on a variety of professional development and career topics, and as graduates become more experienced they are encouraged to mentor less experienced colleagues.

Perhaps the most unusual aspect of a career at Ernst & Young is the view below, explained on the company website when addressing potential recruits:

> *The experience you gain with EY will last you a lifetime. In fact, whatever you go on to do in the future, you'll be able to take the knowledge and insights you've gained with you.*
>
> *EY and you (EYU) is our career development framework, which is designed to provide you with the skills, knowledge and confidence you need to take ownership of your career.*
>
> *Your development is at the heart of our culture, but it centres on giving you the tools to progress in the direction you desire. We believe you'll do the best work you can when you have the freedom to map your own career path. And ultimately that means our clients will benefit too.* (www.ey.com, accessed 11 April 2016)

This provides an unusually strong focus on graduates developing their own career path, and even more unusually the focus on career development for graduates which they can then take with them to a new employer. Mike Cullen, Ernst & Young's Global Managing Partner, People, explains this position thus:

> *For every thousand graduates you recruit, you've only got 250 manager slots . . . Most people who come through our doors (as recruits) now live somewhere out there in the economy. How they feel about E&Y is crucial to our proposition. We want them to feel a lifetime member of one of the best business networks in the world.* (Smedley 2012: 30)

Alumni are positively encouraged to remain in touch through magazines sharing news from past colleagues and personal and business directories to enable searching for past colleagues. Ernst & Young wants people to feel proud of working for it and offer development for people who carry on their careers within or outside the company. Thus it develops future leaders for business and commerce generally and not just Ernst & Young. Cullen explains how external analysts were taken aback by this idea as conventional thinking at the moment is focused on retaining talent. The aim is to create career value for people that will last a lifetime.

Sources: Smedley, T. (2012b) 'On my agenda', *People Management*, August, pp. 28–31; www.ey.com.

Questions

1 What are the dangers and downsides of the Ernst & Young approach to career development?

2 Exactly how can Ernst & Young reap the advantages of its approach to careers?

3 In which type of organisations might this approach to careers be advantageous? What criteria are you using, and why?

4 Assess the potential value of the career development activities that Ernst & Young provides. What other activities would you include, and why?

FURTHER READING

Brewster, C. Houldsworth, E., Sparrow, P. and Vernon, G. (2016) *International Human Resource Management*. London: CIPD, Chapter 14.

This is a very useful all-round text for international HRM, but in particular Chapter 14 on managing expatriation is very useful here and gives an excellent overview of selecting and preparing an individual for an international assignment as well as managing performance and repatriation. It also includes the career perspectives of the expatriates themselves.

Macrae, I. and Furnham, A. (2014) *High Potential*. London: Bloomsbury.

This is a useful book which identifies different types of talent, and highlights how appropriate development can support retention. There is an interesting section on the dark side of high-potentials and possible derailment.

King, K. (2016) 'The talent deal and journey', *Employee Relations,* Vol. 38, No. 1, pp. 94–111.

An academic but highly readable article which provides a model of the talent deal, focusing on employee perceptions of being identified as 'talent'; the perceived deal (psychological contract; interpretation of supervisor and organisation; and of the relationship between the individual and the organisation) and resultant outcome measures such as performance, promotion and retention. A second model summarises the employee's perceptions of their talent journey.

REFERENCES

Bjorkman, I., Ehrnrooth, M., Makela, K., Smale, A. and Sumelius, J. (2013) 'Talent or not? Employee reactions to talent identification', *Human Resource Management,* Vol. 52, No, 2. pp. 195–214.

Chubb, L. and Phillips, L. (2008) 'A global approach to talent: The best of the world congress', *People Management,* Vol. 14, No. 9, pp. 12–13.

Churchard, C. (2014) 'Foreign object', *People Management,* February, pp. 42–3.

Chynoweth, C. (2015) 'Global mobility is "the biggest HR role of 2015"', *People Management,* August, pp. 8–9.

CIPD (2011) *International Learning and Talent Development Comparison Survey, 2011.* London: CIPD.

CIPD (2013) *International Mobility,* Factsheet. London: CIPD.

CIPD (2015a) *Talent Management: An overview,* Factsheet London: CIPD.

CIPD (2015b) *Resourcing and Talent Planning Survey.* London: CIPD.

Cranet (2011) *Cranet Survey on Comparative Human Resource Management.* Cranfield: Cranfield University.

Crawshaw, J., Dick, R. and Brodbeck, F. (2012) 'Opportunity, fair process and relationship value: Career development as a driver of proactive work behaviour', *Human Resource Management Journal,* Vol. 22, No. 1, pp. 4–11.

Crush, P. (2015) 'If you're good enough we'll find you', *People Management,* May, p. 25.

Cunningham, I. (2007a) 'Disentangling false assumptions about talent management: The need to recognise difference', *Development and Learning in Organisations,* Vol. 21, No. 4, pp. 4–5.

Cunningham, I. (2007b) 'Viewpoint: Talent management – making it real', *Development and Learning in Organisations,* Vol. 21, No. 2, pp. 4–6.

Garrow, V. and Hirsh, W. (2008) 'Talent management: Issues of focus and fit', *Public Personnel Management,* Vol. 37, No. 4, pp. 389–402.

Goffee, R. and Jones, G. (2009) *Clever: Leading Your Smartest and Most Creative People.* Boston, MA: Harvard Business School Press.

Hills, A. (2009) 'Succession planning: Or smart talent management?, *Industrial and Commercial Training*, Vol. 41, No. 1, pp. 3–38.

Hills, J. (2012) 'How firms define and execute talent strategy', *People Management*, September, pp. 42–4.

Hirsh, W. (2015) 'The role of the line in talent management', paper from *HR in a Disordered World: IES Perspectives on HR 2015*, Brighton: IES.

Jeffery, R. (2015) 'Telling someone they're talented is disastrous', *People Management*, November, pp. 44–5.

Jones, D. (2015) 'Agile succession planning', *Training Journal*, December, pp. 15–18.

Kirton, H. (2015) 'You're hired. Can you start in five years?', *People Management*, April, pp. 8–9.

Maynardleigh Associates (2009) *Talent Management at the Crossroads: How 20 of the UK's Best Employers are Rising to Meet the Challenge of Turbulent Times.* London: Maynardleigh Associates.

McNulty, Y. and De Cieri, H. (2016) 'Linking global mobility and global talent management: The role of ROI', *Employee Relations*, Vol. 38, No. 1, pp. 8–30.

Michaels, E., Handfield-Jones, H. and Axelrod, B. (2001) *The War for Talent.* Boston, MA: Harvard Business School Press.

Newbery, C. (2015) 'Talent development isn't a process it's a philosophy', *People Management*, March, pp. 18–20.

PA Consulting (2015) *CEOs Views on their Talent Management Challenges and PA's Response. Key Findings.* London: PA Consulting.

Pickard, J. (2007) 'Go with the flow', *People Management*, Vol. 13, No. 8, pp. 46–7.

Pinto, L., Cabral-Cardoso, C. and Werther, W. (2012) 'Compelled to go abroad? Motives and outcomes of international assignments', *International Journal of Human Resource Management*, Vol. 23, No. 11, pp. 2295–314.

Powell, M. and Lubitsh, G. (2007) 'Courage in the face of extraordinary talent: Why talent management has become a leadership issue', *Strategic HR Review*, Vol. 6, No. 5, pp. 24–7.

Smedley, T. (2012a) 'On my agenda', *People Management*, March, pp. 51–3.

Smedley, T. (2012b) 'On my agenda', *People Management*, August, pp. 28–31.

Smedley, T. (2014) 'How should you handle the office genius?', *People Management*, December, pp. 30–1.

Swailes, S. and Blackburn, H. (2016) 'Employee reactions to talent pool membership', *Employee Relations*, Vol. 38, No. 1, pp. 112–28.

Yapp, M. (2009) 'Measuring the ROI of talent management', *Strategic HR Review*, Vol. 8, No. 4, pp. 5–10.

CHAPTER 20

EMPLOYABILITY: SKILLS IN DEVELOPMENT

THE OBJECTIVES OF THIS CHAPTER ARE TO:

1 Explore skills in teaching and learning

2 Explain coaching skills

20.a. Teaching and Learning

This is a follow-up to the section on learning theories (Chapter 17). Different types of learning require fundamentally different approaches by the teacher. One simplified classification of learning is memorising, understanding or doing (MUD). Better is comprehension, reflex learning, attitude development, memory development and procedural learning (CRAMP).

Comprehension involves the learner developing understanding, knowing the why, how and when things happen – not simply what has been memorised. Knowing that WWII began in 1939 and ended in 1945 is a fact that can be memorised, but gives you no knowledge or understanding of what happened between those dates. HR people need to understand how the laws of employment work as well as memorising the rules.

Reflex learning is quite different; it is when skilled movements or perceptual capacities have to be acquired, involving practice as well as knowing what to do. Juggling and playing football are everyday examples, as are using a keyboard or driving a forklift truck.

Attitude development is enabling people to develop their capacity to alter their attitudes and improve their social skills. Much customer care training works on this basis. Dealing with customers requires people to be confident of their ability to deal with others, shedding some of their feelings of insecurity and discovering how they are able to elicit a positive response.

Memory training enables learners to handle a variety of given situations; pharmacists in training learn by rote a series of maximum dosages, police officers remember car registration numbers better than most people and we all need to remember PINs and passwords.

Procedural learning is a variant of memorising in that a drill to be followed does not have to memorised but located and understood, like a cake recipe. Workplace examples include dealing with a safety drill or health and safety routines.

Most training involves more than one type of learning; an apprentice vehicle mechanic will need to understand how the car works as well as practise the skill of tuning an engine. The driver has to learn the skills of coordinating hands, feet and eyes in driving as well as knowing what to do if the car breaks down.

ACTIVITY 20.1

Think of things you have learned in the past and identify whether the learning was comprehension, reflex, attitude development, memorisation or procedural. How would you classify learning for the following:

- swimming selection
- interviewing
- learning Russian
- calorie counting in a diet
- parenting
- running a business
- preparing for retirement
- safe lifting
- skiing

Broadly speaking, *Comprehension*-type learning works best with a method that teaches the whole subject as an entity rather than splitting it into pieces that are taught one at a time. The lecture, instructor's talk or the training manual are typically used. The method of presentation, described at the end of Part I, is appropriate for the lecture or instructor's talk. Attitude change is typically handled by group discussion, as this involves the learners seeing the response of other people to what they are saying and gradually making sense of the manner as well as the content of the individual responses. Reflex learning is often handled by part methods whereby the job to be done is broken down into components, with each being taught separately, before they are combined into the whole. An example is the tennis player who practises the serve, the smash, the forehand, backhand and other strokes before they are combined when playing a match. A variant is when the learner learns part 1 and then combines it with part 2, practises both together and then combines them with part three, practising all three together and progressively builds up the whole task.

WINDOW ON PRACTICE

David teaches a module on a preliminary course in teacher training which has a mixture of students. Most are recent graduates with little working experience but well-developed study skills. A minority are a little older, often mothers with growing children, who have experience, but whose study skills are rusty. He finds that the mature students tend to dominate group discussion early in the course, as they constantly relate everything to their personal experience and circumstances while the recent graduates are at a loss and feel put down. After a few weeks the recent graduates become more assertive in discussion as they gain confidence from their developing understanding, and the mature students become less dominant because they are beginning to question some of the taken-for-granted certainty of their earlier opinions. Mutual respect soon grows and both groups learn from each other.

The structure of a teaching session is for the instructor first to describe what will be taught, including what the learner will be able to do at the end of the individual session. Next the instructor will demonstrate what the learner is to do, with commentary and answering questions, clarification and perhaps repeated demonstration. Then the learner repeats what has been demonstrated under close supervision, encouragement and checking by the instructor, followed by practice, practice, practice until the learner achieves appropriate competence and is rewarded by the approval and congratulation of the instructor, who will no doubt ensure that the learner clears up and puts things away as appropriate.

For memorisation the most common method used is the mnemonic or jingle, whereby a simple formula provides a clue to more complicated data. 'Laser' is much easier to remember than 'light amplification by stimulated emission radiation'. If the initial letters are not easily remembered they can be replaced by a mnemonic. The colours of the spectrum may be remembered by ROYGBIV, but more easily by 'Richard of York gave battle in vain'. 'Arthur spits in Claude's milk' will be remembered by some as the five arthropods – arthropods, spiders, insects, crustaceans and myriapods.

ACTIVITY 20.2

What do the following sets of initials mean: DSS, RADAR, TINA LEA, HMRC, RAM, UNESCO?

Apart from the obvious (but not always accurate) why should anyone remember the phrase, 'Most engineers prefer blondes'?

Finally, *teaching* is always an interaction, with teacher and learner face to face and both active and both responsible for effective learning. There are other ways *of learning*, which is not interactive in the same way. All the initiative is with the learner, who responds to what is on the page of the textbook or the computer screen, the instruction manual or television programme, but at that stage the 'teacher' is inactive and absent so all the initiative, responsibility and motivation comes from the learner.

SUMMARY PROPOSITIONS

20.a.1. Learning can be classified as comprehension, reflex, attitude development, memorisation or procedural.

20.a.2. Appropriate methods for each type are: for comprehension, lecture or instructor's talk; for reflex, part learning, for attitude development, group discussion; and for memorisation, part learning or mnemonic/jingle.

20.a.3. Teaching is an interactive skill with both teacher and learner being responsible for its effectiveness.

GENERAL DISCUSSION TOPICS

What methods of learning would you choose for attitude development, and why would these be suitable?

PUTTING IT INTO PRACTICE

1 For the individual reader, think of some simple task at which you are adept and work out how you could teach it to someone you know; then teach them, using part methods, until both you and they are satisfied with their competence. Examples might be performing an unfamiliar task with a PC or the rudiments of sign language.

➤

2   *For a small group or 3–5 people.* Each member thinks of a similar simple task and takes it in turn to teach the others. Examples here might be how to solve cryptic crosswords or sudoku puzzles. Discuss afterwards what learning has taken place and how supportive group members were to each other.

3   *For a larger group of 10 plus.* Agree who should chair the discussion and then agree on a matter of general interest among members to be discussed. The person chairing then starts the discussion and keeps it going for 10–15 minutes (some advice on doing this is in Chapter 33). Afterwards, consider what any of you have learned about the way people react to you.

4   *For individuals.* Compile a list of 5 mnemonics and 5 jingles that will help you remember things that you need to know.

20.b. Coaching

Although this section is about coaching, we need to remember the frequent close connection with mentoring, which has been explained in Chapter 18. Coaching is not teaching people how to do things, but helping them to do even better things that they have already learned. It is a form of learning that is highly personal and flexible, largely driven by the protégé rather than led by the coach.

Coaching is as important for the expert as it is for beginners. The more expert a person becomes, the more important a coach is to hone performance, to take a broad view of the context in which the learner's career is developing and how it may proceed. Coaching is a skill but more than just an encounter to be managed; it is a skill in managing a relationship.

WINDOW ON PRACTICE

For many years until 2005 the British sporting public was hungry for success in tennis. Wimbledon annually stages the world's greatest tennis tournament and winning it is the greatest achievement in a player's career, yet it was over 70 years since a British man had won the title. A young Scot, Andy Murray, suddenly emerged as the great hope of British tennis; young, skilled and with a great competitive temperament, who had been coached by his mother, but needing a different coach to take him forward to international success, someone with international experience as well as personal authority, who could take the already-acquired skill of this fiery young man and develop it, and him, to greater international achievement. Brad Gilbert was an experienced international coach. He took on the coaching of Andy Murray, whose accomplishments soon began to increase. Gilbert was not personally as good a player as Murray, but had a breadth of international experience and expertise that provided the right complement to Murray's youth, talent and temperament *at that time*. The two would soon part as Andy Murray would seek other mentors, including the 50-year-old Ivan Lendl, who had won Wimbledon himself and guided his protégé to success and an Olympic gold medal at Wimbledon, building on what Gilbert and Mrs Murray had earlier achieved.

Coaching is a part of the job of every manager, but it is an approach being used increasingly in business circles to bring out the effectiveness of people at all levels. Coaching is helping individuals take charge of their own learning: the primary driver becomes the protégé; the coach or mentor provides guidance, insight and encouragement.

Coaching is a central feature of the managerial role; every manager is expected to act as a coach to those for whom the manager has direct line responsibility, developing the skills and capacities of the individual members of the team, enabling them to perform rather than directing their performance. This nice distinction takes account of changes in the types of jobs people have and the moves towards flexible rather than hierarchical organisation structures. It is rarely so clear-cut, as managers have to combine coaching with direction. Not all managers like the coaching role. Carroll and Gillen (2001) identified various barriers to line manager acceptance of a teaching or coaching role, including lack of interpersonal competence, lack of time, performance pressures, a feeling that the teaching role was not valued and that it should be done by the HR department.

Other members of the business may be involved in coaching on particular aspects of the learner's work. Janice Caplan identified the elements of coaching as being:

> to enable, encourage and facilitate so that staff have a stronger sense of control over their own work and their own time, and so that they identify their own options and solutions to problems . . . The manager also needs to act as a role model of the desired . . . behaviours. Nonetheless, there may be times when the manager will still need to be more directive. (Caplan 2003: 20)

Career anchors

Before considering the appropriate qualities of a coach, we note the important concept of the career anchor, identified by Edgar H. Schein, one of the founding fathers of organisational psychology during his 30 years as Sloan Fellows Professor of Management at Massachusetts Institute of Technology. The career anchor is something that is so important to a person's self-confidence that it will be abandoned only reluctantly, and then only if it can be replaced by something else equally rewarding. Schein described career anchors as much broader than motivation and includes the following:

- self-perceived talents and abilities;
- self-perceived motives and needs;
- self-perceived attitudes and values.

Our perception of ourselves in these areas comes from direct experiences of work, from successes, from self-diagnosis and from feedback. The conclusions that we draw both drive and constrain future career development. Career anchors can identify a source of personal stability in the person which has determined past choices and will probably determine future choices.

Schein acknowledges that career anchors are learned rather than reflecting latent abilities and are only reluctantly abandoned. Not only do we all need to identify and understand what our anchors are in order to make sure we are doing the right thing, we also need to appreciate that there are things that we shall continue to need even if we make a career change.

Among the anchors most widely found are technical/functional competence, managerial competence and security. Those who are confident of their technical competence in their job and enjoy those aspects of their duties will move to a job with a lower technical component very reluctantly. For those anchored to managerial competence the exercising of managerial responsibility is an end in itself, and technical/functional jobs just a way of getting there. They are likely to possess three key competences: analytical competence to solve problems characterised by incomplete information in areas of uncertainty; interpersonal competence to influence and control; and emotional resilience, with the ability to be stimulated rather than paralysed by crises. They will readily move away from technical specialisation if they can maintain or enhance their managerial role. Security and stability is an anchor for those who seek this above all else.

All coaches need to identify these anchors for individuals they are coaching. Coaches who spot the anchors correctly have a very good chance of establishing trust, especially if those being coached have never really worked out what their anchors are, nor heard of the concept. If a coach guesses the anchors wrongly, or has strong views on what they should be, then coaching becomes very difficult (Schein 2010).

Anchors can move, and certainly change over time. The person who is technically anchored at thirty may be managerially anchored at forty and security/stability anchored at fifty, but that is a stereotypical assumption only. Coaches have to work out the anchors for each person at the time the coaching conversation takes place, not yesterday or last year.

The qualities of the coach

Coaching is usually a one-to-one activity, for which the coach needs various qualities.

1 **Trust.** Often needing to deal with what are usually very private aspects of someone's life, it is first necessary that the learner has absolute trust in the coach's integrity and commitment to the coaching. The interpersonal chemistry has to be completely correct between the two of them, even though they will probably argue and may not speak to each other for days. If learners, for instance, are highly skilled performers with a shrewd knowledge of their job and a fair understanding of what they can and cannot do, a coach needing to challenge some part of that self-confidence will then be threatening something that seems to be removing one of the things that the learner has previously relied on, a career anchor. There will be a disagreement and it will not be easy for a learner to abandon something that has previously been an anchor, and it will probably not happen unless there is a grounded belief in the coach's trustworthiness.

2 **Respect.** Closely allied to trust and the next requirement of expertise is *mutual* respect. The learner needs to feel that the coach is worthy of respect because he or she is trustworthy, is expert in the job of the learner, is proficient at the job of coaching, has a great deal of broader experience, is good at explaining things and explaining the right things. These 'things' have to be strong enough to overwhelm other possible thoughts about the coach, such as 'has-been', 'past-it', 'couldn't hack it at the sharp end', 'the job is not like it was way back then'. Coaches are nearly always older than learners, so there may be a temptation for ambitious learners to have such thoughts. Equally the coach must have respect for the learner: no condescension or patronising behaviour, but a real respect for the learner's skill, accomplishments and ambitions.

3 **Job expertise.** The coach needs to *know how* to do the learner's job at least as well as the learner; this is not the same as *being able* to do the job as well as the learner. The person training the novice usually has to be expert at actually doing the job of the learner; the coach enhancing the skill of someone who is proficient does not need that

particular level of ability, as long as there is the understanding. It is often important that the coach is *not* as practically skilled; otherwise coaching may become 'watch me; do this' instead of 'listen to what I say and then work out how to do better'.

4 **Listening.** Coaches have to be sensitive and conscientious listeners. The coaching relationship has many similarities with performance appraisal, in that the coach can only work to improve what the learner is able to acknowledge and understand. There will be a lot of explanation and even simple instruction, but the starting point will usually be in the learner's head. The learner will ask questions, express frustrations or describe a problem that the coach may believe to be the wrong problem. All the time the coach listens with close attention and works on understanding the questions, what lies behind the frustrations and why the wrong problem has been identified. What makes the coach so sure it is the wrong problem anyway?

School teachers sometimes say that gifted teachers are able to develop children's understanding almost entirely by getting them to ask the right questions. Coaches who can do this with adults are on the way to being outstanding, although the method has to be rather more subtle and not manipulative. We have already identified some of the basic skills required in this type of listening, especially reflection and reflecting and summarising (see Chapter 6).

5 **Evaluating.** The coach listens to the learner, listens to what other people say and can probably study aspects of the learner's performance, so that there is a collection of information to process. The coach needs to be able to evaluate all of these data dispassionately but effectively, having the advantage of a degree of objectivity which the learner cannot hope to have, and assembling it in a way that will make a constructive contribution to the coaching process.

6 **Challenging.** However true it may be that talking a problem through should enable a learner to solve whatever the career block may be, it is also true that few of us can do this with everything. We tend to construe a situation in a way that puts us in the right. There will be times when the coach simply has to confront the learner with a different interpretation of what is going on and challenge the learner to accept the validity of the criticism. Some coaches who are not the direct line manager say that it is not their role to do that, and that challenging should be left to the manager, but that is just shirking the responsibility. A coach cannot just do the nice, agreeing things with lots of understanding smiles and sympathetic nods of support. The coach is in a privileged position, being trusted by the learner to provide help including guidance on what is wrong, however reluctant they may be to hear it.

7 **Practical help.** A part of the coaching relationship will be to provide straightforward practical suggestions: 'Have you thought of . . . ?', 'Have you spoken to . . . ?', 'Would it help if I went through it with you . . . ?', 'No, that simply won't work.'

Ideally all of these great qualities would be found in any competent manager, so that the learner automatically has the line manager as coach. However, not all managers have all these qualities particularly well developed, and there are advantages in the coach being outside the line. The act of talking with a 'supportive outsider' can be a help to managers in unravelling and evaluating the mixed messages they are hearing in the workplace, where custom and practice are lagging behind policy, which appears to be out of line with organisational culture. However, a line manager may well be suspicious of supportive outsiders who appear to be giving messages that contradict what the manager is saying. After all, coaching is not quite the same as counselling, where an outsider has a better justification for the position.

The solution to this dilemma seems to be to acknowledge that all managers need to adopt a coaching mode of working with individual members of their department, but that other supportive *insiders* could be called upon to act as individual mentors, where there is a good working relationship or prior familiarity between prospective coach and prospective learner. Clutterbuck and Gover (2004) suggest there are seven stages in the coaching process:

1 Identify the need.

2 Gather evidence.

3 Motivate and set targets.

4 Plan how to achieve.

5 Create opportunities to practise.

6 Observe and give feedback.

7 Support through the setbacks.

A further twist is that there are two different ways of focusing on coaching: pre-coaching and post-coaching. Pre-coaching is the main emphasis when you are preparing someone for the event they are about to handle, so lines of questioning may be, 'What difficulties do you anticipate?', 'How will you handle that?' 'What will you do if . . . ?'. All of these look forward. Post-coaching is equally valuable, but has a different nature after the event has happened. There is less intense focus, less adrenaline; it is much more reflective and analytical. It could include questions like, 'How did it go?' 'What happened that you didn't expect?', 'What can you learn from this experience?', and so on. The first focus is on motivation: the second is on learning and embedding the lessons learned.

SUMMARY PROPOSITIONS

20.b.1. Coaching is a way in which one person (the coach) enhances the working performance of another (the protégé) regardless of the level of job skill that the two have and regardless of the hierarchical relationship between them.

20.b.2. The career anchor is something that it is absolutely essential for the protégé to maintain if he or she is to retain self-confidence and the ability to develop. These anchors vary greatly between individuals and a coach has to understand what anchors each protégé.

20.b.3. Essential qualities in a coaching relationship are for there to be mutual trust and respect between the parties.

20.b.4. Required qualities of a coach are: expertise in the job of the protégé, skilled listening, skill in evaluating information, an ability to challenge and a willingness to provide practical help.

20.b.5. Coaching takes place that is pre, looking forward and motivating, or post, looking back to embed lessons learned.

GENERAL DISCUSSION TOPICS

20.b.1. How would you rank (from 1 to 3) the relative importance of the coach being (a) expert in the protégé's job, (b) older than the protégé and (c) the direct line manager?

20.b.2. What are the career anchors held by members of your group? What anchors have changed?

PUTTING IT INTO PRACTICE

Sometimes a friend or relative will introduce a topic of conversation that is an implicit seeking of help in dealing with a problem, although it may be phrased in a different way. Ask yourself the question, 'Does the person just want to express exasperation or annoyance in order "to get it out?"' If you think the person will find a solution having 'got it out', then you need do little apart from nodding and listening sympathetically. If, however, your assessment is of someone still unsure of what to do, and if you think you have the right sort of relationship with your friend, then try a coaching approach, as outlined above.

FURTHER READING

Teaching and learning

Belbin, R.M. (2010) *Management Teams: Why They Succeed or Fail* (3rd edn.). London: Butterworth Heinemann.

This classic has been in print since 1981. It contains material relevant to led group discussion in Chapters 5, 6 and 10.

Miller J. and Stacey, M. (2014) *Practical Teaching Skills for Driving Instructors* (9th edn.). London: Kogan Page.

Although you may not aspire to be a driving instructor, this is an excellent little book on teaching a skill which nearly all adults have learned.

Buzan, T. (2009) *The Memory Book*. London: Pearson

This book claims to teach you how to remember anything!

Coaching

Passmore, J. (2015) *Excellence in Coaching*. London: Kogan Page.

It is what it says it is, by a prolific author.

Schein, E.H. (2010) *Organizational Culture and Leadership* (4th edn.). New York: John Wiley.

The 1990 book by Ed Schein is now not easy to obtain, although it contains the most thorough explanation of the career anchor concept. The 2004 third edition of his classic text contains a perfectly adequate treatment of the topic.

Hawkins, P. and Schwenk, G. (2006) *Coaching Supervision: Maximising the Potential of Coaching, a Change Agenda*. London: CIPD.

Jarvis, J. and Lane, D. (2006) *The Case for Coaching: Making Evidence-based Decisions on Coaching*. London: CIPD.

Both these publications include solid research evidence to produce a thorough assessment of current practice, including examples of good practice and guidelines for managers.

REFERENCES

Caplan, J. (2003) *Coaching for the Future*. London: CIPD.

Carroll, S. and Gillen, D. (2001) 'Exploring the teaching function of the managerial role', *Journal of Management Development*, Vol. 21, No. 5, pp. 330–42.

Clutterbuck, D. and Gover, S. (2004) *The Effective Coach Manual*. Burnham: Clutterbuck Associates.

PART 5
EMPLOYEE RELATIONS

CHAPTERS

The past thirty or forty years have witnessed a sea change in the UK employee relations scene. Most of the once well-established norms in UK industry have been abandoned or have withered away as the nature of the work that we do and the types of workplace in which we are employed have evolved. To an extent, cultural change has accompanied this structural change too, creating a world of work in which employee attitudes towards their employers and employer attitudes towards their employees have developed in new directions. Ongoing change of one kind or another has affected and continues to affect most areas of HRM activity, but it is in the field of employee relations that the most profound transformations have occurred.

That said, it is important to appreciate that change in this field proceeds at a different pace in different places. There remain many workplaces, particularly in the public sector and in the former public-sector corporations, in which more traditional models of employee relations continue to operate despite attempts by successive governments to change them. What we now have, therefore, is a far greater variety of approaches in place across the different industrial sectors than was the case in past decades.

Overt conflict between labour and management representing different *sides* with fundamentally different interests persists, but usually alongside a newer rhetoric that reflects aspirations towards greater partnership and employee involvement in decision making. In these organisations trade union membership remains high, while terms and conditions of employment continue to be established through formal collective bargaining mechanisms. Negotiations are, however, increasingly carried out at local rather than industry level with individual employers and not with employers' associations as was once standard practice.

This model of employee relations, once common across most of British industry, no longer exists in most private-sector organisations where there is little effective collective employee consciousness on the part of employees and where trade unions are irrelevant, if they have any serious presence at all. Here too the rhetoric of partnership and voice is common, but the extent to which there is any meaningful employee involvement in important decision making can be very limited indeed.

Employee relations practices around the world have tended to head in a similar, broad direction of travel as has been the case in the UK, but because the pace of change varies as well as the journey's starting point, we continue to see a wide variety of approaches in operation internationally. Where public policy has offered a degree of protection, as has been the case in some Scandinavian countries, trade unions have retained a significant role. Elsewhere, including most of the major developing countries, collective employment institutions tend either to be weak, to lack independence from management, or both. Here, as is the case in China for example, they are unable to bring much significant influence to bear on management decision making.

Profound though these changes in employee relations may be, it remains the case that all jobs have the potential to be alienating, making the job holder indifferent or hostile both to the job and to management. Employee relations activity continues to be largely concerned with preventing or alleviating that type of alienation (Chapter 21). In doing so, however, managers are increasingly required to take account of regulation (Chapter 22). Indeed, so great has been the growth of employment law that we now have a situation in most countries whereby employment rights, as well as matters of importance to employees such as equality and health and safety in the workplace (Chapter 23), are guaranteed through the law to a much greater extent than they are by trade unions. Chapter 24 explains skills in mediation and in disciplinary and grievance interviewing, which aims to resolve disagreements between employer and employee. At the end of each chapter you will find a case study in Putting it into practice which will help you to put these ideas into context and explore them more thoroughly.

CHAPTER 21
EMPLOYEE VOICE

THE OBJECTIVES OF THIS CHAPTER ARE TO:

1 Introduce the main methods used by employers to involve employees in decision making

2 Assess the extent of information sharing and its purpose

3 Set out the case for formal and informal consultation with employees and their representatives

4 Explore situations in which co-determination occurs in UK and overseas organisations

It is quite possible to run a successful organisation without involving employees in management activities to any meaningful extent, but the chances of sustained success are higher when employees have a 'voice', so that they are involved in and can influence what happens in the organisation. Objectives are more effectively and efficiently achieved if employees have some say in decision making, especially as it affects their own areas of work. This is for two principal reasons:

1 Ultimately it is for managers to make decisions and to be held accountable. Such decisions can be difficult, but the chances that they will make the right decision are enhanced if they listen to the views of others and allow their own ideas to be subjected to a degree of scrutiny and constructive criticism. Moreover, involvement allows managers to tap into the ideas and suggestions of staff. The best new ideas often originate from people lower down organisational hierarchies because they are closest to the operational coalface and often to customers.

2 Employees like having a voice. They appreciate having their opinions listened to and acted upon, particularly in matters that directly concern their day-to-day activities. The chances of their being positively satisfied with their work are thus greatly improved if they are genuinely able to be involved. The knock-on effects include lower staff turnover, lower levels of absence, the ability to attract more recruits and higher levels of performance. The effective management of change is especially enhanced by employee involvement because people are always happier to support what they helped to create.

There is an emerging stream of research to demonstrate these positive outcomes (Holland *et al*. 2012). Jønsson and Jeppesen (2013), for example, demonstrate that voice arrangements improve employee commitment while Park *et al*. (2010) and Kaine (2012) show the effect of voice in reducing labour turnover and absenteeism. Bryson *et al*. (2013) found that workplaces which encourage some forms of voice suffer less conflict and higher levels of productivity, while others have noted the significance of voice to high performance work practices (Harley 2014) and employee engagement (Guest 2015).

Employee voice comes in many different forms. It can be formal or informal, direct or indirect, one-off or sustained over time, central to an organisation's core business or relatively peripheral. In recent years the number and extent of voice mechanisms have increased. This is partly due to the requirements of the law and partly because they have a part to play in many of the more common, contemporary HRM initiatives we have discussed elsewhere in this text – becoming an 'employer of choice', 360-degree appraisal and employee engagement. The exercise of employee influence is also a central element of an effective psychological contract (Guest and Conway 1998).

Our aim in this chapter is to discuss the major forms employee voice takes, to explore the difficulties that can be experienced in the implementation of initiatives and to evaluate their contribution to the achievement of an organisation's objectives.

Terminology

A variety of labels are used to describe employee voice. Although some writers have sought to make distinctions between them, there is no generally accepted usage. Hence you will read about 'involvement', 'employee participation', 'industrial democracy' and 'empowerment'. Each of these terms differs subtly and suggests a different perspective; Urwin *et al.* (2007), for example, suggest that voice mechanisms are associated with trade union representation whereas HR practices tend to give rise to employee involvement. By contrast, Strauss (2006) argues that 'voice' signifies approaches which give employees less power than is suggested by the more established terms. All, however, are used to a greater or lesser extent to describe a situation in which employees are given, gain or develop a degree of *influence* over what happens in an organisation. The extent and nature of that influence, however, vary considerably.

Marchington and Cox (2007) helpfully distinguish between the major categories of voice with their 'escalator' model (Figure 21.1).

At the bottom of the escalator are organisations where there is no voice at all, managers taking all decisions without taking any meaningful account of what employees might think. By contrast, at the top of the escalator are organisations or parts of organisations which are controlled by employees rather than by a distinct group of managers. Employee control is very rare in the UK at the level of the organisation, although there are one or two examples of companies which are communally owned and run by staff in a partnership arrangement. A substantial degree of control is much more often exercised, however, by employees at the level of an individual department or team within a larger organisation.

Between 'no involvement' and 'employee control', there are three further stages, each in turn representing a deepening of the extent of involvement. The first is 'communication', signalling a very limited degree of involvement. At this stage employer and employees simply exchange information. Managers disclose defined classes of information, ensuring that employees are aware of the decisions they are taking, the economic situation and their objectives. Employees are also given an opportunity to respond, to voice concerns or put their own ideas forward. But decision making remains exclusively in the management realm. The next step up the escalator is 'consultation'. Here information is exchanged, often through formalised channels. Decision making is still the responsibility of managers, but full and proper consideration is given to the views expressed by staff (or their elected representatives) before key decisions are taken. Finally, a further step up the escalator takes us to co-determination or joint decision making. This is relatively rare in a formal sense in the UK, although it happens informally all the time. It is very common in Northern European countries where the law requires the agreement of a works council before significant decisions affecting employment can be taken.

At each of these stages voice initiatives can be either direct or indirect in nature. The term 'direct' relates to situations in which managers enter into a dialogue with, consult with or co-determine decisions with employees as individuals. People thus have a direct input in some shape or form. By contrast, the term 'indirect' refers to a situation in which employers take account of employee views through the filter of a representative

Figure 21.1
The escalator of participation

Source: Marchington, M. and Cox, A. (2007) 'Employee involvement and participation', in J. Storey (ed.) *Human Resource Management: A Critical Text* (3rd edn.). London: Thomson Learning, p. 179, fig 10.1.

institution. This may be a trade union, or it may be another kind of body such as a works council, a working party or a consultative committee. Either way, indirect involvement occurs through representatives of the workforce as a collective group. Academic research into employee voice often encompasses payment arrangements such as profit sharing and employee share ownership schemes which are referred to as types of 'financial participation'. These help to develop a community of interest between employers and their staff and can lead to situations in which individual employees cast votes at annual general meetings. We will discuss them later (see Chapter 26). The remainder of this chapter will focus on the major information-sharing, consultation and co-determination initiatives.

Research by Gollan and Lewin (2013) demonstrates that, while voice mechanisms have increased substantially over recent decades (around 82% of UK employees now have access), types of mechanisms have changed. From 1945 to 1975, trade union voice was dominant in the UK and many other western countries. Since this time, trade union representation has declined and less than 20% of UK private-sector employees were covered by collective pay bargaining arrangements in 2011. Even in the public sector, this proportion rose only to just over 50% (van Wanrooy *et al.* 2013). Non-union voice has thus increased markedly with practices like team briefing being adopted by around 70% of UK workplaces (Gollan and Lewin 2013). These changes are not confined to the UK, as we see in the following Window on practice.

WINDOW ON PRACTICE

Changing patterns of employee voice in Australia

Falling levels of union density and the relaxing of employment regulation have led to the continuing growth of non-union representation and direct voice mechanisms in Australia. These have been typically individualistic in nature, allowed a high degree of management prerogative and are now the preferred means of determining terms and conditions of employment and supporting employee involvement in decision making. There has been a particular interest in joint consultative committees which arise from management initiatives (as opposed to legislative provisions) and can vary in terms of the powers they afford to employees, the level of organisational operation, how they are composed and the issues that they deliberate upon.

Source: Holland *et al.* (2012).

Information sharing

According to the 2011 Workplace Employment Relations Survey (WERS) formal systems of communication between managers and employees are present in the vast majority of UK organisations (van Wanrooy *et al.* 2013). In many cases, however, the communication is carried out at the local level (e.g. line managers meeting with employees individually), there being no formal mechanisms provided for more senior managers to communicate directly with their staff or vice versa. Moreover, where a degree of formality is reported it can be limited simply to the posting of important data on noticeboards or ad hoc circulation of information by email.

The extent to which the disclosure of information by managers can be regarded as a form of employee involvement is debatable. After all, merely being told about an organisation's plans or its financial results does not in any way give employees influence. Nonetheless it can help to make employees feel a sense of involvement or at least of inclusion in the circle of those 'in the know'. It also enables employees, either individually or collectively, to exercise informal influence locally, simply because they are in a position to develop and articulate credible alternative approaches to those their immediate line managers would otherwise impose. Alternatively they are in a position to help improve or refine their strategies. It is often rightly stated that 'knowledge is power' and it therefore follows that spreading relevant knowledge beyond the ranks of management to employees is an empowering activity. This is why managers may hold back information from their staff. Except in a crisis situation in which there is a need to promote calm and keep everyone focused on their jobs, often no damage would be done to the organisation by disclosing the information and labelling it 'confidential'. Refusing to disclose it serves to enhance managers' own sense of personal authority and power.

However reluctant line managers may be to share information to which they are privy, there is substantial evidence to back up the view that regular, extensive information sharing has positive outcomes for organisations. This occurs because it improves levels of commitment among staff (Peccei *et al.* 2005) and because in a practical sense it helps everyone to clarify what their roles are in the wider organisation. It thus enhances communication and coordination across divisions. It also helps to prevent false understanding developing among staff due to the inevitable 'rumour mills' that operate in all organisations and can make employees view change initiatives with less cynicism than otherwise might be the case (Brown and Creagan 2008).

Two-way communication, by contrast, especially when it takes the form of a formal exercise, clearly falls into the category of employee involvement. Staff are being asked to respond to a suggested new approach, asked their opinion, being invited to make suggestions for improvements or given an opportunity to point out flaws in current systems or management thinking. Provided the exercise is not merely cosmetic, and that the views of staff are given serious consideration, influence is gained. Trust in management is, however, vital if staff are to become involved in two-way communication, as Kim *et al.* (2009) demonstrate in a South Korean context.

WERS 2011 identified the most common methods of information sharing in the UK as: workplace meetings (80% of organisations); team briefings (66%); disclosure of financial information (55%); employee attitude surveys (37%); and quality circles (problem-solving groups, 14%). We discuss a number of these methods below.

Team briefing

Team briefing is an initiative that attempts to do a number of different things simultaneously. It provides authoritative information at regular intervals, so that people know what is going on, the information is geared to achievement of production targets and other features of organisational objectives, it is delivered face to face to provide scope for questions and clarification, and it emphasises the role of supervisors and line managers as the source of information. It is used to cascade information down the organisation, usually to teams in a common production or service area, for example a shop in a retail organisation. A trained team leader will undertake the briefings on a regular basis and should allow for questions from employees.

With goodwill and managerial discipline, team briefing can be a valuable contributor to employee involvement, as it deals in that precious commodity, information. Traditionally, there has perhaps been a managerial view that people doing the work are not interested in anything other than the immediate and short term and that the manager's status partly rests on knowing what others do not know. For this reason all the managers and supervisors in the communications chain have to be committed to making it a success, as well as having the necessary training.

Team briefing gets easier once it is established as a regular event. The first briefing will probably go very well and the second will be even better. It is important that management enthusiasm and commitment do not flag just as the employees are getting used to the process.

During economic recessions there is a boost to the team briefing process because so many managements have so much bad news to convey. When you are losing money and profitability, there is a great incentive to explain to employees exactly how grim the situation is, so that they do not look for big pay rises (Kersley *et al.* 2006: 135).

Sometimes, instead of cascading information down a management hierarchy, senior managers in larger organisations like to brief larger groups of employees about significant developments directly. Roadshows or 'interactive executive sessions' of this kind are common and are seen by managers as being almost as effective a means of passing information to employees as more conventional forms of team briefing (IRS 2005a: 11).

Quality circles

Originating in Japanese firms, quality circles comprise small groups of employees (10–15 maximum) who meet regularly to generate ideas aimed at improving the quality of products and services and of organisational productivity. They can also be used as problem-solving groups and as a means by which employee opinion is transmitted to senior management. Some quality circles consist of staff who work together within a team or organisational function, others are cross-functional and focus on interdepartmental issues. They have numerous objectives, such as to generate ideas, encourage cooperative working relationships and drive change (Marchington and Cox 2007). Not only, therefore, are quality circles a potential source of useful ideas for improving systems and saving costs, but also they give people a welcome opportunity to contribute their thoughts and experience. A generally positive impact on employee attitudes should thus result. WERS 2011 indicates that they are used by 14% of UK organisations, a small decline of 3% since 2004.

News sheets

Another common form of employee involvement occurs through the regular publication of in-house journals or news sheets in either paper or electronic form. On one level they simply provide a means by which information concerning finances, policy and proposed change can be transmitted by managers to employees. This is a limited form of employee involvement which does little more than improve the extent to which employees are informed about what is going on elsewhere in their organisations. This will engender a perception of greater involvement and belonging, but does not directly involve employees in any type of decision making. For that to occur the news sheet must be interactive in some way. It may, for example, be used as a means by which employees are consulted about new initiatives, or may provide a forum through which complaints and ideas are voiced.

Attitude surveys

Regular surveys of employee opinion are very useful from a management point of view, particularly where there are no unions present to convey to management an honest picture of morale and commitment in the organisation. Indeed, in their study of workplace bullying, Pate and Beaumont (2010) suggest that attitude surveys are one of the leading employee voice mechanisms. In order to be effective (i.e. honest), responses must be anonymous, individuals stating only which department they work in so that interdepartmental comparisons can be made. It also makes sense to ask the same questions in the same format each time a survey is carried out, so that changes in attitude and/or responses to initiatives can be tracked over time.

The major problems with attitude surveys are associated with situations in which they reveal serious problems which are then not properly addressed. This can easily lead to cynicism and even anger on the part of the workforce. The result is a poorer employee relations climate than would have been the case had no survey taken place. It is counter-productive to involve employees if their contribution is subsequently ignored, yet this appears to happen in many of the organisations where regular surveys are conducted. IRS (2005b) found that the main reasons employers in their sample gave for carrying out employee surveys were to 'take the pulse of the organisation' and to 'demonstrate commitment to employee views'. Only a minority subsequently used the information gathered to shape decision making, even in the HR arena.

Suggestion schemes

A common system of formal bottom-up communication employed by organisations involves encouraging staff to make suggestions about how practices and processes could be improved to make them more effective, efficient or safe. Employees are often best placed to observe in detail what happens operationally on the front line because they have the greatest level of interaction on a day-to-day basis with customers, equipment and organisational procedures. Many organisations go to great lengths to encourage suggestions from employees, as we illustrate in the Window on practice that follows.

WINDOW ON PRACTICE

Tube Lines staff are pitching business ideas to a panel of bosses in the style of the BBC2 television programme *Dragons' Den*. The firm, responsible for the infrastructure of three London Underground lines, rewards workers whose schemes save the company money with £1,000 worth of retail vouchers. Runners-up get £500 and £200 in vouchers.

The Change Challenge Cup, which takes place every three months, is designed to encourage employees to improve the way the business operates. The fifteen-strong panel of judges, chaired by Chief Executive Terry Morgan, is made up of the firm's Change Council, which monitors the organisation's improvements.

The first competition was won jointly by two employees. One developed a new way to clean iron filings from the trackside train position detectors, which has the potential to save the company £1.3 million a year in avoided train delays.

The other winning suggestion was to fit a metal platform across the track to the tunnel wall, allowing workers to cross safely. Morgan said: 'Tube Lines can only continue to move forward if employees are encouraged to come up with better ways of working.'

Source: Adapted from *People Management* (2008) 'Tube lines launches "Dragons' Den" scheme', 21 August, p. 14.

Managers often only become aware of problems when their employees report them, and without such reports can have no opportunities for improving things. So it makes sense to encourage staff to put forward suggestions; having a formal scheme enhances the chances that they will do so. IDS (2005) describes several types of scheme and draws together from these examples of some good practice points. IDS argues that employees should be recognised financially or otherwise when they make a suggestion which is taken up, that systems for submitting ideas should be as uncomplicated as possible, that feedback should be given to all who submit ideas, that past suggestions should be revisited periodically and that schemes must be regularly publicised to remind staff of their existence. IDS also found that organisations are increasingly benefiting from schemes which operate electronically. Suggestions are submitted via email or a form placed on an intranet and filed systematically by an evaluator. Feedback is then given electronically and the successes of the whole scheme publicised regularly through email bulletins sent to all staff.

ACTIVITY 21.1

Despite plenty of evidence that demonstrates how beneficial two-way information sharing can be for organisations, only a minority of non-union employers operate formal systems. Why do you think this is? What are the likely consequences? What arguments would you use to persuade a team of managers of the need to listen to the views of staff and to take them seriously?

Consultation

After information sharing, the next step up the 'escalator' is consultation. Here employees are asked either directly or through representatives to express views which management takes into account when making decisions. Such processes fall short of negotiation or co-determination because there is no ultimate expectation of agreement if the views of staff and management diverge. In some organisations regular meetings are held to enable consultation to take place about a wide range of issues. In others consultation exercises take place irregularly and focus on specific areas such as organisational restructuring or policy changes. Consultation is generally regarded as a hallmark of good management and UK employers have legal obligations to consult with employees (see Chapter 22). An employer who fails to consult properly, particularly at times of significant change, is likely to be perceived as being unduly autocratic. The result will be dissatisfaction, low levels of motivation, higher staff turnover and poorer levels of customer service. Moreover, consultation has important advantages as a means by which good ideas are brought forward and weak ones challenged.

In workplaces where unions are recognised it is usual for consultation to take place over a range of issues through permanent consultative institutions. The joint consultative committee (JCC) is the most common form, being a forum in which managers and staff representatives meet on a regular basis. In more traditional unionised organisations JCCs are kept distinct from negotiating forums – despite the fact that the membership is often the same. A clear divide is thus established between areas which are to be the subject of negotiation (typically terms and conditions of employment) and matters which are the subject of consultation such as health and safety or training. In recent years as partnership agreements have become more common (see Chapter 22), there has been a shift from negotiation towards consultation, the aim being to downplay the adversarial nature of the union–employer relationship and to widen the range of topics about which both sides can engage constructively. Butler *et al.* (2011) argue that partnership arrangements have been resilient forms of voice even in difficult economic circumstances.

The WERS 2011 indicates that 7% of workplaces have a JCC. This percentage is the same as in 2004 and halts a previously declining trend (van Wanrooy *et al.* 2013). It is unusual for the very largest workplaces not to have some form of consultative forum which meets periodically, although in some multi-site corporations formal consultation with employee representatives is restricted to the corporate level and does not take place in individual workplaces. JCCs are four times as common in union workplaces than in those where unions are not recognised (van Wanrooy *et al.* 2013), suggesting that they are mostly still used in parallel with collective bargaining machinery. However, some have argued that they are used in some workplaces as a substitute for collective bargaining or as a means of discouraging the development of a union presence. Managers in such workplaces believe that unions are less likely to gain support and request recognition if the employer keeps the staff informed of issues that affect them and consults with them before taking decisions. Consultative forums in non-union firms also provide a means whereby managers can put their case effectively without the presence of organised opposition. Here employee representatives may be appointed who do not have a connection with a trade union and who may indeed not operate within a JCC. This type of employee representative has been increasing and is now to be found in 13% of UK workplaces (van Wanrooy *et al.* 2013).

From a management perspective, the danger with consultation is that people come to believe that management is not genuinely interested in hearing their views or in taking them on board. This is referred to as 'pseudo-consultation' in which managers are really doing little more than informing employees about decisions that have already been taken. This is borne out by WERS 2011 (van Wanrooy *et al.* 2013: 23):

> Half (52%) of employees considered that management were 'Very good' or 'Good' at seeking their views. However, this is just the first step in the decision-making process. Employees were less likely to rate managers as 'Very good' or 'Good' at responding to suggestions and, in particular, allowing employees influence over final decisions (34%).

Cynicism results because there is perceived to be an attempt on the part of managers to use consultative forums merely as a means of legitimising their decisions. They can say that consultation has taken place, when in truth it has not. Pseudo-consultation typically involves assembling employees in large groups with senior managers present. The management message is then put across strongly and a short time is given for others to respond. In such situations employees have no time to give proper consideration to the proposals and are likely to feel too intimidated to articulate criticisms. The result is often worse in terms of employee morale and engagement with the changes than would have been the case had no consultation been attempted.

Even where managers genuinely intend to undertake meaningful consultation, they can very easily create an impression that it is no more than a 'pseudo'-exercise. It is therefore important to avoid the approaches outlined above. Employees should be informed of a range of possible ways forward (not just the one favoured by management) and invited to consider them in small groups. The results of their deliberations can then be fed back to senior managers and given proper consideration. In this way the appearance of pseudo-consultation, as well as the reality, can be avoided.

WINDOW ON PRACTICE

IRS (2006) describes how a marketing company called BI increased its profitability and halved its staff turnover, in part by introducing a range of employee involvement initiatives. The early years had seen company revenues decline markedly, leading to a pay freeze and staff turnover of 60%.

In 2004, following the appointment of a new chief executive and HR director, a wide range of measures was introduced to tackle these problems. Improving employee involvement was a priority, to signal very clearly the adoption of a new management style, to promote a positive culture and to encourage staff to identify problems and possible solutions. The initiatives included the following:

- weekly email bulletins to staff from senior managers explaining major developments;
- annual letters to staff from the managing director thanking them and setting out key achievements;
- quarterly company meetings at which all staff are briefed about financial matters and strategy;
- an intranet site updated daily with fresh information about the company's activities;
- monthly meetings at which the HR director talks in confidence to ten randomly selected employees about their concerns;
- regular meetings of a 'people forum' at which representatives from each team are consulted about developments.

As a result of these involvement activities many changes were made to operational processes and also to HR practices. Hours of work were made more flexible, and staff discouraged from working more hours than was necessary. A scheme was also introduced to allow people to trade some of their salary for additional holiday.

Co-determination

In the UK, important decision making in organisations is nearly always the preserve of managers. Decisions in the employment area are often taken after extensive and genuine consultation, or after negotiation with union representatives, but anything approaching serious co-determination with employees is very rare indeed. Nevertheless, it must be pointed out that at the level of the individual team, a degree of informal co-determination is common. Indeed, in recent years it has become more common as organisations have tended to de-layer, reducing the number of managers and levels of hierarchy. Increasingly employees and team leaders have found themselves 'empowered' to take decisions for themselves that once they would have had to refer to a manager. It is important not to overestimate the significance of this trend, as any discretion that is given operates within tightly defined boundaries. What gets done is still determined by managers, but there is greater flexibility about when and how exactly it gets done.

Elsewhere in Europe the extent of co-determination at the level of the team and of individual empowerment varies from country to country. In Southern European nations such as France, Italy and Spain managers at the local level tend to guard their autonomy more tightly than typical UK line managers. Co-determination at the local level over day-to-day workplace activities is thus rarer than in the UK. In Northern Europe, by contrast, a far greater degree of team-based autonomy is common. The best-known examples of teams assuming responsibility and decision-making authority are in the Scandinavian countries. The approach involves organising a workforce into small groups of about a dozen members, who are mutually supportive and who operate with minimal supervision. Managers set performance targets (often after consultation) and allocate tasks, but it is for the team to decide exactly how these are to be achieved. The team members organise their own activities, appoint their own leaders and work out themselves how to overcome problems. Teamworking can thus be characterised as a form of worker control, even though it operates within heavily prescribed limits. Managers refrain from giving day-to-day supervision, but are on hand to give advice or more direct assistance where necessary. Disciplining staff, for example, is a task carried out by managers and not by team members. Teamworking is often associated with situations in which several regionally based teams compete with each other to meet or exceed performance targets. Team-based remuneration then accounts for a proportion of the total pay received.

While practice varies at the local team level across Europe, at the level of the organisation co-determination is a great deal more established and widespread in most countries than is the case in the UK. It occurs through two distinct mechanisms:

1 through the legal empowerment of works councils or enterprise committees;

2 by reserving places on executive boards for worker directors.

Both approaches are famously used in Germany, where co-determination over employment matters is standard practice in organisations of any size. In the UK most of the activities described in this text are the preserve of managers, while in Germany they are decided jointly between managers and workforce representatives. German managers cannot impose any decision relating to changing workplace rules, disciplinary procedures, working hours, holidays, bonus payments, overtime arrangements, health and safety matters, training or selection methods without first securing the agreement of their organisation's works council. Moreover, their autonomy to make decisions about any changes relating to the nature of the work their employees do or the physical environment in which it is performed is subject to their first consulting with the works council and taking its objections and suggestions into account. In addition the law requires that managers share a great deal of financial and planning information with works councils that goes well beyond the employment sphere (Budd 2004: 129). Seats are also reserved on the supervisory boards of German companies for workforce representatives. In companies employing more than 500 people, a third of the seats are reserved. Where over 2,000 are employed, half the seats are taken by worker representatives. Such national variations are likely to be the cause of some difficulty for multinational corporations operating in a number of companies. A recent study by Marginson *et al.* (2010) showed that such employers are engaging in significant innovations in representation and voice arrangements in order to address these variations.

ACTIVITY 21.2

In many European companies works councils or enterprise committees tend to be dominated by trade unions, even where a majority of the staff are not members. Why do you think this is? What do you think are the major advantages and disadvantages of trade union representatives also acting as works council members or worker directors?

SUMMARY PROPOSITIONS

21.1. Genuine employee voice serves to increase commitment and to improve decision making in organisations.

21.2. Information sharing is common in the UK. Team briefing, news sheets and suggestion schemes are the most common mechanisms adopted.

21.3. The use of formal consultation processes is common in larger UK organisations. Joint consultative committees are found in most unionised workplaces.

21.4. Co-determination at the level of the organisation or workplace is rare in the UK, but common in many other EU countries.

21.5. Co-determination at the level of teams is increasing in the UK, but is limited in the extent to which it empowers employees.

GENERAL DISCUSSION TOPICS

1. Why do you think employers in the UK are more reluctant to involve employee representatives in strategic decision making than is the case in a country such as Germany?

2. How far do you agree with the view that information sharing barely constitutes employee involvement at all?

3. In what ways would you like to see increased or decreased employee involvement in your organisation, and why?

THEORY INTO PRACTICE

Kaufman (2013) reports a study of the Delta Air Lines employee involvement programme, which forms part of the organisation's attempt to maintain a high-commitment model of employment relations. In essence, Delta sees employee involvement as a way to improve efficiency and communication and to ensure that employees feel valued and well treated. Providing voice mechanisms is also seen as a way to reduce the demand for external representation and underpins Delta's partnership and non-union approach. Kaufman argues that the breadth, depth and formal structure of Delta's employee involvement mechanisms make it one of the leading non-union employee involvement companies in the USA, particlarly in respect of representative councils and forums.

Delta adopts a three-stage formal employee involvement strucure:

1 An organisation-wide consultative committee with five employee representatives, one from each of the major divisions.

2 Four employee involvement groups at divisional level, including: flight attendants, customer service and cargo, technical operations and reservation sales/city ticket offices. The first three of these have a two-layered structure with elected representatives at both city/base forums and system-wide forums.

3 In excess of 100 project teams which operate either across divisions or at particular sites, depending on the nature of the project.

These structures are supplemented by six organisation-wide groups to support employee diversity and, in some divisions, by a peer-review dispute resolution system. There are also a substantial number of other employee involvement activities including monthly CEO breakfasts and phone-ins where employees can ask questions of and provide feedback to senior executives.

Employee involvement mechanisms were central to Delta's merger with Northwest Airlines (NA). Twenty-seven project teams were established to address a whole range of matters, from strategic to low-level operational issues. These project teams comprised equal numbers of Delta and NA employees to foster a spirit of shared identity. Employee involvement was also central to integrating NA employees, from a unionised adversarial culture, into Delta's high-commitment culture. Promises made at the time of the merger, for example that pay rises would be made, were kept, NA employees were included in the councils and forums described above, and 'get acquainted' meetings were held. Former NA employees expressed surprise that the forums were able to achieve positive outcomes and offer protection to employees. Indeed, employee involvement is widely seen as a means to build a successful company and ensure that benefits accrue to all stakeholders, rather than a form of 'anti-union' mechanism. Kaufman attributes this to three things:

1 Some forum representatives are also union supporters and will not tolerate anti-union activity.

2 There is recognition that both organisation and employee representatives lose credibility if they tolerate or support anti-unionism.

3 Delta does not want to create an environment where union representation might seem desirable or take action that might prompt calls for union representation.

It is noteworthy that when, post-merger, there were calls for union recognition, the unions lost all the elections by a relatively wide margin.

Kaufman summarises Delta's approach to employee involvement as being quite successful, although he notes that it was introduced in a piecemeal fashion across the 1990s without any overarching HR vision. Nevertheless, employee involvement has supported a transition from employee commitment based upon a paternalistic employment relationship to commitment premised upon a mutual gains scenario in which management and workers cooperate to drive high performance that benefits both parties.

Questions

1 Using Marchington and Cox's 'escalator' model, how would you categorise Delta's approach to employee voice?

2 What other mechanisms could Delta use to offer employee voice?

3 To what extent do you agree that Delta's approach to employee voice makes union representation unnecessary?

Source: Adapted from Kaufman, B. (2013) 'Keeping the commitment model in the air during turbulent times: Employee involvement at Delta Air Lines', *Industrial Relations*, Vol. 52, pp. 343–77.

FURTHER READING

Benson, J. and Brown, M. (2010) 'Employee voice: Does union membership matter?', *Human Resource Management Journal*, Vol. 20, No. 1, pp. 80–99.

In this article, the authors explore the relationship between trade union membership and employee perceptions of voice. Their findings are counter-intuitive, that trade union membership has a significantly negative impact upon employee perceptions of voice, and they set about explaining why this might be the case.

Dundon, T. *et al*. (2005) 'The management of voice in non-union organisations: Managers' perspectives', *Employee Relations*, Vol. 27, No. 3, pp. 307–19.

In this article Tony Dundon and his colleagues explore the views of managers about the role played by consultative forums in seven non-union organisations. They conclude that commentators have often been too hasty to dismiss these practices as inconsequential or ineffective.

Harley, B., Hyman, J. and Thompson, P. (2005) *Participation and Democracy at Work: Essays in Honour of Harvie Ramsay.* Basingstoke: Palgrave Macmillan.

A book of articles by leading academic researchers which covers every aspect of informing, consulting and involving employees.

Gollan, P. and Lewin, D. (2013) 'Employee representation in non-union firms: An overview', *Industrial Relations,* Vol. 52, pp. 173–93.

This special issue of *Industrial Relations* contains eight articles, authored by scholars from the USA, UK, Canada and Australia, that develop understanding of forms of non-union employee representation internationally.

REFERENCES

Brown, M. and Creagan, C. (2008) 'Organisational change cynicism: The role of employee involvement', *Human Resource Management,* Vol. 47, pp. 667–86.

Bryson, A., Willman, P., Gomez, R. and Kretschmer, T. (2013) 'The comparative advantage of workplace voice and high commitment human resource practices in Britain 1980–2004. *Industrial Relations: A Journal of Economy and Society,* Vol. 52, No. 1, pp. 194–220.

Budd, J. (2004) *Employment with a Human Face.* Ithaca, NY: Cornell University Press.

Butler, P., Glover, L. and Tregaskis, O. (2011) '"When the Going Gets Tough" . . . : Recession and the resilience of workplace partnership', *British Journal of Industrial Relations,* Vol. 49, pp. 666–87.

Gollan, P. and Lewin, D. (2013) 'Employee representation in non-union firms: An overview', *Industrial Relations,* Vol. 52, pp. 173–93.

Guest, D. and Conway, N. (1998) *Fairness at Work and the Psychological Contract.* London: Institute of Personnel and Development.

Guest, D. (2015) 'Voice and employee engagement', in S. Johnstone and P. Ackers (eds), *Finding a Voice at Work: New Perspectives on Employment Relations.* Oxford: Oxford University Press.

Harley, B. (2014) 'High performance work systems and employee voice', in A. Wilkinson, J. Donaghey, T. Dundon and R. Freeman (eds), *Handbook of Research on Employee Voice.* Cheltenham: Edward Elgar.

Holland, P., Cooper, B. and Pyman, A. (2012) 'Trust in management: The role of employee voice arrangements and perceived managerial opposition to unions', *Human Resource Management Journal,* Vol. 22, pp. 377–91.

IDS (2005) 'Suggestion schemes', *IDS Study No. 812.* London: IDS.

IRS (2005a) 'Dialogue or monologue: Is the message getting through?', *IRS Employment Review,* No. 834. London: IRS.

IRS (2005b) 'More questions than answers? Employee surveys revealed', *IRS Employment Review,* No. 820. London: IRS.

IRS (2006) 'BI bounces back with culture of employee engagement', *IRS Employment Review,* No. 839. London: IDS.

Jønsson, T. and Jeppesen, H. (2013) 'A closer look into the employee influence: Organisational commitment relationship by distinguishing between commitment forms and influence sources', *Employee Relations,* Vol. 35, pp. 4–19.

Kaine, S. (2012) 'Regulation and employee voice in the residential aged care sector', *Human Resource Management Journal,* Vol. 22, pp. 316–31.

Kaufman, B. (2013) 'Keeping the commitment model in the air during turbulent times: Employee involvement at Delta Air Lines', *Industrial Relations,* Vol. 52, pp. 343–77.

Kersley, B., Alpin, C., Forth, J., Bryson, A., Bewley, H., Dix, G. and Oxenbridge, S. (2006) *Inside the Workplace: Findings from the 2004 Workplace Employment Relations Survey.* London: Routledge.

Kim, T., Rosen, B. and Lee, D. (2009) 'South Korean managerial reactions to voicing discontent: The effects of employee attitude and employee communication styles', *Journal of Organisational Behaviour,* Vol. 30, pp. 1001–18.

Marchington, M. and Cox, A. (2007) 'Employee involvement and participation', in J. Storey (ed.), *Human Resource Management: A Critical Text* (3rd edn.). London: Thomson Learning.

Marginson, S., Edwards, P., Edwards, T., Ferner, A. and Tregaskis, O. (2010) 'Employee representation and consultative voice in multinational companies operating in Britain', *British Journal of Industrial Relations,* Vol. 48, pp. 151–80.

Park, R., Appelbaum, E. and Kruse, D. (2010) 'Employee involvement and group incentives in manufacturing companies: A multi-level analysis', *Human Resource Management Journal,* Vol. 20, pp. 227–43.

Pate, J. and Beaumont, P. (2010) 'Bullying and harassment: A case of success?', *Employee Relations,* Vol. 32, pp. 171–83.

Peccei, R., Bewley, H., Gospel, G. and Willman, P. (2005) 'Is it good to talk? Information disclosure and organisational performance in the UK', *British Journal of Industrial Relations,* Vol. 43, pp. 11–39.

People Management (2008) 'Tube lines launches "Dragons' Den" scheme', 21 August, p. 14.

Strauss, G. (2006) 'Worker participation: Some unconsidered issues', *Industrial Relations Journal,* Vol. 45, pp. 778–803.

Urwin, P., Murphy, R. and Michielsens, E. (2007) 'Employee voice regimes and the characteristics of conflict: An analysis of the 2003 survey of employment tribunal applications', *Human Resource Management Journal,* Vol. 17, pp. 178–97.

Van Wanrooy, B., Bewley, H., Bryson, A., Forth, J., Freeth, S., Stokes, L. and Wood, S. (2013) *The 2011 Workplace Employment Relations Study: First Findings.* London: BIS.

CHAPTER 22

THE LEGAL FRAMEWORK OF WORK

THE OBJECTIVES OF THIS CHAPTER ARE TO:

1 Demonstrate the extent to which the regulation of workplaces and labour markets has increased in recent decades

2 Introduce the contract of employment and its significance in the regulation of employment

3 Explain and illustrate the major principles of discrimination law, dismissal law and family-friendly employment rights

4 Summarise the major principles underpinning the criminal and civil law aspects of health and safety regulation

5 Debate the extent to which employment law is best characterised as a benefit or a burden from the point of view of employing organisations

A regulatory revolution

One of the most important contemporary developments which has shaped HR practice in organisations has been the seemingly relentless increase, year on year, of new employment regulation. Fifty years ago it was commonly and correctly stated that UK workplaces and labour markets were among the most lightly regulated in the industrial world. It was a long-standing tradition for the state to make a virtue of not intervening in the relationship between employers and employees except when it was absolutely necessary to do so. As a result, with the exception of basic health and safety entitlements, laws preventing the exploitation of child workers and the basic principle that the terms of all contracts of employment were legally enforceable, there was hardly any such thing as 'employment law' in the UK. Since then the position has wholly reversed. Though still less tightly regulated by comparison with some European countries, the UK now has one of the most highly regulated labour markets in the world. As far as the regulation of work is concerned, the past five decades can truly be characterised as a revolutionary period. What is more, the pace of regulation has steadily accelerated over this period. Much of the most significant law is relatively recent in origin, and despite ministerial rhetoric, little deregulation of much significance ever seems to occur. The same story holds true for most industrialised countries. Over time, partly due to concerted efforts on the parts of international bodies like the European Union and the International Labour Organization, increasing legal regulation of the employment relationship has been something that HR managers have had to get used to.

As a result, a wide range of legally imposed restrictions now severely limit employers' freedom to manage people and run their organisations as they please. Regulation plays a role in almost every area of HRM from recruitment and selection to arrangements for paying people, managing working time, determining rights to leave from work, ensuring a decent level of health and safety, dealing with trade unions, managing retirements and dismissals. One aim is to provide some rebalancing of the power relationship between employers and employees, helping to restrict the extent to which managers can abuse their power by exploiting their employees unfairly or acting in an unjustly arbitrary manner towards them. Another is to promote good practice in people management via flexible working and partnership with unions and other employee representatives. We do not have the space in one chapter to explore the whole field of employment law in any great depth, so we will focus on employment rights which most matter to employees and which are the most frequent cause of formal legal action. These are those which relate to contracts of employment, unlawful discrimination, dismissal, family-friendly rights and health and safety. We will consider the law on pay and benefits in Part 6.

WINDOW ON PRACTICE

In the UK people who believe that their employer has acted unlawfully in its treatment of them have long had the right to take their case before a specialised form of court known as an employment tribunal, similar systems existing all over the world to help ensure that organisations act within the law in their dealings with employees. In recent years most would-be claimants have had to pay a fee for this privilege and this has led to a large drop in the number of cases being brought. However, the possibility that an employee might bring such a claim and win a good amount of damages remains, ensuring that HR managers cannot afford to take a complacent attitude towards the requirements that the law imposes.

The most costly cases from an employer's point of view are those which are collective in nature. These involve groups of employees bringing joint claims, typically alleging that they have all been underpaid for a number of years contrary to the requirements of equal pay law or the national minimum wage regulations. From time to time though, an individual case hits the headlines on account of the size of the compensation an individual claimant is awarded.

The biggest tribunal award to date was made to Dr Eva Michalek, a consultant physician, by the Leeds Employment Tribunal in 2012. She won over £4.4 million from the Mid Yorkshire NHS Hospitals Trust, having successfully persuaded the panel that she had been both unfairly dismissed and unlawfully discriminated against on account of her gender. She had returned from a period of maternity leave to find that her colleagues had been paid additional sums of money to do minimal amounts of extra work in her absence. When she was denied similar payments she brought a formal complaint alleging that she was being discriminated against on grounds of her sex. This appears to have made her unpopular among senior colleagues who then launched something of a campaign aimed at securing her resignation. Unfounded bullying allegations were made against her, leading to what the tribunal judged to have been 'a lengthy and wholly unjustified period of suspension' before she was dismissed. Dr Michelak then became ill as a result of a serious nervous breakdown which prevented her from working and led to her husband having to give up his job to care for her and their son.

This case is exceptional because of the amount of damages won and both the length and extent of the harassment Dr Michalek suffered prior to her dismissal, but it serves to remind us of the consequences that can result when organisations fail to uphold basic standards of fairness and decency in the way that they manage people.

Source: The Guardian (2011), BBC (2011).

The contract of employment

Although a great deal is written about 'psychological contracts' and 'contracts for performance', the association between employer and employee remains at base a legal relationship governed by 'a contract of employment'. Whatever expectations employers and employees have of one another when the employment begins, the basic terms and conditions will be agreed and understood at the start and may, if necessary, be enforced in a court. In law the existence of such a contract confers on both parties important obligations as well as giving the employee access to significant legal rights which are not available to people who work under different contractual arrangements.

Employment contracts are very varied, and in recent years all industrialised countries have seen a trend away from what are usually described as being 'traditional' arrangements in which employees are employed on an open-ended basis for forty hours or so over a five-day standard 'working week' towards a variety of different alternative types of contract. In some industrial sectors we have seen a move away from employment altogether as people have chosen, or been required, to switch to self-employment or agency working. However, as far as the law is concerned, over 80% of people who work in the UK are employees. This means that they have a contract of employment with their employer, with the duties and privileges that that implies. As far as the law is concerned, they are working under 'a contract of service'. This derives from the old notion of a master and servant relationship and indicates that the employee (or servant) has obligations to the employer or master, and vice versa. In contrast, those who are self-employed or subcontractors have greater autonomy, but no one standing between them and legal accountability for their actions. The law makes an important distinction between the two groups, employees having access to a wider range of legal rights than non-employees. While some areas of employment law apply to all workers, others only apply to employees. Non-employees are deemed to be working under 'a contract for services' rather than 'a contract of service'. In 2016 the main statutory rights that applied to each were those shown in Table 22.1.

In addition to the statutory rights conferred by Acts of Parliament, a range of common law duties are owed by employers to employees and vice versa which do not apply in the case of other forms of relationship. The major obligations are as follows:

Owed by employers to employees:

- a general duty of care
- a duty to pay agreed wages
- a duty to provide work
- a duty not to treat employees in an arbitrary or vindictive manner
- a duty to provide support to employees
- a duty to provide safe systems of work.

Owed by employees to employers:

- a duty to cooperate
- a duty to obey reasonable/lawful instructions

Table 22.1 Access to statutory employment rights

Employment rights which apply to all workers	Employment rights which apply only to employees
Equal pay for equal work	Right to a statement of terms and conditions of employment
Right not to be discriminated against on grounds of sex, race, religious belief, sexual orientation, age or disability	Right to an itemised pay statement
Right not to have unauthorised deductions from pay	Statutory Sick Pay
Basic health and safety rights	Time off for public duties
Minimum wage	Nine months' maternity pay
Working time regulations	Trade union rights
Data protection rights	Minimum notice periods
Time off to care for dependants	Fixed-term employment regulations
Part-time workers regulations	Parental leave (after one year's service)
Twelve months' maternity leave	Unfair dismissal rights (after two years' service)
Agency workers regulations	

- a duty to exercise reasonable care and skill
- a duty to act in good faith.

Owed by employers to employees and vice versa:

- to maintain a relationship of mutual trust and confidence.

Owed by employees and ex-employees:

- duty of fidelity.

A contract of employment, contrary to common perception, need not exist in written form. It is much more satisfactory for both parties if there is documentary evidence of what terms and conditions have been offered and accepted, but a contract of employment exists whether agreed verbally on the telephone or sealed with no more than a handshake. Where there is any doubt about whether someone is an employee or not, the courts look at the evidence presented to them concerning the reality of the existing relationship between the two parties. If they consider, on balance, that it is governed by a 'contract of service' rather than a 'contract for services', they will consider the worker to be an employee and entitled to the full range of rights outlined above.

WINDOW ON PRACTICE

A case heard in the House of Lords (now reinvented as The Supreme Court) illustrates the importance of employee status. Mrs Carmichael and a colleague were employed as tour guides at a power station run by National Power PLC. They started working for the company on a casual basis in 1989, undertaking about four hours' work each week as and when they were needed. By 1995 they each were working around twenty-five hours a week, so they decided to ask for written particulars of their terms and conditions of employment. The company refused on the grounds that they were casual workers and not employees. The women won their case in the lower courts, but the company decided to appeal right up to the House of Lords. At this stage the women lost their case on the grounds that there was no mutuality of obligation. They could have, and indeed had, turned down requests to work without suffering any disciplinary action. They were therefore not employees and not entitled to the rights associated with full employment status.

ACTIVITY 22.1

Substantial and growing groups of people in the UK work under atypical sets of terms and conditions, for example on casual or agency contracts. As a rule such staff are classed as 'workers' rather than 'employees' because they are not deemed to be working under 'contracts of service'. As a result many important employment rights are denied to them (see Table 22.1).

What do you think are the main arguments for and against extending full employment rights to these groups? Where do you stand in this debate, and why?

Discrimination law

Most anti-discrimination law is now covered by European treaties or directives and thus applies in all member states of the EU. (It is unlikely that any significant rights in this area will be changed following the UK's departure from the EU.) In the UK the passing of the Equality Act 2010 brought together in one statute most of these regulations. There remain important differences in the rights that relate to each 'protected characteristic' set out in the Act, but there is now a greater degree of harmonisation as far as core principles and terminology are concerned. The protected characteristics are as follows:

- sex
- race, ethnicity and national origin
- sexual orientation
- religion or belief
- age
- disability
- pregnancy and maternity
- marital status
- transsexuality.

In each case the details differ somewhat, but the same broad principles apply. Below we illustrate these by describing sex discrimination law at some length, going on briefly to explain how and why some of the other fields of discrimination law employ slightly different approaches.

Sex discrimination law

In the UK, extensive law in the area of sex discrimination has been on the statute books since 1975. This has been amended on several occasions since then and has been interpreted in different ways as a result of new case law, but the core tenets have always remained the same. There are four separate headings under which a case can be brought: direct sex discrimination, indirect sex discrimination, sexual harassment and victimisation.

Direct discrimination

Direct discrimination is straightforward. It occurs simply when an employer treats someone less favourably for a reason related to their gender. In judging claims the courts use the 'but for' test, asking whether the woman would have received the same treatment as a man (or vice versa) but for her sex. Examples of direct sex discrimination include advertising for a man to do a job which could equally well be done by a woman or dismissing a woman because she is pregnant.

If an employer is found to have discriminated *directly* on grounds of sex, except in one type of situation, there is no defence. The courts cannot, therefore, take into account any mitigating circumstances or make a judgment based on the view that the employer acted reasonably. Once it has been established that direct discrimination has occurred, proceedings end with a victory for the claimant.

The one exception operates in the area of recruitment, where it is possible to argue that certain jobs have to be reserved for either women or men. For this to be acceptable the employer must convince a court that it is a job for which there is an 'occupational requirement' on grounds such as:

- authenticity (e.g. acting or modelling jobs);
- decency (e.g. lavatory or changing room attendants);
- personal services (e.g. a counsellor engaged to work in a rape crisis centre).

Indirect discrimination

Indirect discrimination is harder to grasp, not least because it can quite easily occur unintentionally. It occurs when a 'provision, criterion or practice' is set or operated which has the effect, in practice, of disadvantaging a significantly larger proportion of one sex than the other. In other words, if substantially fewer women than men can comply with the condition, even if it is applied in exactly the same way to both men and women, it is potentially unlawful. A straightforward example is a job advertisement which specifies that applicants should be taller than six feet. This is indirectly discriminatory because a substantially smaller proportion of women are able to comply than men. The reverse would of course be true if the ad specified a preference for applicants under six feet in height.

Indirect discrimination differs from direct discrimination in that there is a defence that an employer can deploy. An employer can justify the condition or requirement it has set 'on grounds other than sex', in which case it may be lawful. An example might be a job for which a key requirement is the ability to lift heavy loads. It is reasonable in such circumstances for the employer to restrict recruitment to people who are physically able to comply, for example by including a test of strength in selection procedures. The fact that more men than women will be able to do so does not make the practice unlawful, provided the lifting requirement is wholly genuine. In judging cases of this kind the tribunal has to decide whether or not the provision, criterion or practice constitutes 'a proportionate means of achieving a legitimate aim'. If the tribunal decides it does, the employer wins, if not the employee wins.

It is not sufficient for the employer to show that the practice was convenient or administratively desirable – that does not amount to objective justification; to form the basis of an acceptable defence it must be shown to be genuinely necessary for the achievement of a legitimate business objective.

WINDOW ON PRACTICE

The Equality and Human Rights Commission

Employer actions in the area of discrimination are policed to some extent by the Equality and Human Rights Commission (EHRC) which is required to keep the legislation under review, to conduct formal investigations into employer actions where it has reason to suspect there has been a contravention of the law, to issue codes of practice and to provide legal assistance to employees who consider themselves to be victims of unfair discrimination. On occasions the EHRC itself represents employees before employment tribunals. It also brings its own test cases in a bid to push back the frontiers of the law.

The EHRC began operating in 2007, replacing three well-established commissions: the Equal Opportunities Commission, the Commission for Racial Equality and the Disability Rights Commission. However, its remit extends much further than those of the commissions it replaced to encompass fields covered by the Human Rights Act 1998 as well as discrimination law.

Sexual harassment

Sexual harassment is defined as unwanted conduct of a sexual nature or based on sex, which affects the dignity of men and women at work. It can be physical or verbal in nature, leading *either* to material detriment (i.e. it affects promotion, pay, access to training, etc.) *or* to the creation of an intimidating or humiliating work environment.

Although the law applies equally to men and women, the vast majority of cases are brought by women. The employer's liability in harassment cases arises from the application of the doctrine of **vicarious liability,** under which employers are held responsible for the commitment of civil wrongs by employees when they are at work.

In judging cases the courts focus on the reaction of the victim and do not apply any general definitions of what types of conduct do and do not amount to unlawful harassment. Hence conduct which may not offend one person in the slightest can be found to constitute sexual harassment when directed at someone else who is deeply offended.

For an employer the only valid defences relate to the notion of vicarious liability. An employer can, for example, claim ignorance of the incident of which the victim is complaining or can claim that vicarious liability does not apply because it occurred away from the workplace and outside office hours. Finally the employer can defend itself by showing that all reasonable steps were taken to prevent the harassment from occurring or continuing. In order to succeed here, the employer needs to produce evidence to show that initial complaints were promptly acted upon and that appropriate action, such as disciplining the perpetrators or moving them to other work, was taken.

Victimisation

In the field of sex discrimination the term 'victimisation' means the same as it does in other areas of employment law. An employer victimises workers if it disadvantages them in any way simply because they have sought to exercise their legal rights or have assisted others in doing so. An employee would thus bring a claim of victimisation to a tribunal if the employee had been overlooked for promotion having recently successfully settled an equal pay claim. Importantly victimisation covers situations in which someone threatens to bring an action or plans to do so even if no case is ultimately brought.

Other protected characteristics

These same core principles apply across the other fields of discrimination law covered by the Equality Act 2010. There are, however, some significant differences in the case of age discrimination and disability discrimination law:

- In age discrimination law it is permissible to discriminate directly if the act is objectively justified. In such cases the same defence that applies in cases of indirect discrimination must be complied with if the employer is to be able to show that it has acted lawfully, namely that the act of discrimination amounted to 'a proportionate means of achieving a legitimate aim'. This means that, in practice, mandatory retirement at the age of 65 or above remains lawful across most of the EU.

- Disability discrimination law permits employers to discriminate against a disabled person, a job applicant or an existing employee who becomes seriously ill, provided they have first genuinely considered whether any 'reasonable adjustments' could be made to enable that person to work or continue working. This typically involves adjusting working practices to accommodate someone's particular needs or making alterations to premises.

WINDOW ON PRACTICE

Religion or belief

Under EU law it is a requirement that all member states have in place regulations to deter employers from discriminating against their staff on grounds of 'religion or belief'. Back in 2003 when this law was first introduced, the UK government was keen to ensure that members of extreme political organisations could not use it to defend themselves when an employer objected to their views by, for example, refusing to promote them or even dismissing them. The UK law was thus phrased in terms of discrimination on grounds of 'any religion or similar philosophical belief'. This formulation soon proved to be unsatisfactory and hard to justify because it excluded people who did not have any religious belief and who were found, quite lawfully, to have been excluded from work in religious organisations and faith schools on these grounds. The wording was thus altered in 2006 to 'any religious or philosophical belief', the aim being to include people with deeply held beliefs about 'life, the universe and everything', whether or not they were religious in character. The new wording still sought to exclude instances in which people are discriminated against because of their political opinions or stance on an issue, but exactly who and what beliefs met the definition remained unclear.

In 2009 the issue became further confused when the Employment Appeals Tribunal (EAT) gave judgment in the case of *Grainger PLC & others* v. *Nicholson*. Here the claimant, Mr Nicholson, alleged that he had been made redundant from his post as Head of Sustainability at Grainger, in part, because of his belief in climate change – a point of view he expressed and acted on while at work with some passion. The EAT ruled that such a belief did fall within the new definition and found in his favour.

In the process the EAT set out a list of criteria which tribunals will now have to use when determining whether or not 'a philosophical belief' is or is not covered by the regulations. These are as follows:

- it must be a belief and not merely an opinion or viewpoint based on current information;
- the belief must be genuinely held;
- the belief must concern a weighty and substantial aspect of human behaviour;
- the belief must have a 'certain level of cogency, seriousness, cohesion and importance';
- the belief must be 'worthy of respect in a democratic society, not incompatible with human dignity and not in conflict with the fundamental rights of others'.

The aim here is presumably to steer a careful path so that beliefs that are racist, unpleasant or perverse cannot be protected, while 'allowing through' other deeply held and sincere beliefs. The trouble is that it leaves many questions unanswered, hence creating less clarity than was there before. In short, how can an employer now know whether or not it is or is not acting lawfully when faced with decision in this field? A great deal is now left to the subjective opinion of tribunal members.

In 2012 the European Court of Human Rights ruled against the UK government on this issue, finding in favour of a bus driver called Mr Redfearn who had been dismissed when he was elected to his local council as a representative of the British National Party (BNP). The court was concerned that Mr Redfearn had no legal avenue open to him to challenge his dismissal. This case demonstrates that the law probably still has some way to develop before a settled position on the scope of 'religion or belief' is reached.

Remedies

Victorious claimants in discrimination cases are awarded damages of two kinds. First they can claim from the employer compensation for any financial losses they have sustained as a result of the unlawful discrimination they have suffered. This may be very limited, but where someone has resigned or been dismissed there can be extensive sums awarded to compensate for lost earnings and potential future losses. The second category is 'injury to feelings'. The sums awarded here range from £500 for one-off incidents that cause very limited distress (e.g. being turned down for a job at the shortlisting stage when the individual had little expectation of being successful at interview) up to £30,000 where someone has, for example, been subjected to a lengthy campaign of racial harassment.

Unfair dismissal law

The law of unfair dismissal dates from 1971, since when it has been amended a number of times. Although new additions and the outcomes of leading cases have made it more complex than it was originally, the basic principles have stood the test of time and remain in place. In most circumstances the right to bring a claim of unfair dismissal applies to employees who have completed two years' continuous service with their employer on the date their contract was terminated. This probation period allows employers a period of time to assess whether or not an individual employee is suitable before the freedom to dismiss is restricted. The restrictions on qualification apply except where the reason for the dismissal is one of those listed below which are classed as 'automatically unfair.' A further requirement is that the claim form is lodged at the tribunal office before three months have elapsed from the date of dismissal

When faced with a claim of unfair dismissal, and where it is not disputed that a dismissal took place, an employment tribunal asks two separate questions:

- Was the reason for the dismissal one which is classed by the law as legitimate?

- Did the employer act reasonably in carrying out the dismissal?

Where the answer to the first question is 'no', there is no need to ask the second because the dismissed employee will already have won his or her case. Interestingly the burden of proof shifts as the tribunal moves from considering the first to the second question. It is for the employer to satisfy the tribunal that it dismissed the employee for a legitimate reason. The burden of proof then becomes neutral when the question of reasonableness is addressed.

ACTIVITY 22.2

Consider the working activities of some of your colleagues (and perhaps your own working activities).

What examples are there of behaviour that you feel justify dismissal? Make a list of your ideas and check them when you have finished this chapter and see how many might be classified by a tribunal as unfair dismissals.

Automatically unfair reasons

Certain reasons for dismissal are declared in law to be automatically unfair. When a tribunal finds that one of these was the principal reason for the dismissal, they find in favour of the claimant (i.e. the ex-employee) whatever the circumstances of the case. In practice, therefore, there is no defence that an employer can make to explain its actions that will be acceptable to the tribunal. Moreover, the two years' service requirement does not apply, so people can bring cases even if their dismissal occurred on the first day of employment. In 2016 the list of automatically unfair reasons for dismissal was as follows:

- Dismissal for a reason relating to pregnancy or maternity.

- Dismissal for a health and safety reason (e.g. refusing to work in unsafe conditions).

- Dismissal because of a spent conviction.

- Dismissal for refusing to work on a Sunday (retail and betting workers only).

- Dismissal for a trade union reason.

- Dismissal for taking official industrial action (during the first 12 weeks of the action).

- Dismissal in contravention of the part-time workers or fixed-term employees' regulations.

- Dismissal for undertaking duties as an occupational pension fund trustee, employee representative, member of a European Works Council or in connection with jury service.
- Dismissal for asserting a statutory right (including rights exercised under the Employment Rights Act, as well as those connected with the Working Time Regulations, the National Minimum Wage Regulations, the Public Interest Disclosure Act and the Information and Consultation of Employees Regulations; the right to request flexible working, the right to time off for dependents, the right to adoptive, parental or paternity leave, the right to be accompanied at disciplinary and grievance hearings and the claiming of working tax credits).

Potentially fair reasons

From an employer's perspective it is important to be able to satisfy the tribunal that the true reason for the dismissal was one of those reasons classed as potentially fair in unfair dismissal law. Only once this has been achieved can the second question (the issue of reasonableness) be addressed. The potentially fair grounds for dismissal are as follows:

- Lack of capability or qualifications: if an employee lacks the skill, aptitude or physical health to carry out the job, then there is a potentially fair ground for dismissal.
- Misconduct: this category covers the range of behaviours such as disobedience, absence, insubordination and criminal acts.
- Redundancy: where an employee's job ceases to exist, it is potentially fair to dismiss the employee for redundancy.
- Statutory bar: when continuation of employment would be unlawful in itself such as occurs when a driver is disqualified or a foreign national's work permit expires.
- Some other substantial reason: this most intangible category is introduced in order to cater for genuinely fair dismissals for reasons so diverse that they could not realistically be listed. Examples include security of commercial information (where an employee's husband set up a rival company), irresolvable personality clashes and situations in which necessary changes are made to contracts by dismissing and instantly rehiring people on new terms.
- Dismissals arising from official industrial action after twelve weeks have passed.
- Dismissals that occur on the transfer of an undertaking where a valid ETO (economic, technological or organisational) reason applies.

Determining reasonableness

Having decided that potentially fair grounds for the dismissal exist, the tribunal then proceeds to consider whether the dismissal is fair in the circumstances. The test used by the tribunal in reaching decisions about the fairness of a dismissal is that of the reasonable employer. Tribunal members are not required to judge cases on the basis of what they would have done in the circumstances or what the best employers would have done. Instead they have to ask themselves whether what the employer did in the circumstances of the time fell within a possible band of reasonable responses. In practice this means that the employer wins the case if it can show that the decision to dismiss was one that a reasonable employer *might* conceivably have taken.

In assessing reasonableness tribunals always take a particular interest in the procedure that was used. Judges are also keen to satisfy themselves that the employer has acted broadly consistently in its treatment of different employees and that it has taken into account any mitigating circumstances that might have explained a deterioration in an employee's conduct or performance. In addition, they are required to have regard to the size and resources of the employer concerned. Higher standards are thus expected of a large PLC or a public sector body with a well-staffed HR department than of a small owner-managed business employing a handful of people. The former, for example, might be expected to wait for several months before dismissing someone on grounds of ill health, while a small business could justify dismissing after a few weeks because of the operational difficulties the absence was causing.

WINDOW ON PRACTICE

In recent years the Employment Appeals Tribunal (EAT), the court that hears appeals of cases decided in employment tribunals, has made a number of controversial judgments in dismissal cases which remind us of how employer-friendly unfair dismissal law is, provided procedures are followed correctly before a dismissal takes place.

- In *Weston Recovery Services* v. *Fisher (2010)* a tribunal found that a claimant should not have been dismissed on grounds of gross misconduct when he had failed properly to secure some seats in a minibus after he had borrowed it to drive to France on holiday.

- In *Look Ahead Housing & Care Ltd* v. *Rudder (2010)* an employee was overheard by a client making a discriminatory remark. There had been no consideration by the employer of whether an alternative sanction short of dismissal might have been more appropriate. Managers had simply dismissed on grounds of gross misconduct following a disciplinary hearing. So the tribunal found the dismissal to be unfair.

- In *Quadrant Catering* v. *Smith (2011)* the claimant had sworn in the presence of a manager, there being some doubt about whether her words had been directed at the manager. Here the tribunal ruled that dismissal on grounds of gross misconduct was too harsh a sanction in the circumstances and stated that it should be a last resort and not a first resort.

- In *Wincanton Group* v. *Stone (2012)* a driver was dismissed on grounds of misconduct. According to the employer the dismissal was justified despite his breach of the rules being relatively minor because he had already been given a formal warning following another unrelated incident. The first warning was at the time of his dismissal the subject of an ongoing appeal. The Employment Tribunal found the dismissal unfair, mainly because they considered the incidents to be too trivial to justify dismissal.

In all these cases the EAT said that the tribunals had misapplied the law by substituting their own views as to what it would have been reasonable for the employer to have done. That is not the job of an Employment Tribunal. If the facts are clear, a proper procedure has been carried out, and it is the genuine belief of the employer that the employee is guilty of misconduct, they have the right to dismiss. It may be harsh, but if the decision to dismiss falls into the band of possible reasonable responses, then the dismissal should be found to have been fair in law.

Lack of capability

A common reason for dismissal is poor performance on the part of an employee. The law permits dismissals for this reason. It also allows employers to determine for themselves what constitutes an acceptable level of performance in a job, provided of course that a broadly consistent approach is followed between different employees. However, such dismissals are only considered to be reasonable (and hence fair in law) if the employee concerned has both been formally warned about their poor performance at least once and given a reasonable opportunity to improve. Formality in this context means that a formal hearing has been held at which the employee has been entitled to be represented and after which there has been a right of appeal to a more senior manager.

Another aspect of employee capability is health. It is potentially fair to dismiss someone on the grounds of ill health which renders the employee incapable of discharging the contract of employment. Even the most distressing dismissal can be legally admissible, provided that it is not too hasty and that there is consideration of alternative employment. Employers are expected, however, to take account of any medical advice available to them before dismissing someone on the grounds of ill health. Normally, absences through sickness have to be frequent or prolonged in order for dismissal on the grounds of such absence to be judged fair, although absence which seriously interferes with the running of a business may be judged fair even if it is neither frequent nor prolonged. In all cases the employee must be consulted and effectively warned before being dismissed.

The law on ill-health dismissals was affected in important ways by the passing of the Disability Discrimination Act 1995 (the rights now form part of the Equality Act 2010). Dismissing someone who is disabled according to the definition given in the law, without first considering whether adjustments to working practices or the working environment would allow them to continue working, is unlawful. Reasonable adjustments might well include tolerance of a relatively high level of absence, especially where the employer is large enough to be able to cope perfectly well in the circumstances.

ACTIVITY 22.3

Some North American companies evaluate the individual performance of all their employees each year and use the scores to rank everyone in a particular department or division. They then fire the bottom 10% as matter of policy. The approach is known as 'stack ranking'.

Can you explain why such an approach would generally be unlawful in the UK? Should it be made lawful or remain unlawful?

Misconduct

The law expects employers to make a distinction between two classes of misconduct when dismissing employees or considering doing so. Misconduct is defined as a breach of the employers' rules.

Gross misconduct. This occurs when an employee commits an offence which is sufficiently serious to justify summary dismissal. To qualify, the employee must have acted in such a way as to have breached either an express term of their contract or one of the common law duties owed by an employee to an employer (see Chapter 22). In practice this means that their actions must be 'intolerable' for any reasonable employer to put up with.

Ordinary misconduct. This involves lesser transgressions, such as minor breaches of rules and relatively insignificant acts of disobedience, insubordination, lateness, forgetfulness or rudeness. In such cases the employer is deemed by the courts to be acting unreasonably if it dismisses as a result of a first offence. The dismissal would only be fair if, having been formally warned at least once, the employee failed to improve his or her conduct.

Employers have a wide degree of discretion when it comes to deciding what exactly does and does not constitute gross misconduct, and this will vary from workplace to workplace. For example, a distinction can be made between uttering an obscene swear word in front of colleagues (ordinary misconduct) and swearing obscenely to a customer (gross misconduct). While much depends on the circumstances, the tribunals also look carefully at an employer's established policies on matters of conduct. Where the disciplinary rules spell out clearly the type of conduct that will warrant dismissal then a dismissal for this reason may be fair. Conversely, if the rules are silent or ambiguous as to whether particular conduct warrants dismissal, a dismissal for a first offence may be unfair. It is important, therefore, for employers to set out in writing what standards of conduct they expect, to make clear what will be regarded as 'sackable misconduct', and to ensure that everyone is aware of these rules.

The second key principle in misconduct cases concerns procedure. Whether the individual is dismissed summarily for gross misconduct or after a number of warnings for ordinary misconduct, the tribunals look to see if a reasonable procedure has been used and satisfy themselves that the employer has followed any of its own procedures which go beyond the minimum standard set out in the ACAS code of practice. They thus ask questions such as the following:

- Was the accusation thoroughly, promptly and properly investigated by managers before the decision was made to dismiss or issue a formal warning?
- Was a formal hearing held at which the accused employee was given the opportunity to state their case and challenge evidence brought forward by managers?
- Was the employee concerned permitted to be represented at the hearing by a colleague or trade union representative?
- Was the employee treated consistently when compared with other employees who had committed similar acts of misconduct in the past?

Redundancy

Dismissal for redundancy is protected by compensation for unfair redundancy, compensation for genuine redundancy and the right to consultation before the redundancy takes place:

An employee who is dismissed shall be taken to be dismissed by reason of redundancy if the dismissal is attributable wholly or mainly to:

the fact that his employer has ceased, or intends to cease, to carry on the business for the purposes of which the employee was employed by him, or has ceased, or intends to cease, to carry on that business in the place where the employee was so employed,

or

the fact that the requirements of that business for employees to carry out work of a particular kind, or for employees to carry out work of a particular kind in the place where he was so employed, have ceased or are expected to cease or diminish. *(Employment Rights Act 1996, s. 139(1))*

Apart from certain specialised groups of employees, anyone who has been continuously employed for two years or more is guaranteed a compensation payment from an employer, if dismissed for redundancy. The compensation is assessed on a sliding scale relating to length of service, age and rate of pay per week. If the employer wishes to escape the obligation to compensate, then it is necessary to show that the reason for dismissal was something other than redundancy. The inclusion of age in the criteria for calculating redundancy payments has remained, despite the introduction of age discrimination law in 2006.

The employer has to consult with the individual employee before dismissal takes place, but when more than twenty employees are made redundant together there is also a separate legal obligation to consult collectively. Where a trade union is recognised, the consultation must be carried out with its officers. Otherwise some other body of employee representatives must be established for the purpose of consultation.

One of the most difficult aspects of redundancy for the employer is the selection of who should go. The traditional approach provides that people should leave on a last-in-first-out basis, or LIFO, as this provides a rough-and-ready justice with which it is difficult to argue from the point of view of consistency. It frees the employer from any obligation to choose on grounds of merit and is also inexpensive as the people who leave are those entitled to the least compensation. However, employers have tended to prefer other selection schemes in recent years. The preference nowadays is for one of two alternative types of approach.

- A matrix-type system in which a mix of criteria are used to score employees. Typically these include factors such as performance, qualifications, competence, future potential and attendance records.

- A selection-based system in which a new post-redundancy organisation structure is drawn up. Employees are then invited to apply for the jobs that will remain.

WINDOW ON PRACTICE

Packman Lucas Associates v. *Fauchon* (2012) [IRLR 721]

This case was about whether or not a reduction in hours in the absence of any accompanying reduction in headcount represents a 'diminution of work' as defined in redundancy law and can thus give rise to a redundancy situation. According to the Employment Appeal Tribunal the answer is 'yes'.

Mrs Fauchon was asked to work reduced hours and refused. She was therefore dismissed. She argued that while there had been no reduction in the number of employees at Packman, there had nonetheless been a redundancy situation because there was 'a reduced need for employees to carry out work of a particular kind'. In dismissing her for this reason her employers had therefore made her redundant and she was entitled to a redundancy payment.

Health and safety law

In the UK health and safety law can neatly be divided into two halves, representing criminal and civil spheres. The first is based in statute and is policed by the Health and Safety Executive and local authority inspectorates. The second relies on the common law and allows individuals who have suffered injury during the course of employment to seek damages against their employers. The former is intended to be preventative, while the latter aims to compensate individuals who become ill as a result of their work.

Criminal law

Health and safety inspectors potentially wield a great deal of power, but their approach is to give advice and to issue warnings except where they judge that there is a high risk of personal injury. They visit premises without giving notice beforehand in order to inspect equipment and make sure that the appropriate monitoring procedures are in place. They have a general right to enter premises, to collect whatever information they require and to remove samples or pieces of equipment for analysis. Where they are unhappy with what they find, inspectors issue improvement notices setting out recommended improvements and requiring these to be put in place by a set date. In the case of more serious lapses, where substantial risk to health is identified, the inspectors issue prohibition notices which prevent employers from using particular pieces of equipment until better safety arrangements are established. Breach of one of these statutory notices is a criminal offence, as is giving false information to an inspector. Over a thousand prosecutions are brought each year for non-compliance with a Health and Safety Executive Order, leading to fines and, where there is a potential risk of death or serious injury, to prison sentences of up to six months' duration.

The Health and Safety at Work etc. Act 1974 is the source of most health and safety law in the UK, under which more detailed sets of regulations are periodically issued. Its main purposes are as follows:

- to secure the health, safety and welfare of people at work;
- to protect the public from risks arising from workplace activities;
- to control the use and storage of dangerous substances;
- to control potentially dangerous environmental emissions.

The Act places all employers under a general duty 'to ensure, as far as is reasonably practicable, the health, safety and welfare at work' of all workers. In addition there are specific requirements to maintain plant and equipment, to provide safe systems of working, to provide a safe and healthy working environment, to consult with trade union safety representatives, to maintain an accident reporting book and to post on a noticeboard a copy of the main provisions contained in the 1974 Act.

Since 1974 numerous sets of regulations have been issued, many of a very specialised nature, to add to the more general principles established in the Health and Safety at Work Act. The most significant have been the following:

- The First Aid Regulations 1981 place employers under a general duty to provide adequate first aid equipment and facilities.
- The Control of Substances Hazardous to Health (COSHH) Regulations 1988 concern the safe storage and usage of potentially dangerous substances.
- The Management of Health and Safety at Work Regulations 1992 place a variety of duties on employers. Examples include regulations on the safe lifting of heavy loads, the prolonged use of video display units (VDUs) and the particular health and safety needs of pregnant workers.

- The Health and Safety (Consultation with Employees) Regulations 1996 require employers to consult collectively with their employees about health and safety matters irrespective of whether a trade union is recognised.

- The Health Act 2006 bans smoking in public spaces, including most workplaces and company vehicles in England. Equivalent legislation has been passed by the Scottish Parliament and the Welsh and Northern Irish Assemblies.

ACTIVITY 22.4

Draft a health and safety policy for your organisation. Include information about:

- General policy on health and safety.
- Specific hazards and how they are to be dealt with.
- Management responsibility for safety.
- How the policy is to be implemented.

Civil law

While distinct in origin and nature from the criminal sanctions, civil cases relating to health and safety are often brought alongside criminal proceedings in connection with the same incident. When someone is seriously injured or suffers ill health as a direct result of their work the health and safety authorities will bring a criminal prosecution, while the injured party will sue for damages in the civil courts. Most claims are brought under the law of negligence, the injured party alleging that the employer acted negligently in allowing him or her to become injured.

In such cases the courts have to be satisfied that the employer failed to act reasonably and that the injury or illness was sustained 'during the course of employment'. Central here, as in the criminal law, are the notions of foreseeability and risk assessment. Cases often hinge on what the employer knew at the time the injury was sustained and whether or not reasonable precautions in the form of training or the provision of equipment had been taken. Employers can thus defend themselves effectively by satisfying the court that little else could have been done by any reasonable employer to prevent the accident from occurring. Importantly the principle of vicarious liability applies in this field, so employers are legally liable for the negligence if one employee causes another to become injured.

In recent years people suffering from psychiatric injuries brought about from undue workplace stress have successfully brought claims. In practice, however, large sums by way of damages are only won where employees suffer two serious breakdowns, both of which are work related. Otherwise it is very difficult to satisfy a court that the risk of injury was genuinely 'reasonably foreseeable' and hence that the employer is liable.

Working time

Some of the most significant recent developments in the field of health and safety law have derived from the Working Time Regulations (1998), an example of law that was introduced into the UK rather reluctantly in order to meet European treaty obligations. The basic 'headline' entitlements are as follows:

- a limit of forty-eight hours per week;
- twenty-eight days' paid leave each year;
- twenty minutes' rest in any period of work lasting six hours or more
- eleven hours' rest in any one twenty-four-hour period;
- twenty-four hours' rest in any seven-day period;
- night workers limited to eight hours' work in any one twenty-four-hour period;
- free health checks for night workers
- special regulations restricting working time of young workers (i.e. 16–18 year olds).

On the surface this looks clear cut and straightforward, but this is not the case. The regulations are complex, running to more than 100 pages in length. What is more, parts of them do not apply in some situations, meaning that many workers in the UK are, in practice, either unprotected or only partially protected:

- The regulations allow for considerable flexibility because they allow employers to average time worked over a seventeen-week reference period.
- Anyone can if they wish formally 'opt out' of the forty-eight-hour week restriction by signing or writing a written declaration. Employers in the UK are lawfully able to make the signing of such an opt-out a requirement of employment. Staff are able at any time to 'opt' back in by informing their employer in writing and giving notice and cannot be victimised for exercising this right. This 'opt-out' arrangement only applies in the UK, and from time to time other European governments and institutions campaign for its removal.
- Workforce agreements can be established which allow an employer to vary the working time regulations in various ways. Where the majority of the workforce assent to a proposal in a vote, by signing up directly or via a trade union agreement, a workplace can adapt its interpretation of the working time regulations to suit its needs.

ACTIVITY 22.5

What is your view of the opt-out arrangement maintained by the UK? Should employers be able to make it a condition of employment that new starters sign such an agreement? Aside from the cost implications, what other disadvantages might follow from an employer perspective were opt-outs to be outlawed?

Family-friendly employment law

In recent years a significant contribution to the development of workplaces which offer a better work–life balance has been made via the introduction of new and enhanced employment rights which require employers to take account of the needs of people with family responsibilities. These are straightforward but have been highly significant both for employers who have to find ways of accommodating them and for the many employees who have benefited considerably. The key rights are as follows:

- The right for pregnant employees to take reasonable time off work to attend ante-natal medical appointments without losing any pay. Fathers also now have the right to attend up to two such appointments,

- The right for a mother to take time off before, during and after her baby is born. Most employed women are entitled to take six months' 'ordinary maternity leave' followed by a further six months' 'additional maternity leave'.

- The right to Statutory Maternity Pay (SMP) for a period of nine months while maternity leave is being taken. SMP is paid at the 'higher rate' for the first six weeks (90% of salary) and thereafter at the 'lower rate' (£139.58 per week in 2016).

- A right for fathers of new babies to take two weeks' paid paternity leave within the first fifty-six days of the birth.

- Since 2015 a mother has been able to transfer part of her paid maternity leave to the baby's father under a new 'shared parental leave' system. This enables a couple to take extended periods of time off at the same time during the first weeks of a child's life.

- A right for both parents of a child the right to take up to eighteen weeks' unpaid leave during the first eighteen years of a child's life.

- A right for parents and carers to take reasonable amounts of time off during working hours for urgent family reasons, employers being informed of the intention to take the leave 'as soon as is reasonably practicable'.

- Equivalent rights for parents of newly adopted children. Here, irrespective of gender, one parent can choose to take the maternity rights and the other the paternity rights.

Is employment law a benefit or a burden for businesses?

It is common for managers and owners of small businesses, as well as the journalists, politicians and employers' associations who support their interests, to argue that the extent of employment regulation is now so great as to be having a substantial, negative impact. At base this argument concerns economic competitiveness, it being said that regulation both adds unnecessary costs and stifles the capacity of organisations to act flexibly and opportunistically. The result is reduced international competitiveness because so many rival organisations are based in countries which have far less regulation to contend with. It follows, according to its critics, that employment law acts as a disincentive to job creation and also provides an incentive for UK-based organisations to 'export jobs' by relocating aspects of their operations overseas or by subcontracting them to overseas-based suppliers (CBI 2000).

There is no question that employment regulation adds to employers' costs, not least by taking up a good deal of management time. A survey carried out by the Chartered Institute of Personnel and Development found that two-thirds of HR managers in the UK spend over 20% of their time 'dealing with employment law issues', a further 25% spending over 40% of their time in this way (CIPD 2002). In addition to time spent making sure that an organisation is complying, there are further direct costs associated with the introduction of new measures. To this additional cost burden we can plausibly add lost opportunity costs. Although impossible to quantify at all accurately, it is reasonable to ask what benefits could accrue if managers were free to devote the time they spend dealing with employment law matters on value-adding activities instead.

A further argument contends that the effect of employment law, even if it is not the intention of legislators, is to harm the career interests of those groups who are afforded the most legal protection (e.g. ethnic minorities, disabled people and mothers with dependent children). This occurs because it makes organisations less likely to employ them.

The main arguments in favour of employment law relate to social justice and the need to reduce the extent to which people suffer unreasonably at the hands of prejudiced, negligent or bullying managers abusing the power their position gives them. It is necessary to protect employees via the law, just as it necessary to protect other vulnerable groups from injustice. Such arguments are strong, straightforward and accepted by most, although disagreements will always persist about where the balance should lie between protecting the interests of employees and that of employers. However, there are also influential economic arguments in favour of extensive employment protection legislation. The implication here is that regulation of the employment relationship does not just benefit employees, but that organisations and the economy generally have also stood to gain from its extension in recent decades.

There are a number of distinct strands that make up the economic argument in favour of employment law. The first has tended to be used by ministers introducing new legislation in the face of business opposition, it being argued that the most productive workplaces are those in which people are managed effectively and fairly. In requiring managers to treat their staff with dignity, fairness and in an equitable manner, employment regulation helps to raise employment standards. In turn this has positive benefits for businesses in terms of higher levels of motivation and productivity, lower levels of staff turnover and a healthy, high-trust employee relations climate. Employment law, it is argued, should hold no fears whatever for good employers. All it aims to do is to bring all employment practice up to that same broad standard.

The second strand of the argument relates directly to the issue of growing skills shortages among some key professional groups. The starting point here is the view that the inability of many employers to recruit and retain people with the skills and experience that they need constitutes a significant national economic problem which holds back economic growth (see Frogner 2002). It follows that the amelioration of skills shortages should properly be a significant public policy objective. Improving employment standards by forcing employers to treat their employees well helps to achieve this because it makes work more attractive than it otherwise would be. It follows that more people with a choice about whether to work or not choose to do so in a world of regulated employment than would if the employment relationships were unregulated. The result is a higher economic participation rate as women with young children, people with long-term ill-health issues and those who could afford to retire if they wanted to put their skills, at least for part of the time, at the disposal of the economy. High standards also help to attract into the country highly skilled migrant workers from overseas who might otherwise choose to work elsewhere.

The final, third strand of the argument concerns the UK economy's competitive position internationally. It is argued that highly developed economies such as the UK's cannot sustain themselves in the face of competition from developing and newly industrialised countries by competing on the basis of cost. There is no future for such a business strategy because wage levels in China, India and elsewhere are invariably much lower than is the case in Europe and, as a result, the goods and services that they produce will always be far cheaper (see Chapter 2). It follows that the UK, like many other countries, needs clearly to position itself as a high-wage, knowledge-based economy which produces innovative hi-tech goods and provides upmarket services. In order to achieve this organisations need to be encouraged to work in partnership with their employees and, particularly, to invest in their training. There is little economic incentive for employers to devote resources to extensive employee development programmes in environments characterised by high staff turnover and low-trust employment relationships. The government thus needs to intervene to push employers in this direction and employment law is one of several public policy tools that are used to achieve this. The long-term aim is thus to help sustain economic growth in a rapidly changing and highly competitive business environment.

The most persuasive conclusion to reach is that employment regulation is both a burden and a benefit to UK employers, although it is of less benefit to and a much greater burden for smaller businesses without the expertise and resources to ensure that they are managing within its requirements. It is a burden because it adds substantial costs and because it limits the freedom managers have to run their businesses in ways that they might otherwise wish to. However, it is also a benefit because it helps to raise employment standards throughout the country, making work more attractive to people who have skills and experience that they might otherwise choose not to make use of in the employment context. In the process it contributes to reduced staff turnover, helps to encourage later retirement, helps to create the conditions in which superior individual performance is more likely and, crucially, in which low-trust, adversarial industrial relations are less likely to emerge.

ACTIVITY 22.6

Where do you stand in this debate about employment legislation? Does it serve to underpin economic prosperity or reduce international competitiveness? What further measures would you welcome and which would you oppose?

SUMMARY PROPOSITIONS

22.1. In the space of a single generation UK workplaces have gone from being among the least regulated in the world to being among the most highly regulated.

22.2. At base the employment relationship is contractual. A legally binding agreement is formed when an employee starts working for an employer. Neither side can lawfully breach that contract and cause the other some kind of detriment without risking legal action and the requirement to pay some compensation.

22.3. Discrimination law has grown rapidly in recent years, extending to new grounds such as age, sexual orientation and religion or belief. Equal pay law requires men and women to be paid the same wage for doing work which is the same or which can be shown to be of equal value unless the employer can justify a difference on grounds other than sex.

22.4. Unfair dismissal law provides people with a right not to be dismissed for an unfair reason or in an unreasonable manner once they have completed two years' service with an employer.

22.5. The legal framework for health and safety includes both the criminal and civil law. The former is policed by health and safety inspectors; the latter provides a vehicle for those who suffer illness or injury as a result of their work to claim damages.

22.6. Family-friendly employment law has been very much extended in recent years and will be further extended in the future. It aims to help people better combine their work and domestic responsibilities.

22.7. Employment regulation increases the cost burden for employers and reduces their freedom of action, but in helping to ensure that reasonably high minimum standards are maintained in employee relations it also brings some economic advantages to organisations.

GENERAL DISCUSSION TOPICS

1. How far do you think that UK discrimination law is effective in achieving its aims? What could be done to make it more effective?

2. Should all unfair dismissal rights be extended to people who are not employees who have completed two years' service?

3. To what extent do you agree with the view that employment regulation now imposes so many restrictions and costs on employers as to make businesses based in the UK and other European countries uncompetitive internationally?

THEORY INTO PRACTICE

Trouble at the Big Top

All around towns across the country brightly coloured posters proclaim the imminent arrival of Geraldo Pecorino's traditional, family, travelling circus. Geraldo's round red face smiles out inviting all to gaze and wonder at Alice and Maximillian's amazing feats on the flying trapeze, to gasp in amazement as Little Fat Stan the human cannon ball is propelled at speed across the circus ring, to laugh at the crazy antics of Micky the clown and his chums, and to applaud as Daisy the elephant dances daintily on her hind legs. But in reality, Geraldo is not smiling at all. He is very worried about the future of his circus. His star performers may help bring in the crowds, but they are also causing him a variety of managerial headaches.

Alice is his longest-serving artiste. For thirty-five years, partnered by a succession of male trapeze stars, she has nightly swung and somersaulted high in the air above a safety net, before descending to take her bow. Unfortunately, over time the once lissom Alice has become less agile and has put on a great deal of weight. As a result, when she enters the ring in her leotard and climbs up to her trapeze the audience increasingly see her as a figure of fun. When she carries out her final triple somersault and falls into the safety net, the structure wobbles alarmingly, causing the audience to scream with laughter. The contrast with the much younger and very athletic Maximillian is becoming more and more obvious, and he is not happy. 'Find me a new partner,' he says, or 'I will find a better circus to work for.' But what can Geraldo do? Alice is well paid and popular among the troupe. For several months he has been able to placate Maximillian by saying that he cannot find a replacement for Alice, but now a perfect new partner for Maximillian has become available. A beautiful 18-year-old trapeze artist called Melanie who has the rare capacity to carry out a Russian-style, back-flip, quadruple somersault has left a rival circus and is begging Geraldo for a job. Can he sack Alice? Can he redeploy her? Redeployment would be preferable but the only suitable job he has for her would involve performing with Micky and his crazy clowns. Alice would get the laughs, but it would be much less well-paid work and undignified for a senior artiste with years of loyal service behind her.

Geraldo's second managerial headache concerns another long-serving employee. Jethro has for many years acted as keeper and trainer of Daisy the elephant. They are devoted to one another. Every day Jethro feeds her, cleans her wagon, takes her for walks, washes her and then, in the evening, the two of them perform together to the delight of the audience. For many this act is the highlight of the circus. But six months ago an unfortunate accident occurred. In the middle of their act a large light bulb exploded above the circus ring, which gave Daisy a terrible fright. She panicked and instead of continuing to dance, she charged at Jethro and tossed him into the air. He sustained serious back and neck injuries in this accident and has been in and out of hospital ever since. Geraldo now realises that Jethro will not be able to return to work again for many more months. Daisy is back to her old self and has apparently bonded well with her new keeper, Geraldo's daughter Romola. Jethro visits her when he can, but he comes with his carer and is unable to get up out of his wheelchair. What should Geraldo do? He is still paying Jethro but cannot afford to continue doing so for ever. Can he dismiss him? Should he try to reach a financial settlement, and if so would his insurance company reimburse him?

And finally, what is Geraldo to do about Little Fat Stan, his much-loved but increasingly awkward human cannon ball? Stan has worked in the circus for years, delighting generations of audiences with his acts. He started out as a tumbler, then as he got older he turned to fire-eating and knife swallowing, before winding up being fired nightly from a cannon across the ring through several paper hoops, and landing spectacularly in a meticulously placed bouncy castle. Stan is not happy. He feels his life is unfulfilled and he wants to change direction. Stan has dealt with his depression in the past by drinking heavily, but has now managed to stop. Instead he has found great solace by becoming an active Christian. He attends churches in each town that the circus visits and continually regales the other performers with stories about how his faith has changed his life. But this has caused difficulties for Geraldo because Stan has said that he will not in future be available to perform on Sundays or at any time over the Christmas and Easter periods. He has asked Geraldo if he could give up performing and assist him in a management role, taking responsibility for publicising the circus. Failing that he would like to run the box office. But these jobs are already taken and are not, in truth, suitable for Stan. Geraldo insists that he can only employ him as a specialist performer. What should Geraldo do? Mondays and Tuesdays are the days the circus does not put on a performance and on

➤ which everyone takes time off. Two performances are mounted every Sunday, and Easter and Christmas are periods when audiences increase substantially. Should he threaten to sack Little Fat Stan? Could he employ someone else to be a human cannon ball on Sundays, and reduce Stan's wages to compensate?

The worry of what to do about Stan, Jethro, Maximillian and Alice causes Geraldo to suffer many sleepless nights.

Questions

1 Geraldo decides that he has no choice but to employ Melanie as a replacement for Alice. He tells Alice that from next week onwards she will have to perform alongside Micky and his clowns. Her role will be to act as his foil and a victim of his many practical jokes. For the next six months she will be paid the same salary that she currently earns. After this date it will be reviewed.

2 Assuming that she is unhappy with Geraldo's decision, what possible legal claims might Alice be able to bring? What defences might Geraldo be able to deploy were Alice to take her case to an employment tribunal?

3 Geraldo decides to dismiss Jethro, offering him a one-off payment of £25,000 by way of a full and final settlement.

4 What possible legal claims could Jethro bring were he to reject Geraldo's offer? What action could Geraldo take to minimise his chances of losing these cases in court?

5 Geraldo decides to allow Little Fat Stan to take Sundays off and to take his annual leave over the Christmas and Easter periods. Another performer will be trained up to take his place at these times. In return Geraldo will reduce Stan's pay by 20%.

6 What possible legal claims might Stan be able to bring? How might Geraldo be able to defend himself were the dispute to reach a tribunal hearing?

FURTHER READING

An excellent book which analyses UK employment regulation in the round, explaining its purpose and debating its strengths and weaknesses from a variety of perspectives, is *Perspectives on Labour Law* by A.C.L. Davies (2009).

Sandra Fredman has written extensively on discrimination law. The key debates are discussed concisely and effectively in her book entitled *Discrimination Law* (2011).

There are several good textbooks on employment law. Those aimed primarily at management students rather than lawyers include those authored by Janice Nairns (2011), David Lewis and Malcolm Sargeant (2015), Brian Willey (2013) and Stephen Taylor and Astra Emir (2015).

REFERENCES

BBC (2011) 'Doctor Eva Michalak wins £4.5 million over discrimination', BBC New website, accessed 2016.

CBI (2000) *Cutting through Red Tape: The Impact of Employment Legislation*. London: Confederation of British Industry.

CIPD (2002) *Employment Law: Survey Report*. London: CIPD.

Davies, A.C.L. (2009) *Perspectives on Labour Law* (2nd edn.). Cambridge: Cambridge University Press.

Fredman, S. (2011) *Discrimination Law* (2nd edn.). Oxford: Oxford University Press.

Frogner, M.L. (2002) 'Skills shortages', *Labour Market Trends,* January.

The Guardian (2011) 'Doctor is awarded £4.5m compensation for workplace discrimination trauma', *Guardian* website, accessed 2016.

Lewis, D and, Sargeant, M. (2015) *Essentials of Employment Law* (13th edn.). London: CIPD.

Nairns, J. (2011) *Employment Law for Business Students* (4th edn.). London: Longman.

Taylor, S. and Emir, A. (2015) *Employment Law: An Introduction* (4th edn.). Oxford: Oxford University Press.

Willey, B. (2013) *Employment Law in Context* (4th edn.). London: FT/Prentice Hall.

LEGAL CASES

Grainger PLC & others v. *Nicholson* [2010] IRLR 4.

Look Ahead Housing & Care Ltd v. *Rudder* [2010] UKEAT/0163/10/JOJ.

Packman Lucas Associates v. *Fauchon* [2012] IRLR 721.

Quadrant Catering v. *Smith* [2010] UKEAT/0362/10/RN.

Weston Recovery Services v. *Fisher* [2010] UKEAT/0062/10/ZT.

Wincanton Group v. *Stone* [2011] UKEAT/0011/12.

CHAPTER 23

EQUAL OPPORTUNITIES AND DIVERSITY

THE OBJECTIVES OF THIS CHAPTER ARE TO:

1 Review the current employment experiences of employee groups most vulnerable to discrimination

2 Consider the extent to which the characteristics of these groups intersect to create multiple disadvantages

3 Analyse the differing approaches to achieving equality for these groups, in particular contrasting the more traditional equal opportunities approach with the management of diversity approach

4 Explore the implications which managing diversity has for organisations

In today's times of globalisation and demographic change, the workforce is becoming increasingly diverse and it is more important than ever for organisations to develop equal opportunity and diversity strategies to attract, develop and retain employees. Legislation, voluntary codes of practice and diversity and equality initiatives have resulted in some progress towards equal treatment for diverse groups, but there remains inescapable evidence of continuing discrimination. More recent approaches, under the banner of management of diversity, include the economic and business case for equality, the valuing and managing of diversity in organisations, culture change and the mainstreaming of equality initiatives. Such approaches are partly a response to the insufficient progress made from the equal opportunities route, yet there is only limited evidence that they have made a substantial difference. While diversity approaches offer some useful perspectives and practices, the underlying concepts also raise some issues and concerns. We consider issues relating to both equality of opportunity and diversity management in this chapter.

How 'equal' is the workforce?

The workforce in the UK has changed radically in the past fifty years, becoming more diverse in terms of gender, age, race and ethnicity, sexual orientation and political and religious beliefs, to name just some of the criteria against which employees may differ. Diversity can also extend beyond social category to include informational diversity (differences in terms of education, tenure and functional background) and value diversity (which includes differences in personality and attitudes) (CIPD 2011). We have therefore been necessarily selective in the groups we have chosen to discuss here and include the top five equality and diversity issues identified in a CIPD (2012a) survey, namely gender, racial/ethnic minorities, people who are disabled, older people and individuals who are lesbian, gay, bisexual or transsexual/intersex. We present evidence of the (lack of) equality of opportunity available to these diverse employee groups. We also discuss intersectionality, a concept of growing importance, which recognises that equality and diversity issues can combine to create multiple disadvantages that compound one another (see Harnois 2015). In our own work, for example, we have demonstrated how gender and age combine in ways that are problematic for women's career progression (Atkinson *et al*. 2015).

Gender

If **participation** in the labour force is an indication of decreasing discrimination then recent figures are encouraging. From 1971 to 2012, the UK female participation rate in employment increased from 56% to over 70% and 51% of the UK workforce is now female (van Wanrooy *et al*. 2013). Many women, however, work part time and, as we note in Chapter 7, this type of employment is often low paid, low skilled and insecure, so the over-representation of women in this type of employment hardly creates equality of opportunity.

More obvious signs of discrimination, such as in recruitment advertising, have largely disappeared and there is some evidence to suggest that women are beginning to enter some previously male-dominated occupations. For example, women have now been ordained as priests in the Church of England. Similarly, men are beginning to enter some previously female-only occupations, such as midwifery. However, there remains a high degree of subtle discrimination, for example in access to training and support for development and promotion, and not-so-subtle discrimination, as in the continued **gender segregation** in terms of both type and level of work. Care work is, for example, largely a female occupation (Atkinson and Lucas 2012) and senior management, particularly at board level, continues to be dominated by men (Broughton and Miller 2009). This is not simply a UK phenomenon, as both Ross (2010) and Metz and Harzing (2012) demonstrate in their respective accounts of female board-level exclusion in Australia and women's under-representation on international academic journal editorial boards. Board level diversity continues to attract great interest in the UK, as we outline in the following Window on practice.

WINDOW ON PRACTICE

Gender diversity in the boardroom

A recent CIPD (2015) survey reviews progress in appointing women to board level. It suggests that proportions in the period 2011–14 have increased from 12.5% to 22.8% in FTSE 100 companies and from 7.8% to 17.4% in FTSE 250 companies. While this is encouraging, it is still a long way from gender parity and women clearly continue to be under-represented at board level. CIPD argues that continued action is required and that only around one third of organisations take positive steps to increase female board-level representation. The report suggests that diversity across other characteristics including age, experience and culture is also essential to effective boards. Despite this, the report argues against imposition of mandatory quotas, suggested by the EU, in favour of the UK government's voluntary approach. This creates focus on the issue but allows for appointment on merit, rather than to meet some externally set target. Measuring and monitoring female participation is, however, essential to identify the current position and adopt initiatives to improve it. These initiatives include coaching and mentoring, female sponsorship and advocacy schemes and leadership development programmes.

Source: Adapted from CIPD (2015).

Pay differentials between men and women are still evident. While these began to narrow in the UK when the Equal Pay Act 1970 came into force in 1975, progress has been slow, and a gender pay gap still exists. According to 2015 data (http://www.equalpayportal.co.uk/statistics/), the gender pay gap for full-time employees stands at 9.4% and has narrowed slightly, by around 0.2%, since 2011. The average weekly rate for full-time women is £471 as against £567 for full-time men. Similar international patterns are again apparent, for example in Canada (Drolet and Mumford 2012) and Denmark (Gupta and Eriksson 2012). Recent research has also powerfully demonstrated that gender intersects with characteristics such as ethnicity and age to create multiple disadvantage in pay levels (Woodhams and Lupton, 2015).

IDS (2004) identifies a range of unintentional consequences of pay systems which prove to be a barrier to achieving equal pay, and these are shown in Table 23.1.

Equal pay remains high on policy-makers agendas. In recent years, the UK government has encouraged voluntary gender equality reporting via its 'Think Act Report' framework.

Table 23.1 Barriers to the achievement of gender-based equal pay

Starting pay is frequently individually negotiated	As men usually have higher previous earnings this means they can negotiate a higher starting rate
Length of service	Men generally have longer service and fewer career breaks, and while this may result in greater experience early in a career it is less of a performance-influencing factor as general length of service increases
Broadbanding	There is a lack of transparency in such systems and there is a lack of structured progression; managers are likely to have high levels of discretion and may be unaware of biases
Lack of equal access to bonus payments	There is evidence that appraisal ratings and assessments discriminate unfairly against minority groups
Market allowances not evenly distributed	Such allowances are more likely to be given to men
Different pay structures and negotiating bodies	As some jobs are done primarily by women and some primarily by men, direct comparisons are harder to make
Job evaluation	Such schemes often perpetuate old values and may be subject to managerial manipulation

Source: Based primarily on material in IDS (2004) 'Employers move on equal pay', *IDS Report*, No. 897, January, pp. 10–18.

The logic here was that identifying pay concerns would lead to action to address them. This has been much slower than desired and at the time of writing (April 2016), the government is consulting on measures to require organisations with at least 250 employees to report on their gender pay gaps (see www.gov.uk for further information). It is again anticipated that firms with large gender pay gaps will be forced into action through their publication.

Racial and ethnic groups

Racial and ethnic minority groups constitute around 9% of the UK labour market (van Wanrooy *et al*. 2013). Their labour market participation rates are, however, typically lower than for other groups in both the UK and elsewhere. This is thought to result from discrimination and is not restricted to the UK. In the Netherlands, for example, there is evidence of ethnic minority groups being marginalised, stigmatised and discriminated against in the labour market (der Laan Bouma-Doff 2008). There is also segregation in the UK across occupations, with ethnic minority male employees being disproportionately employed in sectors such as hotel and catering and manufacturing. Ethnic minorities further tend to be under-represented at senior levels of organisations, a study by Cook and Glass (2009) even suggesting that the appointment of ethnic minorities to senior positions in organisations can adversely affect share price. Racial discrimination may also happen less blatantly. Rana (2003) reports on a project designed to understand why ethnic minority managers are under-represented in senior levels of local government. The researchers found that in 360-degree feedback results the line managers' assessments of ethnic minority employees were less favourable for each individual than all other assessments, which were generally similar. This discrepancy did not occur when considering the ratings of white employees. Romero and Perez (2016) also show that race and ethnicity frequently intersect with gender to create further disadvantage for employees.

People with a disability

About 2% of the UK workforce is classified as disabled (van Wanrooy *et al*. 2013). Woodhams and Danieli (2000) demonstrate that people who have a disability face common barriers to full integration into society and yet are a very varied group in that impairments can vary in severity, stability and type. People with a disability are more likely to be unemployed than their able-bodied counterparts, and once unemployed they are likely to remain so for a longer period. Choice of job is often restricted for people with a disability, and where they do find work it is likely to be in low-paid, less attractive jobs, although disability discrimination legislation may have improved the lot of the disabled worker in the past decade (Woodhams and Corby 2007).

Age

Demographic changes, legislation and labour shortages have led to an increased recognition of the need for age equality and there is burgeoning research into older workers. In the UK labour market, 24% of workers are over 50 and this proportion continues to grow (van Wanrooy *et al*. 2013). However, research continues to report that age discrimination remains a significant problem (McCarthy *et al*. 2015), with older workers being commonly disadvantaged in terms of promotion and training, and these age biases being deeply ingrained (Riach 2009). For example, line managers have negative perceptions of older workers, seeing them as less able to cope with change, training or technology and less interested in their careers, more likely to be sick and to cost more money to employ. There are also, however, some positive stereotypes depicting older workers as more loyal and conscientious, having better interpersonal skills and lower turnover rates, more efficient and that their experience counteracts any age-related factors lowering productivity. The young also face labour market discrimination (Snape and Redman 2003) with over 1 million young people in the UK being not in employment, education or training (NEETs) (Burnham 2012). Age can again intersect with other equality issues to create multiple disadvantages, as we demonstrate in the following Window on practice.

WINDOW ON PRACTICE

The double disadvantage of gender and age for older women

This paper presents a narrative from a 50-something professional woman who is reflecting on her prospects in the late stages of her career. She outlines how ageism and sexism combine to create difficulty for her in fulfilling her career potential. She argues that her fragmented career, resulting from caring responsibilities, means that her skills and experience are less valued than a man's. She also reflects on her health and body and notes that little is known about managing menopause in the workplace. The stigma and taboo that surround it lead to ill-informed comparisons and negative judgements. Older women are overlooked amidst questions about what they can contribute organisationally that arise from both gender and age.

Source: Adapted from Atkinson *et al*. (2015).

Sexuality

Lesbian, gay, bisexual and transgender or intersex (LGBTI) discrimination is the most difficult to identify due to the fact that group membership may not be revealed, usually due to the anticipation of discrimination. It is therefore difficult to quantify the extent to which these groups experience active discrimination. The Business & Human Rights Resource Centre (www.business-humanrights.org) suggests that, despite policy rhetoric, homophobia and discrimination are still common in certain sectors, for example financial services. Rumens and Broomfield's research (2012), however, reports that gay policemen feel able to disclose their sexuality and are valued organisational members. There is also some evidence of pay discrimination on the grounds of sexuality, although these relationships are not well understood (Ahmed *et al*. 2011).

Stonewall (2016) adopts a Workplace Equality Index analysing the policies of organisations which support LGBTI employees. Each year, it makes awards to the best 100 employers in the UK. While this represents great progress in eradicating discrimination for these groups of employees, there is still a distance to go in achieving equality. Many of the top 100 employers in the Workplace Equality Index are large firms, smaller firms perhaps being slower to respond with formal policies on sexual orientation. Research by Day and Greene (2008), however, suggests that small firms may have advantages in promoting inclusiveness in terms of a positive work climate.

In summary

Discrimination and inequality are difficult to measure. Fevre *et al*. (2011), for example, analyse the UK government's Citizenship Survey to demonstrate that in 2011 nearly half the population felt they had been discriminated against in the previous year, but that most people did not think that they themselves were prejudiced. Nevertheless, discrimination and inequality remain in the workplace and are particularly evident for certain groups. There is also growing recognition that equality issues intersect to create multiple disadvantages for certain workers (Marfelt 2016). We now turn to the theoretical debate which underpins different organisational approaches to tackling discrimination and inequality.

ACTIVITY 23.1

Talk to people you know across a range of socially defined groups – gender, race, disability and older workers, for example. What are their experiences of discrimination in the workplace? To what extent do you think equality for these groups is apparent?

Different approaches to equality

There has been a continuing debate concerning the action that should be taken to alleviate the disadvantages that particular groups encounter. One approach, generally referred to as equal opportunities or a liberal approach, supports legislative action. Most recently in the UK this takes the form of the Equalities Act (2010), which prevents discrimination on the grounds of a number of 'protected characteristics' including race, disability, gender reassignment, sex, marriage and civil partnership, pregnancy and maternity, religion and belief, sexual orientation and age. A second approach, managing diversity, argues that legislation will not be effective and that a fundamental change to the attitudes and pre-conceptions held about these groups is required. The initial emphasis on legislative action was adopted in the hope that this would eventually affect attitudes. A third, more extreme, radical approach, which enjoys less support, comes from those who advocate legislation to promote positive or reverse discrimination to compensate for a history of discrimina-tion against specified groups and to redress the balance more immediately. In the UK, legislation provides for positive action, such as special support and encouragement, for disadvantaged groups, but not positive or reverse discrimination (discriminating in their favour), except for disability legislation. The labels 'equal opportunities' and 'manage-ment of diversity' are used inconsistently, and to complicate this there are different per-spectives on the meaning of managing diversity, so we draw out the key differences which typify each of these approaches, and offer some critique of their conceptual foundations and effectiveness.

The equal opportunities approach

The equal opportunities approach seeks to influence behaviour through legislation so that discrimination is prevented. It has been characterised by a moral and ethical stance pro-moting the rights of *all* members of society. This liberal approach concentrates on the equality of opportunity rather than the equality of outcome found in more radical approaches. The approach is based on the understanding that some individuals are dis-criminated against, for example in the selection process, due to irrelevant criteria. These irrelevant criteria arise from assumptions based on the stereotypical characteristics attrib-uted to them as members of a socially defined group, for example that women will not be prepared to work away from home due to family commitments or that a person with a disability will have more time off sick. The equal opportunities approach therefore seeks to formalise procedures so that relevant, job-based criteria are used (using job descriptions and person specifications) and discrimination is based on fair criteria, that is the ability to do the job.

Its rationale is to provide a 'level playing field' on which all can compete on equal terms. Differences between socially defined groups are glossed over, and the approach is generally regarded as one of 'sameness'. Positive action, not positive discrimination, is allowable in order that some may reach the level at which they can compete equally. For example, an organisation may advertise its vacancies in publications which target particular under-represented ethnic groups. Once it has generated a pool of applicants, however, it must not then use ethnic origin as a selection criterion.

Equal opportunities approaches stress disadvantaged groups, and the need, for exam-ple, to set targets for those groups to ensure that their representation in the workplace reflects their representation in wider society. Targets are needed in occupations where they are under-represented, such as firefighters, police officers and in the armed forces, where small numbers of ethnic minorities are employed or senior management roles where there are small numbers of women. These targets are not enforceable by UK legislation, in contrast to some other countries, but organisations have been encouraged to commit themselves voluntarily to improvement goals, and to support this commitment by putting in place measures to support disadvantaged groups such as special training courses and flexible employment policies.

WINDOW ON PRACTICE

Questioning quotas: diversity management practices in the United Arab Emirates

While not formalised in UK legislation, the use of quota systems to improve diversity is common in many countries. Quotas are, for example, cited in many Northern European countries as having made a substantial contribution to women's board-level representation. In the United Arab Emirates (UAE), quotas have been adopted to force the employment of home nationals who are often unemployed as a result of the appointment of foreign expatriate workers. There are, however, problems with the use of quotas. In the UAE, for example, they lead to the negative stereotyping of home nationals and to insecurity for expatriates, some of whom consider the quotas themselves to be discriminatory. While quotas have been in place in the UAE for over a decade, less than 1% of private-sector employees are home nationals. This failure can be ascribed to numerous causes, central to which are discourses of efficiency, merit and performance amid concerns that the employment of home nationals would negatively impact on business performance. Scepticism about government penalties for non-compliance has largely rendered the quota system ineffective.

Source: Adapted from Forstenlecher *et al.* (2012).

Problems with the equal opportunities approach

There is an assumption in the equal opportunities approach that equality of outcome will be achieved if fair procedures are used and monitored. In other words, if this is done it will enable any minority groups to achieve a fair share of what employment has to offer. Once such minority groups become full participating members in employment, the old stereotypical attitudes on which discrimination against particular social groups are based will gradually change, as the stereotypes will be shown to be unhelpful.

The assumption that fair procedures or procedural justice will lead to fair outcomes has not been borne out in practice. The focus of equal opportunities is on formal processes and yet it is not possible to formalise everything in the organisation. In addition, there has been criticism of the assumption that once members of minority groups have demonstrated their ability to perform in the organisation, this will change attitudes and beliefs in the organisation. Further, there can be a general lack of support within organisations, partly because equality objectives are not linked to business objectives and partly because equal opportunities have often been viewed as the concern of the HR function. A focus on disadvantaged groups may also alienate the large sections of the workforce not identified as such; for example, Atkinson and Hall (2009) demonstrate that workers adopting standard patterns resent the extra burden that colleagues (mainly female) working flexibly imposes upon them.

In summary the equal opportunities approach is often considered simplistic and to be attempting to treat the symptoms rather than the causes of unfair discrimination.

The management of diversity approach

The management of diversity approach concentrates on individuals rather than groups, and includes the improvement of opportunities for *all* individuals and not just those in minority groups. Hence managing diversity involves everyone and benefits everyone, which is an attractive message to employers and employees alike. Separate groups are not singled out for specific treatment.

The CIPD (2011) argues that managing diversity involves recognising the differences in people and valuing, respecting and using these differences to support business performance. So the focus is on valuing difference rather than finding a way of coping fairly with it. Whereas the equal opportunities approach minimised difference, the managing diversity approach treats difference as a positive asset.

This brings us to a further difference between the equal opportunities approach and the managing diversity approach, which is that the managing diversity approach is based on the economic and business case for recognising and valuing difference, rather than the moral case for treating people equally. Rather than being purely a cost, equal treatment offers benefits and advantages for the employer if it invests in ensuring that everyone in the organisation is valued and given the opportunities to develop his or her potential and make a maximum contribution. The practical arguments supporting the equalisation of employment opportunities are thus highlighted. The CIPD (2012a) suggests that business benefits can be summed up in three broad statements: that diversity enhances customer relations and market share; that it enhances employee relations and reduces labour costs; and that it improves workforce quality and performance in terms of diverse skills, creativity, problem solving and flexibility. Recent research also demonstrates that diversity reduces labour turnover (Ali *et al.* 2015).

A company that discriminates, directly or indirectly, against older or disabled people, women, ethnic minorities or people with different sexual orientations will be curtailing the potential of available talent. The financial benefits of retaining staff who might otherwise leave due to lack of career development or due to the desire to combine a career with family are stressed, as is the image of the organisation as a 'good' employer and hence its attractiveness to all members of society as its customers. Although the impact on performance is more difficult to assess, it is reasonable to assume that more satisfied and committed employees will lead to reduced absence and turnover levels. In addition, the value of different employee perspectives and different types of contribution is seen as providing added value to the organisation, particularly when organisational members increasingly reflect the diverse customer base of the organisation. This provides a way in which organisations can better understand, and therefore meet, their customer needs. The business case argument is likely to have more support from managers as it is less likely to threaten the bottom line. While these arguments may hold good in a buoyant economic climate, a recession does pose a threat to the business case argument as labour markets become less competitive. The CIPD (2012b) presents case studies of organisations which have sustained their diversity efforts even where their business case is less compelling, while Fenwick *et al.* (2011) demonstrate acceptance of the business case for diversity in Australia. This business case underpins many diversity initiatives as we outline in the following Window on practice.

WINDOW ON PRACTICE

White men still account for majority of Apple's top jobs in US

Apple has published figures suggesting that its workforce diversity is a matter of concern: almost three-quarters of senior employees are white males and the workforce as a whole similarly lacks diversity. Yet the firm recognises that diversity is fundamental to innovation, at the heart of Apple's business, and has pledged action. Recruitment is now focusing on under-represented groups and this has had some early success. Apple is also engaging in community education schemes to support minority groups in developing technology skills as a longer-term solution to improving its workforce diversity.

Source: Adapted from Churchard (2015).

Organisational culture is also central to managing diversity. Equal opportunity approaches tend to concentrate on behaviour and, to a small extent, attitudes, whereas management of diversity approaches recognise a need to go beneath this. So adopting a culture which treats people as individuals and supports them in developing their potential is critical, although the difficulties of culture change make this a very demanding task. Also, depending on the approach to the management of diversity, the culture of different groups within the organisation comes into play. For example, men and women may need managing and developing in different ways. Attending to the organisation's culture suggests a move away from seeing the individual as the problem, and requiring that the individual needs to change because he or she does not fit the culture. Rather, it is the organisation that needs to change so that traditional assumptions of how jobs are constructed and how they should be carried out are questioned, and looked at afresh.

In summary, managing diversity is considered to be a more integrated approach to implementing equality. Whereas equal opportunities approaches were driven by the HR function, managing diversity is seen to be the responsibility of all managers. And, as there are business reasons for managing diversity, it is argued that equality should not be dealt with as a separate issue, as with equal opportunities approaches, but integrated strategically into every aspect of what the organisation does; this is often called mainstreaming.

Table 23.2 summarises the key differences between equal opportunities and managing diversity.

Problems with the managing diversity approach

While many saw diversity management as revitalising the equal opportunities agenda and as a strategy for making more progress on the equality front, this progress has been slow to materialise. In reality, there remains the question of the extent to which approaches have really changed in organisations beyond changing the label. Redefining equal opportunities in terms of its 'business case' may just be a way of making it more palatable in today's climate. Apart from this there are some fundamental problems with the diversity management approach and different approaches are also apparent internationally, as we outline in the following Window on practice.

Table 23.2 Major differences between 'equal opportunities' approaches and 'management of diversity' approaches

Aspect	Equal opportunities	Managing diversity
Purpose	Reduce discrimination	Utilise employee potential to maximum advantage
Approach	Operational	Strategic
Case argued	Moral and ethical	Business case – improved profitability
Whose responsibility?	HR/personnel department	All managers
Focuses on	Groups	Individuals
Perspective	Dealing with different needs of different groups	Integrated
Benefits for employees	Opportunities improved for disadvantaged groups, primarily through setting targets	Opportunities improved for all employees
Focus on management activity	Recruitment	Managing
Remedies	Changing systems and practices	Changing the culture
Monitoring success	Changed processes	Business outcomes

WINDOW ON PRACTICE

'Hard' diversity policies and ethnic minority representation

Verbeek and Groeneveld's (2012) study investigates the effectiveness of three types of diversity policy in improving ethnic minority representation. These are:

- assigning responsibility for the policy within the organisation;

- tiebreak preferential treatment (i.e. selecting the ethnic minority candidate if the applicants are equally qualified);

- use of quotas.

These policy types are not legislated for in all countries but are legal in the Netherlands where the study was conducted.

The study demonstrated difficulties with all three policy types and their failure to increase ethnic minority representation. Assigning organisational responsibility for diversity matters did not lead to substantial action as it was 'content empty': that is, a policy instrument without a goal. Similarly, the use of quotas was 'form empty': that is, a goal without a policy instrument. Tiebreak preferential treatment was no more effective as it was either not implemented or implemented with effects opposite to those intended.

Source: Adapted from Verbeek and Groeneveld (2012).

Even within a single legislative framework, diversity management is complex and subject to differing interpretations, which we have so far ignored, and which focus on the prominence of groups or individuals. One approach is to identify and celebrate individual differences, and to expose and challenge prejudices via training. The second, more orthodox, approach is where the organisation seeks to develop the capacity of all.

The most common approach to the management of diversity is based on individual contribution rather than on group identity. The *individualism* approach is based on dissolving random differences, not those that accrue due to membership of a particular social group. The advantage of this approach is that it is inclusive and involves all members of the organisation. An alternative emphasis in the management of diversity is that of *valuing differences* based on the membership of different social groups. Following this approach would mean recognising and highlighting differences, and being prepared to give special training to groups which may be disadvantaged and lack self-confidence, so that all in the organisation feel comfortable. This could, however, lead to reinforcement of group-based stereotypes and, indeed, problems which can result from a more diverse workforce, for example increased conflict.

A significant criticism of managing diversity is its basis in the 'business case', which is unreliable because it will only work in certain contexts. For example, where skills are easily available there is less pressure on the organisation to promote and encourage the employment of minority groups. Not every employee interacts with customers, so if image and customer contact are part of the business case this will apply only to some jobs and not to others. Also some groups may be excluded. For example, there is no systematic evidence to suggest that disabled customers are attracted by an organisation which employs disabled people. UK managers are also driven by short-term budgets and the economic benefits of equality may only be reaped in the longer term. Knights and Omanovi (2016) argue that a reliance on the business case may lead to the failure of diversity management if managers are sceptical about it.

In terms of implementation of a diversity approach there are also difficulties. Foster and Harris (2005) in their research in the retail sector found that it was a concept that lacked clarity for line managers in terms both of what it is and of how to implement it within anti-discrimination laws, and some were concerned that it may lead to feelings of unfairness and claims of unequal treatment. There are also concerns about whether diversity management, which originated in the USA, will travel effectively to other countries where the context is different, especially in terms of the demographics and the history of equality initiatives. Indeed, there are concerns about whether diversity can be managed at all given that individual differences derive from complex societal constructions far beyond the organisation's influence.

In a recent Provocation Series article in *Human Resource Management Journal*, Kulik (2014) argues that research evidence into the practical application of diversity policies at the organisational level is lacking. Our discussion so far would seem to indicate limited understanding of some key issues and we echo her call for further research.

Equal opportunities or managing diversity?

Are equal opportunities and managing diversity completely different things? If so, is one approach preferable to the other? For the sake of clarity, earlier in this chapter we characterised a distinct approach to managing diversity which suggests that it is different from equal opportunities. However, as we have seen, managing diversity covers a range of approaches and emphases, some closer to equal opportunities, some very different.

Much of the management of diversity approach suggests that it is superior to and not compatible with the equal opportunities approach. There is, however, increasing support for equal opportunities and managing diversity to be viewed as mutually supportive and for this combination to be seen as important. Dickens (2006) suggests that social justice and economic efficiency are increasingly being presented as complementary, although there is so far a lack of guidance about how this can be done in practice. To see equal opportunities and management of diversity as *alternatives* threatens to sever the link between them and may therefore be detrimental to organisational objectives. Legislation on equality may support diversity approaches in preventing discrimination which arises from market forces (Dickens 2006) and be of value in setting minimum standards (Woodhams and Lupton 2006).

Implications for organisations

Equal opportunities and managing diversity: strategies, policies and plans

The Workplace Employee Relations Survey 2011 (WERS) found that 76% of organisations had equal opportunities or diversity policies or statements, up from 73% in 2004 and 64% in 1998 (van Wanrooy *et al*. 2013). The public sector and larger organisations were more likely to have policies than smaller ones, which means that the majority of the labour force are in organisations where such a policy exists. In addition, a policy was more likely to exist in organisations where there was union recognition and where there was an employment relations specialist (even allowing for size). It would be a mistake, however, to assume that all policies cover all potentially disadvantaged groups: the CIPD (2006) found that while 93% of organisations which responded to its survey did have a diversity policy, the disadvantaged groups covered by these were very variable, and many did not cover all the groups for which there is legislative protection. Similarly, policies may not cover all organisational activity. Woodhams and Corby (2007) suggest, for example, that many organisations have policies in place which cover the recruitment but not the promotion or career progression of those with disabilities. Further, WERS indicates that, despite having a policy, few organisations seek actively to prevent discrimination; for example, the overwhelming majority do not monitor recruitment and selection or promotion policies or review relative pay rates.

Despite the prevalence of policies there is always the concern that having a policy is more about projecting the right image than about reflecting how the organisation operates. For example, reports abound that job applications from those of minority ethnic origin are less favourably received than those from white UK applicants. Creegan *et al*. (2003) investigated the implementation of a race equality action plan and found a stark difference between paper and practice. Line managers who were responsible for implementing the plan were operating in a devolved HR environment and so had to pay for advice, training and support from HR specialists. The consequence of this was that in order to protect their budgets they were reluctant to seek help. Employees felt that there was no ownership of the strategy or the plan within the organisation by senior or middle managers. Further, Kirton and Healey's (2009) study of the use of competencies to promote equality and diversity in the selection of judges suggests that, while competencies can give an impression of fairness, they are nevertheless interpreted by human actors. This gives rise to the continuing exercise of bias and prejudice.

ACTIVITY 23.2

Consider the equal opportunities and diversity policies in your own organisation, or another with which you are familiar.

1 To what extent does practice match policy?

2 Explore the reasons for the achievement of a match or mismatch.

A process for managing diversity

There are many prescriptions for developing diversity policies and strategies. We draw here on the key elements suggested by a recent CIPD report (2012a):

- Strategy: policies must have board- and senior-level support and this must be sustained over a lengthy period, not as a one-off initiative. The strategy should support business goals, support fairness and inclusion and be legally compliant. Line managers should be supported in policy implementation and empowered to take decisions at local level. The strategy should also be integrated with other HR policies and be effective internationally (where applicable).

- Workplace behaviour: respect and dignity must be consistently valued and all organisational members should understand their role in promoting equality. Bullying and harassment must not be tolerated.

- Communication: open communications and consultation are essential and should draw on a variety of methods such as intranets and organisational magazines.

- Training: equality and diversity concepts should be central to all training and awareness-raising programmes may be helpful. The concepts should also be part of induction and line manager training.

- Measurement: regular audits are essential to review and evaluate progress and demonstrate business benefits. Both organisational and employee data, possibly using employee attitude surveys, should be used. Equality and diversity objectives should be built into job descriptions and performance review. Benchmarking, networking and celebrating success will also promote and reinforce equality and diversity.

While the ideal may be for organisations to work on all aspects of diversity in an integrated manner, the reality is often that organisations will target specific issues or groups at different times.

ACTIVITY 23.3

Prepare a strategy for managing diversity which would be appropriate for your organisation, or one with which you are familiar.

SUMMARY PROPOSITIONS

23.1. The essence of much HR work is to discriminate between individuals. The essence of equality is to avoid unfair discrimination. Unfair discrimination often results from people being treated on the basis of limited and prejudiced understanding of the groups to which they belong rather than on the basis of an assessment of them as individuals. People are not always aware when they are discriminating unfairly.

23.2. Legislation can have only a limited effect in achieving equality, and does not change attitudes, beliefs and cultures and structures. Organisations and their cultures, processes and structures are founded on the needs of the dominant group and individuals from other groups are expected to adapt to this norm. This explains why progress towards equality of opportunity has been very slow.

23.3. Equal opportunities approaches highlight the moral argument for equal treatment, whereas managing diversity highlights the business case.

23.4. Actual changes in practice relating to equalising opportunity are taking place very slowly, and only long-term organisational transformation is likely to support equality.

23.5. Equal opportunities approaches and the management of diversity are best viewed not as alternatives, but as complementary approaches which need to be interrelated.

GENERAL DISCUSSION TOPICS

1. To what extent are equality of opportunity and managing diversity mutually supportive?

2. Thinking about Cook and Glass's (2009) findings that the appointment of racial/ethnic minorities to top management positions can have a negative impact on share price:

- Why do you think that this is the case?
- How could organisations try to address this?

THEORY INTO PRACTICE

A key skill of the international manager is harnessing diversity across a huge variety of cultures. This requires consideration of varying legal, cultural and demographic influences and, outside of Europe, anti-discrimination legislation may be lacking. Indeed, there may well be an absence of policy or organisational interventions to promote equality and diversity. Understanding of diversity management is essentially a western concept that may not translate well into other cultural or national contexts. Business strategies that develop understanding of local contexts and circumstances are, therefore, essential to the international manager, as are coping strategies to deal with ethical dilemmas that may arise. There are a series of questions that managers can ask themselves to determine appropriate actions in difficult situations, which include:

- Is the practice of concern acceptable? Different approaches may apply and derive from the host country's level of development. If this is the case, would the manager's home country have tolerated the practice at a similar stage? If so, the practice should be accepted. If it would not have been tolerated at a similar stage of development in the home country, further questioning is required.

- Is it possible to continue to trade in the host country while accepting the practice? Does the practice violate fundamental human rights? Dependent on the answers, the manager may have to refuse to accept the practice and may need to challenge the practice.

The international manager should, however, proceed with caution and take advice as to the implications of this refusal and how best to frame it.

The international manager must draw heavily on diversity as an effective mechanism of team management. A secure environment for the expression of ideas and communication should be created and recognition of cultural differences should again be recognised. In certain cultures, for example, it may be seen as disrespectful to express views that challenge those of the manager. It is also essential to be aware of and account for local cultural influences that may impact on working practices. Religion is a good example in that it may both affect working patterns, given for example the need to pray, and create work group tensions, where for example the group comprises members drawn from different religions. Similarly, if there is a dominant group, they may have undue influence and other important diversity issues may be neglected. It is important to be alert to cultural issues that may influence working relationships in order to build respect and value dignity.

Gender is also a critical issue. Most international managers are men, which may result from organisations' reluctance to send women abroad. This is particularly so where it is unusual for women to work, especially at senior levels, in the host country. This male dominance itself leads to limited diversity understanding among international managers.

Questions

1 What examples of cultural diversity likely to be faced by the international manager can you think of?

2 What impact might these examples have on work groups and how could this be addressed?

3 How could the dominance of men as international managers be addressed?

Source: Adapted from CIPD (2011) *Diversity and International Management: Factsheet*. London: CIPD.

FURTHER READING

Knights, D. and Omanovi, V. (2016) '(Mis)managing diversity: Exploring the dangers of diversity management orthodoxy', *Equality, Diversity and Inclusion: An International Journal*, Vol. 35, pp. 5–16.

The authors challenge the orthodoxy of diversity management, in large part because of its reliance on a business case approach but also because it displaces all other equality approaches and ignores socio-historical context. They argue that the business case tends to overshadow consideration of human rights, equality and justice and that, if managers are sceptical of the business case, they may abandon diversity altogether.

Cook, A. and Glass, C. (2009) 'Between a rock and a hard place: Managing diversity in a shareholder society', *Human Resource Management Journal,* Vol. 19, No. 4, pp. 393–412.

This is a fascinating study examining whether the appointment of racial/ethnic minorities to top management positions has a different impact on share price than the appointment of Caucasians to equivalent positions. The findings suggest that market reaction to the appointment of racial/ethnic minorities in corporate leadership positions is significant and negative, while the market's reaction to the appointment of Caucasians is significant and positive. The authors suggest, however, that the negative market reaction to the appointment of racial/ethnic minorities can be mitigated by the explicit incorporation of diversity into organisation strategy.

Rumens, N. and Broomfield, J. (2012) 'Gay men in the police: Identity disclosure and management issues', *Human Resource Management Journal*, Vol. 22, pp. 283–98.

This is an interesting article which provides a useful counterpoint to much of the more negative literature which reports discrimination and stereotyping of LGBT workers, especially in traditionally masculine cultures such as the police force. The authors argue that gay police officers do not expect to be stigmatised and seek opportunities to disclose their sexuality. They appear to be openly managed and valued as organisational members.

REFERENCES

Ahmed, A., Andersson, L. and Hammarstedt, L. (2011) 'Inter- and intra-household earnings differentials among homosexual and heterosexual couples', *British Journal of Industrial Relations,* Vol. 49, s258–78.

Ali, M., Metz, I. and Kulik, C. (2015) 'Retaining a diverse workforce: The impact of gender-focused human resource management', *Human Resource Management Journal*, Vol. 25, pp. 580–99.

Atkinson, C., Ford, J. and Harding, N. (2015) 'The aspirations and expectations of a late-career professional woman', *Work, Employment and Society,* Vol. 29, pp. 1019–28.

Atkinson, C. and Hall, L. (2009) 'The role of gender in various forms of flexible working', *Gender, Work and Organisation,* Vol. 16, pp. 650–66.

Atkinson, C. and Lucas, R. (2012) 'Policy and gender in adult social care work in England', *Public Administration,* doi: 10.1111/j.1467–9299.2012.02040.x.

Broughton, A. and Miller, L. (2009) 'Encouraging women into senior management positions', *Research Report 462.* London: Institute for Employment Studies.

Burnham, J. (2012) 'Young jobless Neets still top one million' [online]. London: BBC. Available at: www.bbc.co.uk/news/education-20444524 (accessed 24 February 2013).

Churchard, C. (2015) 'Apple's recruiters prioritise diversity as figures show improvement is needed' [online]. London: CIPD. Available: http://www.cipd.co.uk/pm/peoplemanagement/b/weblog/archive/2015/08/17/apple-s-recruiters-prioritise-diversity-as-figures-show-improvement-is-needed.aspx.

CIPD (2006) *Diversity in Business: How much progress have employers made? First findings.* London: CIPD.

CIPD (2011) *Diversity and International Management: Factsheet.* London: CIPD.

CIPD (2012a) *Diversity and Inclusion: Fringe or fundamental?* London: CIPD.

CIPD (2012b) *Game on! How to keep diversity progress on track*. London: CIPD.

CIPD (2015) *Gender-Diversity in the Boardroom: Reach for the Top*. London: CIPD.

Cook, A. and Glass, C. (2009) 'Between a rock and a hard place: Managing diversity in a shareholder society', *Human Resource Management Journal*, Vol. 19, No. 4, pp. 393–412.

Creegan, C., Colgan, F., Charlesworth, R. and Robinson, G. (2003) 'Race equality policies at work: Employee perceptions of the "implementation gap" in a UK local authority', *Work, Employment and Society*, Vol. 17, pp. 617–40.

Day, N. and Greene, P. (2008) 'A case for sexual orientation diversity management in small and large organisations', *Human Resource Management*, Vol. 47, pp. 637–54.

Der Laan Bouma-Doff, W. (2008) 'Concentrating on participation: Ethnic concentration and labour market participation of four ethnic groups', *Journal of Applied Social Science Studies* Vol. 128, pp.153–73.

Dickens, L. (2006) 'Re-regulation for gender equality: From "either/or" to "both"', *Industrial Relations Journal*, Vol. 37, pp. 299–309.

Drolet, M. and Mumford, K. (2012) 'The gender pay gap for private-sector employees in Canada and Britain', *British Journal of Industrial Relations*, Vol. 50, pp. 529–53.

Fenwick, M., Costa, C., Sohal, A. and D'Netto, B. (2011) 'Cultural diversity management in Australian manufacturing organisations', *Asia Pacific Journal of Human Resources*, Vol. 49, pp. 494–507.

Fevre, R., Grainger, H. and Brewer, R. (2011) 'Discrimination and unfair treatment in the workplace', *British Journal of Industrial Relations*, Vol. 49, s207–35.

Forstenlecher, I., Lettice, F. and Ozbilgin, M. (2012) 'Questioning quotas: Applying a relational framework for diversity management practices in the United Arab Emirates', *Human Resource Management Journal*, Vol. 22, pp. 299–315.

Foster, C. and Harris, L. (2005) 'Easy to say, difficult to do: Diversity in retail management', *Human Resource Management Journal*, Vol. 15, pp. 4–17.

Gupta, N. and Eriksson, T. (2012) 'HRM practices and the within-firm gender wage gap', *British Journal of Industrial Relations*, Vol. 50, pp. 554–80.

Harnois, C. (2015) 'Are perceptions of discrimination unidimensional, oppositional, or intersectional? Examining the relationship among perceived racial–ethnic-, gender-, and age-based discrimination', *Social Production of Difference*, Vol. 57, pp. 470–87.

IDS (2004) 'Employers move on equal pay', *IDS Report*, No. 897. London: IDS.

Kirton, G. and Healey, G. (2009) 'Using competency-based assessment centres to select judges: Implications for diversity and equality', *Human Resource Management Journal*, Vol. 19, pp. 302–18.

Knights, D. and Omanovi, V. (2016) '(Mis)managing diversity: Exploring the dangers of diversity management orthodoxy', *Equality, Diversity and Inclusion: An International Journal*, Vol. 35, pp. 5–16.

Kulik, C. (2014) 'Working below and above the line: The research–practice gap in diversity management', *Human Resource Management Journal*, Vol. 24, pp. 129–44.

Marfelt, M. (2016) 'Grounded intersectionality', *Equality, Diversity and Inclusion: An International Journal*, Vol. 35, pp. 31–47.

McCarthy, J., Heraty, N., Cross, C. and Cleveland, J. (2015) 'Who is considered an 'older worker'? Extending our conceptualisation of 'older' from an organisational decision maker perspective', *Human Resource Management Journal*, Vol. 24, pp. 374–93.

Metz, I. and Harzing, A. (2012) 'An update of gender diversity in editorial boards: A longitudinal study of management journals', *Personnel Review*, Vol. 41, pp. 283–300.

Rana, E. (2003) 'Council appraisals discriminate', *People Management,* Vol. 9, p. 11.

Riach, K. (2009) 'Managing difference: Understanding age diversity in practice', *Human Resource Management Journal,* Vol. 19, pp. 319–35.

Romero, M. and Perez, N. (2016), 'Conceptualizing the foundation of inequalities in care work', *American Behavioural Scientist,* Vol. 60, pp. 172–88.

Ross, E. (2010) 'AHRI: Mind the gap', *People Management,* April, www.peoplemanagement.co.uk/pm/articles/2010/04/ahri-mind-the-gap.htm (accessed 5 June 2013).

Rumens, N. and Broomfield, J. (2012) 'Gay men in the police: Identity disclosure and management issues', *Human Resource Management Journal,* Vol. 22, pp. 283–98.

Snape, E. and Redman, T. (2003) 'Too old or too young? The impact of perceived age discrimination', *Human Resource Management Journal,* Vol. 13, pp. 78–89.

Stonewall (2016) *Workplace Equality Index.* London: Stonewall.

Stonewall (2016) *Top 100 Employers.* London: Stonewall.

Van Wanrooy, B., Bewley, H., Bryson, A., Forth, J., Freeth, S., Stokes, L. and Wood, S. (2013) *The 2011 Workplace Employment Relations Study: First Findings.* London: BIS.

Verbeek, S. and Groeneveld, S. (2012) 'Do "hard" diversity policies increase ethnic minority representation? An assessment of their (in)effectiveness using administrative data', *Personnel Review,* Vol. 41, pp. 647–64.

Woodhams, C. and Corby, S. (2007) 'Then and now: Disability legislation and employers' practices in the UK', *British Journal of Industrial Relations,* Vol. 45, pp. 556–80.

Woodhams, C. and Danieli, A. (2000) 'Disability and diversity: A difference too far?', *Personnel Review,* Vol. 29, pp. 402–17.

Woodhams, C. and Lupton, B. (2006) 'Gender-based equal opportunities policy and practice in small firms: The impact of HR professionals', *Human Resource Management Journal,* Vol. 16, pp. 74–97.

Woodhams, C. and Lupton, B. (2015) 'The snowballing penalty effect: Multiple disadvantage and pay', *British Journal of Management,* Vol. 26, pp. 63–77.

CHAPTER 24

EMPLOYABILITY: SKILLS IN EMPLOYEE RELATIONS

THE OBJECTIVES OF THIS CHAPTER ARE TO:

1 Explain skills in mediation, which aims to resolve disagreements between individuals

2 Explain skills in disciplinary and grievance interviewing, which aims to resolve disagreements between employer and employee

24.a. Mediation

Mediation is resolving a disagreement, a misunderstanding or the breakdown of a relationship between two parties with the assistance of a third: the third party acting as honest broker. Sometimes it is a straight alternative to negotiation in industrial relations. The parties are sufficiently estranged that they will not be able to resolve their difficulties on their own, so a mediator is asked to chair joint meetings, partly to clarify the differences and partly to suggest ways forward. This is slightly different from arbitration, which is where the arbitrator proposes a solution rather than a way for the parties to move forward to find their own.

Similar in process, but different in nature, is disagreement and relationship breakdown between individuals, most dramatically seen in divorce but also to be found in employment situations. If colleagues need to work closely together but have a row or begin to suspect the other's motives, then mediation may be helpful.

WINDOW ON PRACTICE

Since the head designer had left suddenly, Barry had been asked to stand in pending a permanent appointment being made. Interviews were held among internal applicants, including Barry, who was surprised and bitterly disappointed when Julia was appointed head designer. As Barry put it to the HR Manager, ' . . . a relative newcomer of 28 with less experience and far too big for her boots.' When Julia had been offered the job she had said, 'Barry won't like it, but it really would be a good idea if he moved on. He's good at the detail, but very old-fashioned.' The Divisional Director believed Barry was essential to the smooth running of the department and asked the HR Manager to mediate. The HR Manager followed the general plan described below.

The format outlined here will sound more formal and rigid than that in most situations in normal working life. Often mediation will occur spontaneously or the need will come at a very difficult time when two people have just had a flaming row and the mediator is inadvertently thrust into a mediator role. Sometimes it will be more like the Barry/Julia situation, but setting it out in this way illustrates a pattern which usually works, despite the need to modify it to suit specific situations.

Mediator briefing

The mediator finds out as much as possible about the problem beforehand, e.g. who has said what? To whom? What are the real points of contention? This will mainly be hearsay.

Introductory remarks

The mediator will wait until both parties are present and then make introductions. The physical setting will be controlled so that no party feels threatened. The mediator then gives an opening statement that outlines the role of the participants and demonstrates the mediator's neutrality. Some mediators will make comments about what they see as the issue and confirm the case data if briefs have been pre-submitted. Next, the mediator defines protocol and sets the timeframe for the process. Then the mediator will briefly recapitulate what it is that he or she has heard as the issues.

The introductory remarks set out the ground rules for the mediation. These are what help the mediation move along smoothly. The mediator will usually ask that if lawyers are present, they can confer, but the clients should speak for themselves. Parties should not interrupt each other; the mediator will give each party the opportunity to fully share their side of the story.

Statement of the problem by the parties

After the introductory remarks, the mediator will give each side the opportunity to tell their story uninterrupted. Most often, the person who requested the mediation session will go first. The statement is not necessarily a recital of the facts, but it is to give the parties an opportunity to frame issues in their own minds, and to give the mediator more information on the emotional state of each party. The rationale behind the statement of the problem is not a search for the truth; it is just a way to help solve the problem.

Information gathering

The mediator will ask the parties open-ended questions to get to the emotional undercurrents. The mediator may repeat back key ideas to the parties, and will summarise often. This helps the mediator build rapport between the parties, especially when a facilitative style is used.

Problem identification

This might also be part of other segments. The mediator tries to find common goals between the parties while figuring out which issues are going to be easiest to settle or those to tackle.

Bargaining and generating options/reaching an agreement

Once the participants are committed to achieving a settlement, the mediator will begin a brainstorming session to explore potential solutions. This can lead to a final agreement, which diffuses the conflict and provides a new basis for future relations.

The mediator may decide to hold private sessions with both parties in order to move things along. The goal is to find some common ground by exploring lots of options, and to bring about possible solutions for the parties to think about. Parties can also entertain alternative solutions to their problems without committing themselves to offering the solutions as concessions.

SUMMARY PROPOSITIONS

24.a.1. Mediation is trying to resolve a damaging disagreement between colleagues by the intervention of a third person, whose neutrality is accepted by the parties.

24.a.2. The intervention is to find a way forward that enables the parties to find their own solution. It is different from arbitration, where the arbitrator has the power to impose a solution.

GENERAL DISCUSSION TOPICS

24.a.1. For a group, select a news report about a disagreement between parties, about which people in the group have at least a superficial knowledge. What would be a fruitful approach to settlement for a mediator to adopt?

24.a.2. For an individual, think of a situation in your own life where you tried to help settling an argument by acting as honest broker. What would you now do differently?

24.b. The Disciplinary or Grievance Interview

If the appraisal interview is the hardest aspect of management for any manager to undertake, disciplinary interviewing is certainly the least popular, talking to people when things have gone wrong and have to be sorted out. At some point this involves a meeting between a dissatisfied manager and an employee who is seen as the cause of that dissatisfaction. Procedures can do no more than force meetings to take place: it is the meetings themselves that produce answers.

Our approach is thorough, step by step, even painstaking, and does not lay down a rigid method that must always be followed: it is to illustrate the processes and it is directed at finding a solution to a problem of dissatisfaction. It is not a quick-fix method of dismissing someone as quickly as possible, but to formulate an approach to the interview that achieves an adjustment in attitude, with the changed attitude being confirmed by subsequent experience. The conflict of interest between the parties is resolved and the interview only succeeds when there is that confirmation. Figure 24.1 maps the processes.

The nature of grievance and disciplinary interviewing

Many grievance or discipline interviews are simple: giving information, explaining work requirements and delivering rebukes, but from time to time every manager will need to use a problem-solving approach, involving sympathy, perception, empathy and the

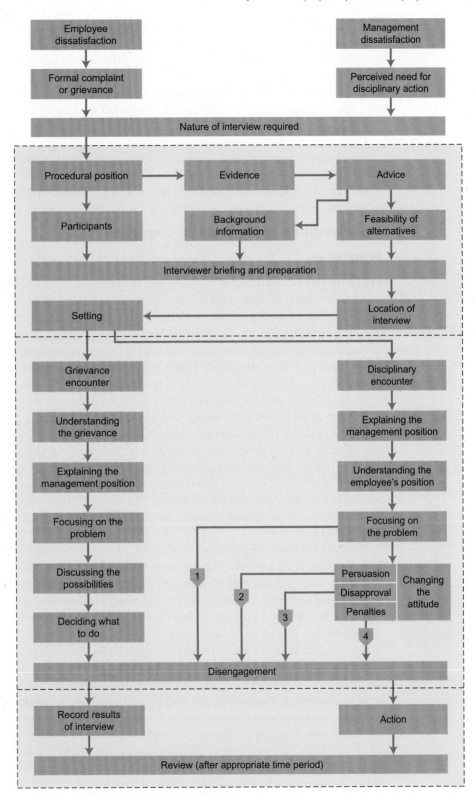

Figure 24.1
The grievance and disciplinary interviews

essential further feature that some managers provide only with reluctance: time. The method is analytical and constructive; not only for the interviews built into the grievance and discipline procedure, but also for interviews that avoid the rigid formality of procedure. Such interviews are one of the means towards self-discipline and autonomy of employees, reducing the need for supervision. The sequence we advocate has discipline and grievance intertwined for much of the process but diverging in the interview itself (see Figure 24.1).

Grievance may be expressed only in *manifest* form, requiring interviewing to understand its *latent content* so that appropriate action is taken to remove the underlying dissatisfaction. Discipline problems will have underlying reasons for the unsatisfactory behaviour which needs to be discovered before solutions to the problems can be found.

The discipline and grievance sequence

Preparation

Check the procedural position to ensure that the impending interview is appropriate. In a grievance situation, for instance, is the employee pre-empting the procedure by taking the matter to the wrong person or to the wrong point in the procedure? This is most common when the first-line supervisor is being bypassed, either because the employee or the representative feels that it would be a waste of time, or perhaps because the supervisor is unsure of the appropriate action and is conniving in the side-stepping of the procedure.

In disciplinary matters even more care is needed about the procedural step, as the likelihood of penalties may already have been set up by warnings, thus reducing the scope for doing anything else in the impending interview apart from imposing a further penalty. In most cases interviews precede procedure, so the parties to the interview are less constrained by procedural rules. The manager will be at pains to explain that the interview is informal and without procedural implications. Alternatively the interview may be one where the likelihood of a move into procedure is so remote that the manager will be at pains to avoid any such reference, for fear of the complainant taking fright.

Who will be there? Here there are similar procedural considerations. In procedure there is the likelihood of employee representation; out of procedure that is less likely, even though the employee may feel anxious and threatened without it. If the manager is accompanied in the interview, the employee may feel even more insecure, and it is doubtful how much can be achieved informally unless the employee feels reasonably secure and able to speak frankly.

What are the facts that the interviewer needs to know? In grievance it will be the subject of the grievance and how it has arisen. This type of information will have been filtered through the management hierarchy and perhaps modified in the process, so it needs careful consideration and any additional background information collected.

Disciplinary interviews always start at the behest of the management so the manager will again collect evidence and consider how it may have been interpreted by intermediaries. This will include some basic details about the interviewee, but mainly information about why the working performance is unsatisfactory. Too often this information exists only in opinions that have been offered and prejudices that are held. This provides a poor basis for a constructive interview, so the manager needs to ferret out details, with as much factual corroboration as possible.

It is almost inevitable that the interviewee will start defensively, expecting to be blamed for something and therefore ready to refute any allegations, probably deflecting blame elsewhere. The manager needs to be prepared to deal with the reaction as well as with facts that have been collected. Unless the interview is at an early, informal stage, the manager also needs to know about earlier warnings, cautions or penalties that have been invoked.

For both types of interview more general information is required, not just the facts of the particular grievance or disciplinary situation, but knowledge to give a general understanding of the working arrangements and relationships. Other relevant data may be the employee's length of service, type of training, previous experience, and so forth.

Most managers will benefit from advice, particularly for anyone who is in procedure, to check the position before starting, as management ability to sustain any action will largely depend on maintaining consistency with what the management has done with other employees previously. The manager may also have certain ideas of what could be done in terms of retraining, transfer or assistance with a domestic problem, and needs to verify the feasibility of such actions before broaching them.

Where is the interview to take place? However trivial this question may seem it is included, because there may be an advantage in choosing an unusually informal situation, or an unusually formal location, according to the manager's assessment. A discussion over a pie and a pint in the local pub may be a more appropriate setting for some approaches to grievance and disciplinary problems, although they are seldom appropriate if the matter has reached procedure. Also employees frequently mistrust such settings, feeling that they are being manipulated or that the discussion 'does not count' because it is out of hours or off limits. If, however, one is trying to avoid procedural overtones, this can be a way of doing it.

Unusual formality can be appropriate in the later stages of procedure, especially in disciplinary matters, when proceedings take on a strongly judicial air. An employee is not likely to take a final warning seriously prior to probable dismissal if it is delivered over a pint in a pub. The large, impressive offices of senior managers can provide appropriate settings for the final stages of procedure.

ACTIVITY 24.1

What incidents have you experienced or heard about where the location of the interview was clearly unsuitable for the nature of the encounter?

The grievance interview

First clarify what the grievance is; a simple way of doing this is to state the *subject* of the grievance and get confirmation from the employee that it is correct. This is important because the manager will probably have a different perspective on the affair from the employee, particularly if it has got beyond the preliminary stage. A supervisor may report to a superior that Mr X has a grievance and 'will not take instructions from me', but when the interview begins Mr X may state his grievance as being that he is unwilling to work on Saturday mornings. In other situations it might be the other way round, with the supervisor reporting that Mr X will not work Saturday mornings and Mr X saying in the interview that he finds the style of his supervisor objectionable. Even where there is no such confusion, an opening statement and confirmation of the subject demonstrate that the two parties are talking about the same thing.

The manager then invites the employee to state the case, explaining the nature and reasons for the dissatisfaction. This enables the employee to explain, citing examples, providing further information and saying not just 'what' but also 'why'. Seldom will this be done well. The presentation of a case is not an easy task for the inexperienced, and few aggrieved employees are experienced at making a case of this type. Furthermore, there is the inhibition of questioning the wisdom of those in authority and some apprehension about the outcome. The manager needs to ask questions in order to fill in any gaps and to clarify some points that were obscure in the first telling. It is better to have an episode of questioning after the case has been made, rather than to interrupt on each point that is difficult. Interruptions make a poorly argued case even more difficult to sustain. There may, however, be disguised pleas for assistance providing good opportunities for questioning to clarify: 'I'm not very good with words, but do you see what I'm getting at?', 'Do you see what I mean?' or 'Am I making myself clear?' Among the strategies the manager needs at this stage could be the method of *reflection* that was mentioned briefly in our introduction to face-to-face skills.

After all the necessary clarification the manager restates the employee's grievance, and gives an outline of the case that has been presented, asking the employee to agree with the summary or to correct it. This is confirming and showing an understanding of the grievance and why it has been brought.

This phase of the interview can be summarised as follows:

Manager	Employee
1 States subject of grievance	
	2 Agrees with statement
	3 States case
4 Questions for clarification	
5 Restates grievance	
	6 Agrees or corrects

The grievance is now understood

The next phase is to set out the management position on the grievance. This is not the action *to be taken* but the action that *has been taken,* with the reasons for the action. This may include an explanation of company policy, safety rules, previous grievances, supervisory problems, administrative methods and anything else which is needed to make clear why the management position has been what it has been. The manager will then invite the employee to question and comment on the management position and its justifications for them to be understood, even if they are not accepted.

The management position is now understood

Setting out the two opposed positions will reveal a deal of common ground, agreement on some things, though disagreement on others. The points on which the parties agree can be ignored, as the need now is to find the outer limits.

Points of disagreement are now in focus

As a preliminary to taking action in the matter under discussion, various possibilities can be put up for consideration. It is logical that the employee's suggestions are put first. Probably this has already been done either explicitly or implicitly in the development of the case. If, however, specific suggestions are invited at this stage they may be different ones, as the aggrieved employee now understands the management position and is seeing the whole matter clearly following the focusing that has just taken place. Then the manager can put forward alternatives or modifications, and these may include, or be limited to, the suggestion that the grievance is mischievous and unfounded so that no action should be taken. Nevertheless, in most cases there will be some scope for accommodation even if it is quite different from the employee's expectation. Once the alternative suggestions for action are set out, there is time for the advantages and disadvantages of both sets to be discussed.

Alternatives have now been considered

The action is to be taken by the manager alone; it is not a joint decision even though the manager will look for a decision that all parties find acceptable. In bringing a grievance the employee is challenging a management decision and that decision will now be confirmed or it will be modified, but it remains a management decision.

Before making the decision the manager may deploy a range of behaviours to ensure that the decision is correct. There may be an adjournment for a while to seek further advice or to give the employee time to reflect further, but the manager has to decide and then explain the decision, not simply deciding and announcing but supporting the decision, with explanation and justification in the same way that the employee developed the case for the grievance at the beginning. There may be employee questions, the employee may want time to think, but eventually the management decision will have to be accepted, unless there is some further procedural step available.

Management action is now clear and understood

The disciplinary interview

Discipline arises from management dissatisfaction rather than employee dissatisfaction, so the opening move is a statement of what the dissatisfaction is, dealing with the *facts* of the situation rather than managerial feelings of outrage about them. This shows that the manager sees the interview as a way of dealing with a problem of the working situation and not (at least not yet) as a way of dealing with a malicious or indolent employee. If an employee has been persistently late for a week, it would be unwise for a manager to open the disciplinary interview by saying, 'Your lateness this week has been deplorable' as the reason might turn out to be that the employee has a seriously ill child needing constant attendance through the night. Then the manager would be embarrassed and the potential for a constructive settlement of the matter jeopardised. An opening factual statement of the problem, 'You have been at least twenty minutes late each day this week . . . ', does not prejudge the reasons and is reasonably precise about the scale of the problem. It also circumscribes management dissatisfaction by implying that there is no other cause for dissatisfaction; if there is, it should be mentioned.

Now the manager asks the employee to say what the reasons for the problem are, perhaps also asking for comments on the seriousness of the problem itself, which the employee may regard as trivial but the manager regards as serious. Getting the employee's reaction is usually straightforward, but the manager needs to be prepared for one of two difficulties. Either there may be a need to probe because the employee is reluctant to open up, or there may be angry defiance. Disciplinary situations are at least disconcerting for employees and frequently very worrying, surrounded by feelings of hostility and mistrust, so that it is to be expected that some ill feeling will be pent up and waiting for the opportunity to be vented.

First possible move to disengagement

If the employee sees something of the management view of the problem and if the manager understands the reasons for the problem, the next step is to seek a solution. It is as likely to be solved by management action as by employee action. If the problem is lateness, one solution would be for the employee to catch an earlier bus, but another might be for the management to alter the working shift to which the employee is assigned. If the employee is disobeying orders, one solution would be to start obeying them, but another might be for the employee to be moved to a different job where orders are received from someone else. Some people regard such thinking as unreasonable, as the contract of employment places obligations on individual employees that they should meet despite personal inconvenience. However, the point is not how people *should* behave, but how they do. Can the contract of employment be enforced on an unwilling employee? Not if one is seeking such attitudes as enthusiasm and cooperation, or behaviour such as diligence and carefulness. The disenchanted employee can always meet the bare letter rather than the spirit of the contract.

Many disciplinary problems require some action from both parties, some require action by the employee only and a small proportion require management action only. The problem-solving session may quickly produce the possibility for further action and open up the possibility of closing the interview.

This simple, logical approach outlined so far may not be enough, due to the unwillingness of employees to respond to disciplinary expectations. They may not want to be punctual or to do as they are instructed, or whatever the particular problem is. There is now a test of the power behind management authority. Three further steps can be taken, one after the other, although there will be occasions when it is necessary to move directly to the third.

Second possible move to disengagement: persuasion

A first strategy is to demonstrate to employees that they will not achieve what they want, if their behaviour does not change:

> You won't keep your earnings up if you don't meet targets.
>
> It will be difficult to get your appointment confirmed when the probationary period is over if . . .

By such means employees may see the advantages of changing their attitude and behaviour. If convinced, there is a strong incentive for them to change, because they believe it to be in their own interests.

Third possible move to disengagement: disapproval

Another strategy is to suggest that continuing the behaviour will displease those whose goodwill the employee wishes to keep:

> The Management Development Panel are rather disappointed . . .
>
> Some of the other people in the department feel that you are not pulling your weight.

A manager using this method needs to be sure that what is said is both true and relevant. Also the manager may be seen as shirking the issue, so it may be appropriate to use a version of 'I think this is deplorable and expect you to do better'.

We asked for a restraint from judgement in the early stages of the interview, until the nature of the problem is clear. The time for judgement has now come, with the proper deployment of the rebuke or the caution.

Fourth possible move to disengagement: penalties

When all else fails or when the behaviour in question is clearly inappropriate, as with serious offences about which there is no doubt, penalties have to be invoked. Usually the first penalty will be a formal warning as a preliminary to possible dismissal. In serious situations summary dismissal is both appropriate and possible within the legal framework.

Disengagement

After one of the four possibilities listed, we come to a stage that is common to both grievance and discipline as a way of describing the process, although the nature of disengagement will obviously differ. The manager now needs to think of the working situation that will follow. In a grievance situation, can the employee now accept the decision that has been made? Are there faces to be saved or reputations to be restored? What administrative action is to be taken? In closing a disciplinary interview, the manager will aim for the flavour of disengagement to be as positive as possible so that all concerned put the disciplinary problem behind them. Where the outcome of the interview is to impose or confirm a dismissal, then the manager will be exclusively concerned with the fairness and accuracy with which it is done, so that the possibility of tribunal hearings is reduced, if not prevented. It can never be appropriate to close an interview of either type leaving the employee humbled and demoralised.

WINDOW ON PRACTICE

The American Eric Harvey reduced what he calls 'positive discipline' to three simple steps:

1 Warn the employee orally.

2 Warn the employee in writing.

3 If steps 1 and 2 fail to resolve the problem, give the employee a day off, with pay (Harvey 1987).

A similar, very positive, approach was outlined in a seminal paper by Huberman in 1967.

SUMMARY PROPOSITIONS

24.b.1. Grievance and disciplinary interviews are central to the process of sorting things out when there is a management/employee problem, but most managers dislike such interviews intensely.

24.b.2. The steps in conducting a grievance interview are first to understand the nature of the grievance, to explain the management position, to focus on the problem, to discuss possibilities and then to decide what to do.

24.b.3. The disciplinary interview starts the other way around, first explaining the management position, then understanding the employee's position and focusing on the problem. If that does not produce a satisfactory result, the manager may have to move through three more steps: persuasion, showing disapproval or invoking penalties.

GENERAL DISCUSSION TOPICS

24.b.1. Do individual grievance and disciplinary procedures weaken trade union organisation in a workplace by enabling the management to deal with employees individually rather than having to face the potential strength of collective action and representation?

24.b.2. In 1791 Edmund Burke, a British statesman, said, 'He that wrestles with us strengthens our nerves, and sharpens our skill. Our antagonist is our helper'. Do trade union officials help HR managers by strengthening their nerves and sharpening their skill?

24.b.3. How would your boss establish a gap between your actual performance and what is expected of you?

24.b.4. Are those lowest in the organisational hierarchy accused of poor performance because it is easier to establish a gap that is clearly the responsibility of the person being accused?

PUTTING IT INTO PRACTICE

In the managerial folklore about discipline there is a type of stereotypically problematic employee which one consultant described as 'the professional weeper'. In other words, some people respond to any dissatisfaction being pointed out by an acceptance that they never have been any good at anything or that what is expected is in some way impossible for them to achieve. They appeal to the manager for enough compassion to just let them carry on as before, but trying really hard. A second stereotype is the counter-attacker, who either flatly denies the allegation or produces vigorous counter-arguments to undermine the management's dissatisfaction. The idea that the counter-attacker actually has a problem that needs to be dealt with is simply not accepted.

How would you deal with both of these stereotypes?

Two different people have complained that the chairs they have are bad for their backs, so could they have better chairs? The supervisor, Barry Jones, who has a better chair, says that they must just get on with it. The matter has been referred to you. You suspect that part of Barry's problem is that he regards his chair as a tangible sign of his status. You also know that one of those complaining (Margaret) does have a bad back and has returned to work after childbirth slightly earlier than her doctor recommended. Apart from the other person who complained (John), everyone else in the office is happy with their chairs.

Margaret has still two weeks' unexpired maternity leave so you suggested that she should take those weeks leave and then try to return to work again. She refuses, claiming that she cannot afford to be 'out of the loop' for any longer and that it is reasonable for her to have a chair 'like that idle slob Barry'.

How would you deal with (a) her request, (b) Barry and (c) John?

FURTHER READING

Mediation

Whatling, T. (2012) *Mediation Skills and Strategies*. London: Jessica Kingsley.
This is particularly suitable for mediation between individuals, with examples drawn from a variety of situations.

Lewis, C. (2012) *Workplace Mediation and Managing Conflict at Work*. London: Globis.
This is similar, but with more discussion about collective issues; written by a consultant.

Dingle, J. and Kelbie, J. (2015) *The Mediation Handbook*. London: The Association of Mediators.
A wide-ranging general text, with very varied examples.

Grievance and discipline

Hook, C.M., Rollinson, D.J., Foot, M. and Handley, J. (1996) 'Supervisor and manager styles in handling discipline and grievance', *Personnel Review*, Vol. 25, No. 3, pp. 20–34.
This study provides further background and discussion of the place of interviewing in employment relations processes.

Cuthbert, C. (2011) *Effective interviewing for Disciplinary, Grievance and Complaints Investigations*. London: Independent Interviewing Ltd.
A short (95 pages), practical book that takes a broad view of the topic.

Borg, J. (2004) *Persuasion: The Art of Influencing People*. Harlow: Pearson Education.

This is a rather different book, popular in style but with solid content on this particular aspect of discipline and grievance handling.

REFERENCES

Discipline

Harvey, E.L. (1987) 'Discipline versus punishment', *Management Review*, March, pp. 25–9.

Huberman, J.C. (1967) 'Discipline without punishment', *Harvard Business Review*, May, pp. 62–8.

PART 6

REWARD: THE CONTRACT FOR PAYMENT

CHAPTERS

Reward is clearly central to the employment relationship. Although there are plenty of people who enjoy working and who claim that they would not stop working even if they were to win a big cash prize in a lottery, most of us work in large part because it is our only means of earning the money we need to sustain ourselves and our families in the style to which we are accustomed. How much we are paid and in what form is therefore an issue which matters hugely to us. These questions are also central ones for the HRM function because money spent on salaries, benefits and other forms of reward typically accounts for well over half an organisation's total costs. For commercial organisations it is thus a major determinant of both profitability and competitive advantage. In the public sector the cost of rewarding staff is determined by, and in turn helps determine, the level of taxes that we pay.

For these reasons, to a greater extent than is the case in other areas of HR practice, the management of reward is heavily constrained by the financial position of the organisation. The aim is to design competitive reward packages which serve to attract, retain and motivate staff, while at the same time keeping a lid on the costs so as to ensure the organisation's commercial and financial viability. This is not an easy task, and it is made harder because of the great significance that employees themselves attach to their pay, and particularly to the level of pay they receive vis-à-vis other people. Getting it wrong has major, negative consequences, because it can demotivate staff in quite serious ways, leading to the departure of good performers, higher absence levels, less effort and the deterioration of the organisation's employee relations climate. Over time, of course, these too serve to reduce an organisation's effectiveness and damage its financial performance.

As markets for goods and services become more competitive and global, the extent to which employers are able to use payment systems as a means of achieving their HR objectives is increasingly constrained. Profit margins are tighter than they used to be in most industries, making it less possible than it once was to tackle skills shortages or to raise the quality of job applications simply by increasing the salaries on offer. The need to restrain labour costs is particularly significant in the public sector as, in recent years, governments have cut their expenditure in order to reduce high levels of public debt. As a result, employers are having to think more creatively and more broadly about the rewards that they offer, looking for ways of motivating and retaining valued staff, without increasing their pay bills. For these reasons the concept of 'total reward' has become attractive and significant in recent years. This involves thinking about the reward package in a very broad sense, not only the aspects that involve payment, but a range of other elements too. Organisations may be increasingly constrained in terms of how much more they can pay someone, but there is a good deal less constraint when it comes to providing them with career development opportunities, flexible working patterns or even a stimulating and pleasant working environment.

The other major contemporary development in this field of HR practice is the increasing prominence in many organisations of well-articulated reward strategies. Over time managers are taking a less reactive approach to the management of their payment systems. Increasingly they are thinking about how the approaches they use to reward staff can be designed so as to achieve specific longer-term objectives. If increasing the level of skills in the organisation is a priority, the response is thus to make salary progression or bonus payments conditional on the attainment of new or increased skills. By contrast, where the overriding aim is to increase productivity, payment systems are developed which reward people or teams for the quantity of their output. Reward strategies are thus about encouraging a confluence of interest between employees and the organisation.

This approach has often been described as 'the new pay' by researchers working in the field of reward management (see Druker and White 2009), and this is an appropriate label because it is only over the past two or three decades that reward management has attained a strategic dimension in the generality of organisations. In the UK, change started in the private sector during the 1980s, later becoming prevalent in many public-sector organisations too. It was associated with the decline in trade union influence we introduced earlier (see Part 5), and in particular with the breaking down of the national collective bargaining system. In the recent past managers in many organisations were thus restricted to deciding who should be employed on which grade, how they should progress up the grade hierarchy, what should be paid by way of an annual increment and how much overtime they worked. In the UK, as in many other countries, this system of multi-employer bargaining has declined steeply since the 1980s. By 2011 only 7% of UK employees had their pay determined by such arrangements, the vast majority of whom work in the public sector (van Wanrooy et al. 2013: 83).

In this part of the text we explore the major elements that make up the reward package, including an introduction to 'total reward' thinking. We will look first at how salaries are determined and at how organisations go about deciding how much each employee should be paid in comparison with others (Chapter 25). Our focus will then turn to incentives and bonus payments of one kind or another (Chapter 26) and to pensions and benefits (Chapter 27). Chapter 28 explains the skills of negotiation and how to reward employees working overseas for the dislocation of their domestic and social arrangements. At the end of each chapter you will find a case study in Putting it into practice which will help you to put these ideas into context and explore them more thoroughly.

REFERENCES

Druker, J. and White, G. (2009) 'Introduction', in G. White and J. Druker (eds), *Reward Management: A Critical Text* (2nd edn.). London: Routledge.

Van Wanrooy, B., Bewley, H., Bryson, A., Forth, J., Freeth, S., Stokes, L. and Wood, S. (2013) *Employment Relations in the Shadow of Recession: Findings from 'The 2011 Workplace Employment Relations Study'.* Basingstoke: Palgrave Macmillan.

CHAPTER 25

TOTAL REWARD AND SETTING PAY

THE OBJECTIVES OF THIS CHAPTER ARE TO:

1 Explain the concept of 'total reward' and the reasons for its increasing prominence

2 Set out the different elements that can make up a reward package

3 Evaluate the alternative methods of setting base pay rates

4 Explore major current developments in the management of salary progression systems

5 Introduce the ways in which regulation affects the level of pay in organisations

6 Explore the ways that reward management practice varies internationally

Introducing reward management

It is helpful to think about reward management in terms of two key decisions:

1 How much should we pay each person in our organisation?
2 How should the payment package be made up?

These are among the most important decisions HR managers have to take because they have such significant outcomes. On the one hand they are a major determinant of organisational profitability vis-à-vis competitors and may help determine whether an organisation thrives or even survives. On the other they also help determine the standard of living that individual employees are able to enjoy, the choices they are able to make about how they and their families live their lives, when they can retire and how many hours a week they are obliged to work. Importantly they also play a large part in determining whether employees are motivated at work and prepared to demonstrate discretionary effort. When poor decisions about pay are made the result is demotivation, higher levels of absence, reduced productivity and an increased chance that an adversarial, low-trust employee relations climate will develop. Finally, of course, these decisions are crucial to an organisation's ability to recruit and retain effective staff in competitive labour markets. Organisations are obliged to compete with one another for good staff as well as for customers, and as Charles Cotton points out in a CIPD survey of reward practices, 'respondents report that employees can be just as discerning as their customers in what they want from their employer' (CIPD 2007: 33). In tight labour markets, where it is harder to recruit and retain the best-qualified people, more pressure there is placed on employers to develop reward packages that suit employees as much as they suit their own needs. By contrast, where labour markets are loose and the skills that employers need to source are in plentiful supply, competitive pressure tends to force wage levels down.

For these reasons great care must be taken when answering the two core questions set out above, and it makes sense to think about how they should be answered in strategic terms. This leads us to asking and looking for answers to a range of further questions:

- What are we seeking to achieve in designing or in redesigning our payment systems?
- What are our competitors doing?
- How do we wish to position ourselves as an employer so as to compete effectively in the labour market?
- What constraints do we face when designing our reward systems?
- How can we avoid demotivating employees when making decisions about how much and in what way we pay them?
- To what extent should employees or their representatives be involved in helping to determine who is paid how much and in what form?

According to Armstrong and Brown (2009: 34) there are four key components in a written reward strategy. First of all there needs to be a statement of intentions setting out, in general terms, what the reward strategy of the organisation is seeking to achieve and which reward initiatives have been chosen in order to achieve these core objectives. Second, these ideas are expanded through a more detailed 'rationale', which explains the objectives in greater depth and shows how the various elements that form the organisation's reward policy support the achievement of those objectives. In effect this amounts to a statement of the business case that underpins the strategy. To that end the rationale should include costings, a statement of the benefits that will accrue, and an indication of the means that will be used to evaluate its success. The third element is an explanation of the guiding principles or values that have been used in developing the initiatives and will be used to adapt them in the future. Typically this will include statements which deal with ethical issues or which reiterate a commitment to core principles such as equality between men and women, fair dealing or rewarding exceptional individual performance. The final component is an implementation plan, setting out exactly what initiatives are being brought forward and when, who has responsibility for their introduction and what their cost will be.

ACTIVITY 25.1

Consider the following list of jobs and job holders. In each case think about how much you think each currently receives annually in basic pay (i.e. excluding benefits, overtime, bonuses, etc.) and about how much you think each *should* be paid. Make a list of the key criteria you are using in making your decisions.

Primary school head teacher

The Prime Minister

Private soldier

Chief Executive of British Telecom

Newly qualified junior doctor

Experienced firefighter

Lollipop lady/man

Wayne Rooney

Total reward

In addition to developing much more clearly articulated strategies in the field of payment, another key contemporary development in this field is a switch in perspective towards 'total reward' thinking on the part of managers. This approach involves giving proper consideration to forms of reward which do not constitute pay, including elements which are neither transactional, tangible nor even financial in nature. Payment remains a significant part of any 'total reward package' that an employer offers, but it also incorporates intangible (or relational) rewards which employees value and which they gain from coming to work. These include opportunities to develop both career-wise and more generally as a human being, the social life which is associated with working in communal settings, recognition from managers and colleagues for a job well done and for the effort expended, and more generally from a sense of personal achievement. Increasingly the opportunity to work flexibly so as to achieve a better 'work–life balance' is discussed in this context too. The idea is effectively illustrated in graphical form by Armstrong and Brown (2009: 25) in their model adapted from work by the Towers Perrin reward consultancy (see Figure 25.1). Here

	Transactional	
Base pay Contingent pay Bonuses Incentives Shares Profit sharing	Pensions Holidays Healthcare Other perks Flexibility
Individual	
	Communal
Learning and development Training Career development	Leadership Organisational values Voice Recognition Achievement Job design Work-life balance
	Relational

Figure 25.1
Job evaluation
analysis.

four distinct categories of rewards are identified, the implication being that each has equal potential significance as a source of reward from the employee perspective.

The change in perspective away from a narrow focus on payment towards a broader focus on 'total reward' has come about largely because of developments in the commercial environment. Year on year, organisations operating in the private sector are facing greater competitive pressure in their product markets leading them to search for ways of reducing their costs while retaining or improving the levels of quality they achieve. In the public sector competitive forces increasingly play a role too, but here pressure to keep costs down comes primarily from government ministers who have a responsibility to taxpayers seeking good value for their money. The trouble is that these pressures are being faced simultaneously with tighter labour market conditions, making it difficult for employers to recruit, retain and motivate the staff they need without substantially increasing pay levels. There are a variety of responses to this conundrum that organisations are embracing. One involves employing fewer, but more highly-paid, people to carry out existing work more efficiently. Another involves keeping a lid on payment levels while simultaneously looking for other ways of rewarding staff effectively. It is this latter approach which has led managers to think about the 'total reward' package that they offer.

As a rule managing the tangible components (i.e. the financial ones) is relatively unproblematic provided basic principles are adhered to and the correct technical decisions are made. While they enable organisations to secure a degree of competitive advantage in their labour markets, these tangible parts of a total reward package are readily imitated by competitors. It is much harder, in practice, to replicate intangible rewards. Over the longer term it is thus in the interests of organisations to improve the perceived value of the intangible elements, but that is a great deal harder both to achieve and to evaluate. Moreover, several important intangible rewards are 'intrinsically' rather than 'extrinsically' motivating, and by definition cannot be directly provided by managers. These are terms used by psychologists to distinguish between sources of positive motivation which are external to individuals and *given* to them by their employer, such as money or praise, and those which are internally generated. An example of intrinsic motivation is someone putting a great deal of effort into a project at work simply because they find it interesting or enjoyable. The result may be very considerable satisfaction on the part of the employee concerned, but this has not resulted directly from any management action. All managers can do is try to create and sustain a culture in which individual employees can achieve intrinsic motivation and hence experience work which is rewarding.

ACTIVITY 25.2

How far do you agree with the proposition that managers should think in terms of 'total reward' as a means of recruiting, retaining and motivating their staff? Are praise and career development as important as pay? Would you trade some of your pay for greater recognition and development opportunities?

WINDOW ON PRACTICE

Total reward at the Crown Prosecution Service

In 2006 the Crown Prosecution Service (CPS) launched a new reward system which was heavily influenced by the 'total reward' concept. Until 1996 when responsibility for reward management was devolved, the CPS's 8,500 staff were paid on standard terms and conditions which were negotiated nationally for civil servants working across all government departments. After devolution incremental changes were introduced that aimed to meet the particular needs of the CPS, culminating in this major overhaul. Labelled 'Invest', the new approach aims to underpin the CPS's evolving agenda.

The first priority for the CPS is to manage successfully a major programme of expansion. New responsibilities taken over from the police require that the CPS employs 300 new lawyers and 500 new administrators. 'Invest' is designed to increase the attractiveness of a career within the CPS and to help retain staff more effectively. An explicit objective of the CPS is to make itself 'an employer of choice' for lawyers and people seeking a career in public administration. A second aim is substantially to improve performance. The CPS has as its central corporate objective a mission to become recognised as 'a world-class prosecution authority'. This requires cultural change and the acquisition by staff of a range of new skills and attributes.

The new strategy aims to meet these objectives in a number of ways. First, a job evaluation system has been introduced to ensure that each job is fairly graded according to the skills its holders require and the responsibilities they shoulder. Second, a new performance appraisal system has come into effect to strengthen links between pay and individual effort and contribution. The existing Civil Service benefits package has been enhanced with new elements such as childcare services and a counselling service, the whole package being promoted with greater coherence at the recruitment stage. A major element is enhanced training and development opportunities for staff, allowing easier career progression within the CPS. Employees are sponsored to attain professional qualifications, and e-learning packages have also been developed to support career development. Finally, flexible working initiatives have been developed, including a great deal more home-working, which aim to meet the needs of both the CPS and its employees. In the future it is intended to introduce long-service awards and to recognise individual achievements with formal letters of recognition from senior managers.

Source: Suff (2006).

The elements of payment

The payment of any individual employee will be made up of one or more elements from those shown in Table 25.1. Fixed elements are those that make up the regular weekly or monthly payment to the individual, and which do not vary other than in exceptional circumstances. Variable elements can be varied by either the employee or the employer.

Basic rate

The irreducible minimum rate of pay is the basic. In some cases this is the standard rate also, not having any additions made to it. In other cases it is a basis on which earnings are built by the addition of one or more of the other elements in payment.

Plussage

Sometimes the basic has an addition to recognise an aspect of working conditions or employee capability. Payments for educational qualifications and for supervisory responsibilities are quite common.

Table 25.1 The potential elements of payment

Bonus	Profit allocation		**Variable elements**
	Discretionary sum		• Irregular
Incentive	Group calculation basis		• Variable amount
	Individual calculation basis		• Usually discretionary
Overtime payment			
Premia	Occasional		
	Contractual		
Benefits	Fringe benefits		**Fixed elements**
	Payments in kind	Other	• Regular
		Accommodation	• Rarely variable
		Car	• Usually contractual
	Benefit schemes	Other	
		Pension	
		Sick pay	
Plussage	'Fudge' payments		
	Special additions		
Basic rate of payment			Basic

Benefits

Extras to the working conditions that have a cash value are categorised as benefits and can be of great variety. The most common are company cars, subsidised meals, childcare vouchers, private health insurance, staff discounts and occupational pensions.

Premia

Where employees work at inconvenient times – or on shifts or permanently at night – they receive a premium payment as compensation for the inconvenience. Sometimes this is built into the basic rate or is a regular feature of the contract of employment so that the payment is unvarying. In other situations shift working is occasional and short-lived, making the premium a variable element of payment.

Overtime

It is customary for employees working more hours than are normal for the working week to be paid for those hours at an enhanced rate, usually between 10% and 50% more than the normal rate according to how many hours are involved. Overtime is earned by 18% of workers in the UK (Kensington 2015), a further 20% apparently working additional hours without being paid (TUC 2015). Where overtime is paid it can account for a significant portion of an individual's gross pay.

Incentive

Incentives are elements of payment linked to the working performance of an individual or working group, usually as a result of prior arrangement. This includes payment by results schemes that reward people for the quantity of their output (e.g. sales commission) as well as other forms of performance-based payment. Incentives are paid to 59% of employees in the UK private sector, compared with only 21% in the public sector (van Wanrooy *et al*. 2013: 96).

Bonus

A different type of variable payment is the gratuitous payment by the employer that is not directly earned by the employee: a bonus. The essential difference between this and an incentive is that the employee has no entitlement to the payment as a result of a contract of employment and cannot be assured of receiving it in return for a specific performance. The most common example of this is the Christmas bonus.

ACTIVITY 25.3

If you could design your own 'remuneration package' which could be made up from any of the items in Table 25.1, what proportion of each item would you choose and why? Does your answer suggest ideas for further development of salary policies?

Setting base pay

One of the most important decisions in the development of reward strategies concerns the mechanism or mechanisms that will be used to determine the basic rate of pay for different jobs in the organisation. There is always a limit on how much any employer can afford to pay if it is to remain competitive in its industry, but on the other hand there is a limit below which it becomes impossible to attract or retain people with the required skills and experience. Hence, as Gerhart (2009: 225) points out, product and labour market pressures effectively set a ceiling and a floor to overall pay levels for any one job or individual.

There are four principal mechanisms for the determination of base pay. They are not entirely incompatible, although one tends to be used as the main approach in most organisations.

External market comparisons

In making external market comparisons the focus is on the need to recruit and retain staff, a rate being set which is broadly equivalent to 'the going rate' for the job in question. The focus is thus on **external relativities.** Research suggests that this is always a major contributing factor when organisations set pay rates, but that it increases in significance higher up the income scale. Some employers consciously pay over the market rate in order to secure the services of the most talented employees. Others 'follow the market', by paying below the going rate while using other mechanisms such as flexibility, job security or longer-term incentives to ensure effective recruitment and retention. In either case the decision is based on an assessment of what rate needs to be paid to compete for staff in different types of labour market. Going rates are more significant for some than for others. Accountants and craftworkers, for instance, tend to identify with an external employee grouping. Their assessment of pay levels is thus greatly influenced by the going rate in the trade or the district. A similar situation exists with jobs that are clearly understood and where skills are readily transferable, particularly if the employee is to work with a standard piece of equipment. Driving heavy goods vehicles is an obvious example, as the vehicles are common from one employer to another, the roads are the same, and only the loads vary. Other examples are secretaries and computer operators. Jobs that are less sensitive to the labour market are those that are organisationally specific, such as much semi-skilled work in manufacturing, general clerical work and nearly all middle management positions.

There are several possible sources of intelligence about market rates for different job types at any one time. A great deal of information can be found in published journals such as the pay bulletins issued by Incomes Data Services (IDS) and Industrial Relations Services (IRS), focusing on the hard-to-recruit groups such as computer staff. More detailed information can be gained by joining one of the major salary survey projects operated by firms of consultants or by paying for access to their datasets. Information on specific types of job, including international packages for expatriate workers, is collected by specialised consultants and can be obtained on payment of the appropriate fee. In addition there are more informal approaches such as looking at pay rates included in recruitment advertisements in newspapers, at job centres and on Web-based job-board sites. There are also now a plethora of salary comparison websites which operate by collecting data about pay rates from people who visit them to establish how well their pay compares with others in their professions (Nagpal 2013:129). These can be useful for employers too. In addition, new staff, notably HR people, often bring with them a knowledge of pay rates for types of job in competitor organisations and can be a useful source of information. Finally, it is possible to join or set up salary clubs. These consist of groups of employers, often based in the same locality, who agree to share salary information for mutual benefit.

Internal labour market mechanisms

Just as there is a labour market of which the company is a part, so there is a labour market within the organisation which also needs to be managed so as to ensure effective performance. According to Doeringer and Piore (1970), there are two kinds of internal labour market: the enterprise and the craft. The enterprise market is so called because the individual enterprise defines the boundaries of the market itself. Such will be the market encompassing manual workers engaged in production processes, for whom the predominant pattern of employment is one in which jobs are formally or informally ranked, with the jobs accorded the highest pay or prestige usually being filled by promotion from within and those at the bottom of the hierarchy usually being filled only from outside the enterprise. It is, therefore, those at the bottom that are most sensitive to the external labour market. Doeringer and Piore point out that there is a close parallel with managerial jobs, the main ports of entry being from management trainees or supervisors, and the number of appointments from outside gradually reducing as jobs become more senior. This modus operandi is one of the main causes of the problems that redundant executives face.

Recent US research has stressed the importance of this kind of internal labour market in determining pay rates. Here the focus is on **internal differentials** rather than external relativities. An interesting metaphor used is that of the sports tournament in which an organisation's pay structure is likened to the prize distribution in a knock-out competition such as is found, for example, at the Wimbledon Tennis Championships. Here the prize money is highest for the winner, somewhat lower for the runner-up, lower again for the semi-final losers and so on down the rounds. The aim, from the point of view of the tournament organisers, is to attract the best players to compete in the first round, then subsequently to give players in later rounds an incentive to play at their peak. According to Lazear (1995: 26–33), the level of base pay for each level in an organisation's hierarchy should be set according to similar principles. The level of pay for any particular job is thus set at a level which maximises performance lower down the hierarchy among employees competing for promotion. The actual performance of the individual receiving the pay is less important.

The second type of internal labour market identified by Doeringer and Piore is the craft market, where barriers to entry are relatively high, typically involving the attainment of a formal qualification. However, once workers are established in the market, seniority and hierarchy become unimportant as jobs and duties are shared among the individuals concerned. Such arrangements are usually determined by custom and practice, but are difficult to break down because of the vested interests of those who have successfully completed their period of apprenticeship. Certain pay rates are expected by those who have achieved the required qualification and it is accepted by everyone that this is a fair basis for rewarding people.

Job evaluation

Job evaluation involves the establishment of a system which is used to measure the size and significance of all jobs in an organisation. It results in each job being scored with a number of points, establishing in effect a hierarchy of all the jobs in the organisation ranging from those which require the most knowledge and experience and which carry a great deal of responsibility to those which require least knowledge and experience and require the job holder to carry relatively low levels of responsibility. Each job is then assimilated to an appropriate grade and payment distributed accordingly. The focus is thus on the relative worth of jobs within an organisation and on comparisons between these rather than on external relativities and comparisons with rates being paid by other employers. Fairness and objectivity are the core principles, an organisation's wage budget being divided among employees on the basis of an assessment of the nature and size of the job each is employed to carry out.

Usage of job evaluation has increased in recent years. It is currently used by over 30% of organisations in the UK, and by a higher proportion still in larger ones (CIPD 2015: 4). It is a well-established technique, having been developed in all its most common forms by the 1920s. In recent years it has received a series of boosts. First, various types of incomes policy between 1965 and 1974 either encouraged the introduction of job evaluation or specifically permitted expenditure above the prevailing norm by companies wishing to introduce it. In the 1980s the use of job evaluation became the hinge of most equal pay cases. More recently organisations have found it useful as part of moves towards single-status contractual arrangements (where everyone is employed on the same basic terms and conditions) and resolving pay issues following organisational mergers. Much of the recent growth has been in the public sector, local authorities and the NHS being examples of major employers establishing new schemes, but the surveys suggest that job evaluation is very widely used in the private sector as well. Moreover, few organisations abandon it, once introduced. The maxim that 'job evaluation is the one management tool that refuses to go out of fashion' thus continues to hold true.

Despite its popularity it is often misunderstood, so the following points have to be made:

- Job evaluation is concerned with the job and not the performance of the individual job holder. Individual merit is not assessed.
- The technique is systematic rather than scientific. It depends on the judgement of people with experience, requiring them to decide in a planned and systematic way, but it does not produce results that are infallible.
- Job evaluation does not eliminate collective bargaining where trade unions are recognised. It determines the differential gaps between incomes; it does not determine pay levels or annual pay rises.
- Only a structure of pay rates is produced. Other elements of earnings, such as premia and incentives, are not determined by the method.

There are many methods of job evaluation in use and they are summarised by Armstrong and Murlis (2007: 129–64). Where a non-analytical or 'whole job' scheme is used a panel of assessors examines each job as a whole, in terms of its difficulty or value to the business, to determine which should be ranked more highly than others. No attempt is made to break down each job into its constituent parts. By contrast, an analytical scheme requires each element or factor of the job to be assessed. The most widely used analytical schemes are based on points-rating systems, under which each job is examined in terms of factors such as skill, effort and responsibility. Each factor is given a weighting indicating its value relative to the others and for each factor there are varying degrees. A score is then given depending on how demanding the job is in terms of each factor, with the overall points value determining the relative worth of each job – hence its grade in the organisation's pay structure.

In recent years there has been great growth in the use of highly sophisticated computer-assisted job evaluation systems marketed by leading firms of consultants which award scores to each job on the basis of information gathered from job analysis questionnaires.

The points values eventually derived for each job can be plotted on a graph or simply listed from the highest to the lowest to indicate the ranking. Then – and only then – are points ratings matched with cash amounts, as decisions are made on which points ranges equate with various pay grades. This process is illustrated in Figure 25.2, each cross representing a job. The most common approach involves using a graph on which one axis represents the *current salary* for each job evaluated and the other the number of *job evaluation points* awarded. A line of best fit is then drawn and each job assigned to a grade. Salary-modelling software is widely available to help with this process.

It is virtually inevitable that some jobs will be found to be paid incorrectly after job evaluation has been completed. If the evaluation says that the pay rate should be higher then the rate duly rises, either immediately or step by step, to the new level. The only problem is finding the money, and introducing job evaluation always costs money. More difficult is the situation where evaluation shows the employee to be overpaid. It is not feasible to reduce the pay of the job holder without breaching the contract of employment. There have been two approaches. The first is buying out. The overpaid employee is offered a large lump sum in consideration of the fact of henceforth being paid at the new,

Figure 25.2
Categories of reward.

lower rate. The second device used is that of the personal rate or 'red circling', so called because the job is circled in red on the job evaluation chart. The outcome is that current job holders continue to be paid at the present level, but their successors are paid at the lower job-evaluated rate.

Collective bargaining

The fourth approach involves determining pay rates through collective negotiations with trade unions or other employee representatives. Forty years ago this was the dominant method used for determining pay in the UK, negotiations commonly occurring at industry level. The going rates for each job group were thus set nationally and were adhered to by all companies operating in the sector concerned. Recent decades have seen a steady erosion of these arrangements, collective bargaining being decentralised to company or establishment level, where it survives at all. The rise of service sector organisations with lower union membership levels has ensured that collective bargaining arrangements now cover only a minority of UK workers. According to van Wanrooy *et al.* (2013: 83) only 13% now have any of their terms and conditions determined via collective bargaining of any kind. The experience of many other countries is similar, but there are regions such as Eastern Europe and Scandinavia where collective bargaining remains a major determinant of pay rates. Where separate clusters of employees within the same organisation are placed in different bargaining groups and represented by different unions, internal relativities become an issue for resolution during bargaining.

In carrying out negotiations the staff and management sides make reference to external labour market rates, established internal pay determination mechanisms and the size of jobs. However, a host of other factors come into the equation too as each side deploys its best arguments. Union representatives, for example, make reference to employee need when house prices are rising and affordable accommodation is hard to find. Both sides refer to the balance sheet, employers arguing that profit margins are too tight to afford substantial rises, while union counterparts seek to gain a share of any increased profits for employees. However good the case made, what ultimately makes collective bargaining different from the other approaches is the presence of industrial muscle. Strong unions which have the support of the majority of employees, as is the case in many public-sector organisations, are able to ensure that their case is heard and taken into account. They can thus sometimes 'secure' a better pay deal for their members than market rates would allow.

ACTIVITY 25.4

Which of the four mechanisms outlined above do you think is usually most efficient for setting the following?

- Base pay
- Annual cost of living increases
- Executive remuneration packages
- Bonus schemes

The importance of equity

Whatever methods are used to determine pay levels and to decide what elements make up the individual pay package, employers must ensure that they are perceived by employees to operate equitably. It has long been established that perceived inequity in payment matters can be highly damaging to an organisation. Classic studies undertaken by Adams (1963) found that a key determinant of satisfaction at work is the extent to which employees judge pay levels and pay increases to be distributed fairly. These led to the development by Adams and others of equity theory, which holds that we are very concerned that rewards or 'outputs' equate to our 'inputs' (defined as skill, effort, experience, qualifications, etc.) and that these are fair when compared with the rewards being given to others. Where we believe that we are not being fairly rewarded we show signs of 'dissonance' or dissatisfaction which leads to absence, voluntary turnover, on-job shirking and low-trust employee relations. It is therefore important that an employer not only treats employees equitably in payment matters, but is *seen* to do so too.

While it is difficult to gain general agreement about who should be paid what level of salary in an organisation, it is possible to employ certain clear principles when making decisions in the pay field. Those that are most important are the following:

- a standard approach for the determination of pay (basic rates and incentives) across the organisation;
- as little subjective or arbitrary decision making as is feasible;
- maximum communication and employee involvement in establishing pay determination mechanisms;
- clarity in pay determination matters so that everyone knows what the rules are and how they will be applied.

These are the foundations of procedural fairness or 'fair dealing'. In establishing pay rates it is not always possible to distribute rewards fairly to everyone's satisfaction, but it should always be possible to do so using procedures which operate equitably.

WINDOW ON PRACTICE

Countries vary considerably in terms of how much different groups are paid, some being a good deal more equal than others in terms of how organisations pay people at different levels and how far income is subsequently redistributed via taxation and state benefits.

International statistics on inequality are published each year by the United Nations in its *Human Development Reports*. The level of equality in a society is measured using the Gini coefficient. Reported as having a Gini coefficient of 100 it would mean that all the wealth was in the hands of a single individual (i.e. as unequal as it is possible to be). By contrast, a Gini coefficient of 0 would indicate a society in which all wealth was distributed wholly equally between everyone. The reported figures for 2015 show that the most unequal country in the world (or at least the most unequal country that reports its figures to the UN) was the Seychelles, with a Gini coefficient of 66. Other African countries also report very high levels of inequality as do most countries in South America. Among the western industrialised countries, the most unequal is the USA (Gini coefficient of 41), the UK following behind with a figure of 36. By contrast some Northern European countries are a great deal more equal. The Gini coefficient in Sweden was just 25, Denmark, Japan and Germany also come close to the top of the equality table.

Although wealth varies across international borders for many reasons, the level of pay plays a major part. The same patterns are reflected in the figures on pay equity in industrialised countries published regularly by the OECD. One measure that it uses is the difference between the gross male full-time average earnings of the top and bottom deciles in a population.

According to the most recent OECD statistics, dating from 2013, the difference in the USA is 5.01, meaning that the top 10% earned just over five times more than the bottom 10%. In the UK the difference in 2013 was 3.6, in Germany it was 3.4 and in France 3.0. Here too the lowest figures are reported in Scandinavian countries: in Finland it was 2.6, and in Sweden only 2.3.

While the precise figures for each country fluctuate from year to year, the overall pattern across most of the world during the past thirty years has been towards greater inequality as measured by both these indices.

Sources: OECD Employment Database, www.oecd.org/employment/emp/onlineo ecdemploymentdatabase; United Nations, *Human Development Report* (2015).

Regulatory restrictions

Governments take action to restrict the extent to which inequality in pay levels occurs. The nature of regulatory restrictions varies from country to country, some governments taking a stronger approach than others. Excessive pay at the top is rarely restricted directly by regulation because it is much easier to tackle the issue through high levels of taxation, but measures are sometimes put in place which have the effect of limiting pay awards to senior people. In the UK, public companies are now obliged to gain the approval of shareholders before they alter any executive remuneration policies and, in any event, must secure their approval for top salary payments every three years. Elsewhere it has been common for governments who are concerned about wage inflation to introduce incomes policies which limit pay increases to a set percentage in a particular financial year. In the UK, as is common in most industrialised countries, there are three major ways in which regulations restrict employer action more directly.

Minimum wages

A National Minimum Wage has been set in the UK for nearly twenty years. This now applies only to people under the age of twenty-five, most of whom qualify for an hourly pay rate of £6.70 (in 2016). Lower rates can be paid to trainees, apprentices and more generally to those who are under 21, but these too are regulated. For older employees a National Living Wage applies. This was set at £7.20 an hour in 2016, the aim being to increase it to at least £9 an hour by 2020.

Equal pay law

A core principle of European employment law is that men and women who work for the same employer should be paid the same amount for doing similar work or work which while different in nature is of equal value or should be graded at the same level. When an employee suspects that this is not the case, he or she (most cases are brought by women) can challenge the practice by bringing an employment tribunal claim. Provided there is evidence of a disparity that cannot be explained by some other factor such as a difference in hours worked, qualification levels or individual performance, the tribunal can require pay levels to be raised and back payments to be made. From 2017 employers with more than 250 staff are being required to publish data about how much their male and female staff are paid as a means of discouraging them from continuing with unequal pay practices.

Unlawful deductions

The third restriction that applies in the UK concerns regulation on when an employer can and cannot lawfully make deductions from a pay packet without first securing the agreement of employees concerned. Some deductions, such as tax and national insurance, are not only permitted, but are legally required. Others which employers might otherwise be tempted to make are not permitted. Importantly this includes any kind of deduction made in response to actual or perceived misconduct and means that it is unlawful to use employee fines as a disciplinary sanction or to suspend someone on reduced pay pending a disciplinary investigation.

International diversity in reward management

Despite globalisation and the rise of multinational corporations, there remain distinct national variations in the way that pay is determined. In a number of industrialised countries there remains resistance to the primacy of market comparisons. Instead, pay scales and/or pay arrangements are agreed/determined at industry level, to a considerable extent removing pay as a factor in labour market competition. To this fundamental divide between national approaches can be added different attitudes towards incentive payments, employee attributes that should be rewarded and huge differences in taxation and social security regulation. The extent of the diversity is best illustrated with some examples.

The US/UK approaches

These approaches are characterised by a high degree of decentralisation. Aside from setting a minimum wage and requiring that men and women are treated equally, the state by and large refrains from interfering in pay determination matters. Even in the public sector, while overall budgets are set by government ministers and while they deal with major public policy questions (like public-sector pension arrangements), ministers leave the detailed negotiation of pay packages to local managers or to pay review bodies which are independent of government. In the private sector, trade unions now play only a limited role, management effectively deciding who should be paid what and in what way. Pay is thus set according to what an organisation can afford and what the market requires. Individual pay negotiation is now the standard approach. Performance-related pay (PRP) is very common in the private sector and is becoming a great deal more common in the public sector too, while the overall value of occupational pensions has been significantly eroded in order to reduce company exposure to financial risk. Meanwhile executive pay has rocketed upwards, way ahead of the increases seen in other countries.

The German approach

In Germany there is a good deal more centralisation, but pay is largely determined at the industry level, not at governmental level. The majority of workers in Germany have their basic pay set through legally sanctioned, industry-level collective bargaining arrangements. The agreements set out the grading structure for each industry and, in many cases, also determine the job evaluation factors to be used in assigning jobs to grades. Employers are not permitted to undercut agreed minima (they are seen as being basic contractual rights), although they can supplement them with locally agreed discretionary emoluments. Typical discretionary payments vary from 5% in the financial sector to 25% in engineering industries. In larger firms, only the most senior managers are employed on individual contracts – equivalent to 2% of the total workforce. Stock option schemes, however, are a good deal less common in Germany than the UK due to unfavourable tax treatment. Incentive payments are common in Germany. There are many piecework and individual performance-based schemes, as well as government-sponsored profit-sharing arrangements. An attractive feature of German remuneration is the wide existence of 'thirteenth-month' bonus payments in December.

The Japanese approach

The Japanese system resembles that of Germany in that it comprises industry-level pay scales agreed between firms. It differs, however, in that it is person based rather than job based. Collective bargaining also plays a lesser role as Japanese unions are all enterprise based. Three separate factors determine each individual's pay:

1 the career category
2 age/seniority
3 rank and class.

There are five accepted career categories into which employees are allocated. Each has its own pay scales. The five are as follows:

- general administration
- scientific/engineer
- secretarial/office
- technician/blue collar
- contingent.

Within each category, base pay is determined with reference to age (around 60% of pay) and skill/effort (typically 40%). In a country with traditions of 'lifetime' or long-term employment in one enterprise, seniority is central to reward. Earnings go up with each year of service until the age of 50, after which they decline steadily. The skill-based element operates in a similar way to traditional UK public-sector grade/incremental systems. In Japan, however, progression is discretionary. Seniority plays a part in the skill-based payments too, as there is usually a minimum time to serve in each class before promotion can be gained. Bonus payments are mostly group based and typically equal two months' pay. The result is a high degree of pay compression and an adherence to the maxim that 'a nail standing too high will be pounded down'.

The Scandinavian approach

In Norway, Sweden and Finland payment arrangements tend to be very much more centralised than elsewhere, the government playing a decisive role that extends across most industries. Collective agreements that cover salaries, benefits and all other conditions of work are negotiated at national level between trade unions and employers associations under the auspices of government agencies. These are typically long-term deals that, once agreed, last three years or more. Government agencies arbitrate when agreement cannot be reached. One result is a high degree of similarity in grading schemes across industries. Another is a relatively low level of social inequality. Top executives in Scandinavian countries are typically paid eleven or twelve times the average wage, whereas in the UK and, especially in the USA, the differential is now typically over fifty times. PRP is very common in Scandinavian countries, but it tends to be team based rather than individual.

SUMMARY PROPOSITIONS

25.1. Until relatively recently many employers in the UK were greatly restricted in their capacity to design reward strategies which met their priorities by the prevailing system of multi-employer or industry-level collective bargaining. The experimentation that followed the disintegration of this system has led to both successful and unsuccessful outcomes.

25.2. Simultaneous competition in product and labour markets has led employers increasingly to think in terms of 'total reward' when developing reward strategies. This involves incorporating all management initiatives which may have the effect of adding value to the experience of working in an organisation.

25.3. The main elements of payment are basic rate, plussage, benefits, premia, overtime, incentives and bonus.

25.4. There are four main alternative methods of setting base pay rates: external labour market comparisons, internal labour market mechanisms, job evaluation and collective bargaining.

25.5. Procedural equity is essential to the design of successful payment systems as is adherence to government regulation in this field.

25.6. The approach taken to payment and the design of remuneration systems varies very considerably from country to country.

GENERAL DISCUSSION TOPICS

1. Can payment ever be truly fair?

2. Do you think it is possible to identify 'best practice' in payment policy? What elements would you consider should make up any such package?

3. 'Job evaluation does not produce equitable payment: it merely produces a ramshackle method of justifying the status quo.' Do you agree with this statement?

4. Why have we seen increased interest in the concept of 'total reward' in recent years? Why might interest grow still further in the future?

THEORY INTO PRACTICE

The following article by Lucy Kellaway is light-hearted and witty, but it also raises several interesting questions about relative pay levels and how we should determine them.

Pandora's pay packet

Imagine if you got into work to find you had been sent an email listing the salaries and bonuses of everybody in your company.

You'd fall on it, read it greedily. And then read it again. You'd scan the list for all those paid more than you. All those paid less. You'd look up the salaries of your most comparable colleagues. You'd look for those of the cocky ones whom you've never rated.

Assuming that you had started the day feeling reasonably content with your salary, by the end it would be a different story. Either you'd be seething at the higher salaries paid to people you think less deserving than yourself, or you'd be feeling sheepish about those talented hard-working people earning considerably less than you.

This is what happens in a case study in the latest *Harvard Business Review*. A disaffected employee unearths a complete salary and bonus list and promptly emails it to the entire staff. Sure enough, all hell breaks loose.

➤ The four labour market experts wheeled on by the magazine to discuss the case agree on one thing. The forced disclosure will do some good – it will bring about a more open culture and a fairer pay system.

I think this is optimistic. Openness is not a good thing *per se*. It is good only when the occasion calls for it.

Pay is the last taboo. Pay is full of iniquities and will always be so. Better, therefore, not to draw attention to it.

If you meet someone at a dinner party, you can ask them about their religion. You can ask them which way they are going to vote. You can ask what they paid for their house. (In fact, I consider this to be the height of bad manners but people ask, nevertheless.)

You may even, if circumstances are right, be able to ask about their sex lives. What you cannot do, under any circumstances, is ask how much they are paid.

You could say that this reticence is misplaced and that in time pay will go the way of all the other taboos.

The reason salaries are so sensitive is that they are the only 'objective' way we have of comparing your labour to mine. Your salary is a clear measure of what someone else is prepared to pay for you.

This makes pay more revealing than other kinds of financial information.

If I know you paid a lot for your house I can conclude any number of things. That your salary is huge. Or that your wife's is. That one or other of you inherited some money. Or that you made a couple of lucky property moves in the past. There are all kinds of possibilities.

But your salary measures only one thing: it sums up your worth. Only as we all know, it does nothing of the kind.

While it may be dangerous to discuss salaries at a dinner party, where bankers may be cheek by jowl with teachers, to discuss them in the office canteen is dynamite.

If salaries in your company were determined fairly, according to some commonly agreed principle, secrecy might not be necessary. But they aren't determined like that, are they? In the real world, your salary reflects a thousand different things, your 'worth' being only one of them.

When did you join the company? Was the job market tight at the time? Which department are you in? How well does your boss like you? How good are you at complaining? All these things affect your pay.

In the public sector people traditionally knew what others were paid, because for each grade and each task there was a rate. But now, thanks to performance-related pay, salary discussion is becoming taboo there too.

Some trendy new companies have experimented with full salary disclosure. This tends to work when the company is very young but as it grows and the outside labour market bears down, transparency seems like less of a good thing.

It could be argued that by publishing all salaries in a company you shock the system into greater 'fairness'. But even if this did happen, it is doubtful whether it would be desirable. Would you want to own shares in a company that could not hire good people from the outside at higher wages for fear of alienating existing employees?

We have, under our noses, a good example of what happens when individual salaries are forcibly outed. For the past few years, directors of public companies have had to disclose in full, gory detail how much they are paid. The aim of this was to rein in the worst of the fat cat pay increases.

Yet it is debatable whether it has in fact achieved that. Pay levels of top directors have continued to soar and the supposed performance criteria they have held up to justify their

➤

> bonuses have proved to be laughably easy to meet. Maybe they would have risen still further if disclosure had not been required; maybe they would not.
>
> What transparency at the top has certainly done is to make everyone else's sense of outrage and envy all the greater. Now that the fat cat is out of the bag, we can all see how fat it really is – and the sight does us no good at all.
>
> So I am not going to tell you what I earn, either. More than anything else, I do not want to share this information with my colleagues.
>
> Yet suppose when I get into work tomorrow I find that email waiting for me. Will I heed the above and simply press the 'delete' button? Like hell. I'll fall on it, read it greedily, then read it again.

Source: FT.com, 14 May 2001.

Questions

1 Is pay really 'the last taboo' as is argued in this article?

2 Why is it only 'dangerous' to discuss salaries at a dinner party, but 'dynamite' to discuss them in the office canteen?

3 Is the author right to argue that more openness in the area of pay is not something to be welcomed?

FURTHER READING

The Chartered Institute of Personnel and Development carries out a big annual survey of reward management policy and practice which is published in February each year. It can be downloaded from the Institute's website. In addition the CIPD publishes the results of other research projects that focus on reward.

Reward management continues to be an area of HRM practice which is heavily researched. Good summaries of the most important recent contributions are the following:

Kessler, I. (2013) 'Remuneration systems', in S. Bach and M. Edwards (eds), *Managing Human Resources* (5th edn.). Chichester: Wiley.

Guthrie, J. (2007) 'Remuneration: Pay effects at work', in P. Boxall *et al.* (eds), *The Oxford Handbook of Human Resource Management*. Oxford: Oxford University Press.

Gerhart, B. (2009) 'Compensation', in A. Wilkinson *et al.* (eds), *The Sage Handbook of Human Resource Management*. London: Sage.

White, G. and Druker, J. (eds) (2009) *Reward Management: A Critical Text* (2nd edn.). London: Routledge.

REFERENCES

Adams, J.S. (1963) 'Towards an understanding of inequity', *Journal of Abnormal and Social Psychology*, Vol. 67, pp. 422–36.

Armstrong, M. and Brown, D. (2009) *Strategic Reward: Implementing more effective reward management*. London: Kogan Page.

Armstrong, M. and Murlis, H. (2007) *Reward Management: A handbook of remuneration strategy and practice*. London: Kogan Page.

CIPD (2007) *Reward Management: Annual survey report 2007*. London: CIPD.

CIPD (2015) *Reward Management: Annual survey report 2014–15*. London: CIPD.

Doeringer, P.B. and Piore, M.J. (1970) *Internal Labour Markets and Manpower Analysis*. Washington, DC: Office of Manpower Research, US Department of Labor.

Gerhart, B. (2009) 'Compensation', in A. Wilkinson *et al.* (eds), *The Sage Handbook of Human Resource Management*. London: Sage.

Kellaway, L. (2001) *Pandora's Pay Packet*. FT.com, May.

Kensington (2015): 'Nearly one in five are paid overtime', press release, www.kmc.co.uk/intermediaries/news/nearly-one-in-five-employees-are-paid-overtime, accessed 15 September 2015.

Lazear, E.P. (1995) *Personnel Economics*. Boston, MA: Massachusetts Institute of Technology.

Nagpal, G. (2013) *Talent Economics*. London: Kogan Page.

OECD (2015) Employment Database. United Nations, *Human Development Report,* www.oecd.org/employment/emp/onlineoecdemploymentdatabase. Suff, R. (2006) 'Investing in excellence at the Crown Prosecution Service', *IRS Employment Review*, No. 841, 17 February, pp. 24–7.

TUC (2015) 'Workers contribute £32 million to UK economy from unpaid overtime', www.tuc.org.uk/economic-issues/labour-market/fair-pay-fortnight-2015/workplace-issues/workers-contribute-%C2%A332bn-uk, accessed 27 February 2015.

United Nations (2015) *Human Development Report*. New York: United Nations.

Van Wanrooy, B., Bewley, H., Bryson, A., Forth, J., Freeth, S., Stokes, L. and Wood, S. (2013) *The 2011 Workplace Employment Relations Study: First Findings*. London: Department for Business, Innovation and Skills.

CHAPTER 26
INCENTIVES

THE OBJECTIVES OF THIS CHAPTER ARE TO:

1 Set out the major choices faced by employers contemplating setting up or reviewing incentive payment schemes

2 Explore the question of how many people are paid different types of incentive in the UK

3 Outline the main forms of payment by results (PBR) schemes and discuss their advantages and disadvantages

4 Debate the merits of individual performance-related pay (PRP)

5 Introduce skills-based pay and discuss its major advantages and disadvantages

6 Outline the major forms of profit-sharing schemes that operate, including those sponsored by the government

Incentive payments remain one of the ideas that fascinate managers as they search for the magic formula. Somewhere there is a method of linking payment to performance so effectively that their movements will coincide, enabling the manager to leave the workers on automatic pilot, as it were, while attending to more important matters such as strategic planning or going to lunch. This conviction has sustained a continuing search for this elusive formula, which has been hunted with all the fervour of those trying to find the Holy Grail or the crock of gold at the end of the rainbow.

Incentives of all kinds have been the source of much debate among HR professionals, consultants, trade unionists and academic writers for a long time. Most attention has been given to the pros and cons of the types of individual performance-related reward systems that have become a great deal more common in recent years, disagreement about them focusing in particular on the public sector and the payment of senior executives. Much has also been written in support of and against the use of team-based incentives and those which reward the acquisition of defined skills. Profit sharing and employee share ownership have been the subject of significant government initiatives and have thus also become topics about which a great deal is written.

Basic choices

While incentive payment systems are common in the UK and in many other countries, there are millions of employees who do not receive this kind of reward and many employers who use them only in a limited way (often in the remuneration of senior managers). It is thus perfectly possible, and some would argue desirable, to recruit, retain and motivate a workforce by paying a simple, fixed rate of pay for each job in the organisation. There is other equipment in the HR manager's toolkit which can be used to reward effort and maintain good levels of job satisfaction. The most fundamental question is therefore whether or not to use an incentive payment system at all. In the opinion of Sisson and Storey (2000: 123–4) many organisations in the UK have introduced schemes for 'ideological reasons' as a means of impressing stock market analysts, reinforcing management control or undermining established collective bargaining machinery. These, they suggest, are poor reasons which have generally met with little long-term success. Incentive schemes should only be used where they are appropriate to the needs of the business and where they can clearly contribute to the achievement of organisational objectives.

There is a long tradition in the academic literature of hostility to incentive schemes in general and those which focus on the individual in particular. In 1966, Frederick Herzberg argued that pay was a 'hygiene factor' rather than a 'motivator'. He claimed that its capacity to motivate positively was limited, and it can very easily demotivate when managed poorly. It follows that there is little to be gained and a great deal to lose from the introduction of incentive schemes. Others (e.g. Thompson 2000) have focused on the way that incentives are perceived by employees as tools of management control which reduce their autonomy and discretion. This, it is argued, causes resentment and leads to dissatisfaction and industrial conflict. In public sector workplaces it is said to undermine the professional ethos and high levels of intrinsic motivation among professional staff (Ray et al. 2014). A third source of criticism is the considerable additional costs which invariably mount up when organisations introduce incentive schemes. Cox (2006: 1493) labels these 'costly side-effects' and shows that they are both considerable and largely unanticipated at the time a new scheme is introduced.

A different school of thought argues in favour of incentives on the grounds that they reward effort and behaviours which the organisation wishes to encourage (Gerhart 2009: 226). As a result they not only are a fair basis for rewarding people, but also can enhance organisational effectiveness and productivity. Advocates of expectancy theory hold this position with their belief that individual employees will alter their behaviour (e.g. by working harder or prioritising their actions differently) if they believe that in so doing they will be rewarded with something they value. Hence, where additional pay is a valued reward, employees will seek it and will work to secure it. A positive outcome for both employer and employee is achievable provided the incentive is paid in return for a form of employee behaviour which genuinely contributes to the achievement of organisational objectives.

In addition, many reward specialists point to a significant sorting effect which leads employees who are willing and able to perform to a higher standard to be attracted to jobs in which their superior relative contribution will be properly rewarded. At the same time, it is argued, existing employees who perform relatively poorly are more likely to seek alternative employment than colleagues who perform well and are rewarded for doing so. Hence, over time, the quality of employees rises as a result of the presence of incentive schemes. Conversely, of course, it can be plausibly argued that employers who fail to recognise superior individual contribution in their payment systems are more likely to lose higher-performing people because they perceive themselves to be inadequately rewarded for their skills and efforts.

The research evidence is patchy on the question of how far incentives actually lead to performance improvements at the organisational level. Some studies suggest a correlation between superior performance and some types of incentive scheme (e.g. Huselid 1995; Lazear 2000; Piekkola 2005; Gielen *et al.* 2006; Cadsby *et al.* 2007; Gerhart and Trevor 2008), while others (e.g. Pearce *et al.* 1985; Thompson 1992; Makinson 2000; Marsden 2004) have found either no significant evidence of any link. A third group of studies reach context-specific conclusions, finding that incentives can have positive and negative effects in different settings (see Hasnain *et al.* 2012 and Ray *et al.* 2014). In any case, as Corby *et al.* (2005: 5–6) point out, there are very few published studies which focus on performance or productivity levels before and after the introduction of a new scheme. What we have are correlation studies which link superior organisational performance to the presence of incentive schemes, but no proof of any causal relationship. Much seems to depend on the circumstances. Incentives are not universally applicable, but can play a role in enhancing individual effort or performance where the conditions and scheme design are right. Problems occur when the wrong system is imposed, on the wrong people, in the wrong circumstances or for the wrong reasons.

Where an incentive scheme is used, the next choice relates to the way the scheme is to operate. There are two basic approaches that can be used: bonus payments and incremental progression. In the case of the former, the employee is rewarded with a single payment (possibly made in stages) at the end of a payment period. In the case of profit sharing it will often be an annual payment, while sales commission is usually paid monthly. Whatever the timing, the key principle is that the pay is variable. Good performance in one period is rewarded, but the same individual could earn rather less in the next if his or her performance deteriorates. Some writers refer to such systems as putting 'pay at risk', because earnings vary from period to period depending on how much incentive is earned.

The alternative approach involves making incremental progression up to the next grade dependent on the individual's contribution. The reward takes the form of a general pay rise over and above any cost of living increment being paid in a particular year. The incentive payment thus becomes consolidated into overall earnings and is not variable or 'at risk' after it has been earned.

ACTIVITY 26.1

What in your view are the main advantages and disadvantages of these alternative approaches from a management perspective? Would you be more motivated by the prospect of a pay rise or a one-off bonus payment?

Another basic choice concerns the extent of the incentive. In practice this is a decision of rather greater importance than the type of incentive scheme to be used, although it is given rather less coverage in the literature. There is the world of difference, in terms of cost and employee perception, between a scheme which rewards people with 3% or 4% of salary and one which pays a sum equivalent to 25%. Studies undertaken in the USA, reported by Bartol and Durham (2000: 14), suggest that the minimum level of bonus or pay rise 'necessary to elicit positive perceptual and attitudinal responses' is between 5% and 7% of salary. Piekkola (2005), in her studies of links between incentives and firm performance in Finland, found that a positive impact on productivity only began to kick in once the incentive exceeded 3.6% of salary. Lesser payments are thus unlikely to provide meaningful incentives and will have only a peripheral impact. According to Hendry *et al*. (2000: 54), this has been a major problem for schemes introduced in the public sector where incentives have tended to be worth a maximum of only 2% or 3% of salary.

The final choice concerns the level at which the incentive will be paid. Some schemes reward individuals for individual performance, others reward a group of employees or team for their collective performance. Finally there are schemes which share incentive payments out among all employees in the organisation or within individual business units. Team-based incentives have tended to get a better press in recent years than individual incentives, a major problem with the latter being their tendency to undermine teamworking in situations where it is an important contributor to competitive advantage (see Pfeffer 1998: 218–20; Gerhart 2009: 232), but the different forms of incentive are by no means mutually exclusive. It is possible, for example, to reward a salesperson with three types of incentive, one from each level. The basic pay would thus be enhanced with commission calculated individually, with a performance-based payment made to all in the person's sales team to reflect excellent customer feedback, and finally with a profit-related bonus paid to all employees in the organisation. Indeed, the more recent research suggests that employers are increasingly mixing different types of incentive scheme so as to enable them to help meet a range of distinct organisational objectives. It is not at all uncommon, as a result, for more senior employees to have an opportunity to earn additional income from three or four different types of bonus, some individual, some group-based, some leading to a pay rise, others resulting in a one-off bonus payment. The schemes themselves also appear to be becoming increasingly sophisticated and administratively complex (IDS 2005: 7).

WINDOW ON PRACTICE

Peter and Patrick are sales consultants for a financial services company and both had business targets for a six-month period. Peter met his target comfortably and received the predetermined bonus of £6,000 for reaching on-target earnings. Patrick failed to reach his target because his sales manager boss left the company and poached two of Patrick's prime customers just before they signed agreements with him, whose bonus was therefore £2,000 instead of £6,250.

Joanne was a sales consultant for the same company as Peter and Patrick. Before the sales manager left, he made over to her several promising clients with whom he had done considerable preparatory work and who were not willing to be 'poached' by his new employer. All of these signed agreements and one of them decided to increase the value of the deal ten-fold without any reference to Joanne until after that decision was made, and without knowing that she was now the appropriate contact. Her bonus for the period was £23,400.

Henry is a production manager in a light engineering company with performance pay related to a formula combining output with value added. Bonus payments were made monthly in anticipation of what they should be. One of Henry's initiatives was to increase the gearing of the payment by results scheme in the factory. Through peculiarities of company accounting his bonus payments were 'justified' according to the formula, but later it was calculated that the production costs had risen by an amount that cancelled out the value-added benefits. Also 30% of the year's output had to be recalled due to a design fault.

Patrick had his bonus made up to £6,250. Joanne had her bonus reduced to £8,000, but took legal advice and had the amount cut restored, whereupon Peter and Patrick both threatened to resign until mollified by ex gratia payments of £2,000 each. Peter resigned three months later. Henry was dismissed.

The extent to which incentives are paid

There is conflicting evidence about how widespread incentive payments are in the UK and about whether or not they are becoming more or less common. Until 2005, each year the government's New Earnings Survey selected a sample of over 100,000 employees from across the country and asked their employers to fill in a form outlining their earnings in the previous tax year. One of the questions asked about incentive payments 'such as piecework, commission, profit sharing, productivity and other incentives/bonuses'. The survey results persistently showed that only around 15–20% of employees were receiving such payments, most of which were accounted for by traditional piecework or PBR systems operated in manufacturing organisations. The incidence of individual incentives paid to non-manual workers was low. However, other surveys have long painted a rather different picture. The authors analysing the 2011 Workplace Employment Relations Survey (van Wanrooy *et al*. 2013: 24–5) concluded that 54% of the workplaces in their sample operated some form of incentive payment system, 40% using schemes that tie pay to individual performance and 38% to group performance. Even allowing for a strong degree of overlap between schemes as a result of employers operating different payment systems simultaneously, these figures show that incentive payments form at least some part of some people's reward packages in a good majority of UK workplaces.

The CIPD's annual survey of reward practice covers a much smaller sample of employers, but it too suggests both high usage of incentives in the UK and considerably increased usage of incentives over recent years. In 2015 the CIPD reported that 57% of its respondents rewarded staff with individual performance-related bonuses, while 51% gave merit pay rises and 40% operated a profit-sharing scheme. While such approaches are used by a sizeable minority of employers in the public and voluntary sectors, it is in the private sector that activity is focused.

It is not easy to reconcile the diverse results produced by these surveys. One possibility is that the different results may reflect the different samples used. The New Earnings Survey covered workplaces of all sizes, including the very smallest, while the others tend to focus on somewhat larger employers. It could therefore be the case that incentive schemes are largely used in bigger firms with more sophisticated management practices. Another possibility is that many of the schemes in operation only apply to senior managers and not to the generality of staff. Either way, there is clear evidence of growth in the extent to which employers make use of incentive payment systems. Most studies also suggest this is very much an international trend and one which is associated with all industrial sectors (Marginson 2009: 103; IRS 2009), but it is important to note the evidence that suggests performance-related pay may now be rather less widely used in the USA than it was a decade ago (Gittleman 2014).

ACTIVITY 26.2

Why do you think the proportion of workplaces using individual incentive payment systems seems to have grown so much in recent decades?

Payment by results (PBR) schemes

Historically, the most widely used incentive schemes have been those which reward employees according to the number of items or units of work they produce or the time they take to produce them. This approach is associated with F. W. Taylor and the phase in the development of personnel management described under the heading 'Humane bureaucracy' (see Chapter 1). Little attention has been paid to the operation of piecework schemes in recent years and there is some evidence to show that traditionally designed schemes are in decline, both in terms of the proportion of total pay which is determined according to PBR principles and in terms of the number of employees paid in this way (Bryson and Forth 2008: 499; CIPD 2015). However, PBR is still widely used in some shape or form by employers of manual workers (Cox 2006) and, in the form of sales commission, continues to account for a good portion of the earnings of people with selling roles. PBR schemes tend to take one of five major alternative forms:

1 **Individual time-saving schemes** involve incentives being paid for time saved in performing a specified operation. A standard time is derived for a work sequence, the employee receiving an additional payment for the time saved in completing a number of such operations. If it is not possible to work due to shortage of materials or some other reason, the time involved is not counted when the sums are done at the end of the day.

2 **Measured daywork schemes** work by paying employees a fixed sum as long as they maintain a predetermined and agreed level of working. Employees thus have far less discretion over the amount of effort they expend. The advantage of measured daywork over time-saving schemes, from the management point of view, is the greater level of management control that is exercised.

3 **Group incentives** involve applying the principles of individual time saving to group rather than individual output to improve group performance and to promote the development of teamworking. Where jobs are interdependent, group incentives can be appropriate, but it may also put great pressure on the group members, aggravating any interpersonal animosity that exists and increasing the likelihood of stoppages.

4 **Plant-wide bonus schemes** ensure that all employees in a plant or other organisation share in a pool bonus that is linked to the level of output, the value added by the employees collectively or some similar formula. Theoretically, employees are more likely to identify with the organisation as a whole when paid in this way and will cooperate more readily with the management and each other. The difficulties lie in the fact that there is no tangible link between individual effort and individual reward, so that those who are working effectively can have their efforts nullified by others working less effectively.

5 **Commission** paid on sales secured is a widespread practice about which surprisingly little is known as these schemes have not come under the same close scrutiny as incentive schemes for manual employees. They suffer from the same drawbacks, except that they are linked to business won rather than to output achieved.

ACTIVITY 26.3

A problem with sales commission is its tendency to reward the quantity of goods sold without having regard to the quality of service provided by sales staff. In which circumstances might this have negative consequences? How could a commission-based incentive scheme be adapted to incorporate measures of quality as well as quantity?

Performance-related pay (PRP)

Arguments about the advantages and disadvantages of individual PRP have been some of the most hotly contested in recent decades. The topic has formed the basis of numerous research studies and remains one which attracts much controversy, as was shown in recent debates about the introduction of PRP for teachers working in state schools and other public sector workers (see Ray *et al.* 2014). The main reason is the apparent contrast between the theoretical attractiveness of such systems – at least from a management perspective – and their supposed tendency to disappoint when operated in practice. While there are many different types of scheme available, all involve the award of a pay rise or bonus payment to individual employees following a formal assessment of their performance over a defined period (normally the previous year). Two distinct varieties of scheme can be identified:

1 **Merit-based systems** simply involve the immediate supervisor undertaking an appraisal of each subordinate's work performance during the previous year. This will typically be done following a formal appraisal interview and often requires the completion of standard documentation drawn up by an HR department. A proportion of future remuneration is then linked to a score derived from the supervisor's assessment. Some systems require supervisors to award a percentage mark against different criteria, while others oblige them to assess individual performance as 'excellent', 'good', 'satisfactory' or 'inadequate'. Merit-based systems are generally regarded as unsatisfactory because they allow considerable scope for assessors to make subjective judgements or to allow personal prejudice to colour their assessments. There is also a tendency to give undue weight to recent events at the expense of achievements taking place early in the appraisal period.

2 **Goal-based systems** are more objective, but are not appropriate for all kinds of job. They are, however, particularly well suited for the assessment of managerial work. Here the supervisor and subordinate meet at the start of the appraisal period and agree between them a list of objectives which the appraisee will seek to meet during the coming months. Examples would be the completion of particular projects, the establishment of new initiatives, undertaking a course of training or making substantial progress towards the solving of a problem. Many employers nowadays seek to link individual objectives directly to defined organisational goals for the year as a means of reinforcing their significance and ensuring that all are pulling in the same direction. At the end of the year the employee is assessed on the basis of which objectives have or have not been met. A score is then derived and a bonus payment or pay rise awarded. Where performance in a job can meaningfully be assessed in this way, such systems are recommended because they are reasonably objective and straightforward to score. Where the nature of the job involves the consistent achievement of a defined level of performance, and cannot usefully be assessed in terms of the achievement of specific objectives, the goal-based approach has less to offer. It may still be possible to assess part of the job in this way, but there will also have to be a merit-based element if the appraisal is to reflect all of a person's activity during the appraisal period.

ACTIVITY 26.4

Make a list of five jobs that you consider would be best rewarded by a merit-based system and five more that are best rewarded via the goal-based approach.

The attractions of PRP

It is not difficult to see why PRP has attracted the interest of managers, consultants and government ministers. Its theoretical attractions are considerable and include the following:

- attracting and retaining good performers;
- improving individual and corporate performance;
- clarifying job roles and duties;
- improving communication;
- improving motivation;
- reinforcing management control;
- identifying developmental objectives;
- reinforcing the individual employment relationship at the expense of the collective;
- rewarding individuals without needing to promote them.

In short, PRP aims to provide a flexible and cost-effective means of distributing rewards fairly between the good and poorer performers while also contributing towards improved organisational performance. Moreover, it is based on principles to which most people, employees as well as managers, seem to adhere (Brown and Armstrong 2000: 11–13). Most of us are very happy to see individuals rewarded for superior performance and/or effort and would like payment decisions to be based on such criteria. The problems arise when attempts are made to put the principles into practice. A system which is fair and objective in theory can easily fail to achieve these objectives when implemented.

Critiques of PRP

PRP attracted a great amount of criticism from academic researchers in the 1980s and 1990s during a period when its virtues were frequently asserted by HR managers and consultants. The attacks came from several quarters. Occupational psychologists tended to question the ability of PRP to motivate positively (e.g. Kohn 1993), while sociologists saw it as a means of reinforcing management control at the expense of worker autonomy (e.g. Hendry *et al.* 2000). A further source of criticism has come from those who suspect that PRP is used as a means of perpetuating gender inequality in payment matters (e.g. Rubery 1995). However, the most colourful and damning criticisms have come from management thinkers such as W. Edwards Deming who advocate total quality management approaches and for whom PRP represents exactly the wrong kind of initiative to introduce. The whole basis of their philosophy is the substitution of 'leadership' for 'supervision', removing organisational hierarchies and managing people with as little direction and control as possible. They see PRP as having the opposite effect. It reinforces the hierarchy, enhances the power of supervisors and strengthens management control.

For many critics, including those cited above, PRP has fundamental flaws which cannot be overcome. Kohn, for example, argues that incentives can only succeed in securing temporary compliance. Their use cannot change underlying attitudes, while the attempt to do so ultimately damages the long-term health of an organisation by undermining relationships and encouraging employees to focus on short-term aims. Managers who insist that the job will not get done right without rewards have failed to offer a convincing argument for behavioural manipulation. Promising a reward to someone who appears unmotivated is a bit like offering salt water to someone who is thirsty. Bribes in the workplace simply cannot work (Kohn 1993: 60).

A second stream of criticism is more moderate, arguing that PRP can have a role to play in organisations, but that its positive effects are limited. Moreover, while not fundamentally flawed, PRP is very difficult to implement effectively in practice. As a result, systems fail as often as they succeed. The arguments are summarised well by Gomez-Mejia and Balkin (1992: 249–55), Cannell and Wood (1992: 66–101), Pfeffer (1998: 203–4), Purcell (2000) and more recently by Armstrong and Brown (2009: 47–9) and Gerhart (2009). The major points made by these authors are as follows:

- Employees paid by PRP, especially where the incentive is substantial, tend to develop a narrow focus to their work. They concentrate on those aspects which they believe will initiate payments, while neglecting other parts of their jobs.

- PRP, because of its individual nature, tends to undermine teamworking. People focus on their own objectives at the expense of cooperation with colleagues.

- PRP, because it involves managers rating employees according to their perceptions of performance, can lead to a situation in which a good proportion of staff are demotivated when they receive their rating.

- Employees are rarely in a position wholly to determine the outcomes of their own performance. Factors outside their control play an important role, leading to a situation in which the achievement or non-achievement of objectives is partially a matter of chance.

- Even the most experienced managers find it difficult to undertake fair and objective appraisals of their employees' performance. Subjective judgements are often taken into account leading to perceptions of bias. Some managers deliberately manipulate ratings for political reasons, allowing their judgement to be coloured by the effect they perceive the outcome will have on particular employees. Low ratings are thus avoided, as are very high ratings, where it is perceived this will lead to disharmony or deterioration of personal relationships.

- In organisations subject to swift and profound change, objectives set for the coming year may become obsolete after a few months. Employees then find themselves with an incentive to meet goals which are no longer priorities for the organisation.

- PRP systems tend to discourage creative thinking, the challenging of established ways of doing things and a questioning attitude among employees.

- Budgetary constraints often lead managers to reduce ratings, creating a situation in which excellent individual performance is not properly rewarded.

- It is difficult to ensure that each line manager takes a uniform approach to the rating of their subordinates. Some tend to be more generously disposed in general than others, leading to inconsistency and perceptions of unfairness.

- When the results of performance appraisal meetings have an impact on pay levels, employees tend to downplay their weaknesses. As a result development needs are not discussed or addressed.

- PRP systems invariably increase the pay bill. This occurs because managers fear demotivating their staff by awarding low or zero rises in the first years of a system's operation. Poorer performers are thus rewarded as well as better performers.

- PRP systems can be too successful, leading people to take unnecessary risks or to act recklessly in order to secure higher rewards.

WINDOW ON PRACTICE

One of the fundamental problems associated with PRP derives from the so-called 'Lake Wobegon Effect' (Guthrie 2007: 350). The label derives from the words the great American humorist Garrison Keillor uses each week on his radio show when completing his monologue about the goings on in his fictional, but archetypal, small rural town:

> And that's the news from Lake Wobegon where all the women are strong, all the men are good looking, and all the children are above average.

Just as it is not mathematically possible for all children to be 'above average', neither is it possible for all employees to be so. Yet whenever people are asked to rate their own performance they have a very strong tendency to rate themselves as being 'above average'. The inevitable consequence is a situation in which most employee ratings of their own performance are considerably higher than those of their managers. The result is disappointment when manager ratings are revealed, and a tendency for most people to be demotivated.

Using PRP effectively

Despite the problems described above it is possible to implement PRP successfully, as is shown by the experience of case study companies quoted by Brown and Armstrong (2000), IRS (2005a; 2005b) and IDS (2005). It will only work, however, if it is used in appropriate circumstances and if it is implemented properly. Part of the problem with PRP has been a tendency in the HR press to portray it as universally applicable and as a panacea capable of improving performance dramatically. In fact it is neither, but is one of a range of tools that have a useful if limited role to play in some situations. Gomez-Mejia and Balkin (1992) specify the following favourable conditions:

- Where individual performance can be objectively and meaningfully measured.
- Where individuals are in a position to control the outcomes of their work.
- Where close teamworking or cooperation with others is not central to successful job performance.
- Where there is an individualistic organisational culture.

A consensus now appears to be emerging in support of the view that PRP does not generally work as well in the public sector as it does in the private sector (OECD 2005; Prentice *et al.* 2007; Hasnain *et al.* 2012). Only a minority of public-sector workers appear to be motivated positively by PRP, while some groups find that it actively undermines their motivation simply because they are not primarily motivated by pay. Introducing PRP thus cuts across the established professional culture and is not compatible with their perceptions of 'the public-sector ethos'. By contrast PRP does seem to fit better with cultures in some of the growing private-sector industries. Armstrong and Brown (2009) focus particularly on knowledge-intensive work and on customer service, finding in both cases that the circumstances are often, if not always, suited to individualised rewards such as PRP.

Brown and Armstrong (2000) also point to the importance of careful implementation and lengthy preparation prior to the installation of a scheme. Moreover, they argue that PRP should not be looked at or judged in isolation from other forms of reward, both extrinsic and intrinsic. Success or failure can hinge on what else is being done to maximise motivation, to develop people and to improve their job security.

Ultimately PRP has one great advantage which no amount of criticism can remove: it helps ensure that organisational priorities become individual priorities. Managers can signal the importance of a particular objective by including it in a subordinate's goals for the coming year. If the possibility of additional payment is then tied to its achievement, the chances that the objective concerned will be met increases significantly. Organisational performance is improved as a result. Where the achievement of such specific objectives forms a relatively minor part of someone's job, PRP can form a relatively minor part of their pay packet. Other rewards can then be used to recognise other kinds of achievement.

WINDOW ON PRACTICE

Many job descriptions for supervisory positions include reference to responsibility for ensuring that the appropriate health and safety at work regulations are adhered to. Few supervisors, however, left to themselves would see this aspect of their work as a priority. In one organisation known to the authors it was decided to try to raise the profile of health and safety issues by including objectives in this field into managers' annual performance targets. It therefore became clear that the level of PRP in the following year would, in part, be determined by the extent to which the health and safety objectives had been met. The result was the swift establishment of departmental health and safety committees and schemes whereby staff could bring safety hazards to the attention of supervisors.

Skills-based pay

A further kind of incentive payment scheme is one which seeks to reward employees for the skills or competencies which they acquire. It is well established in the USA and became fashionable in the UK during the 1990s and early 2000s. Since then interest has waned, most recent texts on reward management paying it relatively little attention. It is most useful as a means of rewarding technical staff, but there is no reason why the principle should not be extended to any group of employees for whom the acquisition of additional skills might benefit the organisation.

There are several potential benefits for an employer introducing a skills-based pay scheme. Its most obvious effect is to encourage multiskilling and flexibility enabling the organisation to respond more effectively and speedily to the needs of customers. A multiskilled workforce may also be slimmer and less expensive. In addition it is argued that, in rewarding skills acquisition, a company will attract and retain staff more effectively than its competitors in the labour market. The operation of a skills-based reward system is proof that the sponsoring employer is genuinely committed to employee development.

Most skills-based payment systems reward employees with additional increments to their base pay once they have completed defined skill modules. A number of such schemes are described in detail in a study published by Incomes Data Services (IDS 1992). Typical is the scheme operated by Venture Pressings Ltd where staff are employed on four basic grades, each divided into ten increments. Employees progress up the scale by acquiring specific skills and demonstrating proficiency in them to the satisfaction of internal assessors. New starters are also assessed and begin their employment on the incremental point most appropriate to the level of skills they can demonstrate. In many industries it is now possible to link payment for skills acquisition directly to the attainment of National Vocational Qualifications (NVQs) for which both the setting of standards and the assessment of individual competency are carried out externally.

A skills-based pay system will only be cost effective if it results in productivity increases which are sufficient to cover the considerable costs associated with its introduction and maintenance. A business can invest a great deal of resources both in training its workforce to attain new skills and in rewarding it once those skills have been acquired, only to find that the cost of the scheme outweighs the benefit gained in terms of increased flexibility and efficiency. Furthermore, in assisting employees to become more highly qualified and in many cases to gain NVQs, an employer may actually find it harder to retain its staff in relatively competitive labour markets.

The other major potential disadvantage is associated with skills obsolescence. Where a business operates in a fast-moving environment and needs to adapt its technology regularly, a skills-based payment system can leave the organisation paying enhanced salaries for skills which are no longer significant or are not required at all. Employers seeking to introduce skills-based systems of payment therefore need to consider the implications very carefully and must ensure that they only reward the acquisition of those skills which will clearly contribute to increased productivity over the long term.

ACTIVITY 26.5

A number of commentators praise skills-based pay as a system which avoids some of the pitfalls associated with PRP schemes. Look back at the list of practical problems with PRP schemes above and consider which do and which do not apply to skills-based incentive systems.

Profit sharing

There are a number of different ways in which companies are able to link remuneration to profit levels. In recent decades governments all over the world have sought to encourage such schemes and have actively promoted their establishment with advantageous tax arrangements. The EU has been particularly interested in promoting these types of scheme. Underlying government support is the belief that linking pay to profits increases the employee's commitment to his or her company by deepening the level of mutual interest. As a result, it is argued that such schemes act as an incentive encouraging employees to work harder and with greater flexibility in pursuit of higher levels of take-home pay. Other potential advantages for employers and governments described by Pendleton (2009) are better cost flexibility, changed attitudes on the part of employees and the discouragement of union membership.

Cash-based schemes

The traditional and most common profit-sharing arrangement is simply to pay employees a cash bonus, calculated as a proportion of annual profits, on which the employee incurs both an income tax and a National Insurance liability. Some organisations pay discretionary profit bonuses on this basis, while others allocate a fixed proportion of profits to employees as a matter of policy. Gain sharing is a variation on cash-based profit sharing which is widely used in the USA and which can be used in non-profit-making organisations as well as those operating in the commercial sector. Here the bonus relates to costs saved rather than profit generated in a defined period. So if a workforce successfully achieves the same level of output at lower overall cost, the gain is shared between employer and employees.

Share-based schemes

There are several methods of profit sharing which involve employees being awarded shares rather than cash. Here too there are government-sponsored schemes in operation which involve favourable tax treatment. There are several distinct schemes available for employers to use, some of which are more tax efficient than others. The current list includes Share Incentive Plans, the Save As You Earn (SAYE) scheme, Company Share Option Plans and Enterprise Management Incentives (EMIs).

Traditionally senior managers have been paid, in part, through share-based reward systems, but companies are increasingly seeing an advantage in extending these arrangements to a greater proportion of their staff. The purpose is to increase commitment by giving employees a significant financial stake in the future of the business they work for, at the same time helping to align employees' interests with those of shareholders. The result should be improved staff retention and higher levels of individual performance, but it is difficult to prove that such outcomes result in practice from the introduction of these schemes. For most ordinary employees the level of reward is too low, and the extent to which their actions impact on a firm's performance too indirect, for there to be a clear-cut incentive effect.

Disadvantages of profit-related schemes

The obvious disadvantage of the schemes described above from the employee's point of view is the risk that pay levels may decline if the company fails to meet its expected profit levels. If no profit is made it cannot be shared. Share values can go down as well as up. Companies are not permitted to make guarantees about meeting payments and will have their schemes revoked by the Inland Revenue if they do so. In any event it is likely that profit-based incentives will vary in magnitude from year to year.

For these reasons it is questionable to assert that profit-sharing schemes do in fact act as incentives. Unlike PRP awards they do not relate specifically to the actions of the individual employee. Annual profit levels are clearly influenced by a whole range of factors which are both internal and external to the company. An employee may well develop a community of interest with the company management, shareholders and other employees but it is unlikely seriously to affect the nature of his or her work. Furthermore, both poor and good performers are rewarded equally in profit-related schemes. The incentive effect will therefore be very slight in most cases and will be restricted to a general increase in employee commitment.

WINDOW ON PRACTICE

For many years government ministers from across the political spectrum in the UK have developed schemes which provide incentives to firms to share profits with their employees. These have often taken the form of plans which make it tax efficient to reward staff with shares. The model operated by the John Lewis Partnership (owners of the John Lewis department stores and the Waitrose supermarket chain) is often cited as one which government would like other companies to imitate.

John Lewis is controlled by a trust which has the task of running the company in the interest of its employees, all of whom are partners in the enterprise for as long as they remain employed by the company. The trust appoints the chairman and deputy chairman, who in turn appoint five members of the executive board. The remaining five places are occupied by people who are nominated by the Partnership Council, an eighty-two-strong body of whom 80% are elected by the partners through a branch network. The result is a company which is highly successful commercially, but which also provides its people with terms and conditions of employment that are very generous by comparison with those provided by other retailers. Each year in January all partners receive a bonus payment which is linked directly to the profits generated in the previous year. This is calculated as a percentage of their annual salary, the same percentage being received by everyone regardless of seniority. Because the company is successful and growing, bonus payments have tended to be quite high in recent years, averaging between 10% and 20% of salary. In 2012–13 the company made a net profit of £406.6 million, of which £210.8 million was distributed to partners in the form of profit sharing. This gave each of them a bonus payment equivalent to 17% of their annual salaries. Pension and holiday entitlements are also very generous, all partners who complete twenty-five years' service being rewarded with a six-month period of paid leave.

SUMMARY PROPOSITIONS

26.1. Incentive schemes should be used where they are appropriate to the needs of the business and where they can clearly contribute to the achievement of organisational objectives.

26.2. The extent to which different types of incentive arrangement are used in the UK is unclear. There is evidence of growth in recent years, but the majority of employees are not covered by such schemes.

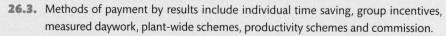

26.3. Methods of payment by results include individual time saving, group incentives, measured daywork, plant-wide schemes, productivity schemes and commission.

26.4. Performance-related pay systems are either merit based or goal based. They have been the subject of notable debate in recent years, many researchers finding a mismatch between their theoretical attractions and practical outcomes.

26.5. Skills-based pay involves linking incentives to the achievement of defined competencies or qualifications. It rewards what people bring to the job rather than the results of their efforts.

26.6. Profit sharing has been promoted by governments for many years. The share incentive plan is one of several government-sponsored schemes aimed at encouraging employees to hold shares in their own companies.

GENERAL DISCUSSION TOPICS

1. What are the relative advantages of: (a) a system of straight salary that is the same each month; and (b) a system of salary with an individual performance-related addition so that the total payment each month varies?

2. In what circumstances might it be appropriate to base individual payment on team performance?

3. What do you think about Peter, Patrick, Joanne and Henry in the Window on practice box early in this chapter?

THEORY INTO PRACTICE

Performance-related pay at the Cavendish Hall Hotel

Daphne Jones has recently been appointed as Personnel Manager of the Cavendish Hall Hotel, a 200-bedroom, four-star country house hotel located in rolling hills a few miles south of a major northern industrial conurbation. The hotel provides a wide range of conference and banqueting facilities and is a popular wedding location. Despite poor reviews from guests concerning the cost of drinks and the quality of the food on offer, the hotel is financially successful, having recently recorded increased annual profits.

Soon after her appointment Daphne decides that it is necessary and desirable to introduce a new payment system which links reward to individual effort and competency. She is concerned that the present system of paying everyone in a job role the same rate irrespective of their individual performance is unfair and tends to demotivate the best performers. She therefore decides to take a different approach when determining this year's annual pay rises:

1 Each member of staff will receive a 1% salary increase regardless of performance to take account of the increased cost of living.

2 Each line manager will be required to score their staff based on their individual performance over the past year. There are four options:

- excellent
- good
- satisfactory
- unsatisfactory.

3 Staff scored as 'excellent' will receive a 4% pay rise (3% plus the 1% cost of living increase), those marked as 'good' will receive 3% and those as 'satisfactory' 2%. People who are marked as 'unsatisfactory' will simply receive the 1% cost of living increase.

The hotel has not hitherto operated any kind of formal performance management system. There are no annual appraisals or development reviews. Managers vary greatly in the extent to which they communicate with their staff at all, let alone to discuss their individual performance. For many the only indicator they have that they are doing a good job is the amount they receive from guests in the form of tips. As a result, when the new scheme is announced in a series of staff meetings, there is enormous excitement. There is massive anticipation among staff in the days and weeks running up to the announcement of the pay awards.

At the last minute, however, there are hitches and as a result the announcement is delayed for a week. This occurs because Daphne finds herself disagreeing profoundly with the scores awarded by two of her managers.

George Clapham, the Head Porter, has awarded all his staff excellent ratings. When Daphne questions him about this, he replies that he thinks all his lads are wonderful, that they have all worked very hard over the last year and that they all deserve the full 4%. Surely, Daphne argues, he cannot give Graham Dudd an excellent rating? Not only has he been absent most of the past year, but he is regularly found away from his post chatting up chambermaids in the staff room?

George argues that Graham means well and is greatly liked by his colleagues. Daphne insists he is downgraded to 'satisfactory'.

Henry Oldham-Down, the Head Chef, has awarded two of his senior staff excellent ratings, but has rated all the commis chefs and kitchen porters as 'unsatisfactory'. When questioned about this, Henry says that they are all 'crap' and a waste of space as far as he is concerned and that giving them the 1% cost of living rise is much more than they deserve. Daphne lists some names of kitchen staff who she thinks do a good job. After each name is mentioned Henry just says 'crap'.

Daphne insists that one or two of the staff are upgraded to 'satisfactory'.

The following week letters are sent to all staff telling them how they have been rated by their managers and what the implications are for their pay. At the end of the letter is a sentence that asks staff who are unhappy with their pay rises to see Daphne Jones.

The following day a long line of disappointed staff forms outside Daphne's office. There is a perceivable drop in morale and this leads to reduced effort. In the coming weeks absence

➤ rates increase and guest complaints rise. There are particular problems in the kitchen, leading several guests to write very strongly worded letters of complaint.

Daphne is not surprised that poor performers are disappointed, but she finds it hard to understand why so many strong performers who have been rated 'good' are so negative about the whole exercise. What is more, she finds herself under fire from the Finance Director of the company which owns the hotel. He says that the pay bill is now too high and that it will have to be cut back next year.

The General Manager of Cavendish Hall thinks that the problems with the scheme have mainly been caused by different managers rating people according to different criteria. Next year, he says, a forced ranking system will be used. This will mean that each line manager will be asked to rank their staff in order of performance. The top 25% will then receive the excellent rating and highest pay rise. Those in the second quartile will be scored as 'good' and those in the third and fourth quartiles as 'satisfactory' and 'unsatisfactory' respectively. This system also means that a budget can be set and that it will be adhered to in practice.

Questions

1 What was wrong with the design of the payment system?

2 What was wrong with the way it was introduced?

3 What do you think of the new 'forced ranking system' that is planned for next year?

4 What alternative type of system would you argue should be introduced and why?

FURTHER READING

Brown, D. and Armstrong, M. (2000) *Paying or Contribution: Real performance-related pay strategies*. London: Kogan Page.

Kohn, A. (1993) 'Why incentive plans cannot work', *Harvard Business Review,* September–October, pp. 54–63.

The debate about the merits of individual performance-related pay is so polarised that it is rare to find a balanced account that sets out the views of those who are for and those who are against. It is best to read the partisan accounts. Kohn's (1993) article contains an eloquent and damning critique of such schemes, while Brown and Armstrong (2000) paint a more positive picture.

Incomes Data Services: various publications.

Industrial Relations Services: various publications.

Information about trends in the design of incentive payment schemes is regularly provided in the IDS and IRS publications. They also commonly feature case studies which show exactly how the various schemes operate in practice as well as regular surveys of current practice that can be used for benchmarking processes.

Gerhart, B. (2009) 'Compensation', in J. Storey *et al.* (eds), *The Routledge Companion to Strategic Human Resource Management*. London: Routledge.

This is a very good, comprehensive summary of academic research on incentives of all kinds, reviewing the major studies and reaching sound, balanced conclusions.

REFERENCES

Armstrong, M. and Brown, D. (2009) *Strategic Reward: Implementing more effective reward management*. London: Kogan Page.

Bartol, K.M. and Durham, C.C. (2000) 'Incentives: Theory and practice', in C. Cooper and E. Locke (eds), *Industrial and Organisational Psychology*. Oxford: Blackwell.

Brown, D. and Armstrong, M. (2000) *Paying for Contribution: Real Performance-related Pay Strategies*. London: Kogan Page.

Bryson, A. and Forth, J. (2008) 'The theory and practice of pay setting', in P. Blyton *et al*. (eds), *The Sage Handbook of Industrial Relations*. London: Sage.

Cadsby, C., Song, F. and Tapon, F. (2007) 'Sorting and incentive effects of pay-for-performance: An experimental investigation', *Academy of Management Journal*, Vol. 37, pp. 554–79.

Cannell, M. and Wood, S. (1992) *Incentive Pay: Impact and Evolution*. London: IPM.

CIPD (2015) *Reward Management 2014–15*. London: CIPD.

Corby, S., White, G. and Stanworth, C. (2005) 'No news is good news? Evaluating new pay systems', *Human Resource Management Journal*, Vol. 15, No. 1, pp. 4–24.

Cox, A. (2006) 'The outcomes of variable pay systems: Tales of multiple costs and unforeseen consequences', *International Journal of Human Resource Management*, Vol. 16, No. 8, pp. 1475–97.

Gerhart, B. (2009) 'Compensation', in J. Storey *et al*. (eds), *The Routledge Companion to Strategic Human Resource Management*. London: Routledge.

Gerhart, B. and Trevor, C. (2008) 'Merit pay', in A. Varma *et al*. (eds), *Performance Management Systems: A Global Perspective*. London: Routledge.

Gielen, A.C., Kerkhofs, M.J.M. and Van Ours, J.C. (2006) *Performance-related Pay and Labour Productivity*, IZA Discussion Paper 2211. Berlin: Institute for the Study of Labour (IZA).

Gittleman, M. (2014) 'Performance-related pay in the United States is becoming less prevalent', *Monthly Labor Review*, February, pp. 1–2.

Gomez-Mejia, L. and Balkin, D. (1992) *Compensation, Organisational Strategy and Firm Performance*. Cincinnati, OH: South Western Publishing.

Guthrie, J. (2007) 'Remuneration: Pay effects at work', in P. Boxall *et al*. (eds), *The Oxford Handbook of Human Resource Management*. Oxford: Oxford University Press.

Hasnain, Z., Manning, N. and Pierskalla, J.H. (2012) 'Performance-related pay in the public sector: A review of theory and evidence', The World Bank Policy Research Paper 6043.

Hendry, C., Woodward, S., Bradley, P. and Perkins, S. (2000) 'Performance and rewards: Cleaning out the stables', *Human Resource Management Journal*, Vol. 10, No. 3, pp. 46–62.

Herzberg, F. (1966) *Work and the Nature of Man*. Cleveland, OH: World Publishing.

Huselid, M. (1995) 'The impact of HRM practices on turnover, productivity and corporate performance', *Academy of Management Journal*, Vol. 38, pp. 635–72.

IDS (1992) *Skills-based Pay*, IDS Study No. 500. London: Incomes Data Services.

IDS (2005) *Bonus Schemes*, IDS Study No. 794. London: Incomes Data Services.

IRS (2005a) 'Pay 4 Performance at Yorkshire Water', *IRS Employment Review*, No. 833, pp. 31–5.

IRS (2005b) 'Performing flexible reward at Severn Trent Water', *IRS Employment Review*, No. 834, pp. 30–3.

IRS (2009) 'Charity employers are turning to performance-related pay', *IRS Employment Review*, No. 914, January.

Kohn, A. (1993) 'Why incentive plans cannot work', *Harvard Business Review*, September–October, pp. 54–63.

Lazear, E.P. (2000) 'Performance pay and productivity', *American Economic Review,* Vol. 90, No. 5, pp. 1346–61.

Makinson, J. (2000) *Incentives for Change.* London: HMSO.

Marginson, P. (2009) 'Performance pay and collective bargaining: A complex relationship', in S. Corby *et al.* (eds), *Rethinking Reward.* Basingstoke: Palgrave.

Marsden, D. (2004) 'The role of performance-related pay in renegotiating the "effort bargain": The case of the British public service', *Industrial and Labour Relations Review,* Vol. 57, No. 3, pp. 350–70.

OECD (2005) *Performance-related Pay Policies for Government Employees.* Paris: OECD.

Pearce, J.L., Stevenson, W.B. and Perry, J.L. (1985) 'Managerial compensation based on organisational performance: A time series analysis of the effects of merit pay', *Academy of Management Journal,* Vol. 28, pp. 261–78.

Pendleton, A. (2009) 'Employee share ownership in Europe', in S. Corby *et al.* (eds), *Rethinking Reward.* Basingstoke: Palgrave.

Pfeffer, J. (1998) *The Human Equation: Building Profits by Putting People First.* Boston, MA: Harvard Business School Press.

Piekkola, H. (2005) 'Performance-related pay and firm performance in Finland', *International Journal of Manpower,* Vol. 7, No. 8, pp. 619–35.

Prentice, G., Burgess, S. and Propper, C. (2007) *Performance Pay in the Public Sector: A Review of the Issues and Evidence.* London: Office of Manpower Economics.

Purcell, J. (2000) 'Pay per view', *People Management,* 3 February, pp. 41–3.

Ray, K., Foley, B., Tsang, T., Waine, D. and Bajorek, Z. (2014) *A Review of the Evidence on the Impact Effectiveness and Value for Money of Performance-related Pay in the Public Sector.* The Work Foundation. www.theworkfoundation.com.

Rubery, J. (1995) 'Performance-related pay and the prospects for gender pay equity', *Journal of Management Studies,* Vol. 32, No. 5, pp. 637–54.

Sisson, K. and Storey, J. (2000) *The Realities of Human Resource Management.* Buckingham: Open University Press.

Thompson, M. (1992) *Pay and Performance: The Employer Experience,* Institute of Manpower Studies Report 218. London: IMS.

Thompson, M. (2000) 'Salary progression systems', in G. White and J. Druker (eds), *Reward Management: A Critical Text.* London: Routledge.

Van Wanrooy, B., Bewley, H., Bryson, A., Forth, J., Freeth, S., Stokes, L. and Wood, S. (2013) *The 2011 Workplace Employment Relations Study: First Findings.* London: Department for Business, Innovation and Skills.

CHAPTER 27
PENSIONS AND BENEFITS

THE OBJECTIVES OF THIS CHAPTER ARE TO:

1 Introduce the different types of pension scheme provided by the state, by employers and by financial services organisations

2 Explain the causes and significance of current trends in the provision of occupational pensions

3 Outline the roles played by HR professionals in the field of occupational pensions

4 Distinguish between Statutory Sick Pay (SSP) and Occupational Sick Pay (OSP)

5 Assess developments in the provision of company cars by UK employers

6 Explore the potential of flexible benefits systems in the UK context

Employee benefits commonly used to be known as 'fringe benefits', suggesting a peripheral role in the typical pay packet. The substantial growth in the value of most benefits packages over the past twenty or thirty years means that the title 'fringe' is no longer appropriate. An increasing proportion of individual remuneration is made up of additional perks, allowances and entitlements which are mostly paid in kind rather than cash. The total value of benefits 'paid' by employers to employees commonly represents between 20% and 50% of an organisation's salary budget, depending on what is included. Pensions alone can easily account for 20%, to which must be added the costs of providing some or all of the following: company cars, sick pay, meals, live-in accommodation, parking facilities, private health insurance, crèche facilities, mobile phones, Christmas parties, staff discounts, relocation expenses and any holiday or maternity allowances paid in excess of the required statutory minima. Wright (2009a: 184) shows that these extra elements of pay are distributed unevenly between members of staff. Those earning at the top of the scale (especially directors and senior managers) tend to gain rather more than average employees, 30% or 50% of their take-home pay being accounted for by benefits of various kinds.

This is an area of HRM policy in which practice varies considerably from country to country. In the USA, for example, there is no legal entitlement to paid holiday and it is usual for people to take just two weeks' leave in a year. Yet the extent and generosity of employer-provided private health insurance and pensions is as good as anywhere in the world. By contrast, in France holiday entitlements and redundancy payments are very generous, but occupational pensions are rarely provided for most employees at all. In the UK statutory paid maternity leave and associated rights are among the most generous in the world, have become increasingly generous in recent years, yet are still exceeded by many employers. Occupational pensions are in decline in the UK, but still cover many more employees than is the case in most European countries. Generally speaking, however, everywhere in the world the long-term trend is towards the provision of a wider range of benefits, and for this element of the total pay package to increase as a proportion of the whole.

Despite these developments, there remains a big question mark over how far employees value the benefits provided to them by their employers or appreciate the extent of the costs involved in their provision. Surveys of both employers and employees regularly demonstrate that staff have little understanding of the value of the benefits they receive and that there is thus little by way of any positive motivational effect generated by their presence (see Accor 2008; Thomson Online 2007). International survey evidence also tends to show that employees often fail to take advantage of the benefits provided for them (Hina *et al.* 2014) and that in some cases there is a preference for pay increases over benefits even when the true value of the benefits package being offered can be shown to be higher (Duda 2011).

This does not mean, of course, that employers can easily stop offering benefits. While the full cost and range of benefits may not be appreciated by employees, they are generally in favour of them and resent their removal. They also appear to be associated with superior organisational performance (Lin *et al.* 2014). Moreover, poor publicity would inevitably follow the withdrawal of rewards such as pensions which are generally seen as being the hallmark of a good employer. The alternative courses of action involve communicating the true value of benefits to employees more effectively and providing them with a degree of choice as to which benefits they wish to receive. The latter approach, involving the provision of 'flexible' or 'cafeteria' benefits, has become very common in the USA and has received a great deal of attention in the UK too.

Pensions

The role of employers in providing pensions has moved up the public policy agenda for several reasons in recent years, but underlying all of them are the long-term demographic trends which have called into question the ability of the established UK pension system to provide an adequate income to older people after they retire. First and foremost, people are living increasingly longer and thus require a bigger pension to provide them with an income across their years of retirement. In 1950 men aged 65 in the UK could expect to live for a further twelve years on average, and women for a further fifteen. The figures are now over nineteen years for men and twenty-two for women, and with rapid developments in medical science there is every reason to expect life expectancy rates to accelerate further in the coming fifty years. It is likely, according to many projections, that over half of the people born in the 1980s will live into their 90s and beyond. Second, fewer children are being born, birth rates in the UK having been at below replacement rates since the late 1960s (Pemberton *et al*. 2006: 4). These trends are soon going to lead to a steady increase in the dependency ratio, by which is meant the proportion of retired people vis-à-vis working people in the economy. At present in the UK 27% of the adult population is aged over 65. By 2050, according to the Government Actuary, the proportion will be 48% (Turner 2004: 4). Demographic trends are thus leading us steadily towards a situation in which the funding of adequate pensions using established approaches is going to become harder and harder to achieve. The trend for more young people to stay at school until the age of 18 and for many more to go on to university makes the problem more acute because it further reduces the proportion of the population which is economically active.

The UK is by no means unique in facing this long-term problem. Indeed, in many other industrialised countries the situation is worse because fertility rates are lower still and there is a tradition of greater reliance on the state to provide pension income than has hitherto been the case in the UK. Everywhere it is increasingly being realised that action needs to be taken now in order to avoid a future scenario in which either the elderly live in unacceptable poverty or taxation has to be increased to economically unsustainable levels in order to fund a decent level of state pension.

In the UK the situation has been made worse over the past seventeen years by some most unwelcome trends in the occupational pensions sector. Until the 1990s the UK could boast that it had one of the most extensive and well-funded systems of occupational pension provision in the world. Well over half of the workforce were members of reasonably generous, well-funded occupational pension schemes provided for them by their employers, while millions of retired employees drew a substantial income from the schemes which supplemented their state pensions. This system was likened by commentators who drew international comparisons to the goose that laid the golden egg. It meant that the UK had a great deal less to worry about from population ageing than other countries because so much more of our pension income was sourced privately through both individual savings and these huge, long-established occupational pension funds. Unfortunately, the goose has now stopped laying the golden eggs and the long-established system is in terminal decline. Employers are less likely to offer membership of occupational schemes than they were, and where they still do, it is on a less satisfactory financial basis when seen from the perspective of most employees.

A combination of factors is responsible, but the core problem is the hugely increased costs that are now associated with the provision of good pensions for staff. This is due to taxation changes, to increased life expectancy and to the need to keep topping up pension funds whenever the stock market suffers falls of the kinds it has in recent years.

The government has responded to this situation in a way that most commentators have welcomed, although some argue that the plans it has put in place do not go far enough. In 2002 Adair Turner (now Lord Turner), a former Director General of the Confederation of British Industry (CBI), was appointed by the Department for Work and Pensions to lead an extensive review of future pension provision in the UK. The Turner Commission has since produced three substantial reports setting out its findings and recommendations. The government accepted the vast majority of these and brought forward legislation in the form of the Pensions Act 2007 to encourage later retirement and significantly greater levels of saving into pension funds. It also makes important changes to the established state pension system which are aimed particularly at improving the position of women. At the same time other steps have been taken by the government to ease the pressures on the pension system caused by demographic trends. The equalisation of state pension ages between men and women is such a step, as in many respects is the recent substantial growth in immigration. Other measures include new incentives for people who are not working (e.g. single parents and early retirees) to re-enter the workforce.

ACTIVITY 27.1

The UK has always been unusual in having such a substantial occupational pensions sector. There is a similar system in the Netherlands and in the Republic of Ireland, but in most EU countries most employers see no reason why they should be involved in the provision of pensions. Why do you think these differences persist? What arguments would you advance to persuade a company based in an EU country of the need to offer occupational pensions to employees in a new UK subsidiary?

State schemes

In the UK the state currently runs two schemes: a basic scheme and the State Second Pension (S2P) scheme, although the latter will soon be phased out and replaced with a single, more generous, basic old age pension benefit. By 2020 the pensionable age for both men and women will be 65 and in the years running up to this date the pensionable age for women is gradually increasing from 60 where it was for many decades. The government has announced plans to push back the state pension age for men and women once equalisation has been achieved. It will increase to 66 from 2024, to 67 from 2034 and to 68 from 2044, but changes may in fact come in considerably earlier than this.

The state pension scheme is organised on a pay-as-you-go basis. This means that there is no state pension fund as such, and the money that is paid to today's pensioners comes from today's taxes and National Insurance contributions. The money that will be paid to today's contributors, when they become pensioners, will come not from the investment of their and their employers' contributions, but from the contributions of the workforce and its employers in the future. This is why there is concern about the ability of future governments to be able to fund state pensions for many more retired people beyond a basic subsistence level, and why a raft of new regulation is currently being introduced which aims to increase pension saving (see below).

Occupational schemes

The UK has had, for many years, one of the most extensive and effective systems of occupational pension provision in the world. According to the most recent government statistics, there are around 44,000 separate schemes in operation with combined assets worth approximately £1.9 trillion. Just over 8 million people are members of occupational pension schemes, while around 9 million pensioners draw an income from their funds (ONS 2012a). Although there has been some reduction recently in the proportion of the workforce covered by occupational pensions, they remain by far the most significant employee benefit in terms of their cost to employers.

Occupational schemes provide an additional retirement pension on top of the state pension, providing better and wider-ranging benefits than the state schemes and a great deal more flexibility. They are most often found in large organisations and the public sector, but some smaller organisations also run such schemes. Men and women have equal access to occupational schemes and, since 1990, have had to be treated equally in respect of all scheme rules. Yet, in spite of this, men and women continue to fare differently in terms of pension benefits due to the typical pattern of women's employment being different from male patterns and women's longer average life expectancy. A higher proportion of managerial and professional workers have occupational pensions than other groups, unskilled workers being the least likely to be in schemes. It is no longer lawful for an employer to exclude part-time or temporary workers.

With the exception of one or two in the public sector, occupational schemes do not pay their pensioners in the pay-as-you-go manner operated by the state, but create a pension fund, which is managed separately from the business. The advantage of this is that, should the organisation become bankrupt, the pension fund cannot be seized to pay debtors because it is not part of the company. The money in the pension fund is invested and held in trust for the employees of the company at the time of their retirement. However, where a company becomes insolvent at a time when its pension fund is in deficit, employees can lose all or part of their pensions. This has happened in one or two high-profile cases recently, leading the government to establish a central fund to provide a measure of compensation to those whose pensions are reduced as a result of their employer's insolvency.

Larger organisations traditionally administer their own pension funds through an investment or fund manager. The manager will plan how to invest the money in the fund to get the best return and to ensure that the money that is needed to pay pensions and other benefits will be available when required. An actuary can provide mortality tables and other statistical information in order to assist planning and must be hired regularly to carry out a formal actuarial assessment of the scheme's assets and liabilities. Smaller organisations tend to appoint an insurance company or a bank to administer their pension funds, and so use their expertise. Pension funds can be invested in a variety of different ways, and are often worth more than the market value of their sponsoring companies. As a result they have come to dominate investment on the stock market.

Defined benefit schemes

Defined benefit schemes dominated in the final decades of the twentieth century, but the number of people with access to them has declined hugely in the last twelve years. Virtually all the public-sector schemes still take this form, but 87% of the private-sector schemes have now been closed to new members (NAPF 2013). They remain operational only for the purposes of paying pensions to retired members and for the benefit of employees who joined before their closure. Here contributions are made into a single organisation-wide fund which is invested on behalf of members by a fund manager. Retired employees then draw a pension from the fund calculated according to a defined formula. Most defined benefit schemes take the final salary form, in which the value of the pension is determined by the level of salary being received by each individual at the time of retirement. In the private sector it is common for this to be calculated on a 'sixtieths' basis, whereby the retiree is paid an annual pension equivalent to $1 \div 60$ (1.67%) of their final salary multiplied by the number of years' pensionable service they have completed. In the public sector it is usual for the figure to be based on 'eightieths', with a tax-free lump sum being paid in addition at the time of retirement. In either case the size of pension is heavily related to the length of scheme membership, the maximum pension payable equalling two-thirds of final salary. Examples of final salary calculations are given in Table 27.1.

Another form of defined benefit scheme bases the pension calculation on the average salary earned over a period of 5, 10 or 20 years prior to retirement rather than on pay in the final year. Unless most of someone's pensionable service has been spent earning close to the final salary level, such schemes are less generous than the final salary variety in terms of the amount of pension paid. High levels of inflation also reduce the value of pensions calculated on an average salary basis. The government has signalled that it wishes over time to convert the public-sector schemes from the final salary to an average salary formula, while also removing the right previously enjoyed by many public-sector workers to retire on a full pension at the age of 60.

Most defined benefit schemes are contributory. This means that monies are paid into the fund on a regular basis by both the employer and the employee. In the case of employees the contribution is fixed as a percentage of salary (typically 5%), a sum which is

Table 27.1 Final salary schemes – examples of various contribution periods with a 1/60th and a 1/80th scheme

Sixtieths scheme:

Final salary	= £24,000
Contributions for 5 years	= 1÷60 × 24,000 × 5
Pension	= £2,000 per year
Final salary	= £24,000
Contributions for 25 years	= 1÷60 × 24,000 × 25
Pension	= £10,000 per year
Final salary	= £24,000
Contributions for 40 years	= 1÷60 × 24,000 × 40
Pension	= £16,000 per year

Eightieths scheme:

Final salary	= £24,000
Contributions for 25 years	= 1÷80 × 24,000 × 25
Pension	= £7,500 per year
Lump sum	= 3÷80 × 24,000 × 25 = £22,500

subject to tax relief. Employers, by contrast, are obliged only to pay in sufficient funds to ensure that the scheme remains solvent. When the pension fund is in surplus, as many were in the 1980s and 1990s, employers can take 'contribution holidays'. By contrast, when the fund is in deficit, the employer has to contribute whatever is necessary to ensure that assets are sufficient to meet possible liabilities.

This means that the amount of employer contribution can vary considerably, year on year, in an unpredictable fashion. In 2012 contribution rates for employers were averaging over 15% of salary (ONS 2012b). However, employers, like employees, gain from tax relief on contributions paid.

In some industries, as well as parts of the public sector, it has been traditional for occupational pensions to be non-contributory. In such schemes the employee makes no contribution at all, but nonetheless draws a pension calculated according to the final salary. Civil servants benefit from this kind of arrangement, as do many employees in the banking and finance sectors. Defined benefit schemes also typically offer extra benefits such as ill-health pensions for those forced to retire early and death-in-service benefits for widows and widowers.

Defined contribution schemes

Defined contribution schemes (also known as money purchase schemes) are organised in a totally different way from defined benefit arrangements. There are no promises about what the final level of pension will be. Instead employees and employers both contribute a fixed percentage of current salary to these schemes, usually 5% to 8% on a monthly basis. The pension benefits received are then entirely dependent on the money that has been contributed and the way that it has been invested. Where investments perform well, a good level of pension can be gained. Where investments are disappointing, the result is a low level of pension. Further uncertainty derives from the way that money purchase schemes result in the payment of a single lump sum to the employee when he or she retires. This is then used to buy an annuity from an insurance company from which a weekly or monthly income is paid for life. Annuity rates vary considerably from year to year, and there is also considerable variation between the deals offered by different providers. In essence this means that the risk associated with pension investments is carried by the employee in a defined contribution arrangement, rather than by the employer as in a final salary scheme. For this reason defined contribution schemes are generally less satisfactory than defined benefit schemes when seen from an employee's perspective. Investments have to perform unusually well while inflation remains low for a money purchase scheme to give an equivalent level of benefit. However, despite these drawbacks, money purchase schemes are more flexible and more easily transferable than defined benefit arrangements. For people changing jobs frequently or working on a self-employed basis for periods of time, particularly during the early years of a career, they can thus be a more attractive option.

In recent years there has been a strong trend away from defined benefit schemes and towards defined contribution provision. The majority of newly established schemes take the defined contribution form, while many organisations now offer only a money purchase scheme to new employees (Dobson and Horsfield 2009). The trend has coincided with a period in which long contribution holidays have come to an end and in which the amount of regulation to which defined benefit schemes are subject has increased substantially. Employers have thus taken the opportunity to reduce their own liabilities and to move to a form of provision which is more predictable financially from their point of view, but which is likely to pay a far lower level of pension to their employees when they retire.

Hybrid schemes

Hybrid schemes too are becoming more common, although as yet they represent a small minority of UK pension funds. These, in various different ways, combine elements of the defined benefit and defined contribution forms of provision. The most common form is the 'money purchase underpin' which is basically a final salary arrangement, but one which calculates pensions and transfer values on a money purchase basis where these are higher. Such schemes seek to combine the best aspects of both main types of scheme. They offer a generous, secure and predictable pension, but also incorporate the flexibility associated with defined contribution schemes.

In the USA some organisations have moved towards the provision of cash-balance pension plans which work on a final salary basis, but pay out a single lump sum at retirement rather than a monthly pension (Field *et al.* 2009: 185). The employee uses the money to purchase an annuity, so the level of pension received varies considerably depending on market rates at the time of retirement. Such schemes make the financial commitment more predictable from the employer's perspective, but tend to result in lower pensions than a conventional final salary arrangement.

ACTIVITY 27.2

Which of these three types of occupational pension scheme would you find most attractive at the current stage in your career? Under what circumstances might you change your preference?

Group personal pensions

Since the 1980s there has been substantial growth in the market for personal pensions. Self-employed people have always used these, but increasingly as employers have withdrawn from occupational pensions, employees have had to start up personal pensions too. More general attention has been focused on this area due to increasing job mobility and the perceived greater portability of personal pensions. A personal pension is arranged, usually through an insurance company, and the individual pays regular amounts into his or her own 'pension fund' in the same way that the individual would with a company fund. The employer may also make a contribution to the fund, but at present there are very few employers who have chosen to do so.

An alternative arrangement is a Group Personal Pension plan (GPP) set up by an employer instead of an occupational pension scheme. From a legal and taxation perspective a GPP is no different from any individual personal pension arrangement, but charges are lower because the employer is able to arrange a bulk discount. The scheme is administered by an insurance company, the employer making contributions as well as the employee. Pensions are calculated on the same basis as an occupational money purchase scheme, but tend to be less extensive because employees are responsible for paying some of the administrative charges. From an employee's perspective a GPP is inferior to an occupational pension scheme, but is better than a situation in which no employer provision is made at all. Such arrangements are mainly entered into by small firms, but one or two big companies have also set them up in place of conventional occupational pensions. A key difference is that a GPP is contract based rather than trust based. This means that unlike an occupational pension there is no board of trustees appointed to oversee the running of the scheme; instead a contract is signed with an external provider.

Auto-enrolment

The Pensions Act 2008 contained a range of measures designed to increase the amount of money being saved in private pension funds and also to encourage employer contributions. At the time of writing (2016) these are in the process of being phased in. The requirements are complex and apply at different times to different organisations depending on their size in terms of staff. The first 'staging date' was 1 October 2012. There are forty-two in all, only businesses employing fewer than five people being exempt for the time being.

Ultimately, once all staging dates have passed in October 2017, all employees in the UK who earn over £9,440 (in 2016) and are over the age of 22 will have to be enrolled either in an occupational pension scheme or in the new government-sponsored 'personal pension account scheme'. People will be able to opt out if they wish, but otherwise they will be automatically enrolled into one scheme or the other, including any new starters after the relevant staging date. Employees will contribute 4% of their earnings (up to £42,385 in 2016) into their fund and employers will contribute 3%, tax relief effectively meaning that a further 1% is contributed by the government.

The aim is to achieve a situation by the middle of the century whereby 60% of retirement income is provided from private sources and only 40% by the state. At present 60% is state provided and only 40% from private sources.

Occupational pensions and HRM

Although occupational pension schemes are governed by a board of trustees which includes member representatives, in most organisations the pensions manager and pensions department are part of the HR function. It is thus important that HR professionals are familiar with the types of scheme offered and the main operating rules so that they can give accurate and timely advice to staff and to potential recruits. They also need to be familiar with the regulatory environment for occupational pensions, which has changed considerably in recent years. Aside from new legislation outlawing discrimination on grounds of sex or against part-time and temporary staff, several other important regulatory changes have been made and new regulatory bodies established. The Pensions Act 1995 sets out in detail what information must be disclosed to scheme members on request and what must be sent to them automatically each year. The Act also requires all occupational funds to meet a defined minimum funding level so that they are always able to meet their liabilities in the event of the employing company being wound up. Moreover, strict restrictions are now placed on 'self-investment', making sure that fund assets cannot be invested in property or other business ventures controlled by the sponsoring organisation.

The Social Security Act 1985 put in place a series of measures to protect 'early leavers', ensuring that people who switch employers during their careers do not suffer substantial loss in the value of their pensions. Early leavers now have one of three options in making their pension arrangements when they begin work for a new employer. One option is to claim back the contributions that the individual has made into the former employer's pension scheme. Deductions are made in accordance with tax laws and, of course, the employer's contribution is lost, but a substantial sum can be reinvested in the new employer's scheme or in a personal pension. Another alternative involves opting for a preserved pension. With a final salary scheme, if there were no inflation, and if the individual progressed very little up the career ladder, a preserved pension from an old employer plus a pension from the recent employer would equate well with the pension the individual would have received had he or she been with the new employer for the whole period. However, if these conditions are not met, which in recent times they have not been, individuals who have had more than one employer lose out in the pension stakes. Past employers are required to revalue preserved pensions in line with inflation (to a maximum of 5%), but the value of such a pension remains linked to the level of salary at the date of leaving.

The third option is usually preferable, but is only open to people who have completed two years' membership of a scheme. This involves the transfer of the pension from the old employer's fund into that of the new employer. The process is straightforward in the case of a money purchase scheme, because the worth of each person's pension is readily calculated. It is simply the value of the employee's contributions, plus those of the employer, together with funds accrued as a result of their investment. The process is more complicated in the case of a final salary scheme, the transfer value being calculated according to standard actuarial conventions which take account of the employee's age, the length of pensionable service, the level of salary at the time of leaving and the current interest rate. All things being equal, 'early leavers' still fare worse than 'stayers' in terms of final pensions, but the difference is a great deal less than used to be the case.

Aside from giving advice and taking overall responsibility for pensions issues, HR managers are concerned with determining their organisations' pension policy. Is an occupational pension to be offered? If so, what form should it take? What level of contribution is the employer going to make? It is quite possible to make a judgement in favour of generous occupational provision simply on paternalistic grounds. Many organisations have thus decided that they will offer pensions because it is in the interests of their staff that they should. Occupational schemes represent a convenient and tax-advantageous method of providing an income in old age; it therefore makes sense to include a pension in the total pay and benefits package. The problems with such a commitment, particularly in the case of defined benefit schemes, are the cost and the fact that the long-term financial consequences are unpredictable. This, combined with the fact that many employees do not seem to appreciate the value of an occupational pension, is one of the reasons that many employers have been questioning their commitment to final salary schemes and to pension provision in general.

Research suggests that interest in and understanding of occupational pensions varies considerably from person to person (Taylor 2009). Older people, professional workers and those working in the financial services sector usually have a clearer perception of their value than other groups of staff. For these groups pensions are important, and their labour market behaviour will be affected as a result. A firm which does not offer a good pension will thus find it harder to recruit and retain them than one which does. By contrast, a firm which largely employs younger people, and/or workers in lower-skilled occupations, may find that it makes more sense to offer additional pay in place of an occupational scheme.

ACTIVITY 27.3

It has been argued that by making occupational pensions readily transferable, by increasing the complexity of the regulatory regime and by increasing taxation levied on pension funds, successive governments have provided a major disincentive to employers considering the establishment of a scheme. To what extent do you agree with this point of view?

Sick pay

As with pension schemes, the provision of sick pay is seen as the mark of a good employer. Sick pay is an important issue due to the need for control and administration of absence. Research suggests that sickness absence represents around 4% of working time (CBI 2008), although there are large differences between sector and job type. The HR manager and the HR department have a variety of roles to play in relation to sick pay, particularly in relation to the administration of Statutory Sick Pay.

Statutory Sick Pay

Statutory Sick Pay (SSP) is a state benefit that has been in existence for several decades. It provides a basic income (£88.45 per week in 2016) to employees who are incapable of going to their normal place of work as a result of illness. SSP, however, is not claimed from a benefit office; it is administered by employers and paid through the payroll according to regulations set out in statute.

Employers are required to take full financial responsibility for SSP for the first four weeks of absence, after which they can claim back a portion of the costs from the state through reduced employer National Insurance contributions. However, the method of calculation used ensures that smaller employers are able to claim back a considerably higher proportion of the costs than larger employers who usually have to fund it all themselves. Most employees are entitled to State Sickness Benefit; however, there are some exceptions: employees who fall sick outside the EU; employees who are sick during an industrial dispute; employees over pensionable age; and part-timers whose earnings are below the lower earnings limit (£112 per week in 2016). These groups, as well as self-employed people, are obliged to claim State Incapacity Benefit instead. SSP is built around the concepts of qualifying days, waiting days, certification and linked periods.

- **Qualifying days** are those days on which the employee would normally have worked, except for the fact that he or she was sick. For many Monday-to-Friday employees this is very straightforward. However, it is more complex to administer for those on some form of rotating week or shift system. Sick pay is only payable for qualifying days.

- **Waiting days** have to pass before the employee is entitled to receive sick pay – at present the number of days is three. These three days must be qualifying days, and on the fourth qualifying day the employee is entitled to sickness benefit, should he or she still be away from work due to sickness.

- **Certification** from a doctor is required after seven days of sickness absence. Prior to this the employee provides self-certification. This involves notifying the employer of absence due to sickness by the first day on which benefit is due – that is, immediately following the three waiting days.

- **Linked periods** of illness mean that the three waiting days do not apply. If the employee has had a period of incapacity from work (PIW) within the previous eight weeks, then the two periods are linked and treated as just one period for SSP purposes, and so the three waiting days do not have to pass again.

The employer does not have to administer SSP for every employee indefinitely. Where the employee has been absent due to sickness for a continuous or linked period of twenty-eight weeks the responsibility for payment passes from the employer to the state. A continuous period of twenty-eight weeks' sickness is clearly identifiable. It is not so clear when linked periods are involved. An employee who was sick for five days, back at work for four weeks, sick for one day, at work for seven weeks and then sick for two days would have a linked period of incapacity of eight days. Alternatively, an employee who was sick for four days, back at work for ten weeks and then sick for five days would have a period of incapacity this time of five days. The DWP requires employers to keep SSP records for three years so that these can be inspected.

Occupational Sick Pay

There is no obligation on employers to pay employees for days of absence due to sickness beyond what is required under the state's SSP scheme. However, most employers choose to do so via a benefit known as Occupational Sick Pay (OSP). The most common approach is to continue paying the full salary for a set period of time, but other schemes involve reducing the pay rate for days taken off as a result of illness. In either case a sum in excess of the statutory minimum is paid, the portion accounted for by SSP being reclaimed from the state where possible. Paying the full salary is straightforward for those staff who receive a basic salary with no additions. It is more difficult to define for those whose pay is supplemented by shift allowances or productivity bonuses.

OSP arrangements tend to be most generous in unionised environments and in the public sector, although professional and managerial employees are usually well covered in most organisations. The common public-sector approach involves paying full pay for the first six months of an illness, once three years' service have been completed, before moving the employee on to half-pay for a further six months. Thereafter OSP ceases. At the other end of the scale are employers who pay no OSP at all. They take the view that OSP will be abused and so pay only what is due under the state scheme. Another approach involves paying a predetermined flat rate in addition to money provided via SSP.

OSP schemes also vary according to the period of service required. Some employers provide sick pay for sickness absence from the first day of employment. Others require a qualifying period to be served. For some this is a nominal period of four weeks, but the period may be three or six months, or a year or more. There is a major difference here between OSP and SSP. With SSP, pay is available immediately after employment has begun.

Company cars

A form of employee benefit which is a great deal more common in the UK than in other countries is the company car, but it is a good deal less common than it used to be. In 2000, 84% of companies offered a car to at least some of their staff. By 2012 the proportion had fallen to 54% (CIPD 2012). Managers from overseas often take some persuading that cars are necessary to attract and retain high-calibre managers, but the received wisdom is that they are. Their importance to employees is demonstrated by the comparative lack of take-up of cash alternatives where these are offered (Smith 2000a: 161). After pensions, they are the second most significant employee benefit in cost terms.

There are a number of sound reasons underlying the provision of company cars. First, for some there is a need as part of their jobs to travel very widely and regularly. Not everyone can be assumed to own a reliable car, so it is sometimes necessary to provide one simply to enable an employee to carry out his or her day-to-day job duties. In the case of sales representatives and senior managers the impression created when travelling on company business can be important. It is therefore often considered necessary to provide them with upmarket and up-to-date models to ensure that clients and potential clients are suitably impressed. A case can also be made on cost efficiency grounds for people who clock up a great number of business miles each year. The cost of paying them a reasonable mileage allowance to drive their own cars is often greater than the cost of providing them with a company vehicle; it costs £9,000 a year to reimburse someone who has travelled 30,000 miles at 30p per mile.

However, most possessors of company cars do not fit either of the above categories. Their car entitlements simply come as an expected part of the pay package for middle and senior managers. As such, they signify the achievement of a certain level of status. Indeed, in many companies the cars offered become steadily more imposing as people climb up the corporate hierarchy. Being upgraded to a more impressive car thus signifies in a very manifest way the company's approval. Downgrading, of course, has the opposite effect.

One of the reasons that company cars are so significant in the UK is historical. Until 1994 they were a highly tax-efficient benefit. It was a good deal cheaper to drive a company car than to purchase one's own out of taxed income, so it made sense for people to be 'paid' in part with a car. This is now far from being the case.

The current tax regime introduced in 2002 encourages employers to lease or purchase cars which are environmentally friendly. Formerly company cars were simply taxed according to the number of miles driven on company business, the annual tax paid by the driver being equivalent to a percentage of the car's list price. The more business miles clocked up, the less tax was paid. In addition there were substantial discounts for people who drove older cars. Since 2002 the tax paid depends on carbon emissions or engine size and there are no reductions for people who drive a great number of miles or use an older vehicle. So there is a substantial incentive for people who drive a great deal as part of their jobs to use smaller cars or larger ones with low carbon emissions. Most employers offer cash alternatives equal to the tax payable on the car, but many of those eligible choose not to take these up despite the fact that there are no longer any obvious tax advantages associated with driving a company car. This is partly because company cars tend to be more expensive than individuals could justify spending from their own income, but mainly because of the substantial savings that still accrue in terms of insurance, maintenance and repair costs. The tax changes have, however, led to a preference for 'trading down'. This means that, where a choice is given, employees are increasingly opting for a smaller car and more cash in their pay packets.

ACTIVITY 27.4

Assume that you have been offered a new job which comes with either the use of a new company car or a cash allowance. The salary is £35,000 per year. The car is worth £15,000, giving you an annual tax bill of £5,250. This is also the amount being offered by way of an annual cash allowance. Which option would you choose and why?

Flexible benefits

Flexible benefits or 'cafeteria plans' have proliferated in the USA over recent years where they are specifically recognised in the tax regime. By contrast, take-up of the idea in the UK has tended to be slow (Wright 2009b: 207). However, several high-profile organisations have now moved towards greater flexibility and there is unquestionably a great deal more interest in the approach developing among UK employers more generally. This has been driven by skills shortages and to initiatives in the work–life balance arena. The CIPD (2012: 41) reports that 24% of the respondents to its reward management survey operated some form of flexible benefits scheme.

The case for flexible benefits from an HRM perspective is strong, but the systems themselves can prove to be very costly to operate. The approach involves giving individual employees a choice as to how exactly their pay packet is made up. The overall value of the package is set by the employer, but it is for employees to choose for themselves what balance they wish to strike between cash and the different kinds of benefit. Those who have children, for example, can opt for benefits that are of value to them, such as childcare vouchers, access to a company crèche or additional holidays. A young person in their first job might well prefer to forgo most benefits in return for higher take-home pay, while an older person may wish to purchase additional years of pensionable service in exchange for cash or perhaps a car.

There are a number of good reasons for considering such an approach. First, it helps ensure that employees are only provided with benefits which they are aware of and appreciate. Resources that would otherwise be wasted by providing unwanted benefits are thus saved. The employer gets maximum value per pound spent, while at the same time allowing employees to tailor their own 'perfect' benefits mix. The result should be improved staff retention and a better motivated workforce.

WINDOW ON PRACTICE

In 1998 a large-scale merger took place between two of the world's largest professional services firms – Price Waterhouse and Coopers & Lybrand. The merged firm, called Price-waterhouseCoopers, employs 150,000 people in 150 different countries. While the two organisations were culturally similar, they had rather different traditions in the provision of benefits. Rather than continue with different people employed on different sets of terms and conditions, the partners decided to harmonise everyone as soon as was possible. This process was made a great deal easier and less contentious by the decision to develop a new flexible benefits scheme called 'Choices'. It allows employees to trade cash for additional holiday, a choice of car, childcare vouchers, retail vouchers, insurance of various kinds and a pension. No one was required to alter their existing benefits package as a result of the merger unless they wished to.

Source: Franks, O. and Thompson, D. (2000) 'Rights and rites of passage', *People Management*, 17 February.

Flexible benefits plans take many different forms, the main distinction being between those that are 'fully flexible' and those that allow a degree of flexibility within prescribed limits. The former allow employees a free hand to make up their own package and to change it at regular intervals. Under such a regime an employee could theoretically swap all benefits for cash, or could double his or her holiday entitlement in exchange for a pay cut. A degree of restriction is more common, a compulsory core of benefits being compulsory, with flexibility beyond that. Under such a scheme everyone might be required to take four weeks' holiday and invest in a minimal pension, but be allowed freedom to determine whether or not they wished to benefit from private health insurance, gym membership, discounts on company products, etc. Typical plans also permit some choice of the make and model of car.

A third approach is administratively simpler but is more restrictive in terms of employee choice. This involves 'pre-packaging' a number of separate benefits menus designed to suit different groups of employees (rather like a pre-set banquet menu in a Chinese restaurant). Employees must then opt for one package from a choice of five or six, each having the same overall cash value. One is typically tailored to meet the needs of older staff, another is for those with young families, a third for new graduates and so on.

A number of disadvantages with flexible benefits systems can be identified which may well explain their relatively slow development in the UK. These are summarised by Smith (2000b) as follows:

> Objections include difficult administration; problems connected with handling individual employee choices; the requirement for complex costing and records; difficulty in getting employees to make effective choices; employees making mistakes (for example leaving themselves with inadequate pension cover); employees' circumstances changing over time leaving his or her package inappropriate and giving the employer the costly headache of re-designing the package; and finally the possible hiring of expensive specialist or consultant skills and financial counselling to support the move to flexibility.

Uncertainty about the future tax position may also be a deterrent, especially where changes have the potential to throw a whole system out of kilter (as happened in 1997 when the Chancellor of the Exchequer substantially extended taxation on pension fund investments).

SUMMARY PROPOSITIONS

27.1. Between 20% and 50% of the typical employer's pay bill is spent on the provision of supplementary benefits. Evidence suggests that most employees do not appreciate the true financial value of such benefits.

27.2. Occupational pensions are a tax-efficient means of providing funds for retirement in excess of what is provided by state and personal pension schemes.

27.3. Employers are required to facilitate the payment of Statutory Sick Pay to employees who are away from work as a result of an illness. Most pay Occupational Sick Pay in addition either as a result of moral obligation or in order to attract, retain and motivate their workforces.

27.4. Company cars are commonly provided by UK employers for senior staff. The tax regime aims to discourage demand for larger cars which are not environmentally friendly.

27.5. In theory flexible benefits plans have a great deal to offer employees. It is likely that their use will grow more widespread in the next few years.

GENERAL DISCUSSION TOPICS

1. Why do you think so few people seem to have an appreciation of the value of their occupational pensions and other benefits? What could be done to raise awareness of the costs involved in their provision?

2. Draw up three flexible benefits packages: one aimed at new graduates; one at employees in their 30s; and one for those aged over 50.

THEORY INTO PRACTICE

According to the 2012 Annual Reward Management Survey carried out by the Chartered Institute of Personnel and Development, the following benefits are provided for employees by over 20% of UK employers:

- Twenty-five paid holiday days a year in addition to bank holidays
- Training and career development
- Childcare vouchers
- Free tea and coffee
- Christmas party
- On-site car parking

> - Eye-care vouchers
> - Employee assistance programme (i.e. counselling advice helpline)
> - Life assurance
> - Enhanced maternity and paternity leave
> - Dress-down days
> - Cycle-to-work loans
> - Subsidised dining
> - Travel season ticket loans
> - Unpaid sabbaticals
> - Discounts on own products and services
> - Flu-jabs
> - Paid leave for military activities
> - Private medical insurance
> - Company picnic or barbeque.

Questions

1 Over time the proportion of employers who offer these benefits is increasing. Why do you think this is?

2 What other benefits might you have expected to see listed here?

3 Which of these benefits would you consider to have value for you personally? How far might their presence or absence from a reward package influence your interest in working for a company?

Source: After *Reward Management: Annual Survey Report 2012*, London: Chartered Institute of Personnel and Development (CIPD 2009), Reproduced with the permission of the publisher, the Chartered Institute of Personnel and Development, London (www.cipd.co.uk).

FURTHER READING

Taylor, S. (2009) 'Occupational pensions', in G. White and J. Druker (eds), *Reward Management: A Critical Text*. London: Routledge.

Wright, A. (2009a) 'Benefits', in G. White and J. Druker (eds), *Reward Management: A Critical Text*. London: Routledge.

Field, S., Olsen, C. and Williams, R. (2009) 'The pensions revolution', in S. Corby *et al.* (eds), *Rethinking Reward*. Basingstoke: Palgrave.

Wright, A. (2009b) 'Flexible benefits', in S. Corby *et al.* (eds), *Rethinking Reward*. Basingstoke: Palgrave.

Between them, these four chapters in two edited books published fairly recently cover the issues raised in this chapter very effectively. All review the contemporary research and explain trends in a clear and concise manner.

The *Turner Report* (2004) *New Pension Settlement for the Twenty-first Century: The Second Report of the Pensions Commission*. London: HMSO, contains several chapters looking at the background to pension provision over the next few decades, including demographic and funding issues.

Incomes Data Services (IDS) regularly publishes issues of its HR Studies that are focused on employee benefits. The approach is practical, case studies being provided to illustrate the approaches that employers are currently choosing to take. Two excellent editions are Study 856 on employee benefits and Study 811 on flexible benefits.

REFERENCES

Accor (2008) *Reward to Engage: Rewards, Benefits and Employee Engagement in Today's Organisations*. London: Accor Services.

CBI (2008) *CBI/AXA Absence Survey 2008*. London: Confederation of British Industry.

CIPD (2012) *Reward Management: Annual Survey Report 2012*. London: CIPD.

Dobson, C. and Horsfield, S. (2009) *Defined Contribution Pension Provision*, Research Report 608. London: Department for Work and Pensions.

Duda, J. (2011) 'Employee benefits or wage increase?', *Acta Universitatis Agriculturae et Silviculturae Mendelianae Bunensis*, Vol. LIX, pp. 65–8.

Field, S., Olsen, C. and Williams, R. (2009) 'The pensions revolution', in S. Corby *et al*. (eds), *Rethinking Reward*. Basingstoke: Palgrave.

Franks, O. and Thompson, D. (2000) 'Rights and rites of passage', *People Management*, 17 February.

Hina, Q., Zamir, S. and Nudari, S. (2014) 'Impact of employee benefits on job satisfaction of teachers at higher level', *Journal of Education and Practice*, Vol. 5, No. 7, pp. 122–9.

Lin *et al*. (2014) [ref needed]

NAPF (2013) 'Final salary pensions shut at record rate in private sector', Press release, 20 January.

ONS (2012a) *Occupational Pension Scheme Survey 2011*. London: Office for National Statistics.

ONS (2012b) *Pension Trends*. London: Office for National Statistics.

Pemberton, H., Thane, P. and Whiteside, N. (2006) *Britain's Pension Crisis: History and Policy*. Oxford: The British Academy.

Smith, I. (2000a) 'Benefits', in G. White and J. Druker (eds) *Reward Management: A Critical Text*. London: Routledge.

Smith, I. (2000b) 'Flexible plans for pay and benefits', in R. Thorpe and G. Homan (eds), *Strategic Reward Systems*. London: Financial Times/Prentice Hall.

Taylor, S. (2009) 'Occupational pensions', in G. White and J. Druker (eds), *Reward Management: A Critical Text*. London: Routledge.

Thomson Online (2007) *Employee Rewards Watch 2007*, available at www.thomsons.com.

Turner, A. (2004) *Pensions: Challenges and Choices. The First Report of the Pensions Commission*. London: HMSO.

Wright, A. (2009a) 'Benefits', in G. White and J. Druker (eds), *Reward Management: A Critical Text*. London: Routledge.

Wright, A. (2009b) 'Flexible benefits: Shaping the way ahead?', in S. Corby *et al*. (eds), *Rethinking Reward*. Basingstoke: Palgrave.

CHAPTER 28

EMPLOYABILITY: SKILLS IN REWARD

THE OBJECTIVES OF THIS CHAPTER ARE TO:

1 Explain the skills of negotiation, a clear conflict of interest between as little as possible on one side and as much as possible on the other

2 Explore how to reward employees working overseas for the dislocation of their domestic and social arrangements

28.a. Negotiation

WINDOW ON PRACTICE

Early in 2016 a simmering disagreement between the British government and junior doctors in the National Health Service reached token strikes and stalemate because the two sides interpreted quite differently a government proposal for a new contract to facilitate better medical coverage in hospitals at weekends. The government proposals were claimed and explained as giving more money, while the doctors claimed and explained how they would get less. The naive observer might believe that it was a simple question of what the facts said, but both sides were convinced that they were right. There was an impasse, so the government announced that the contract would be imposed, and then the doctors would see how much their conditions had improved. At the time of writing the stalemate continues, although the number of doctors taking strike action has declined.

That is a very unusual situation, as doctors rarely strike. The last had been forty years ago. The intractability of the situation is unusual. Negotiation is a way of reaching an accommodation between the parties, typically between management and union(s). The negotiation process is as shown in Figure 28.1.

Agenda

This is no more than a mutual agreement between the parties on what they are going to negotiate about. They may see the issue from different perspectives, but they must agree what the issue is, so that all those attending have the same focus.

Information

Both parties need to assemble facts to support their argument, and each member of their team has to have the same understanding of those facts. Negotiation is not a roundtable discussion about the issue, it is a confrontation of two – and only two – different perspectives on the issue.

Objectives

Both sides need clear and helpful objectives. Specific improvements in efficiency, acceptance of new working practices, staffing levels, flexibility in duties and so on. Whatever the objectives are, they need to be clear, specific and shared by all members of the team. In our conversations with management representatives from a variety of businesses over several years, some hopeless objectives have been: 'Get the best deal we possibly can', 'Remain calm and dignified', ' Hold out for as long as we can', 'Keep them talking until

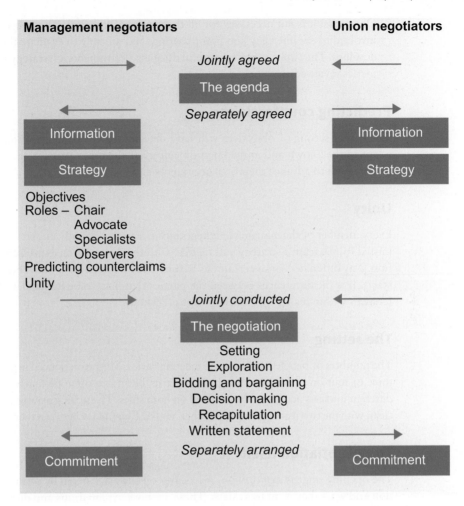

Management negotiators

Union negotiators

Jointly agreed

The agenda

Separately agreed

Information

Strategy

Information

Strategy

Objectives
Roles – Chair
      Advocate
      Specialists
      Observers
Predicting counterclaims
Unity

Jointly conducted

The negotiation

Setting
Exploration
Bidding and bargaining
Decision making
Recapitulation
Written statement

Separately arranged

Commitment

Commitment

Figure 28.1
The negotiating
process

well into lunchtime, when their tummies are rumbling.' They are hopeless objectives because the parties do not want anything, it is just a war of attrition.

Roles

It helps to have defined roles. Except in very large, formal negotiations, it is generally accepted that management will have one of their number to chair the negotiation and control the meeting. Apart from that there are potentially three roles:

1 **Advocate.** This is the person who is the main presenter of the management case and the person who marshals the rebuttal of the opposing arguments. Sometimes the roles of chair and advocate are combined in one person for status reasons, but this is difficult, like bowling and keeping wicket at the same time.

2 **Specialists.** This role is to provide advice as required on the basis of knowing the management position and having a thorough understanding of the facts of the situation. Specialists should *not* get involved in the general debate, as this can become confusing and may undermine the advocate's authority. Negotiating does not benefit from free-for-all general discussion

3 **Observers.** It is not necessary for all those present to speak. They get less emotionally involved in the interplay and point scoring, and are able to evaluate the situation as it develops. They are particularly useful during adjournments as strategy is redefined and tactics reviewed.

Predicting counterclaims

The earlier setting of objectives will have determined the strategy, which then needs to adapt to the known and anticipated objectives of the other party. Negotiators will then be able both to advance their own arguments and respond to the arguments put to them.

Unity

Every member of the management negotiating team has to fully understand, and be committed to, the team's strategy and tactics, with that unity being expressed in the negotiation. Any differences or uncertainties within the team must be handled before the meeting starts. It is the differences between the parties that have to be handled and resolved; differences within teams are a nuisance for everybody.

The setting

The numbers of people present at the meeting varies. Most experienced negotiators feel that three or four on each side is the most effective, but it can often be much more because of different interests needing to be involved on both sides. The seating arrangements need to be clear, with the two teams facing each other, with the boundary between them also being clear.

The negotiation itself

The opening stage is *exploration*. Advocates on each side begin by setting out their position and what they want to achieve. These are both explanations and displays of strength as they convince themselves they are right and impress the opposition, who had previously only been able to see things from their own perspective. The substantive element of this phase is to clarify what the differences are and to assess how important and intransigent each part of the opposing case is. It is an essential part of the process: differentiation precedes integration and the exchanges are kept impersonal, presenting the interests of those represented, not simply the opinions of negotiators.

After the differences have been explored, there is an almost instinctive move to a second, integrative phase of the meeting known as *bidding and bargaining*. Statements are much more tentative than before, as negotiators sound out possibilities, float ideas, ask questions, make non-committal suggestions and move towards a problem-solving mode. Negotiators make comments that are personal and non-committal, as opposed to the impersonal, emphatic mode of the first phase. Typical comments or thrusts are:

'This is just a personal view, and my colleagues will probably not be happy, but I wonder if we could do this . . . if you could move on that . . . ?' and

'We would have to look into the cost implications but there might be a possibility of . . . if . . .' .

The chair could be crucial, for example making a statement such as: 'I was struck by your point about . . . so I think it would help us, Harry (a management side specialist), if you could give us your quick assessment of the implications.'

WINDOW ON PRACTICE

Negotiations usually have breaks or adjournments, which give both parties the opportunity to discuss their strategy among themselves and agree any changes in direction, with the comments from the observers being very useful. Adjournments serve little purpose during exploration, but are almost essential before bidding and bargaining and before decision making.

The third phase is *decision making*, when the parties reach a provisional agreement, which is inevitable in most situations because the employer has no one else to negotiate with and needs the employees to work; the employees need the employer to continue employing them. The employer cannot realistically dismiss the employees and recruit replacements while employees cannot replace the management with a different lot.

The bidding and bargaining phase has uncovered possibilities for a settlement that may well be different from what either party had contemplated, but if the terms are what the negotiators feel they can live with, then a decision can be reached. A proposal from management is needed, probably having first been discussed in an adjournment. It will be received by the employees, perhaps eliciting questions for clarification followed by a further adjournment for the proposal to be discussed. Any proposal has to be carefully and thoroughly discussed before it is put on the table and has to take account of both the exploration phase and bidding and bargaining. You have to answer three questions:

- Are we agreed that this meets our objectives?
- Will we be able to convince our management colleagues?
- Do we all believe that it will probably be accepted by the other party with only small modifications?
- Do we believe that the other party will be able to get it accepted by their members?

Any proposal has to pass the test of those questions. Remembering that you have to agree in the end, you have to make a proposal that is credible to and supportable by both parties and those whose acceptance they need. You need a subsequent working situation that is based on mutual confidence and which produces commitment, otherwise you are approaching the negotiation as if you were buying a secondhand car – if the dealer will not accept your offer, then you go to another dealer.

The response you hear from the other party will usually tell you that you are on the right track. If it is an acceptance subject to modest adjustment, you need another adjournment to consider how you would cope with the suggested adjustments. If the adjustments cannot be accepted for clear and powerful reasons, they should be turned down. If you are resistant to them simply because you don't like them and they are going to create more work, ask yourself if your resistance is strong enough to risk the negotiations breaking down, then discuss it a bit more.

Are there alternatives that could be suggested that might be acceptable to the other party and which would be palatable on your side of the table? If the answer is yes, reconvene the meeting, explain the problem and suggest the alternative and proceed to bidding and bargaining. If the answer is no, reconvene the meeting and tell the other party that their suggestions are not workable (a better word than 'unacceptable'), so your original offer stands. To-ing and fro-ing may continue, but eventually you either reach an agreement or the negotiation stalls.

Recapitulation

Complete breakdown of talks is rare. Ultimately, agreement is the norm but not the end. If an impasse is reached, everyone will want to go away and do something else as the negotiation process is not easy and can be protracted, but do not let the other party go just yet. Summarise, slowly and carefully, what has been agreed and ensure that everyone agrees. Then call for some tea, while the best and quickest typist in the building is summoned and asked to produce a record of the points of agreement and enough copies for all present. This puts a brake on the grapevine, so what has been agreed is less likely to be changed in passing on the news, in confidence of course, to friends and colleagues.

Commitment of the parties

So far you have agreement between a handful of people in one room. They now need the commitment of those on each side to make the agreement work. On the employee side they will have to gain the approval of those they represent. If they reject the offer, the agreement probably fails. Management representatives need the commitment of those they represent, first those in senior positions who need to sanction it, second those in supervisory and middle management roles who will have to make it work; this commitment is difficult and may be glossed over or forgotten unless the changes are painstakingly secured by all concerned.

This activity has been described as a straightforward process. In practice it is often much more messy and erratic. In the last paragraph was the statement that if the agreement is not accepted it *probably* fails. The negotiations with junior doctors have stalled. By the time you read this you will know what eventually happened. At the time of writing there are two foreseeable possibilities, either negotiations will have been resumed and agreement eventually found, or the changed contract terms will have been implemented and produced a reaction.

WINDOW ON PRACTICE

Fisher and Ury (2012) suggest four basic rules to govern any negotiation:

1   Separate the people from the problem; it is not the clash of personalities and the bruised egos that must be addressed, but the problem that needs resolution.

2   Focus on interests, not positions; always look for alternative possibilities.

3   Make the pie bigger. Generate other possibilities beyond what your 'opponent' is asking for by thinking of options that are low cost to you and high benefit to them.

4   Prevent the negotiation becoming a contest of wills by looking for objective criteria that can be used by both parties to test the reasonableness of any position.

SUMMARY PROPOSITIONS

28.a.1. The practice of negotiation is based on the need to resolve or accommodate a conflict of interest between those who employ and those who are employed.

28.a.2. Negotiation can clear the air, introduce new rules, modify an unworkable management initiative or produce a better understanding of respective positions.

28.a.3. Among the drawbacks of negotiation are the waste of time, the stress and the risks of failure.

28.a.4. Preparation involves setting the agenda, collecting information, deciding a strategy, objectives and roles.

28.a.5. The phases of negotiation are exploration, bidding and bargaining, decision making, recapitulation and commitment of the parties.

GENERAL DISCUSSION TOPICS

28.a.1. The British entrepreneur Richard Branson allegedly dislikes trade unions because they bring an adversarial way of dealing with things into a situation which should be harmonious. Do you think that the recognition of unions is a failure of management? Does your answer differ between the public and private sectors?

28.a.2. The eighteenthth-century political philosopher Edmund Burke said in a speech, He who wrestles with us strengthens our nerves and sharpens our skill. Our antagonist is our helper. is this true of negotiations in business?

PUTTING IT INTO PRACTICE

Various activities have been devised to simulate bargaining, but they all suffer from the same problem of artificiality. What follows is something that is at least hypothetically real, although limited in its scope. You will need a close friend to help you.

Identify a personal possession that you might be willing to sell for a suitable price – a car, a home cinema system, an expensive item of clothing or jewellery, two tickets for the theatre or a sporting event. A realistic, although hypothetical, willingness on both sides is essential in selecting the item to be 'sold'.

Plan your negotiation, splitting your objectives into two: first your target points, what you realistically hope to achieve, secondly your resistance points, what you would be prepared to settle for rather than abandoning the sale. Ask your friend to do the same as the prospective buyer.

Conduct the negotiation, trying to avoid simple haggling over the price. When you agree or fail to agree, discuss your feelings about the experience.

28.b. Rewarding overseas employees for dislocation of domestic and social arrangements

How do you adjust pay and expenses for those who travel to, and perhaps reside in, countries other than their own?

The expatriate

This is someone being transferred abroad for a period of years, probably highly skilled, specialised and relatively well paid, but they expect a level of pay and benefits while abroad that exceeds by a large margin what they would receive by staying put. This is against a background of fluctuating currency values, hyperinflation in some countries, changing political circumstances and social conditions. Is the home country house to be sold or rented and, if rented, how will it be managed during the expatriation? Other issues include education for school-age children, return trips on leave, removal expenses and housing costs, and compensation of a spouse needing to interrupt or abandon a career, possibly unable to take up independent employment in the new location. Much of the detail in the arrangement will be contracted out to a specialist company, but the broad principles need to be determined by HR, or in consultation with them.

Salary on return. Concern with this aspect of employment may seem the wrong way round, but is often the first question the potential expatriate asks. The current contract of employment will usually be suspended, but there needs to be a guarantee of the minimum level of salary and pension rights at which the expatriate will return. This requires a formula; adjustment for inflation would be a minimum, but a modest additional uprating is typical, so that an incentive to accept the expatriation is returning to a better position than staying put.

Expatriate salary will rarely be less than at home, even if moving to a country with a lower cost of living, but will have to be raised if moving to a country with a higher cost of living.

Allowances are additional payments made to expatriates to balance what is needed at home with what is needed abroad. A method of doing this was worked out by Dowling and Schuler (1990) and is still used as a format by most specialist companies in this field (see Figure 28.2).

Short-term overseas assignment

Those who travel abroad for short spells will not have their basic salary and benefits altered while they are away, but there have to be arrangements about expenses which are reasonable without getting out of control, not only to monitor expenditure but also to ensure compliance with the tax rules of the home country. If an employee attends an important business meeting in Florida, it is reasonable that all expenses are met by the employer. It is more complicated when there is an accompanying spouse. Can their expenses be claimed if their role is to help with entertaining? Probably not. If they provide other forms of assistance, such as translation or secretarial services, then their expenses probably can be claimed.

Figure 28.2
The balance sheet approach to salary setting

 = Additional company costs

SUMMARY PROPOSITIONS

28.b.1. Someone being transferred abroad for a finite period of years (an expatriate) is probably highly skilled, specialised and relatively well paid, but they expect a level of pay and benefits while abroad that exceeds by a large margin what they would receive by staying put.

28.b.2. Issues to be considered include: fluctuating currency values, political circumstances and social conditions, the home country house, education for school-age children, return trips on leave, removal expenses and housing costs, a spouse needing to interrupt or abandon a career.

28.b.3. Expatriates need to know what their salary and pension rights will be on their return.

28.b.4. Those travelling abroad for short spells need to know the expenses they can claim and claims must be monitored both to guard against unreasonable claims and possible income tax implications.

GENERAL DISCUSSION TOPICS

28.b.1. Sending employees and their families to live and work abroad for several years and then reintegrating them on return is obviously expensive. Why do companies do it instead of employing local personnel?

28.b.2. Imagine you are well placed in a company and now they ask you to go and spend two years working in a branch in Montreal. What incentives would you need to accept? Compare the responses of different group members and discuss how personal circumstances produce different answers.

PUTTING IT INTO PRACTICE

Example 1

Sonia is 45 and has a satisfying job in the international management of an oil company, earning £65,000 pa. She is married to Tom who is 58 and recently retired from a finance post in the City of London with a pension of £40,000 pa. The company wishes to move Sonia to their office in Singapore for a period of three to five years of international experience and exchange of expertise and perspective with Singaporean colleagues before return to London and promotion to a more senior role. The couple has twin sons, one in the Royal Navy and the other a trainee teacher. There is a family home in the home counties, where the trainee teacher still lives with his parents.

Richard is also 45 and is an accountant, working as a senior manager in an international bank. He earns £100,000 pa and is married to Molly, 38, and they have four children between the ages of 11 and 16 attending local schools. They all live in a London suburb. Molly has acted as homemaker since their first child was born, but aspires to write children's books. Richard has been offered a surprise appointment for two years acting as HR Director of the bank's Middle East operations, based in Dubai.

What are the issues that each couple will have to consider?

Example 2

This is a more demanding exercise, involving some arithmetic, but also some further research.

John Smith works as an account executive in a major international public relations company (PR International Ltd). He has worked at their corporate headquarters in London since 2005 when he joined as a graduate trainee.

Since then his career has progressed steadily. He is now a senior account executive earning £55,000 pa plus car and benefits. He is married to Juliet and the couple have two children aged 8 and 6. They live in a Kent commuter town where they have recently purchased a house. Their children attend the local primary school where Juliet works as a teacher. They have a mortgage, costing £700 per month.

Early in 2009 it was announced that PR Ltd had taken over one of its major rivals. Opportunities now exist for established and successful managers from the company's London office to take up management positions in their overseas branches.

➤ John Smith's boss, Alison Jones, is the Chief Executive of the UK business. She has worked for PR International for 17 years, enjoying a meteoric rise to her present position. Previously she worked in the company's offices in New York, Paris and Johannesburg and is consequently a prime candidate for future promotion to a pan-European or international management role.

Alison Jones has decided to offer one of the new expatriate postings to John Smith as a means of developing his career within the company. She regards him highly and believes him to be very competent and ready for a promotion of this kind. The post she decides to offer to John Smith is the deputy directorship of the Canadian branch office in the capital, Toronto, and will last for three years. John will report to the local branch director, a Canadian national.

Your task is as follows:

1 You have been asked by Alison Jones to recommend an appropriate salary package to offer to John Smith for a three-year posting to the company's Toronto office. You need to minimise the total cost and take account of local differentials, while providing sufficient incentive for John and his family to take up the post. Work out the appropriate salary and associated costs in Canadian dollars. You will need to ascertain the current exchange rate and the cost of living difference between the two countries; both are readily available by searching online. This will enable you to make good salary package approximations, although most companies will use a specialist company to make more sophisticated calculations.

2 You are a close friend of John and Juliet Smith. What additional aspects of the move would you advise them to consider expecting the company to provide for, so that the three-year period is worthwhile for all members of the family? Here are some starters:

- medical cover, as there is no free national health service in Canada;
- the children's education;
- costs of services to maintain the family home during their absence;
- opportunities for Juliet to pursue her career aspiration;
- frequency and costs of home leave for all the family;
- accommodation in Toronto.

To complete the exercise, work out two figures: an opening negotiating position and the minimum acceptable.

FURTHER READING

Negotiation

Fisher, R and Ury, W. (2012) *Getting to Yes*. Harlow: Pearson Education.

First published in 1986, this long-awaited revised edition is excellent on the basics and very thorough throughout.

Gates, S. (2016) *The Negotiation Book*. Chichester: John Wiley.

A new practical guide.

Arden, D. (2015) *Win Win*. Harlow: Pearson Education.

Wide-ranging to the point of being superficial, but provides a picture of negotiating in many different situations.

Walton, R. E, and McKersie, R. B. (1965) *Towards a Behavioural Theory of Labour Negotiation*. London: McGraw Hill.

Expatriate reward

Redman, T. and Wilkinson, A. (2013) *Contemporary Human Resource Management*. Harlow: Pearson Education.

This is a well-researched Australian/British book of text and cases that has a single chapter on international HRM, including material on expatriate payment.

Dowling, P.J. and Schuler, R.S. (1990) *International Dimensions of Human Resource Management*. Boston, Mass.: PWS Kent.

Long out of print, but never seriously challenged in over 35 years and still to be found in libraries.

Torrington, D. (1994) *International Human Resource Management: Think Globally, Act Locally*. London: Prentice Hall.

Out of date and out of print, but has a full chapter on overseas compensation.

REFERENCES

Negotiation

Fisher, R and Ury, W. (2012) *Getting to Yes*. Harlow: Pearson Education.

Expatriate reward

Dowling, P.J. and Schuler, R.S. (1990) *International Dimensions of Human Resource Management*. Boston, Mass.: PWS Kent.

PART 7
CONTEMPORARY ISSUES

CHAPTERS

As we come to the close of the text, we have a different sort of Part in which we are not considering activities in a specific functional grouping, but issues that tend to influence all functional areas. We start in Chapter 29 with the ethical dimension of management in general and HRM in particular which has aroused great interest recently.

The management of the HR function, Chapter 30, is undergoing some changes and those engaged in the area need to be aware of these and how changes may move forward. Structures continue to be adapted and the HR function strives to operate strategically. The effectiveness of the HR function is frequently questioned so all HR people need to consider how valuable their contribution is and how it can be effectively measured.

Health and well-being at work continue to be important in terms of an ethical approach to employment and also as a means of encouraging higher performance (Chapter 31).

Then, in Chapter 32, we look at managing an international workforce, as this becomes more prevalent. We need to understand why HR practices may differ across borders and the role of different cultures, and the challenges these provide for organisational integration.

Finally, in Chapter 33, we come to a round-up of skills for those in more senior positions, who now hone their basic skills for a more wide-ranging role. At the end of each chapter you will find a case study in Putting it into practice which will help you to put these ideas into context and explore them more thoroughly.

CHAPTER 29

ETHICS AND REPUTATIONAL MANAGEMENT

THE OBJECTIVES OF THIS CHAPTER ARE TO:

1 Introduce the topic of ethics and corporate social responsibility
2 Consider aspects of ethics that affect HRM and reputational management
3 Review variations of ethical practice across national boundaries
4 Suggest particular ethical questions facing HRM people in the future

The ethical dimension

A female music teacher in an English girls' school was jailed for engaging one of her pupils in a sexual relationship that had begun when the girl was under 15. Two days after the sentence became public an anonymous letter to a national newspaper commented that the letter writer had had a similar relationship as a teacher with a pupil, but had no feelings of guilt, 'It may have been unethical, but it was not wrong'. That makes an alarming distinction implying that rule breaking is wrong, but unethical behaviour is a matter of personal choice and nothing to do with anyone else. So what do we mean by ethics and what are the ethical dimensions of HRM?

In western thought the major set of ideas are those set out by Aristotle 2,300 years ago, that virtues, such as generosity, charity and justice, impel people possessing them to act in a way that benefits them and their surrounding society. This benign concept remains persuasive, perhaps because of its common-sense attractiveness and its reflection in the Judaeo-Christian tradition that has dominated the western world, being further clarified by philosophers such as the German, Immanuel Kant, and Jeremy Bentham and John Stuart Mill, who defined ethical behaviour as that which produces the greatest good for the greatest number. It is relatively simple to see that every member of the business will seek to behave, and to carry out their duties, in a way which they individually regard as ethical although they may find that their personal ethics conflict with aspects of law or company policy.

This suggests perhaps that people comply with the law but can still behave unethically, as in the situation of some large international companies that pay only token amounts if tax in countries of their subsidiaries on profits earned in those countries. A different aspect has been demonstrated in attitudes to aspects of dress with, for instance, schoolgirls in France not being allowed to wear the burka and some UK employers not permitting employees to incorporate religious insignia such as the cross into their clothing. Whatever one may think of a law, it remains the law until it is changed, no matter how offensive to one's personal views. Equally, company official policy overrides anyone's personal ethical stance.

Can a business have ethical standards? Kenneth Blanchard is an American academic and consultant of considerable reputation, who collaborated with Norman Vincent Peale, author of *The Power of Positive Thinking*, which had sold no fewer than 20 million copies. Together they produced a slim, popular book about ethics in management which they described as follows:

> ethical behaviour is related to self-esteem. We both believe that people who feel good about themselves have what it takes to withstand outside pressure and to do what is right rather than do what is merely expedient, popular or lucrative. We believe that a strong code of morality in any business is the first step towards its success. We believe that ethical managers are winning managers. (Blanchard and Peale 1988: 7)

Aristotle would have been proud of them! It is interesting that the idea is 'sold' as a means to an end rather than as an end in itself, and it sounds almost as 'expedient, popular or lucrative' as the alternative that they are disparaging. We can get Blanchard and Peale in clearer perspective if we consider a definition of ethics from the *Oxford English Dictionary:*

a social, religious or civil code of behaviour considered to be correct, especially that of a particular group or profession.

Thinking back to the opening of this chapter, the anonymous letter about sexual relations between teachers and children included the phrase, 'It may have been unethical, but it was not wrong'. The dictionary definition refers to codes *considered to be correct*. Blanchard and Peale spoke of the need for *a strong code of morality*. There is no room for individual variations in the face of collective consent.

Ethics are part of the culture of the individual business corporation that sets norms of behaviour by which people in the business will abide because the norms have some moral authority as well as being convenient and a yardstick of corporate social responsibility.

They can also be a set of guidelines followed by people in a particular group or profession because it makes practical sense in enabling them to do their jobs. CIPD has just such a code; barristers will not represent two different clients if there is likely to be a conflict of interest between the clients. Medical doctors will generally refrain from sexual relationships with their patients. In the latter cases there are sound practical reasons, quite apart from any moral dimension. The medical profession is, however, an interesting point of comparison because the importance of ethics is so obvious, public discussion of medical ethics is regular, academic examination of medical ethics is widespread and there is a history that goes back at least 2,400 years to the Greek 'father of medicine', Hippocrates.

One twenty-first century attempt to formulate a universal code of medical ethics is described by Gillon (2003) as having four principles, their longevity being demonstrated by three of them being given a definition in Latin as well as in English:

Beneficence – a practitioner should act in the best interest of the patient. (*Salus aegroti suprema lex*).
Non-maleficence – 'first, do no harm'. (*primum non nocere*).
Autonomy – the patient has the right to refuse or choose treatment. (*Voluntas aegroti suprema lex*).
Justice – concerns the distribution of scarce health resources, and the decision of who gets what treatment.

Gillon explains how this affects the individual practitioner:

The best moral strategy for . . . a health care worker is first to distinguish whether it is I or an organisation, profession, or society itself that has to make a decision. For example, 'how should I respond to a particular patient who wants an abortion?' is distinct from, 'what is this hospital's organisational view on abortion?' and 'what is the medical profession's collective view on abortion?' and 'what is society's view as expressed in law and practice?'

Firstly, for decisions that I must take myself I must try to exclude decisions that have no moral basis or justification. Neither pursuit of my own self interest – for example, accepting bribes from patients, hospitals, or drug manufacturers – nor action that discriminates against patients on the basis of personal preference or prejudice can provide a just or morally acceptable basis for allocating scarce health care resources or for any other category of justice. Moreover, it is not my role as a doctor to punish patients; withholding antibiotics from smokers who do not give up smoking or refusing to refer heavy drinkers with liver damage induced by alcohol for specialist assessment on the grounds that they are at fault is not a just or morally acceptable basis for rationing my medical resources. (Gillon 2003: 267)

Although these comments are directed at medical practitioners or healthcare workers, it is an interesting intellectual exercise to substitute the word 'employee' for 'patient' to see how helpful and practical they might be. A book by four American academics (Wicks *et al*. 2010: 10) writing for a *business* readership enlarges the Hippocratic principles, *without any reference to their origin,* into a Standards of Conduct Decision Guide:

> *Beneficence* – People should provide help to others.
> *Non-maleficence* – People should avoid doing harm to others, especially intentional and direct harm.
> *Autonomy* – People should be free to make their own choices, particularly when they relate to their own welfare and life projects.
> *Justice* – People ought to give others what they are due and operate with a sense of fair play.
> *Responsibility* – People have certain expectations of themselves, and feel certain obligations to themselves, which they expect in return from others.

This discussion demonstrates four aspects of ethics for managers:

1 Ethics are about behaviour which stems from personal conviction or collective consent.

2 If personal conviction conflicts with law, company policy or collective consent, then personal conviction has to suspended.

3 Managerial interest in ethics is the extent to which they can emphasise, extend or transcend desirable behaviours within the general framework of company policy.

4 Some ethical standards may be determined by a professional body of which an employee is a member, and with which the employee will feel obliged to comply, even if such compliance leads to behaviour in conflict with company policy and practice.

Early management concern with ethics

The early management concern with ethics was led by philanthropic industrialists in the nineteenth century, such as Cadbury, Lever, Salt and Rowntree, later criticised for their intrinsic paternalism. An American contemporary was Andrew Carnegie, who was born in Scotland but made a considerable fortune after emigrating to the USA and devoted the last years of his life to giving most of it away. In 1900 he wrote a book called *The Gospel of Wealth,* which set out a statement of corporate social responsibility that was quite as paternalist as that of his UK counterparts. He believed that corporate social responsibility had two principles, charity and stewardship. The more fortunate in society had an obligation to aid the less fortunate (charity) and those with wealth should see themselves as owning that wealth in trust for the rest of society by using it for purposes which were socially legitimate (stewardship). This was a position adopted by individuals and their personal convictions, and not necessarily about the management of the business. Furthermore it has increasingly been detached from the management of the business by the donor setting up a charitable trust to dispense accumulated funds by the donor and trustees. There are many examples: the best-known and probably most generously funded is the Bill and Melinda Gates Foundation, which has the objective of eradicating malaria worldwide, but there are many more.

Business ethics today

To many people business ethics remains an incongruous concept, on the grounds that any commercially driven activity has dominant motivations that are inevitably opposed to social considerations. Another version of the same view is that those in management positions should not make moral judgements as they have no authority to do so. Instead they should respond to public opinion as expressed by customers' purchasing decisions, demonstrations by pressure groups or trade unions or by government legislation. However, Lord Browne, who was Chief Executive of BP from 1995 to 2007, argues differently:

> Businesses are there to co-operate, to work with society. Businesses have to engage with everyone who is affected by them; and to tell the truth (Browne 2015: 38)

WINDOW ON PRACTICE

One relatively recent form of control on management decision making is whistle-blowing, which describes the practice of an employee metaphorically blowing a whistle to attract attention from the outside to some ethical malpractice within the business. Originally this was done by lone individuals taking great risks with their employment, but the method has now altered through the establishment of a charity, Public Concern at Work, which gives free legal advice to potential whistle-blowers. Its director claims that most issues are now settled within the business.

The need for ethical guidelines

The logic supporting the need for ethical guidelines is that actions in business are the result of decisions by human beings, and human beings tend to seek justification for their actions beyond the rule of value for money. This can be grotesque rationalisation. The various Mafia families apparently have a very robust code of conduct, based on strong family cohesion and a convenient interpretation of the Roman Catholic faith. This 'justification' enables them to peddle drugs, launder money, run large-scale prostitution and extortion rackets, to say nothing of killing people, without a sense of guilt.

Fortunately, most people do not resort to such extreme behaviour, but will still seek to justify to themselves actions they take that can have unpleasant consequences for others. Recent concern about responsibility for fatal accidents has created great interest in the concept of corporate manslaughter. Who is responsible for a train crash, the train driver or those in overall charge of the business who did not arrange for suitable training, supervision or other facilities?

Moral justification

Sometimes the moral justification comes from a value system that is independent of the business itself and where individual opinions can be sharply divided. Some doctors and nurses are happy to work in abortion clinics, while others refuse. Some people are enraged about the destruction of green land to build motorways or high-speed railways, while others are enthusiastic. Other actions and decisions are more generally supported by the external value system. Few would disagree that people at work should be honest and that claims about a product or service should be accurate. Most would also agree with the general proposition of equal opportunity for all, although there may be sharp disagreement about what exactly that means in practice.

Ethical principles

Some standards of ethics derive from voluntary agreement by members of a particular industry, such as editors of national newspapers, or statutory 'watchdogs' such as those monitoring the activities of privatised public utilities. The problem of pensions and similar financial services being mis-sold produced the Personal Investment Authority, which was dissolved in 2009 with its powers being transferred to the Financial Services Authority with swingeing powers intended to prevent a repetition of that sort of problem. Then there are the ethical standards that are generated within a particular business. The Royal Dutch/Shell Group of Companies relies largely for its international effectiveness on the values shared by all its companies and employees. No new joint venture will be developed unless the partner company accepts them.

These principles were first set out in 1976 and were not imposed from the top, but were a codification of already accepted behaviour. The principles are revised from time to time and one of the challenging tasks for the central HR function was to introduce a code of practice relating to drugs and alcohol, which took considerable discussion and consultation before agreement could be reached:

> At the heart of our Business Principles are three core values: honesty; integrity and respect for people. Consistently behaving with integrity requires clear and simple requirements (like our zero tolerance for bribes and fraud); effective procedures to check and reward compliance, and a company culture that does not tolerate dishonest or illegal practices. (Royal Dutch Shell 2009)

Codes of ethics

The key issue with ethical codes is the extent to which they are supported by the people to whom they apply. They are not rules that can be enforced by penalties for non-compliance. It is necessary that they are understood, appreciated and willingly honoured by the great majority of those who are affected. There will then be considerable social pressure on the few who do not wish to comply. Imposing ethics is very tricky. When examining equal opportunities some years ago, researchers found an interesting situation in an American computer company with a rapidly growing UK subsidiary. The company had a high-profile commitment to 'positive action to seek out and employ members of disadvantaged groups'. This was reinforced in the annual appraisal system for managers, who had to indicate what they had done in the previous twelve months to implement a 'programme of employment and development for minorities'. The company annual report made a claim that this initiative was advancing at all international locations. In the UK, however, it was found in practice that:

> Without exception, all managers to whom we spoke ignored that part of their appraisal . . . They put a line through the offending clause and wrote 'not applicable in the UK', despite the corporate objective of 'citizenship', applicable in the UK, requiring recruitment officers to seek out the disadvantaged in the community . . . Suggestions by the researchers that such an active recruitment policy was an obligation on the part of management . . . invoked the reaction, 'we're not a welfare organisation'. (Torrington *et al.* 1982: 23)

Ethics and HRM

HR people have long held a strong interest in ethics, although it was usually caricatured as welfare, looking after employees regardless of the interests of the business. Going beyond welfare, HR specialists are employed in no other capacity than to participate closely in the management process of the business. They do not have the limited degree of independence that, for instance, company accountants have, as their activities are not subject to external audit, although there is a move in that direction since the CIPD became chartered. Nonetheless the simple existence of a code of conduct is a valuable guide to members of the profession and enhances the value of their work in the business.

The change in general management orientation during the 1980s and 1990s towards the idea of leaner and fitter, flexible organisations, downsizing, delayering, outplacement and all the other ideas that eventually lead to fewer people in jobs and fewer still with any sort of employment security has usually been implemented by HR people. HR and personnel managers cannot behave like Banquo's ghost and be silently disapproving of their colleagues' actions. What they can do is to argue vigorously in favour of what they see as the best combination of efficiency and justice, but they can only argue vigorously if they are present when decisions are made. If they are not generally 'on side', they do not participate in the decision making and they probably do not keep their jobs. Either they are a part of management, understanding business needs and priorities, valued by their colleagues, despite their funny ideas, or they are powerless. There are no ivory towers for them to occupy, and no more employment security for them than for any other member of the business.

HR people can still be critical of proposed management actions, if they are valued by their managerial colleagues for the wholeness of their contribution, and if they accept the fact that they will often lose the argument. They have no monopoly of either wisdom or righteousness, and other members of the management team are just as likely as they are to be concerned about social values.

HR managers have moved away from an approach to welfare that was trivial, anachronistic and paternalist. In the HR vocabulary the term 'welfare' is code for middle-class do-gooders placing flowers in the works canteen. HR managers increasingly shun the traditional approach to welfare not for its softness, but because it is ineffectual. It does not satisfy the HR obsession with getting progress in the employment of people, and it certainly does not do enough to satisfy the people who are employed. In many undertakings HR specialists are taking their management colleagues along with them in an enthusiastic and convinced attempt to give jobs more meaning and to humanise the workplace. Their reasoning is that the business can only maintain its competitive edge if the people who work there are committed to its success, and that commitment is volitional: you need hearts and minds as well as hands and muscle. Investment in training and dismantling of elaborate, alienating organisation structures do more for employee well-being than paternalistic welfare programmes ever did.

Corporate Social Responsibility and HR

The beginning of the twenty-first century saw the rise of the idea of Corporate Social Responsibility. This is an interest in a wide range of matters where some companies wish to review their activities and includes topics like climate change, pollution, charitable contributions, customer care and others that are not narrowly the province of HR and therefore lie outside the scope of this text, although Maureen Stapley describes an interesting broad-based approach at Mondial Assistance that has generated the useful byproduct of short-term absence declining from 2007 to 2009 from 3.76 days to 3.2 while staff turnover fell from 22.68% to 6.4%. She offers the obvious reservation:

> While these decreases were driven by a number of factors within the business, our team of executive directors . . . firmly believe that the commitment and focus on CSR were a very strong contributing factor. (Stapley 2010: 55)

Reviewing the development of CSR, Stefan Stern made the following comment:

> CSR is bound to fail in companies where it is adopted simply for reasons of public relations . . . It may be successful in changing attitudes to your company in the short term, but if your activities are morally dubious they will eventually be exposed. CSR, if it is to mean anything, cannot be a bolted-on attitude or a departmental annexe . . . It is not about 'putting something back' – it is about how you make your money in the first place. (. . . In any case, if you really feel the need to 'put something back', doesn't that suggest you have taken too much already?) (Stern 2004: 35)

HR often made a trap for themselves and then fell into it. Protagonist businesses adopted the principle and then looked for someone to make it happen. HR, always keen for enhanced status, offered to take it on and were then blamed for its failure. They failed because the big issues in social responsibility that had a high profile at the time were the environment, bankers' probity and whistle-blowing. HR could only claim any capability in understanding whistle-blowing; they had no more than any layperson's capability to deal effectively with the other two issues and fell into a trap of their own making.

Reputational management

HR has a very specific interest in reputational management as an aspect of recruitment, as explained in Chapter 8. This is a concern that the business's reputation incorporates features which will encourage the 'right' people to come and work there. Generally people are attracted to a business that is seen as sound and deals fairly with its employees. Whether it is ethical is a slightly different question.

Ethics across national boundaries

The international dimension of the social responsibility question has still to be developed. Logging operations in South America are ravaging the rainforests, which are essential to life continuing on the planet. Error, or neglect, in the management of manufacturing processes can produce a tragedy like that of Chernobyl in Ukraine or the various discharges of crude oil that have occurred all over the world. Since the first formal warning by the US Surgeon General about the risks of smoking, tobacco consumption has been falling in western countries, so the tobacco companies have increased their marketing in less developed countries, which is widely regarded as a most dubious practice.

Ethical standards vary. Becker and Fritzsche (1987) carried out a study of different ethical perceptions between American, French and German executives: 39% of the Americans said that paying money for business favours was unethical; only 12% of the French and none of the Germans agreed. In the USA, Japanese companies have been accused of avoiding the employment of ethnic minority groups by the careful location of their factories (Cole and Deskins 1988: 17–19). On the other hand, Japanese standards on employee health and safety are as high as those anywhere in the world (Wokutch 1990). In South East Asia the contrast in prosperity between countries such as Malaysia and Singapore on the one hand and Indonesia and the Philippines on the other means that there are ethical questions in the more prosperous Asian countries about the employment of illegal immigrants from the less prosperous that are superficially similar to those applying to Cubans and Mexicans in the USA, but which do not occur in other parts of the world. There are very low wages and long working hours in China and in much of India.

The various high-profile cases over the last twelve years of offering inducements to individuals in order to obtain business led the UK government to introduce the Bribery Act of 2010. This makes it an offence (a) to offer or pay a bribe, (b) to request or receive a bribe, or (c) to bribe a foreign public service official, and there is also (d) a corporate offence of failing to prevent a bribe being offered or paid on behalf of the business.

The disparate nature of ethical standards between countries will be one of the key HR issues to be addressed in the future. There will gradually be a growing together of national practice on working hours, but it will take much longer for rates of pay to harmonise. One can visualise common standards on health and safety developing much more quickly than equality of opportunity between the sexes and across ethnic divisions.

Some current and developing ethical dilemmas

We conclude this chapter by suggesting some of the ethical dilemmas for those in management positions, where HR could be expected to play a leading role. Issues such as the environment, equalising opportunity and ensuring safe working conditions with fair treatment are extensively discussed, but there are others that receive less attention.

Life in the business

Workplace stress is one of the most common causes of absence and the place of work is an arena where newspapers, TV reports and social media would have us believe that harassment, poor supervision and bullying are rife. We include a piece on dealing with bullying in Chapter 33. In 2015 surveys of job satisfaction in both the UK and the USA showed that half the working population in both countries disliked their jobs. These results echoed research twenty years earlier:

> Few people go off to work these days with a song in their hearts . . . many people dread each day because they have to work in places where they feel abused and powerless. What

is happening to us? Why are talented, productive people being thwarted and sabotaged? Why do we treat each other so badly? Why are tyrannical bosses tolerated? Does the bottom line really justify the hurt and frustration we experience? (Wright and Smye 1996: 3)

We now lack the comfortable feelings of security that the employing organisation used to provide. Whether people really are more or less secure in their jobs is debatable, but there is no doubt that they feel less secure. Furthermore, delayering and downsizing to become leaner and fitter have mainly affected people in middle-range posts, who used to be the most secure and who valued their security most highly.

We shall have to find ways that make work less stressful and more satisfying, despite the decline of its traditionally most attractive features: security and community.

Information technology and the workplace

Managers have long been able to spend more of their time, and make more of their decisions, by rational planning and operational research methods than in fact they do. There continues to be a preference among managers in general and HR managers in particular to spend their time talking with people and to make their decisions as a result of discussion and shrewd judgement.

As we indicated in employability skills for Part 1 (Chapter 6), managers may now begin to eschew face-to-face discussion in favour of face-to-screen interaction and decision making, or will they continue to confer and keep busy while others feed to them an ever-increasing flow of processed information requiring interpretation, evaluation and further discussion? Research findings suggest that managers work in the way that they do at least partly because they like it that way. Nobody saw it more clearly than one of the management greats, Henry Mintzberg:

> The manager actually seems to prefer brevity and interruption in his work. Superficiality is an occupational hazard of the manager's job. Very current information (gossip, hearsay, speculation) is favoured; routine reports are not. The manager clearly favours the . . . verbal media, spending most of his time in verbal contact. (Mintzberg 1973: 51–2)

The date and male gender of that quotation may be significant. Most of the studies of managerial work have been of men and of men and women working in a male-dominated culture. It may be that the increasing proportion of managerial jobs done by women will alter the stereotype. The women authors of *Corporate Abuse* are quite clear about the need to care for souls:

> Studies of work flow suggest there is five times more opportunity to experience joy in the workplace on a daily basis than in the home environment if it is a workplace that is in tune with the needs of the soul . . . Once we have a community of fully nurtured souls, the possibility of creativity is limitless. Everyone in the workforce will be tapped into his or her own power source as well as being part of a larger community of effort and partnership. (Wright and Smye 1996: 248–9)

This rings strangely in management ears, but maybe this is the way to rediscover the sense of community that employing organisations used to provide.

How great will the influence of digitalisation on HRM work actually become? How will we make up for what the computer takes away? If there is a general tendency for people to work at home, taking their laptop with them, how popular will that turn out to be? It is over a century since the household ceased to be the central productive unit and the men, and later the women, began to spend a large part of their waking hours at a different social centre: the factory, shop or office – the organisational entity. To be house-bound has become a blight.

The digital age may not turn everyone into a home-worker, but it is still having a significant impact. There is the slightly isolating nature of the work that computerisation produces. The individual employee is not one of many in a crowded workshop, but one of a few scattered around a mass of busy machines. The clerical employee spends more time gazing at a computer terminal and less talking to colleagues. Current predictions are that a large swathe of management jobs will disappear as robots take over within the next decade or so. For the dwindling number of human beings left at work, what behaviour will this engender and what attitudes will be associated with that behaviour?

ACTIVITY 29.1

What difference has the computer made to your working life so far? What further effect do you expect it to have in the next five years? How readily would you be (or are you) a home-worker?

The central ethical dilemma seems to be that we are allowing information technology gradually to take away the social institution of the organisation on which we have become so dependent. How will this scenario unfold?

Employment

How will people find employment, both as a way of earning their livelihood and as a means of finding their place in society? Some people manage their own careers and concentrate on ensuring their continuing employability. Charles Handy enunciated his concept of portfolio living, whereby people put together a portfolio of different activities so that they could control their own lives without becoming dependent on a single employer. This is fine for the able, well-educated and independently minded, but human society has not evolved to the point where that description fits everyone; it probably fits only a minority. Where large businesses have survived recent economic difficulties as organisational entities, they tend to have fewer levels in the hierarchy and the recent experience of controlled low inflation combine to make promotion rarer and pay increases fewer. Most people at work aspire to a career that involves doing better, making progress, 'going up'. In current circumstances this becomes more difficult and the tendency to begrudge more senior people better conditions becomes greater. A nice HR challenge is to develop novel aspects of corporate culture that will recognise achievement and give a sense of progress for all those who seek it, without generating envy.

Another impact on employment that is yet to be evaluated is robotics. There are predictions that robots will remove up to 40% of routine jobs and up to 20% of administration carried out by humans. Evaluation of this will come in our next edition; perhaps that will be compiled by robots!

The pay divide

Our last suggestion of an ethical dilemma for HR is the divide between the highest-paid in a business and everyone else. This was seen as sufficiently serious for the UK to set up an independent inquiry by a High Pay Commission. Their final report, *Cheques with Balances,* was published at the end of 2015 and included the comment by its chair Deborah Hargreaves:

> There is a crisis at the top of British business and it is deeply corrosive to our economy. When pay for senior executives is set behind closed doors, does not reflect company success and is fuelling massive inequality it represents a deep malaise at the very top of our society. (High Pay Commission 2015)

This may not be a matter that HR people feel they can influence, as top people's pay and conditions are usually dealt with by the top people themselves, perhaps with the advice of a remuneration committee made up of similar people from outside. However, the High Pay Commission has suggested some specific reforms to high pay, one of which is that employees should be represented on remuneration committees. Who better qualified than those HR people who deal with the pay and conditions of employees to assume this role?

Ethics and policy

There has recently been a practice of HR people being described as 'HR Strategic Business Partner' to emphasise the importance of HR taking a strategic perspective, but this may not be wise. An HR perspective on strategy is important in avoiding an ethical misjudgement or in advocating an ethical initiative, but HR involvement in policy is surely crucial. Strategy describes the sense of purpose and overall direction of the business. Policy complements strategy by describing the way in which the objectives will be carried out. Developing overseas by establishing a new subsidiary might be a strategy while a policy might be needed on rates of pay and how they relate to those at headquarters. Some of the main policies in a contemporary business relating to its people are about whether or not all vacancies will be advertised, the avoidance of unlawful discrimination, union recognition or not, health and safety, fairness in dismissal, methods of redundancy, and how people are paid. Other areas that impinge on members of the business and which are more recent are environment and ethics.

Throughout the 1990s a number of large companies produced written ethical policies covering employee affairs and relations with customers, ranging from the simple, 'Never knowingly undersold', to lengthy documents. These frequently included an environmental dimension following concerns about climate change and animal health.

In developing policy it is even more important than with strategy that those who have to implement the policy, or their representatives, are closely involved in its drafting. They will certainly find all manner of reasons why some aspects simply will not work, but they will also have excellent suggestions for improvement. Just make sure you get them hooked on the idea before you get onto the practice.

SUMMARY PROPOSITIONS

29.1. In the business context, ethics are part of the corporate culture that sets norms of behaviour by which people in the business will abide because they have some moral authority as well as being convenient.

29.2. Ethical standards vary between different national cultures, making international standards difficult.

29.3. Ethical codes are only valid if they are appreciated and willingly implemented by the great majority of those to whom they apply.

29.4. Personnel/HR management has always had a strong ethical dimension, although personnel managers and the practice of HRM are regularly criticised for failure in corporate social responsibility.

29.5. Among current and developing ethical dilemmas are the quality of life in the business, information technology and robots in the workplace, employment, self-improvement and the increasing divide between pay at the top of the business and all other employees.

GENERAL DISCUSSION TOPICS

1. The chapter opens by explaining that personnel managers for years played down their ethical/welfare role. Why do you think this was?

2. What examples can you think of that would make you feel that the demands of your job conflicted with what you regarded as being right? How would you deal with this?

3. Most people agree that differences in rates of pay according to value or effort are justified, but that some differences are 'obscene'. What criteria would you suggest for setting pay differentials within a business that are seen as both fair and effective in being able to attract and retain appropriate people from the labour market?

THEORY INTO PRACTICE

Here is an ethical dilemma on HR decisions.

Eric

Thirty years ago, before the days of wheelie bins, Eric was deaf, mute and suffered from cerebral palsy. He had been unemployable all his adult life, but in his late twenties he started to follow round the local authority refuse collectors emptying dustbins. As the lorry reached the end of a street, Eric would go ahead of it and drag dustbins out from behind the houses to the front. His handicap made it a very slow and painful process, but it was something he could do and he was exhausted. This completely unofficial arrangement was accepted by the refuse collectors as they were able to complete their rounds more quickly and they were on an incentive payment arrangement. Eric's participation enabled them to complete their rounds in slightly less time. At the end of the week they had a collection and gave Eric a few pounds. This transformed his life, as he had a purpose and had some mates. Setting aside, for a moment, issues about legal entitlement to benefit . . .

Questions

1 Do you feel that Eric was being exploited by the refuse collectors? Local authority officials heard about what Eric was doing and said it had to stop.

2 Why do you think they made this decision? Do you agree with it? A personnel manager in the neighbourhood heard about Eric and arranged for him to be taught to operate a sewing machine. He was then employed in the personnel manager's factory to maintain and repair all the overalls, a straightforward job carried out skilfully and conscientiously.

3 Do you feel that Eric was being exploited by the personnel manager?

4 As Eric was able to draw invalidity benefit, do you feel that the job should have been offered first to someone who was able-bodied? In the following three years investigations twice demonstrated that the overalls could be repaired more cheaply by subcontracting the work to another company, but that decision was not taken. Eric carried on as an employee.

5 Why do you think that decision was not made? Do you agree with it?

FURTHER READING

Fisher, C., Lovell, A. and Nestor, V-S. (2013) *Business Ethics and Values* (4th ed.). Harlow: Pearson Education.

This is a fairly weighty textbook providing an integrated discussion of ethical issues for managers in general. There are sections of particular interest to HRM people, including some careful treatments of international comparisons and ethical differences as well as some excellent case studies. Chapters 4 and 5 provide an interesting evaluation framework for an individual manager to assess the ethical validity of a particular course of action.

People Management (2003) and (2012).

The first issue, from July 2003, is dedicated to examining corporate social responsibility. The second, from December 2012, pp. 24–7, has an article devoted to whistle-blowing.

Torrington, D.P. (2013) *Managing to Manage*. London: Kogan Page, pp. 33–46.

This short work is a general management book for managers rather than an HR textbook, but has a useful section on the relationship between strategy, policy and procedures.

Wicks, A.C., Freeman, R.E., Werhane, P.H. and Martin, K.E. (2010) *Business Ethics: A Managerial Approach*. Upper Saddle River, NJ: Prentice Hall.

An American text that takes an unashamedly managerial approach and sometimes blurs difficult issues, but still a useful text to provide a distinctly different approach to Fisher *et al*.

REFERENCES

Becker, H. and Fritzsche, D.J. (1987) 'A comparison of the ethical behavior of American, French and German managers', *Columbia Journal of World Business*, Winter, pp. 87–95.

Blanchard, K. and Peale, N.V. (1988) *The Power of Ethical Management*. London: Heinemann.

Browne, J. (2015) *Connect: How Companies Succeed by Managing Radically with Society*. London: Weidenfeld and Nicolson.

Cole, R.E. and Deskins, D.R. (1988) 'Racial factors in site location and employment patterns of Japanese auto Firms in America', *California Management Review*, Fall, p. 11.

Gillon, R. (2003) 'Four scenarios', *Journal of Medical Ethics*, Vol. 29, pp. 267–8.

High Pay Commission (2015) Final Report, *Cheques with Balances*. London: The Stationery Office.

Mintzberg, H. (1973) *The Nature of Managerial Work*. London: Harper & Row.

Royal Dutch Shell (1976–2015) *Statement of General Business Principles* [internal document].

Stapley, M. (2010) 'How HR made a difference at work', *People Management*, February, p. 55.

Stern, S. (2004) 'The perils of CSR', *Royal Society of Arts Journal*, January.

Torrington, D.P., Hitner, T.J. and Knights, D. (1982) *Management and the Multi-Racial Workforce*. Aldershot: Gower.

Wicks, A.C., Freeman, R.E., Werhane, P.H. and Martin, K.E. (2010) *Business Ethics: A Managerial Approach*. Upper Saddle River, NJ: Prentice Hall.

Wokutch, R.E. (1990) 'Corporate social responsibility, Japanese style', *Academy of Management Executive*, May, pp. 56–72.

Wright, L. and Smye, M. (1996) *Corporate Abuse*. New York: Macmillan.

CHAPTER 30

MANAGING THE HUMAN RESOURCE FUNCTION

THE OBJECTIVES OF THIS CHAPTER ARE TO:

1 Identify and explain the purpose, role and competencies of the HR function and potential structures that may be used to manage the function

2 Explore the extent to which the HR function operates strategically

3 Examine the use of self-service HR, shared services, outsourcing and the benefits and drawbacks of these approaches

4 Explore the role of line managers in HRM

5 Debate and critique the current developments in the management of the HR function

The purpose and structure of the personnel/HR function has developed considerably since its earliest welfare function, through a range of different incarnations, and in order to manage the function effectively we need to pay attention to its current purpose. Historically the HR function has been encouraged to gain greater power and credibility, and more recently play a greater strategic role, and become more efficient. In the first two decades of the twenty-first century there has been a great deal of attention on how HR purpose, roles, structures and relationships are changing and much opinion on how they should change in in order to meet future challenges. As Fry and Fishman (2015) point out:

> There seems to be no HR function that is not embarking on, is not part-way through, or has not recently completed major change in the way it organises itself and how it delivers its services to the organisation it supports. (Fry and Fishman 2015: 27)

As we shall see there has been mixed success to date in meeting such challenges and much thought is being devoted to how HR operating models (structure, roles, systems, delivery methods, architecture) need to evolve to meet yet another imperative: the critical importance of driving talent programmes.

In this chapter we will explore recent changes in roles and structures and conclude with a critical review of progress to date, and consider some of the imperatives that are beginning to shape the function for the future

The HR function: purpose, roles and competencies

The purpose of the HR function has historically been expressed as a variety of different roles that the function plays in the organisation, the most well-known typologies, based on the analysis of empirical data, being Tyson and Fell (1985) and Storey (1992). See Truss *et al.* (2012) for more details of these and other typologies.

Following this, on the basis of work with leading-edge organisations in the USA, Ulrich proposed four HR roles in 1997 and, on the basis of further research, Ulrich and Brockbank (2005a; 2005b) provided a view of the way these roles had evolved since, focusing on what an HR professional has to do to create value. In Table 30.1 we list the 2005 role set.

One of the fundamental features of Ulrich's approach is his view that HR effectiveness can only be achieved if all business needs relating to HR are met, and therefore all roles are fulfilled. Thus, Ulrich argues that HR must deliver on both a strategic and an administrative level. This view has been echoed elsewhere, with comments that operational HR excellence is an essential precursor for the involvement of HR professionals at a strategic level (e.g. Caldwell 2003). More recently in a banking case study, Aldrich and colleagues (2015) found that hard-won credibility to contribute strategically can be undermined when basic HR administrative tasks go wrong. The 'business or strategic partner' roles, though, have unsurprisingly attracted most attention in terms of job advertisements and new job titles. However, while making the case for strength from fulfilling all roles, Ulrich does acknowledge the paradox created by this, such as representing employee needs at the same time as implementing a management agenda. We return to this issue in the final section of this chapter.

In parallel work, Ulrich and colleagues (2013) have studied how the competencies required to fulfil HR roles have evolved over time and in the latest iteration six HR competencies are identified, as shown in Table 30.2.

Table 30.1 Ulrich and Brockbank's 2005 HRM role set

Roles in Ulrich and Brockbank (2005b)	Explanation of role
Employee advocate	Caring for, listening to, understanding and responding to employee needs, covering issues such as grievances, the impact of strategy on employees, equality, diversity, health and safety, discipline. All of these are played out in a context of the realities of the firm and the performance standards required of individuals
Human capital developer	Based on the premise that people are a critical asset of the organisation and thus need to be developed proactively with a focus on maximising their potential and contribution in the future. Such human capital developers would be located in Centres of HR Expertise, and often act as coaches working on behaviour and attitudes
Strategic partner	Multiple dimensions including business expert, change agent, knowledge manager and consultant. Aligning HR with business strategy is key, alongside transformation and cultural change
Functional expert	Application of the HR body of knowledge through HR practices. There are two categories of HR practices, those for which HR has direct responsibility (such as recruitment) and those for which responsibility is indirect (such as communications) Some practices are delivered through administrative efficiency and others through policies and interventions.
Leader	Leading the HR function, establishing the function's agenda within the firm and acting as a role model demonstrating the importance of HR in the way they lead their own function. Also contributing to the leadership of the organisation. This role requires that the functions of the four roles above are met

Source: Ulrich and Brockman (2005a; 2005b).

Table 30.2 HR competencies

Competency	Competency includes
Strategic positioner	Speak the language of the business; co-creating strategy; serve key customers; be deeply knowledgeable about the business environment
Credible activist	Build relationships of trust and communicate clear and consistent messages with integrity; use positive influence
Capability builder	Facilitate capability audits to understand what the organisation is good at, for example in terms of culture, process and identity
Change champion	Support the organisation's internal capacity for change; initiating and sustaining change
Human resource innovator and integrator	Know the latest insights on all areas of HRM in order to be innovative and integrate HR practices to impact on business results
Technology proponent	Use technology to deliver HR services efficiently and to support communication. Use technology in relationship building and leveraging social media

Source: Ulrich *et al.* (2013).

An analysis of a large data set, involving results from both inside and outside the HR function, showed that the credible activist domain had the most impact on perceived HR effectiveness and that human resource innovator and integrator had the most impact on business performance. An alternative model of competencies produced by the CIPD can be found on their website at www.cipd.co.uk.

CIPD (2011) research has focused on the fundamental purpose of the HR function, and how it needs to change in new environments, as this is seen to be more important than limited roles and structures. The 'Next Generation' research uncovered a range of HR purposes, generally along the lines of 'people and performance', 'creating a great place to work' and 'landing strategy through people and culture'. However, the CIPD also found some HR leaders who identified the purpose of the HR function as building organisations that would last, focusing on the fitness for purpose of the business now and in the future; in other words, 'supporting sustainable performance'. A key interpretation of the research is that four levels of purpose can be identified which the CIPD arranges in a pyramid:

'actively seeking out growth opportunities' (4) at the top;
'ensuring the business is able to deliver its business strategy' (3);
'seeking competitive advantage through shaping the organisation's culture and people capabilities' (2); and
continuously improving core people processes (1) at the bottom.

The CIPD suggests that the purpose of the HR function has gradually moved up through the pyramid, and that it is most important that the purpose of HR covers all levels. The research suggests that it is more important for HR to take a situational and imaginative approach to the needs and demands of its own organisation rather than merely following generic prescriptions of best practice such as the fulfilment of specific roles.

Structure of the HR function

The purpose and roles of HR in any organisation will have an influence on the structure of the function in any business/business unit, and this becomes more complex in a corporation which comprises several business units, which may or may not be related. Decisions need to be taken about the location of HR professionals between corporate HQ, business HQ and functions and departments, and a range of geographical locations complicates this further. HR professionals and policy/decision making can be either fully centralised or fully decentralised, or any point on this continuum to suit business needs. This is often reflected in reporting lines: for example, does the business HR manager report to the business CEO or to HR at corporate HQ? The level of involvement of line managers in HR is part of this mix and we deal with this specifically later in the chapter. Further complexity is added in global corporations.

WINDOW ON PRACTICE

Getting the structure right for the business

Facilities management company Servest Group has grown quickly through mergers and acquisitions, and J-C. Green, now HR Director, explains that when she joined in 2009 there were 'pockets of people doing HR administration' and the company lacked a formal HR department. Green centralised these small HR teams but did provide an HR Business Partner for each business, recognising that she needed people who were familiar with the characteristics of each separate business in order to improve HR's awareness of how each one operated on a day-to-day basis. She says that while HR is centralised, it retains a local feel. She feels the HR function is accessible to customers as there is one HR team to go to, and underlines the importance of matching HR structure to the nature of the business.

Source: Kirton, H. (2015) 'Anyone can Google . . . understanding the business is harder', *People Management*, May, pp. 20–22.

A second and equally critical aspect of structure is the extent to which the HR function is an integrated department of generalists across the business, or whether there is some segregation on the basis of expertise, such as recruitment or reward or development across the business; or in terms of client departments, such as research or marketing each having their own dedicated HR generalist. The two approaches may, of course, be taken together, so structures may be very complex.

An extreme structure derived from Ulrich's research on roles is a three-legged one comprising:

- strategic/business roles;
- shared service centres/outsourcing/intranet support; and
- centres of HR expertise.

There is evidence that in some large organisations (see e.g. Chesters 2011) a version of this structure has replaced the integrated model where one HR team carried out this full range of roles, and the model has certainly had a huge impact. However, although popular, it is not as prevalent in its pure form as much of the publicity surrounding the model suggests. Ulrich (Stephens 2015) cautions how models evolve over time, and that the model was never intended to be adopted unquestioningly; more important is that the HR structure should match organisation structure. The model has been criticised for fragmenting the HR function and there are now examples of organisations seeking greater collaboration between the different structural parts of HR, as in the Window on practice, next.

WINDOW ON PRACTICE

Amey redesigns its HR structure and philosophy

Amey had grown considerably through Transfer of Undertakings (Protection of Employment), or TUPE, transfers, and the HR function had found the growth in job titles, large numbers of temporary agency workers and unspecified numbers of people managers a complex challenge. There was an HR service centre but this had been badly received. To transform the HR function to become a strategic driver in the business, greater collaboration within the function was needed. Centres of excellence and shared service teams were brought together and there was increased interaction and movement across the business. Communication with line managers was improved and an HR intranet, telephone support and a self-service system introduced. HR career pathways and succession plans were introduced and links made to CIPD competencies. Amey won the CIPD 'Building HR Capability' award in 2011, the judges concluding that it had redesigned the HR structure and philosophy in a go-ahead way which was commercially successful.

Source: Riddoch, V. (2011) 'Built-in success', *People Management*, November, pp. 40–1.

After further work with organisations, Ulrich and his colleagues (2009) developed and expanded the model to better reflect the complexity of modern organisations, and this has five elements which are explained as distinct but overlapping:

- **Corporate HR:** being concerned with corporation-wide integration and initiatives, working with top management.
- **Centres of expertise:** providing specialist support to the service centres, providing expert advice and being involved in the design of HR policy and activities.
- **Embedded HR:** those who focus on the strategic needs of the business unit rather than the corporation, working with the leadership team and sometimes line managers, and having a wide range of role titles such as including 'business partner' and 'HR generalist'.
- **Operational executors:** who are based within the business unit dealing with operational HR issues and occasionally administrative work that cannot be dealt with by service centres, enabling 'embedded HR' to focus on strategic issues.
- **Service centres/e-HR:** focusing on administrative and routine issues.

This suggests more opportunities for strategic and business partner involvement. The emphasis in this work is on the importance of the HR structure matching the structure of the larger business, for example in the extent to which it is decentralised, giving much greater priority to context than the previous model. Ulrich *et al.* also suggest that the five-element model fits most closely with an organisation comprising allied/diversified businesses rather than a single business or a holding company comprising vastly different businesses. However, Ulrich (2015) argues that more important than roles defined on organisational charts are the relationships between different parts of the HR function. His focus here is to increase the operating effectiveness of HR and he proposes six key principles in achieving this: share a common purpose; respect differences; govern, accept, connect (manage problems); care for the other; share experiences together; and grow together.

WINDOW ON PRACTICE

Influences on HR structure in a global setting

A major challenge for global companies is to decide the degree of centralisation in the business and the HR function. High levels of centralisation engender a 'one-company approach' where employees receive the same experience wherever they are in the world. Such standardisation is often cost effective and provides high levels of consistency, as long as centralised policies and practices are not subverted. Alternatively some organisations pay more attention to the local context: for example, as Reilly (2012) points out, there are likely to be differences in attitudes and legal provisions relating to data protection; in attitudes to age and seniority; in the acceptability of nepotism; and in social obligations. There are of course more differences than these and local cultures can be very resilient to corporate dictates. Working with the local culture may be productive in terms of goodwill, flexibility, commitment and performance. Responsiveness to local cultures generally works best with a corporation which is a holding company for a group of very different specific businesses which keep their separate identities. However, it may be more difficult to clarify shareholder expectations and there are greater risks of unacceptable behaviour.

Whatever balance is chosen in terms of centralisation it will impact not only on HR strategies, but also on the positioning and structure of the function and its reporting lines as it works to support corporate and business strategies.

HR strategic contribution

There is much evidence that the strategic or business partner role is the one which has been most attractive, particularly in larger organisations (see for example CIPD 2015a), with these job titles used heavily initially, although a greater variety of titles has now emerged. It is worth bearing in mind, however, that the term 'business partner' is often used as a synonym for strategic partner, and used interchangeably (Francis and Keegan 2006), although this is not what Ulrich was originally suggesting. Business partners may be located alongside line managers, building a relationship with them and helping to solve issues, yet in other organisations partners have a more strategic role, providing consultancy to senior managers and becoming involved in the wide range of business issues. So, different organisations have interpreted the role in a variety of ways.

While some commentators have found a greater HR involvement in strategy, others suggest that there remains a wide gap between rhetoric and reality (see for example Holly 2015). So changes in job titles may not reflect changes in roles. As Holly points out it is often the same people in the role with a rebadged title, yet their capability level does not match what is now required of them. In the banking sector, Aldrich and colleagues (2015) found no cases of HR being involved in joint strategic decision making about HR issues although in around half of the case studies the senior HR person did have an influence over HR policy. In a recent Oracle/IBM study, while there was a will for HR to be involved in strategy, 40% of senior managers felt that HR was too focused on process and rules; over a third felt that HR did not understand the business well enough; and just under a third felt the senior HR person was not of the same calibre as other C level executives (Economist Intelligence Unit 2012).

In addition to the lack of clarity about the nature of the strategic role, another problem with assessing the extent of strategic involvement is that many surveys on the HR role are completed by HR specialists alone, and it has often been demonstrated that others in the organisation will not necessarily share the view of the HR specialist on this and other topics. In a survey which included an assessment of the HR strategic role in India, Bhatnagar and Sharma (2005) found that line managers and HR managers differed significantly in their assessment of the HR strategic partner role, with HR managers having a much more positive view of their involvement in this capacity.

The extent to which the HR function is involved in both organisational and HR strategy development is dependent on a range of factors, including the overall philosophy in the organisation towards the management of its employees, and there are clear examples of organisations where the HR role remains administrative. The presence of an HR director is considered important and this has previously been used as a proxy for strategic involvement. In a survey of HR directors, Caldwell (2011) found that the benefits of board membership were: having greater involvement and influence in business planning; experiencing more positive perceptions of HR performance; anticipating their CEOs to have higher ratings of the HR function; and a belief that there was greater integration between HR and business strategy. Although Caldwell found other mechanisms for involvement in business strategy, such as executive committees and personal networks, board membership appeared to confer 'symbolic capital', which was significant and attractive.

Long-term historical evidence suggests that HR board membership has increased, although HR director roles can come and go depending on the context, and HR does not yet have an automatic right to be on the board – the function has to earn its place. The focus on assessing trends in HR directorships has weakened more recently with the emphasis moving to strategic contributions in a variety of different HR roles, as we have previously seen, the competencies for strategic capability being a key theme.

It is suggested that HR managers need to use business and financial language; describe the rationale for HR activities in terms of added value; use strategic thinking; act as a business manager first and an HR manager second; appoint line managers into the HR function; concentrate on priorities as defined by the business; understand the business they work in, display business acumen; use relationship building (especially with the CEO) and networking skills; and offer well-developed change-management skills that can be used immediately.

To gain strategic influence HR has to be credible and it has been suggested that such credibility needs to come from being involved in a wider range of business agendas, such as branding, ethics, risk management and corporate social responsibility, and there is some evidence of this happening

In response to a list of nine possible factors shaping HR credibility, Aldrich and colleagues (2015) found the four most important were the business manager's trust in, and personal empathy with, the business partner; the business partner's knowledge of the external environment; the track record of the individual business partner in delivering HR services and their part in business plan execution; and the track record of the HR function in delivering HR services to the business manager. Both business partners and senior managers independently identified these as the four most important factors.

WINDOW ON PRACTICE

Establishing HR professionals' influence and credibility

Aldrich and colleagues (2015) studied twenty-one cases in the banking sector and found that strategic influence was very transient and HR had to earn its place. From the interviews they found this was based on personal credibility of the senior HR person rather than on credibility of the function itself. They found that factors which impinged on HR influence were also the views of the CEO on HR itself; the relationship of the most senior HR person with the CEO; and with other members of the Board.

Source: Aldrich, P., Dietz, G., Clark, T. and Hamilton (2015) 'Establishing HR professionals' influence and credibility: Lessons from the capital markets and investment banking sector', *Human Resource Management*, Vol. 54, No. 1, pp. 105–30.

The *Next Generation* research (CIPD 2011) focused on the importance of insight-led HR in making a strategic contribution. Such insight is based on three savvys: business savvy (in-depth understanding of how the business makes money, its current and future commercial health); organisational savvy (in-depth understanding of people and culture and how things get done in this internal context); and contextual savvy (in-depth understanding of context, for example in terms of demographics, competitor behaviour and geo-politics).

Self-service HR

Sometimes referred to as employee self-service (ESS) or manager self-service (MSS), or e-HR, these interactive systems allow employees and managers to update records, or get information to solve their queries online, rather than contacting a service centre. Increasing use of cloud technology means that systems can be downloaded, adapted and accessed from any location.

As with other initiatives, much of the drive for such systems has come from the need to reduce the time that the HR function spends on administrative tasks to allow it to focus on more strategic matters. Improvements in efficiency, service delivery, standardisation and organisational image are commonly cited as reasons for introducing self-service systems. Some organisations cite empowering employees as a reason for introduction. In terms of impact of the system Gainey and Klaas (2008) found improvements in delivery of HR (e.g. time and accuracy); improved communications; cost reductions; HR strategic involvement; and employee involvement.

Facilities can be wide ranging and are summarised in Table 30.3. Clearly some of the items in the table are password protected because confidential information is involved, and employees and their line managers may have different levels of access.

Table 30.3 Self-service HR facilities

Type of facility	Examples
Information and communication	HR policies and procedures Online employee handbooks Induction information Benefits information Available training courses News/newsletters
Downloading of forms	Expenses claim forms Overtime forms Application forms Training request
Interrogation of recorded data	Provision of personal information to employee or line manager such as absence or leave taken to date Pension forecasts
Queries via email to be answered by an HR specialist	Training requests Requests for advice
Uploading information	Change of address and personal details Attendance data Submitting forms such as expenses Choosing flexible benefits from a menu Responding to a staff survey
Managing HR processes	Performance management uses with ongoing recording of performance and development goals, progress and outcomes by employee and manager, maybe including salary review

In addition, such systems may offer cost-saving advantages, but can pose special problems of their own inducing feelings of remoteness, dehumanisation and lack of customer friendliness. Further, there are concerns about the loss of the personal touch and security of information. The success of such systems depends on sufficient communication and training, accessible support, as well as ease of use.

ACTIVITY 30.2

We referred to the 'loss of the personal touch' in this discussion of these alternative means of providing HR services.

How important is 'the personal touch' to the employees of today and why do you think this is so?

HR shared services

Shared services refers to one element out of the five in Ulrich's model of the HR function, and service centre staff deal with transactional HR issues for both line managers and employees. They are usually remote call centres and replace local HR officer/ administrative staff, with service centre staff having electronic access to personal employee details and HR policies and other information, and are sometimes referred to as partnership service centres or insourcing. Reasons for introducing them revolve around costs savings, the creation of more effective HR services for line managers and employees, and enabling embedded HR/business partners to focus on strategic rather than transactional issues. A Towers Watson survey (2012) of 628 global firms found that in nearly half of those businesses surveyed the HR function was to be reorganised over the forthcoming year with 40% of these moving to a shared services environment and just over 30% extending their use of shared services. No firms anticipated moving away from shared services.

WINDOW ON PRACTICE

Strategic reasons for HR shared service centres in the Netherlands

Farndale and his colleagues (2009) contacted all the companies in the Netherlands using HR shared services and found that the four most common reasons for their introduction were:

52% Improve professionalisation – customer orientation

48% Reorganisation of the HR function to be more customer focused

32% Improve quality, flow and management of work processes

32% Cost savings.

Source: Summarised from Farndale, E., Paauwe, J. and Hoeksema, L. (2009) 'In-sourcing HR: Shared service centres in the Netherlands', *International Journal of Human Resource Management*, Vol. 20, No. 3, pp. 544–61.

Service centres may be shared across all geographical locations of a business and some provide services shared with other functions such as IT and finance. HR service centres may provide for transactional needs on an even wider basis, such as across a number of different businesses in a corporation where the businesses have enough in common. Alternatively, in the public sector the most frequent form of shared services is a centre which serves two or more public bodies, such as local councils, and Stevens (2011) provides an example of four councils sharing HR services. Lastly a shared service centre may be an independent unit jointly owned by the organisation and an external supplier. In almost every case this form of HR delivery is supported by a self-service system as the first port of call, and is usually accompanied by a push to devolve operational HR tasks to line managers.

The centre typically has front office staff who deal with phone calls and back office staff who are involved with a variety of other transactional work such as sending out interview invitations, preparing contracts and so on. Work is sometimes structured by specialist function, for example training or recruitment, or by client group. There is usually a system of escalation whereby queries can be fed up to the next level or tier if the original call centre operator cannot resolve them, so for example there would be access to a functional specialist for non-routine or complex queries.

Shared services are a form of centralisation which avoids duplication but which can also be responsive to local needs. Benefits are expected from efficiency savings and lower transaction costs, and a more consistent HR approach across the whole of a company. In addition there are potentially increased opportunities for shared learning. One of the advantages of such centres is the metrics that can be derived to assess their performance. Examples are call waiting time, call count, call length, time taken to resolve queries, accuracy and satisfaction measures from users.

The problems with the service centre structure are that local knowledge and business solutions may be lost in the changeover, many low-level administrative roles are created with little potential for career development and there may be an obsession with measurement at the expense of service delivery. Anecdotal evidence suggests that in some organisations line managers have difficulty getting through to the centre and eventually give up. CIPD (2015b) point up the danger of a 'them and us' attitude between shared service centres and the rest of the business, and in a survey, Reilly (2008) found gaps in service provision and difficulties in defining and communicating the boundary with other parts of HR. He also found that customers did not like standardised services and having various different contact points. Higher staff turnover was also found as employees saw these HR jobs as dull, and cost savings were not always sustained.

Outsourcing HR

Outsourcing is an alternative approach to shared services but typically involves the same delivery channels: self-service HR and an outsourced service centre. Spence (2015) notes that while outsourcing was prompted by the need to do more for less, it has increasingly become standard practice in the drive for continued efficiency.

WINDOW ON PRACTICE

Police forces share and outsource HR services

The first HR services shared between three police forces is between Leicestershire, Derbyshire and Nottinghamshire, in the East Midlands, and is delivered by Capita. It is expected that each force will save £900,000 annually and that the contract will cost £2.3 million over five years.

Source: People Management (2012) 'Strategy and OD', July, p. 8.

HR administration, for example pensions and payroll and recruitment, has typically been outsourced. But more specialist aspects have been subject to outsourcing too, such as training and legal work, and in its 2010 survey IDS found that the most popular activity to be outsourced was health and well-being/occupational health. ACAS (2012) note an increasing trend for higher-value HR processes to be outsourced, such as recruitment and training, in addition to routine transactional activities. The definition of outsourcing is somewhat elastic and there is a lack of consensus as Woodall (2009) points out, but she separates out traditional subcontracting of low-skilled tasks from outsourcing business processes where an external provider owns, manages and administers them. Outsourcing the whole of HR (sometimes called end-to-end outsourcing) is also a very different proposition from outsourcing differentiated activities, which has been happening in an ad hoc manner for a much longer time.

The key drivers for outsourcing HR are usually reducing costs and improving service delivery. Outsourcing appears to encourage the measurement of the value of HR, through the need for service-level agreements and key performance indicators with a greater focus on customer satisfaction. Sometimes current HR inefficiencies drive the move to outsourcing. Most of the publicity surrounding HR outsourcing focuses on larger global companies such as BT and BP, but outsourcing is a slightly different proposition for smaller organisations. According to a CIPD survey (CIPD 2015c) a third of SMEs outsource complex advice and they are also more likely to outsource specialist advice than larger organisations. Outsourcing does appear to be growing overall.

Some of the benefits of outsourcing are that the organisation can concentrate on its core business; potentially save money due to the supplier's economies of scale; and achieve greater numerical flexibility with less risk. Outsourcing has also been introduced as a vehicle for effecting changes that would be hard to implement internally. For example, in large organisations outsourcing has been used to bring different parts of the organisation together to reduce costs, apply common standards, share best practice, and access innovative IT solutions. A further advantage that is claimed is that the internal HR function can now concentrate on driving the direction of HR rather than carry out more mundane tasks. Truss *et al.* (2012) provide a very useful summary of the advantages and disadvantages of outsourcing.

However, time is needed to select and develop a relationship and trust with a service provider, and fit with the service provider is important. There is evidence to suggest that the HR function is not the key mover in outsourcing (Woodall 2009) and the CIPD (2009) found that the involvement of HR professionals in the outsourcing process was limited, although considered important. Decisions were generally made by senior executives in the organisation. Outsourcing providers are more likely to find themselves negotiating with the purchasing department, which is more likely to be concentrating solely on cost, rather than the HR function.

It will be some time before the full impact of such major long-term outsourcing relationships can be assessed. However, a range of problems has emerged and many large contracts continue to be renegotiated due to problems such as suppliers bidding at too low a price and not being able to fulfil the deal, not knowing which processes need to stay in-house and lack of clarification of roles. BP for example (Pickard 2009), in the renewal of its outsourcing deal with Hewitt, expanded the geographical area of outsourcing yet took most aspects of recruitment and ex-pat administration back in-house. There is also evidence that big outsourcing contracts are being replaced by smaller deals. Some companies, such as LV (*People Management* 2009), have brought an outsourced HR function back in-house.

ACTIVITY 30.3

We noted that outsourcing the whole of the HR function is a different proposition from outsourcing some specific aspects. In the context of your own organisation, or one with which you are familiar:

1 If you were to outsource some specific aspects of HR, what would they be and why would you choose them?

Or:

What aspects of HR are already outsourced, how effective has this proved to be and why?

2 If you were to outsource the whole HR function, what reactions would you anticipate from employees and line managers, why do you think they would react like this and what could be done to support them through this change?

Or:

If your organisation has already outsourced the entire HR function, how effective has this proved to be and why?

Sometimes outsourcing has been used as a way to get rid of a problem (such as cost and inadequate computer systems) and the results of this are not always positive, especially if it is believed that once activities are outsourced management responsibility for them ends. Overall problems include the potential loss of skill, knowledge and capacity (limiting the development of a distinctive HR contribution); short-term disruption and discontinuity; and potentially a longer-term reduction in the quality of services (damaging the HR relationship with the line). The loss of HR employee morale and motivation, partly due to more limited career prospects, has also been identified, as has damage to long-term competitiveness. In addition, Woodall (2009) found that rather than cost savings there were sometimes increases in costs.

The role of line managers in HR

For some time there has been an emphasis on the devolution of HR management by integrating HR activities with day-to-day line management. We use the word 'devolution' here to mean the reallocation of HR tasks to managers outside the HR function, focusing on the line taking ownership of HR activities, enabling HR specialists to act as consultant, coach, facilitator and strategic partner. Such devolution of operational day-to-day HR tasks has been described by Hope-Hailey *et al.* (2005) as devolving the employee champion role, and it is considered to be a means of strengthening the relationship between the employee and his or her manager, resulting in a more positive management approach to employee performance. The importance of the role of the line manager in delivering HR is well documented. Line managers translate HR policies into practice and only then do such policies have the power to affect employees' perceptions, behaviour and performance (see, for example, Alfes *et al.* 2013).

However, the difficulties of devolving HR activities to first-line managers have also been consistently highlighted, and Purcell and Hutchinson (2007) identify a gap between what is formally required in the HR policy and what line managers actually deliver, and note that poorly implemented policies, for example appraisal, are worse than no action at all.

WINDOW ON PRACTICE

First Line Managers (FLM) and their HRM role

Evans (2015) studied how FLMs carried out their HR role in two retail settings, focusing on the gap between intended and actual HR practice as discussed in Chapter 4.

In Superco, the FLMs had significant responsibility for HRM but their status and pay in the organisation did not equate to this. They carried out recruitment, selection, training, performance management (including appraisals), staff scheduling and workload allocation. They also had little support from the HRM Department, as even though there was a store HR person, this was not an HR trained professional but a line manager passing through the role. The FLMs were required to meet targets and staffing budgets but, if these were met, how they carried out their HR role was not monitored. For example, FLMs explained where they had deviated from HR policy by recruiting part-timers rather than committed full-timers as required by the HR policy. They did this because part-timers were more flexible and cheaper. There was a lot of variability in HRM across the stores. Due to time constraints, particularly connected with large spans of control, the FLMs felt they could not fulfil their HRM role even though they appeared to be committed in principle to this.

Source: Evans, S. (2015) 'Juggling on the line: Front line managers and their management of human resources', *Employee Relations*, Vol. 37, No. 4, pp. 459–74.

The idea that line managers need to take on more day-to-day HR activities has been countered by line managers' lack of skills and interest in this. Caldwell (2004) for example found that managers resisted taking full ownership of HR and conversely HR professionals wanted to retain control over HR policy. His interviewees were generally reluctant to take devolution 'too far', as ultimately too much devolution may result in the HR role itself being devalued. Alternately, McConville (2006), in the context of the NHS, the armed forces and the fire services, found that middle managers wanted to be proactive in HR, were committed to it, and exceeded their job requirements to carry out HR activities, but their already substantial workload created the greatest barrier. Research suggests that line managers are now more accepting of the HR aspects of their role.

Maxwell and Watson (2007), on the basis of their investigation into line manager and HR manager perspectives of line management involvement in HR in Hilton Hotels, propose three types of line manager buy-in which are key to their active involvement in HR activities. These are:

- a conceptual understanding of the reasons for their involvement;
- the ability to implement these activities effectively through a clear HR role and having sufficient capability; and
- belief that their involvement in HR is valuable.

Interestingly the authors also found a general lack of shared understanding between line managers and HR specialists about the role of line managers in HR, and some indications that the more similar the perceptions of HR and line managers, the better the hotel performance, whereas the more divergent their perceptions, the weaker the hotel performance. The importance of communication and shared understanding is underlined by Keegan *et al.*'s research (2012) in the Netherlands, Austria, UK and USA. They found that line and project managers were more comfortable carrying out HR tasks if they had direct access to an HR specialist as opposed to online support. In McDermott and colleagues' research (2015) one of the difficulties experienced when line managers took on HR roles was that the HR professionals were both geographically distant and cognitively (i.e. gaps in understanding) distant.

Devolution has also been identified as problematic due to the lack of consistency of HR decisions, increased potential for inappropriate decisions, and lack of integration resulting in more difficulties in implementing HR strategy. In addition, roles and boundaries are often not well thought through (see, for example, Gollan 2012), and in a hospital setting McDermott and colleagues (2015) found issues getting lost between FLMs, the HR department and senior clinicians, all of whom had had a part to play in delivering HRM.

Yet in spite of the risks, more devolution to the line is considered key to realising the full potential of the workforce (Churchard 2012), and more recently Shipton and colleagues (2016) found that when line managers genuinely embrace the employee champion role this is associated with higher levels of employee commitment.

Critique of changes in the management of the HR function

There are some examples of the HR function having greater strategic involvement, that line managers are more involved in HR, and that the use of outsourcing and shared services is increasing rather than diminishing. Boroughs (2015) of Orion Consulting found in their 2014 research that over 90% or organisations found that their HR function was more efficient and commercially focused than 10 years previously, with 77% attributing this to the 'Ulrich model'. However, we have also shown that these changes are not universal and are difficult to implement, and sometimes have adverse consequences. It is also important to separate the rhetoric from the reality. In particular the business partner model does not seem to have fulfilled its promise and delivered significantly more strategic involvement overall, and Boroughs reports that the business partner role remains too transactional. Indeed it has been suggested that the word 'partner' is not appropriate as HR specialists need to be integral to the business, not just a partner of the business.

In addition, the focus on the business partner role may cause employee experience to deteriorate. The concentration on strategic roles appears to have gone hand in hand with the abandonment of the role of employee champion or advocate. Evidence suggests that concern for employee well-being is seen as a signal that the HR function is being dragged back to its old welfare role, with consequent loss of status and credibility. In an interview, one senior CIPD adviser stated that 'nobody wants to be an employee champion. They all think it's ideologically unsound' (Francis and Keegan 2006). Sheehan and colleagues (2014) found that HRM specialists experienced tensions when trying to deliver both the strategic partner and the employee advocate roles and that these tensions had a negative effect on how HR professionals were viewed in the organisation. Tensions were reduced when the employee advocate role was delivered elsewhere.

This role may also be undermined by increasing use of self-service and outsourcing (Harris 2006). Harris suggests that as the HR function becomes distanced from the workforce and line managers, the consequent loss of knowledge of operational issues means that the function is less able to act as an employee advocate. She found that employees were less likely to see HR as a form of support and advice and suggests they are more likely to approach the union or use legal redress, making the employment relationship more adversarial. She proposes that this loss of touch hinders rather than enables a strategic role, and that lack of opportunity to build relationships and trust with both the line and employees may have a negative impact on promoting employee commitment (Harris 2007).

McDermott and colleagues (2015), in a hospital setting, argue for 'an enhanced focus on the ward, rather than the board' (p. 828), suggesting that the underperforming business partner role in central HR functions needs to be supplemented by local HR professionals rather than relying so heavily on line managers for local HR. They question the conception that devolution enhances the processes and outcomes of HRM. Similarly Brewster *et al.* (2015) suggest that in order to attain the higher status necessary to be involved in corporate strategy, the HR function has to take a more controlling role in the management of human resources, leaving a smaller role for line managers in this area.

The split between strategic and non-strategic HR roles not only hinders strategic parts of the role and therefore the fulfilment of the HR role overall, but also can create barriers between different groups of HR professionals with those in non-strategic roles experiencing low morale and feeling undervalued (see e.g. Pritchard 2010). Sometimes overlap has been found between business partners and centres of excellence (CIPD 2015a) and we have already noted that some issues can fall between the gaps. Career progression in the function also becomes more problematic.

The fragmentation of the HR function and devolution and decentralisation create problems for consistency and integration. In addition, Caldwell (2003) suggests there is also a risk of the deprofessionalisation of the function, and that decentralisation may cause the HR contribution to shift constantly, thereby diminishing the clarity of its role or function. He suggests that the function remains dogged by ambiguity and conflict.

A focus on more effectively managing the HR function across boundaries (see, for example, ACAS 2012) has emerged, with greater collaboration between different parts of the HR function so that it is better connected, and Ulrich (Stevens 2015) stresses the relationship and integration between its different parts. Bersin (2015) suggests the function needs to be 'less centralized and more "co-ordinated but distributed" into the business' (p. 6), and Riddoch (2011) even suggests reintegrating the HR function.

The emerging consensus appears to be that there is too much emphasis on models and not enough on skills, people and delivery in context, and that there is a need for the HR function to be agile and flexible in response to the needs of the organisation and consequently for the less rigid application of models, with roles being customised to the business. The HRM function needs to go beyond efficiency savings (Boroughs 2015) and while Ulrich's models have been a good starting point, the focus has to move to contribution and effectiveness.

SUMMARY PROPOSITIONS

30.1. For many years categorisations of the HR role have been proposed. Ulrich and Brockbank have identified five roles: employee advocate; human capital developer; strategic partner; functional expert; and leader, with a compound role.

30.2. The focus is moving on from specifying roles to examining the purpose of HR in building a sustainable organisation, with a focus on context and HR capability. The purpose of the HR function and the way the business is organised will influence its structure.

30.3. There is some evidence of larger organisations employing the three-legged HR structure derived from Ulrich's research, but a structure reflecting that of the organisation is increasingly seen as more important.

30.4. The extent to which HR specialists are involved in HR strategy is influenced by the environment of the business, its culture, the perspective of the chief executive, HR board membership and the qualities, characteristics and working relationships of the most senior HR specialist.

30.5. Although there have been some early problems with outsourcing and shared services, these continue to be pursued by many organisations, and often involve cost savings and staff reductions.

30.6. Devolution of HR activities to line managers enables HR professionals to focus on strategic issues. But line managers often do not have the required motivation, skills or time to carry out HR activities effectively, and boundaries are often unclear.

30.7. There are concerns that the focus on the business partner role has been at the expense of the employee champion/advocate role, with the consequence that employee well-being is compromised.

30.8. The current trends in HR roles and structure are fragmenting the HR function, resulting in a lack of integration and consistency, and difficulties in effective strategic HR. Collaboration between different parts of the HR function is very important.

GENERAL DISCUSSION TOPICS

1. Does it really matter whether the most senior HR person is on the board of directors, or are personal work relationships, political alliances and personal track records more important?

2. 'Outsourcing may be an effective solution in the medium term, but it brings short-term disruption and long-term damage to organisational capability and success.' To what extent do you agree or disagree with this statement?

3. Debate the following comment: 'There has always been a debate about the extent to which day-to-day HR activities should be shared between the professional function and the line. In essence nothing has really changed.'

THEORY INTO PRACTICE

ARM Holdings

This is a continuation of the case study we used earlier (see Chapter 4). You should reread this first to remind yourself about the company. Then read the extract below:

> ARM has one centralised way of doing things across 17 countries. 'Twenty years ago, people used to bang on about "Act global, think local"', says Parsons. 'Whereas we fundamentally don't do that. If you join our company community, we have a certain way of doing things. If you operate in many countries and you have many ways of doing the same thing, you are setting yourself up for complexity by definition.' For example, an annual equity stake is paid to ARM employees worldwide. Rather than tweak or change the amount according to local laws, tax regimes, or norms, it is simply one rule for all. Not only does it make it easier to administer but, says Parsons, it 'gives the message that we are one company, one community, one everything'. (Smedley 2011: 26)

Questions

1 What are the potential disadvantages of this approach for ARM?

2 What other potential advantages are there for ARM in addition to the ones noted?

3 How would you structure the HR function in ARM so that it supports ARM's one-company approach? Justify your structure.

Source: Extract from Smedley, T. (2011) 'A light touch', *People Management*, October, pp. 24–8.

FURTHER READING

Brewster, C., Brookes, M. and Gollan, P. (2015) 'The institutional antecedents of the assignment of HRM responsibilities to line managers', *Human Resource Management,* Vol. 54, No. 4, pp. 577–97.

This article reports the analysis of a large dataset covering eleven countries and finds that in any economy organisations which are larger, unionised, and with a strategically positioned HRM department, are the least likely to allocate HRM responsibilities to the line.

Caldwell, R. (2008) 'HR business partner competency models: Re-contextualising effectiveness', *Human Resource Management Journal,* Vol. 18, No. 3, pp. 275–94.

Based on survey and interview evidence Caldwell provides a useful insight into the value of competency models, finding them to be weak at predicting performance in business partner roles. He also highlights the importance of contextual factors such as the degree of change within the HR function, patterns of centralisation/decentralisation, the consistency of the implementation of business partnering and overall levels in the reduction of transactional HR work.

CIPD Factsheets relevant to this chapter: *HR Shared Service Centres* (2015), *HR Outsourcing* (2015), *HR Business Partnering* (2015) and *The Role of Line Managers in HR* (2015).

Each of these factsheets provides useful definitions; a helpful summary of the key issues; an analysis of advantages and disadvantages; and practical guidance on implementation.

REFERENCES

ACAS (2012) *Outsourcing and the Fragmentation of Employment Relations: The Challenges Ahead,* ACAS Future of Workplace Relations discussion paper series. London: ACAS.

Aldrich, P., Dietz, G., Clark, T. and Hamilton, P. (2015) 'Establishing HR professionals' influence and credibility: Lessons from the capital markets and investment banking sector', *Human Resource Management,* Vol. 54, No. 1, pp. 105–30.

Alfes, K., Truss, C., Soane, E., Rees, C. and Gatenby, M. (2013) 'The relationship between line manager behavior, perceived HRM practices, and individual performance: Examining the mediating role of engagement', *Human Resource Management,* Vol. 52, No. 6, pp. 839–59.

Bersin, J. (2015) 'A modern HR operating model: The world has changed', in CIPD (ed.), *Changing HR Operating Models: A Collection of Thought Pieces.* London: CIPD, pp. 5–7.

Bhatnagar, J. and Sharma, A. (2005) 'The Indian perspective of strategic HR roles and organisational learning capability', *International Journal of Human Resource Management,* Vol. 16, No. 9, pp. 1711–39.

Boroughs, A. (2015) 'The future is "centres of expertise": What impact has 18 years of the Ulrich model had on the HR operating model and what does it tell us about the future?', in CIPD (ed.), *Changing HR Operating Models: A Collection of Thought Pieces.* London: CIPD, pp. 8–11.

Brewster, C., Brookes, M. and Gollan, P. (2015) 'The institutional antecedents of the assignment of HRM responsibilities to line managers', *Human Resource Management,* Vol. 54, No. 4, pp. 577–97.

Caldwell, R. (2003) 'The changing roles of personnel managers: Old ambiguities, new uncertainties', *Journal of Management Studies,* Vol. 40, No. 4, pp. 983–1004.

Caldwell, R. (2004) 'Rhetoric, facts and self-fulfilling prophecies: Exploring practitioners' perceptions of progress in implementing HRM', *Journal of Management Studies,* Vol. 35, No. 3, pp. 196–215.

Caldwell, R. (2011) 'HR directors in UK boardrooms: A search for strategic influence of symbolic capital?', *Employee Relations,* Vol. 33, No. 1, pp. 40–63.

Chesters, J. (2011) 'Creating strategic HR impact: It's the how, not what', *People Management,* August, pp. 32–5.

Churchard, C. (2012) 'HR "must devolve to line managers despite risks"', *People Management,* April.

CIPD (2009) *HR Outsourcing and the HR Function: Threat or Opportunity?* London: CIPD.

CIPD (2011) *Next Generation HR: Insight Driven.* London: CIPD.

CIPD (2015a) *CIPD Factsheet: HR Business Partnering.* London: CIPD.

CIPD (2015b) *CIPD Factsheet: HR Shared Services.* London: CIPD.

CIPD (2015c) *CIPD Factsheet: Outsourcings.* London: CIPD.

Economist Intelligence Unit (2012) *C-suite Perspectives of HR.* London: Economist Intelligence Unit

Evans, S. (2015) 'Juggling on the line: Front line managers and their management of human resources', *Employee Relations,* Vol. 37, No. 4, pp. 459–74.

Farndale, E., Paauwe, J. and Hoeksema, L. (2009) 'In-sourcing HR: Shared service centres in the Netherlands', *International Journal of Human Resource Management,* Vol. 20, No. 3, pp. 544–61.

Francis, H. and Keegan, A. (2006) 'The changing face of HRM: In search of balance', *Human Resource Management Journal,* Vol. 16, No. 3, pp. 231–49.

Fry, B. and Fishman, A. (2015) 'Owning our HR operating model: An enterprise-centred organizational design methodology for HR in CIPD', (ed.) *Changing HR Operating Models: A Collection of Thought Pieces.* London: CIPD.

Gainey, T. and Klaas, B. (2008) 'The use and impact of e-HR: A survey of HR professionals', *People and Strategy,* Vol. 31, No. 3, pp. 50–5.

Gollan, P. (2102) 'HR on the line: The contribution of human resource management to organizational value and workplace performance', *Asia Pacific Journal of Human Resource Management,* Vol. 50, No. 3, pp. 263–389.

Harris, L. (2006) 'Have council changes eroded HR's role as employee champion?', *People Management,* Vol. 12, No. 21, p. 72.

Harris, L. (2007) 'The changing nature of the HR function in UK local government and its role as "employee champion"', *Employee Relations,* Vol. 30, No. 1, pp. 34–47.

Holly, N. (2015) 'You can't put in what God left out: Not everyone can be a strategic HR business partner', in CIPD (ed.) *Changing HR Operating Models: A Collection of Thought Pieces.* London: CIPD.

Hope-Hailey, V., Farndale, E. and Truss, C. (2005) 'The HR department's role in organisational performance', *Human Resource Management Journal,* Vol. 15, No. 3, pp. 49–66.

IDS (2010) *The HR Function,* HR Study 928, October. London: IDS.

Keegan, A., Huemann, M. and Rodney Turner, J. (2012) 'Beyond the line: Exploring the HRM responsibilities of line managers, project managers and the HRM department in four project-orientated companies in the Netherlands, Austria, the UK, and the USA', *International Journal of Human Resource Management,* Vol. 23, No. 15, pp. 3085–104.

Kirton, H. (2015) 'Anyone can Google . . . understanding the business is harder', *People Management,* May, pp. 20–22.

Maxwell, G. and Watson, S. (2007) 'Perspectives on line managers in human resource management: Hilton International's UK Hotels', *International Journal of Human Resource Management,* Vol. 17, No. 6, pp. 1152–70.

McConville, T. (2006) 'Devolved RM responsibilities, middle-managers and role dissonance', *Personnel Review,* Vol. 35, No. 6, pp. 637–53.

McDermott, A., Fitzgerald, L., Van Gestel, N. and Keating, M. (2015) 'From bipartite to tripartite devolved HRM in professional service contexts: Evidence from hospitals in three countries', *Human Resource Management,* Vol. 54, No. 4, pp. 813–31.

People Management (2009) 'In-house HR saves £3m for insurance group', 24 September, p. 10.

People Management (2012) 'Strategy and OD', July, p. 8.

Pickard, J. (2009) 'BP and Hewitt renew outsourcing deal', *People Management,* Vol. 15, No. 4, p. 10.

Pritchard, K. (2010) 'Becoming an HR strategic partner: Tales of transition', *Human Resource Management Journal,* Vol. 20, No. 2, pp. 175–88.

Purcell, J. and Hutchinson, S. (2007) 'Front-line managers as agents in the HRM-performance causal chain: Theory, analysis and evidence', *Human Resource Management Journal,* Vol. 17, No. 1, pp. 3–20.

Reilly, P. (2008) 'Should you branch out?', *People Management,* Vol. 14, No. 6, pp. 16–17.

Reilly, P. (2012) 'HR's future in a global setting', *Human Resource Management International Digest,* Vol. 20, No. 3, pp. 3–5.

Riddoch, V. (2011) 'Built-in success', *People Management,* November, pp. 40–1.

Sheehan, C., De Cieri, H., Greenwood, M., and Van Buren III, H. (2014) 'HR professional role tensions: Perceptions and responses of the top management team', *Human Resource Management,* Vol. 53, No. 1, pp. 115–30.

Shipton, H., Sanders, K., Atkinson, C. and Frenkl, S. (2016) 'Sense-giving through HR roles: Line managers and employee commitment in health-care', *Human Resource Management Journal,* Vol. 26, No. 1, pp. 29–45.

Smedley, T. (2011) 'A light touch', *People Management,* October, pp. 24–8.

Spence, A. (2015) 'Will the cloud have a silver lining for HR outsourcing?', in CIPD (ed.) *Changing HR Operating Models: A Collection of Thought Pieces*. London: CIPD.

Stevens, M. (2011) 'Local authority shared services "secure HR's future"', *People Management*, 24 February, p. 9.

Stephens, C. (2015) 'Are HR business partners a dying breed?', *People Management*, February, pp. 36–7.

Storey, J. (1992) *Developments in the Management of Human Resources*. Oxford: Blackwell.

Towers Watson (2012) *Emerging Choices and Enduring Changes: Creating Service Delivery in an Era of New Opportunities*. New York: Towers Watson.

Truss, C., Mankin, D. and Kelliher, C. (2012) *Strategic Human Resource Management*. Oxford: Oxford University Press.

Tyson, S. and Fell, A. (1985) *Evaluating the Personnel Function*. London: Hutchinson.

Ulrich, D. (1997) *Human Resource Champions: The Next Agenda for Adding Value and Delivering Results*. Boston, MA: Harvard Business School Press.

Ulrich, D. and Brockbank, W. (2005a) 'Role call', *People Management*, Vol. 11, No. 13, pp. 24–8.

Ulrich, D. and Brockbank, W. (2005b) *The HR Value Proposition*. Boston, MA: Harvard Business School Press.

Ulrich, D., Younger, J., Brockbank, W. and Ulrich, M. (2013) 'The state of the HR profession', *Human Resource Management*, Vol. 52, No. 3, pp. 457–71.

Ulrich, D., Allen, J., Brockbank, W., Younger, J. and Nyman, M. (2009) *HR Transformation*. Maidenhead: McGraw-Hill.

Ulrich, D. (2015) 'I'll tell you something: The new HR operating model is all about relationships, not partners', *People Management*, April, p. 17.

Woodall, J. (2009) 'Making the decision to outsource human resources', *Personnel Review*, Vol. 38, No. 3, pp. 236–52.

CHAPTER 31
HEALTH AND WELL-BEING

THE OBJECTIVES OF THIS CHAPTER ARE TO:

1 Discuss the nature of health and well-being in an organisational context

2 Outline the range of initiatives that sit within a health and well-being agenda

3 Explain the importance of 'good work' and job design and its role in well-being

4 Explore the business case for health and well-being initiatives

5 Examine criticisms of health and well-being initiatives

The nature of health and well-being

The links between employee health and performance were identified long ago. Indeed, the origins of personnel management lie with social reformers such as the Cadbury family who, in the late nineteenth century, began to provide housing, healthcare and education to their workforces. Welfare officers, the early incarnation of today's HR officers, were appointed to oversee the well-being of the workforce. Although altruism played a part in this paternalistic approach towards employees, there was also a strong business case underpinning these practices. Healthy and well-educated workforces are more productive than those struggling in poor accommodation and with insufficient access to education and healthcare. The impact of this focus on well-being on workers' lives was substantial, as can be seen in Cadbury's museum in Bourneville which documents these early attempts at improving employee health and well-being.

However, HRM's development has had many stages and, since those early days, there has been little enthusiasm to associate the function with what came to be viewed as a 'tea and sympathy role'. Certainly the supposed evolution of personnel into HR management in the 1980s, and its preoccupation with the strategic aspects of business, left little room for considerations of employee health. In recent years, however, health and well-being have again become central to the HR agenda. The CIPD, for example, has demonstrated significant interest in health and well-being, arguing that it is wide-ranging in nature:

> Well-being is more than an avoidance of becoming physically sick. It represents a broader bio-psycho-social construct that includes physical, mental and social health. Well employees are physically and mentally able, willing to contribute in the workplace and likely to be more engaged at work. (CIPD, 2016a: 2)

Health and well-being go beyond the typically narrower concerns of absence management to include a holistic approach to managing employees that recognises links to other important concepts such as engagement. Although a widely agreed definition is lacking, there is a general consensus that employee health and well-being underpins strong performance and productivity: a sound business case clearly underlies attempts to improve the workers' lot.

The re-emergence of health and well-being in the HR agenda can perhaps be explained by the changes to the employment relationship which have been widely reported since the mid-1980s. Changes to the psychological contract have given rise to far less job security for employees, organisational restructuring has led in many sectors to work intensification and the negative consequences for employee morale have been widely reported. Alongside this, there has been an explosion in stress-related illness and absence. An ageing workforce (see Chapter 27) also requires greater consideration of employee health and well-being. A need to refocus on employee well-being to prevent detriment to organisations has become apparent. A further impetus has come from the increasing interest in corporate social responsibility within firms. Employers have a responsibility to create healthy workplaces for reasons beyond performance, bearing a responsibility to society to ensure employees are well treated and healthy. See, for example, IBM's website where information on its wellness programme is presented in its corporate social responsibility section: www.ibm.com/ibm/responsibility/employee_well_being_management.shtml. Promoting the work environment as a source of better health and improving health in the workplace acts as means to reduce social inequality through employment.

In the UK, these developments have coincided with government interest in health and well-being, aimed at reducing sickness absence and tackling developing social phenomena such as obesity. Much of this work arises from Dame Carol Black's (2008) review 'Working for a Healthier Tomorrow'. The government's response to this has been wide-ranging (DWP/DH, 2008) and has led to the establishment of the Health, Work and Well-being Initiative which is coordinated by a number of government bodies including the Departments of Health, Work and Pensions, and Business, Innovation and Skills. Interesting outcomes include the Investors in People Health and Well-being Good Practice Award (IIP 2016) and the Workplace Well-being Charter (http://www.well-beingcharter.org.uk/index .php) in England, with similar initiatives in other parts of the UK. The UK government is also seeking to measure well-being at a national level as a complementary measure to more traditional indictors of performance such as Gross Domestic Product (ONS 2016). Underpinning policy-maker interest is a strong rhetoric that improving public health will increase national productivity. One obvious benefit is reducing working days lost to sickness, which stood at 27.3 million in 2014–15 but has fallen from 39.5 million in 2000–02 (HSE 2016b). The emphasis within UK government programmes has been upon proactive employee support, good employment practice to reduce prospects of ill health and injury, and effective return to work and rehabilitation strategies. As with many other areas of the employment relationship, the government has to a large extent avoided regulation and exhorted employers to action based upon a business case for health and well-being, for example, that it supports increased employee engagement (MacLeod and Clarke 2014), resilience (Brunetto *et al*. 2012) and retention (Soane *et al*. 2013). A corporate social responsibility emphasis is also being advanced as organisations such as CIPD (2016b) argue the ethical basis for employee health and well-being.

Despite burgeoning interest, there is no widely agreed definition of health and well-being. Acas (2014) presents a detailed discussion of definitional differences and we take the position here that well-being comprises both employee health and happiness (subjective well-being) (see, for example, Sutton and Atkinson 2014). This is generally accepted in academic circles but, as we go on to outline in what follows, many practitioner definitions (or at least initiatives) have a narrow focus on health. A wider definition supports the inclusion of a varied range of issues. This breadth is evident, for example, in the Management Standards on workplace stress introduced by the Health and Safety Executive in 2004 (HSE 2016a) which outline six key areas where employers and employees can work together to reduce stress and improve well-being, as shown in the following Window on practice.

WINDOW ON PRACTICE

HSE's Management Standards on managing stress in the workplace

Demands – includes workload, work patterns and the work environment.

Control – how much say a person has in the way they do their work.

Support – includes the encouragement, sponsorship and resources provided by the organisation, line management and colleagues.

Role – whether people understand their role within the organisation and whether the organisation ensures that they do not have conflicting roles.

Change – how organisational change (large or small) is managed and communicated in the organisation.

Relationships – promoting positive working to avoid conflict and dealing with unacceptable behaviour.

Source: www.hse.gov.uk/stress/standards/.

The Standards encourage consideration of relationships, job design, autonomy and employee involvement and support a holistic view of well-being, notwithstanding Acas's (2014) call for them to be updated to reflect the better understanding of mental health that has developed in the decade or more since their introduction. Nevertheless, they support a view of well-being that goes beyond narrow concerns of physical health to address more sophisticated workplace issues.

Health and well-being initiatives

CIPD has published a great deal of work in recent years on health and well-being (cipd.co.uk/research/health-well-being/) reflecting growing practitioner as well as policy-maker interest in the topic. Its most recent report (CIPD 2016a) recognises the wider remit of well-being and presents it as comprising of five elements: health, work, personal growth, collective/social relationships and values and principles. It argues, however, that there is an implementation gap: that is, practitioners are not delivering enough of the right kind of initiatives to substantially improve employee health and well-being. This is perhaps unsurprising as the reports demonstrates that only 8% of organisations have a health and well-being strategy, 37% operate on an ad hoc basis and 9% take no action at all. Data drawn from the report also confirm that the focus remains firmly upon physical and mental health (Table 31.1).

Initiatives also include small numbers of companies that are providing financial well-being schemes like private medical insurance, personal accident insurance and income protection. Indeed, financial well-being is emerging as an area of growing importance.

ACTIVITY 31.1

To what extent do you think that the initiatives set out in Table 31.1 are likely to improve employee health and well-being? Where might they be successful? What issues might they miss?

While there is not a great deal of academic literature on the types of initiatives presented in Table 31.1, entering 'employee health and well-being' into an Internet search engine returns a plethora of consultancies offering advice on the subject, alongside a large number of organisations presenting their own policies and suggesting that employee health and

Table 31.1 Employee well-being initiatives

Employee Support	%
Access to counselling service	60
Employee assistance programme	49
Emotional intelligence training	7
Health Promotion	
Access to physiotherapy	30
Advice on healthy eating	29
Health screening	28
Stop Smoking support	27
Healthy canteen options	21
Subsidised gym membership	18
Onsite massages	17
Well-being days	17
Free fresh fruit	15
Mindfulness	13
In-house gym	13
Relaxation or exercise class	11
Walking/pedometer initiatives	10
Standing desks	7
Personalised health living programmes	6

Source: Adapted from CIPD (2016a), Table 4.

well-being are important to their success. The University of Bath's, for example, can be found at http://www.bath.ac.uk/hr/hrdocuments/staying-safe-well/policies/health-well-being.pdf.

The number of practices which relate to physical health in Table 31.1 is notable. A key concern here is obesity which, with its links to illnesses such as cancer and heart disease, has emerged as one of the most significant threats to health in modern times in the western world. While its causes are complex, diet and exercise are thought to be two major contributory factors and government policy has sought to encourage both individuals and employers to adopt healthier lifestyles. This is clearly reflected in organisational policy that is focused upon healthy eating, mechanisms to promote physical exercise such as gym membership, health checks and support with giving up smoking. A fast emerging concern, however, is mental health and counselling, and employee assistance programmes now top the list of well-being initiatives, coupled on a lesser scale with mindfulness and relaxation programmes.

WINDOW ON PRACTICE

Employers must recognise the scale of the mental well-being challenge

Absence resulting from worker stress and depression runs at about 70 million lost days each year in the UK. Several themes emerged from a recent think tank on the subject:

- It is difficult to talk about mental health in the workplace: greater support is needed for both employees and line managers to encourage open dialogue.

- The consequences of poor mental health are high, costing around £26 billion each year to the UK economy.
- Managers lack the required skills and more emphasis on training is needed.
- HR has an important role and must work to open lines of communication around the issue.
- The workplace can be part of the solution and should be seen as a support mechanism.

It appears to be widely accepted that mental well-being is an area of substantial concern and that organisational interventions in this area are inadequate.

Source: Adapted from Burt (2016).

ACTIVITY 31.2

What mental health support is offered by your organisation or one with which you are familiar? How effective is this in creating the necessary open culture and supportive environment?

The range of practices adopted by organisations in attempts to promote employee health and well-being is vast, and not all are captured in Table 31.1. Our own experiences, and those of colleagues and other contacts, suggest that it is common for employers to offer free cholesterol tests, cycle to work schemes, dance and yoga classes, tai-chi – the list is seemingly endless! A narrow emphasis on physical and mental health, however, over-looks other key aspects of employee well-being. An increasing body of research demonstrates the impact of work overload, role conflict, lack of control or autonomy at work, job insecurity and unsupportive working environments in reducing employee well-being (see e.g. Alfes *et al*. 2012; Greasley *et al*. 2012). 'Good work' (CIPD 2016b) i.e. job quality, is important in alleviating many of these problems and we move on now to explain job design and outline its role in well-being.

'Good work' and well-being: the role of job design

Job quality is central to employee health and well-being (Bryson *et al*. 2014) and is supported by effective job design, that is, the process of putting together a range of tasks, duties and responsibilities to create a composite for individuals to undertake in their work and to regard as their own. It is crucial: not only is it the basis of individual satisfaction and achievement at work, but also it is necessary to get the job done efficiently, economically, reliably and safely. As long as there have been organisations, there has been debate on the best way to design the jobs within them and for much of this time the interest in job design has centred round attempts to improve employee satisfaction with the working situation. The focus has changed from designing jobs which ensure employee compliance to designing those which generate employee commitment. In this way, job design is seen to be integral to efforts to improve employee well-being and thus organisational performance. The most recent WERS (van Wanrooy *et al.* 2013) has reinforced the relationship between elements of job design such as job autonomy and improved employee well-being. This UK-based evidence is supported by international research as we show in the following Window on practice.

WINDOW ON PRACTICE

Stress and health and well-being in a Chinese University

Research into stress in a Chinese university studied the impact of certain 'job stressors' on employee health and well-being. The stressors included work relationships, work–life balance, job control, job overload, job insecurity, resources and communication, and pay and benefits. The overall context was one of increasing staff/student ratios and hard performance management in which academic workloads had increased. The study identified negative relationships between these stressors and both psychological well-being and physical well-being. It also predicted that those with better psychological well-being would have better physical well-being. These findings are clear evidence that job design has an important role to play in overall employee well-being.

Source: Sang *et al.* (2013) 'Modelling occupational stress and employee health and well-being in a Chinese higher education institution', *Higher Education Quarterly*, Vol. 67, pp. 15–39.

The first attempts at job design were influenced by F.W. Taylor and the scientific school of management. This approach was founded on the division of labour into simple jobs and rigid allocations of individuals to narrowly defined tasks. Concerns centred around efficiency, time and motion studies, for example ensuring tasks were structured in a way that allowed workers to conduct them in the most efficient manner. This led to highly specialised jobs, workers at Ford's factories on assembly lines each carrying out, for example, very narrow specified elements of the construction of a motor car. Scientific management was premised upon the idea of 'man as machine', that is rational, unemotional and focused upon economic concerns. Incentives, such as bonuses, were designed to meet the extrinsic motivations of employees. Jobs were, however, routine, repetitive and monotonous, leading to boredom and industrial unrest among workers.

The recognition that workers had needs beyond economic ones led, from the 1940s on, to worker motivation being a key concern within job design. Abraham Maslow, for example, suggested that there was a hierarchy of needs within workers and that job design should meet a range of needs, such as social, rather than simply focusing on economic concerns. In the period 1940–60, a range of motivational theories influenced job design. We do not have the space here to provide a comprehensive review of motivation theory and suggest the reader refers to an organisational behaviour text for further information. We do intend, however, to focus in some detail on one of the most influential pieces of research on job design, namely Hackman and Oldham's (1976) Job Characteristics Model. Despite first appearing in the 1970s, it has resonance and influence to this day (see e.g. Bryson *et al*. 2014).

The JCM specifies certain aspects that must be designed into a job in order to ensure the positive outcomes of meaningful work, responsibility and knowledge. These include skill variety, task identity, task significance, autonomy and feedback. Delivering these will lead to high internal motivation and links to enhanced individual and organisational performance.

Skill variety

Skill variety is the extent to which the tasks in a job require a range of skills and abilities. Jobs designed in accordance with scientific management principles were highly special-ised, requiring a narrow range of skills and abilities, and the negative outcomes arising from the boredom and monotony created by this became evident. The JCM suggested that jobs should require workers to use a wide range of skills and abilities and led to a focus on **job enrichment,** the process of incorporating more skills and abilities into jobs. Wood and Wall (2007) make a case for the continuing importance of job enrichment in job design, arguing that it has been overlooked in strategic HRM and that it should con-tinue to be a key element within HRM endeavour.

Task identity

Task identity refers to the degree to which a job provides the opportunity to undertake a whole and identifiable piece of work. Completing such a piece of work is critical to posi-tive psychological outcomes, the negative impact of not doing this again being apparent from, for example, the alienation caused by working on an assembly line. Car manufactur-ers such as Volvo have over the years experimented with principles such as autonomous work teams, where a team is tasked with the construction of an entire car, rather than individuals being tasked with specified elements of it, in order to provide this task identity. While such experiments have not been unproblematic, they are an attempt to design jobs so as to provide workers with meaningful work.

Task significance

Task significance is the extent to which a job has an impact, whether on the organisation, its employees or customers. The more impact a job is seen to have, the better the psycho-logical outcomes for the worker. A key aspect of job design is thus that workers should understand the contribution made by their job to the organisational endeavour. An oft quoted example in this respect is the hospital cleaner who sees his or her job not as clean-ing but helping to deliver high-quality patient care. When conceptualised in this way, the cleaner's job takes on a high level of task significance.

Together, skill variety, task identity and task significance comprise the 'meaningfulness' of the work undertaken. Job design should aim to achieve all three in order to promote motivation in workers and thus higher performance. Although some organisations have worked to design jobs to achieve this, there are still many contemporary organisations which adopt somewhat Taylorist principles. One only has to think of the level of routine and specialisation in jobs such as call centre operatives or fast food restaurant workers to see that the principles of the JCM are by no means universally adopted. This may go some way to explaining the typically high level of labour turnover in such organisations.

Autonomy

Autonomy describes the extent to which the individual undertaking the job has the discretion to make decisions about how it is done, including scheduling the work and deciding upon the procedures used to carry it out. Autonomy creates the positive outcome of responsibility, which again influences motivation. The flattening organisation structures discussed earlier in this chapter have led, since the mid-1990s, to an organisational preoccupation with worker autonomy in the guise of 'empowerment'. Empowerment devolves responsibility to workers and removes the need for close supervision control – impossible given the removal or reduction of middle managers in many organisations. Working time flexibility, which we discuss below, can also create greater worker autonomy (Hall and Atkinson 2006). More recently, the concern to create worker autonomy has been reflected in high-performance work organisation designs focusing on employee involvement mechanisms, as discussed earlier (see Chapter 25).

Feedback

Feedback is about receiving direct and clear information about levels of performance. This leads to worker knowledge which again, according to the JCM, leads to higher motivation. Krasman (2013) presents an interesting study of feedback in relation to the JCM and its positive outcomes. It is this need for feedback which underpins many contemporary performance management systems (see Chapter 11).

The JCM led to a paradigm shift in which jobs were designed which required a range of skills and abilities, provided greater freedom to workers, who often worked in autonomous teams, and adopted flexible working practices. Its principles impacted on models of the flexible firm in the 1980s, high-performance work systems in the 1990s and through to the organisational development approaches of this century. Job design is, however, still dependent on individual characteristics; some workers will, for example, be more receptive to being stretched and challenged than others. Morgeson and Humphrey (2006) also argue that its effectiveness will depend on organisational context, as we see in the Window on practice below which considers role redesign for midwives in the NHS.

WINDOW ON PRACTICE

The redesign of midwives' roles

A central premise of HRM strategies in the NHS is the need to redesign workforce roles and develop new ones, while at the same time expanding the scope of jobs so that staff can take on new responsibilities and skills. The effect of this for midwives was to design 'extended' roles, expanded to include work traditionally performed by doctors, with some aspects of their previous role being delegated to maternity support workers. Midwives felt, however, that the extended roles often prevented them from providing individualised woman-centred care, as they spent time going from one woman to another performing repetitive technical tasks. Work was often described as a 'production line' and a case of 'get them in, get them delivered, and ship them out'. They also felt that there was greater ambiguity in their role and that its extension reduced autonomy and recognition, de-skilling them as they became reliant on technology rather than expertise. In order to undertake the extended roles, the delivery of care, where midwives obtain the greatest job satisfaction and their highest intrinsic motivation, was delegated to maternity support workers. The professional boundaries of midwifery and its traditional social and emotional skills are thus being eroded or replaced as midwives take on more technical roles previously undertaken by doctors and reluctantly relinquish their traditional social and caring roles to maternity support workers.

Critics of the HRM policies of the NHS suggest that role redesign, rather than improving work satisfaction, is being used to reduce labour costs, de-skill staff and promote greater flexibility of labour. The demotivational effects of this upon midwives raises questions about government assumptions that NHS role redesign will improve midwives' productivity.

Source: Adapted from Prowse, J. and Prowse, P. (2008) 'Role redesign in the National Health Service: The effects on midwives' work and professional boundaries', *Work, Employment and Society*, Vol. 22, No. 4, pp. 695–712.

ACTIVITY 31.3

Thinking of a job you have held, or one you have observed (e.g. your interactions with workers in fast food restaurants), analyse it in terms of the Job Characteristics Model. To what extent does it offer:

- Skill variety
- Task identity
- Task significance
- Autonomy
- Feedback?

What are the implications of your analysis for worker motivation and well-being?

The business case for health and well-being

Despite our own view that job design is central to well-being, many organisations emphasise physical health and fitness in health and well-being initiatives. Such initiatives are not cheap: one university spent £50,000 on a programme to encourage staff to keep fit and this

Table 31.2 Benefits of health and well-being initiatives

Recruitment	Many organisations promote their health and well-being policies in order to attract applicants for vacancies that they advertise. They seek to be 'employers of choice' in demonstrating concern for employees
Improved performance	Achieved through more productive employees and better service via a reduced dependence on replacement employees
Competitive advantage	Some firms argue that investing in health and well-being helps to build competitive advantage through employees, i.e. other firms struggle to replicate the workforce quality that results
Positive employee attitudes	Employees will be more engaged, committed and contented and these positive employee attitudes have been demonstrated to be performance enhancing
Retention	Fewer employees will be lost due to ill health and intention to quit employment is likely to be reduced as a result of positive employee attitudes

level of expenditure is not unusual. Willingness to invest relates back to the business case promoted by UK government that we discussed earlier in the chapter. Employers expect that there will be substantial returns on their investment, often in the form of improved employee attendance (see Chapter 14). But returns are expected to go significantly beyond reduced sickness absence, as we outline in Table 31.2, and one survey suggests that there is a return of £4.17 for every £1 spent on employee well-being (Newman 2010).

Crush (2009) reports on Royal Mail's health and well-being initiatives. While he recognises that their contribution can be hard to assess, he cites an international survey which suggests that well-being is one of the prime drivers of employee engagement. We summarise part of his work in the Window on practice which describes Royal Mail's health and well-being policy and practices and their outcomes and considers the wider implications of health and well-being for economic performance.

WINDOW ON PRACTICE

Royal Mail Group's health and well-being 'blueprint' could provide a £1.45 billion boost to the UK's struggling sectors: innovative measures helped the organisation cut absence by 25% and save £227 million in three years.

Health and well-being initiatives introduced by Royal Mail Group could hold the key to reducing the impact of absence across the UK's worst performing sectors and deliver savings of £1.45 billion a year, a study by the London School of Economics revealed. In its 'Value of Rude Health' report – the result of a unique, year-long study – the London School of Economics also calculated that the value of Royal Mail Group's approach to tackling absence could bring more than 94,000 people absent through illness or injury back into work more quickly.

The study revealed that Royal Mail Group's health and well-being activities have:

- Slashed absence by 25% between 2004 and 2007.
- Brought 3,600 employees absent through illness or injury back into work.
- Saved more than £227 million in terms of direct costs (wages and benefits).

Royal Mail Group's success in cutting absence by a quarter has been achieved through:

- Health screening for employees and occupational support services including physio-therapy and occupational therapy.
- Health clinics in more than ninety Royal Mail Group sites to help people return to work and prevent them getting ill.
- Fitness centres run by trained instructors in larger sites.
- Health promotion campaigns targeting smoking and back pain.
- Increased support and training for managers to improve the effectiveness of absence to attendance policies.

And the business is continuing its activities to improve the health and well-being of its people through two new initiatives – an online health check-in and assessment service and the recruitment of health trainers to help fellow workers improve their health through advice and practical support.

David Marsden, a Professor in the Centre for Economic Performance at the London School of Economics and author of the report, commented:

Our study suggests that the 13 sectors of the economy least effective at addressing employees' health and well-being could benefit significantly from Royal Mail Group's 'blueprint'. Following the organisation's example in bringing high rates of absence in specific sites to average levels would deliver huge financial gains and provide a boost to the performance of a range of companies and organisations.

These include:

- Bringing more than 94,000 workers absent through illness or injury back into work.
- Adding an extra 21 million days worked by UK employees a year.
- Annual cost savings of £1.45 billion to the UK economy.

At a time when absence is an increasing priority for employers, the London School of Economics' 'Value of Rude Health' report has created one of the most compelling invest-ment cases to date for health and well-being policies. One of the UK's largest employers, Royal Mail Group has invested £46 million over three years in approaches that address the biological, social and psychological causes of absence, delivering a return on investment of five to one.

Source: Adapted from Marsden and Moriconi (2009) 'The value of rude health: Employee's well being, absence and workplace performance', *CEP Discussion Paper No. 919*. London: Centre for Economic Performance.

Criticisms of health and well-being initiatives

There are a variety of criticisms of health and well-being initiatives, ranging from questions of definition to challenges of HR's conception of the issue. While health and well-being programmes have grown in popularity in recent years, there is a suggestion that they contain little new, rather that they are a rebranding of absence management programmes. Even where they are seen to contain practices of merit, lack of resources or senior management buy-in can lead them to be largely ineffective. Such initiatives may also be beyond the financial means of many smaller firms, which form the majority of organisations.

A further concern is the extent to which organisations have the right to interfere in employees' lives. While employers may have a responsibility to tackle work-related stress, there is an argument that an employee's weight and fitness levels are nobody's business but the employee's own. Indeed, many employees have expressed concern about information obtained by employers as part of these programmes being put to inappropriate use, in, for example, redundancy or promotion selection decisions. When Walmart launched its wellness campaign, requiring employees to volunteer information on weight and take steps to reduce this if appropriate, there were accusations of heavy-handedness and even fascism from employees and their representatives.

The major criticism of health and well-being initiatives as conceived by the HR community, however, is their narrow focus on concerns such as fitness and healthy eating (see for example CIPD 2016a). As we noted earlier, academic treatments of health and well-being take a much wider view on what it constitutes. Recent work, for example, has defined employee well-being as a combination of employee happiness, health and relationships (see for example Peccei *et al.* 2013) and academic publications on the subject rarely concern the kinds of initiatives outlined earlier. Rather, they consider issues such as job design and the extent to which workers have autonomy and experience job satisfaction (Sutton and Atkinson 2014). It has been suggested that narrow approaches are a facade to conceal the fact that the employer is seeking to get more out of employees for less:

> Overall, 'wellness' is a sham. It is aimed at distracting attention from more stressful work, more bullying and the weakness of unions which means that workers have less 'voice' at work. (Newman 2010: 36)

It is ironic, as we outline in the following Window on practice, that many employees have insufficient time to engage with common health and well-being initiatives.

WINDOW ON PRACTICE

Too busy for well-being

A recent study argues that organisations need to create workplaces which provide the time and space to lead healthy lives. Over one third of the study's participants said that they were too busy to engage in health and well-being activities and many do little or no physical exercise nor commit time to mental well-being practices, although some did seek to address signs of stress in themselves. Organisational support in creating an appropriate environment is essential to avoiding the diseases that could result.

Source: Paton (2015).

A final concern is the effectiveness of the business case that underpins health and well-being. Hamilton (CIPD 2016b), for example, argues that the business case is not easy to establish, particularly as recent research argues for complex measures that combine evaluation (e.g. job satisfaction), experiential issues (e.g. happiness and stress) and eudemonic issues (e.g. how worthwhile is job/career). Bryson *et al.* (2014) further suggest that many organisations do not understand the business case and, perhaps more problematically, also argue that it may not hold good where staff are unskilled and can be easily replaced, i.e. labour turnover is less costly than health and well-being interventions. Employee cynicism is also a concern where the fundamentals of good quality jobs are not in place. A recent CIPD blog, for example, highlighted the practice of providing free pizza when asking people to work late, but a long hours culture is hardly likely to promote well-being.

Our argument thus far has been that current HR initiatives are too narrowly drawn and an article in the UK higher-education press makes the point strongly that there is more to health and well-being than massage and free fruit (Newman 2010). It may also be that this is becoming apparent to HR practitioners and CIPD's most recent report (2016a) certainly seeks to widen the agenda. In the Window on practice below, we draw from two speeches by senior HR professionals, both of whom support the argument that a narrow focus on physical and mental health is unhelpful and that the HR perspective on health and well-being needs to be reconsidered. A greater focus is needed on the fundamentals of the workplace that may create poor health and well-being, rather than presenting solutions to problems that have already emerged.

WINDOW ON PRACTICE

What drives employee well-being?

'What HR professionals need to decide is whether health and well-being is about providing lettuce for lunch or about far less obvious but potentially more effective things,' says David Batman, Group Medical Officer, Nestlé UK. 'Simply giving staff more autonomy in their jobs will reduce the level of stress they suffer. This impacts blood pressure and heart conditions. To me, just giving people the opportunity to do their job will have a far more significant impact on the health of a company's employees than persuading them to give up smoking and eating more healthily in the staff canteen.'

> 'Old-style well-being is like walking downstream of a river, rescuing employees who are flailing around in the water, needing saving,' says Margaret Samuel, Chief Medical Officer at EDF Energy. 'What we need to do is turn around and walk upstream to find out why so many of these employees are ending up in the water in the first place; we need to find the source of the emergency.'
>
> *Source*: Crush, P. (2009) 'Health and well-being: The science of employee well-being', Human Resources, 1 July. Available at: www.hrmagazine.co.uk/hr/features/1014936/health-well-being-the-science-employee-well-being.

ACTIVITY 31.4

What are the key causes of reduced productivity and/or commitment in an organisation with which you are familiar? To what extent do you think that these issues will be improved or resolved by the initiatives outlined in Table 31.1?

SUMMARY PROPOSITIONS

31.1. The links between health and well-being and employee performance were identified long ago, although there was little emphasis on them from an HR perspective for much of the twentieth century.

31.2. For more than a decade there has been a substantial increase in interest in employee health and well-being from both an organisation and a government perspective. This has been driven by social, demographic, economic and political changes.

31.3. Initiatives within a health and well-being policy have typically focused narrowly on employees' physical and mental health. This focus has attracted a great deal of criticism.

31.4. Job quality and effective job design are essential to employee health and well-being.

31.5. It is suggested that health and well-being initiatives have a range of positive outcomes including improvements in recruitment, performance, engagement and retention, more positive employee attitudes and enhanced competitive advantage.

31.6. There are many criticisms of the narrow HR approach to health and well-being. These include assertions that such approaches differ little from traditional absence management, are likely to lack management buy-in and are financially beyond the reach of the many smaller firms in the economy. A business case approach may also be questionable.

31.7. Other concerns surround the argument that an employee's health is no concern of the employer and, most fundamentally, that health and well-being initiatives often tackle the symptoms of poor employment practice. Better job design and more worker autonomy may be much more effective in improving the lot of the employee.

31.8. There is some evidence that HR practitioners are beginning to recognise the need for wider conceptions of health and well-being.

GENERAL DISCUSSION TOPICS

1. 'The positive outcomes from health and well-being initiatives justify their significant cost.' Discuss this statement.

2. 'An organisation does not have the right to concern itself with the weight and fitness levels of its employees.' To what extent do you agree with this statement?

3. Evaluate the suggestion that organisations would obtain more significant benefits from designing jobs well than from providing access to free fruit and low-cost gym membership.

THEORY INTO PRACTICE

Employee stress and burnout

Read: Burt (2016) 'Mental health-related sick leave soars in civil service'.

Questions

1 To what extent do you agree that current mental health absence is likely to be 'the tip of the iceberg'?

2 What pressures are contributing to absence levels? How could job design help to reduce these? How could the type of health and well-being initiatives laid out in Table 31.1 help to address these?

3 Are the issues discussed in the case mainly restricted to the UK or are they to be found internationally? If the latter, find evidence of these issues in other countries.

Source: http://www.cipd.co.uk/pm/peoplemanagement/b/weblog/archive/2016/04/04/mental-health-related-sick-leave-soars-in-civilservice.aspx?utm_medium=email&utm_source=cipd&utm_campaign=pm_daily&utm_term=678405&utm_content=pm_daily_040416–5486–8127-20160404141322-Mental%20health-related%20sick%20leave%20soars%20in%20civil%20service.

FURTHER READING

CIPD (2016a) *Growing the Health and Well-being Agenda* and

CIPD (2016b) *Moving the Health and Well-being Agenda Forward*. London: CIPD.

The first report presents CIPD's latest thinking and findings on health and well-being from a practitioner perspective. The second is a series of thought pieces from policy makers, academics and practitioners that raise some interesting debates and present some novel insights into the health and well-being agenda.

De Voorde, K., Paauwe, J. and Van Velhoven, M. (2012) 'Employee well-being and the HRM–organisational performance relationship: A review of quantitative studies', *International Journal of Management Reviews,* Vol. 14, pp. 391–407.

This paper reviews thirty-six research studies to explore the relationship between employee well-being and organisational performance. A broad conceptualisation of well-being as comprising happiness, health and relationships is adopted. The authors argue that where well-being relates to happiness and relationships, both the individual and the organisation benefit. Where it relates to health, the organisation benefits at the expense of employees. The paper is valuable in reviewing a broad range of literature in the field and in demonstrating the benefit of considering well-being to be more than just health and fitness.

Soane, E., Shantz, A. and Alfes, K. (2013) 'The association of meaningfulness, well-being, and engagement with absenteeism: A moderated mediation model', *Human Resource Management,* Vol. 52, pp. 441–56.

This article introduces a Special Issue linked to a growing body of research that argues employee perspectives are important in linking HR practice and organisational performance. The roles of well-being and engagement are explored in depth in a number of the articles and conclusions drawn as to their relevance in improving performance.

REFERENCES

Acas (2014) *Is it Time Well-Being Grew Up?* London: Acas.

Alfes, K., Shantz, A. and Truss, C. (2012) 'The link between perceived HRM practices, performance and well-being: The moderating effect of trust in the employer', *Human Resource Management Journal,* Vol. 22, pp. 409–27.

Black, C. (2008) *Working for a Healthier Tomorrow: Dame Carol Black's Review of the Health of Britain's Working Age Population Presented to the Secretary of State for Health and the Secretary of State for Work and Pensions*. London: Stationery Office.

Brunetto, Y., Teo, S. and Shacklock, K. (2012) 'Emotional intelligence, job satisfaction, well-being and engagement: Explaining organisational commitment and turnover intentions in policing', *Human Resource Management Journal*, Vol. 22, pp. 428–41.

Bryson, A., Forth, J. and Stokes, L. (2014) *Does Worker Well-being Affect Workplace Performance?* London: BIS.

Burt, E. (2016) 'Employers must recognise scale of mental well-being challenge, says shadow minister', *People Management,* http://www.cipd.co.uk/pm/peoplemanagement/b/weblog/archive/2016÷02÷05/what-we-learned-from-the-bitc-mental-health-first-aid-conference.aspx.

CIPD (2016a) *Growing the Health and Well-Being Agenda: From First Steps to Full Potential.* London: CIPD.

CIPD (2016b) *Moving the Employee Well-Being Agenda Forward: A Collection of Thought Pieces.* London: CIPD.

Crush, P. (2009) 'Health and well-being: The science of employee well-being', *Human Resources,* 1 July.

DWP/DH (2008) *Improving Health and Work: hanging Lives. The Government's Response to Dame Carol Black's Review of the Health of Britain's Working Age Population.* London: Stationery Office.

Greasley, K., Edwards, P., Baker-McClearn, D. and Dale, J. (2012) 'Why do organisations engage in HR initiatives? A test case of a health and well-being intervention', *Employee Relations,* Vol. 34, pp. 443–62.

Hackman, J. and Oldham, G. (1976) 'Motivation through the design of work: Test of a theory', *Organizational Behavior and Human Performance,* Vol. 16, pp. 250–79.

Hall, L. and Atkinson, C. (2006) 'Improving working lives: Flexible working and the role of employee control', *Employee Relations,* Vol. 28, pp. 374–86.

HSE (2016a) *Stress Management Standards* [Online], http://www.hse.gov.uk/stress/standards/index.htm. London: Health and Safety Executive.

HSE (2016b) *Working Days Lost* [Online], http://www.hse.gov.uk/statistics/dayslost.htm. London: Health and Safety Executive.

IIP (2016) *Investors in People, Health and Well-being Good Practice Award* [Online], https://www.investorsinpeople.com/sites/default/files/IIP%20Health%20and%20Well-being%20Framework_0.pdf. London: IIP.

Krasman, J. (2013) 'Putting feedback-seeking into "context": Job characteristics and feedback-seeking behaviour', *Personnel Review,* Vol. 42, pp. 50–66.

Macleod, D. and Clarke, N. (2014) *The Evidence: Well-Being and Employee Engagement.* London: Engage for Success.

Marsden, D. and Moriconi, S. (2009) 'The value of rude health: Employees' well being, absence and workplace performance', *CEP Discussion Paper No. 919.* London: Centre for Economic Performance.

Morgeson, F. and Humphrey, S. (2006) 'The Work Design Questionnaire (WDQ): Developing and validating a measure for assessing job design and the nature of work', *Journal of Applied Psychology,* Vol. 91, pp. 1321–39.

Newman, R. (2010) 'Get happy and get on with it', *Times Higher Education,* 21–27 January, pp. 32–6.

ONS (2016) *Measuring National Well-being: Life in the UK (2016).* London: ONS.

Paton, N. (2015) 'Too busy for well-being', *Occupational Health,* Vol. 67, pp. 7–11.

Peccei, R., Van De Voorde , K. and Van Veldhoven, M. (2013) 'HRM, well-being and performance: A theoretical and empirical review', in Paauwe, J., Guest, D. and Wright, P. (eds.), *HRM and Performance: Achievements and Challenges.* Chichester: Wiley.

Prowse, J. and Prowse, P. (2008) 'Role redesign in the National Health Service: The effects on midwives' work and professional boundaries', *Work, Employment and Society,* Vol. 22, No. 4, pp. 695–712.

Sang, X., Teo, S., Cooper, C. and Bohle, P. (2013) 'Modelling occupational stress and employee health and well-being in a Chinese higher education institution', *Higher Education Quarterly,* Vol. 67, pp. 15–39.

Soane, E., Shantz, A. and Alfes, K. (2013) 'The association of meaningfulness, well-being, and engagement with absenteeism: A moderated mediation model', *Human Resource Management,* Vol. 52, pp. 441–56.

Sutton, A. and Atkinson, C. (2014) 'HR practices, well-being and performance: Testing the "bathtub" model', ESRC Seminar Series/BAM HRM SIG Joint Conference on HRM and Well-being. Manchester: Manchester Metropolitan University.

Van Wanrooy, B., Bewley, H., Bryson, A., Forth, J., Freeth, S., Stokes, L. and Wood, S. (2013) *The 2011 Workplace Employment Relations Study: First Findings.* London: BIS.

Wood, S. and Wall, T. (2007) 'Work enrichment and employee voice in human resource management: Performance studies', *International Journal of Human Resource Management,* Vol. 18, pp. 1335–72.

CHAPTER 32

MANAGING THE INTERNATIONAL WORKFORCE

THE OBJECTIVES OF THIS CHAPTER ARE TO:

1 Provide an overview of research and practice in international HRM

2 Explore how staffing practices vary in international organisations

3 Review aspects of communication and coordination in international organisations

4 Discuss the major steps necessary to ensure the successful deployment of expatriate staff

5 Explain how international HRM practice varies from nationally based HRM practice

Earlier we explained how the globalisation of economic activity over recent decades and, in particular, its acceleration in the last twenty-five years have had a huge impact on the context in which HRM activity now takes place (see Chapter 2). We went on to explore the field of comparative HRM, discussing the very major ways in which practice varies from country to country, reflecting significant and long-standing cultural and institutional differences (see Chapter 3). Here we build on these discussions by turning our attention to the practicalities of managing people effectively in international organisations.

There are no definitive estimates of the number of people who are employed directly in global companies, but it is now likely to be in excess of 200 million worldwide (ILO 2016). The biggest one hundred organisations alone employ 15 million people, of whom 9 million are located in countries other than those where the parent company is based (Dicken 2015:117). This makes them powerful players in many labour markets around the world. Their high profile means that they tend to be seen as 'employers of choice', for whom UK graduates as much as oil workers in Nigeria or hotel receptionists in China are keen to work if they can. In the HRM field it is the bigger, well-resourced multinational corporations which tend to lead the way, developing and implementing new approaches and generally setting the benchmarks that other employers then follow. Most public sector organisations and SMEs tend not to operate internationally, but they have to compete for staff with those that do.

Unsurprisingly, as globalisation has picked up its pace, international HRM has become one of the most widely researched and written about fields of study. Numerous books and articles have been published over the past twenty-five years examining all aspects of practice in international organisations, a number of fascinating debates evolving about what is happening, what should happen and about the longer-term direction of travel. In one short chapter we can only begin to introduce this subject, so we will focus on two or three key issues that have generated considerable interest to date. We start by discussing key issues in the management of people in international corporations, focusing in particular on communication and coordination difficulties. We go on to introduce some specific issues that arise in connection with the employment of expatriate staff. Finally we focus on some particular areas of HRM that pose particular challenges in international organisations.

Structuring international organisations

In terms of its aims and objectives, IHRM (i.e. HRM in an international organisation) is no different from HRM in an organisation based in one country. The purpose is to mobilise an appropriately qualified workforce, and subsequently to retain it, motivate it and develop it. IHRM, however, is more complex and necessarily has a rather different emphasis:

- IHRM involves working with an organisational structure that is more complex.
- There are a greater number of more diverse stakeholder groups to take account of.
- There is greater involvement in people's private/family lives because of the expatriation element.
- Diversity is necessary in terms of management style.
- There are greater numbers of external influences and risks to understand and manage.

IHRM is also harder because of the communication difficulties that arise due to distance and language differences as well as cultural and institutional traditions and assumptions that we discussed in Chapter 3. This makes effective knowledge management and change management harder to achieve in particular. International HR managers thus need to have a somewhat different skill set from domestically focused HR managers and tend to develop their careers largely, if not exclusively, in international organisations.

A particular issue of significance for international organisations concerns the design of internal structures and reporting lines. While these are complex issues at the best of times for large organisations, they are made a great deal more involved when geographically diverse workforces are included. The major alternatives are as follows:

- by product group
- by organisational function
- by geographical region
- matrix structures.

In the latter case individuals may report to two or three different people for different purposes, a direct line manager based in the same geographical location, a regional manager working in the same specialist area of activity but based in another country, and others with responsibility for particular projects and initiatives being run internationally from a corporate headquarters based elsewhere.

Linked to the question of the overall structure is the issue of who should manage plants or other units located in countries other than that of the corporate headquarters. Most international companies are firmly rooted in a home country and wish to appoint home country nationals in sufficient numbers around global operations as a means of exercising financial control. However, in a truly global organisation, where the original location of the corporate headquarters is less relevant to staffing policy, and perhaps where ownership is no longer concentrated in one country, the nationality of each unit manager is less of an issue. This is also true of many international organisations that are not commercial (e.g. the EU, the UN and its associated bodies). Here corporate culture tends to supersede separate national cultures, and it becomes possible simply to promote people to new positions across different countries on the basis of individual merit. Deresky (2008: 343–6) identifies the following three main alternative approaches.

The **ethnocentric approach** involves filling key overseas positions with people from headquarters. This is typical of businesses that are at the internalisation stage of expansion and retain a strong, centralised structure. The people appointed have a full understanding of the company ethos, products and technology, and may be essential where there is a shortage of appropriately skilled and experienced local personnel. This approach, however, denies promotion opportunities to local managers and prevents the business from making use of its full overseas staff potential. It means, for example, that a Japanese car manufacturer always appoints Japanese nationals who have previously worked in its operations to all the most senior posts in its overseas operations.

The **polycentric approach** employs local managers to fill key positions in their own countries. This has the obvious advantage that they are familiar with the culture, language and ways of doing business in their own country and probably already have many useful contacts as a basis of their essential network. Once this step is taken, there is the potential problem of maintaining effective coordination across the business as a whole. The benefits of strong centralisation are lost. The US company, for instance, that has Americans in all its local CEO positions has people with a common national culture and background, as well as familiarity with the company's products and procedures. If that company opts instead to appoint CEOs who are from the local country, there is no longer the same degree of what can be taken for granted in shared values, attitudes and understanding. Will the CEO in Taiwan have the same understanding of the business use of bribes (or 'sweeteners', 'gifts in appreciation', 'special fees' and so on) as the CEO in Kuwait, in Detroit or in Stockholm? If polycentric staffing becomes widespread, will the social understanding and cultural awareness at headquarters become increasingly less effective in relation to the subsidiaries?

The **geocentric** approach is where the most appropriate person for a particular job is recruited from anywhere in the group, or even outside, so that the entire management cadre gradually becomes internationalised, with a shared global view as well as local understanding. This usually works only in a mature and very large business with great international experience.

An alternative approach which is commonly advocated is **inpatriation.** Here a multi-national corporation recruits globally, but then employs these people in its home country HQ for a few years before sending them back to their original countries or regions to manage subsidiary operations. The process takes time and money, but it seeks to ensure that the people who manage the MNC's international activities have *both* local market knowledge and fully understand the company's established approach to doing business internationally.

Communication

Communicating across geographical, ethnic and national boundaries is a major challenge for HR people. There are various ways in which expectation determines communication content and all can impair the accuracy of message transmission. Such problems are compounded by geographical distance, cultural differences and subtleties of language.

Cognitive dissonance does more than lead to misunderstanding; it can also distort or inhibit action. Not only do recipients of information find it difficult to understand, remember and take action, but they will also grapple with the dissonance that the problematical new information presents. One of the ways in which they do this is to distort the message so that what they actually hear is what they expect to hear and can easily understand rather than the difficult, challenging information that is being put to them. There are particular problems with jargon, where a word or a phrase has a specialised meaning that is immediately understandable by those in the know, but meaningless or misleading to those who do not share the specialised knowledge.

There is a need for constant communication throughout the business to disseminate information and to sustain changing values. The organisation must operate holistically. It is not the sum of its parts: the whole exists in every part, like the human body. If you are ill a doctor can obtain information about your illness from any part of you. A sample of your blood or taking your temperature is just as good wherever it comes from. If you are to be protected against cholera, which attacks the intestines, you have an injection in your arm. If you are about to be shot in the chest, your entire body will shiver in fear.

When a company is operating internationally, one logical main channel for communication could be the work flow pattern. If a washing machine is produced by manufacturing electronic components in California, subassemblies and wiring harnesses in Korea and final assembly in Scotland, there is an easy sequence to follow. Job instructions, guidance notes, queries, telephone calls, specifications, requisitions, authorisations, order forms are some of the many ways in which groups of people communicate with those before and after them in the work flow, or critically adjacent to the process, like the HR people. Among the most effective international communicators are airlines, as their entire business is moving not only customers but also staff constantly across national boundaries to different organisational outposts of the business: the business activity creates the communications. All international businesses require centralised, coordinated communications to create common purpose and to share ideas and benefits, but those that do not have a natural work flow link across national boundaries will have this need more highly developed.

The communications management challenge for IHRM is at two extremes. At one is the personal behaviour and skill of individual people in making themselves understood, persuading others to do things, negotiating agreements with people from different cultural backgrounds, overcoming language barriers, appreciating different frames of reference and developing heightened sensitivity to varying behavioural norms and conventions. Communication is an individual activity, reflecting personal style, and the HRM requirement is for cultural awareness and perhaps language training. In this type of communication the manager is a skilled solo performer. The other extreme is impersonal and systemic, more concerned with channels of communication than with individual behaviour, and more concerned with the systematic distribution of carefully chosen information and the organisation of communications opportunities. In this type of communication the manager metaphorically writes the score and then conducts the orchestra.

WINDOW ON PRACTICE

An expression that is often repeated in the French workplace is *Pourquoi le faire simple si l'on peut le faire compliqué?* (Why make something simple if one can make it complicated?) This slightly ironic comment encapsulates the French practice of opting for elaborate and time-consuming work systems rather than less complicated alternatives.

A similar point of view was expressed by Ann Moran (1994), who was involved in a merger between a UK company and a French one. She describes some of the cultural differences and their impact:

> the effort needed to communicate has doubled. The French expect a response from the person to whom a communication was sent and not from a delegated person. To reply otherwise is taken as a slight.
>
> More upwards and more complicated communications are needed whilst keeping [within] the formal hierarchical framework that is normal in French companies. Open questioning of superiors by the French is not common.
>
> In meetings French colleagues do not feel constrained to follow the agenda and sometimes walk out of the meeting for a private discussion. (Moran 1994: 112–13)

Coordination

Managers working internationally give themselves major problems of coordination by adopting measures that they see as necessary for business success. On the one hand they have to encourage diversity of local action, so that what is done fits local circumstances. On the other hand their global thinking requires careful coordination as the way to synergy, so that the global business does more and better together than it could possibly achieve as a number of independent units.

Bartlett and Ghoshal (1989) described three conventional approaches to coordination that were used, stemming from the nationality of the parent company, namely the Japanese, the American and the European.

Japanese centralisation

The typical Japanese approach is where a strong headquarters group maintains for itself all major decisions and frequently intervenes in the affairs of overseas subsidiaries. This appears to stem from its difficulty in dealing with foreigners:

> a major strategic challenge for Japanese firms is to accept that non-Japanese must somehow be given more direct responsibility and opportunity for promotion within the company at local level . . . there has to be letting-go from the centre. But this is no easy thing. For companies must overcome severe impediments associated with wariness, distrust and lack of knowledge about the world beyond Japan. (Holden 1994: 127)

American formalisation

The American approach is described as formalisation. Power is vested not in headquarters or in the managers of local companies, but in formal systems, policies and standards, so that it is the systems that drive the business. Many American businesses went international at the time when the use of control systems was being rapidly developed to cope with the large size of the businesses. The idea of delegation and holding others accountable by means of extensive computerised information systems seemed eminently suitable for operating the increasing number of overseas units, especially when one remembers the apparent unpopularity of overseas postings among American managers (e.g. Tung and Miller 1990).

European socialisation

In European companies the approach to coordination is described as socialisation. There has been a reliance on key, highly skilled and trusted individuals. These people were carefully selected and developed a detailed understanding of the company's objectives and methods. Their personal development included the establishment of close working relationships and mutual understanding with colleagues. Once groomed these key decision makers were despatched to manage the subsidiaries, so that the headquarters and the subsidiaries were both strengthened:

> because it relies on shared values and objectives, it represents a more robust and flexible means of co-ordination. Decisions reached by negotiations between knowledgeable groups with common objectives should be much better than those made by superior authority or by standard policy. (Bartlett and Ghoshal 1989: 163)

These three different approaches worked best for companies headquartered in those three regions of the globe. As the world becomes smaller and companies become more diverse with subsidiaries that are fully mature, more sophisticated methods are needed: companies are not international, but global. The influence of the parent company's national culture remains strong, but there is a cosmopolitan tendency gradually blurring some of the traditional boundaries.

Harmonisation

Across all decision making in IHRM, however organisations are structured, however good the communication systems and however well coordinated they are, there runs an ever-present and highly significant tension. This relates to the degree of harmonisation and centralisation that is possible or desirable.

Organisations want to develop strong corporate cultures and take active steps to manage culture and cultural change in order to achieve this. In nationally based corporations shaping corporate culture is straightforward provided it runs with the grain of the national culture. However, when a strong centralised corporate identity is imposed on an international company, inevitably it will run against the grain of some national cultures. The same is true of HR policies and practices. What works well in one national culture will jar in another, leading to demotivation, reduced performance, lower levels of trust and recruitment/retention problems.

In-depth knowledge of local labour market conditions, expectations and attitudes is the only means of judging where to strike a balance between centralisation and diversity. A long-held mantra which sums up the best approach to take is simple:

Think global, act local.

This means developing HR strategies for the whole global operation, but implementing them differently so as to take account of local cultural and institutional differences.

ACTIVITY 32.1

1 Think of where you work, or where you have worked, and identify three activities where global thinking needs to influence local action. What are the local people management implications of this?

2 In the same situation what aspects of local action influence, or should influence, global thinking?

Managing expatriates

A feature of HRM in international organisations which makes it different from HRM in a nationally based organisation is the need, on a regular basis, to post people overseas. International organisations need to have on their payroll substantial numbers of people who originate in one country, often where corporate headquarters is located, but work elsewhere in an international operation. Overseas employees can be divided into a number of distinct categories:

- Engineers are staff who regularly spend short periods of a week or two overseas, often working on specific projects such as setting up new production processes.

- Cosmopolitans are a small elite group who are familiar with different countries and are comfortable dealing with different cultural contexts all the time. They travel from location to location throughout their working year, spending little more than a week or two in each country before moving on.

- Occasional parachutists are firmly based in one country, but whose work takes them from time to time to sites based in other countries for a few days at a time.

- Expatriates are staff whose normal place of work is in one country, but who are sent on secondment for a period of two or three years to work overseas, usually in a relatively senior position, before returning home to their original workplace.

The management of all these groups requires some specialist knowledge and experience if it is to be carried out well, but it is expatriates who pose the biggest challenge. Unlike cosmopolitans they are not used to living overseas and will often find it hard to adjust, particularly when they take their families overseas with them. But unlike the engineers and occasional parachutists their role is long term and for the duration of their period working abroad they form an integral part of the overseas operation they are being sent to manage or work in. They also expect to be repatriated and anticipate that they will benefit from their overseas experience by gaining promotion to a more senior post.

Complexity arises because whenever an expatriated worker is not single the needs of spouses, partners and dependent children have to be considered as well as those of the individual employee. Sometimes it is possible to employ a couple together in some capacity or another, but more commonly the partner is placed in a position of total or partial dependency by corporate expatriation: one career is subordinated to another. This dependency is not just economic, it affects the social position and status that a couple have while overseas. For expatriate spouses with a professional career in suspension, adapting to this state of affairs can be very challenging. Because of the demands that expatriation makes on both individuals and families, the whole process thus has to be managed carefully and thoroughly.

The truth is that while expatriation is necessary, it is also very expensive and highly risky. While there is some dispute in the published research about how we should define 'expatriate failure' and hence how common it is (Reiche and Harzing 2011), there is no question that the process of sending someone overseas for an extended period can easily go badly wrong. Disappointment of some sort is very common as are situations in which expatriation episodes fail fully to meet expectations. 'Culture shock' is a common experience, as is a situation in which hopes are raised about life in an overseas country, only to be dashed by the reality.

Black and Gregerson (1999) looked at the experience of American managers undertaking expatriate assignments, finding that:

- 10–20% returned before scheduled to do so

- 30% completed the assignment but failed to meet their supervisors' performance expectations

- 25% left soon after returning to their jobs in the US.

When the costs associated with expatriation are considered, there is clearly a very strong business case for taking great care in selecting and preparing people for these kinds of assignments. It should not be assumed, as it often is, that anyone who really wants to go will cope well, nor is it right to take the view that anyone who has senior management potential is suitable to send on an expatriate assignment. Moreover, however urgent the need can sometimes be to fill an overseas posting, it always makes sense to take enough time to select the right person and prepare them properly.

Selection for expatriation

The possibility of an extended overseas assignment can come as a shock, which may or may not be welcome, presenting all the problems of considering the potential career handicap of turning down the opportunity and the potential domestic problems of accepting it. Employers seldom have the luxury of a large number of appropriately qualified people readily available to fill any vacancy, but the most satisfactory general approach to selection for expatriation is through the combination of performance management and career planning.

A feature of annual appraisal can be a discussion of whether people are interested in working overseas at all, the degree of technical expertise and managerial experience they possess and the domestic/social constraints that would affect the timing of such a move. That can then be developed by identifying timings that would be appropriate for such a move, preferred locations and even some language training. As with all career management initiatives, this sets up expectations of the future that the management may not be able to deliver because of changes in business activity, but it provides a cadre of people who would welcome an overseas move.

The particular location is the next most important determinant in matching the person to the job. Among the most important issues are the following:

- **Culture**: How different from home is the culture of the country – religion, the social position of women, the degree of political stability/instability, personal security and petty crime, local press and television, cable television, availability of foreign newspapers, health hazards?

- **Economic development**: How well developed is the economy of the country – standard/cost of living, availability of familiar foods and domestic equipment, transport, post and telephone, internet, local poverty, health and education facilities, availability of international schools?

- **Geographical location**: How far away is it and where is it – climate, in a cosmopolitan city or more remote, the importance/unimportance of language proficiency, the size of the local expatriate community, employment prospects of spouse?

- **The job**. What has to be done and what is the situation – the nature of the organisation, proportion of expatriates, technical, commercial and managerial demands of the job, staffing and support, the extent of role in managing local nationals?

The most important aspect of selection is making sure that the potential appointee and family members have a full understanding of what will be involved. It is essential, however, that those proceeding on an overseas posting should be appropriate for it. If there is not an appropriate person in the organisation, then recruitment from outside is preferable to assigning someone about whose suitability there are doubts. There is no profile of the ideal expatriate, but here are some selection issues arranged under the four headings used already.

Culture

How well prepared is the expatriate family for an unfamiliar culture? In many ways the developed countries of Western Europe present fewer problems than those of further afield, but English is spoken more widely in Singapore than, for instance, in France. Malaysia is a multi-ethnic society, but with a Muslim majority in the population. The Muslim dominance of life in most Middle East countries has profound implications for expatriates, requiring a degree of puritanism that will be unfamiliar and a social role for women that is quite unlike that which western women experience. In the developing countries of the Far East there may be superb hotels, but limited evening entertainment opportunities. Manila and Bangkok have plenty of after-dark facilities for men on their own, but little for couples and even less for women on their own. Whatever the culture is, openmindedness and tolerance are essential qualities for the expatriates to develop.

Economic development

Many Asian countries now enjoy a standard of living and material convenience that matches or surpasses that of people in the west, so that the expatriate will find excellent systems of transportation and postal and telecommunication systems that will be similar to those of the home country. Elsewhere the situation will be very different and everyday life will require a great deal more adjustment once the expatriate is outside the air-conditioned cocoon of the MNC's offices. Medical and dental facilities may be sparse and few expatriate families can avoid being affected by the conditions of those among whom they live. Not only may they be distressed by the living conditions they see in most parts of Africa, for instance, but also they will have to contend with very high rates of urban crime in some places.

Geographical location

This is a further twist to the economic development question. The heat and humidity of tropical climates are supportable when moving from an air-conditioned home, via an air-conditioned car to an air-conditioned office or shopping mall. Those moving to more remote areas have greater problems in coping with the climate and the relative isolation, so they need to be emotionally self-sufficient and not too dependent on outside stimulation. The distance from home is another determinant of personal suitability to the posting. The Parisian working in Brussels could easily contemplate weekly commuting: someone from Brussels working in Madagascar could not. There will be a smaller expatriate community in most Italian cities than in Hong Kong, so that the expatriate family may have to work harder at establishing social contacts, and will therefore require considerable social skill and self-confidence. The geographical location will also determine the importance of local language proficiency for all members of the expatriate family.

The job

In a global business questions about the job may initially seem unproblematic. Many expatriates are simply moving to exercise their well-developed company expertise in a different location. The situation will, however, always be different no matter how similar the conventions and procedures. The various demands of the job need to be thoroughly considered, especially what may be involved in managing local nationals, where the subtleties of response to leadership and expectations of authority will probably still baffle the expatriate when finally on the way home from the tour of duty.

Preparing for expatriation

If circumstances permit a relatively lengthy period of preparation, language training can make real progress. This comes to life most effectively when there is a strong flavour of cultural orientation and familiarisation as well, so that two of the basic requirements of preparation are dealt with simultaneously. The nature of the language training provided is usually slightly different for the expatriate employee and for the expatriate's spouse, partner and family. The employee will concentrate on technical and business terms, while the spouse concentrates on what will be useful in everyday matters like shopping and trying to get the washing machine repaired, or in local social contacts.

More general aspects of cultural familiarisation can be achieved by various means, often depending on the individual. Some will read voraciously, both travel books and the range of novels that have been written about most parts of the world. Others prefer film and video. Can there be any better preparation for Australian suburban life than watching several episodes of *Neighbours*?

Some companies use returned expatriates to write and present case histories about the country, with the obvious advantages that the potential expatriate can discuss with someone face to face personal experiences in a situation which they are about to undergo. It should also be automatic for the potential expatriate to meet socially with any nationals from the country of expatriation who may be visiting the host company during the pre-departure stage. A pre-expatriation family visit is also a good idea when it can be arranged, or even a short working assignment, so that the move becomes more of a process undertaken in stages than a single, sudden, one-off event. If there are children, arrangements for their schooling can also be made along with decisions about housing.

Continuing back-home logistics while abroad can be extensive. There may be children remaining in boarding schools, or elderly relatives to be catered for and pets to worry about, as well as renting the family home and many more arrangements. There may be a need for some company help, especially with financial and similar matters.

Travel arrangements themselves are relatively straightforward, but still have to be organised. There may be a need for family visas and one or more work permits, removal of household effects as well as personal baggage, health checks and whatever range of 'jabs' and medication are required.

Repatriation

Coming back from an overseas assignment seldom receives the attention it needs. It is not expected to be problematic and therefore receives little attention: all the problems are expected to be about getting out and getting settled. Why should there be problems about coming home?

> The long-term implications of ineffective repatriation practices are clear: few good managers will be willing to take international assignments because they see what happened to their colleagues . . . the only people willing to take on foreign assignments in the future will be those who have not been able to succeed on the home front.
>
> (Deresky 2008: 370)

The first potential problem is the nature of the overseas experience. If it has been thoroughly satisfactory, with an enhanced lifestyle, plenty of career development and scope for the employee, plenty of money and exciting experiences for the family in an agreeable climate, then there may not be much initial enthusiasm for returning, so that it will be like coming back from an extended holiday, with all the reluctance about leaving good friends and stimulating experiences to return to dreary old Barnstaple, or Dusseldorf or Des Moines.

On the other hand, if the overseas experience has been difficult, with a loss of social life, disagreeable climate, frustrations and disappointment at work and all sorts of petty inconveniences, then the prospect of returning home can become an obsession, with the days ticked off on the calendar and a great buildup of anticipation. When the day of return to hearth and home at last comes, Barnstaple (or Dusseldorf or Des Moines) may soon seem just a little ordinary compared with the wonderful picture that had been built up in expectation.

The second major problem is the career situation of the returning expatriate. Virtually all repatriated personnel experience some personal difficulty in reintegrating on return. There may be loss of status, loss of autonomy, lack of career direction and lack of recognition of the value of overseas experience. It may not be considered a management responsibility to fuss over a manager's personal readjustment, but an American study (Adler 1991: 238) showed that the effectiveness of expatriates took between six and twelve months to return to an acceptable level on repatriation, so there are some hard-headed reasons for taking it seriously.

ACTIVITY 32.2

Expatriate assignments frequently end in failure, in that the posting is not completed or fails to meet its initial objectives. Briscoe *et al.* (2009: 179) identify three types of expatriate failure:

- dropout (the expatriate returns home early);
- brownout (the expatriate performs poorly while overseas);
- turnover upon repatriation (the expatriate resigns shortly after returning home).

What different factors do you think contribute to each of these three types of failure? What steps can IHRM specialists take to reduce the likelihood of their happening?

HRM issues in international organisations

Our final task in this chapter is to draw your attention to ways in which some common, day-to-day HRM practices become more challenging in an international setting and need either to be adjusted or carried out in a rather different way.

Ethics and corporate social responsibility

Organisations that operate within a single country may or may not choose to adopt policies and practices which have a strongly ethical character, and those that take this path have a variety of motivations, some of which are more altruistic than others. However, they do not generally have to hesitate too much when deciding what is and what is not ethical business behaviour. In the UK context, while there will always be ethical dilemmas faced by managers on a regular basis, there is nonetheless wide agreement that certain practices are ethically unacceptable. This would be true of bribery, for example, not paying payroll taxes that are owed, the employment of children and selecting people for jobs on the grounds of their race or creed rather than their ability. However, these ethical norms are not always shared across the world. In many countries the payment of bribes and the giving of gifts is an entirely accepted feature of business life. It is also very common in a large number of countries for most people to get their jobs through personal and family contacts and for members of an ethnic group, religion or caste to favour one another when it comes to recruitment. Children are expected to work from a young age in many countries, and the very idea that men and women deserve equal pay and equal opportunities in a workplace seems entirely alien in some cultures. While the big ethical differences tend to be between developing and more industrialised societies, subtler differences in ethical norms in the USA and Europe have often been identified as have a number that prevail between southern and northern EU countries (Crawley *et al.* 2013, p:252–3).

Clashes of values are thus an inevitable feature of life in multinational organisations and have to be managed. Most international organisations are now very mindful of the need to protect their reputations and invest a great deal of time and money in maintaining an image of probity and good practice. The last thing they want is to see a valuable global brand's carefully constructed image tarnished in some way thanks to damaging media stories. HR managers have an important role to play in this process. Not only is it necessary to ensure that standards of expected conduct are well-communicated and enforced, but there is also a need to ensure that people with appropriate values are appointed and that extensive training is provided so that everyone knows both what is expected and why. The HR function itself also needs to practise what it preaches, upholding high standards of employment practice in all international operations.

Pay and benefits

Calculating an appropriate pay package for expatriate staff is necessarily complex because of the need to ensure that someone is paid sufficiently well to persuade them to take up an overseas posting, but not so well that they decide not to return home and resume their in-house careers at the end. Here there are also thorny issues to take account of like housing, exchange rates, schooling, flights home and transportation of belongings. You will find more information on this subject, together with an exercise to work through, in the following chapter. Aside from the particular challenges associated with getting expatriate pay right, the whole question of how much to pay people and in what form is often a difficult matter in a multinational corporation. On the one hand there is a need to be fair if good levels of morale and commitment are to be maintained, but on the other there is also a need to remain competitive by paying people a going rate in the place that they are employed. Living standards vary hugely across the world, as do local labour market conditions. So it is quite impossible for any multinational organisation that operates commercially simply to pay everyone who does the same job an equal amount wherever they are based. A fast food chain has to pay its restaurant managers in Europe or the USA much more than their equivalents in China or the Caribbean if it is to be profitable. However, paying people too little, even when it is possible to do so, not only demotivates, but it also tends to undermine the development of a serious sense of shared purpose across an organisation's international operations. Moreover, of course, there is the danger of negative press coverage arising from accusations of unjust exploitation. The same is true of working hours, physical working conditions and practices in areas such as maternity leave, sick pay, job security and health and safety. As is always the case with international HRM, a balance thus has to be found between a need to adhere to global policy principles, while adjusting implementation to suit the needs of a local operation.

The same is true when it comes to the design of payment systems. As Yanadori (2015) demonstrates, the common principles that are used to determine pay differentials and rates vary hugely from one country to another. No MNC can therefore hope to impose a harmonised global approach which fails to take account of local norms. For example, in some parts of the world seniority matters a great deal when it comes to pay. This is true of Japan and China, where the expectation is that loyalty to an organisation will be properly rewarded. The longer you stay, the more you are paid. Elsewhere individual performance tends to play a much bigger role in determining bonuses and pay rises, as tends to be the case in the USA and the UK. Here it seems entirely right and proper that a high performer should be paid more than a weaker one and that pay may vary from month to month depending on achievement. A third model is far more collective in its orientation, it being the norm for everyone who does the same job to be paid the same amount and for trade unions to have a considerable influence over how much each group is paid.

Trade unions

The approaches that MNCs take to trade unions tend to be very much more determined by what happens at corporate HQ in the country of origin than is the case with ethics and pay. This means, in turn, that it is usual for a standard position to be taken which applies across the whole company. Local adaptation only occurs when legal requirements demand that it should or where union bargaining power is too great to be resisted. The preference generally seems to be to replicate overseas the approach taken at home (Lamare *et al.* 2015).

This means that it is common for US-based corporations at least to try to operate a non-union model across their international operations. There is a preference not to recognise unions or to interact with them formally. Instead, many American corporations prefer to adopt high involvement practices, to build healthy psychological contracts with staff in overseas subsidiaries and generally to replicate the kind of 'work-hard, play-hard' culture that is prevalent back in the USA. High performers are rewarded, poor performers are disposed of and unions have little say in the matter. Some Chinese companies operating in Africa take a similar approach in refusing to recognise trade unions and actively discourage them. Here, however, local labour market conditions and weak or corrupt government institutions mean that the MNCs are able to operate using pretty brutal management methods that leave no room for any kind of employee involvement. They do not even aspire to basic standards of fairness. Local employees are hired and fired without restriction, the better paid jobs being occupied almost exclusively by Chinese expatriates (Yaw Baah and Jauch 2009).

By contrast Japanese companies famously like to replicate overseas the single-union, partnership-based arrangements that are the norm in Japan. This is very much the approach that the big Japanese car manufacturers take in their UK factories, requiring UK unions to compete with one another for the right to be recognised as sole representatives of all workers in a plant. It is then typical for the union to be consulted regularly and to have considerable influence, but in return a no-strike arrangement has to be accepted.

Some MNCs take a more contingent approach and vary their approach from country to country, following the 'think global, act local' principle when it comes to decisions about whether or not to recognise trade unions. But these are in the minority (Lamare *et al.* 2015: 104). When it comes to employee relations matters, a harmonised, global approach is far more common than it is in other areas of HRM.

Training and development

Human resource development (HRD) activities clearly have a major role to play if an organisation is to achieve high standards of quality service, productivity and efficiency across its international operations. It follows that a failure to invest sufficiently in HRD initiatives serves to undermine part of the rationale for expanding internationally in the first place. Whenever new systems are introduced, new technologies or new products and services, a significant training effort is always going to be required in order that the benefits can be maximised rapidly in every international subsidiary. In principle this process is no different than would be the case when managing training activities across different workplaces within a single country, but in practice there are big differences in the case of an MNC. First of all there is a need to take account of different preferred learning styles in different countries and to design HRD interventions that are culturally appropriate. Classroom based instruction, for example, goes down better in the eastern Asian countries than it does in the west where employees are used to questioning the people training them and may need persuading that an innovation has some merit. Secondly, there are straightforward language issues to get over. Unless the trainer is able to speak another language fluently, interpreters need to be hired, often doubling at one stroke both the time training takes to deliver and the cost of doing so. Thirdly, there is a need to employ trainers who are willing and able to spend extended periods overseas carrying out the training, potentially moving from location to location each week as a programme is 'rolled out' globally. It may seem exciting at first to be paid to fly from one place to another, staying in comfortable international hotels and having an opportunity to explore overseas locations, but over time the appeal wanes. Recruiting and retaining high quality, international trainers can thus pose a real challenge for multinationals.

Management development can sometimes pose a second major HRD challenge for international organisations. This occurs principally because nascent management talent is likely to reside in people who come from a wide range of cultural backgrounds and who have a similarly broad range of expectations about the natural way to manage operations. Multicultural management teams, because of their diversity, have a great deal to offer organisations. A far wider range of ideas and life experiences can be brought to the table and discussed fruitfully than is typically possible when a management team is culturally homogenous. But there is also a danger that a multicultural team of managers can become dysfunctional, characterised by conflict and undermined by rivalry between people from different backgrounds. It follows that considerable investment needs to be put into selecting people to develop globally. Not everyone with management potential will also be sufficiently culturally sensitive and adaptable to succeed in an international corporation. It is also necessary to build cultural awareness into the training and development opportunities that are provided.

Finally it is worth noting how Web-based HRD tools have a great deal to offer international organisations. Not only do they potentially provide a low cost method of disseminating training internationally and bringing people together in virtual classrooms, but also through the use of wikis, intranets and blogs, people who are carrying out similar activities on the part of the same organisation but in different locations can support one another and share their knowledge. In the future, as Skype-type communication technologies improve in terms of their quality and as reliable simultaneous translation software becomes widely available, the benefits that a global organisation will be able to gain from the use of e-HR technologies can only increase.

SUMMARY PROPOSITIONS

32.1. The rise and proliferation of multinational organisations is both a consequence and cause of globalisation.

32.2. Problems of communication in any international business are made more difficult by different frames of reference, stereotyping, cognitive dissonance and language.

32.3. Traditional forms of coordination can be roughly stereotyped as Japanese centralisation, American formalisation or European socialisation.

32.4. In order to maximise the likelihood that an expatriate posting will be successful, particular care must be taken when selecting, preparing and repatriating expatriate staff.

32.5. HRM activities such as promoting ethics, managing trade union relationships, determining payment arrangements and carrying out HRD activities pose greater challenges in international organisations than they do in those which are mainly based in one country.

GENERAL DISCUSSION TOPICS

1. Multinational companies tend to be unpopular with social activists, who mount demonstrations against their apparent greed and serious impact on some of the societies in which they operate. What are the arguments for and against this point of view?

2. Do you think international HRM is likely to get easier or harder in the future? Justify your answer.

3. Why are global companies much more likely to take a harmonised approach to trade union relations, resisting decentralisation to different localities, than they are in other areas of HR activity?

THEORY INTO PRACTICE

Over the past decade some of the most highly-rated universities in the world have experimented with off-shoring some of their activities. Starting slowly, but gaining pace in more recent years, there is now a strong trend towards the establishment of branch campuses in overseas locations. The main aim is to enable these universities to expand their student numbers significantly and increase their income, but there are other objectives too. Sometimes innovative research opportunities are opened up, particularly where funding is provided by host country governments and corporations. They can also serve to enhance a university's international reputation. In addition, overseas branch campuses provide ready opportunities for exchange programmes whereby students from the university's main campus can study abroad for a period, while students based at the branch can travel to the main campus.

Estimates vary, but it is clear that there are now over two hundred and fifty overseas branch campuses being operated by universities based in the USA, the UK and Australia. They are mainly located in Asia and the Middle East, but one or two have also recently been established in Africa. Two prominent Chinese universities have recently opened campuses in Italy and it is estimated that there will be many more examples of such 'south–north off-shoring' in the higher education sector in the future. There are already known to be considerably more overseas-based students registered on degree programmes offered by UK universities than there are overseas students studying in the UK.

Some branch campuses are wholly owned and operated by the universities concerned, while others have been established through commercial partnership agreements. Either way the mission is to replicate as far as is possible the experience of studying at a university's main home campus. Governance, examination and assessment arrangements are the same, while every attempt is made to ensure that teaching quality and other facilities are also maintained at an equivalent standard.

The establishment of overseas operations, sometimes on quite a large scale, poses some significant human resource management (HRM) and human resource development (HRD) challenges. There are also major risks, both financial and reputational, associated with the HR aspects of setting up and running overseas branch campuses. Moreover, because this whole development is so new, universities rarely have the required stock of specialist HR knowledge or experience to draw on when they first seek to establish an overseas presence.

According to the published research, by far the biggest problem is persuading established academic staff to work overseas for extended periods of time. In the commercial world undertaking an expatriate assignment is widely perceived to be a career-enhancing step, but this is not generally the case in academia. Five years spent in a developing country is often seen as five wasted years without access to home-based academic networks, laboratory facilities and research libraries. The problem is compounded by the long-established practice of appointing academic staff to the main management roles in universities as this makes it hard to fill even the most senior jobs on overseas branch campuses.

In addition to these specific issues, universities are faced with all the usual difficulties associated with the recruitment, retention and engagement of expatriate workers. These include the requirement to take account of family needs as well as those of expatriates themselves and the relatively high likelihood that people will want to return home before their assignment is scheduled to end. Losing staff immediately following their repatriation is another common problem as people find it hard to adjust to life back in their home countries. It is also always difficult to find a balance between paying a sufficient salary to make it worth someone's while to move overseas whilst avoiding overpaying them vis à vis local market rates.

An alternative approach involves hiring local administrators in the host country to support a freshly recruited team of lecturing staff from all over the world. But this model makes it very hard, if not impossible, to replicate overseas the culture and standards that students experience when they study on the home campus. And this is exactly what has to happen if an overseas venture of this kind is to enjoy long-term success. The last thing a well-regarded university wants is to find that its hard-won international reputation is diluted or even contaminated as a result of inadequate performance at a branch campus.

You have been asked to advise a university based in the UK about HRM and HRD matters in connection with their plan to set up a branch campus in one of the Gulf States (i.e. Kuwait, Dubai, Qatar, Bahrain etc.).

Questions

In particular your advice is sought on the following matters:

1 What steps should be taken to ensure that the faculty recruited to teach on the overseas campus are capable of delivering a high-quality learning experience that is as good if not better than that encountered by students studying on its home campus?

2 What steps can be taken to minimise the possibility that expatriate assignments will fail to meet expectations by ending prematurely or provoking resignations at the repatriation stage?

3 What steps can be taken to maximise levels of employee engagement on an overseas branch campus among all kinds of staff?

What key points would you make? How would you justify your recommendations so as to make them as compelling as possible?

FURTHER READING

Numerous books and articles are published each year about the different aspects of HRM introduced in this chapter. Three edited volumes containing articles by academic researchers and which cover the field effectively are:

Handbook of International Human Resource Management, edited by Paul Sparrow (2009).

Handbook of Research in International Human Resource Management, edited by Gunter Stahl and Ingmar Bjorkman (2006).

The Routledge Companion to International Human Resource Management edited by David Collings, Geoffery Wood and Paula Caligiuri (2015).

Communications and cultural issues are introduced and discussed in:

Management Across Cultures by Richard Steers, Carlos Sanchez-Runde and Luciara Nardon (2010).

REFERENCES

Adler, N.J. (1991) *International Dimensions of Organisational Behaviour.* Boston, MA: PWS Kent.

Bartlett, C.A. and Ghoshal, S. (1989) *Managing Across Borders.* London: Random House.

Black, J. and Gregerson, H. (1999) 'The right way to manage expats', *Harvard Business Review,* Vol. 77, No. 2, pp. 52–60.

Briscoe, D., Schuler, R. and Claus, L. (2009) *International Human Resource Management: Policies and Practices for Multinational Enterprises* (3rd edn.). New York: Routledge.

Crawley, E., Swailes, S. and Walsh, D. (2013) *Introduction to International Human Resource Management.* Oxford: Oxford University Press.

Deresky, H. (2008) *International Management* (6th edn.). Upper Saddle River, NJ: Pearson Education.

Dicken, P. (2015) *Global Shift* (7th edn.). London: The Guilford Press.

Holden, N.J. (1994) 'Management language and Euro-communications: 1992 and beyond', in M. Berry (ed.), *Cross-Cultural Communication in Europe,* Proceedings of the Conference on Cross-Cultural Communication, Helsinki. Turku: Institute for European Studies.

International Labor Organization (2016) 'Multinational enterprises', www.ilo.org/global/topics/employment-promotion/multinational-enterprises/lang-en/index.htm (accessed, April 2016).

Lamare, J.R., Farndale, E. and Gunnigle, P. (2015) 'Employment relations and IHRM', in D. Collings, G. Wood and P. Caligiuri (eds), *The Routledge Companion to International Human Resource Management.* London: Routledge.

Moran, A. (1994) 'Ferranti-Thomson sonar systems: An Anglo-French venture in high tech collaboration', in D.P. Torrington, *International Human Resource Management.* London: Prentice Hall International.

Reiche, B.S. and Harzing, A.W. (2011) 'International assignments', in A.W. Harzing and A.H. Pinnington (eds), *International Human Resource Management* (3rd edn.). London: Sage.

Tung, R.L. and Miller, E.L. (1990) 'Managing in the twenty-first century: The need for global orientation', *Management International Review,* Vol. 30, pp. 5–18.

Yanadori, Y. (2015) 'Compensation and benefits in the global organisation', in D. Collings, G. Wood and P. Caligiuri (eds), *The Routledge Companion to International Human Resource Management.* London, Routledge.

Yaw Baah, A. and Jauch, H. (eds) (2009) *Chinese Investments in Africa: A Labour Perspective.* Geneva: African Labour Research Network.

CHAPTER 33
ADVANCED HR SKILLS

THE OBJECTIVES OF THIS CHAPTER ARE TO:

1 Explore the skills of chairing meetings
2 Provide guidance for presentation at tribunal
3 Provide guidance in dealing with bullying and harassment
4 Explain the skills needed to use consultants

We finish our chapters on skills with our final chapter, using the descriptor 'advanced' for two reasons, first because these skills are usually within the function of people with more responsibility than we have been describing previously, and secondly because the *skilfulness* involved is not to be developed unless there is an element of relevant experience and expertise to combine with the suggestions we make.

You will find that the approach we take in this chapter varies, as the skilfulness involved in presentation at tribunal and dealing with bullying and harassment is essentially more in thorough understanding of the issue than in handling simple practical situations.

33.a. Chairing Meetings

An engineering plant manager has on the wall of his office a framed citation confirming that he is a full member of 'The Institution of Meetings Engineers'. This non-existent body was dreamt up by a few engineers who felt that most meetings were a waste of time. The inscription included phrases such as, 'Members shall attend all meetings called, regardless of their value . . . Any member falling asleep shall have membership suspended until he wakes up.'

Meetings are an inescapable part of the management process and they are frequently less successful than they should be, leading to the cynicism of the Institution of Meetings Engineers. They take a lot of time, so how do you at least cope and perhaps make good use of the meetings you attend? The basic necessities are a clear format, purpose and preparation, with the leader being in control. Those attending the meeting can then concentrate on content rather than fretting about the way the meeting is being conducted. People will only attend and make a success of meetings they see as useful. Poor meetings not only fail to achieve objectives, they also do harm, as members become frustrated about lack of progress or about not being able to get their point of view across. It is not just the fault of the person in charge. The analogy of the orchestra is apt. The conductor is responsible for the quality of the coordinated act, but every instrumentalist has to make a distinctive contribution that blends with all the others.

Chairing a meeting is a position associated with authority. Company boards, benches of magistrates, Cabinet committees, employment tribunals, political parties, debating societies are among the many activities that are led by the person in the chair. Professors in universities are appointed to chairs, not because they are too weary or lazy to stand up, but because the occupation of a chair represents authority. If you are chairing a meeting be sure you know the answer to some preliminary questions:

- Does this meeting have the power to take a decision, to make a recommendation, or simply to exchange information? All of these are equally valid objectives, but it helps to be clear on this basic question of what sort of meeting it is.

- What should the agenda be? The content of the agenda is usually drafted and proposed by the chair or, in more formal meetings, the chair in consultation with the secretary. The topics need to be clearly described, so that members of the group can come to the meeting with an understanding of them and with a focus on the key issues. The sequence of items is a question of which chicken needs to come before which egg. Getting the right things early on the agenda can make it easier to resolve later matters, provided they are in the right order; otherwise decisions are half made and then deferred 'until we have dealt with item X'.

- What is the meeting for? It may be to convey information. Then the sole focus is on the chair, who is passing on information, or analysis or news to a gathering of those who need to know. The only role for others attending the meeting is to listen, perhaps ask questions and probably mutter explanations and reiterations to each other to check their understanding. The reason for doing this in a meeting rather than by e-mail or memorandum is to give the opportunity for further clarification through questions; there is also the symbolic impact of information being passed on personally rather than impersonally. It is therefore usually done for matters of weight and significance.

- If a meeting is to share information, the chair is the coordinator rather than the fount of all wisdom. A health or social work case conference is a typical example and the chair needs skill to elicit constructive participation, and to encourage a free flow of information at the same time as preventing such a free flow that the meeting becomes chaotic and loses any sense of direction.

At a meeting to make a decision the expertise needed to make the right decision is distributed among the members of the group, so that much of the time is spent sharing information, but there has to be joint ownership of, or support for, the decision that is eventually made. This is most often by consensus to be identified as the discussion develops so that it can be articulated for everyone to accept or modify until it wins general acceptance and commitment. Some decisions are reached by voting. Although these are not common in management meetings, it is still essential that the chair moves to a vote only when a consensus is apparent. A majority of one is scarcely a majority at all and talking should continue until the weight of opinion is more substantial.

Conduct of the meeting itself

Few people are accustomed to expressing a point of view in a meeting, and many find it inhibiting. They speak best when asked to do so, and when speaking on something about which they are knowledgeable. Leaders of meetings get contributions by asking people to speak, picking up non-verbal cues of a desire to speak or reaction to what someone else has said. Statements of fact rather than expressions of opinion are the easiest way for people to make their first contribution. Experienced members of groups can help the less experienced by 'shaping' the clumsy or overemotional comments of their colleagues and agreeing with them (for example: 'I would like to agree with what Hilary was saying and make the further point . . .' NOT, 'I think Hilary was trying to say . . .').

Curbing the excesses of the verbose is a true test of chairing skill. Making a succinct and focused contribution is a competence rarely found among people attending meetings, so the chair has to be skilled not only in eliciting contributions, but also in closing people down when they are running out of control. Here are some suggestions:

- Use eye contact with the speaker to indicate encouragement or discouragement. When you begin to lose interest, or become mildly irritated, the speaker will receive that silent message and will usually respond to it.

- For those who will not respond, use more direct signals, such as looking away or looking anxiously at your watch.

- Use focus questions. If the speaker is rambling on and on, pinpoint what is being said by interrupting with a question to focus the speaker and to elicit an answer that is likely to be brief.

Bringing people into the discussion at the time when their contribution is most appropriate can be done by picking out someone who you think should have a relevant or constructive comment to make and putting a direct question to them ('What is your view, Will?' or 'I wonder if Sheila could help us with the exact figures . . .' or, 'Well I know that Harry has direct experience of this sort of problem . . .'.)

As the meeting proceeds the chair is constantly listening and looking for relevant contributions as a pattern develops, which they then help everyone to see and concentrate on.

The rank and file member of the committee

Chairing is the key role in a meeting, but what about the rest? First of all the other people are not quite equal. Some are more rank than file. Some are very much involved in dealing with whatever the committee decides, while others may not have any direct interest and may wonder why they are there at all. So first of all you need to work out your role as that will affect how you behave. Are you, for instance sage, brake, technical adviser, synthesiser, stimulus, delegate, diplomat or something else? Probably you may combine two or three of those roles. Whatever you decide will shape your approach and behaviour.

Some general suggestions are:

- Be objective in seeking solutions that others will accept.
- Support and develop contributions from others that you regard as being constructive
- Constantly monitor the mood of the meeting to judge when best to make your contributions, facts, opinions, suggestions or hypotheses.
- Always work through the chair, recognising the authority that the group always invests in that role, even in informal meetings.

SUMMARY PROPOSITIONS

33.a.1. The person chairing a meeting has to be clear beforehand on the purpose of the meeting: to decide, to recommend or to share information. This purpose needs to be clarified for all others attending.

33.a.2. Clarify what the agenda is to be and in what order.

33.a.3. Others attending make their best contributions by looking for solutions that others will support, building on contributions from others that are constructive, timing contributions for when the mood of the meeting is right and working through the chair.

GENERAL DISCUSSION TOPICS

33.a.1. 'It's a waste of time having a meeting if the person chairing it does not control the proceedings tightly.' Discuss.

33.a.2. Discuss the idea that both the chair and the members of the meeting should all have the appropriate training to ensure that meetings are effective and efficient.

PUTTING IT INTO PRACTICE

Attend a meeting that has an obvious purpose, e.g. political meeting, book group, university debate, group of teachers selecting prefects, group of volunteer guides at a stately home being briefed before the season opens.

1 Assess the chairing of the meeting, using the suggestions above.

2 Assess the contributions of other participants, using our classifications of sage, brake, technical adviser, synthesiser, stimulus, delegate, diplomat or something else. Assess the effectiveness of each.

3 If you could attend the meeting with a friend or colleague, compare your assessments *afterwards*.

33.b. Presentation at Tribunal

When employment tribunals were first established in the UK they were called industrial tribunals and intended to resemble traditional courts in their function and power, but with more informality in their style of operation. In particular it was envisaged that the parties should represent themselves, professional lawyers only being present in unusually difficult cases. However, as the amount of employment law has grown and become more complex, lawyers have increasingly briefed both claimants and respondents to advocate their cases and to undertake a proportion of the preparatory work.

Nonetheless anyone is permitted to represent anyone else in the employment tribunal and it is common for claimants either to represent themselves or to be represented by a trade union official, and for respondents to be represented by an HR manager. Employment judges are accustomed to managing such situations by taking a more active role than when the parties are professionally represented. They are also well practised in the art of providing chairing when one party is represented by a confident, knowledgeable lawyer and the other is not and requires some help in presenting their case effectively. Representing your organisation in the tribunal can be challenging and daunting, even where a case is relatively straightforward. But if you prepare thoroughly there is no reason why you cannot do a very effective job and save a lot of money otherwise spent on legal fees.

The key is unquestionably very thorough preparation. You must know all the facts of the case and must fully understand the relevant law and how it is applied by the courts. You need to clearly understand the strengths and weaknesses of your case, what points you need to persuade the tribunal to accept, precisely what you are trying to prove and how you can do so in practice. This level of preparation is necessary throughout the weeks and months beforehand as documents are collated, witness statements prepared and negotiations for a possible out-of-court settlement undertaken.

Settlements

Most cases lodged at a tribunal office are settled prior to a formal hearing, often at the last minute; some because the claimant decided not to fight on with a weak case, some settled via the Advisory, Conciliation and Arbitration Service (ACAS). It is not at all unusual for the parties to settle cases 'on the steps of the courtroom' a few minutes before a hearing is due to start. Sometimes the parties even agree the terms of a settlement after a hearing has commenced and may well be urged in that direction by the judge.

In the months leading up to the hearing the parties or their representatives are often, though not always, contacted by an ACAS conciliation officer, whose role is to explore the possibility of an agreement and to facilitate the drawing up of a full and final, legally binding settlement. Conciliation officers are always keen to advocate a settlement and this is very helpful if your side's case has significant weaknesses and could well be lost if a full hearing goes ahead. However, when your case is strong and you are genuinely confident of a likely, ultimate victory on the key points, you should resist the temptation to 'cut and run' and reject any suggested settlement which is more generous to your opponent than the tribunal is likely to be. You should be resolute when talking to the conciliation officer, stressing the strengths of your case and turning down any suggested offer politely but firmly.

If you decide to negotiate a settlement either through the services of ACAS or directly with the claimant's representative, you need to be aware of what a tribunal would award by way of compensation were your side to lose the case. It is helpful to calculate a worst case scenario and also to work out the most likely outcome. You should then be able to negotiate credibly by demonstrating to the claimant that you are not going to pay him or her off with an overinflated sum simply in order to dispose of the matter quickly. Paying a large sum may be justified as a means of reducing the costs which your organisation will have to shoulder if it goes ahead and fights the case in the tribunal room. But it sends out a bad message to other would-be litigants. An employer known to settle at pretty well any price to avoid tribunal hearings will inevitably attract speculative claims in the future.

Preparing for the hearing

The best advice is to start by preparing your closing statement. This is the statement that the representative of each side makes at the end of proceedings after all the evidence has been presented. It is your opportunity to set out your case clearly, to remind the panel of the main facts of the case as you see them and to explain how you think the law should be applied to the facts when the ruling is made. Representatives also use closing statements to draw the panel's attention to any case law that is relevant to the case and helpful to their arguments. Lawyers extemporise their closing statements and take considerable pride in their ability to do so well, often without recourse to even a few notes. This is not advisable for an inexperienced representative. It is much better to read out a carefully prepared closing statement, even if it is one that has to be adjusted to take account of unexpected developments during the hearing.

Writing a comprehensive, legally credible and clear closing statement is thus an essential stage in the preparation of a successful case. Take plenty of time to get it right and produce several drafts if necessary. Having completed it, you can then use it as your guide when preparing everything else. You need to be able to prove every fact in your closing statement and to be sure of your interpretation of each point of law you make. Facts are proved either with reference to documents in the bundle which is presented to the panel at the start of proceedings, or with reference to the evidence given by witnesses as a hearing proceeds. So you need to make sure, as far as you can, that each fact in the statement is provable with reference to one, the other or both. Points of law are made with reference to the wording of statutes and to published reports of previous cases dealing with the same legal principles. Tribunals are bound to follow precedents on points of law which have already been determined in the appeal courts, so you need to be aware of these and in a position to present copies of case reports to the panel when you start reading out your closing statement.

Your closing statement guides you when thinking about which documents you need to include in the bundle and also when taking statements from your witnesses. At the hearing your witnesses will take it in turn to enter the witness box (actually they just sit behind a table in most tribunal rooms), take their oath and read out their witness statements. This evidence will constitute the core of your case, so it is important that all points on which you want to rely are included in the statements and that they are structured clearly.

The final stage is to prepare your cross-examinations and examinations-in-chief. A week or two before the hearing you will exchange witness statements with your opponents. This needs to happen at the same time (or at least on the same day) so as to ensure that neither side can adjust their statements having had sight of the other's. At the hearing after your opponent's witnesses have read out their statements you will have the opportunity to question them about their evidence. This is known as cross-examination. Your aim is to push them into admitting points that weaken their case and to confirm agreed facts that serve to strengthen yours. A good cross-examination is courteous in style, but persistent. Do not give up a line of questioning if you do not get quite the answers you are hoping for. Instead try another way of asking the same question or putting the same points. By the same token, though, it is important to know when to stop a line of questioning that is having the effect of strengthening your opponent's case or weakening yours. If you get into a hole when cross-examining, stop digging! Sometimes you need to accuse a witness of failing to tell the whole truth or to have lied when giving evidence. This is not easy to do, but is often a necessary feature of an effective cross-examination. The key is to do this in a relatively polite way, avoiding aggression. A good approach involves asking the question with a degree of apparent regret, as in:

I'm afraid I have to put it to you that that statement is untrue.

Or to ask directly about a conflict in the evidence that has been presented, as in:

You stated in evidence that you were not formally warned about your poor performance before you were dismissed. Yet the letter sent to you on 1st April clearly contains a formal warning. Your witness statement was inaccurate, wasn't it?

The stage in proceedings known as examination-in-chief is your opportunity to put questions to your own witnesses after they have read out their witness statements. No new evidence can be presented at this stage, but witnesses can be asked to expand on points or to clarify exactly what they meant by words used in their statement. The most important task, however, is to give your witnesses an opportunity to comment on something, or to contradict a point which has been made in the claimant's witness statement or in that of one of the other witnesses appearing to support the claimant's case.

Remedies

As the respondent employer's representative you will always be anticipating that you are going to win your case on all points and that there will be no need for the tribunal to address the question of the remedy. However well prepared you are, and however strong your case, you can never be sure that you are going to win. Litigation always carries some risks. So you will need to prepare for the possibility that the tribunal will find against you and turn its attention at the end of the hearing to determining appropriate compensation. Sometimes claimants are not looking for compensation, wanting reinstatement for example, or a straightforward declaration that they have been treated unlawfully. Either way you need to be in a position to argue that the remedy the claimant is seeking is overly generous or inappropriate. Here too you will be guided by published precedents and by guidance set out in statutes.

Prior to the hearing the claimant will usually have sent you a copy of the 'Schedule of Loss'. This document sets out what is being sought by the claimant in terms of compensation. In practice, it is rare for victorious claimants to receive every penny they are seeking by way of compensation, but this can only happen if you, as the respondent's representative, argue strongly that a lower sum is appropriate. Here too, thorough preparation is necessary. You may, for example, in an unfair dismissal case be able to argue that the claimant was in part responsible for his or her own dismissal and that compensation should be reduced to take account of that. Alternatively you could argue that the claimant has not mitigated his or her losses adequately by seeking alternative employment and that compensation should be reduced on that account. In a redundancy case you can argue that while the matter was handled unlawfully in terms of procedure, it is likely that the claimant would have been selected and dismissed even if a lawful procedure had been followed. This should be reflected in the compensation. In discrimination cases there is usually an opportunity to argue that what is being sought by way of damages for 'injury to feelings' is too high and out of line with awards in similar cases decided in the past.

SUMMARY PROPOSITIONS

33.b.1. The majority of cases lodged at a tribunal are settled or withdrawn shortly before the tribunal.

33.b.2. The best advice for preparation is to first choose a clear, legally credible and comprehensive closing statement and use this as a focus for other preparation.

33.b.3. It is wise to prepare for remedies in the event that you do not win your case.

GENERAL DISCUSSION TOPICS

The formality and funding for bringing a case to a tribunal results in very small numbers of cases being brought. What alternative system might require less funds and be less daunting? How would it work?

PUTTING IT INTO PRACTICE

Knight and Latreille (2001) reported the results of research they carried out into 'gender effects' in unfair dismissal cases dealt with in UK employment tribunals. Some of their findings were surprising:

- 69% of unfair dismissal cases are brought by men;
- 71% of cases that reach a full hearing are brought by men;
- women are considerably more likely to be offered a settlement by their employers prior to the tribunal hearing;
- 51% of cases brought by women resulted in a settlement, compared with only 44% in the case of male claimants;
- 49% of the women won their cases; only 37% of men won their cases;
- men represented themselves at the hearing in 34% of cases, for women the figure was only 19%;
- women won 57% of cases in which they represented themselves, the figure for men was 36%.

Questions

1 Why are men more likely than women to bring unfair dismissal cases to the tribunal?
2 What could explain the apparent success of women claimants relative to men?

33.c. Dealing with Bullying and Harassment at Work

Defining bullying and harassment

Bullying and harassment are increasingly common in the modern workplace and research suggests that around 20% of employees have experienced it in one form or another (Pate and Beaumont 2010). The consequences can be serious: it has been demonstrated to have a negative impact on employee well-being (Vartia 2001), there are potential legal consequences and one estimate puts the associated costs at around £2 billion a year (Tehrani 2005). Clearly it is an important issue. We first define bullying and harassment, demonstrating that a wide range of behaviours can be classified under this heading. We then consider both employer and employee perspectives on the issue and the skills required to deal with them.

The terms 'harassment' and 'bullying' are used interchangeably by many people but ACAS provides the following definitions:

> Harassment, in general terms, is unwanted conduct affecting the dignity of men and women in the workplace. It may be related to age, sex, race, disability, religion, sexual orientation, nationality or any personal characteristic of the individual, and may be persistent or an isolated incident. The key is that the actions or comments are viewed as demeaning and unacceptable to the recipient. (ACAS 2009a: 2)

> Bullying may be characterised as offensive, intimidating, malicious or insulting behaviour, an abuse or misuse of power through means intended to undermine, humiliate, denigrate or injure the recipient. (ACAS 2009b: 2)

These broad definitions are intended as guidance to both managers and employees about the types of conduct that are unwelcome in the workplace. In practice, examples of what constitute bullying are actions such as gossip, unwelcome jokes, exclusion from social or work groups, or items such as posters and graffiti. Managers misusing power, setting impossible deadlines or blocking promotions may also be classed as bullying employees. Tehrani (2005) presents very detailed examples of bullying behaviours in the workplace that the reader may find useful in establishing what can be classed as bullying. We list two examples in the excerpts in the Window on practice below. D'Cruz and Noronha (2010) also present a fascinating study of bullying in Indian call centres from an employee perspective, demonstrating that bullying and harassment are an issue that has relevance internationally.

WINDOW ON PRACTICE

A secretary joined a media organisation to work for a senior manager. Within a few days, she found that he was behaving very badly towards her. He would criticise her work, pointing out errors in front of visitors. He would become angry whenever he was kept waiting. The secretary then found out that he had behaved in the same way with all his secretaries and that no one stayed with him long.

Two research scientists had been working on a project and when one of the researchers made a breakthrough, he wrote a paper that failed to recognise the work undertaken by his colleague. From that time, the two men would not work together and continually undermined each other. The situation got so bad that they were moved to different locations.

Source: Excerpts from Tehrani (2005).

While the legal definitions of these terms are more precise than the definitions and examples given earlier (see Chapter 24), it can be seen that the parameters of bullying and harassment in the workplace are broadly drawn. Additionally, it is the individual's *perception* of being bullied that is the defining factor in establishing whether bullying has taken place. One employee may, for example, take exception to a joke that another finds inoffensive. This can make dealing with bullying and harassment complex and the CIPD (2007) has, therefore, devised useful self-assessment checklists for assessing and analysing organisational culture to determine whether it is likely to support or suppress bullying. Bullying and harassment may be hard to identify but employers have a legal and moral duty to tackle them. We consider in the following section the means through which employers can do this.

Policies to deal with bullying and harassment

In order to deal effectively with bullying and harassment, employers must have appropriate policies and procedures and ensure that they are enacted. Over 80% of employers in a survey suggest that they do have a policy as a mechanism for tackling these issues (Tehrani 2005). This is likely to be easier for large employers with appropriate resources than for small firms. ACAS (2009a), however, presents a detailed guide to employers on the subject and a helpful checklist (p. 6) on what should be included in a policy to deal with bullying and harassment. In the Window on practice below, we present a similar checklist on the topic from the CIPD (2009).

WINDOW ON PRACTICE

Checklist for a policy on bullying and harassment

- Give examples of what constitutes harassment, bullying and intimidating behaviour including cyber-bullying, work-related events and harassment by third parties.
- Explain the damaging effects and why bullying and harassment will not be tolerated.
- State that bullying and harassment will be treated as a disciplinary offence.
- Clarify the legal implications and outline the costs associated with personal liability.
- Describe how to get help and make a complaint, formally and informally.
- Promise that allegations will be treated speedily, seriously and confidentially and that you will prevent victimisation.
- Clarify the accountability of all managers, and the role of union or employee representatives.
- Require supervisors/managers to implement policy and ensure it is understood.
- Emphasise that every employee carries responsibility for their behaviour.

Source: Adapted from CIPD (2012) *Factsheet: Harassment and Bullying at Work*. Reproduced with the permission of the publisher, the Chartered Institute of Personnel and Development, London (www.cipd.co.uk).

It is important that a policy in some way covers all these steps and also that it is supported, and seen to be supported, by senior management who act in accordance with the policy. It is advisable to deal with issues informally where possible, to prevent escalation of the situation. If this fails, or if the matter is serious, it will be necessary to deal with a complaint formally. Some organisations have procedures specific to the bullying and harassment policy but many simply rely on their usual grievance procedures, as we outlined in Chapter 24. Depending on the outcome of the investigation, disciplinary action may be taken against the perpetrator of the bullying, as we also covered earlier in describing these procedures.

Where policies are robustly drawn and effectively implemented, they can have great effect, as we outline in the Window on practice below.

WINDOW ON PRACTICE

Pate and Beaumont (2010) present a case study which outlines the actions taken by one public-sector organisation to tackle bullying and harassment. In response to attitude surveys which identified bullying as an increasing problem, a new CEO launched a Dignity at Work policy which adopted a two-pronged approach to the problem. First, reported cases of bullying and harassment were vigorously pursued and this led to the dismissal of a number of employees, some of whom were at a senior level. Second, compulsory training for all employees was rolled out. A further attitude survey demonstrated that there was a significant reduction in employee perceptions of bullying and harassment in the organisation. Indeed, those perceiving bullying to be problematic declined from a half to a quarter of employees in a three-year period. Trust in senior management overall, however, was not enhanced. Tackling bullying is not, it seems, a panacea for all ills.

Source: Adapted from Pate, J. and Beaumont, P. (2010) 'Bullying and harassment: A case of success?', *Employee Relations*, Vol. 32, No. 2, pp. 171–83.

Employee perspectives on bullying and harassment

The role of the organisation is critical in influencing employees' responses to bullying and harassment. It is, **as noted above,** important to have an effective policy but there is a danger that this may not be communicated to or believed by employees who may avoid the issue or resign rather than tackle it (D'Cruz and Noronha 2010). In the Window on practice below we illustrate how difficult it can be for employees to assimilate the fact that they are being bullied.

WINDOW ON PRACTICE

It never struck me what was happening. Work pressures are so high and TLs [team leaders] are also caught up with them – they yell and scream abuse to get the work done. So how can one dream that this is harassment. It is only after repeatedly experiencing it and carefully observing that it was only me who was getting the worst, the most frequent, the lousiest treatment from him that I realised what was happening. It just took me off guard because I was a top performer, always at the top of the team . . . so there is no reason for this. Merit, objectivity . . . these are all jargons used to describe the organisation – they are so empty. But at that time, they deceived me well.

Source: Excerpt from: D'Cruz, P. and Noronha, E. (2010) 'The exit coping response to work place bullying', *Employee Relations*, Vol. 32, No. 2, pp. 102–20.

Vartia (2001), however, notes that it is not only the targets of bullying and harassment who suffer, but bystanders also, and that it is the problem of the entire work unit, not just the person targeted. The CIPD (2009) and ACAS (2009b) advocate certain actions for the organisation to ensure that bullying and harassment policies are implemented and taken seriously. For example, employees should be introduced to policies at induction and made aware of their rights and personal responsibilities. There should then be continuous communication of and training in policies and employees should have a point of contact to whom they can turn for advice and information. Many organisations appoint 'champions' as a source of advice for employees with concerns about bullying. Employees should also be made aware of the mechanisms for taking a complaint forward.

While much of the focus is, rightly, on those who suffer bullying and harassment, the impact on those instigating it should not be overlooked. There has recently been a high-profile example of a senior public figure found guilty of bullying. The case involved a Metropolitan Police Commander, convicted and ultimately jailed for serious offences of this nature. Although one may consider the individual involved to be the author of his own misfortune in engaging in this behaviour, a working environment that condones such behaviour protects all parties, not just the victims of it.

ACTIVITY 33.1

Look at an organisation's policy on bullying and harassment, for example the University of Bradford's (2007) policy (www.brad.ac.uk/admin/equalopp/policies/HarassmentandBullyingPolicy07.pdf) or one from an organisation with which you are familiar.

1 What are key aspects of the policy?
2 To what extent do you think it is likely to be successful in tackling bullying and harassment?

Tackling bullying and harassment

Recent research about the dynamics of relationships in management responses to claims of bullying has found that HR people are seen as typically supporting the manager and being suspicious of the employee making the complaint as they are anxious to maintain the goodwill of managers (Harrington *et al.* 2012). **In this text** we have already made the point that HR is inescapably a part of management, but this does not mean being automatically supportive of an individual manager.

As we suggest above, many organisations tackle bullying and harassment using their grievance policies. In brief, the key aspects of dealing with bullying and harassment are:

- To address the issue as quickly as possible. It is often advised that grievances are best resolved informally, but this may not be appropriate for allegations of bullying and harassment. Where the allegations are of a serious or sensitive nature, the formal procedure should be instigated without delay.

- To provide a confidential and supportive environment for both the person who feels bullied and the person accused of bullying. The allegations may or may not be substantiated and both individuals need to be dealt with fairly during the course of the investigations.

- The face-to-face and communication skills we deal with throughout this chapter are vital in what can be sensitive investigations and discussions.
- An open, transparent and fair investigation is essential, as are appropriate feedback mechanisms once the investigation is complete.
- Both parties are likely to need support once the process is completed, unless the outcome leads to dismissal. The provision of counselling can be invaluable in maintaining positive employment relations.

ACTIVITY 33.2

Search the Internet for news stories about cases of alleged bullying at work. Which of the methods described **above** would you regard as especially appropriate to forestall such incidents?

SUMMARY PROPOSITIONS

33.c.1. Bullying and harassment are common and problematic for both employers and employees.

33.c.2. Employers need to decide how to respond to these issues and are advised to do so using policies and procedures which require senior management support.

33.c.3. Employee responses to bullying and harassment often include avoidance and resignation. They need to understand the policy clearly and how to use it if it is to be successful in reducing bullying and harassment.

33.c.4. Dealing with allegations of bullying and harassment can be very sensitive and a wide range of skills must be deployed.

33.c.5. Bullying damages the person, it damages the bully and it damages the organisation within which bullying takes place, especially if it is a way of suppressing dissent from what some people see as examples of sustaining misguided management practice.

GENERAL DISCUSSION TOPICS

33.c.1. To what extent do you believe that setting challenging deadlines can be considered to be bullying?

33.c.2. A robust policy on bullying and harassment will be effective in reducing employee perceptions that these behaviours are tolerated in the organisation.' Discuss this statement.

33.c.3. What actions can be taken to prevent employees resigning as a result of bullying and harassment?

PUTTING IT INTO PRACTICE

The main emphasis in this chapter and most of recent academic and general discussion on this topic has been about the effect on the bullied individual and on the bully, but there is the associated impact on the effectiveness of the business. This was dramatically illustrated by the report of a public inquiry into failings at a Staffordshire Hospital (Frost: www.midstaffspublicinquiry.com) in 2013, where an unusually high death rate caused distress, complaint and outrage. The inquiry produced many explanations, among which was:

> appalling care flourished because managers put corporate self-interest and cost control ahead of patients and their safety.

One salient feature of this was a culture of management disregarding staff complaints and concerns about patient care because of an inward-looking focus on financial targets and the need for 'efficiency' improvements so that the hospital could achieve the objective of becoming a Foundation Trust. Staff members who raised other concerns felt bullied into compliance in 'a climate of fear'. As a business the hospital failed to meet its financial and efficiency objectives because it failed to meet its fundamental and overriding purpose of caring effectively for patients. A month after the report was published the financial situation was so serious that the hospital was put into administration. Although this was a public-sector body with unusual and drastic results of its failure, the same criterion applies to every organisation which is always essentially a business. There is always a 'customer', whose needs have to be met. A culture putting other objectives ahead of that imperative and fosters an atmosphere of harassing or bullying staff members who raise other concerns is in danger; bullying is damaging to the bullied person, but it also damages the business that fosters or tolerates bullying behaviour.

Questions

1. In what ways is a bully damaged by bullying?

2. Discussion topic 2 above invited you to discuss the proposition that 'A robust policy on bullying and harassment will be effective in reducing employee perceptions that these behaviours are tolerated in the organisation.' Would that have been sufficient to deal with the hospital situation in this case?

3. It is quite common that senior or specialist personnel are required to sign agreements that they will not disclose sensitive information about the business if they leave. The reason is to maintain secrecy about matters that would assist a competitor. Can such agreements be reasonable where the information that might be disclosed indicates wrongdoing?

33.d. Using consultants

We begin with some light-hearted scepticism from 1985:

The Preying Mantis

Of all the businesses, by far
Consultancy's the most bizarre.

For, to the penetrating eye,
There's no apparent reason why,
With no more assets than a pen,
This group of personable men
Can sell to clients more than twice
The same ridiculous advice,
Or find, in such rich profusion,
Problems to fit their own solution
The strategy that they pursue –
To give advice instead of do –
Keeps their fingers on the pulses
Without recourse to stomach ulcers,
And brings them monetary gain
Without a modicum of pain.
The wretched object of their quest,
Reduced to cardiac arrest,
Is left alone to implement
The asinine report they've sent . . .

Source: Taken from Ralph Windle (1965). Republished
with consent of the author.

The amount of money spent on consultants by the UK government and its agencies has recently been increasing at a rapid rate, and this has been widely criticised by political opponents and by media correspondents expressing great scepticism about the value for money that has been achieved. Unflattering views of consultants persist, whether justified or unjustified, but the problem can be as much with those who employ them as with the consultancies themselves. Too often the reason for calling in consultants is inappropriate or not properly thought through. Some of the reasons are these (although they are rarely expressed this way):

I really don't know how to handle this, so I'll give the job to a consultant.

We're short-staffed since we had our budget cut, so I'll farm it out.

The MD plays golf with X and thinks he would be really useful to us in a consultancy role. I wonder how long it will be before he gets my job?

I think I will bring in a consultant to do some of this difficult stuff. If they mess things up it will prove that those upstairs should never have introduced this crazy idea in the first place – as I told them.

Consultants can rarely produce useful results if the project is simply parcelled up and given to them to get on with, particularly if it is given to them with the grudging or negative attitude expressed **above**. They may undertake jobs that others do not have the time or skill to do, but their input must always be monitored closely and built in to the rest of what has to be done so that the benefits of their work can be maximised and used in the future, after they have left. Here is an approach to using consultants in HR work.

Describe the problem

What is the issue on which you are thinking of obtaining outside assistance? This is not as obvious as it might seem. If, for example, the marketing director leaves abruptly, the immediate 'problem' presents itself as being to find a replacement, but worrying away at that issue might suggest that the real problem is to find out why the marketing director left so abruptly, especially if the current deputy does not fancy the promotion. You might then reshape your description of the problem as: 'work out why the position of marketing director is untenable.' Be honest. If your motivation is like one of the last three examples quoted **above**, you are heading for trouble. You must be able to present a consultant with a clear and realistic brief, otherwise you are in trouble.

Work out how to do it without using consultants

Consultants are expensive and they take time because they have to find out exactly how your business works, the structure, the ethos and the personalities of the key players, as well as its policies and products. Time and expense could both be saved if you could find an easier way of dealing effectively with your problem. Perhaps a recently retired senior executive from the organisation could come and spend a few days wandering round and chatting to people to give you a different perspective on the issue, or to show that you are dead right? Have one or two people to lunch to talk it over: say, people from your local CIPD branch or from a nearby business school, provided that you know them and have confidence in them. Talk to the marketing director's deputy to find out what makes the obvious promotion unattractive. You now already have the answers to the first questions that a consultant would ask and can work out how to tackle the problem without turning to a consultant. If you can convince yourself that it is a sound answer, and if you can sell it to your key colleagues and organisational superiors, then the job is done. If you are unsure, or cannot get backing, then move to the next step.

Approach consultants

Provided that you have identified and understood the problem accurately, and provided that you can describe it clearly to someone who has never been inside your business, then you can brief one or more outside suppliers of expertise and invite them to bid for the business. Do not start until you can pass all the tests in that sentence!

Keep control of the project at this stage. Beware of the suggestion that they will come and carry out a preliminary study at your expense before they formulate their approach. Any consultancy will want to work within the framework of their own expertise, but also of their own *experience*. You may not necessarily need some well-practised approach that has worked elsewhere, but in situations that are markedly different from your own. Successful experience elsewhere is invaluable but is limited in value if the organisational context or the business situation is dissimilar. Even large and well-regarded consultancies can be unsuitable. Their breadth of experience in all sorts of different situations may gradually generate an excellent standard product, which they may be reluctant to adapt, or even abandon, if they encounter the unfamiliar.

You have to produce a brief that will be the basis of your dealings with them. You should have the basis after going through the steps suggested above, but the brief needs to be reworked so as to make unequivocal sense to outsiders and to form a framework from which they cannot deviate.

Decide between alternatives

You now have to decide whether to continue with the consultants or to pursue your own rough-cut strategy. If the consultants can produce the most desirable outcome, can you afford it? Have you the resources to implement your own plan? How much time do you have?

Own the solution

If you do decide to continue with the consultants, your objective must be to control the next phase and to follow implementation closely, creating a situation in which local ownership of the solution is achieved as quickly as possible. Only when the new arrangements are working well and owned by your own people will the implementation be complete.

SUMMARY PROPOSITIONS

33.d.1. Using consultants can often fail because there is insufficient clarity in briefing them and a reluctance to work closely with them on the project.

33.d.2. Suggested steps in using consultants are (a) describe the problem, (b) work out how to solve the problem without consultants, (c) approach consultants, (d) decide between the alternatives and (e) own the solution.

GENERAL DISCUSSION TOPICS

33.d.1. Earlier we suggested a possible thought would be, 'This is going to be really unpopular, so I'll bring in consultants; they can take the blame.' Is this a manager unfairly and unrealistically avoiding a proper responsibility, or is it a sensible way of dealing with a problem on the grounds that management is weakened by making itself unpopular?

33.d.2. What aspects of HR work do you think are most suitable for using consultants?

PUTTING IT INTO PRACTICE

You have recently been appointed to replace the HR director in an organisation where members of the board felt that HR practice had become over-preoccupied with fashionable ideas and was not meeting the needs of the business and the people who worked there. They have asked you to review the ways in which HRM is being conducted across the entire business, within the line as well as by the HR specialists.

On investigation you find:

1 A scheme of employee involvement in management decision making has foundered because of resistance from two unions with members in the organisation, whose

➤ representatives were excluded from discussions about the proposals; and by reservations held by a number of senior managers, who felt that the scheme had not been properly thought through and that it was too radical.

2 The concept of performance management has been introduced at the same time as moves to empower line managers. Many line managers feel that empowerment means no more than their taking the blame for things that go wrong, and many of their subordinates feel that they are now cut off from the centralised, expert services of the HR function.

3 Members of the HR function say that they have lost credibility and job satisfaction by a series of grandiose schemes that were not fully developed and which could not be fully implemented in a short time.

4 Reporting to you are three people:

- Charles is the long-serving Training Officer, whose opening comment to you was, 'In training I try to see it as establishing a learning community that is separate from the hurly burly of commercial operations.'

- Henry is the Employee Relations Manager, currently on holiday.

- Sunita is the Personnel Manager, a recent appointee of your predecessor with the task of coordinating and developing the HR operation. Your first conversation with her begins with her saying, 'I hope you don't mind if I speak frankly, but I am totally frustrated. Catherine [your predecessor] was off the wall. It was all about changing everything, but she had no grasp of the practicalities of running a business and knew nothing of HR. They hired her because she had a PhD in marketing, but she was hopeless. Henry is all right, up to a point. He certainly has his finger on the pulse on the shop floor, but he has problems with women in positions of authority. He copes with me but Catherine was another matter. She insisted on an employee involvement scheme that was radical to an extreme, and she refused any consultation with the unions. Henry did not simply disagree with her scheme (quite rightly in my view) but it also confirmed his prejudice about women.'

You are now six months into the job and things are going well. Charles has left in order to take a job as a lecturer in a further education college in charge of a group of apprentices. Henry is changing his view of women and is now working very well after you had a long discussion with him about his understanding of Catherine's employee involvement proposals. He is working on a modification to that plan, which he believes will deliver what the members of the board will encourage and for which he thinks he can get shop floor acceptance. He is due to discuss it with you next week. Sunita has calmed down and clearly has a lot to offer.

Questions

1 You need to replace Charles. Who should interview the candidates, and how (e.g. you, Henry and Sunita individually; you and a board member together; you, Henry, Sunita and a board member together; or some other arrangement)?

2 Henry was not making his full contribution because of a poor relationship with Catherine, based on his attitude towards working with women. It is now apparent to you that there are other long-serving employees who share this attitude. Referring to your previous reading in this text, what sort of initiatives will you consider to deal with this problem?

3 What have you learnt from this exercise?

FURTHER READING

Presentation at tribunal

Aside from thoroughly familiarising yourself with the facts of the case and the relevant law, there are a number of good sources of information which are helpful when preparing a case for the first time.

The Legal Action Group (LAG) publishes a number of very user-friendly guides aimed at non-lawyers presenting cases in the employment tribunal, such as Jeremy McMullen, Rebecca Tuck and Betsan Criddle (2004) *Employment Tribunal Procedure: A User's Guide to Tribunals and Appeals* and Naomi Cunningham and Michael Reed (2009) *Employment Tribunal Claims: Tactics and Precedents.*

The Law Society publishes a practical guide by Isobel Manley and Elaine Heslop (2008), *Employment Tribunals,* along with a series of books about the major areas of employment law which put a particular focus on tribunal issues such as compensation and key precedents. An excellent practical guide is Payne, A.R. and Waite, J.-P. (2011) *Employment Tribunals Handbook: Practice, Procedure and Strategies for Success.* London: Bloomsbury.

Brown, D., Forshaw, S., Korn, A. and Palca, J. (2014) *Blackstone's Employment Law Practice* (8th edn.). Oxford: Oxford University Press. This is a vast book edited by a team of leading lawyers who specialise in the field. It includes a detailed guide to the employment tribunal system, different types of hearings and all manner of procedural issues. It also contains copies of all the major employment statutes.

Bullying and harassment

ACAS (2009a) *Bullying and Harassment at Work: A Guide for Employers and Managers,* available at www.acas.org.uk/index.aspx?articleid=797 (accessed 6 February 2016).

ACAS (2009b) *Guidance for Employees: Bullying and Harassment at Work,* available at www.acas .org.uk/index.aspx?articleid=794 (accessed 6 February 2016).

ACAS has produced these two comprehensive and user-friendly guides to explain both employer and employee responsibilities on how to deal with bullying and harassment. The employer guide offers advice on how to establish policies and procedures and the employee guide advises employees on how to manage a workplace situation in which they are being bullied.

CIPD (2007) *Tool: Tackling Bullying at Work – a Good Practice Framework.* London: CIPD.

The CIPD presents a tool that employers can adopt in analysing their workplace culture and establishing an action plan to eradicate workplace bullying.

Frost, R. (2013) *Mid Staffordshire NHS Foundation Trust Public Inquiry.* London: The Stationery Office.

Although this report was produced for general public information and was making recommendations mainly for government action, it is ideal reading for HR people, pointing out how easily major errors can develop from misguided management action, which is usually well intentioned. Written by a lawyer, it has perspectives and uses language that are slightly different from normal management-speak and therefore fresh to management ears.

Using consultants

Two books of general interest on the subject from a US perspective are:

Lewis, H. (2008) *Choosing and Using Consultants and Advisers.* London: Kogan Page.

Zahn, D. (2004) *The Quintessential Guide to Using Consultants*. New York: HRD.

Another US text, but a good account of what consultants believe they can do, is:

Haroun, C.(2016). *What Does a Consultant Do & Best Practice*. San Francisco: Artis Ventures.

Windle, R. (1985) *The Bottom Line*. London: Century Hutchinson.

The full version can also be found in the fourth edition of this text, published by Prentice Hall, Europe in 1998.

REFERENCES

Tribunals

Knight, K.G. and Latreille, P.L. (2001) 'Gender effects in British unfair dismissal hearings', *Industrial and Labour Relations Review*, Vol. 54, No.4, p. 816.

Bullying and harassment

ACAS (2009a) *Bullying and Harassment at Work: A Guide for Employers and Managers*, available at www.acas.org.uk/index.aspx?articleid=797 (accessed 6 February 2016).

ACAS (2009b) *Guidance for Employees: Bullying and Harassment at Work*, available at www.acas .org.uk/index.aspx?articleid=794 (accessed 6 February 2016).

CIPD (2007) *Tool: Tackling Bullying at Work – A Good Practice Framework*. London: CIPD.

CIPD (2009) *Factsheet: Harassment and Bullying at Work*, available at www.cipd.co.uk/subjects/ dvsequl/harassmt/harrass.htm?IsSrchRes=1 (accessed February 2016).

Frost, R. (2013) *Mid Staffordshire NHS Foundation Trust Public Inquiry*. London: The Stationery Office.

D'Cruz, P. and Noronha, E. (2010) 'The exit coping response to work place bullying', *Employee Relations*, Vol. 32, No. 2, pp. 102–20.

Harrington, S., Rayner, C. and Warren, S. (2012) 'Too hot to handle? Trust and HR practitioners' implementation of anti-bullying policy', *Human Resource Management Journal*, Vol. 22, No. 4, pp. 392–408.

Pate, J. and Beaumont, P. (2010) 'Bullying and harassment: A case of success?', *Employee Relations*, Vol. 32, No. 2, pp. 171–83.

Tehrani, N. (2005) *Bullying at Work: Beyond Policies to a Culture of Respect*. London: CIPD.

University of Bradford (2007) *Personal Harassment and Bullying Policy and Procedures*, available at www.brad.ac.uk/admin/equalopp/policies/HarassmentandBullyingPolicy07.pdf (accessed February 2016).

Vartia, M. (2001) 'Consequences of workplace bullying with respect to the well-being of its targets and the observers of bullying', *Scandinavian Journal of Work and Environmental Health*, Vol. 27, No. 1, pp. 63–9.

GLOSSARY

The terms in this glossary have been taken selectively from the text. Rather than repeating definitions we have already given, we have chosen terms which are neologisms that may not appear in a dictionary, or are invented words, like presenteeism, which do not yet appear in a dictionary. We also include terms, like bureaucracy, which can benefit from more interpretation than we have provided in the text.

Absence/attendance. Until quite recently attendance at work was universally accepted as a duty and absence had to be justified by external verification, such as by a medical note or a call to undertake jury service. Without such independent evidence, some sort of punishment was usual. As social attitudes have changed and rights to time off have increased, so the managerial emphasis has changed, requiring managers to manage attendance, by paying attention to reasons for avoidable absence. This has a degree of altruistic concern for employee well-being, where some aspect of the work required from employees is a contributory cause of, for instance, an inability to return to work. There is also an emphasis on trying to minimise disruption to working patterns and persuading people not to be unreasonable. Stress has become a major absence factor since it has become more socially acceptable. Usually it is a perfectly valid feature of a person's working or personal life and can perhaps be alleviated by managerial initiatives. In some other situations it is manipulated by people who place their own interpretation on a right to sick leave. A recent visit to an engineering drawing office in March was surprising as more than half the staff were missing. The drawing office manager explained that the absentees were 'getting in their sick leave' before the end of the leave year. A management attempt to make allowance for understandable sickness absence had been mismanaged in allowing it to become gradually accepted as an additional leave entitlement. In a different, current situation a school teacher has recently shown such unwillingness to implement new professional requirements that there is a risk of the school implementing capability procedure being met with the response, 'If they do that I will simply go off with stress'.

Apprenticeship. The typical idea of an apprentice is of a male who left school as soon as possible and then trained on the job in a manual trade like plumbing or as an electrician, possibly continuing education part time at a local college. Since a university degree has gradually become the must-have qualification for many fields of employment, the number of apprentices had dwindled: certainly not a prelude to a 'nice job'. Currently they are seeing a renaissance, as skills shortages are seen as an impediment to economic growth, but not necessarily for young males. In 2015 more than half of those pursuing an apprenticeship were over 25.

Benchmarking. Originally a benchmark was a mark on a work bench that could be used to measure off a standard size. This idea of comparative measurement is used in HRM to describe the process of checking some aspect of work in one's own business against an external standard, like the average number of days lost through absence across the working population as a whole, or in a particular industry, by age, occupation, gender and so forth. It is slightly different from 'yardstick', which is literally a measuring stick a yard long. This is sometimes used as a rough-and-ready measure for some aspect of management effectiveness, but it lacks the dimension of external comparison.

Best fit/fit. In many fields of human endeavour there is an aim to find and implement the one best way, or the right way, of doing things. An alternative is to work out the best way of doing things in this or that situation. There is no single approach or method that is always right.

Bottom line. A term derived from accountancy, where it is the final total in a profit and loss statement or other financial document. In management generally it is used as the ultimate criterion or most important factor: financial viability.

Brand. A term taken from marketing to describe a company or product name that is very distinctive and powerful. Examples are Coca-Cola, Microsoft, Rolls-Royce or Virgin. It was illustrated by the retail director of a fashion chain who said, 'If I buy a ready meal from X and I don't like it, I take it back. If I buy it from Marks & Spencer, either I haven't followed the instructions or there is something wrong with my cooker.' To HR people the company brand can be very important in matters of commitment and recruitment.

Bureaucracy. This has become almost a term of abuse, describing rigidity, lack of responsiveness by staff, lack of willingness to take responsibility and too much emphasis on the rules. It is, however, a time-honoured method of making any large organisation work. In contemporary business usage it describes a type of centralised social order that makes things happen by having guidelines of policy, procedure and precedent to empower role holders to do their jobs, conferring appropriate authority for action as well as limiting the scope for individual whim or prejudice. It is therefore both more acceptable and more practical as a method of organisation for any large undertaking than relying on the autocratic alternative of everything being decided by a small number of people at the centre, while everyone else waits and grumbles. HR managers are occasionally derided by some of their colleagues in other functions for their apparent preoccupation with the 'rules' of procedure and employment law. These colleagues are, of course, wrong, but bureaucracy has a serious inherent flaw in that it always grows, requiring frequent pruning and review.

Career. The idea of a career involving moving from job to job is relatively recent. For most people a career was an occupation, like nursing or teaching or carpentry or bricklaying. It was only in bureaucracies that people looked for a promotional ladder. In most of the long-standing professions a career was a lifetime of doing the same job, although perhaps introducing a change of emphasis. A clergyman was a clergyman, even though a few might become deans or bishops. A writer was a writer, although there might be moves from writing poetry to writing novels. An architect is an architect, a dentist is a dentist, a driver is a driver. In some areas the idea of moving 'up' has been created artificially by inventing new pay grades and titles. Until the 1970s nursing in the UK had three levels: nurse, sister and matron. In order to provide a career structure, new jobs were introduced: nursing officer, senior nursing officer and principal nursing officer. The flattening of hierarchies is changing the emphasis. There are now a greater number of sideways, cross-functional moves than vertical moves, thus the increasing trend for careers to involve changes in occupation.

Casual work is work where someone is employed on a temporary and probably irregular basis without any obligation on either party of further employment when a spell is complete. A recent form of this is the zero hours contract, whereby someone is 'on the books' as being available for certain jobs, but with no guarantee of security of employment.

Change initiatives are often regarded as invariably desirable, particularly by consultants trying to sell you something. Although constantly advocated in HRM, they have to be balanced against other issues such as stability and security. Furthermore, few changes in HR practice can be made quickly and easily. The ideas are usually easy or obvious. Getting them accepted and making them work requires a great deal of hard work, which means that changes have to be worth the trouble and not just some transitory idea that will have been overtaken by something else in six months' time. 'Initiative fatigue' is a term used to describe the experience of some people who have scarcely got used to one new initiative before another is imposed that contradicts the first.

Clocking on (or in) is a term still in common usage, although the practice is not now widespread. In the heyday of large-scale production businesses, manual employees registered their arrival for work by operating an automatic time-recording machine, usually by punching a hole in a personal card. Sometimes they clocked out as well as on. This gave a reliable record of hours worked and enabled pay calculations to be made. Although initially seen as a way to be fair, it eventually became a symbol of close, overbearing control – 'the tyranny of clocking on'. It has become less common although variants are used by, for example, security staff who clock their arrival at various parts of the premises at regular times during the night, or by managers of motorway service stations to demonstrate that they have recently checked the cleanliness of the toilets. A refinement and extension of clocking is the tachograph in road-haulage vehicles.

Coach/mentor/protégé. A coach is someone who gives specialised training and guidance as well as general support and encouragement. This may be to an individual, like a tennis player, or to a team, as in cricket. A mentor gives the same sort of service to an individual in what is often a very close personal relationship, requiring from the protégé a high degree of trust in the integrity and goodwill of the mentor. A protégé is someone who is guided by a mentor, acknowledging a need for that person's greater standing and expertise. Novak Djokovic is the world's most successful tennis player, but still needs a coach: he is not the coach's protégé. One of the most ghastly bits of management jargon is the word 'mentee', presumably invented by someone who could not cope with three syllables, as an alternative to protégé.

Commitment is widely used in contemporary HR to describe the quality of being dedicated to the cause, and various methods are used (see Chapter 13, for example) to develop this quality among the members of the workforce in their dedication to the cause of company success. Some may be committed to a career or to the employment security that is associated with the success of the business, while others are committed to the success of their career perhaps at the expense of the business, and others have no commitment at all. In these circumstances the value of the brand may be important.

Competitive advantage. Any business has to be competitive, no matter how much many of its members may not like the idea. A school has to be seen by parents to be at least as good as other schools, otherwise parents will remove their children and the pupils will not have self-respect. Commercial

organisations seek competitive advantage for more immediate reasons of survival, but schools, hospitals, charities and churches will all decline and may close if they do not meet the current needs and expectations of their 'clients', although they will quite rightly cavil at the terms 'customers' or 'clients'.

Contingency is a word much used in sociology and organisation theory. Apart from its normal usage of describing a possible future event that cannot be predicted with certainty, in management it is used to differentiate from the absolute. Solutions to problems are seldom invariably right: it depends on the particular circumstances of the event.

Contract/consideration. In this text the use of material about contract is mainly about legal agreements, although there is also the reference to psychological contracts. The fundamental principle of a legal contract is that there must be consideration. A contract is a spoken or written agreement that is intended to be enforceable at law, but the offer of agreement by one party only becomes legally enforceable when there is consideration from the other party, that is an undertaking of some sort, to do something or to stop doing something or to abandon a claim. An offer of employment, for instance, is not legally binding on the employer making the offer until and unless the prospective employee accepts the offer and agrees to provide the work (consideration) that the employer is offering.

Culture/organisational culture. In management circles interest in culture is an attempt to grasp the

realities of collective life in a department or organisation that cannot be easily seen and described with such identifiers as job titles, departments and organisation charts. It is an aspect of the hard/soft distinction. Recently it has been especially important in explaining the differences in management practice in various countries, but organisational culture refers to the beliefs, conventions and general patterns of behaviour that characterise a particular organisation.

Delayering is a method of downsizing that reduces the number of people in a hierarchy by removing a tier in the organisation structure.

Demographics describe statistical data relating to the age and gender structure of the population. They are an important element in understanding the labour market.

Discipline is often seen in the very narrow way as punishment for past misdeeds, with disciplinary procedure being regarded and used as an irritating preliminary to justifiable dismissal. A more constructive view is to see it as a process of trying to deal with unsatisfactory performance in the hope that it can be improved, even if it becomes dismissal after remedies fail.

Diversity is subtly different from equality and refers principally to the value to management of making the most of employees from two distinct groups, women and those from ethnic minorities, rather than assuming that core employees are white and male. Although these two groups have been the main focus of debate and action, greater attention has recently been paid to other groups, such as those who are potentially discriminated against on the grounds of age or disability.

Downsizing describes an approach to increasing organisational efficiency by reducing the number of people employed in the business and therefore reducing the costs associated with their employment. The main methods are delayering and outplacement/outsourcing.

Emotional intelligence is an idea that still lacks validation, but it is popular, especially in relation to effectiveness in leadership, as well as seeming to make sense. Intelligence is well understood, with a dictionary definition as the ability to acquire and apply knowledge and skills. Emotional intelligence is the ability to perceive, control and evaluate emotions; the further aspect is that it includes the ability to perceive and evaluate emotions in other people, with the obvious relevance to HR.

Employee relations/industrial relations are not simply different terms for the same activities; they denote a significant change of emphasis. Concern with industrial relations developed when the emphasis was on collective relationships within an industry, such as engineering, agriculture or teaching. Each business within the ambit of that industry observed the terms and conditions agreed between employers' representatives and unions, which bound every employer. Employee relations have little regard for industry criteria and focus on collective arrangements within an individual business.

Employee voice is a term that has only come into use during the twenty-first century, largely as a result of the globalisation issue. It refers to a wide variety of processes and structures which enable people to contribute to decision making in the place where they work and perhaps to influence decision making in other places that affect the place where they work.

Environment. We typically think nowadays of the physical environment in which we live and the environmental issues that are of concern: pollution, greenhouse gases, GM crops, vulnerable species and so forth. In HRM it is more likely to refer to the social, political and legal environment of the business.

Flexibility is something managers try hard to achieve and trade unions and the legal system try to limit. The flexible workforce makes managerial life easier by giving more scope to managers to manipulate the labour supply, as do flexible hours arrangements. Flexibility agreements with unions reduce rigidity in work practices. All these practices reduce the problems of bureaucracy but the advantages for employees may be more mixed. Flexible hours are probably the most attractive, but there are always disadvantages for employees with flexibility initiatives that at least slightly erode their personal security. Currently we see the rise of another neologism, 'flexicurity'.

Globalisation/internationalisation are both terms coined recently to describe two slightly different aspects of modern business. Many companies work internationally, importing materials and resources and exporting products and services. If their business expands they may appoint agents in overseas countries to represent their interests, or they may establish overseas subsidiaries. The company remains with a distinctive national head office and branding. Globalisation represents a distinctive further step as the company operates major businesses in different countries and regions. Its national identity is submerged beneath its global identity and branding. As these businesses grow larger and therefore more powerful, some commentators and pressure groups grow very concerned that their commercial interests can destabilise and harm the economies of individual countries, especially smaller countries in the developing world.

Grievance/discipline. Everyone who is employed has a contract in two parts. The first part is the wage/work bargain. One party to the contract pays money and provides benefits to the other party, who provides work in exchange. The second part of the contract is the psychological contract, referred to throughout this text, where what is exchanged between the two parties is a less tangible – but no less important – form of satisfaction. Both parts of the contract are maintained through the mutual satisfaction of the parties. When something happens to reduce the level of satisfaction of either party, HRM uses the terms 'grievance' or 'discipline' to describe the processes whereby satisfaction may be restored.

Hard/soft. Hard data is precise and can be accurately measured by numbers and statistical calculation. Soft data is less precise but may be more important in planning. It includes judgement, assessment and informed guesswork.

Hierarchy is the system of organisation which ranks all the people according to their status or authority.

This is used for all manner of purposes, ranging from the trivial, like who has the biggest office and who is allowed to travel first class, to the identification of who is empowered to do what, as the hierarchical system includes titles or labels to make sense of the jobs that people do. In the UK the growth of hierarchy received a boost when an early management theorist, E.F.L. Brech, advanced his theory of the span of control, saying that no manager should supervise directly the work of four or five subordinates *whose work interlocks*. Many people accepted the theory but conveniently forgot the last three words.

Human capital. Economists, rather reluctantly, conceded that any economic analysis of an organisation or an economy needed to include the concept of a value or cost assigned to skills, knowledge or experience of the population. It has proved a more acceptable and useful concept than the sterile accountancy technique of human asset accounting. Its main value to HR practitioners is the idea that human capital requires investment.

Intersectionality is a cumbersome word coined towards the end of the twentieth century by feminist sociologists to make the argument that the social disadvantage of some categories of people is exacerbated by the way various biases against them in one category intersect with the bias against them in another, making them doubly disadvantaged. This has begun to emerge in the management literature with examples such as men's health, which might be seen solely as an aspect of gender, while a richer understanding of this identity could come by its intersection with another social category, such as class or race.

Marketplace/labour market. The importance of both these concepts (taken from economics) in HRM is to emphasise that people management can never be entirely inward in focus. The business has to operate in a context in which there is a market for its products or service, and the business has to survive in that market no matter how inconvenient it may be for the people inside the business. Equally there is an external market for labour and skills, which cannot be ignored. Even employees totally loyal to the business will be aware of prevailing conditions elsewhere, not only how much people are paid but also conditions of work, hours and fringe benefits.

Matrix is a term that has recently come into popular currency because of film and television programmes using it in a very specialised way. In management it has long been used to describe a particular form of organisation in which levels of specialisation, accountability and responsibility are set out in vertical columns crossed by horizontal lines, with points of intersection identifying individual people who have a line of communication in one direction (line management) as well as a distinct accountability to someone else. An office manager, for instance, might be responsible for most things to the immediate superior, but accountable to the HR manager for health and safety issues. 'The line' is often mentioned in this text and refers to the vertical line of accountability.

Meta-analysis is an analysis which combines a number of existing analyses already carried out by others into one summary analysis. 'Meta' is a scientific term indicating a change in condition, such as in

metamorphosis. In social sciences it denotes something beyond, of a higher-order kind.

Mission/aims/objectives/targets. These are all terms used quite loosely in management jargon and are in a rough hierarchy from the broad to the specific. Mission comes from religion and is used in a business to describe what the organisation is for, what its purpose is. A mission statement is typically vague and general, but can be useful in developing commitment. Aims and objectives describe the more specific purposes of individual functions, departments, teams or individuals within the mission framework. Targets are very specific and usually short term as stages on the way for teams and individuals to achieve longer-term objectives. Recently we have seen examples of how targets can be a dangerous distraction from mission, as when some hospitals concentrated so hard on a target of reducing a financial deficit that they lost focus on their clear mission to care for the sick.

Occupational health. Many businesses describe their medical departments as 'Occupational Health' departments, regardless of the skills possessed by the people who work in them, but it is worth bearing in mind that occupational medicine is a defined specialism, not general practice in an occupational setting. Both doctors and nurses can acquire qualifications in occupational medicine, but they are most likely to be needed in a business with specific hazards, like radiation or toxic materials.

Organisation. Few words have attracted so much attention in so many different areas of human enquiry, fascinating administrators, anthropologists, archaeologists, biologists, economists, military strategists, political activists and theorists, psychologists, sociologists, trade unionists and many more. This plethora of perspectives can be confusing or even bewildering when trying to define a management perspective that comes within the purview of this text, especially for those whose education has included a thorough grounding in such widely taught subjects as economics, psychology or sociology. Basically our interest is in two meanings of the word, organisation as an arena in which human activity takes place (an **entity**) and organisation as a way of getting things done in such an arena (a **process**). To most academics the first is of much greater interest than the second; to most managers the second is of more interest than the first.

HR managers need to understand first the contexts within which their organisation or entity operates. There is the political context which provides a legal and broad administrative framework of benefits and limitations. The social context includes the availability of prospective employees, the educational situation and the prevailing ethical standards that govern attitudes and behaviour. Every organisational entity exists within a market, or series of markets. If there is not sufficient demand for the products and services that are offered, the entity will eventually wither and die. This is not only true of commercial activities. In 1780 Robert Raikes started a Sunday School for the children of chimney sweeps in the appropriately named Sooty Alley in the centre of Gloucester. This was the first time that education of any type apart from the memorising of catechisms had been provided for working-class

children and adults. Sunday Schools spread rapidly, so that four years later there were nearly 2,000 pupils in Manchester and Salford and in Leeds. They continued to flourish for a century until their function was taken over by the secular authorities. Sunday Schools steadily declined as centres for general education until the middle of the twentieth century before they finally relinquished that function.

Organisation behaviour, organisational development, organisational psychology all focus on the micro-entity of the individual business or businesses. Organisational psychology, for instance, studies the interaction between working people and their employing organisational entity and the resultant behaviour of those people.

Outplacement/outsourcing. There is a small difference between these two terms. Outplacement describes taking a complete activity and shifting it to a supplier, while outsourcing describes looking outside the business for human resources without the responsibility of being the legal employer.

Peers is an equivocal term in the UK because it has two meanings. One is to describe members of the aristocracy: earls, baronets, dukes, marquesses and viscounts. In this text, and in more general usage, it describes people of the same age, status, ability or qualification as oneself. A peer group is therefore a group of one's equals, not one's superiors.

Performance. Everyone wants effective performance. The individual wants the satisfaction of achievement and results, managers want individuals to be effectively

coordinated and productive, customers want a good product and good service at the right price, governments want efficient businesses in a growing economy. Achieving performance is complicated. It is not simply paying people lots of money, although not paying people enough money may well inhibit performance. It is not simply being nice to people and releasing them from supervision, as without supervision they may do the wrong things. Achieving effective performance also varies according to the work done. A symphony orchestra requires members of great expertise at different instruments, yet all must work to an identical score under the strict leadership of the conductor, with very little scope for individual flair. The jazz quartet is more loosely coordinated, with many individual riffs. Those working for a courier firm or in the operating theatre of a hospital can only perform well by following a tight schedule arranged by someone else. Those working in an advertising agency have a much looser rein in order to encourage their creativity.

Portfolio is a collection of items that represent a person's work. Very familiar for people whose work can best be demonstrated by examples, like painters or cartoonists, it is also now much used by all classes of worker to demonstrate their skills and accomplishments, thereby justifying a qualification to practise.

Presenteeism. Absenteeism is defined in the dictionary as regularly staying away from work without good reason, but is scarcely used in this text. It is included here simply to give point to its antonym 'presenteeism', a term recently coined to describe the practice of people coming to work when they should not, as when unwell, for instance. Some people feel they may lose their job or a promotion opportunity if they are away.

Reactive/proactive. This distinction is important in HRM because there is a natural emphasis in people matters to await developments and deal with them (reactive). Many HR people report that they spend much of their time putting right problems created by the impetuosity or thoughtlessness of their colleagues in other functions. There is also a need, however, to create opportunities for growth and change and to think ahead of issues so that problems can be averted. A well-rounded HR/personnel function is able to maintain a balance between both types of approach, vigorously and calmly sorting out problems or disasters but also taking matters forward in a creative way when the problems are all under control.

Recruitment/selection. Recruitment is the process whereby a business seeks applicants either generally or for particular vacancies. Potential applicants are interested but there is no mutual obligation. Selection is the process whereby not only does the employer choose between two or more interested applicants, but applicants also select, deciding how much further they wish to pursue their original enquiry. The end of the process is a legally binding agreement.

Resourcing. This term has only recently come into common usage and means simply providing the needed resources. For HR people this is providing the human resources that are needed, although some pedantic academics (like at least one of your authors) dislike the term 'employee resourcing'

as it is the employing organisation that is being provided with resources, not the employees. Also employees are not the only source of human resources for the business. Consultants or subcontractors are alternative sources.

Ritual is a series of actions or a type of behaviour that is invariably followed, in accordance with a convention. Developed originally to help people feel secure in the mysteries of religious practices, rituals are widespread in contemporary society (the ritual of going to the pub on Friday after work, the ritual of the pre-match huddle, the ritual of Prime Minister's Question Time). All provide the benefit of enabling people to feel comfortable and accepted in a social situation, and are therefore important in many employment situations where there is a felt need to conform to existing conventions. The selection interview is the most obvious. Other examples are the 'leaving do', collections before a marriage, negotiations, and the office party.

SNS stands for Social Networking Sites. Although these are mainly an element of people's social and personal lives, they are also used in recruitment, as explained in Chapter 9.

Scenario. A method of envisaging the future is to bring together various bits of evidence, both hard and soft, and fit them together in a way that describes a reliable version of the future in X years' time.

Scientific management. The first modern theory of management, formulated by F.W. Taylor and using the principles of industrial engineering to raise productivity by adapting the worker to the machine or the

process. It relied heavily on adjusting the worker's earnings to the level of individual output. The basic ideas remain in place and are at the root of many payment systems, but most management academics and commentators throughout the last three-quarters of the twentieth century disparaged and deplored the 'mechanistic and inhuman' practices spawned by scientific management.

Sex/gender. The word 'sex' is pretty clear in its meaning as describing either a range of interesting activities, or to describe the biological distinction between male and female. Until recently 'gender' was a grammatical term to distinguish between classes of noun or pronoun in some languages, loosely based on natural distinctions of sex: masculine, feminine or neuter. It is now also used to refer to social and cultural differences between the sexes.

SMEs. Small and Medium-sized Enterprises in full. The European Commission has defined SMEs as either micro-entities with fewer than 10 employees, small businesses with fewer than 50 and medium-sized businesses having fewer than 250. Their significance is that they outnumber larger businesses by some distance and they are seen as an engine for innovation and economic growth.

Statutory rights. Rights of the individual citizen or citizens that derive explicitly from a statute or Act of Parliament.

Stress presents managers with two problems. An employee may be absent from work suffering from stress, but this is a condition that is easy to fake and not easy to diagnose. How does a manager detect malingering and take appropriate action? More significantly, a manager may exacerbate or cause stress in someone. How can this be avoided and what remedies are available to employees? A further complication is that stress is not necessarily undesirable. Any football fan will suffer periods of intense stress when the wrong team is winning a match, but this only makes sweeter the euphoria when the right team wins. Stress can be stimulating as well as harmful and some jobs are best done and most enjoyed where there is frequent stress followed by achievement (journalists' deadlines and surgical crises being two examples).

Tells. 'I love you' is a statement by one person to another that is normally accompanied by certain actions and behaviours that demonstrate to the recipient the sincerity of the feeling. Sometimes, however, we say things that we do not believe, or of which we are unsure. Then the listener may try to guess what we really mean, not just what the words say. We give clues to our uncertainty or our truthfulness by what we do, especially what we cannot help doing. These are 'tells'. Blushing shows we are embarrassed, many people put their hands to their mouths when they feel guilty.

HR managers need to learn what tells to look for in situations like selection, where not all candidates are strictly accurate in what they say, or in appraisal, where people may be very guarded in what they say.

Tribunal in this text refers almost exclusively to the three-person panel that makes up the employment tribunal that decides matters of employment law, although it can be any sort of body used to settle disputes. It is not always made up of three people, but it is normal to have an odd number to avoid deadlock.

INDEX